Contents

Second Edition

Population and Society
Essential Readings

Edited by
Frank Trovato

OXFORD
UNIVERSITY PRESS

OXFORD

UNIVERSITY PRESS

Oxford University Press is a department of the University of Oxford.
It furthers the University's objective of excellence in research, scholarship, and education by publishing worldwide.
Oxford is a registered trade mark of Oxford University Press in the UK and in certain other countries.

Published in Canada by
Oxford University Press
8 Sampson Mews, Suite 204,
Don Mills, Ontario M3C 0H5 Canada

www.oupcanada.com

Library and Archives Canada Cataloguing in Publication

Population and society : essential readings / edited by Frank Trovato. — 2nd ed.

ISBN 978-0-19-543978-6

1. Population. I. Trovato, Frank, 1951–

HB871.P653 2011   304.6   C2011-906614-9

Cover image: Harry Malt/Ikon Images/Getty Images

This book is printed on permanent acid-free ∞ paper.

Printed and bound in Canada.

1 2 3 4 — 15 14 13 12

Preface

My intention in compiling this second edition of *Population and Society* was to provide a wide range of works—some classic, others more recent—that reflect important research and theorizing in the field of population studies, broadly speaking. At the same time I also wanted to convey, through these selected readings, the complex ways in which population is interconnected with so many aspects of human society, the environment, and natural resources. I have retained some of the works published in the first edition of this volume, specifically the chapters by Ansley Coale ('How a Population Ages or Grows Younger'), Johan Bongaarts and Joseph Potter ('Fertility, Biology, and Behaviour'), and Wilbur Zelinsky ('The Hypothesis of the Mobility Transition'). These classic readings are foundational and cannot be avoided by introductory students of population studies. The other selections in this volume are no less important, covering a wide range of subjects, from population theory to models of demographic action and changing nuptiality patterns, to international migration, health and mortality, and population policy concerns.

As with the first edition, the present collection can be used as a supplement to any introductory textbook on population. It may also be used fruitfully as a stand-alone text, though clearly in such cases instructors would surely incorporate into their lectures materials from other pertinent sources. Since no edited volume can cover an entire field (especially one as varied as population studies), I have written a brief introductory essay establishing common underlying themes among the constituent readings to accompany each of the ten sections that comprise this volume. I have also included, in each section, learning objectives and questions designed to encourage classroom discussion or to help students review the material. The reader will also find rudimentary methods of demographic analysis at the end of each section, together with suggested print and online resources related to the themes of the section.

The ten topic sections conform to those typically found in most introductory textbooks on population. Section I, The Study of Population, concerns the foundational principles of demography and its nature as a multidisciplinary field. The relationship between individual action and demographic phenomena is the subject matter of Section II, Demographic Processes and Individual Action, while Part III, World Population: Past, Present, and Future, deals with the history of the human population. The fourth section devotes itself to the principles of age composition; it is followed, in Section V, by nuptiality and family processes. Sections VI, VII, and VIII cover, respectively, the three central variables of demography: fertility, mortality, and migration. Issues pertaining to population and its relationship to environment and resources are addressed by the readings in Section IX, while the final part is devoted to population policy concerns.

Acknowledgements

In producing this volume, I have benefited greatly from the expert managerial and editorial guidance of Sarah Carmichael and her esteemed colleagues at Oxford University Press, particularly Mark Thompson and Caroline Starr, both of whom were involved in the early stages of this project. The reviewers for Oxford Press deserve a special acknowledgement for their constructive suggestions towards the successful development of this volume. I am most grateful to the authors whose contributions and permission to allow reprinting of their works have made this volume possible. Last but not least, I wish to express my appreciation to my running group colleagues at the University of Alberta for their patient acceptance of my many absences during the preparation of this volume: Doug H., Doug D., Artin, Val, and Janet. My deepest gratitude is reserved for my family for their unlimited support and understanding.

Frank Trovato
The University of Alberta,
Edmonton, Alberta
20 January 2011

SECTION I
The Study of Population

Learning Objectives

By the end of this section, students should understand and be able to discuss the following:

- the differences between and interconnectedness of formal demography and social demography (i.e. population studies)
- the components of population change
- how demographers explain population processes.

Introduction

Demography is perceived as a field whose principal preoccupation is the rapid growth of the human population. This is certainly one aspect of the discipline. Overpopulation and its implications for the future of humankind—otherwise known as the 'population problem'—have received much attention in both the academic literature and the popular media, and continue to stimulate important scholarly investigations today. Prestigious venues including *Scientific American, National Geographic, Nature,* and *Science* publish on a periodic basis timely feature stories on population and its interrelationships with society, resources, and the environment.[1] Writers such as Paul Ehrlich, in *The Population Bomb* (1968), and Donella Meadows and associates, in *The Limits to Growth* (1972), warned of looming disaster to a world with runaway population growth. They developed complex simulation models purporting to show that continued growth in certain key sectors of the economy combined with the consumption of non-renewable resources and a growing population would ultimately cause the collapse of the earth's ecosystem. They even anticipated when it was likely to happen: pondering the results of their simulation models, the authors of the latter of these two studies concluded that if growth trends in world population, industrialization, pollution, food production, and resource depletion continued unchanged, the limits to growth on this planet would be reached sometime within the next hundred years, with the most probable result being a rather sudden and uncontrollable decline in both population and industrial capacity (p. 23).

At present, however, in spite of continued concerns about overpopulation, the industrialized world is facing a very different 'problem'. For these populations the prevailing predicament is a continued pattern of below-replacement fertility coupled with natural increase rates close to zero, and even at negative figures in some cases. The crisis that looms on the horizon for the more developed countries is depopulation and a rapidly aging population (Teitelbaum & Winter, 1985).

Concerning the developing world, even though population growth rates are declining, many of the poorest countries are experiencing growth rates well above the world average. Countries in sub-Saharan Africa fit this profile. Another factor at play in the demographic situation of these countries is the frequent occurrence of natural and human-made disasters—famines, droughts, sociopolitical conflict, and civil war, not to mention the ongoing HIV/AIDS epidemic, which, along with malaria and other communicable diseases, claims a disproportionate number of lives annually.

These divergent demographic and socioeconomic trends speak to a widening demographic divide between developed and developing countries. A part of the world's population is advancing socioeconomically; their demographic situation having reached a state of maturity, these countries must rely increasingly on immigration as a source of labour. Meanwhile, the poorest countries of the world, those that make up the so-called Third World, are struggling in their efforts to overcome their demographic and economic predicaments, caught in vicious cycles of rapid population growth and poverty.

The Study of Population

Fundamentally, the subject matter encompassed by the study of population stems from common experiences we all undergo as we pass through our lives. Consider these facts: we were all born and will someday die; between these two fateful occurrences we experience a host of formative events throughout the life course—the start of school, graduation, our first full-time job, marriage, parenting, divorce, remarriage, change of residence, widowhood, and so forth. The timing and frequency of these life events in the population, on the aggregate, determine the population's demographic profile, including its growth rate and age–sex composition.

One of the most important aggregate indicators for a population is the birth rate, the incidence of births in relation to overall population. Similarly, the death rate can be understood as the number of deaths occurring in the population at a given point in time. Together with migration, these are the three fundamental variables in demographic analysis. Whether a population is growing or not depends how these rates change, and so, examined over time, these measures mirror population change.

Other variables have an effect on population change, but they do so indirectly through their influence on fertility, mortality, and migration. Two of the most important of these demographic variables are age and sex. At the individual level, they are biological facts; in the aggregate, however, they express a population's age and sex *composition*, the distribution of the population in accordance with these two characteristics. This information can help us establish, for example, whether a population is relatively young or aging, or whether it has a balanced or a distorted sex composition (i.e. in its ratio of men to women). Because they are so closely connected to most demographic phenomena, age and sex are among the most important variables in the study of population.

Population Defined

To demographers, a human population is a dynamic aggregate existing within a defined geographic boundary, which is continuously changing as a result of the complementary processes of *attrition* (i.e. losses through emigration and deaths) and *accession* (i.e. gains through births and immigration). A national population exists through time, and can be projected into the future using mathematical procedures guided both by past knowledge of fertility, migration, and mortality, and by sound assumptions concerning the future direction and magnitude of change in these three demographic variables (Pressat, 1985, p. 176; Preston, Heuveline, & Guillot, 2001, p. 1).

Demography Defined

The term *demography* derives from the Greek words *demos*, meaning 'people', and *graphia*, meaning 'the study of'. Demography, therefore, is the study of people, specifically the scientific study of population

in relation to the changes brought about by the interplay of births, deaths, and migration. Pressat (1985, p. 54) describes the scope of demography neatly when he writes that work within this discipline falls into three main areas:

1. The size and makeup of populations according to different criteria, such as age, sex, marital status, educational attainment, or spatial distribution; in short, pictures of a population at a fixed moment.
2. The different processes (i.e. fertility, mortality, migration) that directly influence this composition.
3. The relationship between these static and dynamic elements and the social, economic, and cultural environment within which they exist.

This last point calls attention to sociology specifically (and, by implication, the social sciences generally) as key to a proper understanding of population phenomena. Keyfitz (1996, p. 1) is explicit in his acknowledgement of this, calling demography 'a branch of sociology [that] uses birth and death rates and related statistics to determine the characteristics of a population, discover patterns of change, and make predictions'.

Formal Demography and Population Studies

Demography, the scientific study of population, is customarily viewed as being made up of two sub-disciplines: *formal demography* and *population studies*. Formal demography deals with the quantitative study of population in terms of growth, distribution, and development (change). As articulated by Yaukey (1985, p. 1), three central questions lie at the heart of formal demography: 'How many people, of what kind, are where?' The first question, *How many?*, refers to the accounting aspect of formal demographic analysis, used, for example, in determining or estimating the size of population and its change over time. The question *What kind?* fixes on population composition. It drives the statistical analysis of population distribution in terms of such key demographic characteristics as age, sex, and marital status; secondary population characteristics encompassed by this question include ethnic origin, language, religion, labour force status (i.e. employed *vs* unemployed), income, and occupation, among others. Finally, the question *Where?* expresses formal demography's concern with the geographic dimension of population analysis, specifically the distribution and concentration of the population across geographic space, and its mobility across geographic boundaries.

Population researchers typically broaden their analyses to include both formal methodologies and conceptual frameworks from various disciplines. An economist, for instance, would emphasize the interrelation of demographic and economic variables across human populations; an ecologist would study how populations develop and change in the context of varying conditions in their natural environments; a sociologist investigates the social forces underlying demographic change, while a geographer looks at spatial dimensions of demographic phenomena; medical scientists and epidemiologists focus on the demographic bases of health and mortality variations across populations. Yet although the scholars from these fields may approach the study of population from the point of view of their own disciplinary lenses, they share a common appreciation of and reliance on formal demographic methods and their proper application to the analysis of population dynamics. They all aim to specify the *determinants and consequences* (broadly speaking) of demographic change. This aspect of the field is often referred to as *population studies*, or *social demography*, in contrast to formal demography.

The demarcation of formal demography and population studies provides a neat division that helps the beginning student gain a better appreciation of the all-encompassing nature of the discipline. In practice, however, adherence to this distinction is often a matter of degree, for the two aspects are seldom separated in real demographic research. The scientific analysis of population usually involves the application or development of formal principles and methods (i.e. statistics and mathematics) in conjunction with substantive conceptual frameworks drawn from the social and natural sciences.

Population Change

The natural processes of fertility and mortality, together with net migration (the net difference in the number of incoming and outgoing migrants), determine the difference in the size of a population between two points in time. This principle is illustrated by the *demographic components equation*, also known as the *demographic balancing equation*:

$$P_{t1} - P_{t0} = (B_{t0, t1} - D_{t0, t1}) + (IN_{t0, t1} - OUT_{t0, t1})$$

Letting P_{t0} and P_{t1} represent the population at the beginning and the end of some specified interval, its numerical change ($P_{t1} - P_{t0}$), can be expressed as a function of the difference in births and deaths ($B_{t0, t1} - D_{t0, t1}$) plus the net exchange in the numbers of immigrants ($IN_{t0, t1}$) and emigrants ($OUT_{t0, t1}$). The component ($B_{t0, t1} - D_{t0, t1}$) is called *natural increase*; the term ($IN_{t0, t1} - OUT_{t0, t1}$) is *net migration*. Therefore, the balancing equation may be rewritten as follows:

$$P_{t1} = P_{t0} + (Natural\ Increase_{t0, t1}) + (Net\ Migration_{t0, t1})$$

The Space and Strategy of Demographic Growth

Population change depends heavily on the process of *reproductivity*. At the individual level, reproductivity is the ability to produce surviving offspring, who may themselves produce their own progeny in adulthood. In his enlightening chapter on the space and strategy of demographic growth, Massimo Livi-Bacci explains in lucid detail the fundamental demographic processes that characterize human populations, aptly illustrated with examples from populations of the past, including an Italian family in seventeenth-century Florence and the remarkable case of the French Canadian pioneers.

What makes Livi-Bacci's analysis especially illuminating is his emphasis on the role of the family, for it must be understood that populations are made up largely of families and households. Therefore, the ability of a population to reproduce itself implies that the society is successful in promoting values and norms that promote the formation of families.

Beside fertility, the level of mortality in the population plays an important role in reproductivity. This is especially so for women: women's survival probabilities in the childbearing ages determine to a large extent the fertility level in a population. Under favourable conditions, more women reach reproductive age and are thus able to have children, whereas under harsh conditions, survival probabilities are lower, and fewer women on the average would survive through their reproductive lifespans.

Stated differently, let us think of a population that is closed to migration (i.e. no in- and out-migration). This population, to the extent that there is an equal number of surviving offspring each year in relation to the number of progenitors, is just replacing itself—in other words, there are equal numbers of parents and offspring. Over the long term, this leads to a state of equilibrium, where the growth rate is zero (thus, a stationary population). However, if in this population the numbers of surviving offspring exceeds the number of parents, the population is doing more than replacing itself: it is growing. The growth rate of the population in this case will depend on the degree to which the number of surviving progeny exceeds the number of parents (the larger the difference, the higher the growth rate). When the number of surviving children falls below the number of progenitors, this situation would lead to population decline and, in the long term, extinction.

How Do We Know the Facts of Demography?

Demographers, whether their preoccupations are formal methodologies or substantive analysis, are principally concerned with explaining real-world situations and how populations change under different structural conditions. This means that population scientists cannot avoid theory in their quest to better understand population dynamics in everyday life; they will often have to develop or apply theoretical models in their work. These models are meant to lay out in a logical manner the conditions under which a particular phenomenon is expected to occur (Giere, 1999).

Almost four decades ago, Canadian demographer Nathan Keyfitz (1975) asked, 'How do we know the facts of demography?' Keyfitz was attempting to highlight the idea that demographic phenomena cannot be fully explained by direct observation of data or statistical relationships among variables. Rather, observing statistical relations is just a starting point towards explanation. In an important article, reprinted in this volume (see Chapter 2), Keyfitz argues that the analyst must have a model in mind—a conceptualization of the causal mechanisms about the phenomenon he or she is trying to understand. A model should specify how change in one variable leads to change in another variable, and stipulate the conditions that lead to change. 'No model,' writes Keyfitz , 'no explanation.'

Keyfitz begins his discussion by explaining the difference between the theoretical approach and the empirical approach. The theoretical approach relies on proven principles concerning how variables in the real world are causally related under clearly specified conditions. The empirical approach is based on observing correlations among variables in the real world. To illustrate the difference between these approaches, Keyfitz considers the relationship between population growth rate and the percentage of population over age 65, which is an important question for demographers. Although somewhat technical, this part of Keyfitz's chapter provides an excellent example of formal demography done well, through the application of mathematical methods and theory to explain demographic phenomena. First, he fits a simple linear regression equation to a set of empirical data for Mexico and the United States. The two countries show very different results for rate of population growth (defined as r) and percentage of population aged 65 and over (defined as P_{65+}). The calculated regression equation is

$$P_{65+} = 11.5 - 2.3r$$

where 11.5 is an overall average value of the percentage over 65 across the countries, and 2.3 the increase in P_{65+} due to a 1 per cent increase in r (thus, in this fitted equation a 1 per cent increase in r is associated with a drop of 2.3 per cent in P_{65+}).

Although the equation is straightforward, Keyfitz warns that different data sets would most likely produce different results. His examination of a larger set of countries produces an equation that is not identical to the one he derived earlier, even though the association between the two variables of interest remained negative (i.e. the higher the growth rate of population, the lower the percentage of population over age 65). This time the fitted equation is

$$P_{65+} = 8.45 - 1.6r$$

Why the difference? Keyfitz explains that countries may differ in the extent to which they experience emigration of young adults, and that this would affect the percentage of their population that is 65 and over. Countries may also differ in the extent to which birth and death rates (both of which, along with emigration, affect P_{65+}) are changing. To uncover these different possibilities would require extensive empirical studies of the specific countries.

But as Keyfitz point out, there is no need for such extensive investigation of the empirical data. The relationship in question can be analyzed theoretically by applying what is known as the *stable population model*. A stable population is a theoretical population that describes the structure and dynamics of a closed population (one with no in- or out-migration) with constant (unchanging) age schedules of fertility and mortality. Given these inherent features, a stable population can, depending on the fertility and mortality schedules assumed, either grow or decline

at a constant rate of change. The growth rate in a stable population is called *the intrinsic rate of growth*. A stable population with an intrinsic growth rate of zero is a *stationary population*.

By varying the age schedules of mortality and fertility in the stable population, one can derive the corresponding age compositions of the stable population. For example, one may increase age-specific fertility rates by a certain percentage but keep mortality unchanged; alternatively, one may hold fertility rates unchanged but vary the age-specific mortality schedule. One can then see how the age composition of the stable population changes with each of these different manipulations of fertility and mortality.

Using the stable population approach, Keyfitz comes up with a new equation to describe the relationship between the rate of population growth and the proportion aged 65 and over. Applying the stable population model to Mexico and the United States, he finds that

$$P_{65+} = 12.5 - 5r$$

Again, the association between the variables is negative (as it should be), though the exact values of the parameters are different than those obtained with the previous equations.

Through this exercise Keyfitz meant to demonstrate the incontrovertible fact that the population growth rate determines the proportion of population aged 65 and over in a population, something that can be proven easily with the stable population model. Thus, the model enables us to say something meaningful about real-world population dynamics while bypassing the vagaries of empirical data (including data errors, insufficient data, biased samples, and so on). As Keyfitz puts it, '[t]hese theoretical relations [in the stable population] largely escape defects of the data' (1975, p. 272).

Later in the chapter, Keyfitz presents other, less technical examples to emphasize the importance of theory in demographic analysis. Among these are the problem of explaining the causal mechanisms related to the increase in breast cancer among

North American women, and the question of how population growth is related to economic development. Concerning breast cancer, he notes that some of the increase may be due to heightened awareness and diagnosis. Or possibly, it may stem from the fact that more women in North America are having babies later in life compared with women in developing countries, where birth rates are higher and women have children earlier in life. Although these theories are consistent with the observed relationship between cancer rates and economic development (breast cancer rates are relatively low in poorer countries and relatively high in wealthier ones), Keyfitz makes it clear that 'no one thinks that having children—early or late—can prevent the disease or account for the differences' (1975, p. 275). According to Keyfitz, such statistical puzzles will remain unsolved until someone comes up with a model that specifies the causal mechanisms underlying the observed differences (e.g., why breast cancer is high in North America and low in developing countries).

On the question of development and population growth, national income is often used as a proxy for a country's level of economic development. In cross-national analyses, researchers have indeed observed a negative correlation between development and population growth rates—the higher the level of economic development, the lower the rate of population growth. But as Keyfitz observes, the correlation is far from perfect. For example, wealthy countries have low birth rates and therefore low rates of population growth; but it also happens that less wealthy countries, such as those in eastern Europe, have similarly low birth rates and low population growth rates. Adding to the inconsistency, there is evidence in the literature that the correlation between household income and fertility is positive in rich countries but negative in less developed nations.

Applying economic theory to these observed correlations provides us with a reasonable explanation: increased affluence causes people to buy more of most things, the exceptions being those labelled 'inferior' goods. The argument goes that since children are not generally viewed as being inferior goods, children and income are positively related. However, the relationship is concealed by the intervention of other factors—that is, the better-off have access to contraceptives, which the poor may be uninformed about or unable to acquire; the better-off have higher standards for their children and therefore seek to spend more money on them, which means they opt for fewer children, though of 'higher quality'. All of this makes for a negative correlation between level of economic development and population growth rate.

Keyfitz also addresses the opposite question: 'In what direction and to what extent does rapid population growth affect development?' This is an important policy-relevant question for developing countries that are trying to curb population growth rates. Here again, Keyfitz's analysis is enlightening. He first presents the classical economic theory linking population growth to development. In accordance with the theory, rapid population growth means people have many children, which have to be fed, clothed, educated, and taken care of. Essentially, this means that the state must take resources away from other investments that could be used to promote economic growth, and in this sense, rapid population growth handicaps economic development. However, the economic theory also specifies that when fertility falls from an initially high level, the *dependency ratio* (i.e. the number of children plus the number of elderly divided by the working-age population) begins to shift in an economically favourable direction (i.e. more workers per dependants), and investments can therefore be greater than before. As well, over the long run—say 20 years hence—young adults entering the labour force will have an easier time finding work, as there will be less competition for jobs (i.e. smaller cohorts of labour-force age due to declining fertility rates in the past). This situation would also be conducive to economic growth.

Now, all this sounds perfectly plausible and conforms to standard economic theory. But if one simply ignored the theory, or pretended not to know it, and instead looked at the empirical correlations concerning population growth rates and economic progress (i.e. change in national income), the data would paint a rather different picture, argues Keyfitz. Among the developing countries, one would find some nations with relatively high population growth rates and relatively high levels of economic progress, and others with low population growth rates and low economic progress. From such empirical correlations, 'the relation that theory predicts is not at all evident', and 'the inverse correlation [of population growth rate] with economic dynamism simply does not appear' (Keyfitz, 1975, p. 281).

Of course, one can come up with an explanation for the unexpected cross-national differences by incorporating into the theory the possible effects of country-specific differences in political conditions, efficacy of governance leadership, type of religion, and degree of resource endowments. But even if the theory is sustained by such *a posteriori* explanatory addendums, none of this would help to answer the question, 'to what extent would naïve examination of population and income data for the poor countries of the world have discovered any clear effect of population on development' (Keyfitz, 1975, p. 281)? In fact, the empirical correlations by themselves would provide a rather chaotic picture. So, theory is essential as a guide to the analysis of complex population dynamics.

Much of demographic analysis involves using empirical data to test theory. Scholars aim to determine the extent to which empirical correlations fit a given theory about a specific phenomenon. As already noted, empirical correlations can often show ambiguous relationships between variables or even relationships that contradict a theory. According to Keyfitz, this problem can be handled by carefully considering what other subsidiary unmeasured variables may be at work to produce the ambiguous correlations. For example, if one finds that among developing countries, higher rates of population growth produce higher levels of economic development in contrast to what the theory predicts, then it would be especially important to think of what unobserved subsidiary variables may be involved in producing this unexpected correlation. In other words, there may be other factors that 'stick' to the observed variables and that need to be taken into account.

The approach of directly correlating the variables of immediate interest is less promising than a search for any subsidiary variables 'sticking' to them. The researcher must possess the knowledge to understand what these auxiliary variables might be. For example, one may find that a positive correlation between population growth and development may be interpreted as being a result of dictatorial regimes placing great emphasis on economic growth on the one hand and little or no emphasis on family planning to reduce fertility on the other. However, Keyfitz correctly warns, the burden of proof on the researcher for this type of interpretation would be quite onerous. One would have to overlook the more reasonable classical economics theory and, beyond that, would need to demonstrate some necessary relation between technocratic dictators and development on the one hand and dictators and large families on the other.

Whenever a challenge to established theory arises, the onus is always on the scientist to present the challenging new evidence to his or her peers. This means that one must be confident of having credible new evidence, and then other scientists must accept the new evidence as a reasonable challenge to a theory. This is a crucial feature of any science. Demography has an abundance of data to draw on, and this allows 'an inappropriate theory or an erroneous prediction to stand out' more so than in other social sciences where data are less bountiful.

Note

1   See, for example, *National Geographic* collector's edition, *State of the Earth 2010* (22 November 2010); *Scientific American, Earth 3.0. Population and Sustainability* (June 2009).

Works Cited

Ehrlich, Paul. (1968). *The population bomb.* New York: Ballantine Books.

Giere, Donald N. (1999). *Science without laws.* Chicago: University of Chicago Press.

Keyfitz, Nathan. (1975). How do we know the facts of demography? *Population and Development Review, 1*(2), 267–88.

———. (1996). Population. *Grolier's Encyclopedia* (CD-ROM).

Meadows, Donella H., Meadows, Dennis L., Randers, Jorgen, & Behrens III, W.W. (1972). *The limits to growth: A report for the Club of Rome's Project on the Predicament of Mankind.* New York: Universe Books.

Population Reference Bureau. (2010). *World population data sheet 2010.* Washington, DC: Population Reference Bureau.

Pressat, Roland. (1985). *A dictionary of demography.* Ed. Christopher Wilson. Oxford: Basil Blackwell.

Preston, Samuel H., Heuveline, Patrick, & Guillot, Michael. (2001). *Demography: Measuring and modeling population processes.* Malden, MA: Blackwell.

Teitelbaum, Michael S., & Winter, Jay M. (1985). *The fear of population decline.* San Diego, CA: Academic Press.

World Health Organization. (2010). Mortality table 1: Numbers and rates of registered deaths, Canada 2004. Retrieved from http://apps.who.int/whosis/database/mort/table1_process.cfm

Yaukey, David. (1985). *Demography: The study of human population.* Prospect Heights, CA: Waveland Publishers.

CHAPTER 1

The Space and Strategy of Demographic Growth

Massimo Livi-Bacci

Divide and Multiply

Many animal species are subject to rapid and violent cycles which increase or decrease their numbers by factors of 100, 1,000, 10,000, or even more in a brief period. The four-year cycle of the Scandinavian lemming is well known, as are those of many infesting insects of temperate woods and forests (4–12 years). In Australia, 'in certain years the introduced domestic mouse multiplies enormously. The mice swarm in crops and haystacks, and literal bucketfuls can be caught in a single night. Hawks, owls and cats flourish at their expense . . . but all these enemies have little effect in reducing the numbers. As a rule the plague ends rather suddenly. A few dead mice are found on the ground and the numbers dwindle rapidly to, or below, normal.'[1] Other species maintain an equilibrium. Gilbert White observed, two centuries ago, that eight pairs of swallows flew round the belfry of the church in the village of Selborne, just as is the case today.[2] There are, then, both populations in rapid growth or decline and populations that are more or less stable.

The human species varies relatively slowly in time. Nonetheless, as we shall see below, long cycles of growth do alternate with others of decline, and the latter have even led to extinction for certain groups. For example, the population of Mesoamerica was reduced to a fraction of its original size during the century that followed the Spanish conquest (initiated at the beginning of the sixteenth century), while that of the conquering Spaniards grew by half. Other populations have disappeared entirely or almost entirely—the population of Santo Domingo after the landing of Columbus, or that of Tasmania following contact with the first explorers and settlers—while at the same time others nearby have continued to increase and prosper. In more recent times, the population of England and Wales multiplied sixfold between 1750 and 1900, while that of France in the same period increased by barely 50 per cent. According to probable projections, the population of the Democratic Republic of Congo will have increased tenfold between 1950 and 2040, while in the meantime that of Italy will remain unchanged.

These few examples should suffice to demonstrate at what different rates the human species can grow even in similar situations (France and England) and over long periods. It should also be clear that here lies the heart of demography as a science: to measure growth, analyze mechanisms, and understand causes.

Population growth (whether positive or negative, rapid or slow) can be described by a simple calculation. In any interval of time, a population (P) varies numerically as a result of renewal or arrivals (births B and immigration I) and elimination or departures (deaths D and emigration E). Leaving aside migration (considering the population 'closed', as is that of the entire planet), the change in population dP in any interval of time t—by convention and for convenience demographers use years—is given by the following:

$$dP = B - D,$$

and so the rate of growth r (where $r = dP/P$) will be equal to the difference between the birth rate b (where $b = B/P$) and the death rate d (where $d = D/P$):

$$r = dP/P = b - d$$

The range of variation of the birth and death rates is fairly wide. Minimum values are 5 to 10 per thousand (possible today with mortality and fertility under control) and a maximum 40 to 50 per thousand. As mortality and fertility are not independent, it is unlikely that opposite extremes should coexist. Over long periods, growth rates vary in practice between −1 and 3 per cent per year. . . .

Fertility and mortality rates are numerical calculations with little in the way of conceptual content, and as such are not well adapted to the description of the phenomena of reproduction and survival on which demographic growth depends.

Jacopo Bichi and Domenica Del Buono, Jean Guyon and Mathurine Robin

Jacopo Bichi was a humble sharecropper from Fiesole (near Florence).[3] On 12 November 1667 he married Domenica Del Buono. Their marriage, although soon ended by the death of Jacopo, nonetheless produced three children: Andrea, Filippo, and Maria Maddalena. The latter died when only a few months old, but Andrea and Filippo survived and married. In a sense, Jacopo and Domenica paid off their demographic debt: the care received from their parents, and their own resistance and luck, succeeded in bringing them to reproductive age. They in turn bore and raised two children who also arrived at the same stage of maturity (reproductive age and marriage) and who, in a sense, replaced them exactly in the generational chain of life.

Continuing the story of this family, Andrea married Caterina Fossi, and together they had four children, two of whom wed. Andrea and Caterina also paid their debt. Such was not the case for Filippo, who married Maddalena Cari. Maddalena died shortly afterward, having borne a daughter who in turn died at a young age. The two surviving sons of Andrea constitute the third generation: Giovan Battista married Caterina Angiola and had six children, all but one of whom died before marrying. Jacopo married Rosa, who bore eight children, four of whom married. Let us stop here and summarize the results of these five weddings (and ten spouses):

- Two couples (Jacopo and Domenica, Andrea and Caterina) paid their debt, each couple bringing two children to matrimony.
- One couple (Jacopo and Rosa) paid their debt with interest, as the two of them produced four wedded offspring.
- One couple (Giovan Battista and Caterina Angiola) finished partially in debt in spite of the fact that they produced six children; only one wed.
- One couple (Filippo and Maddalena) was completely insolvent, as no offspring survived to marry.

In three generations, five couples (ten spouses) produced nine wedded children in all. In biological terms, ten breeders brought nine offspring to the reproductive phase, a 10 per cent decline which, if repeated for an extended period, would lead to the family's extinction.

A population, however, is made up of many families and many histories, each different from the others. In this same period, and applying the same logic, six couples of the Patriarchi family married off 15 children, while five Palagi couples did so with 10. The Patriarchi paid with interest, while the Palagi just fulfilled their obligation. The combination of these individual experiences, whether the balance is positive, negative, or even, determines the growth, decline, or stagnation of a population in the long run.

In 1608 Quebec was founded and the French inhabitation of the St Lawrence valley, virtually abandoned by the Iroquois, began.[4] During the following century, approximately 15,000 immigrants arrived in these virgin lands from Normandy, from the area around Paris, and from central western France. Two-thirds of these returned to France after stays of varying lengths. The current population of 6 million French Canadians descends, for the most part, from those 5,000 immigrants who remained, as subsequent immigration contributed little to population growth. Thanks to a genealogic-demographic reconstruction carried out by a group of Canadian scholars, a considerable amount of information relating to demographic events is known about this population. For example, two pioneers, Jean Guyon and Mathurine Robin, had 2,150 descendants by 1730. Naturally, subsequent generations, including wives and husbands from other genealogical lines,

contributed to this figure, which in and of itself has little demographic significance. On the other hand, the fate of another pioneer, the famous explorer Samuel de Champlain, was very different, and he left no descendants at all. The extraordinary Canadian material also provides measures of significant demographic interest. For example, the 905 pioneers (men and women) who were born in France, migrated to Canada before 1660, and both married and died in Canada, produced on average 4.2 married offspring (see Figure 1.1), a level of fertility which corresponds to a doubling of the original population in a single generation (from two spouses, four married children). The exceptionally high reproductive capacity of the settlers of French Canada was the result of an extraordinary combination of circumstances: the physical selection of the immigrants, their high fertility and low mortality, ample available space, low density, and the absence of epidemics.

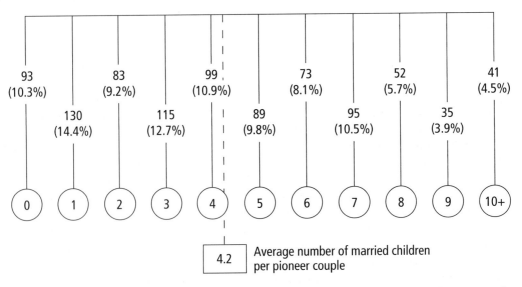

Figure 1.1 Growth of the French-Canadian population (seventeenth century): Pioneers and their children

We have unknowingly touched the heart of the mechanisms of population growth. As we have seen, a population grows (or declines or remains stationary) from one generation to the next if those who gain access to reproduction (here defined by the act of marriage) are in turn successful in bringing a larger (or smaller or equal) number of individuals to marriage. The end result, whatever it might be, is basically determined by two factors: the number of children each individual, or each couple, succeeds in producing—due to biological capability, desire, age at marriage, length of cohabitation, and other factors—and the intensity of mortality from birth until the end of the reproductive period. A familiarity with these mechanisms, which I shall discuss in the following section, is essential for understanding the factors of demographic change.

Reproduction and Survival

The growth potential of a population may be expressed as the function of two measures, whose significance should be intuitive: (1) the number of births, or children, per woman, and (2) life expectancy at birth. These are synthetic measures of, respectively, reproduction and survival. The first describes the average number of children produced by a generation of women during the course of their reproductive lives and in the hypothetical absence of mortality.[5] Below we shall consider the biological, social, and cultural factors which determine the level of this measure. The second, life expectancy at birth, describes the average duration of life (or average number of years lived) for a generation of newborns and is a function of the force of mortality at the various ages, mortality which in turn is determined by the species' biological characteristics and relationship with the surrounding environment. In the primarily rural societies of past centuries, which lacked modern birth control and effective medical knowledge, both of these measures might vary considerably. The number of children per woman ranged from less than five to more than eight (though today, in some western societies characterized by high levels

of birth control, it has declined below one), and life expectancy at birth ranged from 20 to 40 years (today it has exceeded 80 in some countries). The number of children per woman depends, as has been said, on biological and social factors which determine (1) the frequency of births during a woman's fecund period, and (2) the portion of the fecund period—between puberty and menopause—effectively utilized for reproduction. . . .

The Space of Growth

Fertility and mortality, acting in tandem, impose objective limits on the pattern of growth of human populations. If we imagine that in a certain population these remain fixed for a long period of time, then, by resorting to a few simplifying hypotheses, we can express the rate of growth as a function of the number of children per woman (TFR) and life expectancy at birth (e_0).

Figure 1.2 shows several 'isogrowth' curves. Each curve is the locus of those points that combine life expectancy (the abscissa) and number of children per woman (the ordinate) to give the same rate of growth r. Included on this graph are points corresponding to historical and contemporary populations. For the former, life expectancy is neither below 15, as this would be incompatible with the continued survival of the population, nor above 45, as no historical population ever achieved a higher figure. For similar reasons the number of children per woman falls between eight (almost never exceeded in normally constituted populations) and four (recall that these are populations not practising birth control). For the present-day populations included in Figure 1.2, control of fertility and mortality make possible e_0 values of 80 and TFR of 1. Figure 1.3 identifies specific examples within the more restricted boundaries of historical populations. These examples have varying degrees of precision, being in some cases based on direct and dependable observation, in others on estimates drawn from indirect and incomplete indicators, and in others on pure conjecture. Nonetheless, most of these populations fall within a band that extends from growth rates of 0 to 1 per cent, a space of growth typical of historical populations. Within this narrow band, however, the fertility and mortality combinations vary widely. Denmark at the end of the eighteenth century and India at the beginning of the twentieth, for example, have similar growth rates, but these are achieved at distant points in the strategic space described: the former example combines high life expectancy (about 40 years) and a small number of children (just over four), while in the latter case low life expectancy (about 25 years) is paired with many children (just under seven).

Although their growth rates must have been similar, the points for Paleolithic and Neolithic populations are assumed to have been far apart. The Paleolithic, a hunting-and-gathering population, was characterized by lower mortality, owing to its low density, a factor that prevented infectious

diseases from taking hold and spreading, and moderate fertility, compatible with its nomadic behaviour. For the Neolithic, a sedentary and agricultural population, both mortality and fertility were higher as a result of higher density and lower mobility.

Figure 1.4 includes points for some of the most populous countries of the world since 1950. The strategic space utilized, previously restricted to a narrow band, has expanded dramatically. Medical and sanitary progress has shifted the upper limit of life expectancy from the historical level of about 40 years to the present level of about 80, while the introduction of birth control has reduced the lower limit of fertility to a level of about one child per woman. In this much expanded space the populations listed vary between a maximum annual potential growth rate of 4 per cent (many developing countries have a growth rate of over 3 per cent) and a minimum of

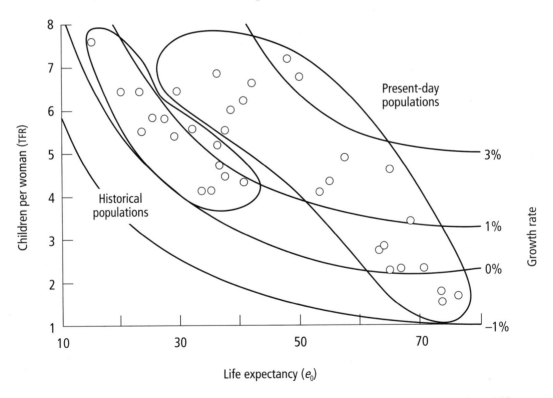

Figure 1.2 Relationship between the average number of children per woman (TFR) and life expectancy (e_0) in historical and present-day populations

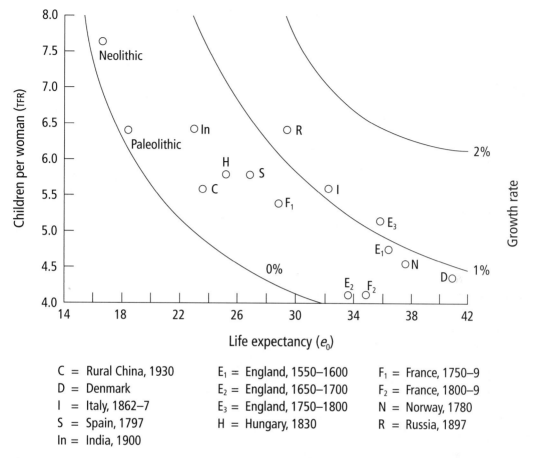

Figure 1.3 Relationship between TFR and e_0 in historical populations

C = Rural China, 1930

D = Denmark

I = Italy, 1862–7

S = Spain, 1797

In = India, 1900

E_1 = England, 1550–1600

E_2 = England, 1650–1700

E_3 = England, 1750–1800

H = Hungary, 1830

F_1 = France, 1750–9

F_2 = France, 1800–9

N = Norway, 1780

R = Russia, 1897

−1 per cent (which will, for example, be realized by many European countries should the current fertility and mortality levels remain unchanged). We are able to recognize the exceptional nature of the current situation if we keep in mind that a population growing at an annual rate of 4 per cent will double in about 18 years, while another declining by 1 per cent per year will halve in 70.[6] Two populations of equal size experiencing these different growth rates will find themselves after 28 years (barely a generation) in a numerical ratio of four to one!

The two situations described in figures 1.3 and 1.4 differ not only in the strategic space they occupy, but also, and especially, in their permanence. The first of the two figures represents a situation of great duration, while the second is certainly unstable and destined to change rapidly, since it implies a rate of growth that cannot in the long run be sustained.

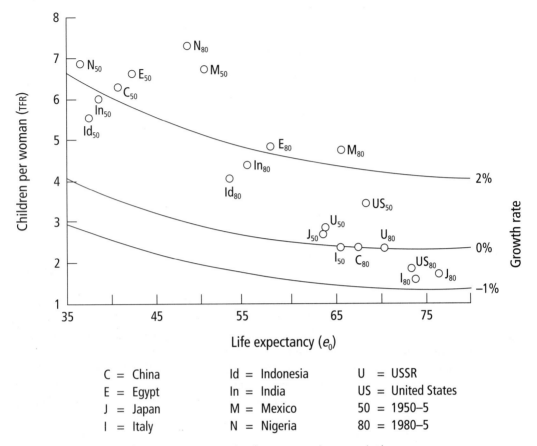

Figure 1.4   Relationship between TFR and e_0 in present-day populations

Notes

1. F. MacFarlane Burnet, *Natural History of Infectious Diseases* (Cambridge University Press, London, 1962), p. 14.
2. R.M. May and D.I. Rubenstein, 'Reproductive Strategies', in *Reproductive Fitness*, ed. C.R. Austin and R.V. Short (Cambridge University Press, London, 1984), pp. 1–23.
3. I am indebted to Carlo Corsini for having supplied me with the following examples taken from family reconstructions for the diocese of Fiesole.
4. The discussion that follows is derived from H. Charbonneau et al., *Naissance d'une population. Les Français établis au Canada au XVIIe siècle* (Presses de l'Université de Montréal, Montréal, 1987).
5. The average number of children per woman, or total fertility rate (TFR), is the sum of age-specific fertility rates for women between the minimum and maximum ages of reproduction, $f_x = B_x/P_x$. B_x is the number of births to a woman aged x, and P_x is the female population aged x.
6. It may be useful to recall a mnemonic device for the calculation of population-doubling times. These can be approximated by dividing 70 by the annual growth rate (expessed as a percentage): a growth rate of 1 per cent implies a doubling time of 70 years, of 2 per cent 35 years, of 3 per cent 23 years. Similarly, if the growth rate is negative, the population-halving time is obtained by the same method: if the population is declining by 1 per cent per year, it will halve in 70 years, if by 2 per cent in 35, and so on.

CHAPTER 2

How Do We Know the Facts of Demography?

Nathan Keyfitz

Demographers know that a population that is increasing slowly has a higher proportion of old people than one that is increasing rapidly, and that differences in birth rates have a larger influence on the age distribution than do differences in death rates. They also often claim that a poor country whose population is growing rapidly will increase its income per head faster if it lowers its birth rate than if it maintains a high birth rate.

How do demographers know these things? Many readers will be surprised to learn that in a science thought of as empirical, often criticized for its lack of theory, the most important relations cannot be established by direct observation, which tends to provide enigmatic and inconsistent reports. Confrontation of data with theory is essential for correct interpretation of such relationships, even though on a particular issue it more often generates an agenda for further investigation than yields useful knowledge. This article will examine how demographers distill knowledge from observation and from theory. It also will try to show how a reigning theory can be successfully challenged.

Let no one think these questions are remote or purely abstract. The resolution of the major policy issues of our time depends on the answers. How much of their development effort should poor countries put into birth control if they deem their rate of population growth excessive? Some would put nothing, in the expectation that rapid increase of income

will by itself bring population under control. Once people have automobiles, once their countryside is paved over with roads, once enough air-conditioned houses are built, they will lower their fertility, but is this not an overly circuitous way of getting people to use pills and IUDs? Surely direct intervention aimed at lowering fertility would help reach desired developmental goals faster.

Any answer to such questions must take into account the degree to which a low rate of population increase promotes development. That is no simple matter to ascertain. Figure 2.1 shows the relation between rates of population growth and increase of income per capita. Even the most imaginative viewer would hardly see the negative relation that the dominant theory (later to be summarized) requires. In the pages ahead, the irregularity of empirical data as they appear in charts and tables will be repeatedly contrasted with the clear-cut mathematical relations of theory. Every such contrast presents a puzzle, and tackling puzzles constitutes demographic research.

The theoretical approach can be described as 'holding unmentioned variables constant'; the empirical, for example in the form of a regression between measured variables, as 'allowing unmentioned variables to vary as they vary in actuality'. The difference is first studied with an example in which we think we know the true nature of the relationship between two variables.

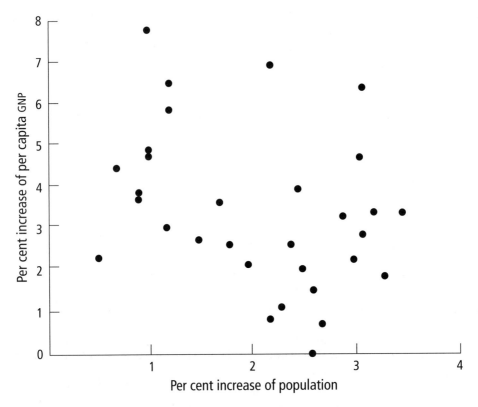

Figure 2.1 Average annual increase of per capita GNP and of population for countries with over 20 million population, 1960–72

Growing Populations Have Smaller Proportions of Old People

The population of Mexico grows at 3.5 per cent per year; its proportion at ages 65 and over is about 3 per cent. The United States has been growing at less than 1 per cent per year; its proportion 65 and over is about 10 per cent. The relation can be expressed as a linear equation. For 1966 the four numbers are:

	Mexico	United States
Rate of natural increase (%)	3.44	0.89
Percentage aged 65 and older (%)	3.31	9.42

Call the annual per cent rate of increase r, and the per cent over age 65 P_{65+}. Then the straight line from the 1966 information on the United States and Mexico is

$$P_{65+} = 11.5 - 2.3r$$

which tells us that for each 1 per cent by which the rate of increase is higher, there is a decrease of 2.3 per cent in the proportion aged 65 and over. With zero increase the per cent over 65 would be 11.5; with 3 per cent increase it would be $11.5 - 6.9 = 4.6$ per cent.

We should be able to obtain a more reliable result with a larger group of countries, so let us try those of Latin America shown in Table 2.1. The result is $P_{65+} = 8.45 - 1.6r$. Apparently the more homogeneous group gives a less steep slope than the United States and Mexico. Now each 1 per cent increase in *r* is associated with a drop of 1.6 in P_{65+}—only two-thirds as much. The scatter diagram (Figure 2.2) shows that we could have chosen two countries that would provide almost any given slope. Moreover, much of what correlation exists is due to three countries of the southern cap—Argentina, Uruguay, and Chile—that are culturally distinct from those farther north, along with Puerto Rico and Martinique. To exaggerate a little, it looks as though countries fall into two groups, those with low *r* and high P_{65+} and those with high *r* and low P_{65+}. In short, much of the pertinent information was contained in the comparison of the United States and Mexico with which we started.

What about taking one country and following changes through time in the two variables? Sweden provides information over nearly 200 years, and also provides a very different regression from any obtained cross-sectionally.

The comparisons and regressions summarizing them are highly inconsistent in reporting how much difference in the proportion over 65 is to be associated with differences in the rate of increase. A large research project could be undertaken to see why they fail to agree; it might reveal that the changing mortality over 200 years in Sweden is confounded by the changing birth rate; that the more homogeneous the group, the lower the correlation and the lower the slope of regression. It happens that in this instance no one will undertake such research because a simple theory is available that will provide a better insight into the nature of the relationship between growth rate and age distribution. Let us use this theory to stand back and take a fresh run at the question.

Table 2.1 Proportion aged 65 and over and rate of natural increase, 18 Latin American countries

Country	Per cent aged 65 and over	Per cent rate of natural increase
Argentina 1964	6.05	1.40
Brazil 1950	2.45	2.80
Chile 1967	4.47	1.89
Colombia 1964	3.00	2.85
Costa Rica 1966	3.18	3.44
Dominican Republic 1966	3.57	2.85
Ecuador 1965	3.16	3.25
El Salvador 1961	3.18	3.81
Guatemala 1964	2.77	2.89
Honduras 1966	1.76	3.55
Martinique 1963	4.96	2.50
Mexico 1966	3.31	3.44
Nicaragua 1965	2.90	3.57
Panama 1966	3.57	3.29
Peru 1963	3.42	2.83
Puerto Rico 1965	5.77	2.36
Uruguay 1963	7.81	1.03
Venezuela 1965	2.99	3.65

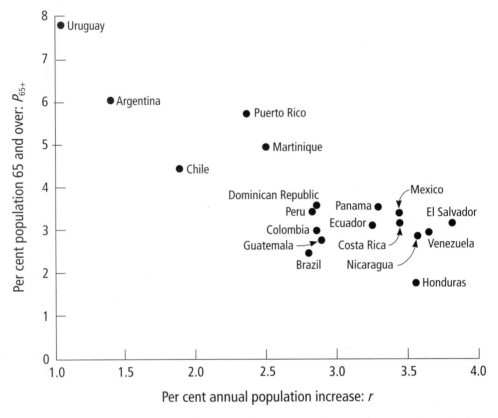

Figure 2.2   Relation of proportion of the population over age 65 to the rate of population increase: 18 Latin American countries

Older Population as a Function of Rate of Increase When All Else Is Constant

For this more abstract consideration we might start with an extreme stylization. Let us imagine a country in which 100,000 births take place each year, everyone lives to age 100, and there is no migration. Then the population at any moment is exactly 10 million, and the fraction over age 65 is exactly 35 per cent at all times. This contains the essence of the stable population model—a model describing the structure and dynamics of a 'closed' population with constant schedules of fertility and mortality. But the assumptions underlying the example just given need generalizing in two directions.

The first is to a more flexible mortality pattern. To suppose that everyone lives to age 100 is to specify a very special kind of survivorship schedule (or life table), and we can easily improve on it by using the mortality of the country in question. With United States 1972 mortality, taking both sexes together, the fraction over 65 comes down to 15.5 per cent.

Let us now also allow for increasing births. Suppose that the fraction of births surviving to age x is given by a fixed survival function $s(x)$, and the annual per cent rate of increase of births is r, so that compared with x years ago the number of births is now $(1 + r/100)^x$ greater. Then for each present birth there were $1/(1 + r/100)^x$ births x years ago, and of these past births a fraction $s(x)$ have survived, the surviving individuals being now aged x. Thus the number of present individuals of age x must be $Bs(x)/(1 + r/100)^x$, where B is the number of current births. This applies for all ages, and suffices to specify the age distribution.[1] Since the expression depends on r, it will tell the relation between any given index of the age distribution on the one hand and the rate of increase on the other.

For example, the proportion aged 65 and over is simply obtained by summing up the number of persons at ages 65, 66, 67, and so on, all the way to the maximum age of life (say 100), and dividing this sum by the total population. The latter is obtained by summing up the number of persons at all ages, beginning at age zero. To express this in percentage terms we must also multiply the result by 100:

$$P_{65+} = 100 \frac{B \sum\limits_{65}^{100} \left\{ s(x) / (1 + r/100)^x \right\}}{B \sum\limits_{0}^{100} \left\{ s(x) / (1 + r/100)^x \right\}} \quad (1)$$

If the $s(x)$ is fixed, equation (1) establishes P_{65+} as a function of r and of nothing else. The equation is not very instructive in this form, for we cannot easily see whether P_{65+} increases or decreases with r, let alone by how much. One way to study the matter is to set up model tables of stable populations, in which stable age distributions are in effect tabulated for many combinations of r and $s(x)$.[2]

Another way is to 'linearize' equation (1). If r is small, one finds that with good approximation:

$$P_{65+} = \left[\frac{r(m_2 - m_1)}{100} \right] \sum\limits_{65}^{100} s(x) \bigg/ \sum\limits_{0}^{100} s(x) \quad (2)$$

where m_2 is the mean age of those 65 and over in the stationary population described by $s(x)$ and m_1 is the mean age of everyone, also in the same stationary population.

Equation (2) can be applied with a minimum of data, as it involves quantities that vary little among populations. Thus $\sum\limits_{65}^{100} s(x) \big/ \sum\limits_{0}^{100} s(x)$—that is, the fraction 65 and over in the stationary population

described by the survival schedule $s(x)$—is 0.127 for Mexican males and 0.123 for United States males; the means m_2 and m_1 are usually not far from 75 and 35, so that $m_2 - m_1$ is about 40. Thus, using information that a demographer carries in his head, the expression (2) comes to about[3]

$$P_{65+} = 100 \left(1 - \frac{r}{100} (40) \right) 0.125$$

or

$$P_{65+} = 12.5 - 5r$$

These theoretical relations largely escape defects of the data. Another advantage of the theoretical approach is that we know exactly its assumptions. In this instance, our model specifies that comparison be among populations closed to migration, with the same life table but different rates of increase; that each of them have had births increasing exponentially during the lifetimes of persons now alive, or alternatively, have had fixed age-specific birth and death rates over a long past period. Consequently, this model does not tell anything about the change through time from one such condition to another.

Instead of supposing fixed rates in a closed population, the empirical regression takes into account migration, in whatever proportion it has been occurring in the populations whose data are included. Insofar as mortality has been falling, the influence of that fall is also incorporated. Thus it is a better description of the state of affairs covered by the data; it is a worse description of the intrinsic relationship between the stated variables.

In another aspect the regression inevitably depends on a data base, and that base is determined by what data are available. One can hardly apply sampling notions to it, since whatever unit is taken, the number of measured populations that are truly independent is small. Moreover, data on many countries are lacking. Even if each entity describable as a nation could be thought of as providing independent evidence, and if all had good data, the collection of nations is not easy to conceptualize as a homogeneous universe.

This simple introductory example shows how uncertain our knowledge would be if analytical tools like the stable model were not available. One can imagine extensive research projects for describing the various extraneous factors, methodological controversies, and schools of opinion, some perhaps taking the view that the relation was really different for different races or different continents. One who has been through the theory would no sooner say that the underlying relation between growth and age composition is different for continents than he would say that the laws of thermodynamics differ from country to country.

No Model, No Understanding

A good deal of data is on hand regarding breast cancer. Despite stepped-up efforts to deal with it, expensive operations and other forms of treatment, and widespread publicity urging women to examine themselves and to see their doctors at once if there is any indication, the increase of deaths from breast cancer is considerable in North America and western Europe, just where the most intensive effort is being made. Breast cancer is the leading cause of death for women aged 35–54 and second only to heart disease for older ages. Some of the increase may be due to more awareness and hence more frequent diagnosis now than in the past, and to better diagnosis in America and Europe than in Asia and Latin America, but apparently this is not the whole cause. Women who bear children early seem to have a lower risk of breast cancer, but no one thinks that having children—early or late—can prevent the disease or account for the differences. Breast cancer is less common in warm climates and among poor populations, but that climate or poverty is a preventive seems unlikely.

Such statistical differentials are mere unsolved puzzles until someone comes along with a model that explains the differences. In the meantime, all that can be done is to continue gathering the data to discriminate among proposed models.

The ratio of male to female births is a similar case, in that there is no obvious model, and no clear-cut result has so far emerged from differentials and correlations. We know that births to young mothers have a higher sex ratio (males to females) than births to older ones, that first births to a mother have a higher sex ratio than later births, and that children of young fathers have a higher sex ratio than children of older fathers. But among age of mother, parity of mother, and age of father, which is the operative cause? The high intercorrelations among the possible causes make it difficult to distinguish. Mechanisms have been suggested involving the relative activity and viability of sperm producing male and female babies, but until some such mechanism is shown to be the operative one, our knowledge has a tentative and uncertain character. Here is just one more question that is unlikely to be solved by any volume of statistics by themselves, although they should be able to discriminate among models based on the biology of the matter, once convincing models are presented.

Effect of Development on Population Increase

This brief article is not the place to take up intricate issues of population economics, which is an entire academic discipline having scores of specialists, a literature running to many hundreds of articles and books, and its own lines of cleavage and of controversy. It is worth saying enough only to show that both theoretical and empirical methods are applied in this field, and that, notwithstanding their extensive and skilled use, much remains to be done in disentangling the lines of causation. The literature speaks of 'development' as the socioeconomic transformation into the modern condition, and of 'income' as sufficiently correlated with development to be used as a proxy.

First the effect of development on population: a quick look at cases suggests a familiar negative relation, with which theory conforms. Development seems sooner or later to have brought a reduction in population growth in all the instances where it has occurred. All of the rich countries have low birth rates today, and the very richest are not replacing themselves. For example, West Germany had fewer births than deaths in 1973, and in 1974 it had fewer births plus net immigrants than deaths, so that its population actually declined by 2 per cent. But the countries of eastern Europe are much less rich, and they also have low birth rates, while in Britain the birth rate first started to fall almost a century after development was underway. Thus the correlation is not perfect, but still history seems to be saying that with more or less lag, industrialization has led to reduced family size.

In theory this may be due to women finding jobs and sources of prestige outside the home, so they do not need to rely on childbearing for their standing, and to children being on the one hand more expensive and on the other less directly useful to their parents as income increases, both effects being related to the decline of the family as a productive unit with the growth of industry. With easy contraception, relatively weak motivation suffices to cut the birth rate. What we ought to believe in this matter, summed up in the concept of demographic transition,[4] is relatively unambiguous because the dominant theories and the most conspicuous anecdotal evidence all point the same way.

Yet even here, the more closely and systematically scholars have looked at the data, the less clear they have found the effect of development on family size. Taking income as a proxy for development, Adelman makes 'an analysis of fertility and mortality patterns as they are affected by economic and social forces'.[5] Her materials, mostly based on national statistics for 1953, show a decidedly *positive* relation between income and fertility. Friedlander and Silver partial out more variables, and find that for developed nations fertility and income are positively related, but for less developed nations negatively.[6] David Heer calculated correlations for 41 countries that suggested that the direct effect of economic development is to increase fertility, and the indirect effects (through education, and so on) are to reduce it.[7] But

it makes a difference when the data for the 24 less developed countries are separated from those for the 17 more developed and more than one point of time is introduced, so that changes rather than levels are correlated. Ekanem used two points of time, the 1950 decade and the 1960 decade, but the effect of his greater care seems to be a less clear-cut result than Heer's.[8] Janowitz follows five European countries and finds that variables shift enough through time that the longitudinal relations, more likely to indicate causation, are decidedly different from the cross-sectional regressions.[9]

It would be too unkind to say that these efforts constitute raw empiricism. They are oriented by an economic theory that increased affluence causes people to buy more of most things, the exceptions being labeled inferior goods. Since no one considers children inferior goods, many argue that children and income 'really' are positively related, but the relation is concealed by the intervention of other factors. The better-off have access to contraceptives of which the poor are ignorant; the better-off have higher quality (that is, more expensive) children, and so can afford fewer of them.[10]

Effect of Population Growth on Development

The writers cited above were trying to find the impact of development on fertility where, despite some complications and contradictions, causation seems clearer than in the inverse problem: in which direction and to what extent does rapid population growth affect development? Among all the questions that demographers seek to answer, this is the one that is truly important for policy.

In the classic theory, rapid growth means many children—40 per cent or more of the population under age 15 years. The children have to be fed, clothed, and educated, and however the cost is divided between parents and the state, it requires resources that compete with industrial and other investments. In addition, growth requires that provision be made for *increasing* numbers, in particular to equip a larger and larger labour force with capital goods. Thus a fast-growing population is doubly handicapped.

So much for the static aspect of the demographic–economic relationship. As to dynamics, when fertility falls from an initially high level, the dependency ratio begins to shift immediately in an economically favourable direction. Thus investment can be greater compared to what it was before. Lagging 15 or 20 years behind is a longer-run dynamic effect; a slackening of the growth of the population in the labour force ages. When relatively fewer children grow up to enter those ages, there is less competition for productive jobs and each entrant may have more capital to work with compared to the situation that would exist if the birth rate had not been cut.[11]

All this is based on the view that development is capital-limited rather than resource-limited. But if it is resource-limited, population is an even more serious drawback, although now the absolute level of population is the problem rather than the birth rate; the more people, the less resources at the disposal of each, on a theory running back to John Stuart Mill and ultimately to Malthus. In the most general statement, certain ratios of labour to the other factors of production—land and capital—are more favourable than others, and most developing countries are moving away from the optimum with present population sizes and birth rates.

But now try to see how matters would look if no theory had ever been presented. Let us try to wipe theory out of our minds, and look at the data with complete naiveté. Among developing countries, Pakistan is increasing at over 3 per cent and India at less than 2.5 per cent, yet Pakistan seems to be making more economic progress. Iran's rate of population increase is much greater than Nepal's, and so is its economic advance. Brazil and Venezuela are not increasing in population less rapidly than their economically stagnant neighbors; indeed, Argentina and Chile, with very low birth rates, may be becoming poorer absolutely. Mexico is advancing economically with an annual population increase of 3.5 per cent per year, one of the highest in the world and higher than that in Paraguay or Bolivia, where

economic dynamism is absent. On the other hand, sub-Saharan Africa has high rates of population increase and low income growth. Figure 2.1 depicts the broad array of relationships between population growth and increase in income for large countries in the contemporary world. As noted at the start of this article, the relation that theory predicts is not at all evident.

It makes a difference if we compare birth rates rather than natural increase and for the theory, births less infant deaths might be the best indicator of the demographic impact. But whatever measure is used, the inverse correlation with economic dynamism simply does not appear.

Of course individual countries can be analyzed, and by making allowance for such non-population aspects as leadership, political conditions, the educational system, religion, the dissolving of patrimonial social relations as expressed in landholding, and other ways, along with resource endowment, we need not be at a loss to account for the observed national differences. This explanation *a posteriori* can be made to sustain the theory, but hardly answers the disturbing question: to what extent would naïve examination of population and income data for the poor countries of the world have discovered any clear effect of population on development? Would the effect have been as blurred as the effect of population increase on age distribution?

It is just this incapacity of the raw data to speak for themselves that permits some to argue that population and its growth do not harm development and should be allowed to take care of themselves. One might expect the facts to silence anyone who could utter such opinions, but as presented either anecdotally as above or in simple correlations they do not. How can the facts be made to speak loudly and clearly to this issue?

How Nature Covers Her Tracks

The reason for bringing these very difficult matters into the present exposition is the hope that their investigation can be aided by going back to some simpler issues, like the relation between age distribution and the rate of increase of a population. There most would agree that theory gives the right answer: the rate of increase determines the proportion of old (as well as middle-aged and young) in the population. Where the relation is obscured by migration or by changing birth and death rates, as it commonly is, these are seen as mere disturbances. Such noise could drown out the relation in the observed data without weakening our conviction that the relation is 'really' as stable theory says it is. Up to this point stable theory has the immutability of the laws of logic: if over a sufficient period of time death rates are the same in two populations, then the one with the higher birth rate will have the lower proportion at ages 65 and over. Belief in this is unshaken by El Salvador being higher than Honduras both in rate of population increase and in per cent over age 65, or by similar cases that might turn up. The supporter of the theory would convincingly argue that the official data must be wrong (perhaps registration of births is differentially incomplete), or there has been age-selective migration, or some other reason underlies the discrepancy between expected and observed relationships.

Although stable theory can never be disproved, it could be deprived of all interest if in the real world certain things that it assumes constant were in fact steadily changing. If death rates were always falling at a certain pace, then the proportion of old people would everywhere be different from that given by stable theory, and a different theory would be required for interpreting reality. Any steady change that was universal would make us want to replace stable theory with its fixed rates by some other, inevitably more complicated, theory that would have equal force of logic but be more applicable. In fact, change is not so uniform under different real conditions, but is rather erratic, a means by which nature covers up her mechanisms, rendering their interpretation not amenable to a universal theory.

But change, whether steady or erratic, is not the means by which the mechanisms of nature are most effectively covered. More deceiving is the clinging together of variables. Suppose all countries of rapid growth were countries of emigration, so that they lost their young people to countries of slower growth; then the conclusion derived from the application of stable theory would be downright misleading. We would want some other theory, perhaps one on which populations tend to spread out evenly in relation to resources. In fact, such a view is held on internal migration, where free movement occurs and people go to distant places unless they are attracted to intervening opportunities.[12] Empirical investigation of the clinging together of variables can strengthen or weaken a theory.

The Oblique Use of Data to Challenge Theory

In short, challenges to theory have to take the form either of showing that some of the variables assumed fixed move in a systematic fashion, or more importantly, that some variables supposed to move independently in reality cling together; that some of the independent variables are not really independent, but are creatures of other hidden variables of quite different nature.

How then can the classical theory that rapid population growth checks development be challenged? The matter is important because a theory that there is no chance of proving wrong has little value for science.

One way is by declaring that there is a trend toward development everywhere in the world, as well as a trend toward smaller families, and that the latter makes no difference to the former. Suppose the trend to development occurs everywhere sooner or later and nothing can either stop it or hasten it. On this comfortable view of development as immanent in human history, no detailed causal theory would be possible, and no policy measures would be sought or needed. Such a view is not entirely absent from contemporary discussion, although in its very nature little evidence can be summoned for or against it.

A more persuasive direction of attack is to adduce evidence that enterprising personalities are more often born into large families and to show quantitatively that this greater enterprise is sufficient to overcome the capital and land shortage due to large families. Or else that couples with more children will have a greater incentive to save and so increase investment funds. Or else that having many children increases consumption but fathers of large families work correspondingly harder and offset this. All of these are statements on the individual level that there is a sticking together of the variables concerned with development-population growth, motivation to work, motivation to save. Nothing in logic proves that the sticking together does not occur, but it is the obligation of anyone who challenges the theory to adduce evidence.

On the national level, the countries that are developing may be the ones in which the authorities are development-minded and persuade their people to make sacrifices that more than offset the disadvantages of population increase. Again, evidence bearing on this specific point would be required.

To take an example that, alas, may not be entirely unrealistic, if dictatorial technocratic regimes are effective in producing development, and if these happen to be lukewarm about population control, then the population effect might be dominated by the dictator effect. But one would only give up the classical theory if there were shown to be some necessary relation between technocratic dictators and development on the one hand and dictators and large families on the other. Otherwise one would still have to insist that the dictator was paying a price for population growth, and the price could be avoided.

Why, then, does the failure of a correlation-type approach to show that development follows on a slowing of population growth present no challenge to the theory? The major difficulty is that many other factors affect the correlations. In principle, the disturbing factor of 'motivation to work', or 'making sacrifices' could be partialled out or held constant while the relation of population to development is examined. Yet even if one or two disturbing factors could be identified and measured, many others would remain. And to partial out a large number of variables simultaneously raises logical difficulties if any of them are correlated with the variable retained.

What part of the observed phenomena is a manifestation of the underlying causal mechanism and what part is the concealment? Even for the most straightforward matters this is not an easy question to answer. For national populations, one assumes, age distributions are really determined by the rate of increase, and migration or correlated death rates merely conceal this true relation. On the other hand, density-dependent growth is in evidence for many animal populations, so high birth rates might cause high death rates or out-migration. If the correlation of high births with out-migration is necessary, if it is an intrinsic part of the causal mechanism that the investigator is attempting to lay bare, then the stable theory of age distribution is downright wrong; if it is a provisional and temporary complication of the observed data, then the stable theory stands. If autocratic regimes produce development and the same autocratic regimes fail to initiate family planning, this may result in a positive correlation between population increase and rise in income per head, and the student who wants to know what is happening must penetrate to the intermediate variable, 'autocratic regime'.

After discovering the existence of this intermediate variable, the student would have to judge whether its operation is necessary or incidental.

To express the conclusion of this argument in its most radical form, no amount of data showing a gross positive correlation between the birth rate and economic growth can substantially weaken the belief that these two variables are causally negatively related under the economic-demographic conditions that characterize the contemporary world. After all, every country is a unique case; cross-sectional correlations do not carry over into longitudinal correlations; nature has many ways of concealing her mechanisms.

Nonetheless, empirical data have to be applied to check theory, and doing so is the heart of demography as of any other science, but data have to be brought to bear in an oblique fashion, If we are going to detect nature's hidden mechanisms, we need a subtlety that approaches hers. The attack by directly correlating the variables of immediate interest is less promising than a search for what other subsidiary variables stick to them. This applies equally to the analysis of age distribution, and population and development.

The Psychology of Research

A footnote on the mental conditions in which research occurs may help illuminate the way we get to know the facts of demography. Faced with a variety of data the investigator listlessly surveys them, in the hope of somehow tying them together. He is swamped by the multiplicity of observations and tries to fit them into a scheme, if only to economize his own limited memory. He becomes more animated when he sees that some general connections do subsist in the data and that a model, however crude, helps him to keep their relations in mind. The model is much more than a mnemonic device, however; it is a machine with causal linkages. Insofar as it reflects the real world, it suggests how levers can be moved to alter direction in accord with policy requirements. The question is always how closely this constructed machine resembles the one operated by nature. As the investigator concentrates on its degree of realism, he more and more persuades himself that his model is a theory of how the world operates.

But now he is frustrated—he has just turned up an incontrovertible observation that is wholly inconsistent with his theory. Such an observation is truly a fact, an exception to the theory that cannot be avoided or disregarded. A struggle ensues as the investigator attempts to force the theory to embrace the exception. As his efforts prove vain he questions the theory, and looks back again at the raw data whose complexity he thought he had put behind him. The intensity of the struggle that ensues is one of the hallmarks of scientific activity, and distinguishes it from mindless collecting of data on the one side and from complacent theorizing on the other.

The problem and its possible solutions have now taken possession of the person. In this phase of his research his unconscious is enmeshed and is working on the question day and night. Sleep is difficult or impossible; eating and the daily round of life are petty diversions. He is irritable and distracted. Whatever he does, the contradiction he has turned up comes into his mind, and stands between him and any normal kind of life.

During the struggle the investigator is like a person with high fever. Then with luck he comes on the answer, or his unconscious does. He finds a model that fits, perhaps nearly perfectly, perhaps only tolerably, but well enough to provide a handle on the varied data. His tension relaxes, and he goes on with the normal and dull work of establishing the details of the fit and presenting his results. He must indeed revert to a calmer state before he can hope to communicate his finding to an audience that is perfectly normal. An immediate test of his result will be whether it makes sense to his contemporaries; an ultimate test is whether it can predict outcomes involving data not taken into account in the establishment of the model.

Only in exceptional cases will one period of feverish concern produce a final theory and permit immediate relaxation. More often a long series of false starts and disappointments will precede the resolution. Sometimes the problem turns out to be unsolvable in the existing state of knowledge, or beyond the capacity of the investigator, and then he has the unhappy task of winding himself down without the desired denouement.

None of the psychological accompaniment of scientific production is special to demography, but that field may show it in heightened form, at least compared with other social sciences. The abundant data of demography cause an inappropriate theory or an erroneous prediction to stand out more clearly than the corresponding failure in writing history or in the general analysis of society. Where that possibility of a sharp rejection by hard data is lacking, the game of research loses its seriousness—it is like playing solitaire with rules that are adjustable to the cards that have appeared.

Notes

1. It is clear that if $r = 0$, the age distribution of the stable population equals the survival function. The special case is known as the stationary population.

2. This is one of the purposes that Ansley J. Coale and Paul Demeny had in mind when they constructed their tables in *Regional Model Life Tables and Stable Population* (Princeton: Princeton University Press, 1966).

[3] [Editor's note] Keyfitz omits the steps between his initial equation and its final form, P65+ = 12.5 − 5r. Here is the worked equation with the intervening steps included:

$$P_{65+} = 100 \left[1 - \frac{r}{100} (40) \right] (0.125)$$

$$= \left[100(1) - 100 \left[\frac{r}{100} (40) \right] \right] (0.125)$$

$$= 100(1)(0.125) - 100 \left[\frac{r}{100} (40) \right] (0.125)$$

$$= 12.5 - r(4)(0.125)$$

$$= 12.5 - r(5)$$

$$= 12.5 - 5r$$

4. For an explication of the demographic transition theory, see Frank W. Norstein, 'Population—The long view', in Theodore W. Schultz (ed.), *Food for the world*, pp. 35–7 (Chicago: University of Chicago Press, 1945).

5. Irma Adelman, 'An econometric analysis of population growth', *American Economic Review*, 53, no. 3 (June 1963): 314–39.

6. Stanley Friedlander & Morris Silver, 'A quantitative study of the determinants of fertility behavior', *Demography*, 4, no. 1 (1967): 30–70.

7. David M. Heer, 'Economic development and fertility', *Demography*, 3, no. 2 (1966): 423–44.

8. Ita Ekanem, 'A further note on the relation between economic development and fertility', *Demography*, 9, no. 3 (August 1972): 383–98.

9. Barbara S. Janowitz addresses the longitudinal aspect in 'An empirical study of the effects of socioeconomic development on fertility rates', *Demography*, 8, no. 3 (August 1971): 319–30. For other aspects of this issue, see Jean-Claude Chesnais & Alfred Sauvy, 'Progrès économique et accroissement de la population: Une expérience commentée', *Population*, 28, no. 4–5 (July–October 1973): 843; and Edward G. Stockwell, 'Some conversations on the relations between population growth and economic development during the 1960s', *Rural Sociology*, 37, no. 4 (December 1972): 628.

10. Gary S. Becker, 'An economic analysis of fertility', in *Demographic and economic change in developed countries* (Princeton: National Bureau of Economic Research, Princeton University Press, 1960); and Harvey Leibenstein, 'An interpretation of the economic theory of fertility: Promising path or blind alley?', *Journal of Economic Literature*, 12, no. 2 (June 1974): 467–79; and H. Liebenstein, 'The economic theory of fertility decline', *Quarterly Journal of Economics*, 89, no. 1 (February 1975): 1–31.

11. Ansley J. Coale & Edgar M. Hoover, *Population growth and economic development in low-income countries: A case study of India's prospects* (Princeton: Princeton University Press, 1958).

12. Samuel A. Stouffer, 'Intervening opportunities: A theory relating mobility and distance', *American Sociological Review*, 5, no. 6 (December 1940): 845–67.

Basic Demographic Measures

1. Crude Birth Rate (CBR)

The crude birth rate (CBR) measures the number of births in a given interval of time in relation to the mid-interval population. If we assume the interval is one year (in this and in all subsequent measures), then the formula for the crude birth rate is

$$CBR = \frac{number\ of\ births}{midyear\ population} \times 1{,}000$$

2. Crude Death Rate (CDR)

The crude death rate (CDR) measures the number of deaths in a given year in relation to the midyear population in the same year. As with the crude birth rate, this rate is usually multiplied by 1,000:

$$CBR = \frac{number\ of\ deaths}{midyear\ population} \times 1{,}000$$

3. Annual Rate of Natural Increase (RNI)

The annual rate of natural increase (RNI) measures population growth in a given year due to the difference between the number of births and the number of deaths in the same year. This rate is usually expressed as a percentage:

$$RNI = \frac{number\ of\ births\ -\ number\ of\ deaths}{midyear\ population} \times 100$$

If only crude birth and death rates per 1,000 population are available, the annual rate of natural increase can be computed as follows:

$$RNI = \left[\frac{CBR}{1{,}000} - \frac{CDR}{1{,}000}\right] \times 100$$

4. Population Growth Rate (r)

Whereas RNI concerns the difference between births and deaths, the growth rate of population is simply the difference in population size between any two points in time expressed as a rate. Consider, for example, the average annual growth rate (r) formula below:

$$r = \left[\frac{P_1 - P_0}{P_0}\right] \Big/ n$$

where P_1 = population at the end of the interval; P_0 = population at the beginning of the interval; and n = the number of years in the interval.

If the interval is one year, then n is 1; if it is 5 years, than n is 5, and so on. This computation can be expressed as a percentage by multiplying the result by 100.

Questions for Critical Thought and Discussion

1. The subject matter of population studies is familiar to all of us. Discuss this proposition. Give some examples to support your discussion.

2. How is population a factor in socioeconomic disparities, environmental stress, and resource sustainability in the world?

Websites of Interest

An important source of demographic data is the *World Health Organization*. The WHO website contains deaths by cause, age, and sex for a large number of countries: www.who.int/healthinfo/morttables/en/index.html

The *United Nations Demographic Population Division* publishes a wealth of demographic information, available at its website: www.un.org/esa/population/unpop.htm

The Population Reference Bureau issues publications on a regular basis, including *Population Bulletin* and its annual *World Population Data Sheet*. The Bureau's publications can be accessed via its website: www.prb.org/

Further Reading

Burch, Thomas K. (2002). Teaching demography: Ten principles and two rationales. *Genus, 58*(3–4), 21–34.

Burch, Thomas K. (2002). Teaching the fundamentals of demography: A model-based approach to family and fertility. *Genus, 58*(3–4), 73–90.

Demeny, Paul, & McNicoll, Geoffrey (Eds). (2003). *Encyclopedia of population* (vols 1 & 2). New York: Macmillan Reference USA/Thompson-Gale.

Hedstrom, Peter, & Wittrock, Bjorn (Eds) (2009). *Frontiers of sociology*. Leiden: Brill.

Hedstrom, Peter, Swedberg, Richard (Eds). (1998). *Social mechanisms: An analytical approach to social theory*. Cambridge: Cambridge University Press.

Le Bras, Hervé. (2008). *The nature of demography*. Princeton: Princeton University Press.

Meadows, Donella, Randers, Jorgen, & Meadows, Dennis. (2005). *Limits to growth: The 30 year update*. London: Earthscan.

Petersen, William. (1975). *Population*, 3rd edn. New York: Macmillan.

Stycos, Mayone. (1989). *Demography as an interdiscipline*. New Brunswick, NJ: Transaction Publishers.

SECTION II

Demographic Processes and Individual Action

Learning Objectives

By the end of this section, students should understand and be able to discuss the following:

- the role of individual action in aggregate population phenomena
- how demographic behaviour can be explained by three models of human action: the utility (rational actor) model, the normative model, and the drift model.

Introduction

Demography is often considered a field principally interested in the systematic quantitative analysis of aggregate population phenomena. To a large extent this is true. However, population scholars also share strong interest in the development of theory as it pertains to both macro-level phenomena and individual behaviour. Gaining a better understanding of individual demographic action is especially important because human behaviour is strongly conditioned by our perceptions of situations in the broader social environment and our sense of the reaction of significant others to our actions (approval, disapproval, indifference, etc.). Just as important, demographic change at the aggregate (macro) level is the expression of action at the individual (micro) level.

Rational Actor, Normative, and 'Drift' Models of Demographic Action

One of the important questions in the study of human behaviour is whether our actions are entirely determined by conscious, rational decision making and whether there may be unconscious processes involved as well. In explaining human action, different schools of thought place different degrees of emphasis on the role of rationality and the unconscious. For instance, psychoanalytic theory would say that behaviour is guided primarily by unconscious motives in the individual. In sharp contrast to this theoretical perspective, the rational actor model of human action (also known as the *microeconomic* or *rational utility* model) describes the individual as a 'rational maximizing agent', one who attempts to minimize the perceived costs (e.g. having to take time off work) associated with an intended action (e.g. to have a baby), while at the same time striving to maximize utility (e.g. increased sense of self-fulfillment from having a child).

Thomas Burch, in his essay reprinted here, elaborates on these ideas by proposing a synthesis of two important models of human decision making—the rational actor (or rational utility) and the normative—under the unifying theme of human decisions being driven principally by rational maximizing principles. While the rational actor model emphasizes the paramount importance of maximizing utility as the basis for human action, the normative model stresses above all the constraining influences of social norms (or 'normative constraints') on the individual in the context of the decision making process (Fishbein, 1972). Norms are constraining because they reflect social expectations regarding what is considered acceptable or not acceptable by others.

Demographic processes such as marriage, divorce, migration, changing residence, and having children can all be explained by examining utility principles in conjunction with the normative evaluations made by the individual. A person's decision with respect to an intended action is conditioned by her perception of the action's utility (e.g. material gain, such as money; psychic gain, such as feelings of satisfaction) balanced by her assessment of the possible reactions (positive and negative) of others who are significant in her life (spouse, children, relatives, co-workers, etc.) to her intended action (behaviour). Synthesis of the two models of action—utility and normative—allows for the possibility that even after having evaluated the costs and benefits of an intended action, the individual may forgo acting on the evaluation because of her expectation of negative evaluations from significant others. On the other hand, it is entirely possible that in other circumstances normative considerations may pose for the individual actor little or no weight whatsoever in her decisions. Thus, in practical terms, utility maximization and normative considerations need not exert equal weight in rational decision making; there will be times when one component might outweigh the other, and vice versa.

The rational actor model inherently assumes that the individual is always consciously and rationally involved in the decision making process, fully aware of his motives, goals, and constraints in relation to his intended actions. However, some authors have raised doubts about whether this conceptualization of action fully captures the complex nature of decision making in humans. Is behaviour always rational? Are individuals always perfectly aware of the potential costs and benefits associated with an intended course of action? Could it be, perhaps, that some aspects of human action—demographic or otherwise—cannot be explained by maximizing and normative principles alone?

These are the kinds of questions that Lincoln Day addresses in his insightful essay. He poses the argument that both the utility and the normative models present an incomplete and in some respects unrealistic picture of how humans make decisions in everyday life. The utility model conjures up an individual who coolly calculates the gains and losses to be anticipated from available possibilities, while the normative model presents the individual as constantly conforming to normative expectations. Day asserts that most human action does not in fact conform to the inherent postulates of these two models, but rather is consistent with what he calls 'drift' principles. He views the rational actor model and the normative model as opposite poles on a continuum, with 'drift' processes somewhere in the middle. Decisions about a vast array of important life matters—whether and when to have a child; whether or not to marry, to divorce, or to move; whether or not to engage in sexual intercourse and to use contraceptives, and so on—are seldom executed in the narrowly calculative and precise manner dictated by the utility model or in automatic adherence to normative constraints as implied by the normative model.

According to Day, people typically make choices within a broad range of normative options that are themselves under limits imposed by society. Society establishes a broad normative framework for what is considered appropriate behaviour under given circumstances and also sets the boundaries for the means by which one can pursue and realize individual goals. In this sense, we can assume, as suggested by Day, that conscious choice is present in behaviour only if we think of conscious choice as being a matter of degree rather than as something that either exists or does not exist in absolute terms. Put differently, Day's 'drift' model assumes that much of human behaviour arises "almost by accident at one or another point within the limited range of socially possible and allowable behaviours, and then is guided gently by underlying influences (but not necessarily inexorably) toward its conclusion in a manner largely imperceptible to the person doing the acting." The degree to which conscious choice is present will differ according to the particular psychological and social milieu occupied by individual actors.

While the 'drift' model may not be totally at odds with the utility and normative perspectives, Day insists that human action often depends on emergent properties of interaction, habit, and even unconscious motivation (on this theme see also Field, 1984; Friedman, Hechter, & Kanazawa, 1994; Leibenstein, 1982; Miller & Godwin, 1977). Thus, it may be possible that in some cases, the desire, for example, to have a child, to change residence, and even to divorce may be driven in part by unconscious motivation acting on the individual. Although difficult to study in an objective scientific manner, the possible role of unconscious motivation in demographic action cannot be ruled out altogether.

Works Cited

Fishbein, Martin. (1972). Toward an understanding of family planning behaviors. *Journal of Applied Social Psychology, 2*, 214–27.

Field, Alexander J. (1984). Microeconomics, norms and rationality. *Economic Development and Cultural Change, 32*(4), 279–93.

Friedman, Debra, Hechter, Michael, & Kanazawa, Sitoshi. (1994). A theory of the value of children. *Demography, 31*(3), 375–401.

Leibenstein, Harvey. (1982). Economic decision theory and human fertility behavior: A speculative essay. *Population and Development Review, 7*, 381–400.

Miller, Warren B., & Godwin, R. Kenneth. (1977). *Psyche and Demos: Individual psychology and the issues of population.* New York: Oxford University Press.

CHAPTER 3

The Structure of Demographic Action

Thomas K. Burch

It is a measure of the growing scientific maturity of demography that Vance's question—'Is Theory for Demographers?'—now seems almost quaint (Vance, 1952). As a science, demography needs theory as well as data, and indeed has always had theory, if only implicitly. But maturity means openness about one's acts and intentions. And what characterizes demography today, in contrast to then, is an increasingly open, unapologetic approach to theory.

At the same time, demography has shifted from an almost exclusive focus on the behaviour of large population aggregates to concern with the behaviour of individuals and small groups. Discussions of individual behaviour that remained implicit or ad hoc in earlier works are now more explicit and systematic.

Nothing better exemplifies these developments than the proliferation of work on the microeconomics of fertility. This has not been a theoretical development *within* demography, so much as an application of existing economic theory to fertility. But it has brought to the study of fertility a new level of theoretical explicitness and rigour.

Attention to, and controversy over, the microeconomic theory of fertility, however, has sometimes obscured a broader, deeper, and more important theoretical development, namely, the increasingly widespread tendency of researchers from a variety of disciplines, writing on a variety of demographic phenomena, to cast their argument in terms of what is essentially an individual decision making model of behaviour. These models resemble the microeconomic theory of fertility in many ways, but they arise in studies of other kinds of behaviour—migration, moving, marriage, divorce—as well as in studies of fertility. They have different intellectual origins—in sociology, social and behavioural psychology, and decision theory rather than microeconomics—and they give different emphases to different determinants of behaviour, often taking a broader, less abstract view than narrowly economic theories.

The aim of this paper is threefold: (a) to illustrate this broader theoretical development by citing several examples of decision making models from a variety of sub-fields of demography; (b) to compare and contrast these examples; (c) to suggest some unsolved problems and directions for future theoretical development.

Microdemographic Theory: Some Current Examples

The Economic Theory of Fertility

The most obvious example of the use of individual decision making models in demography is the large and rapidly growing body of literature on the microeconomics of fertility. Combining traditional theory of consumer choice and newer ideas on household production, this theory views fertility as the outcome of a couple's choice of the number of children, based on their preferences or tastes for children versus other goods, constrained by prices and income, and made so as to maximize their lifetime utility.

By now, the economic theory of fertility appears in several variant forms (Sanderson, 1976; Turchi, 1975). For present purposes, mention can be made of three.

Becker (1976, chs 1 & 9) has developed what might be called a strictly economic theory of fertility, that is, he retains three fairly stringent assumptions from traditional microeconomics, namely, assumptions of: (a) maximizing behaviour; (b) the existence of markets that 'with varying degrees of efficiency coordinate the actions of different participants . . . so that their behaviour becomes mutually consistent' (p. 5); and (c) stable tastes, that is, 'preferences are assumed not to change substantially over time, nor to be very different between wealthy and poor persons, or even between persons in different societies and cultures' (p. 5).

Leibenstein has proposed a reformulation of microeconomic theory (1978) which relaxes all three of the assumptions mentioned above: (a) behaviour is characterized as selectively rational rather than as maximizing ('. . . in some sense individuals have a choice as to how "rational" they are to behave in different contexts'—p. 21); (b) social relationships between participants in the relevant markets are considered important, in contrast to the 'usual assumption in neoclassical theory . . . that every decision making unit is independent of all other decision making units' (p. 20); (c) differing tastes. On the latter point, with specific reference to fertility, Leibenstein comments:

The alternative that we shall employ is to view populations as composed of social status groups that have different tastes, and who especially see the whole cost structure of their expenditures, including expenditures for children, from the viewpoint of vastly different preference structures. (p. 126, fn. 2)

A particularly useful formulation of the microeconomic theory of fertility for present purposes is that of Easterlin (1975; see also 1978). In his model,

a couple limits births when their motivation to do so exceeds the costs (both monetary and psychic) of limitation. Motivation is defined as the difference between the number of surviving children the couple would want if fertility control were costless (C_D) and the number they are likely to have in the absence of fertility control (C_N). That is, motivation = $C_N - C_D$.

The desired number of surviving children (C_D) is arrived at by a decision process in which the couple balance their *tastes* for children as compared to other goods against the constraints imposed by *income* and the relative *price* of children. The potential number of surviving children (C_N) is defined as a function of natural fertility, and the probability of a newborn child surviving to adulthood (mortality). Natural fertility is defined as a function of fecundity and fetal mortality, as determined by nonvoluntary factors, and by the frequency of intercourse (see Easterlin, 1975).

Easterlin argues that a couple's material aspirations and therefore their tastes for children will reflect the level of living they experienced in the parental home.

The basic structure of the Easterlin model is worth emphasizing, before taking up other decision models in other realms of demographic behaviour. The couple compare one future situation (the number of surviving children they want) and another (the number of children they are likely to have if they take no steps to limit births). If the discrepancy between these two is large enough, they are motivated to do something to remove it. But removing it by the practice of fertility control involves costs. And the couple will actually limit births only when motivation to do so is strong enough to outweigh costs.

Theories of Migration

For a look at micro-theories of migration, we turn to Lee's classic article on 'A Theory of Migration' (Lee, 1966), and to Uhlenberg (1973), where the individual decision making model is more explicit.

Lee's 1966 article sets forth a model of migration to explain observed patterns of migration in regard to volume, stream and counterstream, and characteristics of migrants. The model involves four classes of factors: (1) factors associated with the area of origin; (2) factors associated with the area of destination; (3) intervening obstacles; (4) personal factors (pp. 49–50). Factors at the areas of origin and destination may be positive (attractive), negative (repelling), or neutral from the standpoint of a prospective migrant. And though they clearly have some basis in objective reality, what is important is the individual's subjective perception and evaluation of these factors: 'It is not so much the actual factors at origin and destination as the perception of these factors which results in migration' (p. 51).

But if conditions at origin and destination as perceived and evaluated by the individual set the stage for migration—assuming the net positive balance is greater for destination than for origin—they do not assure it:

> The balance in favour of the move must be enough to overcome the natural inertia which always exists. Furthermore, between every two points there stands a set of intervening obstacles which may be slight in some instances and insurmountable in others. (p. 51)

If motivation to migrate is defined as the difference between expected net satisfactions at destination and those at origin, and costs of migration as intervening obstacles, Lee's model may be summarized by saying that migration occurs when motivation to migrate exceeds the costs of doing so.

A more explicit framework is found in Uhlenberg (1973): 'I suggest using a framework which examines *motivation* for and *constraints* upon migration for individuals as a starting point in developing migration theory' (p. 296, emphasis added).

Motivation is determined by '. . . perception of social and economic conditions at the place of residence . . .' and '. . . information (accurate or inaccurate) of conditions elsewhere' (p. 303). Motivation is a necessary but not sufficient condition for (voluntary) migration, since '. . . one cannot predict actual

behaviour until the various migration constraints have also been examined' (p. 303).

Constraints on migration include: (a) political and legal barriers; (b) economic constraints, including the direct costs of the move and those associated with liquidation of investments at origin; and (c) social constraints related to '. . . the extent of integration into and dependence upon the local community . . . and the potential for assimilation into the new community' (p. 304).

It is the balance between motivation and constraints that determines finally whether migration occurs:

> One would not expect migration to occur just because opportunities appear superior at some place other than the area of residence. . . . the perceived advantages of moving must be at least greater than the perceived economic costs involved in migration. (p. 304)

Theories of Moving

In geographical literature on moving or 'intraurban migration', considerable use has been made recently of the notion of *place utility,* and of an associated theory of individual decision making. Much of this work derives from Wolpert (1965, 1966), but for present purposes it is convenient to focus on representative formulations by Brown (for example, Brown, Horton, & Wittick, 1970).

In these formulations, moving is seen as the result of a two-step decision. First, there is a decision to seek a new residence, one of several possible responses to dissatisfaction arising from a comparison of 'experienced place utility'—satisfactions derived from one's current place of residence—with one's aspirations. The second decision concerns where to relocate. It involves 'two simultaneous endeavors—the search for available vacancies and the evaluation of each vacancy encountered'. Its outcome depends upon '. . . the comparative place utility associated with each vacancy, and the migrant household will naturally choose to *maximize* its gain in experienced place utility' (Brown, et al., p. 176).

Costs in this model include both the time and effort of the search for alternatives and the costs of a delay in moving, as well as the actual costs of moving as measured by the physical and social distance between two places of residence within the community.

The move is assumed to take place in such a way that households are '. . . minimizing migration distance and search effort . . .' (i.e. the costs of a move), and '. . . maximizing the household's gain from migration as measured by the increase in realized aspirations tempered by the search effort involved in acquiring a new vacancy . . .' (p. 180). If costs are perceived to exceed any possible increase in place utility, then a move will not take place. Some other resolution to the original dissatisfaction will be sought.

A similar model has been used by Speare (1974). A household is viewed as tied to a particular location through various bonds, whose strength '. . . is reflected in a general level of satisfaction . . .' (1974, p. 175). Satisfaction is a subjective concept, and a 'highly satisfied person will not even consider moving despite the fact that he might be better off somewhere else . . .' (p. 175). If dissatisfaction develops and crosses a threshold, a person begins to consider moving: 'he will search for alternatives and will evaluate these alternatives relative to his current location' (p. 175). Dissatisfaction does not always lead to moving, however, since there are other forms of adjustment, and because costs of moving enter in. If the costs of moving, both monetary and non-monetary, are reckoned as too high in relation to benefits, a move will not take place.

Marriage and Divorce

The decision to marry has been modelled by Becker (1976) in rigorous microeconomic terms, and by Fawcett (1976) using a psychological cost–benefit or 'value of marriage' approach. Levinger has treated divorce as a special case of the breakdown of group cohesiveness, formulating the process in terms of *attractions*, *barriers* or costs, and *alternative attractions* (1976). The marital partners are seen as comparing the net attractiveness of their current relationship with the net attractiveness of some other situation, including perhaps another relationship. When the net attractiveness of the alternative seems greater, there is motivation for marital dissolution. But now, 'barrier forces' come into play. These include legal barriers; the money costs of marital dissolution; psychic costs and feelings about effects on dependent children; and 'symbolic costs' associated with feelings of obligation toward the marital bond, religious beliefs, and pressures from primary groups or the community as a whole (p. 29). For the divorce to take place, motivation must be strong enough to overcome the barrier forces.

Fishbein on Fertility and Fertility Control

Discussions of fertility by Fishbein and his colleagues are especially interesting in the present context because of the explicit manner in which they introduce (a) subjective perceptions and evaluations of consequences of acts, and (b) normative influences on behaviour (Fishbein, 1972).

According to the underlying model, behaviour follows closely on intention to perform that behaviour and:

> . . . an individual's intention to perform any specific behavior is a function of: (1) his beliefs about the consequences of performing that behavior and the evaluative aspects of those beliefs—that is, his subjective judgment of the 'probability' or 'improbability' that performing the behavior will lead to certain consequences or outcomes, and his evaluation of those outcomes. (2) His 'normative' beliefs and his motivation to comply with those 'norms'—that is, his beliefs about what 'others' expect him to do, or say he should do, and his desire or lack of desire to do what he believes 'others' think he should do. (p. 216)

The first component is what has come to be known in social psychology as a 'value times expectancy' model of attitude. The second refers to social norms, so long as this concept is defined narrowly to refer to '. . . a specific behavioral expectation attributed to a given social agent . . .' rather than more broadly (p. 217).

Thus, '. . . there are two major factors influencing behavioral intentions and behaviour: (a) there is a personal or attitudinal influence; and (b) there is a social or normative influence.' The relative importance of the two '. . . will systematically vary across types of behavior *and* across different individuals . . .', and must be established empirically (p. 218).

Costs are contained in the model as negatively evaluated consequences of the act, including those inherently associated with its performance, and as perceived negative reactions of significant others. If the positive rewards and approval of significant others do not outweigh the negatives, then intention to act will be nil, and the act will not occur.

Similarities and Differences

A comparison of the above conceptualizations of demographic behaviour shows striking similarities.

First, they are theories of decision making, in which an individual, couple, or household is seen as making a choice, a decision to perform or not perform some demographic act, by balancing personal preferences against perceived costs and constraints. In psychological terms, they are *cognitive* rather than *behavioural* theories; in sociological terms, they are *individual* rather than *sociologistic* theories.

Second, motivation to act derives from a more or less explicit comparison by the actor of two states (situations, conditions) and the discovery of a discrepancy between them. Stated most generally, the discrepancy is between what one wants or thinks one should want on the one hand, and what is or is likely to be on the other.

Third, a specific behaviour occurs when motivation far exceeds the costs of that behaviour.

Fourth, it is assumed that the decision making process is rational, at least in some broad and minimal sense of that word. Based on information available to them about conditions of action, constraints, means, alternatives, the future, and

so forth, individuals will choose in such a way as to further their desires, tastes, values, satisfaction, happiness. In the words of the economists, they are either 'mazimizers' or at least 'satisficers' (Simon, 1957). This is not to attribute any particular, precise notion of rationality to any of the above authors, only to say that none of them emphasizes the irrational, non-rational, self-defeating, or altruistic in human behaviour.

Of the differences among the above theories, the *first* and most striking is their immediate intellectual origins, and the apparent self-consciousness with which the models of demographic behaviour are related to more general theoretical traditions. The economic theories flow directly from the standard theory of consumer choice, although each of the authors mentioned above has made distinctive modifications. Brown and Wolpert derive their basic ideas from works on decision making in managerial science and from organization theory (Cyert & Marsh, 1963; McGuire, 1964; Simon, 1963). Levinger refers to Lewin's 'field theory', to social psychological studies of group cohesiveness (Cartwright & Zander, 1960; Festinger, Schachter, & Back, 1950; Lewin, 1951), and to psychological exchange theory (Thibaut & Kelley, 1959). Fishbein builds on work by Dulany on 'propositional control' (1968), and a more general tradition of social psychological research on the relations between attitudes and behaviour (Ehrlich, 1969; Triandis, 1967; Wicker, 1969). Speare uses a cost–benefit approach and Simon's notion of 'satisficing behavior' (Simon, 1957). Of the authors reviewed above, only Lee and Uhlenberg fail to make explicit reference to a more general body of theory, perhaps another reflection of the atheoretical tradition in mainline demography.

The fact that the models derive from such disparate scientific origins makes their core similarities all the more striking.

A *second* difference lies in the theories' characterization of the extent of the actor's knowledge, the certainty with which it is held, and its validity. The economists' actor is portrayed as well informed about matters relevant to the fertility decision. In

[handwritten margin note: re creation of potential scientific theories even when there are clear shortfalls or probs of validity]

Easterlin's model, for example, there is an implied understanding of how current conditions will affect the number of surviving children, the likely costs of various methods of fertility control, and the effects of given family sizes on one's happiness and fulfillment ('lifetime utility').

For Brown, et al., by contrast, an important part of the overall decision process is a search for alternatives and the knowledge needed to evaluate them. Speare's assumption that the actor will choose the first satisfactory alternative discovered suggests lack of knowledge about objectively better alternatives. For Fishbein's actor, knowledge of consequences of one's acts is explicitly probabilistic; even highly valued or highly feared consequences will have little influence on behaviour if they are seen as highly unlikely.

In short, while all the theories envision an actor who is rational, in terms of perceptions of present and future realities, there are differences in the quality of perceptions attributed to that actor.

A *third* difference is in the extent to which the theories emphasize *adjustments other than* the particular demographic behaviour at issue. For Morris and Winter (1975, fig. 1, p. 85), the decision to move is but one of several explicit outcomes in a repetitive adjustment process. Adjustment to a perceived discrepancy between what one has and what one needs or wants or thinks one should have may take the form of a move, but it may also lead to a re-evaluation of one's needs or wants, to a modification of one's present dwelling, or even (although they do not discuss it) inertia, a 'decision' to put up with the strain for some indefinite period. In some of the other theories, the image is rather that of a threshold beyond which the only adjustment likely is the demographic behaviour at issue. In Easterlin's formulation, for example, given the right combination of potential fertility, tastes, prices, and income, fertility control seems almost inevitable. For Fishbein, too, given the right values and expectancies, including those relating to social norms, a certain course of behaviour seems determined. Neither of these formulations evoke images of an untidy decision process in which perceptions of cost lead to rationalization or to a downward revision of aspirations, an adjustment of tastes, or in which a perception of difficulties ahead may lead to an exaggerated view of one's potential resources (see Miller & Godwin, 1977).

A *fourth* difference relates to different emphases on individual choice versus conformity to social norms. For Easterlin, norms are relevant primarily insofar as they are embodied in individual tastes or in psychic costs of fertility control. At the moment of decision, the actor is largely autonomous and independent of outside pressures. For Fishbein, individual choice is only part of the matter. Actual behaviour may be just as much a result of social constraint, which may run contrary to one's individual wishes. Indeed, the balance between individual attitudes and social conformity as determinants of a specific behaviour becomes a key issue in empirical research. It can be argued that this distinction is unnecessary or even false on the grounds that ultimately individuals choose to conform or deviate with social norms and the expectations of significant others. While perhaps true at the most general level, this approach runs the risk of neglecting the role of social influences on behaviour. One merit of the Fishbein model is that it gives equal conceptual, though not empirical, weight to individual and social processes.

Discussion

The similarities in the models surveyed above suggest theoretical convergence in form and to some extent in substance.

The differences in the models suggest opportunities and a need for a synthesis and generalization. Why so many themes? Why separate theories of fertility, marriage, divorce, migration, moving? Why not one unified theory of demographic behaviour? Indeed, why a separate theory of demographic behaviour, except as a specific application of a general theory of human behaviour? It could be argued that the convergence described above, insofar as it has not systematically tapped more general work on human behaviour, has been wasteful, involving the needless reinvention of several theoretical wheels—sociologists and psychologists rediscovering rational calculation, economists rediscovering culture or social class, and so forth.

Synthesis need not involve the elimination of all differences, but at least initially only those that are accidental and superficial, often merely verbal. It would involve recognition that different models often focus on and elaborate *one part* of a full model of human behaviour (e.g. economists on prices and income, psychologists on subjective perceptions, sociologists on norms and conformity); the synthesis would attempt to combine what may well be complementary strengths.

At the same time synthesis of this sort would actually help to emphasize deeper and more important differences, whether of substance or style. By showing what is common to various models, it would put into bolder relief what is not. Becker's assumption of unvarying tastes, for example, is not just a different conceptualization of an idea common to all the models reviewed above. It is a flat contradiction of the assumption held by most social and behavioural scientists that there are systematic differences in tastes among individuals and social groups and that these often play a large part in explaining individual or group differentials in behaviour. Synthesis cannot remove such a disagreement, but only genuine theoretical or empirical advance.

Such advance seems likely to result not from an uncritical borrowing of more general theories of human behaviour from any of the disciplines, but from a borrowing that recognizes several special, though not unique, characteristics of demographic behaviour. Thus, the specific behaviours studied by demography are not repeated very often in an individual's lifetime, so that opportunities for direct learning are few. Important consequences of acts are often slow to materialize. In behavioural terms, the reinforcements of childbearing or of marriage decisions often occur when the possibility of more childbearing or another marriage no longer exists. The individual cannot so easily learn through trial and error, but must rely on the experience of others, either directly observed or embodied in culture.

In human terms, demographic choices are often what Westoff has somewhere called 'fateful choices' and their consequences for the individual are immense. What are the implications of this fact for the applicability of social psychological findings derived from laboratory experiments in which choices are both contrived and trivial?

The time span over which the direct consequences of demographic choices may be observed is vast, lasting a lifetime or even more. Do actual human beings work with the whole time frame (as suggested by economists' notions of lifetime utility), or do they foreshorten it (Homans, 1974, p. 49), and if so how and how much?

The lack of repetition in demographic behaviour and the long delay in the experience of some of its important consequences make it doubly hard for the individual to judge likely outcomes. How do individuals manage this uncertainty?

Who is the demographic decision maker? Often it is not an individual at all, or even a group unified by common interests (for example, members of a firm trying to maximize profits). Demographic actors act with, but also partly against, other demographic actors with whom they have close and enduring social ties. Hill and Hill (1976) have recently modelled the decision of a young adult to leave home in terms of the partially opposing interests of the adult and the parents. And Bagozzi and Van Loo (1978) have argued that the focus of attempts to understand and explain demographic behaviour should be precisely on those processes of social exchange and negotiation that take place *within* couples, and by implication other small units of demographic behaviour.

The scope for further theoretical and empirical work in this area is vast. The promise of further synthesis seems unlimited. Demography, compared to many sub-fields of social and behavioural science, is richly endowed with a fund of empirical generalizations, mostly at the aggregate level, for many populations and over long periods of time. If these aggregate findings could be firmly anchored in micro-theories of human behaviour, the resulting scientific structure would be impressive.

References

Bagozzi, R.P., & Van Loo, M.F. (1978). Toward a general theory of fertility: A causal modeling approach. *Demography, 15,* 301–20.

Becker, G.S. (1976). *The economic approach to human behavior.* Chicago: University of Chicago Press.

Brown, L.A., Horton, F.E., & Wittick, R.I. (1970). On place utility and the normative allocation of intraurban migrants. *Demography, 7,* 175–84.

Cartwright, D., & Zander, A. (Eds). (1960). *Group dynamics.* Evanston: Row, Peterson.

Cyert, R.M., & Marsh, J.G. (1963). *A behavioral theory of the firm.* Englewood Cliffs, NJ: Prentice-Hall.

Dulany, D.E. (1968). Awareness, rules, and propositional control; A confrontation with S–R behavior theory. In D. Horton & T. Dixon (Eds), *Verbal behavior and general behavior theory.* Englewood Cliffs, NJ: Prentice-Hall.

Easterlin, R.A. (1975). An economic framework for fertility analysis. *Studies in Family Planning, 6,* 54–63.

———. (1978). The economics and sociology of fertility: A synthesis. In Charles Tilly (Ed.), *Historical studies of changing fertility.* Princeton: Princeton University Press.

Ehrlich, H.J. (1969). Attitudes, behavior, and the intervening variables. *American Sociologist, 4,* 29–34.

Fawcett, J.T. (1976). Psychological determinants of nuptiality. In S.H. Newman & V.D. Thompson (Eds), *Population psychology: Research and educational issues.* Washington: Government Printing Office.

Festinger, L., Schachter, S., & Back, K. (1950). *Social pressures in informal groups.* New York: Harpers.

Fishbein, M. (1972). Toward an understanding of family planning behaviors. *Journal of Applied Social Psychology, 2,* 214–27.

Fishbein, M., & Ajzen, I. (1975). *Belief, attitude, intention and behavior: An introduction to theory and research.* Reading, MA: Addison-Wesley.

Hill, D., & Hill, S. (1976). Older children and splitting off. In G. Duncan & J. N. Morgan (Eds), *Five thousand families: Patterns of economic progress.* Ann Arbor, MI: Institute for Social Research.

Homans, G.C. (1974). *Social behavior: Its elementary forms* (rev. edn). New York: Harcourt Brace Jovanovich.

Lee, E.M. (1966). A theory of migration. *Demography, 3,* 47–57.

Leibenstein, H. (1978). *General X-efficiency theory and economic development.* New York: Oxford University Press.

Levinger, G. (1976). A social psychological perspective on marital dissolution. *Journal of Social Issues, 32,* 21–47.

Lewin, K. (1951). *Field theory in social science.* New York: Harper.

McGuire, J.W. (1964). *Theories of business behavior.* Englewood Cliffs, NJ Prentice-Hall.

Michelson, W. (1977). *Environmental choice, human behavior, and residential satisfaction.* New York: Oxford University Press.

Miller, W.B., & Godwin, R.K. (1977). *Psyche and Demos: Individual psychology and the issues of population.* New York: Oxford University Press.

Morris, E.W., & Winter, M. (1975). A theory of family housing adjustment. *Journal of Marriage and the Family, 37,* 79–88.

Parsons, T. (1968). *The structure of social action.* New York: The Free Press.

Sanderson, W. (1976). On two schools of the economics of fertility. *Population and Development Review, 2,* 469–78,

Simon, H.A. (1957). *Models of man.* New York: John Wiley.

———. (1963). Economics and psychology. In S. Koch (Ed.), *Psychology: A study of a science.* New York: McGraw-Hill.

Speare, A., Jr. (1974). Residential satisfaction as an intervening variable in residential mobility. *Demography, 11,* 173–88.

Thibaut, J.W., & Kelley, H.H. (1959). *The social psychology of groups.* New York: John Wiley.

Triandis, H.C. (1967). Toward an analysis of the components of interpersonal attitudes. In C.W. Sherif & M. Sherif (Eds), *Attitude, ego-involvement and change.* New York: John Wiley.

Turchi, B. (1975). Microeconomic theories of fertility. *Social Forces, 54,* 107–25.

Uhlenberg, P. (1973). Noneconomic determinants of nonmigration: Sociological considerations for migration theory. *Rural Sociology, 38,* 296–311.

Vance, R.B. (1952). Is theory for demographers? *Social Forces, 31,* 9–13.

Wicker, A.W. (1969). Attitudes versus actions: The relationship of verbal and overt behavioral responses to attitude objects. *Journal of Social Issues, 25,* 41–78.

Wolpert, J. (1965). Behavioral aspects of the decision to migrate. *Papers of the Regional Science Association, 15,* 159–69.

———. (1966). Migration as an adjustment to environmental stress. *Journal of Social Issues, 22,* 92–102.

CHAPTER 4

Illustrating Behavioural Principles with Examples from Demography: The Causal Analysis of Differences in Fertility

Lincoln H. Day

Introduction

Demographic behaviour not only offers the theorist of human behaviour and motivation a rich store of illustrative material, it also offers a high degree of intellectual challenge. This is particularly evident in behaviour giving rise to differences in fertility. But the analysis of fertility differences is useful for a further reason: if extended to a questioning of the appropriateness of the two frames of reference most commonly used in analyzing it, the analysis of fertility differences can also provide an opportunity to argue for greater use of a third frame of reference that, as a supplement to (not a replacement for) the other two, holds out the possibility of increasing understanding not only of fertility behaviour but, by implication, of various other human behaviours, as well. It is to this that I wish now to turn.

Analyzing Differences in Human Fertility

Introduction

The three general frames of reference used in seeking an understanding of the non-physiological origins of human fertility differences are: utility, normative, and what for want of a better term I shall label 'drift'. The first two have been much discussed, but the third, which I view as being potentially the

most useful, seems to have been considered, if at all, only by implication.

None of these three is entirely separable from the others; the overlap among them is, in fact, fairly substantial. Nor is any of them so robust that it can explain everything explicable in terms of either of the other two. And, if only by implication, each of the three recognizes that a particular act performed at one time can affect the alternatives available later: by foreclosing some and opening up others, or by altering the probabilities that one or another of the available alternatives will eventually be followed.

Although the differences among them are in some respects matters of mere emphasis, the normative is the most inclusive and the utility the least; while, in the degree of their dependence upon the assumption of conscious decision making, the utility model is at one end of the continuum and the drift model at the other.

The Utility Model

In its application to fertility, the utility model has received its greatest emphasis and elaboration at the hands of economists—those of the social science community whose particular expertise lies in the analysis of what has been termed the 'calculus of choice'. Implicit in this model is the assumption that people's behaviour is an expression of their preferences among available alternatives. Whether or not they realize the fact—so the utility model has it—their purchase of apples (or, for that matter, their 'purchase' of a third child, or of an interval of 30 months between successive births) indicates a preference for this particular 'commodity' over the others that may be available. Availability is defined, of course, in more than merely monetary terms: considerations regarding the expenditure of one's time are frequently introduced into analyses using this model, and, at least by implication, so also are norms and social sanctions. Norms can, in fact, sometimes be integrated into the utility model approach if penalties attending the transgression of norms are regarded as psychic costs.

The utility model is applicable to the analysis of means (including strategies) no less than ends. It has occasionally been applied in consideration of patterns of use of the various means of birth control, and also with reference to the timing of childbirth in response to such considerations as household financial status and mother's health. But for the most part its application, so far as fertility is concerned, has related to ends—particularly respecting desired numbers of children, desired intervals between successive births, and the desired age by which to have borne all of one's children.

The utility model is also applicable to analyses distinguishing between long- and short-term assessments of gains and losses. However, it has only occasionally been applied to this aspect of fertility—despite the fact that actors do, to at least some extent, make such distinctions in the course of their fertility behaviour. Judging from findings about other kinds of behaviour, in fact, actors who tend toward longterm assessments differ significantly emotionally and socially—from those who tend toward short-term assessments.

While the suitability of the utility model for the analysis of human behaviour does not depend on each individual's consciously expressing preferences among alternative 'commodities', the way the model has been applied certainly implies that this is the case. In application, the model posits a kind of rational cost-benefit assessment by the individual, first, of what is 'best' for himself or herself and, second, of the likely outcome of the various behaviours presumably available to employ toward attainment of this 'best' end. The model makes no claim that one's individual assessment of what is best for oneself will necessarily coincide with what is best for society. It is recognized that the two may, in fact, be in conflict. Occasionally it is even admitted that the individual may be in error concerning where his or her own best interests lie—whether the perspective is the long run or the short run. Nonetheless, it is at least implicit in the utility model that the individual has a genuine choice; that he or she possesses or has available:

- a range of possible behaviours (e.g. with respect to fertility, whether to become married, whether to engage in sexual intercourse at a particular time, whether to permit impregnation to take place);
- reasonably adequate means to the attainment of the behavioural goals chosen (e.g. some degree of access to means of contraception, if the choice is to prevent pregnancy; or to abortion, if the choice is to terminate pregnancy); and
- a measure of reliable information concerning the likely consequences for himself or herself of choosing one behaviour in preference to another (e.g. a reasonable idea of the respective economic costs and benefits associated with having or not having an additional child).

Just how much choice actually exists is always open to question. It is also subject to change over time and to differentiation in terms of the individual actor's experience and status (Mixon, 1980). Certainly, what is actually possible (the 'context of opportunity', in Sarver's [1983] terms) at any particular behavioural moment will be a highly significant determinant of the behaviour that takes place. Certainly, also, this fact is frequently overlooked. A 'fundamental attributional error', Ross (1977) writes, is 'the tendency for attribution to underestimate the impact of situational factors and overestimate the role of dispositional factors in controlling behavior'.

However, any society in which fertility is substantially controlled (irrespective of the actual level of that fertility—for controlled fertility is not necessarily low fertility) is arguably a society in which the extent of available choice concerning fertility is going to be fairly substantial. And yet, despite a rather frequent—and I should suggest, largely unnecessary—tendency toward mathematical expression, the proponents of the utility model in the analysis of fertility, even when they apply it to countries in which fertility is largely controlled, seldom give expression to precisely defined and measurable relations between variables. As it is for the rest of us, the nature of both the data and the variables they work with permits resort only to expressions of general probability and direction.

At some risk of overstatement, it seems to me that the conclusion to be derived from application of the utility model to the analysis of fertility reduces to little more than a truism: namely, that to the extent individuals exercise conscious control over their childbearing, they do so in terms of what they expect to gain (or avoid losing) from it; what they expect, that is, to gain from having *no more than* or *as many as* a certain number of children, what they expect to gain from *having* or *not having* a child at a particular time.

Any contribution to fertility analysis inherent in the utility model would thus seem to lie primarily in its use as a tool to specify (a) whether—and, if so, what sorts of—costs and benefits, gains and losses (both material and non-material) accrue to parents or non-parents in consequence of bearing or not bearing children; and (b) the extent to which anticipation of these gains and losses actually affects the frequency and timing of childbearing (to the extent that 'dispositional' factors hold sway, what one decides to do is determined, after all, not so much by the actual facts of the situation as by what one *thinks* those facts are [e.g. Landesman, 1981]). That something is beneficial (or harmful) is not necessarily the reason for its existence (or nonexistence).

But in this respect the yield of the utility model (at least as far as fertility is concerned) has been rather limited. Possibly because most of its proponents have been economists, there has been in its application a rather parochial concentration on essentially economic concerns: income, social security, the monetary costs of rearing and educating a child, the opportunity gained or lost for a woman to undertake employment (notable exceptions to this parochial concentration are: Hull, 1975, and Caldwell, 1976b). Yet, surely there are other than purely economic costs and benefits so associated with childbearing that they could be presumed to have some effect on the fertility decisions of parents and potential parents. What of the desire for affection and response for intellectual stimulation, for the approval of one's peers, for a sense of continuity with the past and future—or, perhaps, for simply putting an end to the incessant nagging of a mere parent hopeful of becoming a multiple grandparent? From the policy standpoint—if none other—it would seem essential to recognize the possibility that, for the parent or potential parent, the costs and benefits associated with the various patterns of childbearing might extend over a considerable range; and that only some of these costs and benefits would be even marginally economic in nature.

People doubtless weigh costs and benefits, both economic and noneconomic, to at least some degree in the course of their fertility behaviour. But the process varies widely between societies, and, within societies, it varies widely among persons of different personality types and statuses (Bonoma, 1975). Nor do the results of this weighing necessarily conform in specific instances to what an 'objective' analysis might conclude was 'appropriate' or 'rational' in the circumstances (e.g. Mamdani, 1972; Caldwell, 1976b). To the extent that people do exercise conscious control over childbearing, any non-repressive policy designed to reduce fertility would need to incorporate alternative means to the attainment of those ends presumably met by childbearing in excess of the number desired by the policy-makers (for more extended discussion of this point, see Day

& Day, 1964, ch. 10; A. Day, 1968). It would also need, in its specific provision, to take cognizance of the fact of human variation both in what might be considered costs and benefits and in the ways in which these costs and benefits might be differentially assessed and weighted.

The Normative Model

While the utility model seems almost to posit an individual apart from society and responsible to no one, the normative model emphasizes the individual's group affiliations and social roles—particularly the constraints (both prescriptive and proscriptive) that arise out of these affiliations and roles to influence individual behaviour. To the extent that people do, indeed, exercise choice, they do so within limits imposed by the social systems of which they are a part. In fact, even where one 'chooses' to act in a 'deviant' manner, that deviancy and the form it takes will be very largely a matter of social definition (Cohen, 1955, chs 3 & 5; Sprott, 1954, ch. 6).

Paradoxically, then, it is precisely the defining attribute of the utility model, namely, its emphasis on the individual—as actor, as decision maker—and its corresponding lack of emphasis on that larger setting within which individual behaviour perforce takes place, that constitutes this model's major shortcoming. Duesenberry's famous quip that economics (in this instance, the utility model) is all about how people make choices, while sociology (here, the normative model) is all about why they have no choices to make, is not, it would seem, all that wide off the mark (Duesenberry, 1960, p. 232).

The applicability of the normative model can, perhaps, be more easily understood if we think in terms of the existence of several possible behaviours in any particular instance, with these several behaviours differentially evaluated by the society—and subsectors within the society. For an illustration relating to fertility, consider the following abbreviated list of possible behaviours with respect to a particular opportunity to engage in sexual intercourse:

a) abstinence
b) intercourse with no effort to avoid conception and no intention of resorting to abortion should conception take place
c) intercourse using a moderately effective contraceptive, but with no intention of resorting to abortion should conception take place
d) intercourse using a highly effective contraceptive, but with no intention of resorting to abortion should conception take place
e) intercourse using a highly effective contraceptive, and with a willingness to resort to abortion
f) intercourse using a moderately effective contraceptive, and with a willingness to resort to abortion
g) intercourse with no effort to avoid conception, but with a willingness to resort to abortion.

While behaviours (a)–(g) represent the range of *possible* variation, behaviours (a)–(d) would represent the range of *allowable* variation in a society (or subsector of society) that strictly forbade abortion, while behaviours (c) and (d) might, in a particular instance, be the only ones to lie within that society's still more narrowly circumscribed range of *desirable* variation.

The extension and contraction of ranges of 'allowable' and 'desirable' variation respecting different types of behaviour is an important measure of the extent and direction of cultural change. While society always pre-exists for individuals—which accounts for the coercive power it has over them (Manicas, 1980)—it is also the actions of individuals that necessarily reproduce and transform society. To some extent then, the ranges of 'allowable' and 'desirable' behaviour are to be seen as always in something of a state of flux, and also as somewhat fuzzy at the edges.

Inevitably, however, what constitutes the ranges of 'allowable' and 'desirable' variation within any particular social system will vary with circumstances; for norms are specific, not universal. Norms are, moreover, specific as to both *occasion* and *social position*. In a society that proscribed abortion, for example, the range of allowable behaviour might extend to (e) in the case of an older woman or a woman already encumbered with a numerous progeny; and even to (f) and (g) in the case of a woman in demonstrably poor health or pregnant as a result of rape. No norm is universal: applicable, that is, with equal force to all persons under all circumstances.

But just as no norm is universal, so also is there no assurance that the norms of any particular social system will be logically consistent with one another. Norms in support of higher fertility (e.g. the absence of an acceptable female role alternative to that of wife and mother) may well coexist with norms in support of lower fertility (e.g. a high value attached to giving one's children a 'good start' in life in the form of schooling, land, or mobile wealth). Nor is there any reason to expect all the members of a sub-sector of the society either to adhere to essentially the same hierarchical ordering of norms or to attach essentially the same degree of importance to individual norms.

This lack of integration among norms constitutes not only a stimulus to change in the normative system but also an area—within the range of allowable variation—in which application of the utility model might afford some insight into what behaviour actually takes place. Further opportunity for a possibly fruitful application of the utility model within the normative framework is provided by role conflict. At any one time, each individual simultaneously occupies a number of social positions—wife, mother, daughter, friend, worker, Catholic . . . Each of these will have a set of behavioural prescriptions and proscriptions associated with it; each set probably incorporating some logical inconsistencies within itself, and certainly in some measure being at variance with the blueprints for behaviour associated with the various other positions. Moreover, because the positions one occupies will vary over time and with age, there is the further possibility of role conflict arising out of a lingering adherence to the norms associated with some previous position. But whatever its origin, role conflict is an area within the broader normative system where application of the utility model could be expected to bear some fruit.

But conflict with behavioural consequences can also occur among interacting individuals, and not merely among the different norms associated with an individual actor's various roles. No man is an island—not even an island in a normative sea. We are forever interacting, directly or indirectly, with others; others playing different roles, possibly marching to the beat of a different drummer, with their own personalities, their own histories, their own needs and goals. With fertility, for example, we can hardly expect husbands and wives always to be in agreement as to the number and spacing of their children, let alone as to whether or not to interrupt a particular instance of lovemaking in order to employ a contraceptive. But analysis of behaviour in terms of the influence of this sort of conflict would appear more appropriately undertaken with a perspective different from that provided by either the utility or the normative model. This perspective I have labelled 'drift'.

The Drift Model

It is one thing to note that people make conscious choices, and that they make them within a broad normative framework that establishes limits and guidelines respecting both the goals to be sought and the means appropriate to the attainment of those goals, but it is quite another to declare that conscious choosing is the characteristic form of human behaviour or, more germane to the present discussion, that it is the characteristic form with respect to the frequency and timing of childbearing. Both the utility model and the normative model put rather undue stress on such behaviour as a determinant of levels of reproduction. Surely conscious choice is present in fertility behaviour, especially if we think of conscious choice as being a matter of degree, rather than as something that either exists or does not exist in an absolute sense. But is it present to the extent implied by the users of these two models?

If use of the utility model seems often to conjure up an individual actor rather too coolly calculating the gains and losses to be anticipated from the available possibilities, use of the normative model seems frequently to present an individual actor buffeted by constant winds of social pressure and forever trimming his or her sails to conform to them. Both models need to be modified in recognition of the twin facts that: (a) most human behaviour—fertility and otherwise—entails little conscious decision making among well-defined alternatives, and (b) in any particular instance, the individual actor is ordinarily but dimly aware of why he or she is behaving in one way rather than another. Human beings may be calculating and reflective animals; there may, in fact, be 'nothing more central to, and distinctive of, human life than the reflexive monitoring of behavior' (Giddens, 1976, p. 114). But one need hardly conclude from this that all—or even most—of human behaviour is truly cognitive. There is need, in short, for a model that acknowledges the fact of behavioural 'drift'.

While the 'drift' model emphasizes rather more than either of the other two the 'ongoing', 'developmental', 'incremental' character of human behaviour—particularly the significance of interaction with others in determining its course—the single most distinguishing characteristic of this model is its emphasis on the relative ease with which individuals make the countless 'decisions' by which they influence their lives and those of others. This constant element of human behaviour is not so much denied in the utility and normative models as it is unacknowledged.

The drift model is an extension of both the utility and the normative model. As already noted, so far as conscious choice is concerned, it is at the opposite pole from the utility model: for it posits a behaviour that commences almost by accident at one or another point within the limited range of possible and allowable behaviours and then, 'guided gently by underlying influences' (Matza, 1964, p. 29) moves (but not necessarily inexorably) toward its conclusion in a manner largely imperceptible to the person doing the acting. Obviously, not all behaviour is like this and, respecting particular behaviours, the degree to which conscious choice is present will differ according to the particular psychological and social milieux occupied by individual actors. But a very high proportion of human behaviour is like this—even a very high proportion of behaviour likely to have profound long-run consequences, such as those acts (or failures to act) that result in different fertility levels.

Not only are the 'choices' one makes very much constrained by the normative setting, and adherence to norms largely unconscious, but one's 'selection' among available alternatives is ordinarily in terms of behaviours actually (or at least seemingly) but little differentiated from one another. The term 'calculus of choice', implying as it does selection among infinitely small degrees of difference, is perhaps an apter depiction of the actual process than its coiners may have originally suspected.

There are several reasons for this seemingly slight differentiation among alternatives. For one thing, the actor, in any particular instance, is unlikely to perceive that he or she has even as wide a range of choices as that provided by the normative setting and, for this reason, is likely to act within a narrower range of alternatives than normatively incumbent upon him or her. This could result from ignorance of what others in the social system would, in fact, be willing to allow; or from ignorance (originating in inexperience) of what the form and likely consequences of alternative behaviour might actually be (Mayer, 1969, pp. 291–3).

There is also the likely tendency to continue behaving in one's accustomed manner, a tendency reinforced by either a psychic comfort in doing the familiar or an actual or anticipated psychic discomfort in doing the unfamiliar. Even where one is discontented with, or has doubts about, what one is doing (or not doing) in any particular situation, acquiescence in the continuation of present behaviour would seem to come more easily than the enterprise necessary to undertake a change. Such behavioural inertia can also be reinforced by one's consciously or unconsciously seeking out—and obtaining—support for what one is doing and, conversely, avoiding what might work to discourage it, instead. For example, in trying to account for the observation that, among industrialized countries, Catholic fertility was higher where Catholics were a numerical minority than where they were a numerical majority, Day concluded:

If there is, in fact, a causal connection between [pronatalist] Catholic doctrine and Catholic [fertility], it would seem to work through an intervening variable: a variable the presence of which is indicated by the two national attributes of a relatively high level of economic development and a minority status for the Catholic population. In countries where nearly everyone else is at least nominally Catholic, and scant likelihood of real or imagined threats to Catholics as such . . . there is no need to feel threatened or at bay *as a Catholic,* and hence, no particular incentive either to seek out co-religionists for support and example, or to attach oneself more closely to the Church and its teachings on account or the slights (or worse) one feels oneself to have suffered on its behalf. (L. Day, 1968, pp. 45–6)

Behavioural inertia can also originate from one's continuing to live within essentially the same setting of supports and constraints. At the risk of being tautological, to the extent that no competing forces arise to encourage alternative behaviours, we should expect continuation of a particular setting to reinforce and encourage the persistence of those behaviours that it originally brought forth.

In a similar vein is the role of the taken-for-granted in human behaviour. It is easier to be acquiescent (or even, in some instances, positive) about a behaviour that is abundantly present; or conversely, about the absence of a behaviour of which there are hardly any examples. Even if one's perception of the situation is somewhat removed from statistical reality, a society where, say, 2 out of 3 women ultimately have at least 5 births must surely, *in that fact alone* and quite apart from any other supports there might be, provide greater encouragement (or, at least, less discouragement) to further childbearing among 4-parity women than a society in which this ratio is but 1 out of 20, instead.

But if the differences between alternative behaviours can be made to appear negligible by the way people behave—that is, by their merely continuing in accustomed ways or confining their behaviour to a narrower range than normatively necessary—there

remains the possibility that some of these differences are negligible in fact, or that they at least appear so to the actor at the time of acting. Demographic examples abound: pregnant women are not ordinarily in a constant state of decision making as to whether to continue their pregnancies; women with IUDs in place are not likely to be constantly choosing whether to leave them there; it hardly takes much calculation on one's own part to engage in behaviour appropriate to participation in, say, the marriage or labour market if one's age and class peers are so occupied; nor is having another child likely to appear such a departure from present behaviour if one's time is already taken up with the care of a young child and there are no competing activities in the offing.

Along the same lines, a perceptive student describes how women in the American setting often drift into premarital sexual experiences:

[M]ost girls in the course of their lives prior to marriage alter their moral standards and sexual behavior, generally becoming more permissive. This process can be viewed as an anticipation of marriage, as a coming to some terms with intimacy and sexuality. . . .

While many girls do manage to come to an open and unconflicted acceptance of premarital sexual intercourse, most are not likely to have begun their dating careers with this view and will have experienced uncertainty in reaching this view. . . .

The central figure of premarital sexual careers is the experience of coming to view as acceptable what was previously viewed as unacceptable, of acting in ways which are not yet acceptable to oneself, but which will come to be acceptable. (Rains, 1971, pp. 10, 12–13)

One could doubtless write in much the same way about taking on the role of a combat soldier, or of a husband, an employee, or a friend. A similar perception—by those doing the acting—of but a negligible behavioural difference is reported by Caldwell, who found that the 'demographic innovators' (i.e.

women who had consciously and successfully restricted fertility to fewer than 6 births) in Ibadan, Nigeria, in the early 1970s, while constituting only 2 per cent of the adult female population, were for the most part 'unaware that they [had] done anything unusual' (Caldwell, 1976a).

Acquisition of the behaviour associated with taking on a different role, or with altering one's behaviour in a role already being performed, is made easier by any actual or apparent similarity among the behaviours at each successive position along the range of possibilities. Yet, each of these slight (or seemingly slight) differences in behaviours possible at any particular time may ultimately lead to markedly different results: for the individual, of course, but if enough people are involved in similar behaviour, for the larger society as well (as, for example, with the cessation of childbearing at an average of but one less—or one more—child per mother).

While changes in behaviour can be analyzed in terms of any of these three models, only the drift model would seem to place much emphasis either on change itself or the manner in which change actually takes place. In application, both the utility and the normative model tend to be rather static.

Changes in fertility levels can be seen in the perspective of all three models as arising either in response to change in what may be termed 'exterior' conditions—such as employment opportunities (Easterlin, 1968) or social attitudes (Sweezy, 1971)—or in the processes of cohort succession (Ryder, 1965) and immigration. But we should not rule out as factors occurrences so little touched by any structuring process as to deserve the appellation 'chance', whether at the individual or the broader social level; nor should we rule out role conflict or the imperfect integration of norms. Childbearing is no exception to the fact that explanation of anything requires, in some degree, an explanation of everything.

Conclusion

It is recognized that in the analysis of childbearing all three frames of reference—utility, normative, and drift—can be useful. But the utility would appear in most applications to be too restrictive, while both the utility and the normative would appear to be too static, and also to imply the existence of rather more conscious rationality in human behaviour than actually exists. It is suggested that introduction of the idea of 'drift', of behaviour moving by small degrees along the continuum of possibilities—behaviour that in some instances would, of course, represent a response to utilitarian or normative considerations—does much to overcome these limitations in the other two models, and provides, also, a closer approximation to behavioural realities.

References

Bhaskar, Roy. (1978). On the possibility of social scientific knowledge and the limits of naturalism. *Journal for the Theory of Social Behaviour, 8*(1), 1–28.

Bonoma, Thomas V. (1975). A methodology for the study of individual and social choice behaviour. *Journal for the Theory of Social Behaviour, 5,* 49–62.

Caldwell, John C. (1976a). Fertility and the household economy in Nigeria. *Journal of Comparative Family Studies* (special issue).

———. (1976b). Toward a restatement of demographic transition theory. *Population and Development Review, 2,* 321–66.

Cohen, Albert K. (1955). *Delinquent boys: The culture of the gang.* Glencoe, IL: Free Press.

Day, Alice T. (1968). Population control and personal freedom: Are they compatible? *The Humanist, 29,* 7–10.

Day, Lincoln H. (1968). Natality and ethnocentrism: Some relationships suggested by an analysis of Catholic–Protestant differentials. *Population Studies, 22,* 27–50.

Day, Lincoln H., & Day, Alice T. (1964). *Too many Americans.* Boston: Houghton Mifflin.

Duesenberry, James S. (1960). Comment. In National Bureau of Economic Research, *Demographic and economic change in developed countries.* Princeton: Princeton University Press.

Easterlin, Richard A. (1968). *Population, labor force and long swings in economic growth.* New York: National Bureau of Economic Research.

Giddens, Anthony. (1976). *New rules of sociological method.* New York: Basic Books.

———. (1979). *Central problems in social theory.* London: Macmillan.

Hull, Terence H. (1975). *Each child brings its own fortune: An enquiry into the value of children in a Javanese village.* PhD thesis, Department of Demography, Australian National University, Canberra.

Journal of Political Economy (1973). *81*(2), March/April.

Landesman, Charles. (1981). Conduct and rational causation. *Journal for the Theory of Social Behaviour, 11,* 241–52.

Layder, Derek. (1981). *Structure, interaction and social theory.* London: Routledge & Kegan Paul.

Mamdani, Mahmood. (1972). *The myth of population control: Family, caste, and class in an Indian village.* New York: Monthly Review Press.

Manicas, Peter. (1980). The concept of social structure. *Journal for the Theory of Social Behaviour, 10,* 65–82.

Matza, David. (1964). *Delinquency and Drift.* New York: Wyley.

Mayer, John E. (1969). Non-observability of family life. In Jeffrey K. Hadden & Marie L. Borgatta (Eds), *Marriage and the family: A comprehensive reader.* Itasca, IL: Peacock.

Mixon, D. (1980). The place of habit in the control of action. *Journal for the Theory of Social Behaviour, 10,* 169–86.

Rains, Prudence Mors. (1971). *Becoming an unwed mother: A sociological account.* Chicago: Aldine-Atherton.

Ross, L. (1977). The intuitive psychologist and his shortcomings: Distortions in the attribution process. In L. Berkowitz (Ed.), *Advances in experimental social psychology,* vol. 10. New York: Academic Press.

Ryder, Norman B. (1965). The cohort as a concept in the study of social change. *American Sociological Review, 30,* 843–61.

Sarver, Vernon Thomas, Jr. (1983). Ajzen and Fishbein's 'theory of reasoned action': A critical assessment. *Journal for the Theory of Social Behaviour, 13,* 155–63.

Sprott, W.J.H. (1954). *Science and social action.* London: Watts & Co.

Sweezy, Alan. (1971). The economic explanation of fertility changes in the United States. *Population Studies, 25,* 255–67.

Questions for Critical Thought and Discussion

1. How does society influence the demographic behaviour of individuals? Is the individual actor completely free of societal influences? Why is there so much uniformity in the demographic behaviour of individuals in society?
2. In what ways do demographic rates (e.g. birth rate, death rate) reflect individual action?

Websites of Interest

The University of Minnesota's Center for the Study of the Individual and Society conducts theoretical and empirical studies on why and how individuals become actively involved in 'prosocial activity'—doing good toward others and for society at large. Notes on current research projects are provided on its website: http://csis.psych.umn.edu/

The World Database of Happiness is an ongoing register of scientific research on 'the subjective enjoyment of life', which is defined as 'the degree to which an individual judges the overall quality of his life-as-a-whole positively'. It brings together findings that are scattered throughout many studies, including 'three homogenous collections of research findings; two collections of distributional findings (Happiness in Nations and Happiness in Publics) and one collection of correlational findings (Correlates of Happiness)'. The project is directed by Professor Ruut Veenhoven of Erasmus University, Rotterdam: http://worlddatabaseofhappiness.eur.nl/

Social Networks is an interdisciplinary and international quarterly that publishes theoretical and empirical articles on the structure of social relations and associations that may be expressed in network form. The principal aim of the journal is to uncover the processes by which social networks emerge, evolve, and have consequences for other aspects of behaviour. A description of the journal, with a list of recent and popular articles, may be found on the publisher's website: www.elsevier.com

Further Reading

Blossfeld, Hans-Peter, & Prein, G. (Eds). (1998). *Rational choice theory and large-scale data analysis.* Boulder, CO: Westview Press.

Freud, Sigmund. (1930). *Civilization and its discontents.* New York: Norton.

Hedstrom, Peter. (1995). Rational choice and social structure: On rational choice theorizing in sociology. In B. Wittrock (Ed.), *Social theory and human agency.* London: Sage.

Jaccard, James, & Dittus, Patricia J. (2000). Adolescent perceptions of maternal approval of birth control and sexual risk behavior. *American Journal of Public Health, 90,* 1426–30.

Jorgensen, Stephen R., & Sonstegard, Janet S. (1984). Predicting adolescent sexual and contraceptive behavior: An application and test of the Fishbein model. *Journal of Marriage and the Family, 46*(1), 43–55.

Liebovitz, Arleen, Eisen, Marvin, & Chow, Winston K. (1986). An economic model of teenage pregnancy decision making. *Demography, 23*(1), 67–78.

Miller, Warren B. (1986). Proception: An important fertility behavior. *Demography, 23*(4), 579–94.

Mills, Melinda, & Trovato, Frank. (2001). The effect of pregnancy in cohabiting unions on marriage in Canada, the Netherlands, and Latvia. *Statistical Journal of the United Nations, ECE, 18,* 103–18.

Sapir, Edward. (1929). The unconscious patterning of behavior in society. In E.S. Drummer (Ed.), *The unconscious: A symposium* (pp. 114–42). New York: Knopf.

Sarver, Vernon Thomas, Jr. (1983). Ajzen and Fishbein's theory of 'reasoned action': A critical assessment. *Journal for the Theory of Social Behaviour, 13,* 155–63.

SECTION III
World Population:
Present, Past, and Future

Learning Objectives

By the end of this section, students should understand and be able to discuss the following:

- population growth trends for the more developed countries, the less developed countries, and the world overall
- world population growth patterns through history

Introduction

Notwithstanding declines in world population growth rates since the early 1970s, in absolute terms the population of the world has been increasing steadily and will continue to do so for some time into the future. According to the *World Population Data Sheet* issued by the Population Reference Bureau, the world's population reached nearly 6.9 billion in 2010. Given crude birth and death rates of, respectively, 20 and 8 per 1,000 population, there is an annual rate of natural increase of 1.2 per cent. This seems like a small rate, yet applied to the total world population, it translates into annual increase of about 82 million persons— nearly equivalent to the population of Germany. Should this rate remain constant, the population of the world will double in about 58 years.

As Table III.1 shows, rates of natural increase vary considerably across the world's regions. The more developed countries[1] are growing at an annual rate of just 0.2 per cent; at this rate, their population will double in about 350 years. The developing countries, as a whole, are growing substantially faster, with annual growth rates in the order of between 1.4 and 1.7 per cent, depending on whether or not China is included in the calculations. The poorest nations among the developing countries show a natural rate of growth of 2.3 per cent. Using the idea of doubling time, this part of the world's population is projected to double in approximately 30 years— just one generation. Not shown in Table III.1 are certain specific industrialized countries—Germany, Italy, Japan—that have been experiencing near-zero or negative natural growth rates in recent years. Certain developing countries, meanwhile, including Nigeria, Ethiopia, Congo, and Guatemala, are growing at rates above 2 per cent per year (Population Reference Bureau, 2010).

In 2010, the developing countries accounted for 81 per cent of the world's total population. (If China is excluded from this figure the proportion falls to 63 per cent.) The wide gap in average national incomes throughout the world suggests that a large proportion of the earth's population endures a standard of living that is quite distant from that enjoyed by the more developed countries. Indeed, the average income per capita of the more developed countries is almost six times greater than the average per capita income of the less developed countries, and 26 times greater than that of the least developed countries. Compounding the gravity of this situation in the less developed world are higher levels of population density. These three factors—rapid population growth, low average income, and high population density—combine to produce a situation of diminishing resources for the average citizen of less developed countries.

The world's highest crude birth rates occur in sub-Saharan Africa, where there are 39 births per 1,000 population. This figure is substantially larger than the next two highest rates, for western Asia (24) and southeastern Asia (20). Europe, North America, and eastern Asia, have the lowest birth rates in the world, all in the range of between 11 and 13 per 1,000 population. These regions also experience very low rates of natural increase.

Crude death rates show less variation across the regions. The magnitude of this measure is largest across Africa, where in some areas crude death rates are as high 20 (Zambia) and 17 per 1,000 (Zimbabwe). These high death rates are attributable to the combined effects of poverty and the devastating contribution of the HIV/AIDS epidemic.

From the Past to the Present

Throughout most of human history, the world's population comprised just a few hundred thousand individuals at most. It was not until 30,000–40,000 years ago—a very short period in broad historical terms—that the population passed the 1 million mark (Biraben, 2003). Coale (1973) has divided population history into two broad segments of time: the first, from the beginning of humanity to around 1750 CE, was a very long era of slow population growth; the second is a very recent stage of explosive

Table III.1 Demographic data for the world, more developed countries, and less developed countries, 2010

Region	Population mid-2010 (millions)	% of world total	Births per 1,000 population	Deaths per 1,000 population	RNI (%)	Population doubling time (yrs)	GNI PPP per capita 2008 (US$)	Population per km²
World	6,892	100.00	20	8	1.2	58	$10,030	51
MDCs	1,237	17.90	11	10	0.2	350	32,370	23
LDCs	5,656	82.10	22	8	1.4	50	5,150	68
LDCs less China	4,318	62.70	25	8	1.7	41	4,880	59
Least DCs	857	12.40	35	12	2.3	30	1,240	41
Africa	1,030	14.90	37	13	2.4	30	2,630	34
Sub-Saharan Africa	865	12.60	39	14	2.5	28	1,930	36
N Africa	209	3.03	26	7	1.9	37	5,370	25
W Africa	309	4.48	41	15	2.6	27	1,600	50
E Africa	326	4.73	40	13	2.7	26	1,030	51
Middle Africa	129	1.87	44	16	2.7	26	1,710	20
S Africa	57	0.83	22	13	1.0	70	9,390	21
North America	344	4.99	13	8	0.6	117	45,890	16
L. America/Carib.	585	8.49	19	6	1.3	54	10,140	28
C America	153	2.22	21	5	1.6	44	11,910	62
Caribbean	42	0.61	19	8	1.1	64	n/a	177
S America	391	5.67	18	6	1.2	58	10,150	22
Asia	4,157	60.32	19	7	1.2	58	6,000	130
Asia (excl. China)	2,819	40.90	22	7	1.5	47	5,990	126
W Asia	235	3.41	24	5	1.9	37	10,590	49
SC Asia	1,755	25.46	24	7	1.6	44	3,130	163
SE Asia	597	8.66	20	7	1.3	54	4,510	133
E Asia	1,571	22.79	12	7	0.5	140	9,080	134
Europe	739	10.72	11	11	0.0	*	25,580	32
N Europe	99	1.44	13	9	0.3	233	36,120	55
W Europe	189	2.74	10	9	0.1	700	36,440	170
E Europe	295	4.28	12	13	−0.2	350**	14,440	16
S Europe	156	2.26	10	9	0.1	700	26,740	118
Oceania	37	0.54	18	7	1.1	64	24,380	4

GNI PPP per capita 2008 ($US) is gross national income in purchasing power parity (PPP) divided by midyear population; it refers to gross national income converted to international dollars using a purchasing power parity conversion factor. International dollars indicate the amount of goods and services one could buy in the United States with a given amount of money.

'MDCs' means more developed countries; 'LDCs' means less developed countries; 'Least DCs' means least developed countries.

* means doubling time cannot be computed (division by zero).

** means number of years to reach half the current population size.

Source: Population Reference Bureau, 2010.

gains in human numbers. Coale (1973) estimates that the average annual growth rate between 8,000 BCE and 1 CE was only 0.036 per cent. Between 1 and 1750 CE, the average rate of growth rose to 0.056 per cent per year, and from 1750 to 1800 it went up to 0.44 per cent. Since the early 1800s, each successive billion of world population has arrived in less time than the previous one. It took humankind until about 1750 CE to reach a population of roughly 800 million. The world's population surpassed the 1 billion mark in 1804, topping 2 million just 126 years later in 1930, and 3 million a mere 30 years after that. The fourth billion occurred just 14 years later in 1974, the fifth billion just 13 years after that in 1987. It was in 1999—12 years later—that the earth welcomed its 6 billionth person (see Table III.2).

From the beginnings of modern human life to the start of the agricultural revolution (the Neolithic period, from about the tenth to the fifth century BCE), and through the Middle Ages (from roughly 500 to 1500 CE), repeated cycles of population growth, decline, and recovery were common, resulting from the combined effects of 'crisis mortality' (famine, pestilence, epidemic diseases), birth deficits, and subsequent birth surges (Bocquet-Appel & Bar-Yosef, 2009; Cipolla, 1962; Herlihy, 1997; Wrigley, 1969; Wrigley & Schofield, 1981). In his contribution to this volume, Jean-Noël Biraben confirms that the human population has passed through periods of abrupt upturns and downturns, though increasing over the very long term. From 400 BCE to 1 CE, population increased across all the

Table III.2 World population growth through broad historical periods and projections

Period	Estimated population at end of period	Estimated average annual growth rate (%) at end of period	Years to add 1 billion
1,000,000–8,000 BCE	8.0 million[1]	0.010[1]	
8000 BCE–1 CE	300.0 million[1]	0.036[1]	
1 CE–1750	800.0 million[1]	0.056[1]	
1804	1.0 billion[1]	0.440[1]	all of humanity
1930	2.0 billion[1]	0.540[1]	130
1950	2.5 billion[1]	0.800[1]	—
1960	3.0 billion[1]	1.700–2.000[1]	30
1974	4.0 billion[2]	2.000–1.800[3]	14
1987	5.0 billion[2]	1.800–1.600[3]	13
1999	6.0 billion[2]	1.600–1.400[3]	12
2011 (projected)	7.0 billion[2]	1.010[3]	12
2024 (projected)	8.0 billion[2]	0.850[3]	13
2045 (projected)	9.0 billion[4]	0.480[3]	21

[1] Population and range of growth rates between specified periods (adapted from Coale, 1974, and Population Reference Bureau, 2010, p. 3).

[2] Population Reference Bureau (2010, p. 3). The projected populations for 2011 and 2024 are based on "medium range" assumptions.

[3] United Nations, Department of Economic and Social Affairs, Population Division (2009: 3).

[4] Interpolated figure based on United Nations 'medium range' projection (United Nations, Department of Economic and Social Affairs, Population Division, 2009: x).

regions of the world; however, since that point, the start of the Common Era, there have been many episodes of depopulation and recovery. As Biraben notes, a sizable drop in population occurred between 1300 and 1400, from approximately 429 million to about 364 million. This decline seems to have been especially marked in China, India, and Europe. In the case of Europe, it is believed that from 1347 to 1353, between a quarter and a third of the population perished due to the plague, or Black Death (Mac Evedy & Jones, 1978).

Biraben identifies three great population surges, each associated with a major technological revolution that helped move humans away from the vulnerabilities brought on by the 'vagaries of nature' and a harsh unpredictable environment, towards a state of increasing control over nature. The first of these revolutions was the acquisition of clothing and of hunting and fishing tools during the Upper Paleolithic period (*c.* 30,000-10,000 BCE). The second technological stage of great significance to human evolution was the sedentarization of the population that occurred with the onset of agriculture, animal husbandry, and maritime navigation in the Neolithic period (*c.* 8,000–5,000 BCE). The third, and most recent, major development in the history of humanity is the industrial revolution, which began in the eighteenth century and will likely conclude sometime in the twenty-first century, as the postindustrial age spreads to all corners of the globe.

Demographic and Epidemiological Transitions

Over time, the human population has undergone two major transitions: the *demographic* and the *epidemiological*. The first of these transitions is the historical shift in birth and death rates and the consequent population explosion experienced by nations during the course of socioeconomic modernization. Occurring in tandem with this demographic development is the epidemiological transition, which involves a longterm shift in the major causes of death in the population, from a prehistoric stage (the *age of pestilence and famine*) characterized by a predominance of infectious and parasitic diseases, famine, and violence, to an intermediate stage (the *age of receding pandemics*) in which societal conditions improved significantly and life expectancy increased, to a third stage (the *age of degenerative and man-made diseases*) where the major killers are chronic/degenerative afflictions, most notably cancer and vascular diseases (Omran, 1971).

This process of concurrent demographic and epidemiological transitions is usually described as involving three successive stages: an early stage of high birth and death rates, a transitional phase of high fertility and declining death rates, and a final stage of low fertility and mortality. Throughout most of human history up until around the nineteenth century, mortality and fertility rates were both very high; however, since the difference between the two rates was small, the rates of natural increase were low. The harsh and unpredictable environment and the 'underdeveloped' social structure contributed to these extreme demographic conditions in the first stage of demographic transition. As society gained gradual improvements in agriculture and attained better standards of living, the death rate declined sharply, though fertility rates remained high. This imbalance, occurring roughly between the mid-1800s and the early part of the 1900s, was responsible for the modern rise of population (Kirk, 1996; McKeown, 1976). Gradually, as Europeans achieved greater levels of modernization and socioeconomic development, birth rates began to fall, and by 1930 mortality and fertility in most Western nations had reached historically low levels, bringing a return to low rates of natural increase. Unlike the situation throughout most of human existence, the return to low rates of population growth, marking the end of the demographic transition, was achieved by incremental control of humans over nature through industrialization, economic growth, modern science and medicine, and widespread contraception to regulate family size.

In response to the early formulations of demographic transition theory (see, for example, Davis,

1945; Landry, 1934, 1945; Notestein, 1945, 1953; Thompson, 1929, 1944), Coale (1969, 1973) undertook a major investigation to examine key propositions about the causes of the European fertility transition. Among the early propositions were suggestions that in pre-transition societies family limitation was absent; that economic development and urbanization preceded fertility decline; and that a drop in mortality occurred before longterm fertility declines. In fact, the vast and diverse body of empirical evidence uncovered by Coale failed to provide unequivocal support for any of these assumptions about the European demographic transition. For instance, one of his most important discoveries was that economic development was not a sufficient condition for fertility decline—in fact, in some national settings, fertility decline occurred first. In the course of his investigation, Coale (1973) identified three preconditions that a society must meet before it would sustain longterm fertility declines:

1. Fertility decisions must be within the calculus of conscious choice; that is, societal beliefs and norms should not forbid family planning, nor should they favour very large families.
2. Reduced fertility must be viewed by couples as economically advantageous.
3. Effective methods of fertility control must be known and be available to couples.

In some settings, only one or two of these preconditions may be present, thus explaining the persistence of high fertility (see, for example, Davis, 1963; Caldwell, 1976). For example, in some contemporary developing countries, social norms favour large families. In such cases, although methods of family planning may be available, pronatalist norms impede the widespread adoption of contraception. Moreover, in highly insecure socioeconomic environments, children represent a form of security for parents, making large families desirable.

Teitelbaum (1975) has delineated a number of important differences in the demographic histories of the West and the developing countries. For the purpose of illustration, we may turn to a few of his more salient points.

1. *The pace and source of mortality decline.* In Europe, mortality declined gradually; in contemporary developing nations, the pace of decline has been quite rapid. Whereas the sources of the improvements in the West were largely endogenous (i.e. they were developments produced from within the society), in developing countries many of the improvements have been exogenous in nature, for example, health technologies and public health programs attained through the aid of the more developed countries, including family planning.
2. *Fertility levels before the decline.* In contemporary developing nations, fertility rates, before they decline, are generally higher than at similar points in the history of the western European fertility transition.
3. *International migration as an outlet to relieve population pressure.* Western Europe was able to export tens of millions of its citizens to the Americas, Oceania, and other overseas colonies. This possibility is radically limited in contemporary developing countries.
4. *Rate of population growth.* European nations undergoing their demographic transitions rarely experienced doubling times of less than fifty years. In contrast, doubling times in some developing nations can be as low as thirty years or less. At no point in their transitions did European nations sustain growth rates found in the experience of developing countries, which even today can be near 3 per cent in some cases.
5. *Momentum for further growth.* As a result of the relatively high fertility and young age structures of developing nations, the potential for further significant population growth exceeds, by a wide margin, that of nations that have long completed the demographic transition.

The Future

In his extensive overview of the demographic transition, Lee reminds us that since about 1800, the world has seen an increase in numbers by a factor of six; he anticipates that by 2100, when the demographic transition comes to an end, the world's population will have risen by a factor of 10. Unlike the situation in the past, however, the future will see a disproportionate growth of the elderly population. This is due to fertility declines throughout the world coupled with steadily rising survival probabilities in general and in particular among those over the age of 60. For Lee, these trends raise many questions:

- Did population grow so slowly for most of human history because of the Malthusian checks of war, famine, and disease?
- Did mortality begin to decline because of medical progress, increasing incomes, or perhaps some other reason?
- What were the causes of fertility decline?
- Will fertility rates around the world continue to fall? If so, what will be the lower limit of fertility decline?
- Is humanity approaching a biological limit to life expectancy, or can we expect further advances in longevity?
- Will the rise of the elderly population be financially catastrophic for governments?
- What will be the effects of continued population growth on the ecology of the earth?

As aptly discussed by Lee, the timing of onset and the duration of the demographic transition can be especially important for developing countries, particularly from the point of view of socioeconomic development. Lee explains that some of the developing countries have benefited from a one-time 'demographic bonus', while certain others—including the world's least developed countries—are expected to pass through the 'bonus' stage within the next four decades. The demographic bonus occurs when a country has a large and youthful labour force

(because of previously high birth rates) combined with reduced rates of population growth (due to fertility declines). The result is a dramatic fall in the dependency ratio—the number of children and elderly in relation to the working-age population—producing conditions that are highly favourable to economic development. A youthful labour force that is large and expanding in relation to the number of dependants means that governments are in a better position to generate investments to safeguard the wellbeing of their population and stimulate further economic growth. The developing countries that gained a demographic bonus are those that by the 1960s and 1970s had successfully lowered their fertility rates owing to a large extent to the vigorous promotion and acceptance of family planning programs. The world's more developed countries are now out of the 'bonus' phase.

What are the foreseen consequences of the end of the demographic transition worldwide? As shown in Figure III.1, based on the United Nations' 'middle-range' set of assumptions about future changes in fertility and mortality, the earth's population is projected to reach just over 9 billion by 2050, and by 2100, this total may reach 9.5 billion before possibly starting to decline slowly. But whether and when this happens will depend heavily on future trends in fertility, especially whether it will continue to decline and, if so, at what speed (Bongaarts, 2009). Nonetheless, given past, current, and anticipated demographic developments for the world, two things seem certain: that the population will get older (in some countries more than in others), and that most of the population growth will occur in the developing countries, whose proportionate share will grow while that of the more developed countries will continue to drop (see Figure III.2).

Beyond these future demographic patterns, Lee anticipates there will be sociological changes as well, affecting such areas as family structure, retirement, health and disability, and investment patterns. As people live longer, we are faced with two contrasting possibilities: on the one hand, people may remain healthy and vigorous into their later years and may

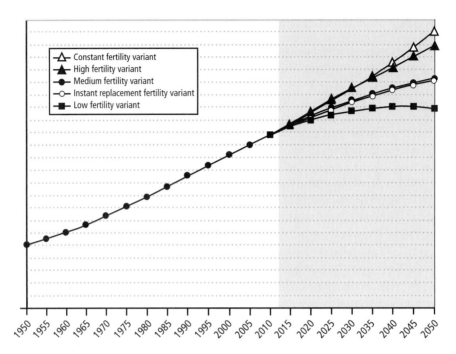

Figure III.1 Population of the world, 1950–2050, according to different projection variants (in billions)

Source: United Nations Department of Economic and Social Affairs, Population Division, 2009, fig. 1.

thus require relatively little healthcare; on the other hand, as the elderly population grows, the dependency ratio may rise, presenting serious difficulties for governments charged with providing adequate public pensions to seniors. This latter scenario may affect the age at retirement: people may need to stay in the labour force longer, past usual retirement age, either to accumulate sufficient income to see themselves through their retirement years or because of government-legislated changes to the official retirement age. Moreover, as labour forces in wealthy countries age and fertility rates remain low, governments will feel increasing pressure to allow more immigrant workers into their countries. While this may have positive economic consequences, the sociological implications of immigration will be much more complex. The less wealthy countries will face serious challenges, too. Among the most serious will be the dual problems of unemployment and underemployment, which will rise as the working-age population swells. The government must provide economically productive roles for a large labour force; failure to meet this challenge may create unsupportable conditions that could lead to unprecedented levels of social and political instability (Cleland, 1996; Potts, 2009). From a global perspective, achieving a suitable ecological balance with a population of over 9 billion may turn out to be the most challenging problem facing the planet (Short, 2009).

Note

1.   The United Nations classifies countries as follows:
   • *more developed* – all of Europe and North America, plus Australia, Japan, and New Zealand
   • *less developed* – all other regions and countries
   • *least developed* – 49 countries with especially low incomes, high economic vulnerability, and poor

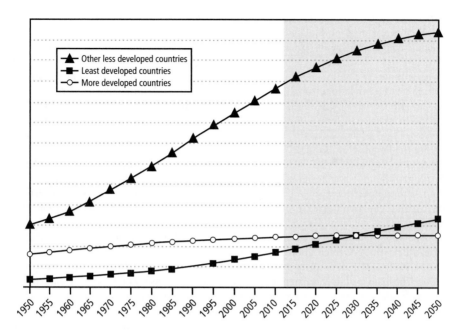

Figure III.2 Population by development region, 1950–2050, medium variant (in billions)
Source: United Nations Department of Economic and Social Affairs, Population Division, 2009, fig. 2.

human development indicators (Afghanistan, Angola, Bangladesh, Benin, Bhutan, Burkina Faso, Burundi, Cambodia, Central African Republic, Chad, Comoros, Democratic Republic of the Congo, Djibouti, Equatorial Guinea, Eritrea, Ethiopia, Gambia, Guinea, Guinea Bissau, Haiti, Kiribati, Laos People's Democratic Republic, Lesotho, Liberia, Madagascar, Malawi, Maldives, Mali, Mauritania, Mozambique, Myanmar, Nepal, Niger, Rwanda, Samoa, Sao Tome and Principe, Senegal, Sierra Leone, Solomon Islands, Somalia, Sudan, Timor-Leste, Togo, Tuvalu, Uganda, United Republic of Tanzania, Vanuatu, Yemen, Zambia).

Least developed countries are determined by three criteria:

1. *low-income criterion*—based on a three-year average estimate of the gross national income (GNI) per

capita: under $745 for inclusion; above $900 for graduation

2. *human capital status* — a composite human assets index (HAI) based on indicators of (a) nutrition: percentage of population undernourished; (b) health: mortality rate for children aged five years or under; (c) education: the gross secondary school enrolment ratio; (d) adult literacy rate)

• economic vulnerability — a composite economic vulnerability index (EVI) based on indicators of (a) population size; (b) remoteness; (c) merchandise export concentration; (d) share of agriculture, forestry, and fisheries in gross domestic product; (e) homelessness owing to natural disasters; (f) instability of agricultural production; (g) instability of exports of goods and services. (United Nations Statistics Division, www.un.org/en/development/desa/policy/cdp/ldc/ldc_definitions.shtml)

Works Cited

Biraben, Jean-Noël. (2003, October). The rising numbers of humankind. *Population and Societies, 394.* Paris: INED.

Bocquet-Appel, Jean-Pierre, & Bar-Yosef, Ofer (Eds). (2009). *The Neolithic demographic transition and its consequences.* New York: Springer.

Bongaarts, J. (2009, October 27). Human population growth and the demographic transition. *Philosophical Transactions of the Royal Society of London (Series B: Biological Sciences), 364*(1532), 2985–90.

Caldwell, John C. (1976). Toward a restatement of demographic transition theory. *Population and Development Review, 2*(3–4), 321–66.

Cipolla, Carlo. (1962). *The economic history of world population*. Baltimore: Penguin.

Cleland, John. (1996). Population growth in the 21st century: Cause for crisis or celebration? *Tropical Medicine and International Health, 1*(1), 15–26.

Coale, Ansley J. (1969). The decline of fertility in Europe from the French Revolution to World War II. In S.J. Berhman, Leslie Corsa, & Ronald Freedman (Eds), *Fertility and family planning: A world view* (pp. 3–24). Ann Arbor, MI: University of Michigan Press.

————. (1973). The demographic transition reconsidered. In *International Population Conference. Volume 1: International Union for the Study of Population* (pp. 53–72). Liège, Belgium : The International Union for the Scientific Study of Population (IUSSP).

————. (1974). The history of the human population. *The Human Population*. Special issue of *Scientific American*. San Francisco: W.H. Freeman.

Davis, Kingsley. (1945). The world demographic transition. *Annals of American Academy of Political and Social Sciences 237*, 1–11.

————. (1963). The theory of change and response in modern demographic history. *Population Index, 29*(4), 345–56.

Herlihy, David. (1997). *The black death and the transformation of the west*. Cambridge: Harvard University Press.

Kirk, Dudley. (1996). Demographic transition theory. *Population Studies, 50*, 361–87.

Landry, A. (1934). *La revolution demographique*. Paris: Sirey.

————. (1945). *Traité de demographie*. Paris: Payot.

Lee, Ronald. (2003). The demographic transition: Three centuries of fundamental change. *Journal of Economic Perspectives, 17*(4), 167–90.

Mac Evedy, Colin, & Jones, Richard. (1978). *Atlas of world population history*. Middlesex, UK: Penguin.

McKeown, Thomas. (1976). *The modern rise of population*. London: Edward Arnold.

Notestein, Frank W. (1945). Population—The long view. In Theodore W. Schultz (Ed.), *Food for the world* (pp. 36–57). Chicago: University of Chicago Press.

————. (1953). Economic problems and population change. In *Proceedings of the Eighth International Conference of Agricultural Economists* (pp. 13–31). London: Oxford University Press.

Omran, Abdel R. (1971). The epidemiological transition: A theory of the epidemiology of population change. *Milbank Memorial Quarterly / Health and Society, 49*, 507–37.

Population Reference Bureau. (2010). *World population data sheet for 2010*. Washington, DC.

Porter, Roy. (1997). *The greatest benefit to mankind: A medical history of humanity from antiquity to the present*. London: Harper-Collins.

Potts, Malcom. (2009). Where next? *Philosophical Transactions of the Royal Society B 364*: 3115–24.

Short, Roger. (2009). Population growth in retrospect and prospect. *Philosophical Transactions of the Royal Society of London (Series B: Biological Sciences), 364*, 2971–4.

Teitelbaum, Michael S. (1975, May 2). Relevance of demographic transition theory for developing countries. *Science, 188*, 420–5.

Thompson, Warren S. (1929). Population. *American Journal of Sociology, 34*, 959–75.

————. (1944). *Plenty of people*. Lancaster: Jacques Cattel Press.

Trewartha, Glenn T. (1969). *A geography of population: World patterns*. New York: Wiley.

Turner, Adair. (2009). Population priorities: The challenge of continued rapid population growth. *Philosophical Transactions of the Royal Society of London (Series B: Biological Sciences), 364*, 2977–84.

United Nations Department of Economic and Social Affairs, Population Division. (2009). *World population prospects. The 2008 revision*. New York: UN. Retrieved from http://esa.un.org/unpd/wpp2008/index.htm

Wrigley, E.A. (1969). *Population and history*. New York: McGraw-Hill.

Wrigley, E.A., & Schofield, Roger. (1981). *The population history of England, 1541–1871: A reconstruction*. Cambridge, MA: Harvard University Press.

CHAPTER 5

The Rising Numbers of Humankind

Jean-Noël Biraben

For a very long time, humankind comprised just a few hundred thousand individuals at most, and it was not until 30,000 to 40,000 years ago—almost yesterday in human history—that the population passed the 1 million mark. It has continued to grow since, reaching a billion in about 1800, and 6 billion in 1999 (see Figure 5.1). But how exactly did it get there?

Population in Ancient Prehistory

About 3 million years ago, the genus *Homo* emerged from the primates of East Africa. What set it apart was the ability to make and purposefully use tools from wood and flint, and especially its new form of social behaviour: no longer did it eat food on the spot, but took it back to a family encampment for sharing with the group. The territory occupied by these first humans, evidenced by the stone tools they have left behind, stretches over little more than 4 million square kilometres of savannah shrubland between Ethiopia and Zimbabwe.

The likely approximate size of this first human population was 100,000, probably already divided into distinct groups. They emerged just as the earth was entering an ice age, which, like any climatic change, resulted in the disappearance of many species and the emergence of new ones. Human genetic evolution was very rapid, and related mainly to the brain. Weighing less than 500 grams at the start, it added a kilogram in under 3 million years. This development of the brain gave its owners such an advantage in natural selection that at each stage, their closest rivals were eliminated. So, *Homo habilis* disappeared as *Homo ergaster* emerged, spreading throughout Africa, and thence across Europe and Asia in the form close to *Homo erectus*.

The standard method for estimating prehistoric population distribution is to attribute to a given area the population density recorded in a recent period among people of a similar culture living in a similar environment and climate. In the Paleolithic era, population distribution was much more closely linked to the size of the territory populated and to climatic variations than to the still very primitive technology. It therefore remained very sparse despite odd technical leaps like learning to control fire. The total numbers of *Homo ergaster* and *Homo erectus* may be very roughly estimated at between 500,000 and 700,000 in the Old World (Eurasia and Africa), which were the only populated areas at the time. Then, between 300,000 and 200,000 BCE (before Christian/Common era), three distinct, hominid population groups developed at the same time but far apart, separated by the oceanic rise in the last two interglacial periods: modern man (*Homo sapiens*) in Africa and southern Asia (perhaps 800,000 individuals), Neandertal man in Europe (perhaps 250,000), and Java man in Indonesia (perhaps 100,000).

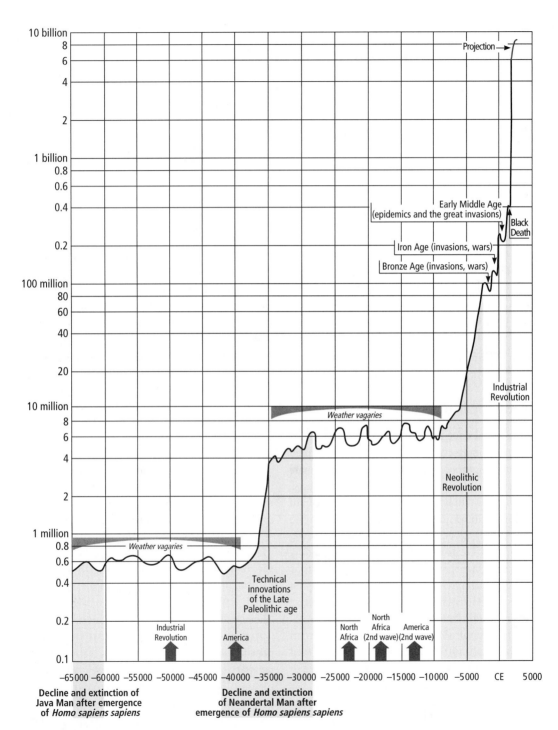

Figure 5.1 Population growth over 65,000 years

With the last ice flood, around 70,000 BCE, falling sea levels brought the three hominid population groups into contact. *Homo sapiens* asserted his supremacy everywhere, squeezing out first Java man, then Neandertal man, and spreading between 50,000 and 40,000 BCE across the as yet unpopulated continental land masses: Australia, the two Americas, and later on, Siberia. The world population at this time may have totalled 1.5 million, including 1 million in Africa and Asia, 50,000 in Australia, 300,000 in America, and 150,000 in Europe, the latter two continents being still largely under ice.

Population in Recent Prehistory

Around 40,000 BCE, technological progress in the form of the invention of the spear-thrower, the harpoon, and the bow and arrow vastly improved the efficiency of hunting and fishing, and became the main engine of population growth, especially in Europe. Taking advantage of the falling sea level, which greatly narrowed the strait between Sicily and Tunisia, two waves of Europeans migrated to North Africa, around 20,000 BCE and 12,000 BCE. They populated it from the Canaries to Egypt, stretching even as far as Arabia. At the height of the Late Paleolithic age, from 10,000 to 9000 BCE, the population of Europe may have stood at 200,000 people. The sudden climatic warming which occurred around 8650 BCE halted their growth, and the beginning of the Mesolithic era saw the population decrease then increase rapidly with the cultural adaptation to the new climate and the repopulation of northern Europe as the ice melted. Around 7000 BCE, it is likely that Europe had close to 400,000 inhabitants.

With the Neolithic era in the Middle East—from 10,000 to 8000 BCE—came sedentariness, hand-hoe cropping, stock rearing, pottery making, and navigation, resulting in a tenfold increase in the population from 0.5 to 5 million inhabitants. From Anatolia, Neolithic peoples migrated to Greece, settling near what would become Thessaloniki, and from this densely populated settlement sent out two streams that propagated Neolithic culture in Europe: one seaborne, investing the coastal regions as far as England, the other across land, moving up the Danube to occupy the central part of the continent. By around 4000 BCE, the Neolithic culture had spread across Europe, with a population of perhaps 2 million, rising so rapidly that it could well have topped 23 million by around 2000 BCE, when the advent of the Bronze Age brought a population decline.

India has been little studied. Neolithic culture first emerged there in the Punjab, which also rapidly developed into a major population centre, rising from perhaps 0.7 to 20 million between 4000 and 2000 BCE. From 8000 BCE, a Neolithic culture also developed in the Huang Ho river basin (China), extending towards the east, then the south where corn gave way to rice. Here, again, the population rose from 0.8 to 20 million between 4000 and 2000 BCE. Other Neolithic civilizations developed somewhat later in Mexico and on the high plateaus of the Andes, likewise bringing a population surge. Finally other partial civilizations developed around pottery and primitive farming from 12,000 BCE in Japan and 8500 BCE in the African Sahel. Between 6000 BCE and 4000 BCE, therefore, the Earth's population is thought to have risen from just short of 7 million to over 30 million, and may even possibly have reached 100 million by 2000 BCE.

Population Settlement from Antiquity to the Modern Day

Since antiquity, the emergence of writing in a region has been rapidly followed by enumeration of all countable things—temple workers, taxpayers, soldiers, citizens, etc. A part of these enumerations—albeit vanishingly small, and hard to interpret—have come down to us, giving us our first documentary data to work on, and thorough, methodical studies enable estimates to be made for the countries concerned, especially the Chinese and Roman empires. These are more substantive than estimates of the prehistoric eras could ever be. Unfortunately, the same copious, detailed data are not available for India, Japan, and Iran, even less so for the Americas, and are virtually non-existent for sub-Saharan Africa. It can be estimated that, after rising to 250 million in the first century CE (Christian/Common era), the total world population decreased to 200 million by the end of antiquity, around 500 CE.

Evidence for the Middle Ages is very patchy. With some gaps, China has the most consistent series; the data in Japan and India remain unreliable; European data is sparse and very disparate. What little is available for the Early Middle Ages is almost always given in hearths (families), and is not easy to interpret, especially after the Black Death in the mid-fourteenth century. From this point on, however, there is more plentiful evidence. Likewise the Middle East and North Africa. Sub-Saharan Africa, however, remains an elusive case. By the end of the fifteenth century, then, the world population was nearing an estimated half-a-billion people. From 1500 onwards, we have for almost all countries in the world, if not censuses, then at least descriptions which give some idea of population distribution; and estimates for the period from 1500 to 1700 are more reliable: China maintains its census system, India has its first documented estimates, enabling its population to be estimated at 145 million in 1595, Japan begins producing reliable documents like the shumon-aratamechô—temple registers that record all individuals living in the village or district. Not only does the number of censuses in Europe increase, but parish registers now recording Protestants as well as Catholics (but not until the eighteenth century for the Orthodox Church) enable microchanges in

population to be investigated. In the Middle East and North Africa, the Ottoman Empire's taxation returns provide increasingly reliable and usable information. Sub-Saharan Africa remains unexplored territory apart from the coastal regions, and there mainly through the slave trade, which is itself an obstacle to any significant development. As for America and Australia, while some schools of thought have placed credence in a high pre-European population density, further examination of the documents they have used reveals very significant biases in their work. It is a legitimate conjecture that the two Americas had barely more than 40-odd million inhabitants, and Australia little over 300,000. Having regard to the significant population losses of both continents, and the relatively slow increases in India and Europe, it can be mooted that notwithstanding the doubling in the Chinese population, the world population was still less than 700 million in 1700.

The population of China more than doubled in the eighteenth century, like those of Europe and the Americas, while those of Japan, India, the Middle East, and North Africa stagnated. Sub-Saharan Africa's population also stagnated, or declined, but here because of the growing slave trade. All centuries combined, the volume of captives shipped to America can be estimated at 12 million, plus 6 million to the Arab countries. The world population is estimated to have been close to 1 billion by 1800.

In the eighteenth century, humankind entered a new era—demographic transition—which was to lead it into a phase of unprecedented growth. This

Population Fluctuations down History: The Example of China

World population totals are usually given at selected dates at sufficiently long intervals between prehistory and modern times, and the curve connecting these points gives a mistaken impression of near-exponential steady growth. In fact, if the points are more tightly plotted, the curve ceases to display any regularity. Looking at the large totalities whose development has been best recorded

since antiquity, like China, Europe, the Middle East, or Japan (which between them account for over half of humankind), it is clear that these populations have fluctuated widely.

China is the best-known example, where a remarkable set of censuses dating from the start of the 'common era' have recorded quite bewildering alternating periods of growth and decline over

2,000 years (see Figure 5.2)[1]. Periods of peace, in which the spread of technical progress and trade are easier, tend to be periods of prosperity, whereas destructive periods of war, which exacerbate severe food shortages and facilitate the spread of epidemic diseases, are frequently periods of economic and demographic decline. Occasionally, but not often, epidemics may be suspected, like that of 70 CE, which slashed China's population by 30 per cent within the space of years. The description left by a doctor, Ko-Hong, suggests that this may have been smallpox, which had recently arrived in China. It is reasonable to assume that it had the same effects on the rest of the world population at the time.

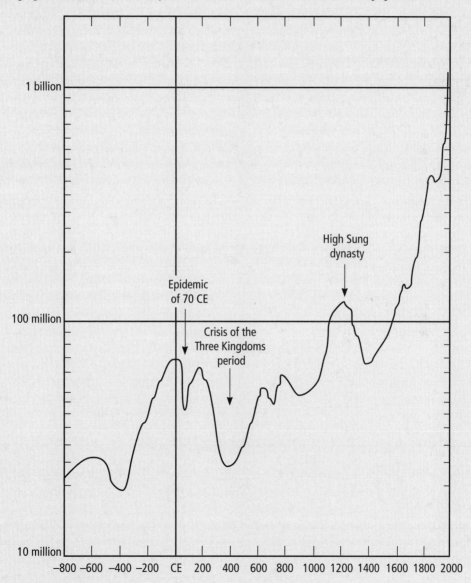

Figure 5.2 Population trends in China over 3,000 years

vital revolution, which would stretch out over three centuries, would take humankind from a high-fertility, high-mortality, pre-transitional stage into a low-fertility, low-mortality, post-transitional stage. Almost wherever it occurred, the population transition began with a mortality decline driven by economic and medical progress, while fertility remained high for one or two generations. This produced an excess of births over deaths, driving rapid population growth. Once birth limitation had become more widespread, the lower birth rate would again more or less offset the death rate and the excess would be reduced or eliminated.

Population growth in beleaguered nineteenth-century China, then still in its pre-transitional stage, slowed to a halt in mid-century, then began to fall. Although likewise still pre-transitional, Japan, India, the Middle East, and North Africa saw their populations grow by one-half. Despite the abolition of the slave trade, sub-Saharan Africa, prey to colonization and much beleaguered, continued to stagnate, whereas the Americas experienced a population boom due to mass immigration from Europe, rising fourfold in South America and eighteenfold in North America. Australia's population tripled for the same reason. Despite this migration drain, Europe, in mid-demographic transition with significantly falling mortality, would more than double its population over the century, and by 1900, the world population topped 1.6 billion.

In the first half of the nineteenth century, China's population was still stagnating, but mainly as a result of revolutions and wars. Despite conflicts, the populations of Japan, India, the Middle East, and North Africa experienced rapid growth due to mortality decline. Likewise sub-Saharan Africa, where the big endemic diseases were on the wane. Despite suffering the highest death tolls of the two world wars, and an all-round sharp drop in fertility, Europe's population increased as the result of a mortality decline. North America mirrored that trend, but to a lesser extent, due to its lesser involvement in the world wars and a steady, if reduced, flow of immigration. Likewise Australia. By mid-century, the world had 2.5 billion people. The sharp all-round mortality decline, especially from its still-high levels in the developing world, produced a growth spurt which peaked at 2 per cent a year in the 1960s. As birth limitation gained a rapid foothold in almost all countries, growth slowed, but still remains at 1.2 per cent a year today. The total world population stood at just over 6 billion in 2000. The developments described here are illustrated in Table 5.1. The figures make no pretense of accuracy; they are merely orders of magnitude. By around 2040 or 2050, the world population could be approaching 9 billion, and if fertility continues to decline, could be posting very much slower, at zero or even negative growth.

Table 5.1 World population by broad regions at different dates (millions)

Region/date	−400	CE	500	1000	1300	1400	1500	1700	1800	1900	2000
China (incl. Korea)	19	70	32	56	83	70	84	150	330	415	1,273
India (incl. Pakistan and Bangladesh)	30	46	33	40	100	74	95	175	190	290	1,320
Southwest Asia	42	47	45	33	21	19	23	30	28	38	259
Japan	0.1	0.3	2	7	7	8	8	28	30	44	126
Rest of Asia	3	5	8	19	29	29	33	53	68	115	653
Europe (incl. Russia)	32	43	41	43	86	65	84	125	195	422	782
North Africa	10	13	12	10	9	8	8	9	9	23	143
Rest of Africa	7	12	20	30	60	60	78	97	92	95	657
North America	1	2	2	2	3	3	3	2	5	90	307
Central and South America	7	10	13	16	29	36	39	10	19	75	512
Oceania	1	1	1	1	2	2	3	3	2	6	30
World	152	250	205	257	429	374	458	682	968	1,613	6,062

Reference

Cartier, M. (2002). La population de la Chine au fil des siècles. In Isabelle Attane (Ed.), *La Chine au seuil du XXIe siècle, questions de population, question de société. Collection* 'Les cahiers de l'Ined', 148, 21–31.

CHAPTER 6

The Demographic Transition:
Three Centuries of Fundamental Change

Ronald Lee

Before the start of the demographic transition, life was short, births were many, growth was slow, and the population was young. During the transition, first mortality and then fertility declined, causing population growth rates first to accelerate and then to slow again, moving toward low fertility, long life, and an old population. The transition began around 1800 with declining mortality in Europe. It has now spread to all parts of the world and is projected to be completed by 2100. This global demographic transition has brought momentous changes, reshaping the economic and demographic life cycles of individuals and restructuring populations. Since 1800, global population size has already increased by a factor of six and by 2100 will have risen by a factor of ten. There will then be fifty times as many elderly, but only five times as many children; thus, the ratio of elders to children will have risen by a factor of ten. The length of life, which has already more than doubled, will have tripled, while births per woman will have dropped from six to two. In 1800, women spent about 70 per cent of their adult years bearing and rearing young children, but that fraction has decreased in many parts of the world to only about 14 per cent, due to lower fertility and longer life.

These trends raise many questions and controversies. Did population grow so slowly before 1800 because it was kept in equilibrium by Malthusian forces? Did mortality begin to decline because of medical progress, because of rising per capita income, or for some other reason? Did fertility begin to fall

because of improved contraceptive technology and family planning programs, or were couples optimizing their fertility all along and reduced it in response to changing economic incentives? Are we approaching a biological limit to life expectancy, or can we expect to see continuing or even accelerating longevity gains? Some predictions suggest that global fertility is projected to fall to 2.0 children per woman, but in Europe it has been only 1.4 for some time, and in East Asia it is 1.8; why should we expect fertility decline to stop at 2.0? Low fertility and increasing longevity cause a dramatic change in the population age distribution, with a tenfold increase in the ratio of elderly to children. Will the societal costs of the elderly be catastrophic? In the past, there has been great concern that rapid population growth in Third World countries would prevent economic development, but most economists have downplayed these fears. Similarly, environmentalists fear that world population is already above the carrying capacity of the biosphere, while most economists are complacent about the projected 50 per cent increase in population over this century. In this paper I will describe these demographic changes in greater detail, and I will also touch on these questions and controversies.

Before the Demographic Transition

According to a famous essay by Thomas Malthus, first published in 1798, slow population growth was no accident. Population was held in equilibrium with the slowly growing economy. Faster population growth would depress wages, causing mortality to rise due to famine, war, or disease—in short, misery. Malthus called this mortality response the 'positive' check. Depressed wages would also cause postponement of marriage, resulting in prostitution and other vices, including contraception; this he called the 'preventive' check. Since population could potentially grow more rapidly than the economy, it was always held in check by misery and vice, which were therefore the inevitable human lot. Economic progress could help only temporarily since population could soon grow to its new equilibrium level, where misery and vice would again hold it in check. Only through moral restraint—that is, the chaste postponement of marriage—did Malthus believe that humanity might avoid this fate, and he thought this an unlikely outcome.

For pre-industrial Europe at least, Malthus seems to have been right. Population was held weakly in equilibrium by the positive and preventive checks. When weather, disease, or political disturbance knocked population out of equilibrium, real wages and rents reacted strongly (Lee, 1987, 1997; Lee & Anderson, 2002), and the checks brought population slowly back to equilibrium.

In western Europe in the centuries before 1800, marriage required the resources to establish and maintain a separate household, so age at first marriage for women was late, averaging around 25 years, and a substantial share of women never married (Flinn, 1981, p. 84; Livi-Bacci, 2000, pp. 99–107). Although fertility was high within marriage, the total fertility rate (TFR) was moderate overall at 4–5 births per woman (Livi-Bacci, 2000, p. 136). Mortality was also moderately high, with life expectancy at birth between 25 and 35 years (Flinn, 1981, pp. 92–101; Livi-Bacci, 2000, pp. 61–90), but this was heavily influenced by high mortality in infancy and childhood. Population growth rates were generally low, averaging 0.3 per cent per year before 1700 in western Europe, but sometimes rising above 1 per cent in the nineteenth century. In Canada and the United States, marriage was much earlier because land was abundant, and population at first grew rapidly, but then decelerated in the nineteenth century.

Outside of Europe and its offshoots, fertility and mortality were higher in the pre-transitional period, and change in fertility and mortality came later. Data on mortality or fertility are only occasionally available for Third World countries before World War II (Preston, 1980). In India in the late nineteenth century, life expectancy averaged in the low twenties and was highly variable, while fertility was 6 or 7 births per woman (Bhat, 1989). In Taiwan, the picture was similar around 1900. Widespread data on fertility for the decades after World War II confirm that total fertility rates in the Third World were typically 6 or higher. However, recent work suggests that the demographic situation in China may have been closer to the European experience than previously thought (Lee & Feng, 1999).

Although pre-transitional fertility was typically high in Third World countries, its levels were far below the hypothetical biological upper limit for a population (as opposed to an individual), which is around 15 to 17 births per woman (Bongaarts, 1978). The contraceptive effects of prolonged breastfeeding, often combined with taboos on sex while breastfeeding, led to long birth intervals and reduced fertility. Abortion was also important, and sometimes the practice of coitus interruptus had an important effect. In some settings, marriage patterns also limited fertility, although not as strongly as in western Europe.

At the aggregate level, population growth throughout the regions of the world was slow over the past millennium, but there was a puzzling similarity in long swings about the growth path, such as stagnation in the fourteenth and seventeenth centuries and more rapid growth in the fifteenth and eighteenth centuries. While exchanges of disease through exploration and trade may have played some role, global climatic change was probably the main driving force (Galloway, 1986).

Mortality Declines, Fertility Declines, and Population Growth

The classic demographic transition starts with mortality decline, followed after a time by reduced fertility, leading to an interval of first increased and then decreased population growth and, finally, population aging. I will consider these major stages in turn.

Mortality Declines

The beginning of the world's demographic transition occurred in northwestern Europe, where mortality began a secular decline around 1800. In many low-income countries of the world, the decline in mortality began in the early twentieth century and then accelerated dramatically after World War II.

The first stage of mortality decline is due to reductions in contagious and infectious diseases that are spread by air or water. Starting with the development of the smallpox vaccine in the late eighteenth century, preventive medicine played a role in mortality decline in Europe. However, public health measures played an important role from the late nineteenth century, and some quarantine measures may have been effective in earlier centuries. Improved personal hygiene also helped as income rose and as the germ theory of disease became more widely known and accepted. Another major factor in the early phases of growing life expectancy is improvements in nutrition. Famine mortality was reduced by improvement in storage and transportation that permitted integration of regional and international food markets, smoothing across local variations in agricultural output. Secular increases in incomes led to improved nutrition in childhood and throughout life. Better-nourished populations with stronger organ systems were better able to resist disease. Life expectancy is still positively associated with height in the industrial country populations, plausibly reflecting childhood health conditions (Barker, 1992; Fogel, 1994).

The high-income countries of the world have largely attained the potential mortality reductions due to reductions in infectious disease and increases in nutrition. In recent decades, the continuing reduction in mortality is due to reductions in chronic and degenerative diseases, notably heart disease and cancer (Riley, 2001). In the later part of the century, publicly organized and funded biomedical research has played an increasingly important part, and the human genome project and stem cell research promise future gains.

Many low-income populations did not begin the mortality transition until some time in the twentieth century. However, they then made gains in life expectancy quite rapidly by historical standards. In India, life expectancy rose from around 24 years in 1920 to 62 years today, a gain of .48 years per calendar year over 80 years. In China, life expectancy rose from 41 in 1950–1955 to 70 in 1995–1999, a gain of .65 years per year over 45 years. Such rapid rates of increase in low-income countries will surely taper off as mortality levels approach those of the global leaders.

There is a range of views on where mortality is headed during the coming decades. On the optimistic side, Oeppen and Vaupel (2002) offer a remarkable graph that plots the highest national female life expectancy attained for each calendar year from 1840 to 2000. The points fall close to a straight line, starting at 45 years in Sweden and ending at 85 years in Japan, with a slope of 2.4 years per decade. If we boldly extend the line forward in time, it reaches 97.5 years by mid-century and 109 years by 2100.

Less optimistic projections are based on extrapolation of trends in age-specific death rates over the past 50 or 100 years. This approach implies more modest gains for the high-income nations of the world, with average life expectancy approaching 90 years by the end of the twenty-first century (Lee & Carter, 1992; Tuljapurkar, Li, & Boe, 2000).

Oddly, some of the most pessimistic estimates of the future improvement in life expectancy come from official government projections. For example, actuaries for the US Social Security Administration project life expectancy of 83 years for 2080 (sexes combined). Their projections are in line with the views of researchers who believe that it will become increasingly difficult to achieve gains as we approach biological limits to human longevity (Olshansky & Carnes, 2001). However, past projections by official government agencies of longevity gains have been systematically too low relative to actual outcomes (Keilman, 1997; National Research Council, 2000). Indeed, old-age mortality has been declining at an accelerating rate in recent decades (Kannisto, Lauritsen, Thatcher, & Vaupel, 1994). It is at the younger ages that declines have been slower.

For a closer look at mortality trends, it is convenient to use the United Nations classification of countries according to their recent economic development status as *more developed countries, less developed countries*, and *least developed countries*. The more developed countries, with 1.2 billion people, include all of Europe, plus North America, Japan, Australia, and New Zealand. The least developed countries, with 0.7 billion, include most of sub-Saharan Africa, plus Bangladesh, Cambodia, and a few other countries. All other countries are less developed countries, including India, China, and the bulk of the world's population—4.2 billion people. One can question the relevance of using membership based on recent experience to categorize groups of countries in earlier periods or far in the future, but on net, this division seems useful.

Figure 6.1 plots global trends in life expectancy since 1950 and UN projections to 2050. For the least developed countries, life expectancy rises from 35.7 years in 1950–4 to 48.7 years in 1995–9, or .29 years per year. For the less developed countries, the increase has been from 41.8 to 65.4 years, or .52 years per year—a very rapid increase, indeed. For the more developed countries, the increase has been from 66.1 to 74.8, or .19 years per year.

While the overall increase in life expectancy is marked, two recent countervailing trends deserve mention. Figure 6.1 shows stagnation in mortality gains for the least developed countries in the 1990s, reflecting increasing mortality from HIV/ AIDS in sub-Saharan Africa. In the past 20 years,

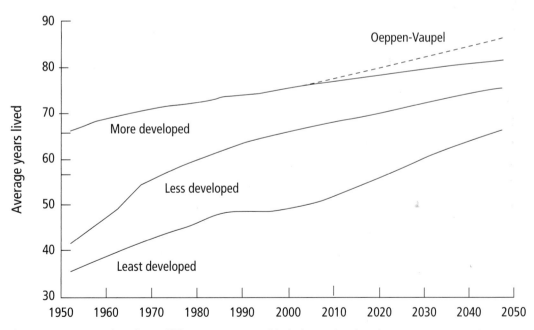

Figure 6.1 Past and projected life expectancy at birth, by major development groups, 1950–2050

Source: Historical and Middle Series forecasts are taken from United Nations (2003). Record life expectancey trend is taken from Oeppen & Vaupel (2002).

more than 60 million people have been infected by HIV/AIDS worldwide, of whom 40 million are still alive. Of these cases, only 6 per cent are in more developed countries, while in sub-Saharan Africa, HIV/AIDS has become the leading cause of death. The United Nations projects that in some African countries more than two-thirds of children aged 15 years in 2000 will become infected with HIV/AIDS before they reach 50 years of age (United Nations, 2002). For the 35 countries in Africa most affected, life expectancy at birth has been reduced on average by 6.5 years in the late 1990s, an effect that is projected to rise to 9.0 years in 2000–5.

The other main exception to the generally favourable recent trends in mortality is found in countries of eastern Europe and former territories in the Soviet Union, which have experienced stagnating or declining life expectancy over the past two or three decades, predating the difficulties of the transition to market economies. Male life expectancy in the Russian Federation is now 60 years, equal to its level in the early 1950s (United Nations, 2002) and similar to that of India; Russian women have done somewhat better.

As longevity has increased, the female advantage in life expectancy has also risen. In the more developed countries, the sex gap in life expectancy has increased from 5.0 years in the early 1950s to 7.4 years today. In the less developed countries, it has grown from 1.7 years to 3.6 years today. In the more developed countries, these trends are partly explained by the later date at which women took up smoking, and we can expect some reversal of the growing gap, as is now happening in the United States, where smoking-related deaths of women were rising rapidly from 1975 to 1995, while they fell rapidly for men (Pampel, 2002, pp. 98–9). The sex difference in life expectancy causes an increasing ratio of women to men at older ages and, combined with a younger female age at marriage, causes a disproportionate number of widows. Worldwide, there are 76 per cent more women than men at ages 80 to 89, and there are five times as many women as men over 100 (United Nations, 2002, p. 196).

Fertility Transition

Between 1890 and 1920, marital fertility began to decline in most European provinces, with a median decline of about 40 per cent from 1870 to 1930 (Coale & Treadway, 1986, p. 44). The preceding decline in mortality may have been partly responsible, although it cannot explain the timing.

Most economic theories of fertility start with the idea that couples wish to have a certain number of surviving children, rather than births per se. If this assumption holds, then once potential parents recognize an exogenous increase in child survival, fertility should decline. However, mortality and fertility interact in complicated ways. For example, increased survival raises the return on post-birth investments in children (Meltzer, 1992). Some of the improvement in child survival is itself a response to parental decisions to invest more in the health and welfare of a smaller number of children (Nerlove, 1974). These issues of parental investment in children suggest that fertility will also be influenced by how economic change influences the costs and benefits of childbearing.

Bearing and rearing children is time-intensive. Technological progress and increasing physical and human capital make labour more productive, raising the value of time in all activities, which makes children increasingly costly relative to consumption goods. Since women have had primary responsibility for childbearing and -rearing, variations in the productivity of women have been particularly important. For example, physical capital may substitute for human strength, reducing or eliminating the productivity differential between male and female labour, and thus raising the opportunity cost of children (Galor & Weil, 1996). Rising incomes have shifted consumption demand toward non-agricultural goods and services, for which educated labour is a more important input. A rise in the return to education then leads to increased investments in education. Overall, these patterns have several effects: children become more expensive, their economic contributions are diminished by school time, and educated parents have higher value of time, which raises the opportunity costs of childrearing. Furthermore, parents with higher incomes choose to devote more resources to each child, and since this raises the cost of each child, it also leads to fewer children (Becker, 1981; Willis, 1974, 1994).

Beyond these tightly modelled theories of fertility, more highly developed markets and governments can replace many of the important economic functions of the traditional family and household, like risk sharing and provision of retirement income, further weakening the value of children.

The importance of contraceptive technology for fertility decline is hotly debated, with many economists viewing it as of relatively little importance. The European fertility transition, for example, was achieved using coitus interruptus. This debate extends from the interpretation of the past to prescriptions for current policy (Gertler & Molyneaux, 1994; Pritchett, 1994; Schultz, 1994).

Figure 6.2 plots fertility for countries by development status since 1950, with United Nations projections to 2050. The transition in the more developed countries occurred before this chart begins. Thus, for the more developed countries, the chart reflects their baby booms and busts after World War II, followed by what is sometimes called the 'second fertility transition', as fertility fell far below replacement level in many industrial nations (Van de Kaa, 1987). The less developed countries began the fertility transition in the mid-1960s or somewhat later. Fertility transitions since World War II have typically been more rapid than those for the current more developed countries, with fertility reaching replacement in 20 to 30 years after onset for those countries that have completed the transition. Fertility transitions in East Asia have been particularly early and rapid, while those in South Asia and Latin America have been much slower (Casterline, 2001). In the 25 years between 1965 and 1990, their total fertility rate fell

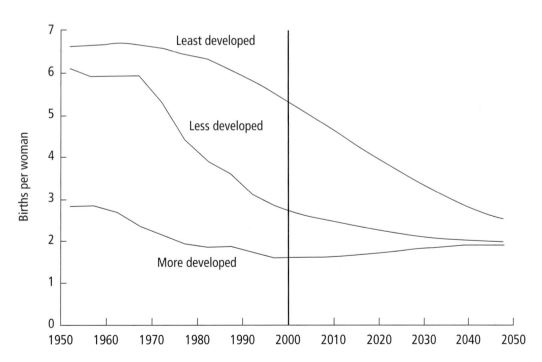

Figure 6.2 Past and projected total fertility rate by major development groups, 1950–2050

Source: Historical and Middle Series forecasts are taken from United Nations (2003).

from 6 children per woman to 3. The least developed countries started from a slightly higher initial level of fertility and started their fertility transition later. By now, it is clear that they, too, have begun the transition, and the question about their fertility transition is no longer 'whether', but rather 'how far' and 'how fast'.

Currently, 60 countries with 43 per cent of the world's population have fertility at or below the replacement level of 2.1 children per woman. Of these, 43 are more developed countries and 17 are less developed countries. The total fertility rate has fallen well below replacement for almost all the industrialized countries and for many countries of East Asia, including Taiwan, South Korea, and China.

When fertility declines, it declines most at the youngest and oldest ages and becomes concentrated in the twenties and early thirties. Currently, two-thirds of childbearing occurs between ages 20 and 35 in the least developed countries, whereas 80 per cent occurs in this age range in the more developed countries. Birth rates above age 35 are only one-seventh as high in the more developed countries as in the least developed countries and only one-fifth as high below age 20. Despite this general reduction in fertility at older ages, age at first marriage and first birth are generally moving to older ages throughout the industrial and much of the developing world. The rising age of childbearing itself depresses the total fertility rate, which is a synthetic cohort measure, below the underlying completed fertilities of generations. When the average age of childbearing stops rising, as it must sooner or later, the total fertility rate should increase to this underlying level. In many countries of Europe, women's mean age at birth of the first child has been rising by 0.1 to 0.4 years of age per calendar year in recent decades, distorting the total fertility rate downward by 10 to 40 per cent relative to the eventual completed fertility of generations (Bongaarts, 2001).

The UN fertility projections in Figure 6.2 show a continuing slow transition in sub-Saharan Africa and the other least developed countries, while fertility decline for the less developed countries decelerates as it approaches replacement level. The fertility

of the more developed countries is projected to return toward replacement levels. These projections are plausible, but fertility has proven very difficult to forecast in the past. Most of the theories of fertility, as well as the experience of the more developed countries, imply that the demand for children will continue to decline in the future. But these theories point to no natural lower bound for fertility. Nor do they provide a mechanism for fertility to respond to economic signals in such a way that population would equilibrate, as I have argued it did in the pre-industrial past. In much of the world, fertility has, in fact, fallen to levels well below the 2.1 births per woman that would just replace one generation by the next, and it is not yet clear whether it will fall farther, rebound toward replacement, or stay at current levels.

Population Growth

The combination of fertility and mortality determines population growth, as shown in Figure 6.3. The horizontal axis of the figure shows life expectancy at birth. The vertical axis shows the total fertility rate. The contours illustrate the steady-state population growth rate corresponding to constant fertility and mortality at the indicated level, where the dark contour represents zero population growth and movement toward the upper right corner indicates increasingly rapid growth. (Caveat: steady-state growth rates will differ from actual growth rates due to evolutions in the age distribution and to net migration.) On this graph, the demographic transition will first appear as a move to the right, representing a gain in life expectancy with little change in fertility and a movement to a higher population growth contour, then, as a diagonal downward movement toward the right reflecting the simultaneous decline in fertility and mortality, re-crossing contours toward lower rates of growth.

Between 1950 and 2050, the actual and projected trajectories for the more, less, and least developed countries are plotted. To add more historical depth, I have added two historical trajectories. One is a trajectory for Europe from 1800 to 1950. The end point

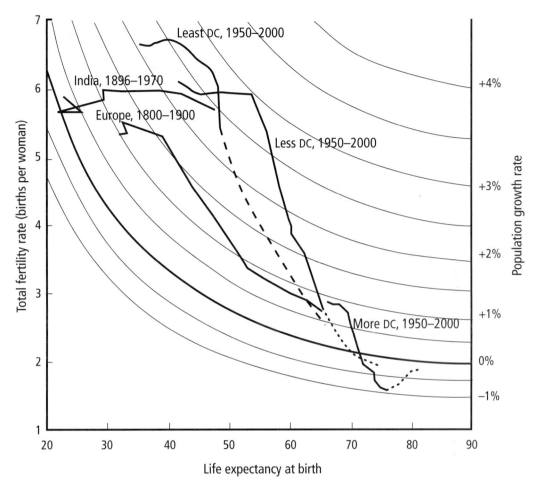

Figure 6.3 Life expectancy and total fertility rate with population growth isoquants: Past and projected trajectories for more, less, and least developed countries

Sources: Historical and Middle Series forecasts for least, less, and more developed countries are taken from United Nations (2003). Data for India are taken from Bhat (1989) for the period 1891–1901 to 1941–51, and from United Nations (2003) for the period 1950–70. Data for Europe are based on tables 6.2–6.5 in Livi-Bacci (2000) for the period 1800–1900 and Mitchell (1975) for the period 1900–50. For the period 1800–1900, European total fertility rate and e_o are derived as a population-weighted average of country-specific data. Where unavailable, these data are estimated based on regression using the crude birth rate and death rates to predict total fertility rate and e_o, respectively, for other European countries in this period. For the period 1900–50, a single series of crude birth rates and death rates for all Europe are assembled. A regression based on data from 1900 to 1950 is used to predict total fertility rate and e_o based on the crude birth rate and death rate, respectively. The growth isoquants are derived from Coale & Demeny (1983) using the Model West Female life table when the mean age of childbearing is 29.

of this trajectory in 1950 is quite close to the start point for the more developed countries. I have also added the trajectory for India from 1896 to 1970, illustrating the earlier stages of the demographic transition that are missing for the less and least developed countries before 1950.

The starting points of these demographic paths differ somewhat. India had higher initial fertility and mortality than Europe, as did the least developed countries relative to the less developed countries in 1950, which in turn had far higher mortality and fertility than the more developed countries in that

year. Except for India, the starting points all indicate moderate (for Europe) to rapid (for least and less
developed countries) population growth. But in all
cases, the initial path is horizontally to the right—
most strikingly for India—indicating that mortality
decline preceded fertility decline, causing accelerating
population growth approaching 3 per cent for the less
and least developed countries. After fertility begins
to decline, the trajectories slope diagonally down
toward the right, re-crossing contours toward lower
rates of population growth. Europe briefly attains 1.5
per cent population growth, but then fertility plun-
ges, a decline picked up after 1950 by the group, ending with population decline at 1 per cent annually.
However, the actual European population growth rate
is very near zero: slightly higher than hypothetical

steady-state growth rate due to changes in the age
distribution and in immigration. All three groups
are projected to approach the zero-growth contour
by 2050, the more developed countries from below
and the less and least developed countries from above.

There has been rapid global convergence in fertility
and mortality among nations over the past 50 years,
although important differences remain. This convergence of fertility and mortality is in marked contrast to per capita GDP, which has tended to diverge
between high-income and low-income countries
during this time. Today, the median individual lives
in a country with a total fertility rate of 2.3—barely
above the 2.1 fertility rate of the United States—and a
median life expectancy at birth of 68 years compared
to 77 years for the United States (Wilson, 2001).

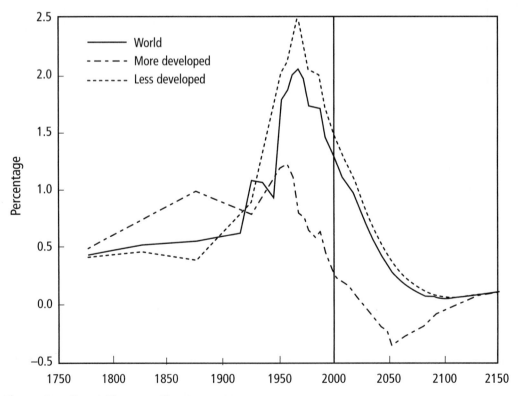

Figure 6.4 Population growth rates, 1750–2150

Source: The population growth rates are calculated as instantaneous rates based on population data. The data for 1750–1950
are taken from tables 1 and 2 of United Nations (1999) and for 1950–2150 are taken from United Nations (2000).

Actual trends in population growth rates can be seen over a longer time period in Figure 6.4. Data before 1950 for the less developed countries (which here include the least developed countries) are particularly uncertain. Population growth rates in the more developed countries rose about a half per cent above those in the less developed countries in the century before 1950. But after World War II, population growth surged in the less developed countries, with the growth rate peaking at 2.5 per cent in the mid-1960s, then dropping rapidly. The global population share of the more developed countries is projected to drop from its current 20 per cent to only 14 per cent in 2050. Longterm UN projections suggest that global population growth will be close to zero by about 2100.

Global population projections are regularly prepared by the United Nations and the US Census Bureau. The method could be described as common sense, informed by careful measurement and inspection of trends and current levels and a distillation of historical patterns of decline for fertility and mortality. The central current projections from the United Nations, which are consistent with some other global

projections, anticipate that global population will reach 8.9 billion by 2050 and just below 9.5 billion by 2100—a 50 per cent increase from its current size (see Figure 6.5). The National Research Council (2000, p. 213), based on a careful analysis of past forecasting errors by the United Nations, concluded that there is a 95 per cent probability that the actual population in 2050 will fall between 8.2 and 10.2 billion. A comparable analysis cannot be done for the 2100 forecasts, but the United Nations' high–low range extends over a very wide interval from 5.2 to 16.2 billion. This great uncertainty must be kept in mind when considering all the projections of fertility, mortality, and population size for the twenty-first century.

The population projection for the more developed countries' population is nearly flat, with population decrease in Europe and Japan offset by population increase in the United States and other areas. Most of the projected population increase takes place in the less developed countries, which gain 1.8 billion, or 43 per cent. However, the greatest proportional gain comes in the least developed countries, with their higher fertility and more rapid growth. These

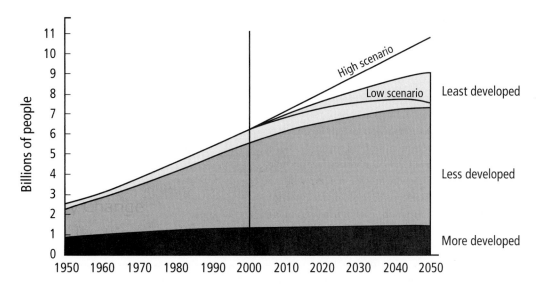

Figure 6.5 Population by major development groups, 1950–2050, with high- and low-scenario forecasts for total world population

Source: Historical and Middle Series forecasts are taken from United Nations (2003), as are high and low scenarios.

countries gain 1 billion in population, or 151 per cent. The relative shares of the three groups will change a good deal over the next 50 years.

Shifts in Age Distribution: The Last Stage of the Demographic Transition

The patterns of change in fertility, mortality, and growth rates over the demographic transition are widely known and understood. Less well understood are the systematic changes in age distribution that are an integral part of the demographic transition and that continue long after the other rates have stabilized.

A Classic Example: The Case of India

The panels of Figure 6.6 display a classic demographic transition, using India as an example. The starred points in the figures are actual data from India from 1896 to 2000. The hollow points are based on the UN projections for India's mortality, fertility, and population up through 2050. The lines in panels A and B are simple analytic functions fit to the historic fertility and mortality data, and the lines in the other panels are simulated, based on these and the initial population. In India, the pre-transitional total fertility rate is about 6 births per woman (panel A), and life expectancy is about 25 years (panel B). India's mortality decline leads its fertility decline by 50 years. The fertility transition here is slow relative to East Asia's, but similar to Latin America's. These trends interact to create a population growth rate that rose from less than 0.5 per cent per year in 1900 to more than 2 per cent per year by 1950 before starting to decline (panel C). India's total population quadrupled in the twentieth century and is projected to increase by another 60 per cent in the twenty-first century, with the growth rate of the population levelling out to near zero by 2100 (panel D).

But the focus here is on shifts in the age distribution that result from the demographic transition. These shifts can be seen in the 'dependency ratios', which take either the younger or the older

population and divide by the working-age population. For example, the child dependency ratio is the population aged 0–14 divided by the population aged 15–64. The old-age dependency ratio is usually defined as the number of those 65 and older divided by the population aged 15–64. The 'oldest-old' dependency ratio looks at those 85 years and older, divided by the working-age population. Finally, the total dependency ratio takes the sum of the population under 15 and over 55 and divides it by the population in the intermediate range of 15–64.

In the first phase of the transition, when mortality begins to decline while fertility remains high, mortality declines most at the youngest ages, causing an increase in the proportion of children in the population and raising child dependency ratios, as shown in panel E. Thus, counter to intuition, mortality decline initially makes populations younger rather than older in a phase that can last many decades and here lasts 70 years. During this phase, families find themselves with increasing numbers of surviving children. Both families and governments may struggle to achieve educational goals for the unexpectedly high number of children.

Next, as fertility declines, child dependency ratios decline and soon fall below their pre-transition levels. The working-age population grows faster than the population as a whole, so the total dependency ratio declines. This second phase may last 40 or 50 years. Some analysts have worried that the rapidly growing labour force in this phase might cause rising unemployment and falling capital labour ratios (Coale & Hoover, 1958). Others have stressed the economic advantages of having a relatively large share of the population in its working years, calling these a demographic gift or bonus (Bloom, Canning, & Malaney, 2000; Williamson & Higgins, 2001). In India, the bonus occurs between 1970 and 2015. If income per person of working age is unaffected, the decline in dependants per worker would by itself raise per capita income by 22 per cent, adding 0.5 per cent per year to per capita income growth over the 45-year span. There is considerable controversy about whether this demographic bonus really affects

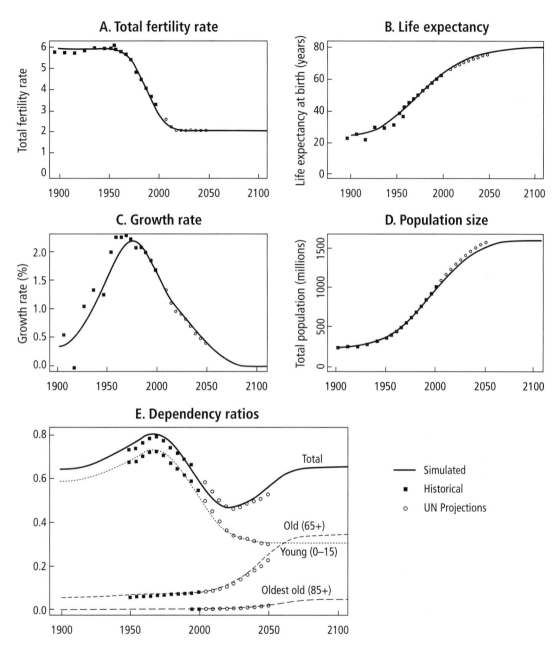

Figure 6.6   A classic demographic transition: Actual and projected for India and simulated, 1900–2100. The simulation is based on a fertility transition in which the total fertility rate follows a quintic path declining from 5.9 in 1953 to 2.1 in 2025 and a mortality transition in which the mortality index follows a sinusoidal path as e_0 increases from 24.7 in 1900 to 80.0 in 2010.

Source: Actual India data for the period 1891–1901 to 1941–51 are taken from Bhat (1989). Actual and projected data are taken from United Nations (2003).

economic development, continuing debates from the 1980s (Birdsall, Kelley, & Sinding, 2003; Kelley, 1988; National Research Council, 1986).

In a third phase, increasing longevity leads to a rapid increase in the elderly population, while low fertility slows the growth of the working-age population. The old-age dependency ratio rises rapidly, as does the total dependency ratio. In India, this phase occurs roughly between 2015 and 2060—and it would last longer if mortality decline were not assumed to cease in the simulation. If the elderly are supported by transfers, either from their adult children or from a public sector pension system supported by current tax revenues, then a higher total dependency ratio means a greater burden on the working-age population. To the extent that the elderly contribute to their own support through saving and asset accumulation earlier in their lives and dissave in retirement, population aging may cause lower aggregate saving rates as life cycle savings models and some empirical analyses suggest (Lee, Mason, & Miller, 2000; Williamson &

Higgins, 2001; but also see Deaton & Paxson, 2000). Nonetheless, even with lower savings rates, the capital labour ratio may rise, since the labour force is growing more slowly (Cutler, et al., 1990; Lee, et al., 2000). This pattern of saving and wealth accumulation may arise either through individual life cycle savings or institutional requirement, as in Singapore. The net effect would then be to stimulate growth in labour productivity due to capital deepening.

At the end of the full transitional process for India shown in Figure 6.6, the total dependency ratio is back near its level before the transition began, but now child dependency is low and old-age dependency is high. Presumably, mortality will continue to decline in the twenty-first century, so that the process of individual and population aging will continue. No country in the world has yet completed this phase of population aging, since even the industrial countries are projected to age rapidly over the next three or four decades. In this sense, no country has yet completed its demographic transition.

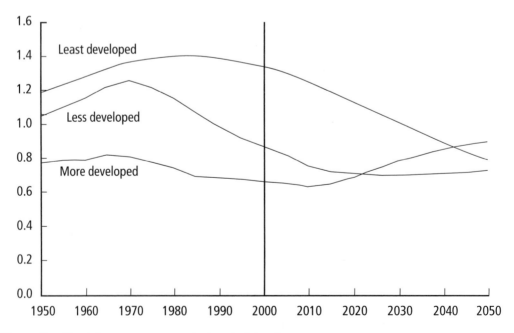

Figure 6.7 Total dependency ratio by level of development, 1950–2050

Source: Historical and Middle Series forecasts are taken from United Nations (2003).

The Transition in Age Distribution by Current Development Category

The past and projected total dependency ratios for the least, less, and more developed countries are shown in Figure 6.7; that is, the sum of the population under 15 and over 65 years divided by the population in the intermediate range of 15–64 years. Remember that even in 1950, the least developed countries had higher fertility and higher mortality than the less developed countries, and change since then has been slower for them. The least developed countries moved slowly out of the phase of rising youth dependency and entered the bonus phase around 1980. For these countries, the total dependency ratio is projected to fall sharply from 2000 to 2050. At the same time, the median age is projected to rise by nine years by 2050, from 18.1 to 27.1 years.

The less developed countries entered the bonus phase earlier, around 1970, and will finish it around 2020, after which the total dependency ratio will be rather flat, since declining child dependency will offset rising old-age dependency. Their median age is projected to rise strongly by 13.3 years between 2000 and 2050, from 25.2 to 38.5 years.

The more developed countries are out of the bonus phase and have already aged considerably. They already have the median age that the less developed countries are projected to achieve by 2050, at which time the median age in the more developed countries will have risen another 8 years to 45.2 years. The total dependency ratio in the more developed countries is projected to rise sharply over the next 50 years as their low fertility increasingly affects labour force size and the baby boom generations move into old age.

Lower Fertility or Longer Life Expectancy?

Both low fertility and longer life contribute to the aging of the population. But the implications of these factors for causes of shifts in the population distribution and for how society might react to the aging of the population are rather different.

When population aging is due to declining fertility, it raises the share of the elderly population without altering the remaining life expectancy (or the health status or vigour) of older individuals. Such aging reflects a choice made by individuals to raise fewer children. The desire to have fewer children may be related to the rise of public sector pensions, which disconnect old-age support from individual fertility, and may have played some role in causing low fertility in industrial nations. The least developed countries as a group are in the midst of their fertility decline, which is causing a substantial proportion of their population aging. While lower fertility may go with reduced total parental expenditures on children, it also raises the ratio of elderly to working-age people, other things being equal, with no corresponding improvement in health to facilitate a prolongation of working years. For this reason, population aging due to reduced fertility may well impose important resource costs on the population, regardless of institutional arrangements for old-age support.

By contrast, population aging due to declining mortality is generally associated with increasing health and improving functional status of the elderly. While such aging is putting pressures on pension programs that have rigid retirement ages, that problem is a curable institutional one, not a fundamental societal resource problem, since the ratio of healthy, vigorous years over the life cycle to frail or disabled years has not necessarily changed.

Some Consequences of the Demographic Transition

The three centuries of demographic transition from 1800 to 2100 will reshape the world's population in a number of ways. The obvious changes are the rise in total population from 1 billion in 1800 to perhaps 9.5 billion in 2100—although this longterm estimate is highly uncertain due largely to uncertainty about future fertility. The average length of life increases by a factor of two or three, and the median age of the population doubles from the low twenties to the low forties. Many more developed countries already have negative population growth rates, and the United Nations projects that the population of Europe will decline by 13 per cent between now and 2050. But many other changes will also be set in motion in family structure, health, institutions for saving and supporting retirement, and even international flows of people and capital.

At the level of families, the number of children born declines sharply and childbearing becomes concentrated into a few years of a woman's life. When this change is combined with greater longevity, many more adult years become available for other activities. The joint survivorship of couples is greatly increased, and kin networks become more intergenerationally dense, while horizontally more sparse. These changes appear to be quite universal so far. However, whether childbearing is concentrated at younger ages or at older ages and whether age at marriage rises or falls seems to vary from setting to setting, and patterns are still changing even in the populations farthest along in the transition. Parents with fewer children are able to invest more in each child, reflecting the quality–quantity tradeoff, which may also be one of the reasons parents reduced their fertility (Becker, 1981; Willis, 1974).

The processes that lead to longer life may also alter the health status of the surviving population, but the change could go either way. For example, mortality decline may permit less healthy or more disabled people to live longer, thereby raising age-specific disability rates. Alternatively, the decline in damage from trauma and disease in earlier life may reduce rates of disability and illness as people age. For the United States, it appears that years of life added by declining mortality are mostly healthy years, and that at any given age, the health and functional status of the population are improving (Costa, 2002; Freedman, Martin, & Schoeni, 2002; Manton, Corder, & Stallard, 1997). Apparently, years of healthy life are growing roughly as fast as total life expectancy, although this is more clearly true for years free of mild disability than severe. In other industrial populations, the story is more mixed, and no general conclusion is yet possible. Trends in health, vitality, and disability are of enormous importance for

the economic and social consequences of aging and, indeed, for human welfare more broadly.

The economic pressures caused by the increasing proportion of elderly are exacerbated in the more developed countries by dramatic declines in the age at retirement, which for US men fell from 74 years in 1910 to 63 years in 2000, with the average age of retirement measured by the age at which the male labour force participation rate fell below 50 per cent (Burtless & Quinn, 2001). Generous public pension programs permitting early retirement, combined with heavy implicit taxes on those who continue working, have played an important role in causing earlier retirement in industrial nations since the 1960s (Gruber & Wise, 1999). The growing ratio of retirees to workers is bringing various policy responses. So-called 'parametric' reforms tinker with pay-as-you-go defined benefit programs, reducing benefits, raising taxes, and eliminating the incentives for early retirement. Sweden, Italy, and some other European countries have introduced 'notional defined contribution' pension systems, whereby pay-as-you-go systems mimic defined contribution programs, removing incentives for early retirement and passing on to individual retirees the financial risks of rising longevity. Other countries, particularly in Latin America, are making the painful transition to funded public systems. Often these policy changes encounter fierce opposition from workers, but population aging makes reform inevitable. In some countries, like the United States, population aging will generate more intense financial pressures on publicly funded healthcare systems than it does on pension systems. Overall, the proportion of US GDP spent on government programs for the elderly is projected to nearly triple over the next 75 years without reforms, while the public expenditure shares for the children and working-age people remain relatively flat (Lee & Edwards, 2002).

Population aging, together with the growth of age-related public transfer systems for pensions, education, and health, creates massive positive fiscal externalities to childbearing. In aging high-income nations with generous support for the elderly, the net present value of future taxes minus benefits for an incremental birth may be several hundred thousand dollars (Lee, 2001), giving governments a powerful incentive to encourage childbearing. In developing countries with younger populations and public programs focused on children, the fiscal externalities and incentives run in the opposite direction (Lee & Miller, 1990).

At the international level, there are intriguing issues about the extent to which the flow of people and capital across borders may offset these demographic pressures. As population growth has slowed or even turned negative in the more developed countries, it is not surprising that international migration from Third World countries has accelerated. Net international migration to the more developed countries has experienced a roughly linear increase from near zero in the early 1950s to around 2.3 million per year in the 1990s. Of course, these net numbers for large population aggregates conceal a great deal of offsetting international gross migration flows within and between regions (United Nations, 2002). For example, prior to 1970, Europe was a net sending region, but since then it has been a net receiver of 17 million immigrants. During the past decade, repatriation of African refugees reversed the net flows from the least developed countries. But overall, while more developed countries may seek to alleviate their population aging through immigration, UN simulations indicate that the effect will be only modest, since immigrants also grow old, and their fertility converges to receiving country levels.

If inflows of immigrants only partially offset population aging, might international flows of capital offer a way of cushioning the financial effects of population aging? Population aging may cause declining aggregate saving rates, but with slowing labour force growth, capital/labour ratios will probably rise nonetheless and profit rates fall, particularly if there is a move toward funded pensions. Capital flows from the more developed countries into the less and least developed countries might help to keep the rate of return earned on pension funds from falling. However, simulations indicate that exporting capital to the younger less developed economies would help the industrial economies only slightly. The much smaller size of Third World economies would limit the gains (Borsch-Supan, et al., 2001).

Dramatic population aging is the inevitable final stage of the global demographic transition, part and parcel of low fertility and long life. It will bring serious economic and political challenges. Nonetheless, life in aging, capital-intensive, and culturally diverse high-income countries should be pleasant, provided our institutional structures are sufficiently flexible to allow us to adapt our life cycle plans to the changing circumstances and provided we are willing to pay for the healthcare and the extended retirement that we apparently want.

References

Barker, D.J.P. (Ed.). (1992). *Fetal and infant origins of adult disease.* London: British Medical Journal.

Becker, Gary. (1981). *A treatise on the family.* Cambridge, MA: Harvard University Press.

Bhat, P.N. Mari. (1989). Mortality and fertility in India, 1881–1961: A reassessment. In Tim Dyson (Ed.), *India's historical demography: Studies in famine, disease and society* (pp. 73–118). London: Curzon Press,

Biraben, Jean-Noël. (1980, December 4). An essay concerning mankind's evolution. *Population, Selected Papers*, pp. 1–13.

Birdsall, Nancy, Kelley, Allen C., & Sinding, Steven (Eds). (2003). *Population matters: Demographic change, economic growth, and poverty in the Developing World.* Oxford: Oxford University Press.

Bloom, David, Canning, David, & Malaney, Pia. (2000). Demographic change and economic growth in Asia. In Cyrus Chu & Ronald Lee (Eds), *Population change in East Asia, transition*, supplement to *Population and Development Review, 26*, 257–90. New York: Population Council.

Bongaarts, John. (1978). A framework for analyzing the proximate determinants of fertility. *Population and Development Review, 4*(1), 105–32.

———. (2001). Fertility and reproductive preferences in post-transitional societies. In Rodolfo Bulatao

& John Casterline (Eds), *Global fertility transition,* supplement to *Population and Development Review, 27,* 260–81. New York: Population Council.

Borsch-Supan, Axel, & Winter, Joachim. (2001). Aging and international capital flows. Institut für Volkswirtschaftslehre und Statistik No. 605–01.

Burtless, Gary, & Quinn, Joseph F. (2001). Retirement trends and policies to encourage work among older Americans. In P.P. Budetti, R.V. Burkhauser, J.M. Gregory, & H.A. Hunt (Eds), *Ensuring health and income security for an aging workforce* (pp. 375–415). Kalamazoo, MI: Urdohn.

Casterline, John. (2001). The pace of fertility transition: National patterns in the second half of the twentieth century. In Rodolfo Bulatao & John Casterline (Eds), *Global fertility transition,* supplement to *Population and Development Review, 27,* 17–52. New York: Population Council.

Chamie, Joseph. (2001). World population in the 21st century. Paper presented at the Twenty-Fourth IUSSP General Population Conference, Salvadore, Bahia, Brazil, August 18–24.

Coale, Ansley, & Demeny, Paul. (1983). *Regional model life tables and stable populations.* New York: Academic Press.

Coale, Ansley J., & Hoover, Edgar M. (1958). *Population growth and economic development in low-income countries.* Princeton, NJ: Princeton University Press.

Coale, Ansley J., & Treadway, Roy. (1986). A summary of the changing distribution of overall fertility, marital fertility, and the proportion married in the provinces of Europe. In Ansley. J. Coale & Susan Cotts Watkins (Eds), *The decline of fertility in Europe* (pp. 31–181). Princeton: Princeton University Press.

Costa, Dora. (2002, February). Changing chronic disease rates and long-term declines in functional limitation among older men. *Demography, 39*(1), 119–38.

Cutler, David, Poterba, James, Shemer, Louise, & Summers, Lawrence. (1990). An aging society: Opportunity or challenge? *Brookings Papers on Economic Activity, 1,* 1–73.

Deaton, Angus, & Paxson, Christine. (2000), Growth, demographic structure, and national saving in Taiwan. In Cyrus Chu & Ronald Lee (Eds), *Population change in East Asia, transition,* supplement to *Population and Development Review, 26,* 141–93). New York: Population Council.

Flinn, Michael W. (1981). *The European demographic system, 1500–1820.* Baltimore, MD: Johns Hopkins University Press.

Fogel, Robert. (1994, June). Economic growth, population theory, and physiology: The bearing of long-term processes on the making of economic policy. *American Economic Review, 84*(3), 369–95.

Freedman, Vicki A., Martin, Linda G., & Schoeni, Robert F. (2002). Recent trends in disability and functioning among older adults in the United States: A systematic review. *Journal of the American Medical Association, 288*(24), 3137–46.

Galloway, Patrick. (1986, March). Long-term fluctuations in population and climate in the preindustrial era. *Population and Development Review, 12*(1), 1–24.

Galor, Oded, & Weil, David N. (1996). The gender gap, fertility, and growth. *American Economic Review, 86*(3), 374–87.

Gertler, Paul, & Molyneaux, John W. (1994, February). How economic development and family planning programs combined to reduce Indonesian fertility. *Demography, 31*(1), 33–64.

Gruber, Jonathan, & Wise, David. (1999). *Social security programs and retirement around the world.* Chicago, IL: University of Chicago Press.

Kannisto, Vaino, Lauritsen, Jens, Thatcher, A. Roger, & Vaupel, James W. (1994). Reductions in mortality at advanced ages: Several decades of evidence from 27 countries. *Population and Development Review, 20*(4), 793–810.

Keilman, Nico. (1997). Ex-post errors in official population forecasts in industrialized countries. *Journal of Official Statistics, 13*(3), 245–77.

Kelley, Allen C. (1988, December 26). Economic consequences of population change in the Third World. *Journal of Economic Literature,* pp. 1685–728.

Lee, James, & Feng, Wang. (1999). *One quarter of humanity: Malthusian mythologies and Chinese realities, 1700–2000.* Cambridge, MA: Harvard University Press.

Lee, Ronald. (1987, November). Population dynamics of humans and other animals. *Demography, 24*(4), 443–66.

———. (1997). Population dynamics: Equilibrium, disequilibrium, and consequences of fluctuations. In Mark Rosenzweig & Oded Stark (Eds), *Handbook of population and family economics,* vol. 1B (pp. 1063–115). Amsterdam: North Holland.

———. (2001). Externalities to childbearing. In Neil J. Smelser & Paul B. Baltes (Eds), *International encyclopedia of the social and behavioral sciences,* vol. 3 (pp. 1686–9). Oxford: Elsevier.

Lee, Ronald, & Anderson, Michael. (2002). Malthus in state space: Macro economic demographic relations in English history. *Journal of Population Economics, 15*(2), 195–220.

Lee, Ronald, & Carter, Lawrence. (1992, September). Modeling and forecasting the time series of US mortality. *Journal of the American Statistical Association, 87*(419), pp. 659–71.

Lee, Ronald, & Edwards, Ryan. (2002). The fiscal effects of population aging in the US: Assessing the uncertainties. In James Poterba (Ed.), *Tax policy and the economy*, vol. 16. Cambridge, MA: MIT Press.

Lee, Ronald, Mason, Andrew, & Miller, Timothy. (2000). Life cycle saving and the demographic transition: The case of Taiwan. In Cyrus Chu & Ronald Lee (Eds), *Population change in East Asia, transition*, supplement to *Population and Development Review, 26*, 194–222. New York: Population Council.

Lee, Ronald, & Miller, Timothy. (1990). Population growth, externalities to childbearing, and fertility policy in the third world. In *Proceedings of the World Bank Annual Conference on Development Economics, 1990*, supplement to *The World Bank Economic Review* and to *The World Bank Research Observer* (pp. 275–304). Oxford: Oxford University Press.

Livi-Bacci, Massimo. (2000). *The population of Europe.* Oxford: Blackwell.

Manton, Kenneth, Corder, Larry, & Stallard, Eric. (1997, March). Chronic disability trends in elderly United States populations: 1982–1994. *Proceedings of the National Academy of Science, 94*, 2593–8.

Meltzer, David. (1992, December). Mortality decline, the demographic transition, and economic growth. PhD dissertation, University of Chicago, Department of Economics.

Mitchell, Brian R. (1975). *European historical statistics, 1750–1970.* New York: Columbia University Press.

National Research Council. (1986). *Population growth and economic development: Policy questions.* Working Group on Population Growth and Economic Development. Washington, DC: National Academy Press.

———. (2000). *Beyond six billion: Forecasting the world's population.* In John Bongaarts & Rodolfo A. Bulatao (Eds), *Panel on population projections.* Washington, DC: National Academy Press.

Nerlove, Marc. (1974). Household and economy: Toward a new theory of population and economic growth. *Journal of Political Economy, 82*(2), 5200–18.

Oeppen, Jim, & Vaupel, James. (2002). Broken limits to life expectancy. *Science, 296*(5570), 1029–30.

Olshansky, S. Jay, & Carnes, Bruce A. (2001). *The quest for immortality.* New York: W.W. Norton & Company.

Pampel, Fred. (2002, March). Cigarette use and the narrowing sex differential in mortality. *Population and Development Review, 28*(1), 77–104.

Preston, Sam. (1980). Causes and consequences of mortality declines in less developed countries during the twentieth century. In Richard Easterlin (Ed.), *Population and economic change in developing countries* (pp. 289–360). Chicago, IL: University of Chicago Press.

Pritchett, Lant H. (1994, March). Desired fertility and the impact of population policies. *Population and Development Review, 20*(1), 1–55.

Riley, James. (2001). *Rising life expectancy: A global history.* Cambridge, MA: Cambridge University Press.

Schultz, Paul. (1994, May). Human capital, family planning, and their effects on population growth. *American Economic Review, 84*(2), 255–60.

Tuljapurkar, S., Li, N., & Boe, C. (2000, June). A universal pattern of mortality decline in the G7 countries. *Nature, 15*(405), 789–92.

United Nations. (2002). *World population prospects: The 2000 revision. Volume 3 analytical report.* Sales No. E.01.XIII.20.

United Nations, Population Division. (1999). *The world at six billion.* New York: United Nations.

———. (2000). *Long-range world population projections: Based on the 1998 revision.* CD-ROM. New York: United Nations.

———. (2001). *World population prospects: The 2000 revision. Disk 2: Extensive set.* CD-ROM. New York: United Nations.

———. (2003). *World population prospects: The 2002 revision.* Retrieved from www.un.org/popin/data.html

van de Kaa, Dirk. (1987). Europe's second demographic transition. *Population Bulletin, 42*(1), 1–57.

Williamson, Jeffrey, & Higgins, Matthew. (2001). The accumulation and demography connection in East Asia. In Andrew Mason (Ed.), *Population change and economic development in East Asia* (pp. 123–54). Stanford, CA: Stanford University Press.

Willis, Robert. (1974). A new approach to the economic theory of fertility behavior. In T.W. Schultz (Ed.), *The economics of the family* (pp. 14–25). Chicago, IL: University of Chicago Press.

———. (1994). Economic analysis of fertility: Microfoundations and aggregate implications. In Kerstin Lindahl Kiessling & Hans Landberg (Eds), *Population and economic development and the environment* (pp. 139–72). Oxford: Oxford University Press.

Wilson, Chris. (2001). On the scale of global demographic convergence 1950–2000. *Population and development review, 27*(1), 153–72.

Basic Demographic Measures

1. Doubling Time of Population

In the absence of migration, a population will grow if the birth rate exceeds the death rate. The difference between these two rates is the rate of natural increase (RNI). The RNI can be used to calculate the doubling time of population. The greater the value of the RNI, the fewer years it would take for a population to double its size, assuming the RNI remains constant and there is no in- or out-migration. The lower the value of the RNI, the greater the doubling time of the population. A simple formula for calculating doubling time is the 'law of seventy', which is expressed as follows:

$$\text{doubling time (years)} = \frac{70}{\text{RNI}}$$

Therefore, if the RNI is 2 per cent, the doubling time will be approximately 70/2.0 = 35 years. If the RNI is 1.5 per cent, the doubling time will be approximately 47 years. As Table III.3 shows, there is a clear inverse nonlinear relationship between the rate of natural increase and the doubling time.

Table III.3 Doubling time (years) for various RNIS

RNI (% per annum)	Doubling time (years)
0.5	140
1.0	70
2.0	35
3.0	23
4.0	17
5.0	14
7.0	10
10.0	7

When a population's RNI is negative, it is in decline. One way to express this is through the concept of 'half life'—that is, how many years would it take for the population to reduce to one-half of its current size, assuming the RNI remained constant. The formula is:

$$\frac{\ln 0.5}{r}$$

where ln means 'natural logarithm', and r is the rate of natural increase.

For example, if r is −0.3 per cent, then according to this formula, the number of years for the world's population to reduce by one-half of its current size, assuming this RNI remained constant, would be:

$$\frac{-0.69315}{-0.003} = 231 \text{ years}$$

2. Dependency Ratio

The dependency ratio is a measure of the number of youth and elderly in the population in proportion to the number of people in the working ages. This can be expressed as follows:

$$Dependency\ Ratio = \frac{P_{0-14} - P_{65+}}{P_{15-64}} \times 100$$

where P is population.

Questions for Critical Thought

1. In what ways are historical changes in population growth and the health of the population inter-related?

2. Given the varying patterns of population growth throughout the history of the developed and developing nations, what is the future of contemporary countries of the developing world with respect not just to their demography but to their social, economic, and sociopolitical prospects?

3. What are some of the major sociological consequences of a world increasingly divided along demographic and socioeconomic dimensions?

Websites of Interest

The United Nations Population Division has an important database on population for countries, regions, and the world overall. It may be found online via the UN's website: http://esa.un.org/unpd/wpp/unpp/panel_indicators.htm

The *United States Bureau of the Census* population clock gives continuous updates on the population of the United States and the world: www.census.gov/main/www/popclock.html Statistics Canada maintains a population clock for Canada, as well as for each province and territory: www.statcan.gc.ca/ig-gi/pop-ca-eng.htm

The *Population Reference Bureau* (PRB) is one of the leading demographic institutions in the world. It publishes the annual *World Population Data Sheet* and Population Bulletins on various demographic topics, all available on its website: www.prb.org

Further Reading

Carr-Saunders, A.M. (1964). *World population: Past growth and present trends* (2nd edn). London: Frank Cass.

Chesnais, Jean-Claude. (1992). *The demographic transition: Stages, patterns, and implications*. Oxford: Clarendon Press.

Crenshaw, Edward M., Christenson, Mathew, & Oakey, Doyle Ray. (2000). Demographic transition in ecological perspective. *American Sociological Review, 65*(3), 375–91.

Discover Magazine. (2010, Summer). *Discover Presents. Origins: Are we still evolving?* (special issue).

Goldewijk, Kees K. (2005). Three centuries of global population growth: A spatial referenced population (density) database for 1700–2000. *Population and Environment, 26*(4), 343–67.

National Geographic. (2010, November 22). *State of the Earth 2010* (collector's edn).

Richerson, Peter J., Boyd, Robert, & Bettinger, Robert L. (2009). Cultural innovations and demographic change. *Human Biology, 81*(2–3), 211–35.

Richerson, Peter J., & Boyd, Robert. (1998). Homage to Malthus, Ricardo, and Boserup: Toward a general theory of population, economic growth, environmental deterioration, wealth, and poverty. *Human Ecological Review, 4,* 85–90.

Scientific American. (2009, June). *Earth 3.0. Population and Sustainability.*

Scientific American. (2005, September). *Crossroads for Planet Earth.*

Wrigley, E. Anthony. (2004). *Poverty, progress, and population.* Cambridge: Cambridge University Press.

SECTION IV
Age–Sex Composition

Learning Objectives

By the end of this section, students should understand and be able to discuss the following:

- the importance of age and sex in demographic processes
- how age composition may be viewed as a key factor in social change
- the demographic determinants of age composition.

Introduction

All demographic phenomena are either directly or indirectly associated with age and sex. Birth, death, and migration—the three key demographic processes—vary strongly with these two variables. Age and sex are also factors in the incidence of many other demographic processes, including cohabitation, marriage, divorce, remarriage, widowhood, labour force activity, and unemployment. At the aggregate level, demographers often refer to these variables in the context of age and sex composition. The term 'composition' in this sense refers to the distribution of the population in accordance with the intersecting characteristics of age and sex. The statistical association between age and these other variables does not follow a linear relationship. For example, across populations the probability of death is relatively high in infancy, drops substantially in childhood, and rises thereafter with increasing age (gradually throughout adulthood and faster at the older ages). Birth rates tend to be highest among women between the ages of 20 and 30 and relatively low at younger and older ages. And in virtually all populations, the geographical mobility propensities of young adults typically exceed those of other age categories.

Demographic Determinants of Age Composition

In a series of important works, Coale (1957a, 1957b, 1964, 1972) examined the demographic dynamics of age composition. As described in his chapter, Coale showed that fertility change is the major determinant of change in age composition, and that the effect of mortality change is relatively minor (though clearly not unimportant). Young populations result mainly from sustained high fertility rates. Under a high fertility regime, there are proportionately more people below the age of 15, and the median age of the population will be relatively young. Declining fertility would have the opposite effects on the age structure—proportionately fewer people below age 15 and an increasing proportion

of elderly people, combining to produce an older median age. The effect of migration on changes in the age composition of national populations is minor (Preston, Heuveline, & Guillot, 2001).

The role of mortality in age composition is not as straightforward. Although typically it has a relatively minor effect, under certain demographic conditions mortality change can have a substantial impact on age composition, either by increasing or by reducing the median age of the population. In contemporary advanced societies, where fertility rates have been at below-replacement levels for some time, producing an increasingly aging composition, mortality improvements are mainly concentrated in the older ages (because infant, childhood, and adult mortality rates are generally low in such contexts). This type of demographic situation serves to further 'age' the population because there would be more elderly people living longer. In contrast, in a young population—for example a transitional society undergoing socioeconomic modernization—mortality rates would normally fall from originally high levels while birth rates would remain high for some time before they decline. Usually in such contexts, the survival improvements occur first among infants and children, and then among women in the reproductive ages. This type of condition would have a 'younging' effect on the age structure because the mortality improvements among infants and children would have the effect of broadening the base of the age pyramid.

The Future Course of Global Population Aging

The future path of worldwide population aging will be determined by specific combinations of declining fertility and increasing life expectancy in different parts of the world. In their chapter of this volume, Lutz, Sanderson, and Scherbov expand on this idea by introducing a series of new measures of population aging, some of which take into account the fact that the remaining average lifetime of a population (i.e. the average length of life that remains to be lived) has been expanding due to survival improvements, and should continue to increase in the future.

These authors explain that conventional measures of aging, such as median age and percentage over the age of 65, do not take into account longevity increases in the population. Such measures are based on chronological age. They assume, for example, that a 60-year-old person in 1900 was just as old as a 60-year-old person in 2000, because each has lived the same number of years. Chronologically, that may be true; however, the rate of aging of these two hypothetical persons would differ considerably—it would be faster for the former and slower for the latter. The contemporary individual would age more slowly because of significantly improved socioeconomic conditions in his lifetime (e.g. better nutrition, better healthcare, new medical therapies, and improved standards of living). Compared with the person in 1900, the average 60-year old in 2000 would have many more remaining years of life and would die at a much older age (see also Manton, Gu, & Lamb, 2006). This is an important qualification for the study of demographic aging, because, as pointed out by Lutz and colleagues, population aging is about more than just increases in the number of older people—it's also about people living longer lives.

Using the conventional measures, Lutz and associates project that population aging follows a rising trend throughout the twenty-first century; the median age rises from 26.6 years in 2000 to 37.3 years in 2050 and then to 45.6 in 2100. But when anticipated longevity increases are taken into consideration, the adjusted indexes of aging show less pronounced increases. For example, the median age changes from 26.6 in 2000 to 31.1 in 2050 and just 32.9 in 2100. This suggests that after about the middle of the twenty-first century, the world will simultaneously experience lower rates of population growth and a slower pace of population aging. It seems likely, then, that over the course of the twenty-first century, the world population will see periods in which it actually grows younger. The regions of the world will vary in the extent of these anticipated trends because of differences in past levels of fertility and mortality.

Societal Implications of Changing Age Composition

A youthful population implies, among other things, governments having to plan for and devote considerable resources to the needs of children and youth, such as daycare and education. In an aging society, the dependency burden shifts away from youth and towards the elderly. Consequently, the government's concerns become issues of retirement, pension security and management, geriatric healthcare and services, and labour force growth (Day, 1992; Magnus, 2009). Such shifts in age composition can have far-reaching implications for the welfare of the young and the elderly alike in society. For example, the aging of the population may induce governments to devote more public spending and resources to the growing elderly population, who, in their growing numbers, exercise increasing political influence on government (Preston, 1984).

Welfare Regimes for Aging Populations

According to Lee (2007), two of the most consequential societal implications of future demographic aging will be as follows:

1. the overwhelming burden on the working-age population of supporting growing numbers of dependent elderly; and
2. a decline in aggregate saving rates in the society because, as the share of elderly rises, there will be more seniors who will not save relative to savers in the working ages.

The dependency costs of an aging population will be larger in countries with persisting low fertility. The most substantial costs will be concentrated primarily in the areas of public pensions, healthcare, and longterm care. Lee (2007) warns that national governments will need to restructure their tax and benefits systems accordingly if they are to successfully meet these challenges.

Magnus (2009) adds that challenges associated with changing age composition will not be confined to the most advanced countries. Especially burdensome for the developing countries will be the challenge of providing sufficient education and productive work for a rapidly expanding working-age population (Cleland, 1996). Developing countries are facing an even more rapid pace of population aging than are the industrialized countries, as Magnus's findings (2009, pp. 159–161) indicate: while the proportion of 'over-65s' in industrialized countries took almost fifty years to double to its current rate of about 15 per cent, this age group in most developing countries will double in just over twenty years. It is anticipated that by the year 2030, the developing world's over-60s will be three times as numerous as in the developed world, and four times as numerous by 2050. Consider China as an example. The country currently has 144 million people aged over 60, representing roughly 11 per cent of its population. By 2050, it is expected to have 438 million—a figure exceeding the entire population projected for the United States in that year and representing 31 per cent of China's overall population, compared with America's 27 per cent. The speed with which developing countries are aging will have material financial consequences, explains Magnus (2009, p. 161):

> Industrialized counties have had a long time to accumulate wealth, and industrial and social infrastructure, build institutions, and realize high levels of income. It is against this backdrop that they are now on the verge of experiencing the challenges and consequences of aging. Developing countries, on the other hand, are going to encounter rising median age, rapidly growing numbers of elderly citizens, and eventually sharply rising dependency ratios at much lower levels of income and development.

Lee, as noted in the introduction to Section III, believes that the success of developing countries in confronting the challenges of changing age distribution is contingent on whether these countries are capable of benefitting from the one-time 'demographic bonus' (or 'dividend'). This 'bonus' presents itself as a function of a youthful and rapidly expanding labour force generated by high rates of fertility in the past, coupled with government efficiency in generating economic growth and investments (see also Bloom, Canning, & Sevilla, 2002).

In the industrialized countries, the severity of the public pension crisis will depend on the extent to which governments succeed in persuading their populations to retire later, and on the ability of these governments to create work for those over the age of 65 (Bongaarts, 2004). Later retirement should ease the burden on the public pension system, as will the continued labour activity of the elderly. It is likely, however, that the probable solution will also entail the option of governments reducing the value of public pension benefits per retiree. This implies that today's workers may have to save more, work longer, retire later, receive less generous benefits, and perhaps pay more taxes (Bongaarts, 2004).

Given their common demographic profiles (all are aging populations), the countries of the Organisation for Economic Co-operation and Development (OECD) share similar pressures on pension reforms. Following an extensive analysis of the situation in these countries, Aysan and Beaujot (2009) have concluded that there does not appear to be a single path for pension reform; rather, welfare states tend to follow their varied traditional paths, each one limited in the kinds of policies it can implement by the country's own institutional arrangements. Specifically, Aysan and Beaujot have found that Canada, Ireland, New Zealand, the United Kingdom, and the United States (all Anglo, liberal regimes) tend to focus on a strategy of cost containment and re-commodification (i.e. cutting back in an attempt to reverse dependence on the state by imposing on citizens tighter eligibility criteria and by cutting some benefits altogether); Denmark, Finland, Norway, and Sweden (social democratic regimes) rely largely on cost containment and recalibration (i.e. rationalizing/modifying social policies to bring them in line with new ideas for achieving welfare targets and by updating/adapting social programs to changes in the economy and society); Austria, France, Germany, and the Netherlands (continental regimes) and also Greece, Italy, and Spain (southern European regimes) apply a mix of policies, including cost containment, recalibration, and re-commodification. Among these different welfare regimes, the continental and southern European regimes appear to have the most difficulty in achieving reforms, and they also face the highest rates of population aging. However, notwithstanding these differences, Aysan and Beaujot (2009) argue that there are important uniformities across regimes. In the interest of achieving sustainability, the reforms include increasing the length of the working life (delay retirement); placing more of the pension responsibilities on the individual (converting pensions to defined-contribution plans); and increasing citizens' dependence on private plans.

Sex Composition

A population's sex ratio is simply its balance of males and females. In human populations the sex ratio is seldom exactly 100 (representing an equal balance). In most cases, especially in the more developed countries, the value of this index is a little below 100, with females outnumbering males. Why is this so?

In order to answer this question let us first distinguish between three types of sex ratios. The *primary sex ratio* is the ratio of male conceptions to female conceptions. In general, more males are conceived, but the intrauterine mortality of male fetuses is much greater than that of females, so that at birth, the imbalance favouring male infants falls to about 105 boys for every 100 girls (Perls & Frets, 1998). This is the *secondary sex ratio*—the sex ratio of live births. The *tertiary sex ratio* is the sex ratio at ages beyond infancy. As Teitelbaum (1972, p. 90) explains, this is an indeterminate measure because it covers so many possibilities. In other words, sex ratios can be computed for any age category or combination of age groups, such as, for example, the sex ratio at ages 20–24, or the sex ratio of males aged 20–29 to females aged 15–24.

Age-specific sex ratios in adulthood are determined mainly by sex differences in mortality, though in some cases migration can also play a role (Guttentag & Secord, 1983). In virtually all societies females have lower age-specific death rates than do males, and on the average women live longer than men (Perls & Frets, 1998). On the basis of the sex mortality differential alone, therefore, one would expect the ratio of males to females in the population to decline gradually with age, and more rapidly among the elderly. In industrialized countries such Canada, Japan, and Italy, where death rates are relatively low, the balance of males and females begins to approach parity at around age 25 or 30, and with increasing age—especially after about 60—it begins to favour females disproportionately. In the ages beyond 60, the sex ratio can be as imbalanced as 25 males to every 100 females, depending on the population. A final point to note: sex differentials in age-specific mortality are the main factor underlying the overall sex ratio being below 100 in many populations.

Sociological Ramifications of Sex Composition

Changes in the three demographic variables—fertility, mortality, and migration—can affect the balance of men and women in society. For instance, high male mortality during times of prolonged national war will usually result in a male deficit. Similarly, high rates of out-migration for either sex can have an impact on the overall sex ratio. In some settings, death and migration rates for males in the prime marriageable ages (typically 20–34) surpass those of females by a considerable margin. If the gender imbalance due to these demographic conditions is sufficiently severe, the marriage market can be affected. Research has shown that marriage and divorce probabilities are partly explained by sex-ratio imbalances in the prime marriageable ages (Guttentag & Secord, 1983; Messner & Sampson, 1991; Schoen, 1983; South and Lloyd, 1992).

In some national contexts, the culture favours males, and families share a strong preference for sons (China and India are examples). In such contexts secondary sex ratios can be severely distorted in favour of boys (Clarke, 2003; Jha, et al., 2006). In some parts of the developing world, couples are increasingly pursuing the option of sex-selective abortion with the aid of screening technologies such as amniocentesis, chorionic villi sampling (CVS), and ultrasound (Bannister & Coale, 1994; Klasen, 2003).

This situation in China, and in some other countries in Asia, the Middle East, and North Africa, has helped create a phenomenon known as 'missing girls'. Estimates of the number of 'missing girls' worldwide range from 89 million to 100 million (Clarke, 2003; Economist, 2010a, 2010b; Klasen & Wink, 2002). Son preference, if it exists at all, is rare in contemporary industrialized populations (Hank & Kohler, 2003).

Works Cited

Aysan, Mehmet F., & Beaujot, Roderic. (2009). Welfare regimes for aging populations: No single path to reform. *Population and Development Review, 35*(4), 701–20.

Bannister, Judith, & Coale, Ansley J. (1994). Five decades of missing females in China. *Demography, 31*, 459–79.

Bloom, David E., Canning, David, & Sevilla, J. (2002). *The demographic dividend: A new perspective on the economic consequences of population change.* Santa Monica, CA: Rand.

Bongaarts, John. (2004). Population aging and the rising cost of public pensions. *Population and Development Review, 30*(1), 1–24.

Clarke, John I. (2003). Sex ratio. In Paul Demeny & Geoffrey McNicoll (Eds), *Encyclopedia of population* (pp. 875–8). New York: Macmillan Reference USA.

Cleland, John. (1996). Population growth in the 21st century: Cause for crisis or celebration? *Tropical Medicine and International Health, 1*(1), 15–26.

Coale, Ansley J. (1957a). How the age distribution of a human population is determined. *Cold Spring Harbor Symposia on Quantitative Biology, 22*, 83–9.

———. (1957b). A new method for calculating Lotka's *r*—the intrinsic rate of natural increase in a stable population. *Population Studies, 11*(1), 92–4.

———. (1964). How a population ages or grows younger. In Ronald Freedman (Ed.), *Population: The vital revolution* (chap. 3). Garden City, NY: Anchor Books, Doubleday.

———. (1972). *The growth and structure of human populations: A mathematical investigation.* Princeton, NJ: Princeton University Press.

Day, Lincoln H. (1992). *The future of low-birthrate populations.* London: Routlege.

Economist. (2010a, March 4). Gendercide: Killed, aborted or neglected, at least 100m girls have disappeared—and the number is rising. *The Economist.* Retrieved from http://www.economist.com/node/15606229

Economist. (2010b, March 4). The worldwide war on baby girls: Technology, declining fertility and ancient prejudice are combining to unbalance societies. *The Economist.* Retrieved from http://www.economist.com/node/15636231

Esping-Andersen, G. (1990). *The three worlds of welfare capitalism.* Cambridge: Policy Press.

Guttentag, Marcia, & Secord, Paul F. (1983). Introduction: The sex ratio question. In Marcia Guttentag & Paul F. Secord, *Too many women? The sex ratio question* (pp. 13–33). Beverly Hills, CA: Sage.

Hank, Karsten, & Kohler, Hans-Peter. (2003). Sex preference for children revisited: New evidence from Germany. *Population, 58*(1), 133–44.

Jha, Prabhat, Kumar, Rajesh, Vasa, Priya, Dhingra, N., Thiruchelvam, D., & Maoineddin, R. (2006, January 9). Low male-to-female sex ratio of children born in India: National survey of 1.1 million households. *Lancet.* doi:10.1016/So14-6736(06)

Klasen, Stephan. (2003). Sex selection. In Paul Demeny & Geoffrey McNicoll (Eds), *Encyclopedia of population* (pp. 879–81). New York: Macmillan Reference USA.

Klasen, Stephan, & Wink, Claudia. (2002). A turning point in gender bias in mortality: An update on the number of missing women. *Population and Development Review, 28*, 285–312.

Lee, Ronald D. (2007). *Global population aging and its economic consequences.* The Henry Wendt Lecture Series. Washington, DC: AEI Press.

Magnus, George. (2009). *The age of aging: How demographics are changing the global economy and our world.* Singapore: John Wiley and Sons (Asia).

Manton, K.G., Gu, X., & Lamb, V.L. (2006). Long-term trends in life expectancy and active life expectancy in the United States. *Population and Development Review, 32*(1), 81–106.

Messner, Steven F., & Sampson, Robert J. (1991). The sex ratio, family disruption, and rates of violent crime: The paradox of demographic structure. *Social Forces, 69*(3), 693–713.

Perls, Thomas T. & Frets, Ruth C. (1998, summer). Why women live longer than men. *Scientific American Presents.*

Pierson, Paul. (2001). The new politics of the welfare state. Oxford: Oxford University Press.

Preston, Samuel. (1984). Children and the elderly in the United States. *Scientific American, 251*(6), 44–9.

Preston, Samuel H., Heuveline, Patrick, & Guillot, Michel. (2001). *Demography: Measuring and modeling population processes.* Oxford: Blackwell.

Schoen, Robert. (1983). Measuring the tightness of a marriage squeeze. *Demography, 20,* 61–78.

South, Scott J., & Lloyd, K.M. (1992). Marriage opportunities and family formation: Further implications of imbalanced sex ratios. *Journal of Marriage and Family, 54,* 440–51.

Teitelbaum, Michael S. (1972). Factors associated with the sex ratio in human populations. In G.A. Harrison & A.J. Boyce (Eds), *The structure of human populations* (pp. 90–109). Oxford: Clarendon Press .

CHAPTER 7

How a Population Ages or Grows Younger

Ansley J. Coale

The age of the whole human population could, I suppose, be measured from the moment the species originated, and the age of a national population could be measured from the country's 'birthday'. The age (in this sense) of the human population has been estimated as at least a hundred thousand and no more than a million years, and the age of national population ranges from several thousand years for Egypt or China to a year or so for some of the emerging nations of Africa.

In this chapter, however, when we speak of the age of a population, we refer to the age of its members, and to be precise we should use the term *age distribution* of a population—how many persons there are at each age—rather than the age of a population. The only way a single age can be given for a group of persons is by using some sort of average. A *young* population, then, is one that contains a large proportion of young persons, and has a low average age, while an *old* population has a high average age and a large proportion of old people.

The ages of various national populations in the world today are very different, and in many countries the present age distribution differs markedly from the past.

The oldest populations in the world are found in northwestern Europe. In France, England, and Sweden, for example, 12 per cent of the population is over 65, and half of the population in these countries is over 33, 36, and 37 respectively. The youngest

populations are found in the underdeveloped countries—those that have not incorporated modern industrial technology in their economies—the populations of Asia, Africa, and Latin America. Half of the population of Pakistan is under 18 years, of the Congo under 20 years, and of Brazil under 19 years. The proportion over 65 in Brazil is less than one-fourth what it is in France. The proportion of children under 15 is twice as great in Pakistan as in England. Paradoxically enough, the oldest nations—China, India, and Egypt—have very young populations.

The highly industrialized countries all have older populations than the underdeveloped countries, and also older populations than they did fifty to a hundred years ago. Since 1900 the median age has risen in England from 24 to 36, in the United States from 23 to 30, in Japan from 23 to 26, and in Russia from 21 to 27. In the underdeveloped countries, however, the age distributions have changed only slightly, and they have, if anything, become slightly younger. In Taiwan, for example, the median age has declined from 21 to 18 since 1915.

What accounts for these differences and these trends in the age distribution of populations? One obvious factor to consider is migration. A famous spa has an older population because old people come there for the cure, and university towns like Princeton have young populations because young people come there to study. But the age distribution of most national populations is not much affected by migration, especially today when almost everywhere international migration is restricted.

Whether a national population is young or old is mainly determined by the number of children women bear. When women bear many children, the population is young; when they bear few, the population is old.

The effect of fertility (as the rate of childbearing can be called) on the age distribution is clearest when a population continuously subject to high fertility is compared to one continuously subject to low fertility. The high-fertility population has a larger proportion of children relative to adults of parental age as a direct consequence of the greater frequency of births. Moreover, by virtue of high fertility a generation ago, today's parents are numerous relative to their parents, and hence the proportion of old people is small. Conversely, the population experiencing a prolonged period of low fertility has few children relative to its current parents, who in turn are not numerous relative to *their* parents. Prolonged high fertility produces a large proportion of children, and a small proportion of the aged—a population with a low average age. On the other hand, prolonged low fertility produces a small proportion of children and a large proportion of the aged—a high average age.

It is the small number of children born per woman that explains the high average age now found in industrialized western Europe, and the high birth rate of the underdeveloped countries that accounts for their young populations. The increase in average age and the swollen proportion of old people in the industrialized countries are the product of the history of falling birth rates that all such countries have experienced.

Most of us would probably guess that populations have become older because the death rate has been reduced, and hence people live longer on the average. Just what is the role of mortality in determining the age distribution of a population? The answer is surprising: mortality affects the age distribution much less than does fertility, and in the opposite direction from what most of us would think. Prolongation of life by reducing death rates has the perverse effect of making the population somewhat younger. Consider the effect of the reduction in death rates in the United States, where the average duration of life has risen from about 45 years under the mortality conditions of 1900 to about 70 years today. Had the risks of death prevailing in 1900 continued unchanged, and the other variables—rates of immigration, and rates of childbearing per mother—followed the course they actually did, the average age of the population today would be greater than it is: the proportion of children would be less and the proportion of persons over 65 would be greater than they are. The reduction of the death rate has produced, in other words, a younger American population.

These statements seem scarcely credible.

Does not a reduction in the death rate increase the average age of death? Are there not more old people as a result of reduced mortality than there would be with the former high death rates? How then can it be said that reduction in the death rate makes a population younger?

It is true that as death rates fall, the average age at which people die is increased. But the average age of a population is the average age of living persons, not their average age at death. It is also true, as we all immediately realize, that as death rates fall, the number of old persons in a population increases. What we do not so readily realize is that reduced mortality increases the number of *young* persons as well. More people survive from birth to ages 1, 10, 20, and 40, as well as more living to old age. Because more persons survive to be parents, more births occur.

The reason that the reduced death rates, which prolong man's life, make the population younger is that typical improvements in health and medicine produce the greatest increases in survivorship among the young rather than the old.

There is one kind of reduction in death rates that would not affect the age distribution of the population at all, that would lead to the same proportion of population at every age as if mortality had not changed. This particular form of reduced mortality is one that increases the chance of surviving one year by a certain amount—say one-tenth of 1 per cent—at every age. The result would be one-tenth of a per cent more persons at age 1, 5, 10, 60, and 80—at every age—than there would have been had death rates been unaltered. Because there would be one-tenth per cent more parents, there would also be one-tenth per cent more births. Therefore the next year's population would be one-tenth per cent larger than it would otherwise have been, but the proportion of children, of young adults, of the middle-aged, and of the aged would not be altered—there would be one-tenth per cent more of each.

Reductions in mortality of this singular sort that would not affect the age of the population at all are not found in actual human experience. However, there has been a tendency for persons at all ages to share some of the increased chances of survival, and the effect of reduced death rates on the age distribution has consequently been small—much smaller than the effect of reduced birth rates, in countries where both fertility and mortality have changed markedly.

As the average duration of life has risen from lower levels to 65 or 70 years, the most conspicuous advances in survivorship seem always to have occurred in infancy and early childhood. It is for this reason that reduced mortality has had the effect of producing a younger population, although the effect has usually been obscured by the much more powerful force of a falling birth rate that has occurred at the same time. Thus the population of the United States has actually become *older* since 1900, because of falling fertility; but falling mortality (with its tendency to produce a younger population) has prevented it from becoming older still.

The younger-population effect of reduced mortality is not an inevitable feature of all increases in length of life. The countries with the greatest average duration of life have by now about exhausted the possibility of increasing survivorship in a way that makes for a younger population. In Sweden today, 95 per cent survive from birth to age 30, compared to 67 per cent in 1870. At best, survivorship to age 30 in Sweden could approach 100 per cent. No important increase in population at younger ages would result. If there are further major gains in the chances of prolonged

life in Sweden, they must occur at older ages and, if they occur, will make the population older.

Every individual inexorably gets older as time passes. How old he gets depends on how long he avoids death. American president Dwight D. Eisenhower remarked after his retirement that he was glad to be old, because at his age, if he were not old, he would be dead.

Populations, on the other hand, can get older or younger. They get older primarily as the result of declining fertility, and younger primarily as the result of rising fertility.

The most highly industrialized countries have all experienced a decline of fertility of about 50 per cent since their pre-industrial phase, and they all have older populations than they used to have. In France and the United States, for example, the number of children each woman bore declined for more than a century, reaching a minimum just before the Second World War. In each country during this period the population became progressively older. In fact the 'aging' of the population continued for a time after fertility had passed its minimum. Between 1800 and 1950 the median age of the French population rose from 25 to 35 years, and in the United States in the same interval the median age increased from 16 to 30. In both countries there has been a substantial recovery in fertility during the past 25 years from the low point reached in the 1930s. This rise in fertility has produced the first decrease in median age recorded in the statistics of either nation. Between 1950 and 1960 the median age in France fell from 35 to 33 and in the United States from 30.2 to 29.6.

This reversal in the trend towards an older population in the United States has been accompanied by a more pronounced reversal in the way proportions of children were changing. The longterm decline in fertility in the United States meant that the proportion of children to adults steadily shrank from about .85 children (under 15) per adult (over 15) in 1800 to .33 per adult in 1940. By 1960 the proportion had rebounded to .45 children per adult. In fact, the increase in the *number* of children in the population between 1950 and 1960—more than

15 million—was greater than the increase between 1900 and 1950.

The abrupt reversal of the longterm trend towards an older population has meant the first increase in the relative burden of child dependency in the history of the United States. The very productive American economy can certainly afford to support this burden, but it has not been painless. The extremely rapid increase in the number of children in the past decade has required the construction of many new schools and the training of many teachers. In some communities where foresight, willingness to pay increased taxes, or resources were inadequate, schools have been overcrowded and the quality of instruction has suffered.

The countries that have not undergone intensive industrialization have experienced no major changes in fertility, no trends of sustained decline and recovery such as occurred in France and the United States. Rather they have experienced a largely unbroken sequence of high birth rates. There has been in consequence little change in the age composition of underdeveloped areas. All have 40 per cent or more under age 15, only 2 to 4 per cent over 65, and a median age of 20 years or less.

The age distributions of the industrialized countries on the one hand and of the pre-industrial countries on the other are ironically mismatched with what each sort of country seems best equipped to accommodate. As we have noted before, the contrast in age of population is striking. In Pakistan or Mexico nearly one person of every two a visitor might encounter would be a child, and only two or three of every hundred would be old (over 65); while in England only one in four would be a child and about one in eight would be old. In the industrialized countries, where the proportion of the aged is so large, the importance of the family in the predominantly urban environment has diminished, and consequently the role of respected old patriarch or matriarch has nearly vanished. The wealthy industrial countries can readily afford to support a sizable component of old people but have not in fact always done so adequately. The aging of their populations has been accompanied by a weakening or a disappearance of the traditional claims of the aged on their descendants for material support and, perhaps more tragically, by a weakening or disappearance of a recognized and accepted position for old people in the family.

In the underdeveloped countries, on the other hand, the relatively few old people are accorded traditional respect and whatever economic support their families have to offer, and hence the aged are less subject to special economic and social deprivation.

Because of extremely young age distributions, adults in the impoverished underdeveloped countries must support a disproportionately large dependent child population—twice as great a burden of dependency per adult in the working ages of 15 to 65 as in typical industrialized countries—a burden these poor countries can scarcely afford. The enormous proportion of children makes it extraordinarily difficult, where incomes are extremely low, to provide adequate shelter, nourishment, and education for the young.

Moreover, the pre-industrial countries can expect no relief from dependency as a result of the spectacular drop in death rates now occurring. Unless fertility declines, this drop in mortality will only make the populations younger, adding to the already extreme burden of dependent children.

In sum, it is the industrialized countries that, better able to afford a high burden of child dependency, have only half the proportion of children found in underdeveloped areas, and that, having abandoned the institutions giving a meaningful role to the aged, have four times the proportion of the elderly found in pre-industrial countries.

The last considered in this brief survey of the age of population is the past trend in age distribution from man's origin to the present, and what alternative trends may possibly develop in the future.

The human population as a whole has always been, and is now, a young population, consisting of at least 40 per cent children, and having a median age of no more than about 20 years, because the overall human birth rate has always been about 40 per 1,000 or higher. It is almost certain that until perhaps two hundred years ago all sizable national or regional populations likewise were young, with about the same age characteristics as the populations of the world.

These statements can be made with confidence, even though no reliable records of the age distribution of the world, or of birth rates, or even records of many national populations, exist for most of man's history. We can be confident that the world's population has always been young because until that last two centuries it was not possible for any population to achieve low mortality for any sustained period, and any population with a low birth rate would therefore have become extinct.

It is simply not possible for a population to have a birth rate much below its death rate for a prolonged period, as can be shown by the following example. The population of the world has grown from about a quarter of a billion to about 3 billion from the time of Julius Caesar to the 1960s—it has been multiplied by about 12. But the average annual rate of increase has been very little—about 1 per 1,000 per year. If the world birth rate has averaged 40 per 1,000 (a reasonable guess), the world death rate by logical necessity has averaged 39 per 1,000. A world birth rate only two points lower (38 instead of 40 per 1,000) would have led to an annual decrease of 1 per 1,000, and the current population would be only one-twelfth instead of 12 times that population of Caesar's day. A birth rate of 35—that of England or the United States in 1880—would have reduced the 250 million of 2,000 years ago to less than 100,000 today.

The industrialized countries have been able to reduce their birth rates without having their population shrink drastically because they first reduced their death rates. Beginning in the late eighteenth century some countries made preliminary steps in the improvement in living conditions and sanitation that has continued until today, and in the latter half of the nineteenth century there began the remarkable development of modern medicine and public health that so greatly extended the average duration of life in the industrially more advanced countries.

In the past few decades modern medical techniques and public health methods have been introduced into the underdeveloped countries, causing an extraordinary drop in death rates, and since birth rates have not changed, the growth of world population has sharply accelerated so that it is now 2 per cent per year.

Just as it is not possible for a population to maintain for long a birth rate much below its death rate, because such a population would shrink to extinction, it is not possible to maintain for long a birth rate much *above* a death rate, because then the population would grow to a physically impossible size. For example, had the current 2 per cent rate of growth existed since the time of Caesar, the population of the world would have been multiplied by about 135 quadrillion instead of by 12, and there would be more than 30,000 times the entire world's current population on each square mile of land area on the earth. Starting with today's 3 billion persons, it would take only about 650 years for a 2 per cent rate of increase to produce one person per square foot, and about twice that long to produce a total that would outweigh the earth.

In short, the present combination of a high world birth rate and a moderate and rapidly falling death rate can only be temporary. The only combinations that can long continue are birth and death rates with the same average levels.

If man chooses to continue the high birth rate that he has always had, the human population will remain a young one—but in the long run it can remain young only by returning to the high death rate and short average life it has always had. Sustained geometric increase is impossible.

If, on the other hand, mankind can avoid nuclear war, and bring the fruits of modern technology, including prolonged life, to all parts of the world, the human population must become an old one, because only a low birth rate is compatible in the long run with a low death rate, and a low birth rate produces an old population. In fact, if the expectation of life at birth of 70 years—now achieved or exceeded in many industrialized countries—becomes universal, the average number of children born per woman must decline to about two from five or more in the underdeveloped areas, slightly more than three in the United States, and some two-and-a-half in Europe. Such a decline in fertility would give the whole world as old a population as any country has had to date—only about 21 per cent under 15, at least 15 per cent over 65, and as many persons over 36 as under.

A world population with the age composition of a health resort is a mildly depressing prospect. Such a population would presumably be cautious, conservative, and full of regard for the past. A young, vigorous, forward-looking population perhaps appears more attractive, but in the long run the world can keep its young only by tolerating premature death.

We find at the end, then, that although the birth rate determines how old a population is, the death rate determines what the average birth rate in the long run must be. If prolonged life produces by its direct effects a younger population, it is nevertheless compatible only with an older population.

CHAPTER 8

The Coming Acceleration of Global Population Aging

Wolfgang Lutz, Warren Sanderson, and Sergei Scherbov

The future paths of population aging result from specific combinations of declining fertility and increasing life expectancies in different parts of the world.[1] Here we measure the speed of population aging by using conventional measures and new ones that take changes in longevity into account for the world as a whole and for 13 major regions. We report on future levels of indicators of aging and the speed at which they change. We show how these depend on whether changes in life expectancy are taken into account. We also show that the speed of aging is likely to increase over the coming decades and to decelerate in most regions by mid-century. All our measures indicate a continuous aging of the world's population throughout the century. The median age of the world's population increases from 26.6 years in 2000 to 37.3 years in 2050 and then to 45.6 years in 2100, when it is not adjusted for longevity increase. When increases in life expectancy are taken into account,[2,3] the adjusted median age rises from 26.6 in 2000 to 31.1 in 2050 and only to 32.9 in 2100, slightly less than what it was in the China region in 2005. There are large differences in the regional patterns of aging. In North America, the median age adjusted for life expectancy change falls throughout almost the entire century, whereas the conventional median age increases significantly. Our assessment of trends in aging is based on new probabilistic population forecasts. The probability that growth in the world's population will end

during this century is 88 per cent, somewhat higher than previously assessed.[4] After mid-century, lower rates of population growth are likely to coincide with slower rates of aging.

Conventional measures of aging are based on chronological age. They assume that a 60-year-old person in 1900 was just as old as a 60-year-old person in 2000 because each has lived the same number of years. However, would we say that the two have aged at the same rate? After all, the 60-year-old in 2000 would, on average, have many more remaining years of life. Population aging is not only about there being more old people (by today's definition of what is old), it is also about people living longer lives.[5] To capture this important impact of increasing life expectancy on our lives, and on the definitions of what is age and what is old, we introduce and quantify three new indicators of age that explicitly take changes in the remaining life expectancy into account. Although traditional age still greatly matters for institutional arrangements such as pension systems in most countries, the alternative measures tell us more about the changing human condition in which more people can plan for a longer and healthier life with consequences for their behaviour.

The conventional measures considered here are the proportion of the population aged 60+ (Prop. 60+), the median age of the population (MA), and its average age (aver. age). The alternative approach to measuring the proportion of elderly people in the population does not depend on a fixed age boundary but, rather, on a fixed remaining life expectancy. We define Prop. RLE 15− as the proportion of the population in age groups that have a remaining life expectancy of 15 years or less (see ref. [6] for the suggestion of a similar measure). If longevity increases, the minimum age of people included in Prop. RLE 15− increases. The adjusted version of the median age is called standardized, or prospective, median age (PMA).[2,3] It is the age of a person in the year 2000 who has the same remaining life expectancy as a person at the median age in the year under consideration. The change in the prospective median age over some time period is roughly the change in the median age minus the change in life expectancy at the median age.

The adjusted version of the average age is the population average remaining years of life (PARYL). It is the weighted average of age-specific remaining life expectancies, where the weights are the proportions of the population at each age.[7,8] PARYL gives us the average remaining years of life of population members. Unlike the other measures, PARYL goes down as a population ages. We intuitively think of populations being younger when, on average, its members have more years left to live and PARYL is higher.

Figure 8.1 shows four of these measures of aging as they evolve over time for the global population. All six measures are listed in Table 8.1 for selected regions and dates (information for all regions is given in Supplementary Table 8.2). All of them indicate that aging will continue throughout the century. The two most rapidly increasing indicators, the proportion of the population 60+ years old and the median age of the population, are based on the traditional definition of age, hence suggesting the need for institutional adjustments to cope with these expected increases. The proportion of the global population 60+ years old increases from 10.0 per cent in 2000 to 21.8 per cent in 2050 and then to 32.2 per cent in 2100. The three measures that are adjusted for longevity change show a slower pace of change. Prop. RLE 15− goes from 7.4 per cent in 2000 to 12.0 per cent in 2050, and then to 15.6 per cent in 2100. As

to regional differentials, Table 8.1 shows that Japan/Oceania is the oldest region today and is likely to keep this position throughout the century with its median age likely to increase to above 60 years. It is closely followed by the European regions. North America shows much slower aging and is likely to be surpassed by China for every indicator of aging by 2030–40.

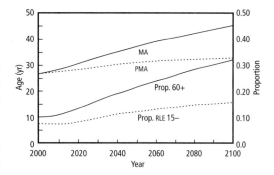

Figure 8.1 Projected changes in the level of aging for the world population over the course of the century for four indicators of aging as defined in the text

Figure 8.2 shows the accelerating and then decelerating speed of aging at the global level. It plots decadal changes in the level of the indicator divided by the maximum increase (speed) projected over the century. For all indicators, the speed accelerates over the coming years, reaching the highest rate of increase before 2035. After that, the speed of aging is expected to decelerate, although there will be further increases in the level of aging throughout the century. This analysis clearly shows that, even under widely differing definitions of aging, the world is expected to experience a significant acceleration in the speed of population aging over the coming years.

How certain are these projected future trends in aging? Is the expected rapid increase in aging in many parts of the world a near certainty or just one out of several possible scenarios? The probabilistic nature of our population projections explicitly addresses this issue. Figure 8.3 shows the cumulative probabilities that different world regions reach one-third of

Table 8.1 Indicators of aging

Region	Indicator	2000	2005	2010	2020	2030	2040	2050	2075	2100
North America	Aver. Age	36.5	37.0	37.7	39.5	41.3	42.6	43.6	46.5	49.5
	Prop. 60+	0.16	0.17	0.18	0.23	0.27	0.28	0.30	0.35	0.39
	PARYL	43.0	43.3	43.4	43.5	43.6	44.1	45.0	46.3	48.4
	MA	35.6	36.7	37.2	38.4	40.3	41.9	43.0	47.0	50.0
	Prop. RLE 15–	0.11	0.10	0.10	0.11	0.13	0.15	0.14	0.15	0.15
	PMA	35.9	35.8	35.4	34.7	34.8	34.6	33.7	33.0	30.9
Middle East	Aver. Age	24.2	25.1	26.0	28.3	31.4	34.4	37.1	42.6	46.6
	Prop. 60+	0.06	0.06	0.06	0.08	0.10	0.14	0.19	0.28	0.34
	PARYL	48.8	48.8	48.7	48.3	47.0	45.8	44.9	43.5	43.7
	MA	19.9	21.2	22.6	25.5	28.7	32.3	35.9	42.4	47.4
	Prop. RLE 15–	0.04	0.04	0.04	0.05	0.06	0.07	0.09	0.13	0.16
	PMA	19.9	20.3	20.9	22.0	23.5	25.5	27.6	30.0	30.6
South Asia	Aver. Age	26.5	27.1	27.8	29.8	32.2	34.6	37.0	42.4	47.3
	Prop. 60+	0.07	0.07	0.08	0.09	0.45	0.14	0.17	0.26	0.35
	PARYL	44.1	44.1	43.9	43.2	42.1	41.2	40.4	38.6	37.6
	MA	22.7	23.4	24.5	26.9	29.6	32.8	35.9	42.6	48.5
	Prop. RLE 15–	0.06	0.06	0.06	0.07	0.08	0.10	0.11	0.16	0.19
	PMA	22.7	22.9	23.4	24.7	26.3	28.3	30.2	33.7	36.2
China Region	Aver. Age	31.2	33.2	35.1	38.6	42.3	45.5	47.7	50.7	51.2
	Prop. 60+	0.10	0.11	0.12	0.17	0.24	0.30	0.35	0.41	0.42
	PARYL	43.4	42.1	41.0	39.0	36.9	35.5	35.0	36.1	39.3
	MA	29.6	32.3	34.7	38.5	43.0	47.5	50.7	53.7	54.0
	Prop. RLE 15–	0.04	0.05	0.05	0.11	0.14	0.19	0.21	0.24	0.22
	PMA	39.6	31.7	33.5	36.0	39.3	42.3	44.1	43.0	38.6
Pacific Asia	Aver. Age	28.2	29.3	30.5	33.0	35.4	37.6	39.5	43.2	47.5
	Prop. 60+	0.08	0.08	0.09	0.12	0.16	0.20	0.23	0.29	0.36
	PARYL	44.7	44.4	43.9	42.9	42.1	41.5	41.2	41.2	41.1
	MA	25.3	26.9	28.4	31.4	34.0	36.4	38.6	43.3	48.7
	Prop. RLE 15–	0.06	0.06	0.07	0.08	0.10	0.12	0.14	0.15	0.17
	PMA	25.3	26.2	27.1	28.7	29.9	30.9	31.6	32.4	33.7

Japan/Oceania	Aver. Age	40.4	41.6	43.0	45.7	47.9	49.7	51.3	54.1	57.7
	Prop. 60+	0.22	0.24	0.27	0.31	0.35	0.40	0.42	0.47	0.51
	PARYL	41.3	41.0	40.6	39.7	39.5	39.5	39.6	41.1	43.0
	MA	40.0	41.3	42.8	46.7	49.9	52.1	53.9	57.6	61.1
	Prop. RLE 15–	0.13	0.13	0.14	0.17	0.18	0.18	0.20	0.21	0.21
	PMA	40.0	40.3	40.9	42.9	44.3	44.6	44.5	43.3	41.7
Western Europe	Aver. Age	38.3	39.1	40.1	42.4	44.7	46.8	48.4	51.0	53.5
	Prop. 60+	0.20	0.20	0.21	0.25	0.31	0.34	0.37	0.42	0.46
	PARYL	41.0	41.0	40.8	40.3	39.8	39.6	39.7	41.1	43.5
	MA	36.8	38.3	40.0	43.1	45.8	48.2	50.2	53.5	56.5
	Prop. RLE 15–	0.13	0.13	0.13	0.14	0.16	0.18	0.19	0.20	0.19
	PMA	36.8	37.5	38.3	39.6	40.5	41.1	41.3	39.8	37.7
Eastern Europe	Aver. Age	37.0	38.4	39.8	42.7	45.6	48.2	50.3	52.4	52.4
	Prop. 60+	0.18	0.18	0.20	0.25	0.29	0.36	0.42	0.44	0.44
	PARYL	39.7	39.1	38.5	37.3	36.0	35.3	34.9	36.9	40.6
	MA	35.6	37.1	38.9	42.9	47.3	51.3	54.0	55.7	55.7
	Prop. RLE 15–	0.13	0.13	0.13	0.15	0.18	0.19	0.22	0.24	0.21
	PMA	35.6	36.4	37.4	39.9	42.8	45.2	46.3	43.5	38.6
World	Aver. Age	29.7	30.4	31.3	33.1	35.2	37.1	38.8	42.3	45.5
	Prop. 60+	0.10	0.10	0.11	0.13	0.17	0.19	0.22	0.27	0.32
	PARYL	43.8	43.6	43.3	42.8	42.1	41.6	41.3	41.0	41.2
	MA	26.6	27.5	28.4	30.8	33.2	35.3	37.3	41.4	45.6
	Prop. RLE 15–	0.07	0.07	0.07	0.08	0.10	0.11	0.12	0.14	0.16
	PMA	26.6	27.0	27.6	28.6	29.4	30.4	31.1	32.1	32.9

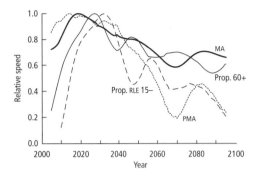

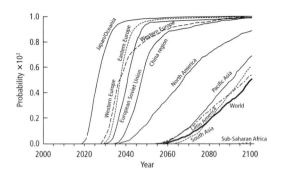

Figure 8.2 The changing speed of increase in selected indicators of aging. This is calculated as increases per decade in the level of the indicator divided by the maximum increase projected over the century; on the time axis, values are allocated to the middle of the decade considered.

Figure 8.3 Cumulative probabilities of reaching a proportion 60+ of one-third or more for the world and selected world regions by calendar year

their population 60+ years old (Prop. 60+) over the course of the century. By mid-century, the chance of having passed this specific aging threshold is 98 per cent in Japan/Oceana, 82 per cent in western Europe, and even 69 per cent in the China region. Uncertainty is so low in these regions because past fertility and mortality declines have already altered the age structures significantly. North America has a 50 per cent chance of crossing this threshold in the 2060s owing to its currently still-younger age structure and anticipated future migration gains. For sub-Saharan Africa, which still has an extremely young population with 44 per cent of the population below age 15, the chance of Prop. 60+ being more than a third of the population is close to zero, even by the end of the century. For all other regions the chances start to increase over the 2060s and 2070s, and reach around 50 per cent by the end of the century. For the world as a whole, the cumulative probability turns out to be exactly 50 per cent in 2100.

Figure 8.4 demonstrates another advantage of studying aging from a probabilistic viewpoint. It shows predicted distributions of the proportion above age 80 for western Europe (see Supplementary Table 8.2 for data on all regions), The proportion 80+ is almost certain to increase significantly over

the coming decades. The projected increase in this indicator is very sensitive to the assumptions about future trends in old-age mortality where our assumed uncertainty ranges reflect tremendous disagreement among scientists.[9-16] Figure 8.4 shows that the 95 per cent prediction interval is 5.5–20.7 per cent by 2050 and 5.0–42.8 per cent by 2100. The small lines inserted in 2100 give the results from the high and low variants of the most recent United Nations long-range projections.[17] These only reflect alternative fertility levels because the United

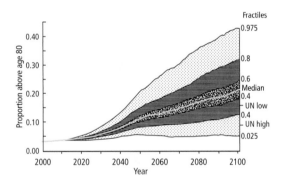

Figure 8.4 Fractiles of the projected uncertainty distribution of the proportion of the population above age 80 in western Europe. Straight lines in 2100 indicate the values given by the high and low variants of the United Nations (UN) longterm population projections.

Nations does not publish variants considering mortality uncertainty. That approach leads to a gross underestimation of the uncertainty of the future proportions of elderly.

Population aging has many dimensions that will affect individuals and societies alike. When we supplement the conventional measures of aging with ones that incorporate longevity change, we obtain a more complete understanding of how these dimensions are expected to evolve. In addition to changes in its level, the speed of aging matters because, generally, the difficulties of adaptation to demographic change increase with the speed of change. In this the world as a whole and the low-fertility countries in particular face the challenge of an accelerating speed of aging over the coming decades with the prospect of a slower speed of aging at a higher level towards the second half of the century.

Notes

1. United Nations. (2007). *World Population Ageing 2007*. New York: United Nations.
2. Sanderson, W., & Scherbov, S. (2005). Average remaining lifetimes can increase as human populations age. *Nature, 435*, 811–13.
3. Sanderson. W., & Scherbov, S. (2006). A new perspective on population aging. *Demog. Res., 16*, 27–58.
4. Lutz, W., Sanderson, W., & Scherbov. S. (2001). The end of world population growth. *Nature, 412*, 543–5.
5. Harper, S. (2006). *Ageing Societies: Myths, Challenges and Opportunities*. London: Hodder Arnold.
6. Ryder, N. (1975). Notes on stationary populations. *Popul. Index, 41*, 3–28.
7. Hersch, L. (1944). De la démographie actuelle à la démographie potentielle. *Melange des Études Economiques Offertes à William Rappard*. Geneva: Georg.
8. Panush, N., & Peritz, E. (1996). Potential demography. *Eur. J. Popul., 12*, 27–39.
9. Bongaarts, J. (2006). How long do we live? *Popul. Dev., Rev. 32*, 605–26.
10. Oeppen, J., & Vaupel, J. (2002). Broken limits to life expectancy. *Science, 296*, 1029–31.
11. Carnes, S. & Olshansky, S.J. (2007). A realistic view of aging, mortality and future longevity. *Popul. Dev. Rev., 33*, 367–81.
12. National Research Council. (2000). *Beyond Six Billion: Forecasting the World's Population* (Eds Bongaarts, J. & Bulatao, R., Panel on Population Projections, Committee on Population, Commission on Behavioral and Social Sciences and Education). Washington, DC: National Academy Press.
13. Lee, R. & Carter, L. (1992). Modeling and forecasting US mortality. *J. Am. Stat. Assoc., 87*, 659–71.
14. Manton, K., Stallard, E. & Trolley, H. (1991). Limits to human life expectancy: Evidence, prospects and implications. *Popul. Dev. Rev., 17*, 603–37.
15. Fries. J. (1980). Aging, natural death, and the compression of morbidity. *N. Engl. J. Med., 303*, 130–35.
16. Kellman, N. (1997). Ex-post errors in official population forecasts in industrialized countries. *J. Off. Stat., 13*, 245–77.
17. United Nations. (2004). *World Population to 2300* (and associated database). New York: United Nations.

Supplementary Information

Supplementary Table 8.2   Six alternative aging measures (derived from the mean scenario) for all world regions

Region	Indicator	2000	2005	2010	2020	2030	2040	2050	2075	2100
North Africa	Ave. Age	25.5	26.4	27.3	29.7	32.5	35.2	37.5	41.7	44.6
	Prop. 60+	0.06	0.06	0.07	0.09	0.12	0.15	0.19	0.27	0.31
	PARYL	46.2	46.2	46.1	45.4	44.3	43.4	42.7	42.2	43.2
	MA	21.6	22.9	24.3	26.9	30.0	33.2	36.3	41.2	44.8
	Prop. RLE 15–	0.05	0.05	0.05	0.06	0.07	0.09	0.11	0.14	0.16
	PMA	21.6	22.0	22.6	23.7	25.2	27.1	28.8	30.0	29.3
Sub-Saharan Africa	Ave. Age	22.1	21.6	21.6	22.2	23.7	25.4	27.3	32.9	38.0
	Prop. 60+	0.05	0.04	0.04	0.05	0.05	0.05	0.07	0.13	0.20
	PARYL	37.7	37.2	36.5	37.7	39.6	40.1	40.1	39.1	38.1
	MA	17.4	17.0	16.9	17.9	20.2	22.2	24.3	30.2	36.8
	Prop. RLE 15–	0.05	0.05	0.05	0.05	0.05	0.05	0.05	0.10	0.13
	PMA	17.4	18.0	18.8	17.6	16.1	15.9	16.2	16.8	18.1
North America	Ave. Age	36.5	37.0	37.7	39.5	41.3	42.6	43.6	46.5	49.5
	Prop. 60+	0.16	0.17	0.18	0.23	0.27	0.28	0.30	0.35	0.39
	PARYL	43.0	43.3	43.4	43.5	43.6	44.1	45.0	46.3	48.4
	MA	35.9	36.7	37.2	38.4	40.3	41.9	43.0	47.0	50.0
	Prop. RLE 15–	0.11	0.10	0.10	0.11	0.13	0.15	0.14	0.15	0.15
	PMA	35.9	35.8	35.4	34.7	34.8	34.6	33.7	33.0	30.9
Latin America	Ave. Age	27.8	28.8	29.8	32.2	34.7	37.0	38.9	42.3	44.7
	Prop. 60+	0.08	0.08	0.09	0.11	0.15	0.19	0.22	0.28	0.32
	PARYL	46.4	46.2	45.9	45.1	44.3	43.7	43.5	44.2	45.9
	MA	24.4	25.8	27.2	30.1	32.9	35.5	37.8	41.6	44.6
	Prop. RLE 15–	0.06	0.06	0.06	0.07	0.08	0.10	0.12	0.14	0.14
	PMA	24.4	25.0	25.7	27.1	28.4	29.4	30.1	29.6	28.0
Central Asia	Ave. Age	26.9	27.8	28.7	30.7	33.4	35.7	37.9	42.4	46.0
	Prop. 60+	0.08	0.08	0.08	0.10	0.13	0.16	0.20	0.28	0.33
	PARYL	46.4	46.2	46.0	45.4	44.4	43.7	43.2	42.8	43.4
	MA	22.8	24.0	25.3	28.4	31.4	33.8	36.6	41.8	46.4
	Prop. RLE 15–	0.06	0.06	0.05	0.06	0.08	0.09	0.10	0.14	0.16
	PMA	22.8	23.2	23.8	25.6	27.1	28.1	29.4	30.6	30.8

Region	Metric									
Middle East	Ave. Age	24.2	25.1	26.0	28.3	31.4	34.4	37.1	42.6	46.6
	Prop. 60+	0.06	0.06	0.06	0.08	0.10	0.14	0.19	0.28	0.34
	PARYL	48.8	48.8	48.7	48.3	47.0	45.8	44.9	43.5	43.7
	MA	19.9	21.2	22.6	25.5	28.7	32.3	35.9	42.4	47.4
	Prop. RLE 15–	0.04	0.04	0.04	0.05	0.06	0.07	0.09	0.13	0.16
	PMA	19.9	20.3	20.9	22.0	23.5	25.5	27.6	30.0	30.6
South Asia	Ave. Age	26.5	27.1	27.8	29.8	32.2	34.6	37.0	42.4	47.3
	Prop. 60+	0.07	0.07	0.08	0.09	0.12	0.14	0.17	0.26	0.35
	PARYL	44.1	44.1	43.9	43.2	42.1	41.2	40.4	38.6	37.6
	MA	22.7	23.4	24.5	26.9	29.6	32.8	35.9	42.6	48.5
	Prop. RLE 15–	0.06	0.06	0.06	0.07	0.08	0.10	0.11	0.16	0.19
	PMA	22.7	22.9	23.4	24.7	26.3	28.3	30.2	33.7	36.2
China Region	Ave. Age	31.2	33.2	35.1	38.6	42.3	45.5	47.7	50.7	51.2
	Prop. 60+	0.10	0.11	0.12	0.17	0.24	0.30	0.35	0.41	0.42
	PARYL	43.4	42.1	41.0	39.0	36.9	35.5	35.0	36.1	39.3
	MA	29.6	32.3	34.7	38.5	43.0	47.5	50.7	53.7	54.0
	Prop. RLE 15–	0.07	0.08	0.08	0.11	0.14	0.19	0.21	0.24	0.22
	PMA	29.6	31.7	33.5	36.0	39.3	42.3	44.1	43.0	38.6
Pacific Asia	Ave. Age	28.2	29.3	30.5	33.0	35.4	37.6	39.5	43.2	47.5
	Prop. 60+	0.08	0.08	0.09	0.12	0.16	0.20	0.23	0.29	0.36
	PARYL	44.7	44.4	43.9	42.9	42.1	41.5	41.2	41.2	41.1
	MA	25.3	26.9	28.4	31.4	34.0	36.4	38.6	43.3	48.7
	Prop. RLE 15–	0.06	0.06	0.07	0.08	0.10	0.12	0.14	0.15	0.17
	PMA	25.3	26.2	27.1	28.7	29.9	30.9	31.6	32.4	33.7
Japan/Oceania	Ave. Age	40.4	41.6	43.0	45.7	47.9	49.7	51.3	54.1	57.7
	Prop. 60+	0.22	0.24	0.27	0.31	0.35	0.40	0.42	0.47	0.51
	PARYL	41.3	41.0	40.6	39.7	39.5	39.5	39.6	41.1	43.0
	MA	40.0	41.3	42.8	46.7	49.9	52.1	53.9	57.6	61.1
	Prop. RLE 15–	0.13	0.13	0.14	0.17	0.18	0.18	0.20	0.21	0.21
	PMA	40.0	40.3	40.9	42.9	44.3	44.6	44.5	43.3	41.7
Western Europe	Ave. Age	38.3	39.1	40.1	42.4	44.7	46.8	48.4	51.0	53.5
	Prop. 60+	0.20	0.20	0.21	0.25	0.31	0.34	0.37	0.42	0.46
	PARYL	41.0	41.0	40.8	40.3	39.8	39.6	39.7	41.4	43.5
	MA	36.8	38.3	40.0	43.1	45.8	48.2	50.2	53.5	56.5
	Prop. RLE 15–	0.13	0.13	0.13	0.14	0.15	0.18	0.19	0.20	0.19
	PMA	36.8	37.5	38.3	39.6	40.5	41.1	41.3	39.8	37.7

Supplementary Table 8.2 Six alternative aging measures (derived from the mean scenario) for all world regions *(continued)*

Region	Indicator	2000	2005	2010	2020	2030	2040	2050	2075	2100
Eastern Europe	Ave. Age	37.0	38.4	39.8	42.7	45.6	48.2	50.3	52.4	52.4
	Prop. 60+	0.18	0.18	0.20	0.25	0.29	0.36	0.42	0.44	0.44
	PARYL	39.7	39.1	38.5	37.3	36.0	35.3	34.9	36.9	40.6
	MA	35.6	37.1	38.9	42.9	47.3	51.3	54.0	55.7	55.7
	Prop. RLE 15–	0.13	0.13	0.13	0.15	0.18	0.19	0.22	0.24	0.21
	PMA	35.6	36.4	37.4	39.9	42.8	45.2	46.3	43.5	38.6
European Soviet Union	Ave. Age	37.2	38.5	39.7	42.3	45.1	47.4	49.1	50.1	48.6
	Prop. 60+	0.19	0.18	0.19	0.24	0.29	0.33	0.40	0.41	0.39
	PARYL	37.3	36.9	36.7	35.6	34.4	33.8	33.8	36.7	41.4
	MA	36.4	37.9	39.0	42.4	46.5	50.7	52.4	52.2	50.1
	Prop. RLE 15–	0.14	0.15	0.14	0.15	0.19	0.21	0.22	0.23	0.19
	PMA	36.4	37.0	37.2	39.2	42.0	45.0	45.2	40.8	33.9
World	Ave. Age	29.7	30.4	31.3	33.1	35.2	37.1	38.8	42.3	45.5
	Prop. 60+	0.10	0.10	0.11	0.13	0.17	0.19	0.22	0.27	0.32
	PARYL	43.8	43.6	43.3	42.8	42.1	41.6	41.3	41.0	41.2
	MA	26.6	27.5	28.4	30.8	33.2	35.3	37.3	41.4	45.6
	Prop. RLE 15–	0.07	0.07	0.07	0.08	0.10	0.11	0.12	0.14	0.16
	PMA	26.6	27.0	27.5	28.5	29.4	30.4	31.1	32.1	32.9

Basic Demographic Measures

1. Age Pyramid

Age–sex-specific percentages can be plotted on a graph to create an *age pyramid*, which is a pictorial representation of the age and sex composition of a population. Essentially, a population pyramid displays the percentage distribution of males and females separately on opposite sides of the graph. For each age–sex intersection, one computes a corresponding percentage based on the overall total population size (the denominator). To illustrate, in 2001 in Canada, there were 1,051,455 males aged 10–14, and the total size of the population as a whole was 30,007,090. The corresponding percentage for males aged 10–14 is therefore 1,051,455 / 30,007,090 × 100 = 3.50 per cent. There were 1,001,665 females aged 10–14; the corresponding percentage is 1,001,665 / 30,007,090 × 100 = 3.34 per cent. These computations are executed individually for all age–sex groups in the population, from age 0–4 to 85+ (the upper-terminal age category may vary, e.g. 90+). Thus, in general we write:

$$\% \text{ males in age group } x = \frac{\text{number of males in age group } x}{\text{total population}} \times 100$$

$$\% \text{ females in age group } x = \frac{\text{number of females in age group } x}{\text{total population}} \times 100$$

2. Dependency Ratios

Demographers are interested in three broad age segments of the population:

1. the population below age 15
2. the population aged 15–64
3. the population aged 65 and older.

This is true generally, though certainly not exclusively, since certain demographic measures are best undertaken on the basis of a more detailed age classification of the population, usually involving either single- or five-year age classes. However, the broader age groups are useful because they represent, respectively:

- the youth, who are typically not engaged in full-time economic activity and who consequently require basic services and assistance from society (education, for example);
- the labour force population, or that part of the population that is assumed to be principally engaged in the paid workforce and paying taxes to government for the purposes of societal maintenance; and
- the post-retirement component of society.

The overall youth and old-age dependency ratios are expressed as follows:

$$\text{total dependency ratio} = \frac{P_{0-14} + P_{65+}}{P_{15-64}} \times 100$$

$$\text{youth dependency ratio} = \frac{P_{0-14}}{P_{15-64}} \times 100$$

$$\text{old-age dependency ratio} = \frac{P_{65+}}{P_{15-64}} \times 100$$

where, P_{0-14} is the population below age 15, P_{65+} is the population aged 65 and over, and P_{15-64} means the working age population.

A dependency ratio greater than 100 would indicate that there are more dependants than workers in the population—the greater the ratio, the greater the dependency 'burden' on the working population. A ratio below 100 signifies the opposite situation. Naturally, the overall dependency ratio is the sum of the youth and old age dependency ratios.

Typically, if a society has a high youth dependency ratio, its corresponding old-age dependency ratio will be relatively low, and vice versa. In some situations, however, the youth and old-age components of the overall dependency ratio can be approximately equal. In developing countries, youth dependency ratios are in general substantially larger than the old age dependency ratios. By contrast, the more developed countries have long passed through the demographic transition and have reached a state of demographic maturity. In such countries, old-age dependency ratios have been increasing steadily, accompanied by gradual declines in youth dependency.

3. Median Age of Population (M_d)

Arithmetic averages are highly sensitive to extreme values. For this reason, the median is preferred as a measure of average age of the population. Populations with a large proportion of members below the age of 15 generally have relatively young median ages. High old-age dependency ratios imply aging populations and an older median age. The *median age* is the age that divides the population distribution in half, such that half of the people in the population are above the median, and half are below that value. The corresponding formula for the median age (M_d) is:

$$M_d = l_{Md} + \frac{\frac{P}{2} - \sum P_x}{P_{Md}} i$$

where l_{Md} is the lower limit of the age group containing the median; P is total population; $\sum_{Px}$ is the population in all age groups preceding the age group containing the median; P_{Md} is population in the age group containing the median; and i is the width of the age interval containing the median.

4. Sex Ratio of Population

The sex ratio of population is the balance of males to females, typically multiplied by 100:

$$\text{sex ratio} = \frac{\text{number of males}}{\text{number of females}} \times 100$$

We can illustrate the computation of this measure with actual data. The 2001 census of Canada enumerated 14,706,850 males and 15,300,245 females. Therefore, the resulting sex ratio for the population was 96.1 males for every 100 females. This indicates the presence of about 4 per cent more women than men.

Questions for Critical Thought

1. Is population aging a critical issue for the world in the twenty-first century? Critically discuss this question.

2. How are sex-ratio imbalances related to social demographic phenomena such as marriage and divorce? Can you think of how sex-ratio imbalances may be connected to other sociological phenomena, such as crime?

3. What are other possible longterm effects of skewed sex ratios in societies where son preference is prevalent?

Websites of Interest

The *United Nations Demographic Yearbook* contains a wealth of demographic information by age, sex and country; it is available at the website of the UN's Statistics Division: http://unstats.un.org/unsd/demographic/products/dyb/dyb2.htm. See the website of the United Nations Population Division for additional data by age and sex for countries of the world: www.un.org/esa/population/

The *US Central Intelligence Association* (CIA) provides useful demographic data by country on their World Factbook page: www.cia.gov/library/publications/the-world-factbook/index.html

Further Reading

Carlson, Elwood. (2009). 20th century US generations. *Population Bulletin*, 64(1). Washington, DC.

Cleland, John. (1996). Population growth in the 21st century: Cause for crisis or celebration? *Tropical Medicine and International Health*, 1(1), 15–26.

Crenshaw, Edward M., Ameen, Ansari Z., & Christenson, Matthew. (1998). Population dynamics and economic development: Age-specific population growth rates and economic growth in developing countries. *American Sociological Review*, 62(6), 974–84.

Denton, Frank T., Feaver, Christine H., & Spencer, Byron G. (2000). The future population of Canada and its age distribution. In Frank T. Denton, Deborah Fretz, & Byron G. Spencer (Eds), *Independence and economic security in old age* (pp. 27–56). Vancouver: UBC Press.

Easterlin, Richard A. (1980). *Birth and fortune: The impact of numbers on personal welfare*. New York: Basic Books.

Foot, David K., & Stoffman, Daniel. (1996). *Boom, bust and echo: How to profit from the coming demographic shift*. Toronto: Macfarlane, Walter and Ross.

Garenne, Michael. (2008). Sex ratio at birth and family composition in sub-Saharan Africa: Inter-couple variations. *Journal of Biosocial Science*, 41, 399–407.

Haub, Carl. (2010, May). Japan's demographic future. *Population Reference Bureau*, retrieved from www.prb.org/Articles/2010/japanesedemography.aspx

Kinsella, Devin, & Phillips, David R. (2005). Global aging: The challenges of success. *Population Bulletin*, 60(1). Washington, DC: Population Reference Bureau.

Nichiporuk, Brian. (2000). *The security dynamics of demographic factors. Population matters.* Santa Monica, CA: Rand.

Sanderson, Warren, & Scherbov, Sergei. (2005). Average remaining lifetimes can increase as human populations age. *Nature, 435*(7043), 811–13.

———. (2008). Rethinking age and aging. *Population Bulletin, 63*(4). Washington, DC: Population Reference Bureau.

South, Scott J. (1988). Sex ratios, economic power, and women's roles: A theoretical extension and empirical test. *Journal of Marriage and Family, 50,* 19–31.

Uhlenberg, Peter (Ed.). (2009). *International handbook of population aging.* New York: Springer.

Zhu, Wei Xing, Lu, Li, & Hesketh, Therese. (2009, April 9). China's excess males, sex selective abortion, and one child policy: Analysis of data from 2005 national intercensus survey. *British Medical Journal 338,* b1211. doi:10.1136/bmj.b1211

SECTION V
Nuptiality and Family Processes

Learning Objectives

By the end of this section, students should understand and be able to discuss the following:

- the meaning of nuptiality in demographic analysis
- the relationship between nuptiality processes and other demographic processes
- explanations of nuptiality change
- variations in cohabitation regimes across industrialized countries.

Introduction

The term *nuptiality* refers to the demographic study of union formation and dissolution and associated sociological processes. It encompasses singlehood, marriage, divorce, remarriage, widowhood, cohabitation, and other types of conjugal arrangements in their varied manifestations (same-sex unions, polygyny, and so on). From a strictly demographic standpoint, nuptiality affects population growth indirectly, through its influences on fertility, mortality, and migration. For this reason, demographers pay particular attention to the interconnections of nuptiality processes as antecedent factors to these three key demographic variables. All societies have established norms that govern the formation of and timing of entry into sexual unions, however varied their form (Bongaarts, 1978; Davis & Blake, 1954). Consequently, there is considerable societal variation in the degree to which childbearing may be tolerated outside of traditional marriage. Consider, for example, the situation among highly developed societies today. In the Scandinavian countries, births to unmarried women make up 45 to 65 per cent of total births. In Canada, the likelihood of a child's being born in a cohabiting union is significantly greater in Quebec than in the other provinces (Le Bourdais & Lapierre-Adamcyk, 2004). These cases contrast sharply with the situation in Japan, Greece, and Italy, where extramarital births comprise only 1 to 9 per cent of all births (Wolfe, 2003).

Beside its link to fertility, nuptiality is connected in complex ways to both mortality and migration. In the late nineteenth century, the sociologist Émile Durkheim (1951 [1897]), in an influential study, showed that marriage acts as protective institution against the risk of suicide. This has been confirmed by numerous subsequent studies across a large number of international settings (Stack, 2000a, 200b). It has also been established that married people, compared with single and unmarried people, have reduced odds of mortality overall and from most major causes of death (Goldman, 1993; Gove, 1973; Waite & Gallagher, 2001). It is important to point out also that the family institution itself has been affected by

longterm mortality declines. Today people live longer, and for the average person this means enjoying more years as a member of a family, whether as a parent, as a child, as a spouse, or in the combination of these statuses that define a family (Aries, 1974; Uhlenberg, 1980; Watkins, Menken, & Bongaarts, 1987).

Concerning the association of nuptiality with geographic mobility, family factors have again been shown to be important. For example, the literature suggests that wives are often 'tied migrants', compelled to follow their emigrating husbands. Traditional gender roles within the family together with the unequal share of economic power held by husbands and wives are thought to be key factors underlying this phenomenon (Bielby & Bielby, 1992; Mincer, 1978; Shihadeh, 1991).

At a more general level, major changes in nuptiality patterns in a society usually point to profound socioeconomic transformations and also ideational shifts (i.e., change in values) concerning the nature of conjugal life and the family institution (Jayakody, Thornton, & Axinn, 2008). Some research has shown that economic cycles are correlated with changes in marriage rates (Kirk, 1960). Meanwhile, the example of cohabitation provides an instructive illustration of how nuptiality is tied to broader shifts in society. In many national contexts, cohabitation was once viewed as deviant and unacceptable. Today, however, this form of conjugal union has become commonplace and highly accepted, so much so that in some cases it may be displacing traditional marriage.

Decline in Marriage and the Rise of Cohabitation in Industrialized Countries

Since about the mid-1970s, marriage rates in industrialized countries, especially those in the West, have fallen to historically low levels, while cohabitation trends have moved in the opposite direction, increasing steadily in most countries. An indication of how far marriage rates have declined can be gained by looking at the proportion of never-married women in the prime marriageable ages of 20–24 and 25–29. Increases in these age categories suggest either that marriage is being postponed until later in life or that it is being forgone altogether. According to a recent United Nations report on the subject, from the mid-1970s to 2000, the percentage of never-married women aged 20–24 increased by almost 20 per cent in Japan, by 35 per cent in the United States, and by almost 40 per cent in western Europe as a whole. At the same time, the proportion of single women aged 25–29 has reached new heights, ranging from about 40 per cent in the United States to 60 per cent in western Europe. What these figures imply is that by the end of the twentieth century, on average, more than half of all women in the countries with established market economies were not married before the age of 30, as compared with one-quarter in 1975 (United Nations Population Division Department of Economics and Social Affairs, United Nations Secretariat, 2003).

Changing economic conditions for young adults may explain the retreat from marriage over recent years. An equally plausible explanation is that ideational change is a root cause. Traditional marriage may have lost its centrality for a growing proportion of young adults, while singlehood and cohabitation have become increasingly attractive, more suitable to a secular lifestyle. As we shall see below, theories of nuptiality place varying degrees of emphasis on economic and ideological causes in the decline of marriage and the rise of cohabitation in industrialized countries.

Explanations of Nuptiality Change
Sociological Theory

A key proposition of the modernization perspective in sociology is that contemporary family patterns in the West are the product of profound longterm changes brought on by the Industrial Revolution. As the prevailing agrarian economic system changed to one based largely on industrial production, the family institution was stripped of many of its traditional functions. In the past, the family was the focus of economic production. People grew or made whatever they needed for survival on the farm. Children were born, raised, socialized, and educated within the confines of the family. The elderly were taken care of by the members of the extended family. Gradually, as the processes of modernization intensified, some of the traditional functions of the family were lost, its economic function displaced by factory-based industrialism, its educational function displaced by mandatory school-based education; its caretaking function towards the elderly delegated to outside institutions. In 1948, Davis (p. 426) asserted that, 'there is one function remaining to the family that is clearly institutional and incapable of being shifted to any other institution without a revolutionary change in society. This is the bearing and rearing of children.' By the later part of the twentieth century, the revolutionary change that Davis intimated had already taken form, and increasingly since then, more and more children are born to parents in cohabiting unions.

Decline of the 'Male Breadwinner System'

Industrialization shifted the economic domain of men from the farm to the factory, creating the 'male breadwinner system', characterized by men cast in the role of chief earner and provider, with women as wife and mother. Following the Industrial Revolution this became the predominant system of gender roles. The pattern shifted for a brief period during the two world wars, when women were called upon to perform typical 'male' work in the factories, but most of them returned to their domestic roles soon after the Second World War ended. Betty Friedan (1963) picks up the story here in her account of the 'feminine mystique', in which she describes women's preoccupation with family life and success through marriage in the 1950s. During this time, marriage patterns depended primarily on the economic opportunities available to men—in times of prosperity, men would marry relatively early, while in times of economic hardship, men would marry late.

The gradual decline of the male breadwinner system began in the 1950s and early 1960s, when women started seeking alternatives to marriage and total commitment to their reproductive and childrearing roles (Davis, 1984). Women's entry into the labour force meant that they no longer needed to rely exclusively on matrimony for economic security. This is a core idea of the sociological school that looks at the causes of family change in industrialized countries (Davis & van den Oever, 1982; Westoff, 1983). The collapse of the breadwinner system is thought to be a root cause of the decline of marriage, with critics such as Davis (1984) suggesting that the large-scale entry of women into the labour force and their growing economic independence have introduced a new challenge to the stability of the marital institution.

Second Demographic Transition Perspective

For second demographic transition theorists (Bernhardt, 2003; Lesthaeghe, 2010; Lesthaeghe & Neels, 2002; Lesthaeghe & Surkyn, 1988; van de Kaa, 1987), late marriage, declining rates of remarriage, increased divorce rates, and rising incidence of cohabitation (and, lately, same-sex unions) are phenomena that stem from a common source: the depreciation of the institutional aspects of the family in favour of more personal, individualistic values. In postmodern societies these tendencies are pervasive among the young, arising from a quest for greater individual self-fulfillment coupled with a greater tolerance for diversity in lifestyles. Tradition has been displaced by this ethos of individualism, complemented by growing secularism (detachment from religion) and post-materialistic values. The latter refers to the tendency among the young to reject many of the features that came to define the life and aspirations of the bourgeoisie, such as high income, technological progress, and consumerism.

Above all else, post-materialists place emphasis on spontaneity, self-reliance, and meaningful

personal relationships, or what Giddens (1992) refers to as 'the pure relationship', entered into for its own sake in a search for emotional intimacy, a kind of relationship to which external criteria (i.e. traditional norms) have no relevance. However, as Giddens points out, such relationships are, generally speaking, highly unstable and impermanent. It is a characteristic feature of this type of relationship that it can be terminated more or less at will by either party at any particular point. To the extent that the 'pure relationship' has come to represent the primary model of intimacy and a pervasive feature of today's youth culture, it undermines the centrality of traditional marriage. While it presents itself as an attractive alternative to marriage (i.e. cohabitation), it also encourages a mindset of impermanency in the participants.

In sum, according to second demographic transition theory, these new orientations, in combination, have paved the way for a growing preference among young adults for alternative lifestyles, particularly in the arenas of sexuality and conjugal behaviours, and as such there has been a growing 'destandardization' of family formation patterns.

Demographic Theory

In the early 1970s, Dixon (1971) proposed that the timing and extent of marriage in society are determined by three factors:

1. the availability of potential mates in the prime marriageable ages
2. the feasibility of marriage for young adults
3. the desirability of marriage.

The first of these factors relates to sex ratios in the prime marriageable ages; the second pertains to young adults' ability to afford marriage; the third corresponds to social attitudes and orientation towards marriage, that is, the degree to which it is a desired option among young men and women.

The idea underlying the first factor, availability,

is that gross imbalances in the sex ratio of people in the prime ages for marriage would create a context that either facilitates marriage or discourages it. Dixon (1971, p. 22) hypothesized that masculinity ratios (i.e. the ratio of men to women), 'should be positively correlated with marital delays among men and with bachelorhood [i.e. with more men marrying later in life and remaining single], and negatively correlated with marital delays among women and with spinsterhood'. Subsequent studies on the 'sex ratio question' confirm that imbalances in the number of men and women in the prime marriageable ages can indeed have important effects on marriage opportunities and divorce probabilities (Guttentag & Secord, 1983; South, 1988; South & Lloyd, 1995).

Economic Theory

Easterlin–Oppenheimer Thesis

Easterlin (1969, 1980) has proposed that marriage rates are conditioned mainly by the extent to which economic opportunities are available to young men. Oppenheimer (1988, 1994, 1997) agrees with this proposition, adding that the social demographic literature must 'bring men back in[to]' the explanation of family change, reversing the overwhelming emphasis on women as principal actors.

Change in marriage rates is a function of whether cohorts of young adult men are economically secure and thus able to afford their material aspirations along with marriage and family-building. The marriage boom of the post-war years and the subsequent marriage bust today are products of the same set of factors, though operating in different directions to cause a rise in marriage from the 1950s through the early 1970s and a decline thereafter. Marriage rates increased after World War II because jobs were plentiful for young men during a period of sustained economic growth. Young male workers enjoyed good access to opportunities, facilitated by the relative small size of the cohorts of entry-level workers born during the low fertility period of the 1930s. These cohorts were fortunate. Their members experienced less competition for entry-level jobs and greater advancement opportunities in the workplace.

The ensuing marriage bust can be attributed to the same set of factors, but this time working in the opposite direction. High fertility rates in the 'baby boom' period culminated in large cohorts of entry-level workers in the 1980s and 1990s, thus generating increased levels of competition in the workplace. The economic aspirations of these generations have been thwarted to such a degree as to discourage marriage. To make matters worse, the economy has been more volatile that it was at the height of the boom years after the Second World War. The world has seen several recessions since the 1973 oil crisis. Economic globalization has intensified the level of competition among corporations for consumer markets and profits. Businesses have restructured as a means to cut costs. Many jobs in the manufacturing sector have been moved to developing countries, where manufacturing and labour costs are substantially lower. Thus, the decline in marriage rates may have less to do with changes in the status of women and more with the erosion of economic security among young adult men.

Economic insecurity and instability among men also account for increased levels of family strain and higher divorce rates. As far as cohabitation is concerned, many young men are drawn to this type of conjugal arrangement because it is seen as an inexpensive alternative to marriage and therefore an adaptation to socioeconomic uncertainty (Oppenheimer, 2003).

Becker's Gains to Marriage Thesis

As we have seen, Dixon (1971) argued that marriage propensities are affected by its feasibility, the supply of potential marital partners, and the extent to which this institution remains desirable to young adults. Gary Becker's thesis elaborates on this third feature of Dixon's proposition. According to Becker (1973, 1974, 1991), the gains associated with traditional marriage have waned over time for both men and women, but mostly for women. Women, traditionally, are viewed as the principal agents of family change. In earlier times, when a man and a woman married, the husband specialized in market work and the wife in home production. The wife traded part of her domestic services, including childbearing and childrearing, to the husband in exchange for economic security provided through his income. Today, however, lower fertility rates and increased levels of female earning power in the labour force have helped reduce the gains available to women through marriage by affording them greater degrees of economic autonomy than they experienced during earlier times. Thus, whereas single men and women once acted as trading partners in marriage, with both parties benefiting from a traditional gendered division of labour in and outside the home, women today will enter marriage only if doing so will bring them sufficient benefits, or at least leave them no worse off than if they were to remain single.

Although it is not the only factor involved, the secular growth in wages, which has contributed significantly to the growth in the labour force participation of women has factored significantly in the rise of divorce rates, according to Becker and others. Many marriages today dissolve because for women the utility expected from staying married falls below the utilities expected from divorce. In other words, given increased access to economic self-sufficiency, contemporary women have less reason for staying in an unrewarding marital relationship (Becker, Landes, & Michael, 1977; Booth et al., 1984; Ermisch, 1981; Grossbard-Schechtman, 1995; Hess, 2004; Hiedemann, Suhomlinova, & O'Rand, 1998; Preston and Richards 1975). As divorce has become more common and an increasing proportion of women have gained economic self-sufficiency, society has seen a cultural shift grounded in an increasing preference among a younger generation of women (and men) to opt for cohabitating unions instead of traditional marriage (Goldscheider & Waite, 1986).

Cohabitation Regimes in the United States and 16 Other Countries

In their study of cohabitation regimes, Heuveline and Timberlake note that although nonmarital cohabitation is steadily increasing in the United States, much of the existing literature in this area has concerned itself with comparisons between individuals who cohabit and those who do not. In an effort to ascertain what type of cohabitation regime is most applicable to the experience of the United States and how it compares with the situation in 16 other industrialized countries with varying levels of cohabitation, the authors propose a typology that encompasses six conceptually distinct ideal types of cohabiting regimes. The regimes and the countries believed to fit each type are as follows:

a) cohabitation is a marginal phenomenon and is socially discouraged (Italy, Poland, Spain)
b) cohabitation is a prelude to marriage (Belgium, Czech Republic, Hungary, Switzerland)
c) cohabitation represents a stage in the marriage process, and thus children are likely to be born in these unions (Austria, Finland, Germany, Latvia, Slovenia)
d) cohabitation serves as an alternative to singlehood, is typically brief in duration, and usually ends in separation instead of marriage (New Zealand, United States)
e) cohabitation is an alternative to marriage (Canada, France)
f) cohabitation is indistinguishable from marriage (Sweden).

As reflected by the variety of cohabitation regimes, characterizing countries as having either high or low levels of cohabitation is inadequate in describing the reality of this phenomenon.

Is Cohabitation Gradually Replacing Marriage in Canada?

The scope of Heuveline and Timberlake's analysis is cross-national and therefore does not speak to within-country variations in cohabitation. It may be that regions within a given country present radically different patterns and levels of both marriage and cohabitation than what is expressed by national averages. Regions within a country may vary in the distribution of individual traits related to the propensity to cohabit, marry, and raise children out of wedlock, and also to the contextual factors that affect these propensities. There is a need for further research along these lines.

In their effort to address the question of regional variations in nuptiality, and specifically cohabitation, Le Bourdais and Lapierre-Adamcyk examined the Canadian context, comparing the experience of Quebec with that of the rest of the country. In doing so, they tackled a question raised frequently in the nuptiality literature (Bumpass, Sweet & Cherlin, 1991; Wu, 2000): has cohabitation become an alternative to traditional marriage, or does it represent a kind of trial marriage for young couples?

Le Bourdais and Lapierre-Adamcyk begin their study by describing trends in marriage and cohabitation across Canada's regions before assessing whether cohabitation constitutes a new stage in the progression to marriage or an alternative to marriage altogether. Their research shows that while marriage has declined and divorce rates have increased across Canada as a whole, there are significant regional differences. In Quebec as compared with the rest of Canada:

- there is less marriage and much more cohabitation
- the risk of cohabiting women eventually marrying is much lower
- cohabiting unions last longer but are less likely to develop into marriages.

Cohabiting unions have become widely accepted in Quebec and form the basis of family life for an increasing proportion of conjugal unions. In the rest of Canada, cohabitation represents predominantly a childless prelude to marriage—a step in the marriage process. Thus, Quebec experiences a much larger proportion of births to cohabiting couples, and this type of arrangement has become the family setting for a rising proportion of children. The question that remains is, how stable are such unions for children?

In keeping with much of the literature in this area, Le Bourdais and Lapierre-Adamcyck find that in Quebec, as in other parts of Canada, cohabiting unions are much more unstable than marriages are. They also discover that the risk of dissolution in Quebec and the rest of Canada is strongly conditioned by whether a couple is married or cohabiting at the time when they have their first child. Among cohabiting couples that have had a first child, the risk of union dissolution is actually lower in Quebec than it is in the rest of Canada. In other words, even though cohabiting couples throughout Canada share a generally high risk of dissolution, it seems the risk is somewhat lower in Quebec if one considers cohabiting couples that have experienced a first birth.

Is it possible to conclude that cohabitation in Quebec has become indistinguishable from traditional marriage? Not according to Le Bourdais and Lapierre-Adamcyk, who point out that there remain important differences between marital and cohabiting unions (for example, cohabiters are more individualistic in their orientations than those who marry). They conclude, therefore, that in Quebec, 'cohabitation remains an alternative to rather than a true substitute for marriage'.

Works Cited

Aries, Philippe. (1974). *Western attitudes toward death: From the Middle Ages to the present.* Trans. Patricia M. Ranum. Baltimore, MD: Johns Hopkins University Press.

Becker, Gary S. (1973). A theory of marriage: Part I. *Journal of Political Economy, 81*(4), 813–46.

———. (1974). A theory of marriage: Part II. *Journal of Political Economy, 82*: S11–S26.

———. (1991). *A treatise on the family* (enlarged edn). Cambridge, MA: Harvard University Press.

Becker, Gary S., Landes, Elisabeth M., & Michael, Robert T. (1977). An economic analysis of marital instability. *Journal of Political Economy, 85*(6), 1141–87.

Bernhardt, Eva. (2003). Cohabitation. In Paul Demeny & Geoffrey McNicolls (Eds), *Encyclopedia of population* (pp. 153–5). New York: Macmillan Reference USA/Thompson Gale.

Bielby, William T., & Bielby, D.D. (1992). I will follow him: Family ties, gender-role beliefs, and reluctance to relocate for a better job. *American Journal of Sociology, 97*(5), 1241–67.

Bongaarts, John. (1978). A framework for analyzing the proximate determinants of fertility. *Population and Development Review, 4*(1), 105–32.

Booth, Alan, Johnson, D., White, L.K., & Edwards, J.N. (1984). Women, outside employment, and marital instability. *American Journal of Sociology, 90*, 567–83.

Bumpass, Larry L., Sweet, James A., & Cherlin, Andrew. (1991). The role of cohabitation in declining rates of marriage. *Journal of Marriage and Family, 53*, 913–27.

Davis, Kingsley. (1948). *Human society.* New York: Macmillan.

———. (1984). Wives and work: The sex role revolution and its consequences. *Population and Development Review, 10*, 397–417.

Davis, Kingsley, & Blake, Judith. (1954). Social structure and fertility: An analytic framework. *Economic Development and Cultural Change, 4*(4), 211–35.

Davis, Kingsley, & van den Oever, Pietronella. (1982). Demographic foundations of new sex roles. *Population and Development Review, 8*(3), 495–511.

Dixon, Ruth B. (1971). Explaining cross-cultural variations in age at marriage and proportions never marrying. *Population Studies, 25*, 215–33.

Durkheim, Emile. (1951 [1897]). *Suicide.* Trans. J.A. Spaulding & G. Simpson. New York: Free Press.

Easterlin, Richard A. (1969). Towards a socio-economic theory of fertility: A survey of recent research on economic factors in American fertility. In S.J. Berham, et al. (Eds), *Fertility and family planning: A world view.* Ann Arbor, MI: University of Michigan Press.

———. (1980). *Birth and fortune: The impact of numbers on personal welfare.* New York: Basic Books.

Ermisch, John F. (1981). Economic opportunities, marriage squeezes, and the propensity to marry: An economic analysis of period marriage rates in England and Wales. *Population Studies, 35*, 347–56.

Friedan, Betty. (1963). *The feminine mystique.* New York: Norton.

Giddens, Anthony. (1992). *The transformation of intimacy: Sexuality, love and eroticism in modern societies.* Stanford, CA: Stanford University Press.

Goldman, Noreen. (1993). Marriage selection and mortality patterns: Inferences and fallacies. *Demography, 30*(2): 189–208.

Goldscheider, Frances Kobrin, & Waite, Linda J. (1986). Sex differences in the entry into marriage. *American Journal of Sociology, 92*(1), 91–109.

Gove, Walter R. (1973). Sex, marital status, and mortality. *American Journal of Sociology, 79*, 45–67.

Grossbard-Shechtman, Shoshana. (1995). Marriage market models. In K. Ierulli & M. Tomassi (Eds), *The new economics of human behaviour.* Cambridge: Cambridge University Press.

Guttentag, Marcia, & Secord, Paul F. (1983). Introduction: The sex ratio question. In Marcia Guttentag & Paul F. Secord, *Too many women? The sex ratio question* (pp. 13–33). Beverly Hills, CA: Sage.

Hess, Gregory. (2004). Marriage and consumption insurance: What's love got to do with it? *Journal of Political Economy, 112*(2), 290–313.

Heuveline, Patrick, & Timberlake, Jeffrey M. (2004). The role of cohabitation in family formation: The United States in comparative perspective. *Journal of Marriage and Family, 66*, 1214–30.

Hiedemann, B., Suhomlinova, O., & O'Rand, A.M. (1998). Economic independence, economic status, and empty nest in midlife marital disruption. *Journal of Marriage and Family, 60*, 219–31.

Jayakody, Rukmalie, Thornton, Arland, & Axinn, William (Eds). (2008). *International family change: International perspectives.* New York: Lawrence Erlbaum/Taylor and Francis.

Kirk, Dudley. (1960). The influence of business cycles on marriage and birth rates. In National Bureau of Economic Research, *Demographic and economic change in developed countries* (pp. 257–76). Princeton, NJ: Princeton University Press.

Le Bourdais, Céline, & Lapierre-Adamcyk, Évelyne. (2004). Changes in conjugal life in Canada: Is cohabitation progressively replacing marriage? *Journal of Marriage and Family, 66*, 929–42.

Lesthaeghe, Ron. (2010). The unfolding story of the second demographic transition. *Population and Development Review, 36*(2), 211–51.

Lesthaeghe, Ron, & Neels, Karel. (2002). From the first to the second demographic transition: An interpretation of the spatial continuity of demographic innovation in France, Belgium and Switzerland. *Population and Development Review, 9*(3), 325–60.

Lesthaeghe, Ron, & Surkyn, Johan. (1988). Cultural dynamics and economic explanation of fertility change. *Population and Development Review, 14*(1), 1–45.

Locoh, Thérése. (2006). Factors in couple formation. In Graziella Caselli, Jacques Vallin, & Guillaume Wunsch (Eds), *Demography—analysis and synthesis: A treatise in demography* (pp. 373–96). Amsterdam: Elsevier and Academic Press.

Mills, Melinda. (2000). *The transformation of partnerships: Canada, the Netherlands, and the Russian Federation in the age of modernity.* Amsterdam: Thela Theses, Population Studies.

Mincer, Jacob. (1978). Family migration decision. *Journal of Political Economy, 86*, 749–73.

Oppenheimer, Kincade V. (1988). A theory of marriage timing. *American Journal of Sociology, 94*(3), 563–91.

———. (1994). Women's rising employment and the future of the family in industrial societies. *Population and Development Review, 20*, 239–342.

———. (1997). Women's employment and the gain to marriage: The specialization and trading model. *Annual Review of Sociology, 23*, 431–53.

———. (2003). Cohabiting and marriage during young men's career-development process. *Demography*, 40, 1, 127-49.

Preston, Samuel H., & Richards, Alan Thomas. (1975). The influence of women's work opportunities on marriage rates. *Demography, 12*(2), 209–22.

Ravenera, Zenaida R., Rajulton, Fernando, & Burch, Thomas K. (1998). Early life transitions of Canadian women: A cohort analysis of timing, sequences, and variations. *European Journal of Population 14*, 179–204.

Shihadeh, Edward S. (1991). The prevalence of husband-centered migration: Employment consequences for married women. *Journal of Marriage and Family, 43*, 432–44.

South, Scott J. (1988). Sex ratios, economic power, and women's roles: A theoretical extension and empirical test. *Journal of Marriage and Family, 50*, 1931.

South, Scott J., & Lloyd, Karen M. (1995). Spousal alternatives and marital dissolution. *American Sociological Review, 60*(1), 21–35.

Stack, Steven. (2000a). Suicide: A 15-year review of the sociological literature. Part I: Cultural and economic factors. *Suicide and Life-Threatening Behavior, 30*(2), 145–62.

———. (2000b). Suicide: A 15-year review of the sociological literature. Part II: Modernization and social integration perspectives. *Suicide and Life-Threatening Behavior, 30*(2), 163–76.

Uhlenberg, Peter. (1980). Death and the family. *Journal of Family History, 5*(3), 313–20.

United Nations Population Division Department of Economics and Social Affairs, United Nations Secretariat. (2003). *Partnership and reproductive behaviour in low-fertility countries.* New York: UN (ESA/P/WP.177).

van de Kaa, Dirk J. (1987). Europe's second demographic transition. *Population Bulletin, 42*(1). Washington, DC: Population Reference Bureau.

Waite, Linda J., & Gallagher, Maggie. (2001). *The case for marriage: Why married people are happier, healthier, and better off financially.* New York: Broadway Books.

Watkins, Susan Cotts, Menken, Jane A., & Bongaarts, John. (1987). Demographic foundations of family change. *American Sociological Review, 52*, 346–58.

Westoff, Charles F. (1983). Fertility decline in the West: Causes and prospects. *Population and Development Review, 9*, 99–104.

Wolfe, Barbara L. (2003). Fertility, nonmarital. In Paul Demeny & Geoffrey McNicoll (Eds), *Encyclopedia of population* (vol. 1, pp. 409–12). New York: Macmillan Reference USA and Thomson Gale.

Wu, Zheng. (2000). *Cohabitation: An alternative form of family living.* Toronto: Oxford University Press.

CHAPTER 9

Changes in Conjugal Life in Canada: Is Cohabitation Progressively Replacing Marriage?

Céline Le Bourdais and Évelyne Lapierre-Adamcyk

In the last 30 years, most Western countries have witnessed formidable changes in the foundation of the family institution. Demographic indicators point to a postponement of marriage and to a decline in the proportion of individuals who are likely to marry during their lifetime.

Marriage has also been characterized by growing levels of instability, with divorce rates showing that it is not that uncommon among these countries to find that one marriage out of two is likely to dissolve. The dramatic increase in cohabiting unions over the last 30 years—first as a way for young adults to start their conjugal life, and more recently, as an environment in which to start and raise a family—further led researchers to question the 'future of marriage' (title of Jessie Bernard's well-known book, and the theme of the 2003 National Council on Family Relations [NCFR] annual conference). Currently, the recognition of same-sex marriage has prompted debates about the meaning of marriage. How has the institution of marriage changed in recent decades, and how do these changes vary across cultures and across countries? These are some of the questions that were raised at the 2003 NCFR conference.

One of the ways to document the weakening of marriage and its change in meaning is to look more closely at the progression of cohabitation over time. This was the focus of the plenary session 'Cohabitation and Marriage in Western Countries', in which we were invited to present a paper. More specifically, we

were asked first to describe the demographic trends of marriage and cohabitation in Canada, and second, to assess whether cohabitation constitutes a new stage in the progression to marriage or an alternative to marriage altogether. After addressing these issues, we close by discussing possible explanations underlying the observed changes. By contrasting the evolution of demographic behaviour adopted across the different regions in Canada, we show that cohabitation has reached different stages of development in Quebec as opposed to elsewhere in Canada, as formulated by Kiernan (2001). In the former, cohabitation seems now to be nearly indistinguishable from marriage, as it is in Sweden, whereas in the latter, cohabitation is still accepted predominantly as a childless phase of conjugal life, as is the case in the United States.

The Decline of Marriage

Profound changes have transformed the conjugal life of Canadians in recent decades. Figure 9.1 presents the evolution of total female marriage rates, calculated by combining marriage vital statistics and census population counts, and exemplifies the fall of marriage over the last 30 years. These rates show the proportions of women within synthetic cohorts who would marry at least once if the behaviours observed in any given year were to last.

As can be seen in Figure 9.1, marriage was still very popular throughout the 1960s; more than 9

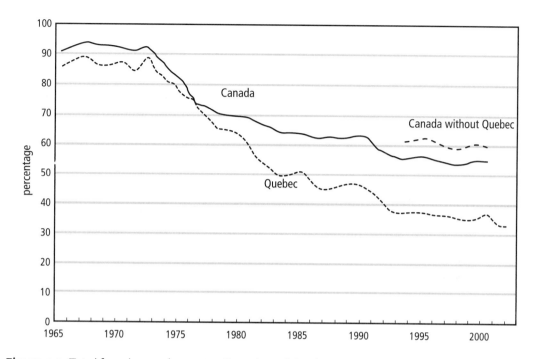

Figure 9.1 Total female marriage rate, Canada and Quebec, 1965–2002

Sources: Quebec: Duchesne (2003). Canada, 1965–87: Dumas & Péron (1992). Canada, 1988–92: Dumas & Bélanger (1994). Canada and Canada without Quebec, 1993–2000: Bélanger (2003).

women out of 10 would marry over the course of their life. In the mid-1970s, marriage started to lose ground progressively, and by the turn of the century just slightly over half of women were expected to marry in Canada. In Quebec, the fall was far more drastic. From nearly 90 per cent in the 1960s, the proportion of women who would marry at least once in their life fell to 50 per cent in 1984, and only one woman in three is now expected to marry according to most recent data. The gap separating Quebec's women from their counterparts living elsewhere in Canada widened throughout the period studied as Quebecers deserted marriage. By 2000, 60 per cent of women living outside Quebec were expected to marry at least once, compared with less than 40 per cent of those living in Quebec. When measured for men, total marriage rates are generally slightly lower but follow similar trends.

The decline of marriage has also been accompanied by a postponement of the age at first marriage. When marriage was widespread, it was relatively precocious, with an average age of 25.4 years among men and 22.5 years among women in Canada in 1960 (26.0 and 23.5 in Quebec, respectively: Dumas & Péron, 1992; Duchesne, 2003). Now that marriage has become less popular, individuals marry approximately 5 years later. In 2001, the age at first marriage was 30.2 and 28.2 years, respectively, for men and women in Canada (30.6 and 28.8 years in Quebec in 2002: Duchesne, 2003; Statistics Canada, 2003a).

Not only has marriage become less popular but it has also become more unstable since the adoption of the Divorce Law by the Canadian Parliament in 1968. In 1970, the total divorce rate was approximately 10 per cent, indicating that 1 marriage in 10 would eventually end in divorce. Although fluctuating depending on the courts' availability and because of modifications to the Divorce Law introduced in 1985, the divorce rate increased steadily in the following years until it reached a plateau in the 1990s. Thirty years after divorce became more easily accessible, the rate has multiplied by four. In Canada as a whole, nearly 40 per cent of couples are expected to divorce. Interestingly, in Quebec, where marriage is least popular, it is most fragile, with nearly one couple out of two likely to divorce (Lapierre-Adamcyk & Le Bourdais, 2004).

Although marriage is on the decline and divorce is on the rise, one cannot conclude that conjugal life has receded to the same extent. From survey data, we know that the majority of Canadian men and women wish 'to have a lasting relationship as a couple' (Lapierre-Adamcyk, Le Bourdais, & Marcil-Gratton, 1999). Hence, the decline of marriage has been mostly offset by the growth of cohabiting unions that began in western Europe after May 1968. In this first phase, cohabitation emerged as an 'avant-garde phenomenon' that was adopted by a small fraction of the young, and often well-educated, population (Kiernan, 2001).

The Growth of Cohabitating Unions as a Form of Conjugal Life

Because of its informal and unstable nature, the importance of cohabitation is often difficult to measure and varies depending on point of view. In Canada, cohabiting unions were recognized as an alternative form of conjugal life from the beginning. As early as the 1971 census, long before cohabitation had become commonplace, cohabiting couples were instructed to consider themselves as 'married'; they were thus counted as *couples,* but they remained invisible among the larger number of married couples (Le Bourdais & Juby, 2001). In 1981, Statistics Canada maintained this instruction on marital status, and included *common-law partner* as a category to describe the relationship

of individuals with the householder, permitting estimation of the number of cohabiting unions for heads of household. The 1986 census was the first to collect direct information on both marital and common-law status of all household members, and to allow a full count of cohabiting couples. In the United States, the practice has been quite different. It was only in the 1990 decennial census that the US Census Bureau introduced the category *unmarried partner* to identify a person's relationship with the householder, thus excluding cohabiting couples in which one partner was not the householder (Seltzer, 2000). And it was not until the mid-1990s that family researchers began to consider unmarried couples with children as couples—that is, as *two-parent* rather than *one-parent* families (Bumpass & Raley, 1995; Bumpass, Raley, & Sweet, 1995). In Canada, they were classified as such as early as 1971.

Figure 9.2 presents the percentages of couples who were identified as cohabiting across Canada in three different censuses. In 1981, 6 per cent of couples were cohabiting in Canada. The proportion varied from 3.4 per cent in the Atlantic region to roughly 7 per cent in the provinces of Quebec and British Columbia. In the 1970s, cohabitation was still a relatively new phenomenon. Consensual unions were usually short-lived; after a few years, cohabiters had either married or separated, explaining the relatively low percentage in the 1981 census.

From that point on, the evolution of cohabitation took a very different course in Quebec from the rest of Canada. During the 1980s, the percentage of couples who were cohabiting in Quebec more than doubled to 19 per cent in 1991. The increase continued unabatedly throughout the 1990s. In 20 years, the proportion of couples who were cohabiting was multiplied by more than 4 in Quebec, but only by 1.9 in British Columbia. Consequently, although both provinces began at a similar level, the percentage of cohabiting couples is now nearly 2.5 times higher in the former than in the latter. As of 2001, the popularity of cohabitation in Quebec is as widespread as it is in Sweden, where 30 per cent of couples are cohabiting, and clearly greater than in

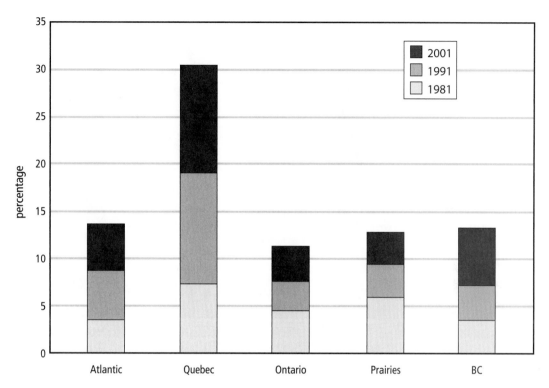

Figure 9.2 Percentage of couples cohabiting in Canada by region of residence: 1981, 1991, and 2001

Source: Statistics Canada for 1981; *Canadian Families: Diversity and Change* (cat. 12F0061XPF). For 1991, 1996 *Census* (table 93F0022XDB96008). For 2001, 2001 *Census* (table 97F0005XCB01006).

France (17.5 per cent) or the United States (8.2 per cent; Statistics Canada, 2002b). The percentage in Canada outside Quebec (12 per cent) falls between these two countries.

Census data give an idea of the percentage of individuals who are cohabiting at a given point in time. In large part, these percentages are composed of young individuals who chose cohabitation to start their conjugal life, but they underestimate the extent to which this phenomenon occurs because cohabiting individuals can marry or separate before the census date. Moreover, as divorce rose, census data also increasingly included proportions of individuals who opted for a consensual union after a first marriage dissolved.

Figure 9.3 presents the cumulative probabilities (derived from life table estimates) that women

experience a first union, through marriage or cohabitation, in five different cohorts. This figure first shows that the vast majority of individuals across all cohorts still form conjugal unions; well above 90 per cent of women born in the 1960s or earlier had formed a union at least once in their life, and 84 per cent of those born in the 1970s had already done so by age 29.

How women started their conjugal life changed drastically across cohorts, however. In the oldest cohort born in the 1930s (ages 60–69 in 2001), 93 per cent of women married directly, and only 2 per cent began by living with a cohabiting partner. The percentage of women cohabiting in their first union throughout the 1970s rose to 27 per cent among those born in the 1950s, and to 42 per cent among those

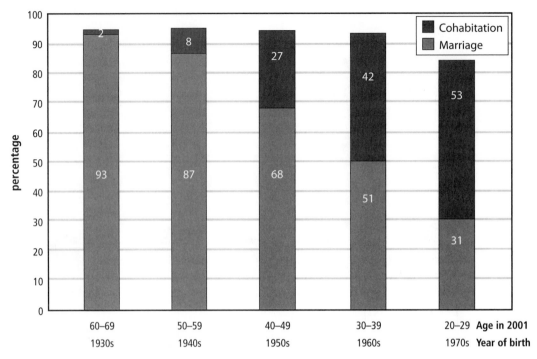

Figure 9.3 Cumulated probabilities that women in Canada enter their first union through marriage or cohabitation, by age cohorts

Source: 2001 General Social Survey on Family; Statistics Canada (2002a), Figure 1.

born in the 1960s. Among the youngest cohorts who entered their first union during the 1990s, cohabitation has become the favoured way to start conjugal life. By age 29, 53 per cent of women had formed a consensual union, as compared with only 31 per cent who had married directly. The percentage of women who will eventually marry directly in the youngest cohorts should be slightly higher as they get older, however, because age at first marriage is increasing as individuals postpone marriage. The figures presented for Canada as a whole are similar to those observed in the United States, where 43 per cent of the first unions concluded by women in the early 1980s and 54 per cent of those formed in the early 1990s began with cohabitation (Bumpass & Lu, 2000).

The trends observed in Canada vary tremendously across the country. As can be seen in Figure 9.4,

marriage was the typical way to start a first union in the early 1970s. It characterized 85 per cent of first unions in Canada outside Quebec, and 80 per cent of those in Quebec. Twenty years later, the situation has totally reversed in Quebec. Four times out of five, Quebec women opted for cohabitation to start their first union in the early 1990s, compared with one in two for their counterparts living elsewhere in Canada. Quebec women now increasingly resemble their Swedish counterparts who, 9 times out of 10, choose cohabitation to start conjugal life (Kiernan, 2001), whereas other Canadian women have similar behaviours to those of their southern neighbours.

Choosing marriage (or cohabitation) to begin conjugal life affects, but does not preclude, the likelihood that women experience cohabitation (or marriage) subsequently. On the one hand, although only

Figure 9.4 Type of first unions formed by women in the early 1970s and 1990s, Quebec and Canada without Quebec

Source: 1995 General Social Survey on Family; Dumas & Bélanger (1997).

8 per cent of women born in the 1940s experienced cohabitation at the beginning of their conjugal life (see Figure 9.3), another 11 per cent did so after their first marriage dissolved (Statistics Canada, 2002a). On the other hand, 78 per cent of women born during the 1960s had married at least once, compared with 51 per cent who had married without first cohabiting. Put differently, older generations of women were more likely to experience cohabitation later in the course of their life, after marrying young, whereas more recent generations are more inclined to marry later—if they ever do—after having first cohabited. It is difficult to forecast the proportion of women who will eventually marry among the youngest cohorts. One thing is certain, though, it is likely to remain quite low in Quebec, where the total marriage rate has been well below 40 per cent for more than 10 years.

As we have seen, cohabitation has progressively replaced marriage, at least in Quebec, as a way to start conjugal life. We know from various studies, however, that cohabiting unions are more short-lived than marriages, and that they have become even less stable over time (Bumpass & Lu, 2000; Dumas & Bélanger, 1997; Statistics Canada, 2002a). A partial explanation for the rising instability of cohabiting unions can perhaps be found in the wide diversity of existing unions. For a significant proportion of couples, cohabitation has replaced 'going steady' relationships, which do not necessarily involve any longterm engagement. For another group, cohabiting unions constitute a 'prelude to marriage' or a 'trial marriage'—that is, a period in which to test the solidity of the relationship while completing schooling and attaining professional achievement (Villeneuve-Gokalp, 1991). As cohabitation has become more socially acceptable, it seems to have attracted larger numbers of less committed couples. As a result, the proportion of cohabiters who married their partners within 3 to 5 years of the beginning of the union has decreased, while the proportion of those who separated has increased (Bumpass & Lu, 2000; Turcotte & Bélanger, 1997; for a review, see Smock & Gupta, 2001). Concomitantly, the percentage of cohabiting unions that endured longer than 3 to 5 years has increased, both in Canada and in the United States, partly countervailing the trend toward rising instability. Again, the situation in Quebec differs from that observed elsewhere in Canada. Cohabitations are of longer duration in Quebec, and they are less likely to transform into marriage (Le Bourdais & Marcil-Gratton, 1996; Turcotte & Bélanger, 1997).

Transitions outside cohabiting unions tend to occur relatively early after the union starts. Hence, 2 years after the beginning of the union, the likelihood of experiencing separation or marriage falls quite abruptly (Brown, 2000). These results tend to suggest that cohabitation, in Canada as in the United States, has successfully completed its second phase; it is 'either a prelude to or a probationary period where the strength of the relationship may be tested prior to committing to marriage and is predominantly a childless phase' (Kiernan, 2001, p. 5). The passage to the next stage requires cohabitation to become an alternative to marriage, allowing individuals to fulfill both conjugal and parental roles.

The Growth of Cohabitating Unions as a Form of Family Life

The percentage of nonmarital births has increased sharply over the last 20 years. In the early 1980s, approximately one birth in six occurred outside marriage in Canada (Marcil-Gratton, 1998). By 2000, nearly one child in three was born to an unmarried mother (Statistics Canada, 2003b). These figures roughly compare to those observed in the United States (Cherlin, 2004), yet increasingly differ from the situation experienced in Quebec, where nearly 60 per cent of all registered births in 2000 were to unmarried mothers (Duchesne, 2003). Clearly, marriage no longer constitutes the sole acceptable way to become a parent, and nonmarital pregnancies do not automatically bring social reprobation, forcing young mothers to either rapidly marry the child's father or place the child for adoption.

To be born outside marriage does not necessarily mean to be born to a single mother. In fact, the percentage of children born to an unknown or nondeclared father was only 3.4 per cent in 2002 in Quebec, a slight decrease from previous years (Duchesne, 2003). This suggests that nonmarital births are more closely associated with the decline of marriage and the progression of cohabitation than with an increase of formerly 'illegitimate' births.

Survey data rather than vital statistics allow a better description of the family environment in which children are born. Figure 9.5 presents the distribution (in percentage) of various cohorts of children according to type of parents' union at the time of their birth. First, this figure shows that the vast majority (over 85 per cent) of children born in 1971–3 were born to married parents who had not previously cohabited; this was the case in Quebec and elsewhere in Canada. Only between 6 per cent and 7 per cent of children were born outside a union—that is, to a single mother.

As we saw earlier, cohabitation began to emerge during the 1970s as a way to enter conjugal life. Hence, it is not surprising to discover, 10 years later, that the proportion of children born to parents who had married after first cohabiting has increased tremendously. In Quebec, as elsewhere in Canada, this situation concerned a quarter of the children born in 1983–4, compared with 5 per cent or less of those born in the early 1970s. Outside Quebec, in the early 1980s, the percentage of couples who gave birth to a child within a cohabiting union remained relatively low (7 per cent). If, by the 1980s, cohabitation had become accepted as a form of conjugal life, it was not yet recognized as a way to start a family.

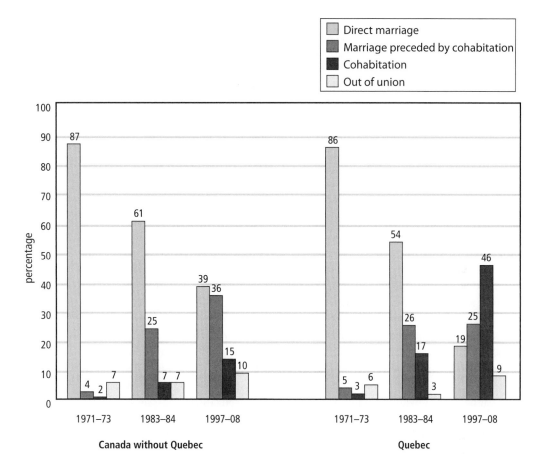

Figure 9.5 Type of parents' union at birth for different cohorts of children, Quebec and Canada without Quebec

Source: Cohorts from 1971–3 and 1983–4 adapted from Marcil-Gratton & Le Bourdais (1999). Cohorts from 1997–8 from Juby, et al. (forthcoming).

By contrast, in Quebec, cohabitation had become the family setting for a rising proportion of children, with 17 per cent born to cohabiting parents. The 1980s thus marked the beginning of a shift that has not yet ended. In 1997–8, nearly half (46 per cent) of all births in Quebec were to cohabiting parents, and well beyond 50 per cent of first-born children. An equivalent proportion (45 per cent) of children was born to married parents who, most often, had previously cohabited; only 19 per cent were born to parents who had married directly. This situation contrasts with that observed elsewhere in Canada,

where three-quarters of births still occurred within marriage. Among those, approximately half (39 per cent) were to parents who married directly without first cohabiting.

In Kiernan's third stage of the partnership transition, cohabitation is socially acceptable, and 'becoming a parent is no longer restricted to marriage' (Kiernan, 2001, p. 5). Now that cohabitation has become the modal way in which to give birth, the transition to this third stage seems to have been successfully achieved in Quebec. Elsewhere in Canada, however, if half of children born in the late

1990s were born to parents who had cohabited, only 30 per cent (15 per cent out of 51 per cent) were born within a cohabiting union (see Figure 9.4). This suggests that cohabiting unions have not yet become an alternative setting in which to become a parent, and that women who become pregnant while living with a cohabiting partner will tend to legalize their union before the birth of the child. In a way, the evolution of family life in Canada outside Quebec parallels that observed in the United States, where only a small fraction of the increase in nonmarital births was due to a decline in the likelihood that pregnant cohabiting mothers will marry before the birth of their child (Raley, 2001). The greatest portion of the increase seems to be attributable to rising percentages of women cohabiting, and to the greater likelihood that single pregnant women start cohabiting (rather than marry). These results led Raley to conclude, along with Manning (1993), that cohabitation was perhaps becoming a trial marriage among singles, but that it was still too early to conclude that it had become a substitute for marriage.

If cohabitation is to be considered a substitute for marriage, it needs to provide not only a family setting in which to give birth, but also a lasting arrangement in which to raise children. Previous studies have shown that cohabiting couples giving birth to a child appear to be more stable than childless unions (Wu & Balakrishnan, 1995). But are these couples as solid as married couples with children? Can we expect the risk of family disruption to vary according to historical context—that is, in relation to the importance and acceptance of cohabitation as a way to start family life? Can we expect the gap in family disruptions between marriages and cohabitations to narrow as cohabitation has become the modal way in which to form a family in Quebec?

The distribution of children according to the family setting in which they live at a given moment provides an indirect indication of the duration of families across the country, depending upon the type of parental union. In 2001 in Canada, over 80 per cent of children aged 0–14 years were living with two parents who were either their biological parents, adoptive parents, or step-parents. Census data do not allow distinction among biological families, adoptive families, and stepfamilies because respondents are instructed to declare as 'son' or 'daughter' their biological children, adopted children, or stepchildren. Between 17 per cent and 20 per cent were living with a single parent, usually the mother (8 times out of 10). Outside Quebec, the percentage of children living with cohabiting parents was relatively low, ranging between 7 per cent in Ontario and 11 per cent in the Atlantic provinces. It was clearly higher in Quebec, where it reached 30 per cent, reflecting the longer duration of cohabiting unions in this province (Statistics Canada, 2002c). Some of the higher percentage of children living in a nonmarried two-parent family in Quebec is also probably due to the greater propensity of couples to choose cohabitation rather than marriage when they form a union after having seen their first family collapse. Hence, according to the 2001 General Social Survey, nearly 75 per cent of Quebec stepfamilies were headed by a cohabiting couple, whereas this percentage was slightly below 50 per cent elsewhere in Canada (Statistics Canada, 2002a).

The only way to directly compare the stability of marriages and cohabiting unions with children is to use longitudinal data and to begin at the moment a child is born. This is precisely the approach we took in two studies of family disruption in Canada (Desrosiers & Le Bourdais, 1996; Le Bourdais, Neill, & Marcil-Gratton, 2000). The most recent study was based on retrospective information collected from respondents to the 1995 General Social Survey, who had become mothers for the first time in an intact family (i.e. within a union with their child's father) between 1970 and 1995. We examined the relative risks of family disruption faced by these women, according to their conjugal situation at the time of first birth and their region of residence (Quebec vs elsewhere in Canada). We used a proportional hazards model to control for a series of variables that were shown to be associated with conjugal and family instability (age of the mother at the beginning of the union, period in which the child was born, mother's level of education and presence in the labour market), and we introduced an interaction variable that combined the effects of region of residence and type of union to allow the effect of conjugal status on the risk of separation to vary across the two regions of residence. We wanted to evaluate whether the higher risks of separation attached to cohabiting families were similar across the country, even though this family type is far more numerous in Quebec, and to check how they compared, within each region, in relation to married families.

Table 9.1 presents the results of this analysis. Compared with the families formed directly through marriage in Canada outside Quebec (the reference category), married couples who lived together before marriage appeared to have a 1.66 greater chance of separating following the birth of their first child. In other words, starting conjugal life through cohabitation rather than marriage increased by two-thirds the risk of separation among parents who had already married by the time their first child was born. Conjugal instability was much greater among cohabiting-couple families. For those who were still cohabiting at the birth of the child, the risk of disruption was nearly five times higher than that observed for those who had married directly, even after controlling for mothers'

Table 9.1 Relative risks of family disruption among 'intact' families, by type of union and region of residence at birth of first child

Type of union	Region of residence	
	Quebec	Canada without Quebec
direct marriage	1.45	1.00
marriage following cohabitation	1.46	1.66
cohabitation	3.47	4.94

The coefficients represent the relative risk of family breakdown after controlling for the effect of a series of mothers' sociodemographic characteristics. All coefficients are significantly different at $p < .05$ from the reference category (i.e. direct marriage outside Quebec).

Source: Statistics Canada, 1995 General Social Survey. Reproduced from Le Bourdais et al., 2000, Table 2.

sociodemographic characteristics (i.e. highest level of education completed at the time of the survey; preconjugal conception; age and school enrolment status at the beginning of the union; period of family formation; employment status; cumulated duration of employment; and cumulated number of work interruptions through the family episode).

Compared with their counterparts living elsewhere in Canada, Quebec families formed within direct marriage appeared more unstable, with a risk of separation that is 45 per cent greater. In Quebec, however, married couples who lived together before marriage formed equally stable families as those who did not. Cohabiting families in Quebec appeared to be more fragile than those whose parents had married by the time the first child was born, but the difference between the two groups was not nearly as large as that observed elsewhere in Canada. In Quebec, cohabiting-couple families were 2.5 times (relative risk of 3.47 compared with 1.45) more likely to separate than those married directly, whereas they were 5 times more likely to do so in the rest of Canada.

As the context in which families are formed changed—that is, as cohabitation became progressively more acceptable and widespread—the risk of separation associated with the different types of unions also changed. We cannot assume the risks of separation across unions to remain invariant over time, as the nature of both cohabitation and marriage is also changing over time (Manting, 1996). The comparison of the relative risks of family disruption among parents who married directly without first cohabiting in Quebec and elsewhere in Canada is instructive, as is the comparison between married and cohabiting parents within each given region. Both comparisons show that, as direct marriage becomes increasingly unusual, it no longer provides a guarantee of stability, and as cohabitation becomes more widespread, it becomes more stable. For these reasons, the promotion of marriage as the only way to raise a family may have little value and, of greater importance, could well result in the opposite—that is, in a desertion of family life altogether, as seems to have occurred in countries such as Italy or Japan, where fertility has fallen to a very low level (Livi-Bacci & Salvini, 2000).

Cohabitating Unions in Canada: Rights and Benefits for Adults and Children

Canada adopted a very pragmatic approach in relation to the growth of cohabitation. Just as the statistical agency was prone to recognizing cohabiting couples as the equivalent of married couples from the beginning, cohabiters rapidly gained access to social programs and benefits. In the absence of a contract or ceremony to clearly mark the start of the union, a criterion of duration (usually 1–3 years) of living together is usually used before cohabiting couples can access benefits, but this criterion is often waived if the couple has a child. As long as they live together, cohabiting couples now seem to have the same benefits and advantages as married couples; they have a right to 'equality' of treatment, a right that was confirmed by the Supreme Court of Canada in 1995 (Goubau, 2004).

Many areas of family law, however, such as laws governing union dissolution and child support, remain under provincial jurisdiction. Some differences exist across provinces, mostly the way that cohabiting couples are treated at separation. Some provinces, such as Alberta and Quebec, have been reluctant to provide total equality for married and cohabiting couples in terms of sharing assets at separation, but for opposite reasons. On the one hand, in Alberta, where marriage was judged the ideal family context, it was felt that additional recognition of cohabitation would undermine marriage. In Quebec, on the other hand, the justification for not assimilating cohabitation to marriage was based on the respect of the freedom of choice of cohabiting partners, who deliberately preferred cohabitation to marriage in order to avoid the rights and obligations attached to the latter (Le Bourdais & Juby, 2001). In December 2002, the Supreme Court of Canada reinforced this latter interpretation by overruling a provincial decision rendered earlier in Nova Scotia. The Supreme

Court argued that if cohabiting partners had not previously signed a contract or written agreement, upon separation, they could not ask for alimony, nor count on sharing equally most assets accumulated through the union, as married spouses do. At separation, the legal system thus respects the private nature of the arrangements made by cohabiters, and during the union, it invokes the right of equality of treatment to justify that cohabiting and married couples be treated in the same way when dealing with a third party.

Although respecting the conjugal choices of adults, the courts and governments have aimed to ensure the protection of children irrespective of their parents' situation. In Canada, children now have the same rights and privileges, no matter the family circumstances of their birth, and birth statistics no longer classify as 'illegitimate' births that occurred outside marriage. Parents, whether married or cohabiting, together or separated, have the same responsibilities and obligations toward their children. As much as possible, policies and laws have aimed to reduce the effect of parental separation on children's wellbeing. In December 2002, a new initiative, the Child-Centred Family Justice Strategy, was developed, aimed at the needs of children and at the reduction of the level of conflict between parents. It eliminated the terms *access* and *custody* included in the Divorce Act and replaced them with the less conflicting notions of *parental responsibilities* and *parental time*, and developed services (mediation, parental education courses) to ease the process of separation (Le Bourdais, Marcil-Gratton, & Juby, 2003).

Officially, children are entitled to the same rights and benefits, irrespective of the conjugal status of their parents. Interestingly, though, the reality appears to be slightly different. Because cohabiting parents are not required, at separation, to share the assets accumulated through the union, children are likely to suffer more difficult economic conditions following parental separation if they were living in a cohabiting rather than married family (Dubreuil, 1999). Moreover, cohabiting fathers are less likely to maintain frequent contact with their children or provide child support on a regular basis following separation

(Marcil-Gratton & Le Bourdais, 1999). Sole custody to the mother, rather than joint custody, has also been shown to be more frequent after the dissolution of a cohabiting union. Consequently, children and adults are likely to experience different living conditions following family disruption, depending on whether the parents were married or cohabiting.

The Divergent Evolution of Cohabitation in Quebec and Elsewhere in Canada

The data presented here have revealed profound changes in the processes of union and family formation and dissolution in Canada, and show how institutions such as the law and the national statistical agency have adapted to these transformations. Our analysis has contrasted the evolution of the demographic behaviours adopted in Quebec with that elsewhere in Canada, and led us to conclude that cohabitation has reached different stages of development across the country.

Outside Quebec, cohabitation seems to have successfully achieved the second stage of Kiernan's (2001) model of partnership transition, and to have not yet attained the third. It has become widely accepted as a form of conjugal life—that is, as a prelude or probationary period in which to test the strength of the relationship before marrying—but not yet as an environment in which to become a parent. In that respect, Canada without Quebec closely resembles the United States, where cohabitation still predominantly remains a childless phase of conjugal life.

In Quebec, though, the progression of cohabitation is far more advanced. Now that cohabitation has become the modal way in which to give birth in Quebec (i.e. an alternative to marriage in order to have children), clearly the transition to the third stage of development appears to have been fully completed. Has Quebec also achieved the transition to the fourth stage of Kiernan's model in which 'cohabitation and marriage become indistinguishable with children being born and reared within

both' (2001, p. 5)? To help distinguish between these two stages, Heuveline and Timberlake (in press) have introduced a further criterion to those advanced by Kiernan. Unlike unmarried couples who, in the previous stage, opted for cohabitation as an *alternative* to marriage, those formed in the latter stage would be *indifferent* to marrying, because of the widespread acceptability of cohabitation and the provision of institutional supports that discriminate little between married and cohabiting families.

Some of the evidence presented here tends to suggest that the transition to this last stage of development is well underway in Quebec. Except for the sharing of assets and the right to alimony after separation, cohabiting families are entitled to the same rights and benefits as married families, and they do not suffer from discrimination. Moreover, the number of cohabiting families is steadily progressing as a result of the increasing duration of these family episodes and the declining likelihood of cohabiting couples marrying following the birth of a child. As the propensity of cohabiting couples with children to marry becomes closer to that of childless couples, cohabiters can be seen as being 'indifferent' to marriage in the sense that the timing of marriage is not closely linked to the presence of children. Yet, in spite of these developments, we cannot conclude that cohabitation is indistinguishable from or a substitute for marriage. As we have seen above, cohabitation still leads to different outcomes from marriage concerning custody and child support following a family disruption. Thus, cohabitation is still, to a certain extent, 'selective' of individuals with given characteristics.

We cannot end this article without raising some hypotheses to explain the divergent evolution of cohabitation in Quebec as compared with elsewhere in Canada. Part of the answer probably lies in the different religious and cultural backgrounds of the two societies (for a similar argument, see Laplante, 2004; Pollard & Wu, 1998). Up to the 1960s, Quebec society was under the yoke of the Catholic Church, which controlled most aspects of Quebecers' lives. During the 1960s, a vast movement of secularization, known as the Quiet Revolution, touched all aspects of society, including health, education, and social services, and led to the development of a modern state. Individuals rapidly embraced this revolution and progressively deserted the Church and abandoned its precepts. In the wake of this movement, Quebec women, who had maintained traditional behaviours in terms of contraception and family life, enthusiastically adopted the pill as a contraceptive method, and couples progressively did away not only with religious marriage but also with the 'institution' of marriage altogether. Consequently, the total fertility rate and the total marriage rate plunged rapidly in Quebec, as it did in other Catholic societies, such as Spain, Italy, and, to a lesser degree, France (Le Bourdais & Marcil-Gratton, 1996). Elsewhere in Canada, the Protestant Church exerted less control over civil society and adapted more easily to the changes observed in family behaviours. Non-Catholic Canadians thus did not feel that they had to break away from their church to fulfill their personal aspirations for conjugal and family life.

This cultural difference partly explains the divergent trends in cohabitation observed in Quebec and in the rest of Canada, but cannot account for the fact that Quebecers now closely resemble their Swedish counterparts, who were not influenced by the Catholic Church. We argue that much of the evolution observed in Quebec has to do with changes in men's and women's roles. As Théry (1993) argued, the principal motor of recent conjugal changes is to be found in the redefinition of men's and women's roles in society and in conjugal relationships. Families remain, to this day, the last places where equality between men and women does not seem to be fully recognized. As societies are promoting greater equality within families, deep changes are likely to occur and lead to ongoing family transformations. Interestingly, the few studies that aimed to document existing differences between marriage

and cohabitation have found that the organization of daily life is more egalitarian within the latter than in the former. Cohabiting partners are more prone than married couples to sharing domestic work (Shelton & John, 1993). They are also more likely to share paid work, as cohabiting women are more involved in the labour market (Le Bourdais & Sauriol, 1998). By contrast, married couples are more inclined than cohabiting partners to pool their financial resources (for a review, see Seltzer, 2000), These studies suggest that cohabitation and marriage constitute two different forms of conjugal engagement, each characterized by different forms of relationships, Cohabitation is based on a greater equality and professional autonomy of partners, whereas marriage rests on greater specialization and complementarity between spouses (Villeneuve-Gokalp, 1991). This interpretation is further supported by Brines and Joyner's (1999) study that showed that similar levels of earnings were associated with greater stability among cohabiting couples, whereas marital stability was more closely linked to specialization of labour, and thus, to unequal earnings.

In Quebec, we argue that the tremendous progression of cohabitation has to do with profound changes in men's and women's roles and expectations brought about in large part by the feminist movement that is stronger and more deeply rooted than elsewhere in Canada. Quebec couples strive for greater equality between men and women, and cohabitation perhaps offers them the best opportunity in this regard. In that sense, cohabitation is probably here to stay, because both Quebec men and women express attitudes more favourable to a redefinition of conjugal unions than other Canadians (Lapierre et al., 1999). As long as cohabitation and marriage represent two different models of conjugal and family life, however, cohabitation remains an alternative to rather than a true substitute for marriage.

References

Bélanger, A. (2003). *Report on the demographic situation in Canada 2002* (cat. 91-209-XPE). Ottawa, ON: Statistics Canada.

Brines, J., & Joyner, K. (1999). The ties that bind: Principles of cohesion in cohabitation and marriage. *American Journal of Sociology, 64*, 333–55.

Brown, S.L. (2000). Union transitions among cohabiters: The significance of relationship assessments and expectations, *Journal of Marriage and Family, 62*, 833–846.

Bumpass, L.L., & Lu, H.-H. (2000). Trends in cohabitation and implications for children's family contexts in the United States. *Population Studies, 54*, 29–41.

Bumpass, L.L., & Raley, R.K. (1995). Redefining single-parent families: Cohabitation and changing family reality, *Demography, 32*, 97–109.

Bumpass, L.L., Raley, R.K., & Sweet, J.A. (1995). The changing character of stepfamilies: Implications of cohabitation and nonmarital childbearing. *Demography, 32*, 425–36.

Cherlin, A.J. (2004). The deinstitutionalization of American marriage. *Journal of Marriage and Family, 66*, 848–61.

Desrosiers, H., & Le Bourdais, C. (1996). Progression des unions libres et avenir des familles biparentales [The rise of cohabitation and its impact on two-parent families]. *Recherches féministes, 9*, 65–83.

Dubreuil, C. (1999). L'union de fait au Québec: Inexistence dans Le Code civil [Consensual union in Québec: Non-existence in the Civil Code]. *Cahiers québécois de démographie, 28*, 229–36.

Duchesne, L. (2003). *La situation démographique au Québec, bilan 2003* [The demographic situation in Quebec, 2003]. Québec: Institut de la statistique du Québec.

Dumas, J., & Bélanger, A. (1994). *Report on the demographic situation in Canada 1994* (cat. 91–209E). Ottawa, ON: Statistics Canada.

———. (1997). *Report on the demographic situation in Canada 1996* (cat. 91– 209E). Ottawa, ON: Statistics Canada.

Dumas, J., & Péron, Y. (1992). *Marriage and conjugal life in Canada* (cat. 91–534F). Ottawa, ON: Statistics Canada.

Goubau, D. (2004). La notion de conjoint: La loi et la société avancent-elles au même pas? [The notion of couples: Are law and society progressing at the same speed?]. In *Actes de la XVIᵉ Conferénce des juristes de l' État* (pp. 39–60). Cowansville, QC: Éditions Yvon Blais.

Heuveline, P., & Timberlake, J.M. (in press). The role of cohabitation in family formation: The United States in comparative perspective. *Journal of Marriage and Family* (special issue).

Juby, H., Marcil-Gratton, N., & Le Bourdais, C. (in press). *When parents separate: Further findings from the National Longitudinal Survey of Children and Youth.* Phase 2 research report of the project 'The Impact of Parents' Family Transitions on Children's Family Environment and Economic Well-Being: A Longitudinal Assessment'. Ottawa, ON: Department of Justice Canada, Child Support Team.

Kiernan, K. (2001). Cohabitation in western Europe: Trends, issues and implications. In A. Booth & A.C. Crouter (Eds), *Just living together: Implications of cohabitation on families, children, and social policy* (pp. 3–31). Mahwah, NJ: Erlbaum.

Lapierre-Adamcyk, É., & Le Bourdais, C. (2004). Couples et familles: Une réalité sociologique et démographique en constante évolution [Couples and families: Sociological and demographic arrangements in constant evolution]. In *Actes de la XVIᵉ Conferénce des juristes de l' État* (pp. 61–86). Cowansville, QC: Éditions Yvon Blais.

Lapierre-Adamcyk, É., Le Bourdais, C., & Marcil-Gratton, N. (1999). La signification du choix de l'union libre au Québec et en Ontario [The meaning of choosing cohabitation in Quebec and in Ontario]. *Cahiers québécois de demographie, 28*, 199–227.

Laplante, B. (2004). *The diffusion of cohabitation in Quebec and Ontario and the power of norms in religion.* Montreal, QC: Institut national de la recherche scientifique (INRS)—Urbanisation, Culture et Société.

Le Bourdais, C., & Juby, H. (2001). The impact of cohabitation on the family life course in contemporary North America: Insights from across the border. In A. Booth & A.C. Crouter (Eds), *Just living together: Implications of cohabitation on families, children, and social policy* (pp. 107–18). Mahwah, NJ: Erlbaum.

Le Bourdais, C., & Marcil-Gratton, N. (1996). Family transformations across the Canadian/American border: When the laggard becomes the leader. *Journal of Comparative Family Studies, 27*, 415–36.

Le Bourdais, C., Marcil-Gratton, N., & Juby, H. (2003). Family life in a changing world: The evolution of the Canadian family in a context of marital and economic instability. In M.J. Kasoff & C. Drennen (Eds), *Family, work, and health policy in Canada: Proceedings from the 16th Annual Reddin Symposium* (pp. 17–38). Bowling Green, OH: Canadian Studies Center, Bowling Green State University.

Le Bourdais, C., Neill, G., & Marcil-Gratton, N. (2000). L'effet du type d'union sur la stabilité des familles dites 'intactes' [The effect of union type on the stability of 'intact' families]. *Recherches sociographiques, 41*, 53–74.

Le Bourdais, C., & Sauriol, A. (1998). *La part des pères dans la division du travail domestique au sein des familles canadiennes* [Father's share in the division of domestic labour among Canadian families] (Études et Documents No. 69). Montreal, QC: INRS-Urbanisation.

Livi-Bacci, M., & Salvini, S. (2000). Trop de famille et trop peu d'enfants: La fécondité en Italie depuis 1960 [Too much family and too few children: Fertility in Italy since 1960]. *Cahiers québecois de démographie, 29*, 231–54,

Manning, W.D. (1993). Marriage and cohabitation following premarital conception. *Journal of Marriage and Family, 55*, 839–50.

Manting, D. (1996). The changing meaning of cohabitation and marriage. *European Sociological Review, 12*, 53–65.

Marcil-Gratton, N. (1998). *Growing up with mom and dad? The intricate family life courses of Canadian children* (cat. 89–566–XIE). Ottawa, ON: Statistics Canada.

Marcil-Gratton, N., & Le Bourdais, C. (1999). *Custody, access and child support. Findings from the National Longitudinal Survey of Children and Youth*. Retrieved May 27, 2004, from the Department of Justice Canada, Child Support Team website: http://canada.juslice.gc.cajen/ps/pad/reports/index.html#res

Pollard, M.S., & Wu, Z. (1998). Divergence of marriage patterns in Quebec and elsewhere in Canada. *Population Development Review, 24*, 329–56.

Raley, R.K. (2001). Increasing fertility in cohabiting unions: Evidence for the second demographic transition in the United States? *Demography, 38*, 59–66.

Seltzer, J.A. (2000). Families formed outside of marriage. *Journal of Marriage and Family, 62*, 1247–68.

Shelton, B.A., & John, D. (1993). Does marital status make a difference? *Journal of Family Issues, 14*, 401–20.

Smock, P.J., & Gupta, S. (2001). Cohabitation in contemporary North America. In A. Booth & A.C. Crouter (Eds), *Just living together: Implications of cohabitation on families, children, and social policy* (pp. 53–84). Malwah, NJ: Erlbaum.

Statistics Canada. (2002a). *Changing conjugal life in Canada* (cat. 89–576–XIE). Ottawa, ON: Author.

———. (2002b). *Profile of Canadian families and households: Diversification continues* (cat. 96F0030XIE2001003). Ottawa, ON: Author.

———. (2002c). *2001 census* (Table 97F0005 XCBOlO02). Ottawa, ON: Author.

———. (2003a, November 20). Marriages. *The Daily* (pp. 11–12, cat. II–001–XIE). Ottawa, ON: Author.

———. (2003b). *Annual demographic statistics 2002* (cat. 91–213–XIB). Ottawa, ON: Author.

Théry, L. (1993). *Le démariage* [Unmarrying], Paris: Odile Jacob.

Turcotte, P., & Bélanger, A. (1997). *The dynamics of formation and dissolution of first common-law unions in Canada*. Ottawa, ON: Statistics Canada.

Villeneuve-Gokalp, C. (1991). From marriage to informal union: Recent changes in the behavior of French couples. *Population: An English selection, 3*, 81–111.

Wu, Z., & Balakrishnan, T.R. (1995). Dissolution of premarital cohabitation in Canada. *Demography, 32*, 521–32.

CHAPTER 10

The Role of Cohabitation in Family Formation: The United States in Comparative Perspective

Patrick Heuveline and Jeffrey M. Timberlake

Normative attitudes on family formation have been changing rapidly in the United States since at least the 1960s (Pagnini & Rindfuss, 1993; Thornton, 1989). As shown by Axinn and Thornton (1993), these attitudinal trends have both contributed to and resulted from concomitant declines in the prevalence of a traditional family connation sequence in which adults first get married, then live together, and finally have children. The deviation from this sequence that has received the most attention in the United States is undoubtedly childbearing before marriage. The increase in the proportion of births to unmarried mothers—from 4.0 per cent in 1950 to 33.0 per cent in 1999 (Ventura & Bachrach, 2000)—is indeed one of the most impressive trends, and a large literature now documents the effects on children of growing up with a single parent (e.g. McLanahan & Sandefur, 1994).

Until recently, living together before marriage generated much less public attention, although family scholars have debated whether to interpret unmarried cohabitation as a prelude to marriage—that is, a simple inversion in the timing of two events (marrying and cohabiting)—or as an alternative to marriage—that is, a decision not to marry. This scholarly debate might have remained just that, as long as unmarried cohabitation was not publicly perceived as a childbearing institution. In fact, Rindfuss and VandenHeuvel (1990) found that unmarried cohabiting couples in the United States exhibited much of the same characteristic behaviours as single dating people, and suggested that cohabitation was an alternative to being single rather than to marriage.

Although cohabiting couples postpone childbearing longer than married couples do (Manning, 1995), cohabitation is nevertheless becoming a significant feature of the modem reproductive landscape. In the early 1990s, births to cohabiting mothers represented more than 10 per cent of all births, and nearly two-fifths of out-of-wedlock births (Bumpass & Lu, 2000). More recent data from the Fragile Families and Child Wellbeing Study suggest that nearly half of all out-of-wedlock births are to cohabiting mothers (J.O. Teitler, personal communication, 30 April 2003). The presence of children has brought cohabitation into public discourse, leading concerned policy makers to propose incentives to incite unmarried cohabitating partners to marry. Although we know relatively little about the consequences for children of parental cohabitation (Smock, 2000)—with the possible exception of economic circumstances (Manning & Lichter, 1996; Morrison & Ritualo, 2000)—cohabitation is generally less stable than marriage and thus presents higher risks for children to experience parental separation. Cohabitation is also spreading as a post-marital institution. The proportion of births occurring to cohabiting mothers nearly doubles to 20 per cent of births among previously divorced mothers (Brown, 2000), and children are more likely to experience cohabitation in a stepfamily than with their two biological parents. Accounting for types of parental cohabitation, Graefe and Lichter (1999) found that one-fourth of all children live with a cohabiting parent at some point during childhood, whereas Bumpass and Lu (2000), using a different data set, estimated the same proportion at nearly two-fifths.

To understand the role of cohabitation in the landscape of family formation in the contemporary United States, several studies compare the characteristics of individuals forming different types of partnerships (e.g. Blackwell & Lichter, 2000; Brown & Booth, 1996; Manning, 1993; Rindfuss & VandenHeuvel, 1990). Cross-sectional studies of individual characteristics cannot provide insight into the contextual factors that affect all individuals, however, and may have contributed to the departure from the sequence of marriage, then coresidence, and finally, childbearing. Looking backward, it is tempting to link this departure to contemporaneous cultural, social, and economic changes in the United States. Even a cursory review of the comparable trends in other Western nations that have experienced many of the same changes, however, renders such an interpretation of recent trends in the United Stales unconvincing. Comparative European research (e.g. Kuijsten, 1996) has found little evidence of convergence on several indicators of the 'second demographic transition' (van de Kaa, 1987), and cohabitation is no exception (Kiernan, 2001; Prinz, 1995).

In this article, therefore, we attempt to contribute to the literature that compares individuals in different living arrangements in the contemporary United States by comparing US patterns of cohabitation formation and fertility among women, and exposure to cohabitation among children, with those in 16 other nations. Our goal is to understand cohabitation in the United States by situating it in a larger context of other Western industrialized societies.

Our analysis proceeds in several steps. In the next section, we identify six conceptually distinct ideal-typical ways in which couples experience unmarried cohabitation, derived from the sociological and demographic family literature. We next adduce a set of empirical indicators, as well as predictions about the relative magnitudes of those indicators, that should yield sufficient cross-national variation to enable identifying the presence of these ideal types in different countries. A key factor in our scheme is the fertility behaviour of cohabiting adults, because the more cohabitation enters 'the arena for reproduction', the more it is likely to be a substitute for marriage (Smock, 2000, p. 10). Using data from 17 nationally representative Family and Fertility Surveys, we then employ single- and multiple-decrement life table analysis to estimate the incidence of, duration in, and routes of exit from cohabitation for female respondents and the children of childbearing female respondents. Comparing these indicators with the patterns corresponding to each ideal type, we draw conclusions about the presence or absence of a dominant orientation toward cohabitation in the different countries.

Theoretical Background

Early research on cohabitation was framed by the *prelude to marriage* versus *alternative to marriage* dichotomy. Rindfuss and VandenHeuvel (1990) conceptualized cohabitation instead as an alternative to being single. Casper and Bianchi (2002) proposed four cohabitation types, essentially introducing one more distinction within the prelude to marriage type: (a) alternative to marriage, (b) precursor to marriage, (c) trial marriage, and (d) coresidential dating. In this typology, the two main dimensions are the expectation to marry (present in *b*, absent in *a* and *d*, and undecided in *c*), and the expected duration of the relationship (long in *a* and *b*, short in *d*, and undecided in *c*), Several researchers (e.g. Manning, 1993; Raley, 2001; Smock, 2000) have also emphasized differences in the arena of reproduction, showing, for instance, how a pregnancy may affect the future of a relationship, especially in the trial-marriage type of cohabitation. Kiernan (2001) recently introduced the idea that in the final stage of development, 'cohabitation and marriage become indistinguishable with children being born and reared in both' (p. 3), which can be seen as a further distinction within the alternative to marriage type. Integrating these critical distinctions, we identify and describe six ideal, typical ways in which cohabitation contributes to family formation in Western societies based on actual behaviour (duration of cohabitation and childbearing) rather than on expectations at the start of cohabitation. More specifically, we define these ideal types by considering unmarried couples' decisions (a) to live together, (b) to have children together, and (c) to stay together.

In any given society at any given time, we expect all combinations of decisions corresponding to each of these ideal types to be found; however, we also expect cross-national variation in the prevalence of these different combinations. Research on cohabitation in the United States has tended to focus on documenting the differences in individual characteristics that explain why some couples pursue or do not pursue particular sequences of partnership formation, marriage, childbearing, and childrearing (e.g. Bumpass & Lu, 2000; Manning, 1993). Kiernan (2000) compared individual differences in the likelihood to marry before ever cohabiting in 14 European countries. Although these comparisons reveal modest education and religion gradients, subgroup differences within countries are small compared with international differences. In other words, although within countries the more educated and those never attending church are less likely to marry without prior cohabitation, members of these subgroups in Spain or Italy are still much more likely to marry without prior cohabitation than the least educated and most religious subgroups in Sweden or Finland.

Cross-national differences in underlying individual characteristics therefore contribute to differences in national-level prevalence, but differences at the national level likely depend much more on the cultural norms, expectations, attitudes, and institutional supports that families encounter in each society. As long as marriage continues to be a socially approved arrangement for family formation, we should find institutional and cultural rewards for living together, having children, and staying together within marriage in all societies. Reher (1998), for instance, documented persistent cultural differences in the subjective contours of family life across western Europe. In addition, Western countries feature different welfare policies (Esping-Andersen, 1990) that have different impacts on families in general (Gauthier, 1996), and families with children in particular (Bradshaw, Ditch, Holmes, & Whiteford, 1993). Individual characteristics may explain who might be more or less likely to forgo these rewards and benefits and form a family outside wedlock, but the nature of these rewards and benefits likely affects the overall proportion of couples who decide to form a partnership outside marriage. Selection into unmarried cohabitation may exist in all countries, but the strength of this selection should vary and be revealed in part by the prevalence of decisions to bear children and to remain unmarried for a substantial length of time.

Ideal Types of Cohabitation

A. Marginal

In countries where unmarried cohabitation continues to be culturally frowned upon and institutionally penalized, cohabitation will attract only a small minority of couples. In these countries, the incidence and duration of adulthood cohabitation should be low, and children's exposure to and duration in cohabitation should be even lower.

B. Prelude to Marriage

Family formation may be initiated by unmarried cohabitation as a 'testing' ground for a relationship. Couples may feel a greater need for this premarital experience when they observe high rates of divorce. Choices to cohabit first may also depend on access to affordable housing, or to reliable contraception to postpone childbearing. If norms or institutions continue to be unsupportive of unmarried couples with children, however, couples would be expected either to end the relationship or to marry before children are born. This implies that the average duration of an episode of unmarried cohabitation should be fairly short, cohabitation should frequently transition into marriage, and children's exposure to cohabitation should remain relatively low.

C. Stage in the Marriage Process

This ideal type is closely related to the previous one. Although Casper and Bianchi (2002) distinguished between trial marriage and precursor to marriage based on the motivation of individuals entering cohabitation with respect to marriage, we distinguish this type from the previous one, based on the actual timing of marriage and childbearing. We see cohabitation as a stage in the marriage process rather than a prelude to marriage when cohabiting couples who decide to have a child do not feel strongly about the precise order and timing of childbearing and marriage. Birth followed by marriage should become more frequent when there continues to be institutional incentives to raise children within marriage, and when cultural sanctions against out-of-wedlock childbearing have eroded. In this scenario, couples may increasingly experience competing opportunities that they could pursue by briefly postponing marriage, as long as it is understood that they intend to marry eventually. When this behaviour becomes more prevalent, we should observe a slightly longer average duration than in the strictly ordered prelude to marriage, and substantially more childhood exposure to cohabitation. The average duration of children's exposure should be relatively short, however, with the assumption being that once children are born, cohabiting adults fairly quickly formalize their relationships as marriages.

D. Alternative to Single

Following Rindfuss and VandenHeuvel (1990), we include this ideal type to capture cohabiting partners who want to postpone forming a family, and instead prefer cohabiting rather than living separately during courtship. As with the prelude to marriage ideal type, increased access to affordable housing and to efficient contraception should

increase the prevalence of this behaviour when children are still expected to be born within marriage. The behaviour should also be more frequent when young adults consider themselves 'too young' to seriously consider marriage, and hence enter cohabitation with no immediate intention to marry. Because the commitment of these cohabiters is more like a dating relationship than a marital one, the presence of this form of cohabitation should depress the average duration of cohabitation episodes and increase the proportion of these episodes ending in separation.

E. Alternative to Marriage

The alternative to marriage corresponds to the choice to cohabit instead of marrying, but simultaneously to form a family as a married couple would. As in the marginal ideal type, we expect population heterogeneity to be manifest, and individual characteristics to determine which couples choose to form a family outside rather than within marriage. We also expect that a greater cultural approval of, and better institutional support for, children raised entirely out of wedlock would reduce the strength of selectivity, however, and lead to a greater proportion of couples opting for cohabitation as compared with the previous types. When these conditions are met, cohabitation should become more prevalent and should last longer, on average, than in the marginal ideal type, and should transition into marriage less frequently than in the prelude to marriage or stage in the marriage process ideal types. Children should also be exposed to cohabitation more frequently, and should remain longer with cohabiting parents, when the prevalence of this type of cohabitation increases.

F. Indistinguishable from Marriage

Following Kiernan (2001), we introduce one more ideal type that shares many similarities with the alternative to marriage type, in the sense that in both, unmarried couples form families as married couples do. In this ideal type, however, couples are not driven to an *alternative* to marriage by their own characteristics and attitudes toward marriage, but in fact are *indifferent* to marrying because of the general acceptability of unmarried cohabitation, and institutional supports for parents that essentially ignore marital status. We expect the incidence of cohabitation among adults and exposure to cohabitation among children to be even higher than in the alternative to marriage type because unmarried cohabitation is less constrained by individual characteristics. We also expect the duration of cohabitation episodes with and without children to be slightly shorter, and a larger proportion of cohabitation episodes to transition into marriage as compared with the alternative to marriage type. This is because cohabitation is not viewed as antithetical to, or something to be done instead of marriage; thus, couples may become more pragmatic in their decision to marry.

Indicators and Empirical Predictions

The foregoing discussion suggests that cross-national variation in the incidence of, duration in, and route of exit from cohabitation for both adults and children should provide insights into the different ways that couples approach unmarried cohabitation as a component to their family formation strategies. Thus, our key indicators for adults are the percentage of women expected to experience at least one cohabitation between ages 15 and 44, the expected duration of such cohabitations, and the route of exit, either marriage or separation. For children, our indicators are the percentage of children expected to experience a parental cohabitation from birth to age 16, the expected duration of exposure to a parental cohabitation, and the route of exit, either the marriage or separation of the child's parents. We describe these measures and their estimation in greater detail below. The measures are indicators of the central tendency of the distribution across women, children, or episodes of cohabitation. As noted above, however, when the prevalence of one type of cohabitation increases, the average indicators are expected to behave in a corresponding manner.

Table 10.1 summarizes the ideal types identified above and lists the empirical predictions for the relative magnitudes of the indicators corresponding to the significant presence of any of these types. Table 10.1 illustrates in particular the importance of considering both women's and children's experiences. We see that according to several of these ideal types, cohabitation could be fundamentally altering the way that couples are partnering, but may have little implication for the family structures in which children are born and raised (Timberlake & Heuveline, in press).

Method

Data: The Family and Fertility Surveys

The Family and Fertility Surveys comprise an international sample survey program focusing on fertility and family change in the member countries of the United Nations Economic Commission for Europe. The list of participants includes over 20 European countries, of which we analyze 14, as well as Canada, New Zealand, and the United States. The program did not fund ad hoc data collection, so participating countries typically included survey modules within their regular survey-taking activities. For example, in Canada, survey questionnaires appeared in cycles 4 and 5 of the General Social Survey, whereas they were included in the 1994 Annual Employment Surveys in France, and in cycle 5 of the National Survey of Family Growth in the United States.

Most important for the present analyses, the data provide histories of all births and partnerships for female respondents. The partnership histories provide the dates of coresidence (beginning and end) for up to nine cohabiting relationships, if and how the partnership ended, and the date of marriage, if applicable. For women, we kept track of transitions to and from cohabiting status directly from these histories. We reconstruct children's exposure to cohabitation by combining the partnership and fertility histories of the female respondents. For each natural-born child, we combined these two histories to create an early life course record of living arrangements with the mother and her partners from birth to exact age 16. As long as the child was living with

Table 10.1 Ideal-typical roles of cohabitation, descriptions of types, and empirical indicators and predictions

| Role | Description | Empirical Indicators and Predictions | | | | | |
| | | Adults | | | Children | | |
		Incidence of own cohabitation	Median duration	Per cent ending in marriage	Exposure to parental cohabitation	Median duration	Per cent ending in marriage
A	Marginal	Cohabitation is not prevalent and is likely discouraged by public attitudes and policies.	lower	shorter	higher	lower	shorter	higher
B	Prelude to marriage	Exists as a pre-reproductive phase for adults. Unions tend to be brief and non-reproductive, and end in marriage.	higher	shorter	higher	lower	shorter	higher
C	Stage in marriage process	Exists as a transitory phase in reproduction. Unions tend to be longer, and children are more likely to be born into a cohabitation than in *B*, yet with short duration of exposure.	higher	shorter	higher	higher	shorter	higher
D	Alternative to single	Cohabitation primarily for brief, non-reproductive unions that end in separation instead of marriage.	higher	shorter	lower	lower	shorter	lower
E	Alternative to marriage	Is a discrete family component. Adulthood cohabitation prevalent, and for longer duration than in *C*. Low proportion leading to marriage. More exposure to cohabitation during childhood than in *C*, and for longer duration.	higher	longer	lower	higher	longer	lower
F	Indistinguishable from marriage	Little social distinction between cohabitation and marriage. Children more likely than in *E* to experience the marriage of parents because cohabitation not seen as alternative to marriage.	higher	longer	lower	higher	longer	higher

Note: In the table layout, columns B and C of row headings are read with values aligned as: Incidence of own cohabitation / Median duration / Per cent ending in marriage (Adults); Exposure to parental cohabitation / Median duration / Per cent ending in marriage (Children).

the mother, we knew whether she also lived with a partner and, if so, whether the couple was married.

The Family and Fertility Surveys data represent an unparalleled source of information about differences in family-formation trends across these Western nations, but fitting the survey into existing national data collection programs introduced idiosyncrasies into the sampling designs. Respondents' age ranges vary across countries (upper limits from 40 to 60 years), as do the years of data collection (1989–97). Further differences in survey design, data quality, and comparability, and reasons for excluding certain countries have been described elsewhere (Heuveline, Timberlake, & Furstenberg, 2003; Kveder, 2002; Macura & Klijzing, 1992). Although overall the surveys' data vary in content, they are fairly standardized in terms of the information on births and partnerships that we use for the present analyses. Dates of birth (of self and own children) and marriage are among the most accurately reported items in retrospective surveys, especially by women (Poulain, Riandey, & Firdion, 1991). Retrospective reports on the incidence and timing of cohabitation might be less reliable, so some early and short partnerships might have gone unreported (Casper & Cohen, 2000; Murphy, 2000). This could tend to bias the estimates of the overall incidence of cohabitation downward, and the estimates of the median duration in cohabiting spells upward. These biases are likely to be extremely small, however, because as explained below, we limited our observations to a period shortly before the interview.

Analyses

Our primary analytic tools in this article are single- and multiple-decrement period life tables, which we use to estimate the incidence of, duration in, and route of exit from cohabiting relationships for the female survey respondents and their natural-born children. Life tables are a general class of demographic models that describe the transition over time of a cohort of individuals from one life state to another (Preston, Heuveline, & Guillot, 2001).

For adult women, our state of interest is to live in an unmarried, cohabiting partnership between ages 15 and 44. We had to settle for a younger upper age limit in several countries because of sampling age restrictions at the time of the survey (age 40 in Germany, age 42 in Belgium and Hungary). In addition, because the surveys were fielded in different years, we attempted to make the reference period more comparable by observing rates several years before the survey in some countries. Variations in the lower age limit are a lesser concern. When the lower age limit is greater than age 15—say, age 18— we only observe period rates from age 18 on, but we also observe cohort rates before age 18 from the retrospective histories. We then use the reference period rates to estimate the experience of a synthetic cohort from age 18 on, and complete it with the experience of the actual cohorts turning 18 during the reference period.

For children, the state of interest is to be under exact age of 6 and living with a mother who is unmarried and cohabiting. Retrospective data on children reported by reproductive-age mothers are known to be subject to selectivity biases with respect to maternal age at birth (Rindfuss, Palmore, & Bumpass, 1982). The risk of bias is present here because younger mothers are less likely to be married at the time of birth (Morgan & Rindfuss, 1999). Little bias would be expected in countries where the adult age range for the period of observation reached age 44, because children up to exact age 16 would include children born to mothers up to the age of 28. Selectivity problems could be more severe in the countries with younger age limits, so we also estimated child life tables with an upper age limit of 12 instead of 16. The two sets of tables proved to be sufficiently comparable, so we only present here the tables ending at age 16.

For adults and children, we estimated two types of life tables to study entries into and exits from cohabitation. For adult women, the single decrement 'entry' life tables start at age 15 and follow, ideally up to exact age 45, the 'risk' of forming an unmarried cohabitation. To allow us to distinguish between first cohabitations being formed before or after any marriage, two 'at-risk' states are considered among women who have never cohabited: never married and ever married. For children, the entry life tables start at birth and follow, up to exact age 16, the probability of experiencing a maternal cohabitation.

From the entry tables, we estimate the percentage of adult women expected to live in an unmarried cohabitation by exact age 45 (or younger when required by sampling restrictions) before or after any marriage, and the percentage of children expected to live with an unmarried, cohabiting mother at birth, by exact age 1, and by exact age 16. For both adults and children, we present from the exit tables the median duration in the relationship, that is, how long adults and children are expected to live in premarital (adults) or parental (children) cohabitation before half of these partnerships end, and the percentage that by then would have ended in marriage or separation. The reason for using median duration for the adult tables rather than the more conventional life expectancy indicator is that the latter depend on how we would 'close' the life table (Preston et al., 2001, p. 48). Because our observations are based on retrospective histories, we in effect remove the risk of death for adult women. This is not particularly problematic because that risk is extremely low at the ages under consideration, but it does allow for the possibility that a partnership 'survives' forever, unless we impose arbitrary rules to end partnerships at very long durations. For children, the use of median duration also limits the analyses to younger ages and reduces the potential selectivity bias due to maternal age at the time of birth.

The 'exit' tables are multiple-decrement life tables that account for the different ways that the observation of a spell or episode of interest may end, and in particular, distinguish between the observations ended by an event that effectively terminates the spell (referred to as an *event of interest*) and those ended by an event that removes the possibility of further observing a spell that is still unfinished (referred to as *censoring*; Preston, et al., 2001, pp. 80–6). These life tables can then be re-estimated under the assumption that spells whose observation was ended by a censoring event at a given duration would have had the same likelihood to survive the events of interest as those that can be observed to survive past that duration. Adult women reaching the maximum observable age for the period while in an unmarried cohabitation are treated so, for instance. In contrast, the entry life tables are simply closed at the upper age limit because events are not observed past that age.

For both adults and children, the temporal dimension of the exit life tables is the duration of the cohabiting relationship rather than the age of either the adult or the child. For adults, the table starts either when a premarital cohabitation partnership is formed, or at exact age 15 for never-married women who are already cohabiting at age 15. For children, the table starts either at birth for children born to a cohabiting mother, or at the time that the cohabitation begins for children born to mothers living alone who formed a partnership before the child's first birthday. Although these data do not allow a direct test of the new partner's relationship to the child, we assume that the partner is most likely the child's father and refer to cohabitations started at birth or before age 1 as parental cohabitations.

Taken together, the entry and exit life tables depict what would happen to a synthetic cohort exposed at each duration or age to the estimated duration or age-specific transition probabilities of a reference period. To avoid excessive year-to-year variations, we selected a 3-year reference period in each country. Because these surveys were fielded in different years with different sampling age restrictions, imposing exactly the same age range and the same reference period would have wasted valuable information in countries that had more recent data on a more extended age range. Our choice of reference period and age range across countries reflects several compromises between scope, selectivity (on maternal age), timeliness, and comparability. Although our objective was to estimate adult rates from ages 15 to 44 during a 3-year period in the early 1990s, the actual reference period thus varies across countries. With the exception of those of Finland (1984–6) and Sweden (1987–9), the reference period of all countries include 1 to 3 years in the early 1990s (1990–5). Whereas all values presented below are therefore estimates based on the probabilities observed in a somewhat variable reference period, we sometimes describe those estimates by resorting to the shorthand expression *at early 1990s rates.*

RESULTS

Adulthood Cohabitation

We first examine the incidence of, duration in, and route of exit from cohabitation for adult women.

Figure 10.1 shows the life table estimates of the percentage of 15-year-old female cohorts who enter a cohabiting partnership at least once by exact age 45, by prior marital status—that is, never or ever married. A comparison of these latter two estimates, depicted in the differently shaded sections of the bars, suggests that at early 1990s rates, the overwhelming majority of women who experience a first cohabitation do so before their first marriage. This confirms a recent transformation in the nature of cohabitation, because cohabitation following marital breakdown was likely the principal form of cohabitation through the 1950s and 1960s (Kiernan, 2001, p. 2).

The total percentage of adults forming a pre- or post-marital cohabitation is likely reaching

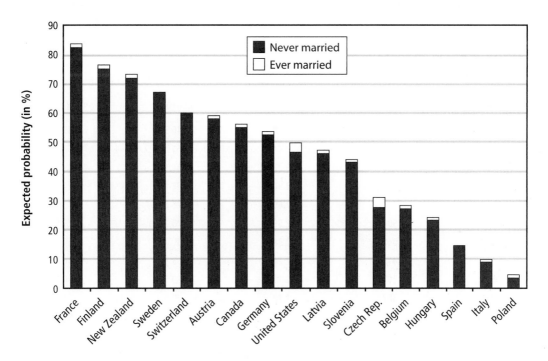

Figure 10.1 Expected probability (%) of experiencing at least one adulthood cohabitation by age 45[a], by previous marital status: Female respondents in Family and Fertility Surveys. Countries sorted in descending order by total percentage expected to cohabit. Estimates derived from single-decrement life tables.

[a] Age 36 in Germany, 37 in Belgium and Hungary, 38 in Sweden, 40 in the Czech Republic and the United States, 41 in Slovenia, and 43 in Italy and Switzerland.

record levels, although high cross-national variation remains. By imposing the same upper age limit across the board, we found that the different upper age limits do not contribute much to this cross-national variation. This is because most women between the exact ages of 15 and 45 experience cohabitation before marriage, and because most women who marry between those ages are married by their late thirties. At early 1990s rates, this percentage ranges from 4.4 per cent in Poland to 83.6 per cent in France. Between these extremes, quantifying exactly which percentages are high or low is somewhat arbitrary. The lower end of the distribution exhibits a clear cutoff point, however, with three countries at 15 per cent or less (Spain, Italy, and Poland), while the next country (Hungary) is at 24 per cent. Cohabitation therefore continues to contribute relatively little to family formation in these three countries.

Table 10.2 shows the median estimated duration of cohabitation spells involving never-married women (i.e. not just the first cohabiting partnership, but all cohabiting partnerships before first marriage)—that is, the number of years it would take, given the transition probabilities observed during the reference period, for 50 per cent of these cohabitation spells to end with the couple either separating or transitioning into marriage.

Table 10.2 also breaks down the route of exit for these first 50 per cent. The estimation has to be restricted to the countries that provide enough cohabitation years of observation during the reference period. Setting a lower limit at 500 cohabitation years, 11 countries are left and there is again

Table 10.2   Expected duration of and route of exit from adulthood cohabitation: Never-married women aged 15–44[a]

Country	Cohabitation years	Median duration[b]	Route of exit[c]	
			Marriage	Separation
France	1,490	4.28	46.3	53.7
Sweden	1,799	3.44	61.2	38.8
Canada	1,310	3.32	36.1	63.9
Slovenia	707	2.90	78.1	21.9
Austria	1,218	2.69	76.8	23.2
Belgium	504	2.39	76.2	23.8
Finland	1,045	2.38	80.7	19.7
Germany	1,470	2.24	53.3	46.7
New Zealand	801	2.18	39.5	60.5
Switzerland	1,367	1.78	75.6	24.4
United States	2,171	1.17	48.0	52.0
Country median		2.39	61.2	38.8

Table sorted in descending order by expected median duration, excluding countries with fewer than 500 observed cohabitation years during the reference period. Estimates derived from multiple-decrement life tables, adjusted for the risk of reaching the upper age limit before the end of a cohabitation spell (see Preston, et al., 2001. pp. 80–4).

[a]Actual age ranges vary across countries.

[b]Duration by which half of the premarital cohabitation spells have ended in either marriage or separation.

[c]Figures relate to the 50 per cent of the cohabitation spells that are ended by the median duration.

substantial variation in both duration and route of exit. Three countries exhibit median durations of 3 years or more (France, 4.28 years; Sweden. 3.44 years; and Canada. 3.32 years), whereas the median duration of premarital cohabitation spells is distinctly shorter in the United States (1.17 years) than in other countries.

When most cohabitation spells are initiated as a prelude to marriage or as a stage in the marriage process, the median duration of these spells should be relatively short, and a fairly high proportion of them should transition into marriage. We find that for 5 of these 11 countries, the percentage of cohabitation spells transitioning into marriage is indeed above three-fourths, with a high of 80.7 per cent in Finland. The percentage is lowest in Canada (36.1 per cent), and relatively low as well in the other two countries with long median duration (France, 46.3 per cent; Sweden, 61.2 per cent). Two other countries with relatively low median durations also exhibit percentages ending in marriage under 50 per cent, however: New Zealand (39.5 per cent) and the United States (48.0 per cent). In contrast to Canada, France, and Sweden, where low likelihood of marriage, combined with relatively long duration, suggests stable cohabitation regardless of marriage, the combination of low likelihood of marriage and short durations in New Zealand and in the United States suggests unstable cohabitation unless they are *converted* into marriages.

Childhood Cohabitation

We now turn to children's experience of cohabitation. Figure 10.2 presents life table estimates of the percentage of early 1990s birth cohorts expected to experience a maternal cohabitation at least once by exact age 16. These estimated percentages are further broken down into three parts: those born to cohabiting parents, those born to single mothers who then transition into a parental cohabitation by age 1, and those whose first experience of maternal cohabitation is between exact ages 1 and 16, which we treat as step-cohabitations. Again, we observe

wide variation in childhood experiences of maternal cohabitation, ranging from 4.7 per cent in Poland to 53.5 per cent in Sweden.

Not surprisingly, at the low end of the distribution of children's exposure we find the three countries with low adulthood exposure, but three other countries (Hungary, Belgium, and Switzerland) also exhibit childhood proportions below 15 per cent (see Figure 10.2). For Switzerland, the contrast between adulthood and childhood percentages is remarkable, with 59.9 per cent of women and only 9.6 per cent of children experiencing maternal cohabitation. According to our estimates based on early 1990s rates, women in Switzerland are thus six times more likely to experience cohabitation than children during the ages under consideration.

At the high end of the distribution, Sweden is an outlier with more than half of a birth cohort expected to experience maternal cohabitation during childhood, followed by France at near 40 per cent. More surprisingly, the United States, which is about average on the adult cohabitation scale, is next, with about one-third of a birth cohort expected to experience maternal cohabitation by exact age 16. Our estimate is higher than Graefe and Lichter's (1999) one-fourth estimate based on a different survey, the 1997 National Longitudinal Survey of Youth, but it is slightly lower than Bumpass and Lu's (2000) two-fifths estimate using the US Family and Fertility Survey and a broader reference period (1990–4). In any event, the relatively high exposure to maternal cohabitation in the United States is due in part to the higher exposure to maternal cohabitation between exact ages 1 and 16, which we infer to be with step-parents rather than with biological parents. The proportion of children experiencing their first maternal cohabitation between exact ages 1 and 16 is the largest in the United States (more than one-fifth of a birth cohort), and accounts for more than one-half of children's first exposure to maternal cohabitation. By contrast, the proportion is about 5 per cent in Sweden, only accounting for about one-tenth of children's first exposure to maternal cohabitation. In part, children in the United States

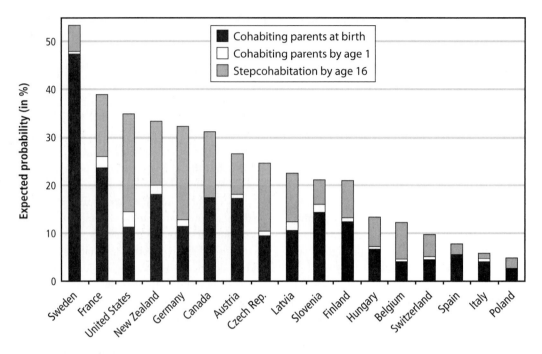

Figure 10.2 Expected probability (%) of exposure to at least one maternal cohabitation by age 16, by route of exposure: Children of Family and Fertility Surveys female respondents. Countries sorted in descending order by total percentage expected to experience maternal cohabitation by age 16. Estimates derived from single-decrement life tables.

are more at risk of experiencing maternal cohabitation between age 1 and age 16 because they are more likely than children in other countries to be living with a single mother at some point during their childhood, most often as a result of parental separation (Heuveline et al., 2003).

Table 10.3 presents children's median durations in and routes of exit from parental cohabitations (begun either at birth or by age 1) for the nine countries that had a sufficient number of observed cohabitation years to enable reliable estimation. As for adults, median durations for children are shortest in the United States and longest in France, ranging among the remaining countries from 2.11 years to 9.48 years (compared with 1.17 years to 4.28 years for adults). Although children are less likely to experience cohabitation than adult women, the median duration of a childhood parental cohabitation is generally longer than the median adult premarital cohabitation. We find the four countries with percentages of parental cohabitation ending in marriage under 50 per cent to be those with percentages of premarital cohabitation ending in marriage also under 50 per cent: Canada, France, New Zealand, and the United States. Perhaps more surprisingly, the highest proportion of parental cohabitations ending in marriage at the median duration among the remaining nine countries is found in Sweden (81.6 per cent).

Summary

Table 10.4 summarizes national indicators and compares them to the ideal types presented in Table 10.1. Several countries exhibit indicators that do not conform entirely to one of the patterns. These countries

Table 10.3   Expected duration of exposure to and route of exit from parental cohabitation: Children aged 0–16

Country	Cohabitation years	Median duration[a]	Route of exit[b]	
			Marriage	Separation
France	1,583	9.48	23.8	76.2
Slovenia	591	6.11	76.9	23.1
Canada	724	4.16	30.5	69.5
Finland	444	3.48	69.7	30.3
New Zealand	660	3.03	34.5	65.5
Austria	6(5	2.82	76.0	24.0
Sweden	2,401	2.71	81.6	18.4
Germany	1,085	2.62	63.3	36.7
United States	1,630	2.11	48.2	51.8
Country median		3.03	63.3	36.7

Table sorted in descending order by expected median duration, excluding countries with fewer than 500 observed cohabitation years during the reference period. Estimates derived from multiple-decrement life tables (see Preston, et al., 2001, pp. 80–4).

[a] Duration by which half of the parental cohabitation spells have ended in either marriage or separation.

[b] Figures relate to the first half of the parental cohabitation that are ended by the median duration.

are classified in Table 10.4 on the basis of the preponderance of fit between the observed values and the patterns. We mark cells that clearly do not conform to that pattern with a boldface. First, we find a few countries where cohabitation remains relatively rare and continues to play a marginal role in the landscape of family formation. We estimate that at early 1990s rates, fewer than 15 per cent of women will experience cohabitation in Italy, Poland, and Spain. As a result, childhood experience of cohabitation is even rarer, which generates an insufficient sample of cohabitation spells to estimate other indicators reliably, such as median duration or percentage transitioning into marriage.

At the other end of the distribution, we estimate that 83.6 per cent of adult women will experience cohabitation between ages 15 and 45 in France, and 53.5 per cent of children will experience maternal cohabitation by age 16 in Sweden. In both countries, the median duration of an adult premarital cohabitation is relatively long (3.44 years in Sweden, 4.28 years

in France), and the proportion of these premarital cohabitations ending in marriage is relatively low (61.2 per cent in Sweden, 46.3 per cent in France). Yet indicators for these countries differ when we estimate the likely trajectories of parental cohabitation. Although fewer children are expected to be born to cohabiting parents in France, half of them can expect to remain with unmarried cohabiting parents for at least 9.48 years, and only 23.8 per cent of those who left parental cohabitation did so through marriage rather than through separation. In Sweden, the median duration is shorter, 2.71 years, but more important, the proportion exiting through parental marriage is much larger: 81.6 per cent. Sweden thus appears to fit Kiernan's (2001) description of the end point in the emergence of cohabitation as a family-building institution, when cohabitation eventually evolves to be almost indistinguishable from marriage. Children are born to cohabiting parents nearly as frequently as to married parents, and when they are, their parents are quite likely to marry later on.

Table 10.4   Family and Fertility Surveys countries by ideal-typical role of cohabitation

		Empirical indicators					
		Adulthood	Premarital	Cohabitation	Childhood	Parental	Cohabitation
Role	Country	Incidence	Median duration	Proportion ending in marriage	Incidence	Median duration	Proportion ending in marriage
A	Marginal						
	Italy	9.4	n/a[a]		4.7	n/a[a]	
	Poland	3.6	n/a[a]		2.6	n/a[a]	
	Spain	14.7	n/a[a]		5.5	n/a[a]	
B	Prelude to marriage						
	Belgium	27.5	2.39	76.2	4.5	n/a[a]	
	Czech Republic	28.2	n/a[a]		10.4	n/a[a]	
	Hungary	23.2	n/a[a]		7.1	n/a[a]	
	Switzerland	59.4	1.78	75.6	5.0	n/a[a]	
C	Stage in marriage process						
	Austria	58.3	2.69	76.8	18.0	2.82	76.0
	Finland	75.4	2.38	80.7	13.1	4.08[b]	74.1
	Germany	53.0	2.24	53.3	12.7	2.62	63.3
	Latvia	47.0	n/a[a]		12.4	n/a[a]	
	Slovenia	43.2	2.90	78.1	15.9	6.11	76.9
D	Alternative to single						
	New Zealand	46.6	2.18	39.5	14.6[b]	3.03	34.5
	United States	71.9	1.17	48.0	20.1[b]	2.11	48.2
E	Alternative to marriage						
	Canada	55.2	3.32	36.1	17.4	4.17	30.5
	France	83.3	4.28	46.3	25.9	9.48	23.8
F	Indistinguishable from marriage						
	Sweden	66.7	3.44	61.2[b]	48.0	2.71[b]	81.6
Median values		47.0	2.39	61.2	12.7	3.03	63.3
Cutoff values (higher/lower, longer/shorter; see Table 10.1)		15.0	3.00	50.0	12.0	4.00	50.0

[a] 'n/a' indicates non-available indicators in countries where we observed fewer than 500 cohabitation years during the reference period.
[b] Denotes indicators whose respective position relative to the corresponding cutoff value is contrary to the expectation for that type (see Table 10.1).

Children born to cohabiting parents in France can expect to remain with unmarried cohabiting parents much longer than in Sweden, and are much less likely to see them marry. A substantial minority of French parents thus seem to choose longterm cohabitation as an alternative to marriage. Although his study focuses on adult cohabitation, Toulemon's (1997) title also accurately describes childhood experience of parental cohabitation in asserting that 'Cohabitation Is Here to Stay' in France. This seems to also be the case in Canada, where parental cohabitations are also fairly long (median duration 4.17 years), with only 30 per cent ending in marriage. The incidence of both adulthood and childhood cohabitation is significantly lower than in either France or Sweden, however. The intermediate values for Canada likely result from the sharp difference in propensity to cohabit between Quebec and the other provinces (Lapierre-Adamcyk, Le Bourdais, & Marcil-Gratton, 1999).

In the majority of countries studied here, most unmarried couples appear to enter cohabitation with the intention of marrying. Most cohabitation spells are relatively short and frequently result in marriage. For those resulting in marriage and childbearing, the normative sequence of marriage first, then birth is respected to a variable extent across countries. On one hand, cohabiting parents in Switzerland seem to conform to this timing, with 59.9 per cent of adult women experiencing cohabitation, 75.6 per cent of cohabiting partnerships resulting in marriage, and only 5.0 per cent of a birth cohort experiencing a parental cohabitation by age 1. This characterization of family formation in Switzerland is consistent with previous studies (e.g. Charton & Wanner, 2001).

On the other hand, Austria may best represent the stage in the marriage process ideal type. Compared with Switzerland, roughly the same percentage of women experience unmarried cohabitation (58.8 per cent vs 59.9 per cent), and roughly the same percentage of these cohabiting partnerships are expected to result in marriage (76.8 per cent vs 75.6 per cent). The percentage of children experiencing parental cohabitation by age 1 is substantially higher in Austria, however (18.0 per cent vs 5.0 per cent), suggesting that some of the cohabiting couples who eventually marry do so after rather than before their first birth. This particularity of the Austrian family system has also been described in previous studies (e.g. Prinz, 1995). Most couples in the remaining countries also seem to cohabit as a more or less timed transition to marriage; the indicators for these countries are intermediate between the Swiss and the Austrian values, with the notable exceptions of New Zealand and the United States.

Cohabitation is not negligible in the United States; about one-half of adult women are expected to experience cohabitation at least once between ages 15 and 45, and one-third of children are expected to experience maternal cohabitation by age 16, but the median duration of the cohabitation spells was the shortest of all of the countries reviewed here for adults (1.17 years) and for children (2.11 years). Couples who cohabit as a durable alternative to marriage are clearly a minority. However, couples who enter cohabitation as a prelude to marriage or even a stage in the marriage process do not clearly dominate either, because about as many cohabitation spells end in separation as in marriage for adults and for children. Rindfuss and VandenHeuvel (1990) described this cohabitation pattern of short duration and relatively high separation frequency as *alternative to single*. An indicator perhaps less consistent with this characterization of cohabitation in the United States is the non-eligible percentage of children experiencing parental cohabitation. As noted above, this is largely due to the contribution of step-cohabitation, which likely results from the higher incidence of divorce in the United States than in European countries, and subsequent partnership formation out of marriage. Another American characteristic is the substantial percentage of children born to single non-cohabiting mothers (Heuveline, et al., 2003). Recent data from the Fragile Families project show that nearly two-thirds of these mothers are romantically involved with the father, who is not living with the mother but visits more or less regularly (J.O. Teitler, personal communication, 30 April 2003). We may hence retain the alternative to single characterization of cohabitation in the United States, as long as we take into account the evolution of being single as a state that involves dating, sexual intercourse, and frequently, childbearing.

Discussion

As noted by Smock (2000), it is difficult to understand cohabitation by comparing it with other living arrangements, and to marriage in particular, because marriage itself is a moving target rather than a stable reference point. It is thus debatable whether the different contours of cohabitation found here to separate the United States and New Zealand from other countries reveal a lesser tendency of cohabiting partners in these two countries to behave as married partners rather than as single adults, or a fading of traditional characteristics of marriage, such as childbearing and expected durability. One interpretation of the relatively short median duration and high separation frequency of cohabitation spells in the United States and New Zealand is that cohabitation resembles being single, yet being single does not preclude childbearing in these two countries. An alterative interpretation would point to the differences in the reference institution, because marriage is not the same across countries and appears particularly vulnerable to disruption in these two countries. Life table estimates from the same data suggest that the relative risk of experiencing parental disruption for children born to cohabiting versus married parents is not higher in the United States or New Zealand than in other countries (Heuveline, et al., 2003). Thus, cohabitation in these two countries could be as much a stage in the marriage process as it is in other countries, a process that exhibits a higher failure rate in these countries regardless of how it is started.

It is noteworthy that the three non-European countries are more difficult to characterize than their European counterparts, perhaps due to their internal diversity. As mentioned above, regional differences are sharp in Canada, and both New Zealand and the United States are ethnically diverse countries, with well-documented ethnic differences in family behaviour in the United States (e.g. Bumpass & Lu, 2000; Manning, 1993). More generally, within-country heterogeneity is clearly important and not captured by the summary indicators presented here. It would be problematic if one interpreted these indicators as applying to whole populations rather than to use them for what they are: mono-dimensional indicators of the central tendency of a whole distribution. In the above analyses, our argument is simply that when a behaviour becomes prevalent enough (e.g. adulthood cohabitation, childbearing while cohabiting before marriage, remaining together but unmarried following a birth), average indicators can detect it even if it remains a minority behaviour. The presence of partners who cohabit as an alternative to marriage in France is a case in point. Although we see evidence of this behaviour from the fact that after 9.48 years, half of the children whose parents were cohabiting at birth or by age 1 were still together and unmarried, these children only constitute 25.9 per cent of a birth cohort; hence, less than 13 per cent of a birth cohort can actually expect to live 9.48 years or more with cohabiting parents.

We are therefore not claiming that the patterns of family formation for which we found evidence in one country or another apply to the whole population of these countries, nor do we claim that these differences represent permanent national characteristics. The snapshot of cross-national differences in cohabitation presented here likely catches many of these countries in the midst of substantial transition. Because the age limit of the survey respondents is typically around age 45, we cannot go backward in time without encountering some well-known selectivity biases related to maternal age at birth (Rindfuss, et al., 1982). Even with these limitations, the Family and Fertility Surveys data provide clear evidence of fast-paced changes (Heuveline et al., 2003). It is possible that the differences found here relate more to differences in the timing of a common transition from the traditional Western family system to a new family regime rather than to stable differences in family formation across countries. From these data, however, there is arguably more evidence of path dependency (e.g. postnatal marriage in Austria) than clear signs of convergence.

In any event, we believe that the single period differences presented here should be attributed partly to cross-national variation in the underlying distributions of individual traits related to the propensity to cohabit, marry, and raise children out of wedlock, and also to the contextual factors that affect these propensities for all or part of a population. As mentioned above, earlier work (e.g. Kiernan, 2000) has shown that within-country differences influenced by individual traits (e.g. education) are small compared with between-country differences. Although the identification of the macro level factors responsible for these differences is beyond the scope of this article, the rise of cohabitation has generated different institutional responses across the countries considered here. For example, the current US administration has launched a 'marriage initiative' to facilitate the transition from cohabitation to marriage. In contrast, the French government recently instituted the *Pacte Civil de Solidarite* as an alternative living arrangement, removing some of the requirements of marriage while providing social protections more comparable with that of married couples (Martin & Théry, 2001). Although we have learned a great deal about differential propensities to cohabit from individual-level survey data and cross-sectional analyses (see Smock 2000, for a review), there remains a great need for complementary comparative research on the effects of contextual-level factors on these propensities.

References

Axinn, W.G., & Thornton, A. (1993). Mothers, children, and cohabitation: The intergenerational effects of attitudes and behavior. *American Sociological Review, 58*, 223–46.

Blackwell, D.L., & Lichter, D.T. (2000). Mate selection among married and cohabiting couples. *Journal of Family Issues, 21*, 275–302.

Bradshaw, J., Ditch, J., Holmes, H., & Whiteford, P. (1993). A comparative study of child support in fifteen countries. *Journal of European Social Policy, 3*, 255–71.

Brown, S.L. (2000). Fertility following marital dissolution: The role of cohabitation. *Journal of Family Issues, 21*, 501–24.

Brown, S.L., & Booth, A. (1996). Cohabitation versus marriage: A comparison of relationship quality. *Journal of Marriage and Family, 58*, 668–78.

Bumpass, L.L., & Lu, H.H. (2000). Trends in cohabitation and implications for children's family contexts in the United States. *Population Studies, 54*, 29–41.

Casper, L.M., & Bianchi, S.M. (2002). *Continuity and change in the American family.* Thousand Oaks, CA: Sage.

Casper, L.M., & Cohen, P.N. (2000). How does POSSLQ measure up? Historical estimates of cohabitation. *Demography, 37*, 237–45.

Charton, L., & Wanner, P. (2001). La première mise en couple en Suisse: Choix du type d'union et devenir de la cohabitation hors mariage [First union formation in Switzerland: The choice of a union type and outcome of extramarital cohabitation]. *Population, 56*, 539–68.

Esping-Andersen, G. (1990). *The three worlds of welfare capitalism.* Princeton, NJ: Princeton University Press.

Gauthier, A.H. (1996). *The state and the family: A comparative analysis of family policies in industrialized countries.* Oxford, UK: Clarendon Press.

Graefe, D.R., & Lichter, D.T. (1999). Life course transitions of American children: Parental cohabitation, marriage, and single motherhood. *Demography, 36*, 205–217.

Heuveline, P., Timberlake, J.M., & Furstenberg, F.F., Jr. (2003). Shifting childrearing to single mothers: Results from 17 Western countries. *Population and Development Review, 29*, 47–71.

Kiernan, K.E. (2000). European perspectives on union formation. In L.I. Waite (Ed.), *The ties that bind: Perspectives on marriage and cohabitation* (pp. 40–58). Hawthorne, NY: Aldine de Gruyter.

———. (2001). The rise of cohabitation and childbearing outside marriage in western Europe.

International Journal of Law, Policy and the Family, *15*, 1–21.

Kuijsten, A.C. (1996). Changing family patterns in Europe: A case of divergence? *European Journal of Population, 12*, 112–43.

Kveder, A. (2002). Data quality issues in comparative Fertility and Family Surveys. In E. Klijking & M. Corijn (Eds), *Dynamics of fertility and partnership in Europe* (vol. 11, pp. 145–55). New York: United Nations.

Lapierre-Adamcyk, E., Le Bourdeais, C., & Marcil-Gratton, N. (1999). Vivre en couple pour la première fois: La signification du choix de l'union libre au Québec et en Ontario [First union: The meaning of choosing non-marital cohabitation in Quebec and Ontario]. *Cahiers Québécois de Démographie, 28*, 199–228.

Macura, M., & Klijking, E. (1992). *Fertility and Family Surveys in countries of the ECE region.* Unpublished manuscript. Geneva: Population Activities Unit of the Economic Commission for Europe.

Manning, W.D. (1993). Marriage and cohabitation following premarital conception. *Journal of Marriage and Family, 55*, 839–50.

———. (1995). Cohabitation, marriage, and entry into motherhood. *Journal of Marriage and Family, 57*, 191–200.

Manning, W.D., & Lichter, D.T. (1996). Parental cohabitation and children's economic well-being. *Journal of Marriage and Family, 58*, 998–1010.

Martin, C., & Théry, I. (2001). The Pacs and marriage and cohabitation in France. *International Journal of Law, Policy, and the Family, 15*, 135–58.

McLanahan, S., & Sandefur, G. (1994). *Growing up with a single parent: What hurts, what helps.* Cambridge, MA: Harvard University Press.

Morgan, S.P., & Rindfuss, R.R. (1999). Reexamining the link of early childbearing to marriage and to subsequent fertility. *Demography, 36*, 59–71.

Morrison, D.R., & Ritualo, A. (2000). Routes to children's economic recovery after divorce: Are cohabitation and remarriage equivalent? *American Sociological Review, 65*, 560–80.

Murphy, M. (2000). The evolution of cohabitation in Britain, 1960–95. *Population Studies, 54*, 43–56.

Pagnini, D.L., & Rindfuss, R.R. (1993). The divorce of marriage and childbearing: Changing attitudes

and behavior in the United States. *Population and Development Review, 19*, 331–47.

Poulain, M., Riandey, B., & Firdion, J.M. (1991). Enquête biographique et registre Beige de population: Une confrontation des données [Retrospective survey and Belgium population register: Confronting data sets]. *Population, 46*, 65–88.

Preston, S.H., Heuveline, P., & Guillot, M. (2001). *Demography: Measuring and modeling population processes.* Oxford, UK: Blackwell.

Prinz, C. (1995). *Cohabiting, married or single: Portraying, analyzing and modeling new living arrangements in the changing societies of Europe.* Brookfield, VT: Ashgate.

Raley, R.K. (2001). Increasing fertility in cohabiting unions: Evidence for the second demographic transition in the United States? *Demography, 38*, 59–66.

Reher, D.S. (1998). Family ties in western Europe: Persistent contrasts. *Population and Development Review, 24*, 203–34.

Rindfuss, R.R., Palmore, J., & Bumpass, L.L. (1982). Selectivity and the analysis of birth intervals with survey data. *Asian and Pacific Census Forum, 8*, 5–16.

Rindfuss, R.R., & VandenHeuvel, A. (1990). Cohabitation: A precursor to marriage or an alternative to being single? *Population and Development Review, 16*, 703–26.

Smock, P.J. (2000). Cohabitation in the United States: An appraisal of research themes, findings, and implications. *Annual Review of Sociology, 26*, 1–20.

Thornton, A. (1989). Changing attitudes toward family issues in the United States. *Journal of Marriage and Family, 51*, 873–93.

Timberlake, J.M., & Heuveline, P. (in press). How much have changes in adult nonmarital cohabitation affected the family structure experiences of children? *Sociological Studies of Children and Youth.*

Toulemon, L. (1997). Cohabition is here to stay. *Population: An English Selection, 9*, 11–56.

van de Kaa, D.J. (1987). Europe's second demographic transition. *Population Bulletin, 42*, 1. Washington, DC: Population Reference Bureau.

Ventura, S.J., & Bachrach, C.A. (2000). *Nonmarital childbearing in the United States, 1940–99* (National Vital Statistics Reports No. 16). Hyattsville, MD: National Center for Health Statistics.

Basic Demographic Measures

1. Crude Marriage Rate (CMR)

Although one can easily obtain the annual number of marriages or divorces that take place in a country, these data would be of limited analytical use because they do not relate to the size of the population that is in a position to marry or divorce. One would need to control for the possibility that, for example, small populations might produce relatively few marriages compared with larger populations. For this reason, it is best to work with rates of marriage and divorce. The most fundamental rate for marriage is the *crude marriage rate* (CMR):

$$CMR = \frac{M}{P} \times 1{,}000$$

where M is the number of marriages (including first marriages and remarriages) that take place in a given interval (e.g. one year), and P is the mid-interval (i.e. midyear) population.

Note: to simplify the presentation, it will be assumed in all measures below that the interval is one year.

2. Crude Divorce Rate (CDivR)

An analogous measure is the *crude divorce rate* (CDivR):

$$CDivR = \frac{D}{P} \times 1{,}000$$

where D stands for the number of divorces in a given year, and P is the midyear population.

3. General Marriage and Divorce Rates (GMR, GDR)

Even though they are used widely in the literature, the crude marriage and divorce rates are not entirely satisfactory. The main problem concerns the denominator, since it consists of individuals who cannot possibly be in the risk set for either marriage or divorce, specifically persons under the age of 15 and, in the case of divorce, people who have never been married and those who are widowed. Sometimes, if the appropriate data are available, it is possible to refine the denominator by using the midyear population aged 15 years of age and older as the risk set, and to confine this to either men or women (typically the denominator is females). The resulting formulae yield the *general marriage rate* (GMR) and the *general divorce rate* (GDR), which can be computed as follows:

$$GMR = \frac{M}{P_f^{15+}} \times 1{,}000$$

$$GDR = \frac{D}{P_f^{15+}} \times 1{,}000$$

where P_f^{15+} is the number of females aged 15 and older at midyear.

These two general rates are usually expressed as per 1,000 population.

4. First Marriage Rate (FMR)

Order-specific marriage rates are of particular interest for demographic analysis because of their varying correlation with the birth rate. The *first marriage rate* (FMR) is the number of marriages occurring for the first time in a given year divided by the midyear never-married (i.e. single) population:

$$\text{FMR} = \frac{M_1}{P_{nm}^{15+}} \times 1{,}000$$

where M_1 is marriages of order 1 (i.e. first marriages) and P_{nm}^{15+} is the midyear never-married population 15 years of age and older.

Second and higher-order marriage rates can be computed by using this same approach. In the case of the second-order marriage rate, the numerator would be the number of second marriages, and the denominator would be the population aged 15 and older that is widowed or divorced.

Questions for Critical Thought

1. Why are young adults in some countries today more likely to cohabit than to enter into marriage? Why in some countries does cohabitation remain generally uncommon?

2. Is cohabitation in some contemporary industrialized societies a replacement for legal marriage, or is it simply a stage in the family-building process?

3. What are the sociological implications of declining marriage rates in contemporary industrialized societies?

Websites of Interest

The *Vanier Institute of the Family* is a Canadian non-profit organization dedicated to promoting the wellbeing of Canadian families. Their website offers information about their research and analysis on a variety of issues concerning families, making it an excellent source of information on this topic: www.vifamily.ca/

The *Child and Family Research Institute* is committed to world-class research spanning a wide range of children's and women's health concerns. Based in Vancouver, BC, it is the largest research institute of its kind in Western Canada. Its website features information about the institute's research and links to news items relevant to the study of family issues: www.cfri.ca/

UCLA's *Center on Everyday Life of Families* is an interdisciplinary center where anthropologists, applied linguists, education specialists, and psychologists study how working parents and their children approach the challenges of balancing the demands of work, school, and family life using detailed, ethnographic research of everyday life. Its research aims and current research are described on its website: www.celf.ucla.edu/

The Government of Canada's *Policy Research Initiative* (PRI) conducts research in the areas of Canada's labour market, population change, and the life-course. Its flagship policy research journal, *Horizons*, is now available online via the PRI's website: www.policyresearch.gc.ca/

Further Reading

Axin, William G., & Thornton, Arland. (1996). The influence of parents' marital dissolution on children's attitudes toward family formation. *Demography, 33*(1), 66–81.

Bianchi, Suzanne, Robinson, John P., & Milkie, Melissa A. (2006). *Changing rhythms of American family life.* Chicago: University of Chicago Press / Russell Sage Foundation.

Blankenhorn, David. (2007). *The future of marriage.* New York: Encounter Books.

Blossfeld, Hans-Peter, & Timm, Andreas (Eds). (2003). *Who marries whom? Educational systems as marriage markets in modern societies.* Dordrecht: Kluwer Academic Publishers.

Burguiere, Andre, Klapisch-Zuber, Christiane, Segalen, M., & Zonabend, F. (Eds). (1996). *A history of the family* (2 vols). Cambridge: Belknap Press.

De Beer, Joop, & Deven, Fred (Eds). (2000). *Diversity in family formation: The 2nd demographic transition in Belgium and the Netherlands.* Dordrecht: Kluwer Academic Publishers.

Esping-Andersen, Gosta. (2009). *The incomplete revolution: Adapting to women's new roles.* Cambridge: Polity Press.

Fincham, Frank D., & Beach, Steven R. H. (2010). Marriage in the new millennium: A decade in review. *Journal of Marriage and Family 72*, 630–49.

Jacobs, Jerry A., & Gerson, Kathleen. (2004). *The time divide: Work, family, and gender inequality.* Cambridge, MA: Harvard University Press.

Kneip, Thorsten, & Bauer, Gerrit. (2009). Did unilateral divorce laws raise divorce rates in western Europe? *Journal of Marriage and Family, 71*, 592–607.

Lichter, Daniel T., & Qian, Zhenchao. (2008). Serial cohabitation and the marital life course. *Journal of Marriage and Family, 70*, 861–78.

Lyngstad, Torkild Hovde, & Jalovaara, Marika. (2010). A review of the antecedents of union dissolution. *Demographic Research, 23* (art. 10), 257–92.

National Research Council and Institute of Medicine. (2005). Growing up global: The changing transitions to adulthood in the developing countries. Panel on transitions to Adulthood in developing countries. In Cynthia B. Lloyd (Ed.), *Committee on population and board on children, youth, and families.* Division of Behavioral and Social Sciences and Education. Washington, DC: The National Academies Press.

Nock, Steven L., Sanchez, Laura A., & Wright, James D. (2008). *Covenant marriage: The movement to reclaim tradition in America.* New Brunswick, NJ: Rutgers University Press.

Potts, Malcom, & Campbell, Martha. (2008). The origins and future of patriarchy: The biological background of gender politics. *Journal of Family Planning and Reproductive Health Care, 34*(3), 171–4.

Presser, Harriet B. (2003). *Working in a 24/7 economy: Challenges for American families.* New York: Russell Sage Foundation.

Rindfuss, Ronald R. (1991). The young adult years: Diversity, structural change, and fertility. *Demography, 28*(4), 493–512.

Ruggles, Steven. (2007). The decline of intergenerational coresidence in the United States, 1850–2000. *American Sociological Review, 72*, 964–89.

Teachman, Jay. (2004). The childhood living arrangements of children and the characteristics of their marriages. *Journal of Family Issues, 25*(1), 86–111.

Wu, Lawrence L., & Wolf, Barbara (Eds). (2001). *Out of wedlock: Causes and consequences of nonmarital fertility.* New York: Russell Sage Foundation.

Zimmerman, F. Klaus, & Vogler, Michael (Eds). (2003). *Family, household and work.* Berlin: Springer.

SECTION VI
Fertility

Learning Objectives

By the end of this section, students should understand and be able to discuss the following:

- the difference between fecundity and fertility
- the proximate determinants of fertility
- evolutionary and sociological explanations of fertility transition.

Introduction

Fertility is the variable most responsible for population growth and the principal determinant of change in the age composition of any population. Although it is an inherently biological process, human fertility is strongly influenced by societal and cultural factors, making it both an individual and a collective matter. A population's continuity over the long term is contingent on its fertility. Its fertility, in turn, depends on the interplay of biological, social, and behavioural factors. The selected readings in this part of the volume reflect, in different ways, this important theme in both contemporary and historical contexts.

Biosocial Aspects of Human Fertility

Fecundity and Fertility

Fecundity describes the physiological capability of a woman, a man, or a couple to reproduce. As noted by Trussell (2003, p. 397), logically, fecundity depends on a sequence of events: the female must produce an egg capable of being fertilized, the male must produce sperm that can fertilize the egg, fertilization must occur, the fertilized egg must survive to implant in the uterus, and once implantation has occurred, the pregnancy must result in a live birth.

The opposite of fecundity is *infecundity*—the total inability to reproduce (i.e. the condition of being sterile). Infecund individuals may be sterile as a result of having been born with a genetic or biological condition that interferes with their ability to conceive or bring about a conception. Sterility can also develop among those who in the past were fecund (and perhaps even had children) as a result of some acquired disease that damages the reproductive system (McFalls, 1979, p. 4).

Subfecundity describes the condition of couples with impairments of any of the biological aspects of reproduction, including the following problems:

- *coital inability* – the inability to perform normal heterosexual intercourse because of physical or psychological disease, which can be temporary or permanent
- *conceptive failure* – the diminished ability to conceive or to bring about conception
- *pregnancy loss* – the involuntary termination of a pregnancy before a live birth, including spontaneous abortion, late fetal death, and stillbirth, but not induced abortion nor neonatal mortality (McFalls, 1979).

The extent of subfecundity can vary, from situations where one of the partners, but not the other, may have a reproductive impairment, to cases in which both partners may have some impairment; in either case, the impairment is thought to be medically treatable. Thus, such cases differ from infecundity, which involves conditions that cannot be reversed through medical treatment. The realization of fecundity is referred to as *fertility*—this term is used to describe the actual reproductive output of a woman, a man, or a couple, as measured by the number of offspring. At the aggregate level, this term implies the computation of a summary measure of reproduction for a population (e.g. total fertility rate).

Proximate Determinants of Fertility

Total fertility rates in many contemporary developing countries, though high by contemporary standards, fall well below the biological upper limit for a human population (Bongaarts, 1975). A reasonable estimate of the maximum level of fertility in humans is about 15 births per woman (Bongaarts, 1978). Married Hutterite women (the Hutterites are an Anabaptist religious sect living in the north-central area of the United States, mainly South Dakota, North Dakota and Montana, and across the southern part of the Canadian prairies) have the highest recorded level of reproduction among humans. In the early twentieth century, married Hutterite women bore an average of 12.4 children (Coale, 1969, p. 4; Coale and Treadeway, 1986, p. 154). Presently, the most prolific nation in the world is Niger in western Africa, which has an average fertility rate of 7.4 children per woman (Population Reference Bureau, 2010). Yet even in this case and that of the Hutterites, the gap between observed levels of fertility and potential maximum fertility is considerable. What accounts for this?

In 1956, Davis and Blake proposed that social structure and culture affect fertility indirectly through a series of *intermediate variables*. These intermediate variables were subsumed under three broad sets of factors:

1. variables that affect exposure to intercourse (e.g. age at entry into sexual unions)
2. variables that affect exposure to conception (e.g. use of contraception)
3. variables affecting gestation and successful parturition of pregnancies (e.g. fetal mortality from voluntary causes, i.e. abortion, and from involuntary causes, i.e. spontaneous loss of pregnancy).

The fundamental idea behind the Davis and Blake framework is that change in the observed level of fertility for a population is the result of change in the intermediate variables. If any one of the intermediate variables changes (contraceptive use, for instance), then fertility necessarily changes in response, assuming of course that the other intermediate variables remain constant (that is, that change in one variable is not offset by change in the others). This principle does not apply to background societal factors. For example, an overall increase in income would affect fertility only indirectly through one or more of the intermediate variables.

As Bongaarts and Potter explain in their chapter of this volume, virtually all of the variability in fertility rates across populations can be accounted for by differences in four proximate (i.e. intermediate) variables:

1. *the extent of non-marriage* – the greater the level of non-marriage in society, the lower the potential fertility

2. *the level of contraceptive use* – the more couples there are using contraception, the lower the potential fertility
3. *the extent of voluntary abortion* – the greater the level of induced abortion, the lower the potential fertility
4. *the average duration of breastfeeding* – the longer the period of breastfeeding, the lower the potential fertility (extended lactation lengthens the period of postpartum amenorrhea—the absence of menstruation—and thus reduces potential fertility).

Other proximate variables have been listed under the category of 'natural marital fertility factors'; these include the frequency of intercourse, sterility, spontaneous intrauterine mortality, and duration of the fertile period. These 'natural fertility' variables have been shown to play a relatively minor role in explaining fertility variations across populations (Bongaarts, 2003).

Fertility Change

Theories of fertility change can be classified under a number of different headings: economic, sociological, social-psychological, anthropological, and even evolutionary. Some of the theories emphasize economic forces (e.g. Becker, 1960), while others place more emphasis on sociological determinants (e.g. Lesthaeghe, 2010; Lesthaeghe & Surkyn, 1988), and yet others combine economic and sociological concepts (e.g. Butz & Ward, 1979; Easterlin, 1969, 1983). Some of the theories apply mainly to the industrialized countries, while others are chiefly suited to developing societies (e.g., Caldwell, 1976; Easterlin, 1983). A full survey of the vast theoretical literature on fertility is not possible here. The selected works in this part of the volume represent important studies in this area. Kingsley Davis's essay is a sweeping account of fertility change over the very long span of human evolution. Caldwell and Schindlmayr offer an overarching explanation for the low fertility of contemporary industrialized countries. Finally, Bongaarts examines the state of fertility transition in the contemporary developing countries. We begin with a summary of Kingsley Davis's explanation of why the contemporary pattern of low fertility in the advanced societies is unusual when examined from the long-run perspective of human evolution.

Low Fertility in Evolutionary Perspective

The current trend of below-replacement fertility in the more developed countries seems anomalous. Never before in human history has fertility fallen so low. But, according to Davis, even more anomalous is the high fertility that characterized these countries at the inception of the Industrial Revolution and that characterizes many of the less developed countries today. In fact, over the course of human evolution, the normal pattern has been one of low to moderate fertility. From this perspective, today's low fertility in the highly advanced societies is not an aberration; it is, in Davis's words, 'an approximation of a *sine qua non* for human evolution', by which he means that throughout most of human history, fertility must have been low. Davis points to four indicators that, albeit indirectly, support this proposition:

1. Over the long haul, hominids had virtually zero population growth; in fact, all of the hominid species eventually became extinct except for modern humans, *Homo sapiens sapiens*.
2. Over the course of evolution, the human reproductive system became vulnerable to many pathologies and lost two of its pronatalist traits: sexual promiscuity and *estrus* (or *oestrus*). The latter refers to the recurring physiological changes induced by reproductive hormones in placental females and continuing until death (in animals, the process known as being 'in season'); human females, instead of estrus, experience a menstrual cycle that starts at puberty and ends at menopause.

3. Primates, our closest kin in the animal world, also exhibit low fertility.
4. Hunter–gatherer societies such as the Dobe !Kung of the Kalahari desert (a society that approximates pre-industrial conditions) have shown only moderate completed fertility. Their rate of 4.7 children per woman is well below the total fertility rate for Niger, which in 2010 was 7.4.

Even in the absence of birth control, our remote ancestors did not have very high fertility. Indeed, writes Davis, '[t]he highest birth rates are found, not under primitive, but under modern circumstances.' What kept the birth rate low throughout hominid evolution? For Davis, the answer lies in the quest for survival by a primitive society living under harsh conditions with high mortality. In order to survive, our distant ancestors had to invest heavily in the extended care of offspring. This meant that births were widely spaced, a situation aided by prolonged breastfeeding and even infanticide when necessary. Wide spacing of births allowed parents to devote to their progeny the time and attention necessary to help guarantee their survival into adulthood.

Thus, for most of human history, the story was one of homeostatic balance between high death rates and fertility levels kept low enough to ensure the continuity of the human species. A significant departure from this type of homeostatic balance would not appear until about 6 to 8 million years ago with the advent of agriculture (the 'Neolithic Revolution'). The ability to grow abundant quantities of food allowed humans to lift 'the traditional brakes on fertility', allowing fertility, for the first time in human evolution, to begin to surpass the death rate, thus creating conditions for rapid population growth.

The next momentous event in human history was the Industrial Revolution, which brought improved standards of living. The development of new medical technologies helped to further reduce the death rate, and following this, fertility rates rose to unprecedented levels, much higher than ever experienced in human history. Once the homeostatic balance around a growth rate of zero was broken, the world began to experience a 'population explosion'.

More recently, the advanced nations of the world have reached a new equilibrium. By bringing down their fertility to levels commensurate with very low mortality, they have achieved population growth rates again close to zero (reaching negative rates in some cases). Sociologically, these post-industrial societies have become grounded on the principles of upward social mobility, complex bureaucracy, and increasing levels of formal schooling for men and women. For Davis, below-replacement fertility rates in this type of context represent yet another human adjustment to the structural conditions that characterize these societies, where people find it advantageous to actualize small families. Moreover, Davis tells us that low fertility is the future not just of the industrial advanced societies but also of the developing countries, once they, too, attain the structural conditions inherent in industrial societies: '[u]nless these [structural] traits are somehow reversed or overcome, the industrial countries will continue to have fertility rates near or below replacement, and as other countries become developed, they too will record low fertility'.

Of the specific traits of post-industrial society most responsible for low fertility, Davis highlights the following four, all of which he linked to an increasingly precarious family institution:

1. postponement of marriage, owing to the growing number of alternatives to marriage available to young adults
2. the rise of nonmarital unions, which are much less prolific than marital unions
3. high divorce rates, which undermine the stability of marriage, reduce the amount of reproductive time spent in marriage, and encourage women to seek economic security by spending more time in education and employment
4. rising participation of women in the labour force, which produces a 'double burden' for working mothers, usually resolved by having fewer children.

As to the root cause of these developments, Davis is quite clear where the blame lies: post-industrial society, by its very nature and structure, penalizes commitment to marriage and marital reproduction. The traditional family has been so badly eroded by modernity, Davis contends, that it is failing to fulfill its reproductive function, as reflected in a number of trends: high levels of abortion, the universal prevalence of contraception, high divorce rates, rising levels of cohabitation, and a growing percentage of children born into cohabiting unions or to single women. In contemporary society,

[a]ny catalogue of 'liberal' or 'enlightened' views will include numerous anti-family attitudes. Homosexuality is only a matter of 'sexual orientation' and must be accepted; no-fault divorce is a good thing because it reduces recrimination; women bearing children out of wedlock should not be blamed for their situation but given financial help and special attention; abortion is a matter for the woman and her doctor to decide (the husband is ignored); teenagers should have access to contraceptives and abortions without their parents' knowledge; cohabitation without marriage is acceptable. (p. 193).

Low Fertility in Modern Societies: The Search for Commonalities

As we have already noted in connection with Davis's insightful analysis, the industrialized countries today, with few exceptions, all have low birth rates, below the 2.1 replacement level. Indeed, some of these countries have been defined as 'lowest-low fertility societies' (Billari & Kohler, 2004; Goldstein, Sobotka, & Jasilioniene, 2009; Kohler, Billari, & Ortega, 2002). Evidence presented by Frejka and Sardon (2004, p. 2) concerning longterm trends in period and cohort completed fertility rates points to the conclusion that below-replacement fertility in most European countries is likely to be a permanent condition, and that a reversal of the trend to fertility rates beyond an average of 2.1 seems highly unlikely. These countries may have fallen into what Lutz, Skirbekk, and Testa (2006) refer to as a 'low fertility trap'.

Caldwell and Schindlmeyr (2003), much like Davis, aim for an all-encompassing explanation for the persistence of low fertility in postmodern societies. Even though countries may differ in how they enter a low-fertility regime, there seems to be a common underlying force. It is, they explain, 'the creation of a world economic system where children are of no immediate economic value to their parents'. They suggest, as Davis earlier argued, that the reproduction of the species may simply be incompatible with advanced industrial society:

> This is a consequence of that society's rewards in the form of a career for women outside the home and the almost measureless temptations of the modern consumer society. . . . Children do not easily fit in it with a great deal of travel, and the entertainment they provide can be replaced by the electronic media and other pleasures. (p.208)

Peter McDonald (2000), in an illuminating study of gender equity, turns to another feature of highly advanced societies: their gender role regimes. He argues that societal variations in gender systems explain why some highly advanced societies have very low fertility rates and others have birth rates close to the replacement level. He draws a distinction between 'gender equity in individual-oriented institutions' and 'gender equity within the family and family-oriented institutions'. These two types of gender equity may not coincide, and that, he argues, can create conditions that are unfavourable to fertility.

Gender equity in individual-oriented institutions has to do with equal access to higher education, careers, and jobs in the paid economy. Societies with greater levels of gender equity in this aspect of social organization allow women greater socioeconomic opportunities in the workplace. But McDonald explains that in some advanced societies,

notwithstanding substantial gains made by women in the sphere of work, the family institution maintains a traditional gender role structure, where women are expected to take care of the children and the domestic chores of cooking and cleaning, all the while holding a job. This situation seems to be characteristic of Mediterranean countries, according to McDonald, and is conducive to very low fertility because women are less able to cope with the dual demands of work and family. In contrast, societies in which individual-oriented institutions are equitable and women have access to jobs and careers, and where family-oriented institutions are also equitable, fertility rates are typically higher (though not necessarily at replacement level) than in societies characterized by high gender equity in individually based institutions but low gender equity in family-oriented ones. Examples of societies that meet both gender equity conditions are the Scandinavian countries and, to some extent, the United States. McDonald's thesis is that birth rates in low-fertility populations could be increased by implementing policies aimed at easing parenthood, especially for women who must negotiate the dual worlds of work and family obligations.

The State of Fertility Transition in Developing Countries

Nearly all developing countries had high fertility levels during the 1950s. Since then, and especially since the 1970s and 1980s, many developing nations have seen substantial fertility declines. Population projections by the United Nations typically assume that this trend will continue until replacement-level fertility is reached. All this is in accord with the historical record, based on the experience of countries that have passed through their fertility transitions. Once a fertility decline is established, it usually progresses toward replacement-level fertility without significant interruptions. Stalls in this type of progression are rare.

Based on a series of demographic health surveys of developing countries conducted between the late

1980s and early 2000s, Bongaarts has found that ongoing fertility declines may have slowed or stalled in a number of countries in transition. In particular, there have been notable stalls in sub-Saharan countries, where the average pace of decline in fertility was lower around 2000 than in the mid-1990s. In all, fertility declines have slowed in more than half of the countries in transition in sub-Saharan Africa, according to Bongaarts.

Although he does not examine the causes of the stall in fertility transition in detail, Bongaarts suggests that two factors in particular may have played a key role. First, unlike much of the rest of the world, economic growth in sub-Saharan Africa declined rather than increased during the 1990s. Life expectancy fell in this region, owing to the devastating effects of the HIV/AIDS epidemic, while the rest of the world enjoyed longevity improvements. The second factor, according to Bongaarts, is the lower priority that family planning has been assigned in sub-Saharan African countries. Ezeh and colleagues (2009) agree with Bongaarts on the role of declining family planning services in the fertility stall. They point out that there have been increases in unwanted fertility and a decline in access to family planning services, especially among adolescents. According to Bongaarts, given these stalls in fertility decline, the population of sub-Saharan Africa will likely more than double in size by 2050, from 769 million (as of 2005) to 1.76 billion (even after the effect of the AIDS pandemic has been taken into account). This anticipated trend in population growth is bound to have significant negative effects on future levels of social and economic development in this region.

Works Cited

Becker, Gary S. (1960). An economic analysis of fertility. In National Bureau Committee for Economic Research, *Demographic and economic change in developed countries*. Universities–National Bureau Special Conference series, 11. Princeton: Princeton University Press.

Billari, Francesco, & Kohler, Hans-Peter. (2004). Patterns of low and lowest-low fertility in Europe. *Population Studies, 58*(2), 161–76.

Bongaarts, John (1975). Why high birth rates are so low. *Population and Development Review*, 1 (2), pp. 289–96.

———. (1978). A framework for analyzing the proximate determinants of fertility. *Population and Development Review, 4*, 105–32.

———. (2003). Proximate determinants of fertility. In Paul Demeny and Geoffrey McNicholl (eds), *Encyclopedia of Population*. New York: Macmillan Reference USA/Thomson Gale, 412–17.

Butz, William, & Ward, Michael. (1979). Will US fertility remain low? A new economic interpretation. *Population and Development Review, 5*(4), 663–88.

Caldwell, John C. (1976). Toward a restatement of demographic transition theory. *Population and Development Review, 2*, (3/4), 321–66.

———. (1981). *Theory of fertility decline*. New York: Academic Press.

Caldwell, John C., & Schindlmayr, Thomas. (2003). Explanations of the fertility crisis in modern societies: A search for commonalities. *Population Studies, 57*(3), 241–63.

Coale, Ansley J. (1969). The decline of fertility in Europe from the French Revolution to World War II. In S.J. Behrman, Leslie Corsa, Jr, & Ronald Freedman (Eds), *Fertility and family planning: A world view* (pp. 388–412). Ann Arbor, MI: University of Michigan Press.

Coale, Ansley J. and Roy Treadway. (1986). A summary of the changing distribution of overall fertility, marital fertility, and the proportion married in the provinces of Europe. In A.J. Coale and S.C. Watkins (Eds), *The decline of fertility in Europe* (pp. 31–162). Princeton: Princeton University Press.

Davis, Kingsley, & Blake, Judith. (1956). Social structure and fertility: An analytic framework. *Economic Development and Cultural Change, 4*(4), 211–35.

Dyson, Tim, & Murphy, Mike. (1985). The onset of fertility transition. *Population and Development Review, 11*(3): 399–440.

Easterlin, Richard A. (1969). Toward an economic theory of fertility: Survey of recent research on economic factors in American fertility. In S.J. Behrman, Leslie Corsa, Jr, & Ronald Freedman (Eds), *Fertility and family planning: A world view* (pp. 127–56). Ann Arbor, MI: The University of Michigan Press.

———. (1983). Modernization and fertility: A critical essay. In Rodolfo A. Bulatao & Ronald D. Lee (Eds), *Determinants of fertility in developing countries* (vol. 2, pp. 562–86). New York: Academic Press.

Ezeh, Alex C., Mberu, Blessing U., & Emina, Jacques O. (2009). Stall in fertility decline in eastern African countries: Regional analysis of patterns, determinants and implications. *Philosophical Transactions of the Royal Society*, B 364-2991-3007.

Frejka, Tomas, & Sardon, Jean-Paul. (2004). *Childbearing trends and prospects in low-fertility countries.* Dordrecht: Kluwer Academic Publishers.

Goldstein, Joshua R., Sobotka, Tomas, & Jasilioniene, Aiva. (2009). The end of lowest-low fertility? *Population and Development Review, 35*(4), 663–99.

Kohler, Hans-Peter, Billari, Francesco, & Ortega, Antonio. (2002). The emergence of lowest-low fertility in Europe during the 1990s. *Population and Development Review, 28*(4), 641–80.

Lesthaeghe, Ron. (2010). The unfolding story of the second demographic transition. *Population and Development Review, 36*(2), 211–51.

Lesthaeghe, Ron, & Surkyn, Johan. (1988). Cultural dynamics and economic theories of fertility change. *Population and Development Review, 14*(1), 1–45.

Lutz, Wolfgang, Skirbekk, Vegard, & Testa, Maria T. (2006). The low-fertility trap hypothesis: Forces that may lead to further postponement and fewer births in Europe. *Vienna Yearbook of Demographic Research 2006*, pp. 167–92.

McDonald, Peter. (2000). Gender equity and theories of fertility transition. *Population and Development Review, 26*(3), 427–40.

McFalls, Joseph, Jr. (1979). Frustrated fertility: A population paradox. Population Reference Bureau, Washington, DC. *Population Bulletin, 34*(2).

Population Reference Bureau. (2010). *World Population Data Sheet, 2010.* Washington, DC: Population Reference Bureau.

Trussell, James. (2003). Fecundity. In Paul Demeny & Geoffrey McNicoll (Eds), *Encyclopedia of population* (pp. 397–9). New York: MacMillan Reference USA/ Thompson Gale.

CHAPTER 11

Fertility, Biology, and Behaviour: An Analysis of the Proximate Determinants

John Bongaarts and Robert G. Potter

Studies of the causes of fertility trends and differentials often seek to measure directly the impact of socioeconomic factors on fertility. This approach has been used widely, partly because measures of socioeconomic variables such as income, education, and place of residence are readily available and partly because policy makers in many countries are interested in identifying the factors that may be manipulated to influence fertility. Unfortunately, the results of these studies are far from conclusive. Not infrequently, relationships are found to differ not only in magnitude, but even in direction in different settings and at different times (Cochrane, 1979; Rodriguez & Cleland, 1981).

To improve understanding of the causes of fertility variation it is necessary to analyze the mechanisms through which socioeconomic variables influence fertility. In response to this need, demographers have turned to the study of the proximate determinants of fertility. The proximate determinants of fertility are the biological and behavioural factors through which social, economic, and environmental variables affect fertility. The principal characteristic of a proximate determinant is its direct influence on fertility. If a proximate determinant—such as contraceptive use—changes, then fertility necessarily changes also (assuming the other proximate determinants remain constant), though this is not necessarily the case for a socioeconomic determinant. Consequently, fertility differences among

populations and trends in fertility over time can always be traced to variations in one or more of the proximate determinants. The following simple diagram summarizes the relationships among the determinants of fertility:

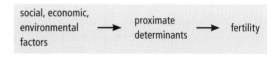

These relationships were first recognized in a now classic study by Davis and Blake (1956). Starting from the premise that reproduction involves the three necessary steps of intercourse, conception, and completion of gestation, Davis and Blake identified a set of 11 proximate determinants[1] which they called 'intermediate fertility variables'. A somewhat different approach to the analysis of the proximate determinants was taken by Henry (1953, 1957), who constructed the first detailed mathematical models of the reproductive process. Following this pioneering work, the investigation of the proximate determinants was pursued during the 1960s by a number of researchers, most notably Potter, Sheps, and Tietz. Much of their efforts focused on the construction of increasingly more realistic but sometimes highly complex models for the relationship between fertility and the proximate determinants. This development has continued into the 1980s, and relatively simple yet quite realistic fertility models now exist. The construction of these models and their validation have been made possible by the greatly increased availability of empirical measures of the proximate variables in many populations. The resulting improvement in the understanding of the fertility effects of the proximate variables has led to a more frequent inclusion of the proximate factors in studies of socioeconomic and environmental determinants of fertility (e.g. Bongaarts, 1980; Cochrane, 1979; Lesthaeghe, Shah, & Page, 1981).

Terminology

Before proceeding, it is useful to briefly discuss the basic terms, *fertility, fecundity*, and *fecundability*. Fertility refers to actual reproduction, whereas fecundity denotes the ability to reproduce. A woman who is bearing children is fertile; a woman is considered fecund if she is capable of bearing live offspring. The opposite terms are *infertility*, also called childlessness, and *infecundity*, which is synonymous with sterility. Sterility (or infecundity) implies the existence of infertility but the reverse is not necessarily the case. A fecund woman may choose to remain infertile by not marrying or by practising highly effective contraception. Infertility, then, either is due to a voluntary decision not to have children or is caused by (biological) infecundity.

The term fecundable refers to the ability to conceive. Fecund and fertile women are necessarily fecundable, although they may experience temporary periods of infecundability. However, some fecundable women are infecund, and consequently infertile, because they are physiologically unable to successfully complete a pregnancy. The term fecundability has taken on a specific meaning as the probability of conceiving per month (among cohabiting women who are not pregnant, sterile, or temporarily infecundable).

These definitions are given in the *Multilingual Demographic Dictionary* (United Nations, 1959) and are consistently used in the English demographic literature. It should be noted that in French and in other romance languages the terms fertility and fecundity are reversed; that is, *fecondité* is the equivalent of fertility and *fertilité* equals fecundity. To add further to the confusion, the words fertility and fecundity are used virtually synonymously in the biological and medical literature.

More specific meaning can be given to the terms fertility and fecundability by adding adjectives. For example, *natural fertility* is found in populations where no contraceptive or induced abortion is practised; *controlled* or *regulated fertility* is observed in societies where fertility-controlled practices are widespread. Similarly, *natural fecundability* is the monthly probability of conception in the absence of contraception, and *residual* or *controlled fecundability* refers to the conception risk in the presence of contraception.

The Proximate Determinants

Davis and Blake (1956) identified the first list of proximate determinants, but their set has not found wide acceptance in quantitative fertility studies because it is not easily incorporated into reproductive models. Extensions and variants of this set have been proposed by other researchers (e.g. Mosley, 1978; Yaukey, 1973). Model builders, however, have based their work largely on Henry's analysis of the reproductive process. This approach has produced a different, but closely overlapping, list of proximate determinants that has greatly simplified the task of constructing fertility models. It is this alternative set that will be presented here.

Figure 11.1 summarizes the various events that most immediately influence the duration of the reproductive period and the rate of childbearing during it. An examination of these events allows the identification of a complete set of proximate determinants. The potential reproductive years start at *menarche*, the first menstruation in a woman's life. Socially sanctioned childbearing, however, is in virtually all societies limited to women in relatively stable sexual unions. For convenience the term *marriage* will be used here to refer to all such

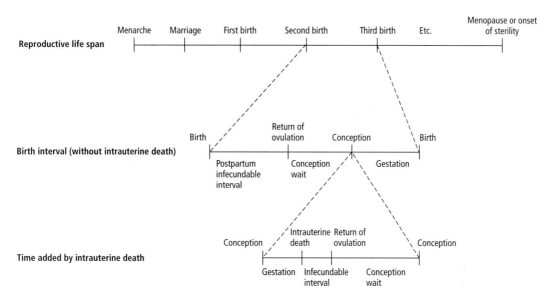

Figure 11.1   Events determining the reproductive lifespan and the rate of childbearing

unions. Marriage (or the first cohabitation) may in practice be taken as the starting point of the actual reproductive years, since it takes place, with few exceptions, after menarche. As a consequence, any changes in age at menarche can generally affect fertility only by influencing age at marriage. Once married, a woman may be considered at risk of childbearing until the onset of permanent sterility or menopause, unless a marital disruption intervenes. Childbearing can of course resume again after a marital disruption if the woman remarries.

While married and fecund, women reproduce at a rate inversely related to the average duration of the birth interval. Short birth intervals are associated with high fertility and vice versa. In the absence of intrauterine mortality, the length of birth interval is determined by its three components (see Figure 11.1):

1. The postpartum infecundable interval. Immediately after a birth, a woman experiences an infecundable period during which the normal pattern of ovulation and menstruation is absent. The duration of this birth interval segment is primarily a function of breastfeeding behaviour. (In a few societies, prolonged postpartum abstinence is practised and the postpartum infecundable interval then exceeds the anovulatory interval to the extent that abstinence lasts beyond the resumption of ovulation.)

2. The waiting time to conception, also called the fecundable or ovulatory interval, from the first postpartum ovulation to conception. The length of this interval is inversely related to the natural fecundability (which, in turn is largely determined by the frequency of intercourse) and to the use and effectiveness of contraception. Short conception delays are observed when natural fecundability is high and no contraception is practised. The waiting time to conception lengthens with declining natural fecundability and with higher prevalence and effectiveness of contraception.

3. A full-term pregnancy. Because the duration of pregnancies ending in a live birth varies little, it is convenient to assume this birth interval segment to have a constant duration of nine moths.

In case a pregnancy ends prematurely in a spontaneous or induced intrauterine death, the birth interval is lengthened by the following additional components: a shortened pregnancy, a brief infecundable period, and a conception delay (see Figure 11.1).

In sum, this short review has identified the following seven proximate determinants: (1) marriage (and marital disruption); (2) onset of permanent sterility; (3) postpartum infecundability; (4) natural fecundability or frequency of intercourse; (5) use and effectiveness of contraception; (6) spontaneous intrauterine mortality; and (7) induced abortion. The first two of these factors determine the duration of the reproductive period, and the other five determine the rate of childbearing and the duration of birth intervals. The seven variables together constitute a complete set in the sense that socioeconomic and environmental factors can affect fertility only through one or more of these proximate variables.

Fertility and the Proximate Determinants

As already noted, observed variations in fertility levels of populations are necessarily due to variations in one or more of the proximate determinants. To describe how the proximate determinants influence fertility, we will present here examples of fairly typical reproductive patterns in a few selected populations, including a modern developed, a traditional developing, and a historical European society. The results will then be compared with the fertility of the Hutterites and with the maximum level of reproduction that is theoretically possible. The average timing of reproductive events in these populations is summarized in Figure 11.2. To simplify this figure and the discussion of the findings, it is assumed that there is no marital disruption and the short period added to the average birth interval by spontaneous intrauterine mortality is included in the waiting time to conception.

A Modern Developed Society

In contemporary Western populations, women bear on average around two births during their reproductive years. A not unrepresentative timing of relevant events (summarized in Figure 11.2) would

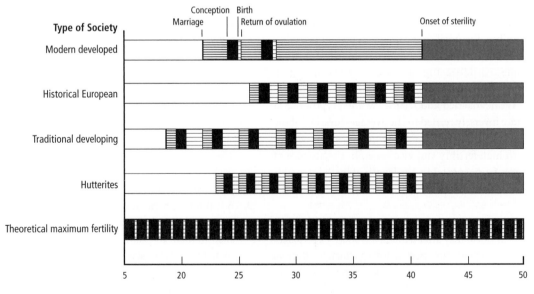

Figure 11.2   Average timing of reproductive events in selected types of societies

involve marriage in the early twenties and about two years between marriage and the first birth and two to three years between births. As the duration of postpartum infecundability is rather short, the spacing of the births is due to the use of contraception, which prolongs the conception wait. The last child would be born in the middle to late twenties. To avoid having further births thereafter requires highly efficient contraceptive use or the practice of induced abortion until the onset of sterility, which on average occurs in the early forties.

A Historical European Population

In seventeenth- and eighteenth-century Europe, fertility was much higher than today, because little or no contraception or induced abortion was practised. In a fairly typical case, women would average about six births between marriage in the mid-twenties and the end of the reproductive years. An average birth interval of around 2.5 years might consist of approximately equal segments for postpartum infecundability, conception delay, and gestation. Compared with the present, the age at marriage was later in the past and duration of postpartum infecundability was longer because breastfeeding was more prevalent. Both factors would have caused a reduction in fertility. Fertility was nevertheless about three times higher than at present because these fertility-reducing effects are more than compensated by the absence of contraception, which is associated with an average waiting time to conception of well under a year.

A Traditionally Developing Society

Over the past decades, the fertility of many of the least developed nations in Africa, Asia, and Latin America has remained relatively unchanged at about seven births per woman. In these societies, marriage usually takes place while the woman is in her teens and average birth intervals around three years are often observed. This average birth interval is longer than in most historical European populations because more prolonged and frequent breastfeeding causes longer periods of postpartum infecundability. Fertility is high despite these prolonged birth intervals because marriage takes place at an early age.

The Hutterites

The Hutterites are members of an Anabaptist sect descendent from Swiss settlers in the northern United States and in Canada. They live in small communities in which strict social and religious control exists over most aspects of daily like. Demographers have a strong interest in their society because the fertility rate of the Hutterites is higher than that of any population with reliable records. In 1950, women who had reached the end of the childbearing years had born an average of about nine children (Eaton & Mayer, 1953). Their high fertility was made possible by spacing births about two years apart throughout their reproductive years, beginning with marriage in their early twenties. The average birth interval of the Hutterites is substantially shorter than in traditional developing countries because breastfeeding is less prolonged so that their period of postpartum infecundability is only about six months.

Theoretical Maximum Fertility

Although the Hutterites have the highest observed fertility rate, it could theoretically be much higher. Reproduction can start in the mid-teens and can continue until near age 50. In addition, birth intervals lasting one year or even less are biologically possible because a full-term gestation takes only nine months. Theoretically then, in the absence of all biological and behavioural constraints on reproduction, a woman could have 35 births (not counting multiple births) between ages 15 and 50, if birth intervals were to average one year. Hutterite fertility is far short of this biological maximum for several reasons, including delayed marriage, the practice of breastfeeding, a moderate frequency of intercourse, a substantial risk of intrauterine mortality, and the onset of sterility of either the male or female in the early forties.

An alternative way to summarize the reproductive patterns of these five populations is presented in Table 11.1 which gives the average proportions of the reproductive years spent in various reproductive states. Five reproductive states are being distinguished:

1. single
2. postpartum infecundable
3. fecundable (including time added by spontaneous intrauterine mortality)
4. pregnant before a live birth
5. permanently sterile

The estimates in Table 11.1 should be considered illustrative, especially as no allowance is made for marital disruption. Except in the hypothetical case with biological maximum fertility, about a quarter of the potential reproductive years between ages 15 and 50 is, on average, spent in the sterile state. This is caused by the fact that the average age at onset of sterility is in the early forties. As expected, the time in the pregnant state rises proportionately with the level of fertility (total fertility rates are assumed to be 2, 6, 7, 9, and 15 respectively in the five populations in Table 11.1). No clear pattern emerges in the estimates of the time in the three remaining reproductive states. It is noteworthy that women in contemporary developed societies are fecundable for nearly half of their reproductive years. This is the consequence of the widespread use of contraception that reduced fecundability to a fraction of its natural level.

Variations in Individual Fertility

The description of fertility patterns in the preceding section dealt strictly with the population averages of the timing of reproductive events. In reality, few women bear children at the regular average rate outlined in Figure 11.2. Not only does the timing of reproductive events differ substantially among women, but there is also wide variation in the number of births women have. This is clear from Figure 11.2, which plots the distribution of the number of past births among ever-married women at the end of the reproductive years in selected populations. In each of these four cases, the number of children ever born ranges from zero to well over ten, although there are admittedly few of these high-parity women in the United States as of 1970. The other three examples are from populations with natural fertility. Their parity distributions have a large standard deviation, and fewer than one in six women had the modal number of births.

As in the aggregate case, variations in the fertility of individual women are caused by variations in the proximate determinants. In the United States and

Table 11.1 Approximate percentage of the potential reproductive years (15–50) spent in different reproductive states in selected types of societies

Society	Reproductive states				
	Single	Postpartum infecundable	Fecundable	Pregnant	Sterile
Developed	20	1	49	4	26
Historical European	31	15	15	13	26
Contemporary developing	10	30	19	15	26
Hutterites	23	13	19	19	26
Theoretical maximum fertility	0	16	9	75	0

other modern societies one can expect to find differences in the number of children born because the desired family size varies among women and contraception is available to help achieve these objectives. In addition, some women will have fewer or more than the desired number of births for nonvoluntary reasons, such as the premature onset of sterility or contraceptive failure.

In natural fertility populations, contraception and induced abortion are virtually absent, and the remaining proximate variables must, therefore, be responsible for the large variance of the parity distributions shown in Figure 11.3. In fact, both the duration of the reproductive years and the length of birth intervals vary widely among women. As an example, the distributions of the age at first marriage and the age at the onset of permanent sterility in Tourouvre-au-Perche, in the seventeenth and eighteenth centuries (Charbonneau, 1970), are plotted in the upper panel of Figure 11.4. The age at first marriage ranged from below 20 to over 40, and the age of onset of sterility had an equally large range. As a consequence, the number of years actually available for childbearing ranged from zero for the women (couples) who were sterile at marriage to over thirty

for those who married early and remained fecund until their late forties. The former will by necessity have no offspring whereas the latter have a good chance of bearing more than ten children.

The duration of the birth interval is also highly variable. The distribution of the interval between first and second births in Tourouvre-au-Perche, plotted in the lower panel of Figure 11.4, shows that the length of birth intervals ranged from less than one year to over four years. Systematic differences

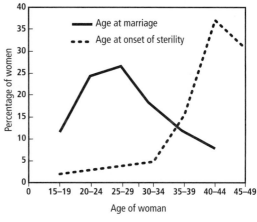

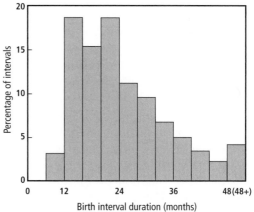

Figure 11.4 Distribution of age at first marriage and age at onset of permanent sterility, and the distribution of the interval between first and second births for Tourouvre-au-Perche, seventeenth and eighteenth centuries

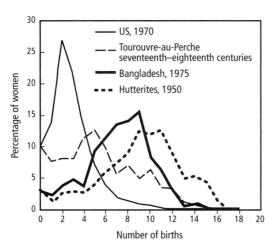

Figure 11.3 Distribution of percentage of ever-married women at the end of the reproductive years, by number of children ever born, in selected populations

in breastfeeding behaviour, frequency of intercourse, and risk of spontaneous intrauterine mortality are major causes of this finding, but an important random element is also present. For example, the conception delay would still be highly variable even if couples all had the same frequency of intercourse, because conception depends on unpredictable events such as the exact timing of ovulation and the successful implantation of the fertilized ovum. Similarly, some women may experience no spontaneous abortions, whereas others have several despite a biologically equal risk of a spontaneous intrauterine death.

Age-Specific Fertility

Fertility varies with the woman's age in all human societies for which measurements exist. The rate of childbearing is lowest in the youngest and oldest age groups, and fertility reaches a maximum in the central childbearing years. The causes of this variation are the age patterns in the proximate determinants. For example, the marriage pattern is of major importance in explaining the shape of the age-specific fertility curve because the proportion married varies substantially with age. This proportion is lowest in the 15–19-year-old age group. The proportions married usually decline in the older age groups as the effects of marital disruption cumulate, thus contributing to the reduction of fertility rates towards the end of the childbearing years.

Even though the marriage pattern has a major impact on the age pattern of fertility, the other proximate determinants also have an effect. This is evident from the changes with age in the fertility of married women. Two examples of age-specific marital fertility rates—one from the United States and the other from the Hutterites—are plotted in Figure 11.5. In both cases, marital fertility declines after age twenty. The difference between the United States and the Hutterite levels of marital fertility are almost entirely due to differences in the practice of contraception and induced abortion. (This conclusion is based on findings which show that the incidence of sterility and the risk of spontaneous intrauterine

mortality vary little among populations and that the slightly longer postpartum infecundability of the Hutterite women is largely compensated by a shorter natural waiting time before conception.)

Hutterite women use virtually no contraception or induced abortion, and the age pattern of their marital fertility rates must consequently be caused by the four remaining proximate determinants: sterility, postpartum infecundability, natural fecundability, and spontaneous intrauterine mortality.

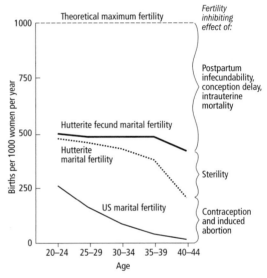

Figure 11.5   Age-specific marital fertility rates of the United States (1967) and Hutterites (marriages 1921–30), and estimated age-specific marital fertility rates of fecund Hutterite women

Unfortunately, direct age-specific measures of these factors are not available. However, a standard age-specific sterility pattern proposed by Henry (1965) may be applied as a good approximation because populations differ little in their prevalence of natural sterility. By dividing the age-specific marital fertility rates by the nonsterile proportion in each age group, we obtain estimates of the age-specific marital fertility rates of the fecund Hutterites. The results are also plotted in Figure 11.5. There is only a modest decline with age in the fertility rate of married women. This finding indicates that the sterility pattern is an important determinant of the marital fertility schedule. It also suggests that any age-related increase in the risk of intrauterine mortality, decline in frequency of intercourse, and rise in postpartum infecundability have only a modest impact on the age pattern of fertility. This conclusion does not imply that these three proximate variables are not important determinants of the overall level of fertility. In fact, they are the reason that the fecund marital fertility rate averages only about 500 rather than the theoretical maximum of 1,000 births per 1,000 women per year.

Only fecund women bear offspring. The average birth interval is therefore inversely related to the age-specific fecund marital fertility rate in populations with natural fertility. For example, the average birth interval of the Hutterites was earlier estimated to be two years; this duration is consistent with the average fecund marital fertility rate of about 500 births per 1,000 women per year (or .5 births per woman per year) found in Figure 11.5.

The Determinants of the Proximate Variables

Socioeconomic factors and health and nutrition are the determinants of the proximate variables. Health and nutrition are, in general, relatively unimportant determinants of fertility. Socioeconomic factors must therefore be the principal causes of fertility trends and differentials. But it should be noted that there is no general agreement on how socioeconomic and cultural factors operate to affect the proximate determinants and fertility. Reviews are available elsewhere (e.g. Andorka, 1978; Cassen, 1976; Freedman, 1975; Hawthorn, 1970; International Research Awards Program 1981; Miro & Potter, 1980; National Academy of Sciences, 1982; United Nations, 1973). Although social scientists and demographers have studied the socioeconomic determinants of fertility for some time, relatively little attention has been given to the potential effects of nutrition and health. A short overview of this subject follows.

Nutrition

Frisch (1975, 1978) has suggested that malnutrition inhibits reproductive performance by delaying menarche and reducing the age at menopause, and by causing increases in the incidence of anovulatory cycles, the risk of spontaneous intrauterine mortality, and the duration of postpartum amenorrhea. This hypothesis has stimulated a growing number of investigations designed to establish its validity. The results of these studies are summarized in three reviews of the evidence (Bongaarts, 1980; Gray, 1983; Menken, Trussel, & Watkins, 1981). The current consensus is that moderate chronic malnutrition such as prevails in many poor developing countries has only a very minor influence on fertility. On the other hand, the acute starvation found in famines causes a substantial reduction of fertility. The weak effect of chronic malnutrition apparently operates primarily through two of the proximate variables: the age at marriage as affected by the timing of menarche and the duration of postpartum infecundability.

Several types of direct and indirect evidence indicate that malnutrition is associated with a higher age of menarche (Bongaarts, 1980):

1. In contemporary developed countries, the mean age at menarche is near 13 years, whereas it is generally higher in the developing countries (e.g. 13–14 in India and 15.7 in Bangladesh). Estimates for nineteenth-century European populations are also high—around 16 years.
2. In one US study, well-nourished girls reached menarche two years earlier than undernourished girls (Frisch, 1972).
3. Nutritional status as measured by anthropometric indicators, such as body weight, is positively correlated with the probability of reaching menarche by a given age.
4. In Western societies with relatively reliable historical data on age at menarche, a decline in age at menarche of about three years has taken

place since the end of the nineteenth century. This decline is associated with an increase in body size and an improved diet.

5. Socioeconomic status and age at menarche are negatively related in a number of countries. Differences ranging from a few months to about two years have been found between urban and rural populations and between high- and low-income groups.

Although there can be little doubt that malnutrition is associated with later age of menarche, the demographic impact of this effect can be shown to be quite small. Age at menarche signals the beginning of potential childbearing, but actual reproduction starts at marriage. The mean age at marriage is almost always higher than the mean age at menarche. The differences range from about two years in some traditional societies to more than ten years in a number of contemporary populations. In populations where the mean age at marriage is near 20 or higher, one can hardly expect a fertility effect from the nutritional variations in age at menarche, whereas the effect on the total fertility rate is only of the order of 5 per cent following a large change in nutrition, even if marriage takes place shortly after menarche and if ages of the two events are correlated (Bongaarts, 1980).

In discussing the relationship between nutrition and lactational infecundability, it is important to make a distinction between changes in maternal and infant nutrition. The provision of dietary supplements to a nursing infant shortens the interval of lactational anovulation because the intensity of breastfeeding declines. The question of interest here is whether the duration of lactational infecundability is influenced by the maternal nutritional status if breastfeeding behaviour remains unchanged. Studies in Bangladesh and Guatemala provide tentative estimates of the importance of moderate chronic malnutrition. Women were divided into groups of high, medium, and low nutritional status on the basis of anthropometric measures. The difference in the duration of lactational infecundability between the groups of high and low nutritional status were 1.1

and 1.0 months in the two studies in Bangladesh (Huffman, et al., 1978; Chowdhury, 1978) and 1.6 months in Guatemala (Bongaarts & Delgado, 1979). Only the latter difference was statistically significant. It should be noted that these analyses did not control for the duration of lactation. It is unlikely, however, that this substantially affects the results, because women in these countries usually breastfeed their infants until the next pregnancy occurs, and, for nearly all women, ovulation resumes during lactation. A direct comparison of the relative importance of breastfeeding duration and nutritional intake as determinants of amenorrhea is available for a Guatemalan population (Delgado, et al., 1978). The results presented in Table 11.2 clearly indicate that the duration of lactation is the primary determinant. There is a fairly consistent, but not statistically significant, difference of the order of one month between the amenorrhea periods of women with high and low caloric intake. A nutritionally induced variation of the order of one month between the amenorrhea periods of women with high and low caloric intake would result in a difference of only a few percentage points between the total fertility rates of well- and poorly nourished groups of women because this change in duration of lactational infecundability represents only a small fraction of the typically average birth interval of 2.5 to 3 years in this population.

The small differences in the duration of amenorrhea of nutritional status groups are not necessary caused by a direct physiological effect of malnutrition on the mother. It is possible that unmeasured differences in the pattern of breastfeeding between the poorly and well-nourished women in these populations are responsible. For example, if malnourished mothers have less food available for supplementing infant diets, or are later in introducing supplementation, then their infants would require more intense breastfeeding, thus prolonging amenorrhea.

In contrast to the apparently small effects of chronic moderate malnutrition, acute starvation causes drastic reductions in fertility. Famines are invariably followed by large but temporary reductions in fertility nine months later. The exact causes of this

Table 11.2   Mean duration of postpartum amenorrhea (months) in groups differing in caloric intake and in duration of lactation (number in parentheses)[a]

Daily caloric intake[b]	Duration of lactation (months)			
	7–12	13–18	19–24	25 or more
Low	6.54(13)	12.03(35)	16.44(45)	19.93(14)
Middle	6.31(13)	11.64(33)	15.47(57)	18.90(10)
High	5.47(14)	11.13(30)	14.60(47)	19.64(11)
High–low differences	1.07	0.90	1.84	0.29

[a] From Delgado, et al. (1978).

[b] Low caloric intake = <1309 calories a day; middle = 1309–1630 calories; high = >1630 calories.

decline remain to be determined, and several factors are involved. It is evident that fecundity is impaired during a famine because a substantial proportion of women become amenorrheic. It is not clear, however, whether this amenorrhea is entirely due to malnutrition or is in part caused by the fear of death and the anxiety that accompanies the crisis. Psychological stress alone can induce amenorrhea. Other factors that may contribute to the decline in fertility during a famine are the separation of spouses in the search for food or work, a decline in libido, and voluntary birth control through contraception, induced abortion, or abstinence. A lack of sufficiently detailed data makes it impossible to estimate accurately the contributions from each of these factors. They would in any case vary in their impact in different famines.

Health

In a review of the available evidence, Gray (1982) concluded that general poor health is unlikely to have a substantial impact on fecundity because morbidity severe enough to inhibit reproduction afflicts only a minority of the disadvantaged women. An important exception to this generalization is the relatively high prevalence of pathological sterility in a few populations, primarily in parts of tropical Africa. The apparent cause of this sterility is pelvic inflammatory disease, which in most cases is the consequence of sexually transmitted infections such as gonorrhea (Gray, 1983).

In addition to the minor direct effect of poor health on reproductive capacity, there are two indirect effects of improved health on fertility. The first is the result of the lengthening of breastfeeding, yet with fewer such deaths these interruptions will occur less frequently. The second indirect effect of changing health operates through a decline in the risk of widowhood. As adult mortality declines, so does the incidence of widowhood. The extent of the resulting increase in the proportions married in a population depends on the remarriage frequency. If most widows remarry quickly, then a change in adult mortality would have little effect on overall fertility, and in the absence of remarriage, the impact can be substantial. It should be noted that the two indirect effects of improved health and mortality tend to compensate one another. That is, improved infant mortality and the consequent lengthening of the birth interval causes a reduction in the total fertility rate, whereas a decline in widowhood would raise it. In fact, in one simulation of fertility patterns characteristic of the population of India by Ridley et al. (1967), it was found that the combined impact of those two indirect effects was very small.

Note

1. Davis and Blake (1956) proposed the following set of intermediate fertility variables:

I. Factors affecting exposure to intercourse ('intercourse variables')
   A. Those governing the formation and dissolution of unions in the reproductive period
      1. Age of entry into sexual unions
      2. Permanent celibacy: proportion of women never entering sexual unions
      3. Amount of reproductive period spent after or between unions
         a. When unions are broken by divorce, separation, or desertion
         b. When unions are broken by death of husband
   B. Those governing the exposure to intercourse within union
      4. Voluntary abstinence

   5. Involuntary abstinence
   6. Coital frequency (excluding periods of abstinence)

II. Factors affecting exposure to conception ('conception variables')
   7. Fecundity or infecundity, as affected by involuntary causes
   8. Use or nonuse of contraception
      a. By mechanical and chemical means
      b. By other mean
   9. Fecundity or infecundity, as affected by voluntary causes (sterilization, sub-incision, medical treatment, etc.)

III. Factors affecting gestation and successful parturition ('gestation variables')
   10. Fetal mortality from involuntary causes
   11. Fetal mortality from voluntary causes

References

Andorka, R. 1978. *Determinants of Fertility in Advanced Societies.* New York: Free Press.

Bongaarts, J. 1980. 'Does Malnutrition Affect Fecundity? A Summary of Evidence'. *Science, 208,* 565–9.

Bongaarts, J., & H. Delgado. 1979. 'Effects of Nutritional Status on Fertility in Rural Guatemala'. In H. Leridon & J. Meken (Eds), *Patterns and Determinants of Natural Fertility.* Liège, Belgium: Ordina.

Cassen, R.H. 1976. 'Population and Development: A Survey'. *World Development* 4(10–11), 785–830.

Charbonneau. H. 1970. 'Tourouvre-au-Perche aux XVII et XVIII Siècles'. INED, Travaux et Documents, Cahier No. 55. Paris: Presses Universitaires de France.

Chowdhury, A.K.N. 1978. 'Effect of Maternal Nutrition on Fertility in Rural Bangladesh'. In W.M. Mosley (Ed.), *Nutrition and Human Reproduction.* New York: Plenum Press.

Cochrane, S.H. 1979. 'Fertility and Education: What Do We Really Know?' World Bank Staff Occasional Papers, No. 26. Baltimore: Johns Hopkins University Press.

Davis, K., & J. Blake. 1956. 'Social Structure and Fertility: An Analytic Framework'. *Economic Development and Cultural Change* 4(4), 211–35.

Delgado, H., A. Lechtig, E. Brineman, R. Martorell, C. Yarbrough, & R.E. Klein. 1978. 'Nutrition and Birth Interval Components: The Guatemalan Experience'.

In W.M. Mosley (Ed.), *Nutrition and Human Reproduction.* New York: Plenum Press.

Eaton, J.W., & A.J. Mayer. 1953. 'The Social Biology of Very High Fertility among the Hutterites: The Demography of a Unique Population'. *Human Biology, 25*(3), 206–64.

Freedman, R. 1975. *The Sociology of Human Fertility.* New York: Irvington Publishers.

Frisch, R.E. 1972. 'Weight at Menarche: Similarity for Well-Nourished and Undernourished Girls at Different Ages and Evidence of Historical Constancy'. *Pediatrics, 50,* 445–50.

———. 1975. 'Demographic Implications of the Biological Determinants of Female Fecundity'. *Social Biology, 22*(1), 17–22.

———. 1978. 'Population, Food Intake and Fertility'. *Science, 199,* 6 January, 22–30.

Gray, R. 1983. 'The Impact of Health and Nutrition on Natural Fertility'. In Rodolfo A. Bulatao, Ronald D. Lee, with P.E. Hollerback & J. Bongaarts (Eds), *Determinants of Fertility in Developing Countries. Volume 1. Supply and Demand for Children* (pp. 139–62). New York: Academic Press.

Hawthorn, G. 1970. *The Sociology of Fertility.* London: Collier-Macmillan.

Henry, L. 1953. Fondements Théoriques des Mesures de la Fecondité Naturelle. *Revue de l'Institut International de Statistique 21*(3); 135–252. Translated in *On the Measurement of Human Fertility*. Amsterdam: Elsevier, 1972

———. 1957. 'Fecondité et Famille, Models Mathematiques'. *Population 12*(3), 413–44. Translated in *On the Measurement of Human Fertility*. Amsterdam: Elsevier, 1972.

———. 1965. 'French Statistical Research in Natural Fertility'. In M.C. Sheps & J.C. Ridley (Eds), *Public Health and Population Change*. Pittsburgh: University of Pittsburgh Press.

Huffman, S.L., A.M.U. Chowdhury, I. Chakborty, & W.H. Mosley. 1978. 'Nutrition and Postpartum Amenorrhea in Rural Bangladesh'. *Population Studies, 32*(2), 251–60.

International Research Awards Program. 1981. 'Research on the Determinants of Fertility: A Note on Priorities'. *Population and Development Review, 7*(2), 311–23.

Lesthaeghe, R.H., I.H. Shah, & H.J. Page. 1981. 'Compensating Changes in Intermediate Fertility Variable and the Onset of Natural Fertility Transition'. In Proceedings of the IUSSP General Conference, Manila. Liège, Belgium: Ordina.

Menken, J., J. Trussell, & S. Watkins. 1981. 'The Nutrition–Fertility Link: An Evaluation of the Evidence'. *Journal of Interdisciplinary History, 9*, 425–41.

Miro, L.A., & J.E. Potter. 1980. *Population Policy: Research Priorities in the Developing World*. London: Francis Pinter.

Mosley, W.M. 1978. 'Issues, Definitions and an Analytic Framework'. In W.M. Mosley (Ed.), *Nutrition and Human Reproduction*. New York: Plenum Press.

National Academy of Sciences. 1982. 'The Determinants of Fertility in Developing Countries: A Summary of Knowledge. Report of the Panel on Fertility Determinants'. In Ed. Rodolfo, A. Bulatao, Ronald D. Lee, with P.E. Hollerback & J. Bongaarts (Eds), *The Determinants of Fertility in Developing Countries: A Summary of Knowledge. Volume 2. Fertility Regulation and Institutional Influences*. New York: Academic Press.

Ridley, J., M. Sheps, J. Linger, and J. Menken. 1967. 'The Effects of Changing Mortality on Natality'. *Milbank Memorial Fund Quarterly, 45*, 77–97.

Rodriguez, G., & J. Cleland. 1981. 'Socio-economic Determinants of Marital Fertility in Twenty Countries: A Multivariate Analysis'. World Fertility Survey Conference 1980, Record of Proceedings. Voorburg, Netherlands: International Statistical Institute.

United Nations. 1959. Multilingual Demographic Dictionary. *Population Studies, 29*. New York: United Nations.

———. 1973. 'The Determinants and Consequences of Population Trends'. Department of Economic and Social Affairs, *Population Studies, 50*, United Nations, New York.

Yaukey, D. 1973. *Marriage Reduction and Fertility*. Lexington, MA: Lexington Books.

CHAPTER 12

Low Fertility in Evolutionary Perspective

Kingsley Davis

Looked at in the long-run perspective of human evolution, the below-replacement fertility now characterizing most of the industrial countries is anomalous. Never before in recorded history—not in the Great Depression, not in the eighteenth and nineteenth centuries, and not in ancient times has fertility been so low for whole societies as it is now in the industrial world. And never has it been so low during the millions of years of hominid evolution.[1]

Low Fertility in Hunting-and-Gathering Societies

But in another sense, the low fertility of today in advanced countries is less anomalous than the high fertility that characterized these countries at the inception of the Industrial Revolution and that characterizes most of the less developed countries today. The total fertility rate (TFR) of the white population of the United States in 1800 has been estimated as 7.04 births per woman (Coale & Zelnik, 1963, p. 36). This is more than four times the TFR (1.65) for 1976. The TFR for Jordan in 1979 was 8.34 (United Nations, *Demographic Yearbook*, 1983, p. 323). Although such high fertility rates characterize modern agrarian populations, they are evidently not the norm in human evolution. Instead, for millions of years extending back in prehistoric times, a special feature of hominid groups was their moderate fertility.

The evidence for this is indirect and varied, but taken together it is persuasive. First, over the long haul, the hominids had virtually zero population growth, and all of the hominid species eventually became extinct except modern man, *Homo sapiens*. Second, on the biological side, the human reproductive system became vulnerable to an extraordinary number of pathologies, and it lost two pronatalist traits—sexual promiscuity and estrus, the second of which in most mammals binds copulation closely to ovulation. Third, according to field observation, our closest kin in the animal world, the subhuman primates, exhibit low fertility. Jane Goodall (1971, p. 12) found that female chimpanzees in the Gombe Reserve gave birth 'about once every three-and-a-half to five years'. In another chimpanzee group (the pygmy chimpanzee), Michael Chiglieri (1984, p. 61) reported only two births in 17 months of observation, yielding an annual birth rate of 31 per thousand animals. Even gorillas, which mature at about seven years, have birth intervals of about four years (Schaller, 1965, p. 333). Fourth, reproduction among recently observed hunter–gatherers is even lower. Nancy Howell (1979, p. 123) found that 62 Dobe !Kung women aged 45 years and older had borne only 4.69 offspring on average. Even this, she says, may have been an overstatement, due to a tendency of childless women to migrate out of the territory and hence fall out of the sample. An analysis of registration data for Australian aborigines of the Northern Territory in

1958–60 showed a TFR of 4.23 (Jones, 1965, p. 242). In a survey of population control among hunter–gatherers in general, Brian Hayden (1972) found that these societies use only a fraction of the reproductive potential available to them. 'Out of a maximum possible fertility of 20–30 living offspring per female,' he says (p. 209), 'this is reduced to 5–6 or fewer primarily by prolonged lactation, physiological controls, abstinence and abortion.' Progeny are further curtailed by infanticide, especially female infanticide, which is surprisingly widespread in hunter–gatherer societies (Hausfater & Hrdy, 1984).

Clearly, the idea that our remote ancestors had a high, biologically determined 'natural' fertility, because they did not use modern contraception, is false. The highest birth rates are found, not under primitive, but under modern circumstances. Among 94 married Hutterite women aged 45–49 in 1950, Joseph Eaton and Albert Mayer (1954, p. 20) found that the mean number of births per woman was 9.9; T.E. Smith (1960, p. 95) found that the average number per woman in the Cocos-Keeling Islands was 8.4; and as mentioned already, the UN *Demographic Yearbook* reports the TFR for Jordan in 1979 as 8.34. Compared with such examples, the fertility of hunter–gatherers or of ancient man seems quite moderate. If we imagine a TFR scale with ten births per woman at the top and one birth per woman at the bottom, our pre-agricultural hominid ancestors would probably fall somewhere near the middle, with four to six births per woman. That is not low compared with TFRs in today's industrial countries, which would fall near the bottom of the scale, but it shares with them a common outcome—namely, zero or negative natural increase.

In other words, the circumstantial evidence suggests that throughout hominid evolution the long-run birth rate was kept as low as possible consistent with survival—as low, that is, as the death rate. Why? The answer seems to be that the hominids were exploiting a unique evolutionary niche by relying on culture, learning, and social organization as their mode of adaptation. To do this, they had to invest heavily in prolonged care and training of offspring.

They succeeded best in this task when the offspring were widely spaced. Helpless infants were particularly burdensome in hunting-and-gathering societies because of the nomadism generally characterizing those groups (Lee, 1979, ch. 11; Carr-Saunders, 1922). Present-day hunter–gatherers frequently give as reasons for wide spacing of offspring the burden of trying to carry two nursing infants at one time and the danger to an older child if the mother has a new birth too soon. A similar motivation often underlies infanticide following the birth of twins, most often of one infant only (Daly and Wilson, 1980, pp. 492–3; Hausfater & Hrdy, 1984, pp. xiii–xiv, xxvi–xxxii; Lee, 1979, ch. 11; Lee & DeVore, 1968, pp. 11, 236ff.; Scrimshaw, 1984, p. 446).

There was a limit, however, on how low the birth rate of ancient man could be. It could not be regularly lower than the death rate. Of the two processes—mortality and fertility—hominids found it far easier to control fertility. As a result, the prehistoric birth rate was determined by the death rate. This meant that to attain the advantages of moderate fertility, our remote ancestors had to achieve a moderate mortality as well, something they found difficult to attain.

The Struggle against Death

The hominids' best approach to combating mortality was to maximize production, which they did by strengthening the very possession (culture) that comprised their evolutionary advantage. They gradually created and improved a cultural system that could satisfy basic needs for food, shelter, clothing, and security. This achievement, peculiar to humans, evolved with extreme slowness at first (during at least 2 million years: Washburn & Lancaster, 1968b), but it was cumulative and increasingly had the potential for keeping the death rate low compared with rates among other animals. This approach, however, had its own limitation. Beyond a certain point, improvement of the means for exploiting the environment meant a degradation of the environment. In some cases this may have meant outright extinction of prey fauna (Martin, 1973; Martin & Klein, 1984; Nitecki, 1984), but more often it meant a local or seasonal scarcity.

Another strictly human method of combating mortality was care of the sick and wounded (Jolly, 1972, pp. 289–90; Washburn & Lancaster, 1968a). This behaviour, which may have arisen as part of the food-sharing complex early in human evolution, must have saved lives because rest and food were often all that an incapacitated individual needed to get well. It did require, however, a home base or at least a temporary shelter or campsite. If the sufferer was permanently injured or sick, and therefore a complete drain on the group, he or she was probably left to die. In present-day hunting-and-gathering societies, the care of the sick and wounded is generally the responsibility of close kin.

A third development that saved lives was the use of fire for cooking and warmth, for protection from predators, and for stampeding prey (Fagan, 1979, pp. 87–9). But a fourth method—also unique to man—proved singularly unsuccessful. This was the development of medicine, a deliberate effort to prevent and cure illness. The emergence of medical practitioners—the shaman, a combined priest, showman, and doctor; the midwife; the diviner—doubtless was among the earliest examples of a division of labour based on presumed skill rather than gender, age, or kinship (Corlett, 1935; Landy, 1977, chs 14, 15, 17, 22; Maddox, 1923). Unfortunately, these specialists, by and large, never developed much ability to benefit the patient.

Significantly, all four of early man's strategies for combating mortality were cultural and therefore unique to humans. Taken together, these efforts must have given the hominids a death rate that was high by today's standards but nevertheless low in comparison with that of other animals of equal size (see Cohen & Armelagos, 1984; Johansson & Horowitz, 1985). These strategies did, however, run up against severe limitations. One of these (environmental degradation) has already been mentioned. Another, much more long-run in character, was deterioration of the hominid genetic constitution.

During hundreds of millennia our distant ancestors tended to lose through relaxed selection what they gained in cultural adaptation.

Another barrier to lowering the death rate was the inability to control infectious and parasitic diseases. Since these, under primitive conditions, usually comprise the main causes of death, this failure guaranteed a rather high mortality compared with present-day societies (Acsádi & Nemeskéri, 1970, ch. 4; Schaller, 1965, p. 334).

In sum, the barriers to mortality control acted as feedback mechanisms. If under favourable conditions a hunting-and-gathering population expanded, it would become more dense, the environment would become depleted, contagious diseases would spread, or warfare would set in. The result would be a rise in the death rate and a return to the status quo ante. In some instances where local resources were great, Late Pleistocene man could become sedentary, but in general, through millions of years, the evolving hominid species remained scarce creatures. They were equipped by their cultural apparatus to spread to new environments, but as hunter–gatherers they were not equipped to multiply within the same area. Overwhelmingly, their population expansion depended on geographical expansion. Spreading out first, apparently, in Africa, they moved into Europe and Asia, and eventually invaded Australia and the Americas. Population numbers must have grown, but since this worldwide dispersion took millions of years, the rate of human population increase was virtually zero. There was apparently some acceleration of population growth after the appearance of modern man around 40,000 years ago as the hunting and foraging technology became more efficient, but a significant departure from zero growth did not occur until the agricultural revolution.

Agriculture and Population Imbalance

If this description is correct, our low fertility in contemporary society is not an aberration. It is rather an approximation of a *sine qua non* for human evolution.

The genius of the species has not been to rely on a birth rate so high that it can overcome almost any death rate, no matter how high. The genius of the species is rather to have few offspring and to invest heavily in their care and training, so that the advantages of a cultural adaptation can be realized. Throughout 99 per cent of hominid history, then, fertility was kept as low as it could be, given the current mortality. Zero population growth was the rule, not the exception. The abnormal situation is that of present-day less developed countries—Bangladesh, the African states, many countries of the Middle East—where death rates have been rapidly reduced but total fertility rates have stayed at, or risen to high levels such as six to nine births per woman. These are societies demoralized by a drastic reduction in mortality without compensating changes in economic and social institutions. They illustrate the principle that an excess of reproduction militates against trained skills in a population.

What happened to the longterm balance of births and deaths that characterized the hunting-and-gathering way of life?

The answer in a word is 'agriculture'. But that response is inadequate. What were the mechanisms by which agriculture destroyed the demographic balance?

According to my estimates, the growth of the human population for some 12,000 years preceding the Industrial Revolution—the period of the rise and spread of agriculture—was 4.4 per cent per century. This was a snail's pace by present-day standards, but it was nine times faster than the estimated growth during the 40,000 years preceding the agricultural epoch.

As a technological change, the agricultural revolution was remarkable for its speed and impact. Although some Upper Paleolithic peoples had reached an impressive level of technological sophistication, no antecedent technological advance was so great or so rapid as the domestication of plants and animals. Among other things, it destroyed some of the feedback mechanisms of the hunting-and-gathering economy. There, if fertility exceeded

mortality for a period, the balance tended to be restored by contagious disease, warfare, and or deterioration of the environment. But under agriculture the improvement of the productive apparatus was so fast (in terms of human evolution) that it temporarily suspended some of the important feedback mechanisms. With respect to fertility, for instance, women no longer needed long birth intervals, because they did not need to carry their infants for long distances. They could wean their offspring earlier, because cultivation provided more reliable alternative food sources. Also, insofar as cultivation increased per capita food consumption, it may have hastened menarche and improved the likelihood of conception. In any case, children were more useful in an agrarian than in a hunting-and-gathering economy, because the variety of tasks suitable to the young was greater. The traditional brakes on fertility were therefore lifted.

On the mortality side, there is considerable evidence that initially the switch to agriculture may have raised mortality, owing to increased reliance on starchy staples and increased density of settlement, but later, as agriculture provided more reliable food sources, better shelter, and greater resistance to disease, the death rate was probably no higher than it had been in hunting-and-gathering societies and may have been lower. The symposium volume edited by Mark Cohen and George Armelagos (1984) adduces evidence for most parts of the world that the transition to agriculture at first meant a worsening rather than an improvement in mortality. The somewhat stepped-up rate of population growth must therefore have been due to a rise in fertility.

Eventually, the demographic imbalance created by the speedy adoption of agriculture would have righted itself, and it probably did in many worn-out farming areas. But once the genie was out of the bottle, further technological progress and the spread of agriculture to new areas compensated for feedback mechanisms that otherwise would have driven up mortality or depressed fertility and thus have halted population growth. At last the reliance on a cultural mode of adaptation was beginning to pay off in an evolutionary sense—in the sense of permitting, for the world as a whole and for a much longer period than ever before, a birth rate higher than the death rate.

The Industrial Revolution

If left alone, the agricultural revolution would doubtless have spun itself out and eventually would have ceased to sustain population growth. As it was, the main stimulus to growth came from expanding agriculture into new areas, not from piling up ever more people in the same area. But the industrial age came along while the expansion of agriculture around the world was still going on. It thus did not permit a return to the zero population growth rate that would eventually have characterized a world limited to agriculture; instead, it sharpened the imbalance between birth rates and death rates that agriculture had already fostered.

Despite temporary exceptions in particular cases, industrialism generally produced a lower death rate in several ways. First, it facilitated the improvement of agricultural output per man and per worker through irrigation, plant breeding, machinery, and fossil fuel. Second, it improved the efficiency of transportation, permitting more varied diets and more secure supplies around the world. In other words, the agricultural age did not disappear when faced with industrialization, the way hunting-and-gathering societies disappeared in the face of agricultural encroachment; instead, agriculture was enormously improved by the advent of industrialism. Third, man's age-old effort to develop a specialized medical technology finally began to bear fruit after about 1850 (Starr, 1982, ch. 3). With continued improvement of economic production, and with medical technology rapidly diffused to all nations, man could control mortality as he had never done before. The speed of this control was unique, and the later it occurred in a country the faster mortality fell.

In all modern societies there were, and are, off-setting factors tending to nullify the mortality improvements (warfare, self-destruction through drugs and alcohol, new diseases), but these are weak in the face of the continued drive to save lives. Consequently, in the advanced nations most of the burden of restoring a balance between births and deaths has fallen, as it did in hunting-and-gathering societies, on the fertility side. After a century or more of rapid population growth and the resulting congestion, the advanced nations have finally adjusted their fertility to their mortality. Since their mortality is now extremely low, the adjustment has given rise to birth rates so low as to be unprecedented for entire nations. The advanced countries have reached these low rates by pushing the principle underlying human social organization—reliance on a division of labour based on acquired skills—to its limit. The destiny of the child (and hence of the parent) has come to depend on the child's training and education. The social structure that generates this kind of adaptation is characterized by social mobility, planned innovation, formal schooling, urbanization, separation of home and workplace, and bureaucracy. Unless these traits are somehow reversed or overcome, the industrial countries will continue to have fertility rates near or below replacement, and as other countries become developed, they too will record low fertility.

Causes of Below-Replacement Fertility

When we ask why industrial societies eventually exhibit below-replacement fertility, the answer can be given in more than one universe of discourse. For instance, from a global point of view it would be impossible for these societies to do otherwise. A hunting-and-gathering technology enabled people to live modestly by harvesting the wild bounty of nature, but, except as it expanded into new areas, the population could not grow. By contrast, the agricultural and especially the modern industrial societies have learned how to alter and manipulate nature in order to increase its bounty. The result is a miraculous gain in the level of consumption and, initially at least, an equally miraculous increase in the human population. It needs little perspicacity, however, to see that in a finite world the twin forces of population and per capita consumption cannot both long continue to increase. Neither one can grow indefinitely, but the two together can grow for only a brief moment in history. To see this, one can take any basic resource and calculate the drain on it under certain assumptions regarding growth. For example, if the entire world were to consume energy at the rate the United States did in 1980, total world consumption would be 5.6 times what it actually was. If one assumes that the world not only reaches the US 1980 level but surpasses it by a rate of increase corresponding to that for the United States between 1950 and 1980, one finds that by 2010 the world consumption would be more than 12 times the actual 1980 level. Even if quantities of coal, oil, and uranium, or new substitutes, could be found sufficient to meet this enormous demand, it is doubtful whether the environment could withstand the assault of the resulting contaminants.

In industrial societies, then, the combination of ever more goods and services per person and ever more persons is creating an impossible situation in terms of congestion and environmental damage. It is this situation to which below-replacement fertility is an adjustment. People cannot, or will not, limit the goods and services supplied by their ever more complex technology, but they can forgo children, who, if produced in abundance, would greatly add to the congestion.

Ordinarily, however, people do not curb their fertility out of concern for society at large. They may invoke environmental problems as a rationalization, but their main motivation is more personal. To understand today's extremely low fertility, then, one must turn to the special features of industrial societies that dampen the individual's enthusiasm for childbearing. Since these features are interrelated, it makes little difference where we start. Let us begin with marriage.

Postponement of Marriage

In the past, marriage was the approved institutional arrangement for bearing and rearing offspring.

With remarkable persistence, from hunting-and-gathering societies to modern times, it was a focus of public interest and ritual. But in today's advanced nations it is in trouble (Davis, 1986). One sign of this is that it is increasingly being postponed. In the United States in 1960, for example, only 19.2 per cent of women aged 20–39 had never married; the corresponding figure in 1984 was 37.1 per cent (US Bureau of the Census, 1970, p. 11; *Statistical Abstract of the United States 1986*, p. 36). The latter figure may seem high, but in Sweden (in 1981) 49.6 per cent of women aged 20–39 had never married.

It is difficult to predict how far marital postponement will eventually go. In the past some countries, such as Ireland and the Scandinavian nations, approached female marital ages as high as 30 on average, and a high proportion of women (26 per cent in Ireland and 22 per cent in Sweden in 1940) reached menopause without ever marrying (Sklar, 1977, p. 360). Today, marriage is again being postponed, this time with a rising per cent of births that are illegitimate.

Postponement is not being used as a respectable mode of birth control, as it long was in western Europe, but rather as a means to reduce uncertainty with respect to marriage and parenthood.

If one asks why marriages are being postponed, the answer lies largely in the other traits of modernity that we shall consider. High rates of divorce make marriage a risky business; widespread cohabitation and numerous births out of wedlock provide alternatives to marriage; wives' employment disturbs the division of labour between husband and wife. These changes decrease the need for marriage, especially for the young, at the same time that they increase the penalties.

The Rise of Nonmarital Reproduction

Of course, postponement of marriage does not necessarily bring a commensurate decline in births, because illegitimate births may wholly or partially offset the decline. In most advanced countries, the percentage of all births that are illegitimate has been rising. In the United States in 1960, the fraction was 5.3 per cent; by 1984 the per cent had reached 21.0 (US National Center for Health Statistics, 1985, p. 31). With such a speedy rise, illegitimate reproduction can compensate for a considerable portion of the loss of legitimate births. In the United States there were 1.1 million fewer legitimate births in 1983 than in 1960, but there were 0.5 million more illegitimate births. Illegitimacy thus offset 45 per cent of the decline in legitimate births, the rest being accounted for by marital postponement and reduced marital fertility.

In general, a similar pattern seems to characterize other developed nations. Married women still have higher fertility than unmarried women (nearly six times higher in the United States), but the difference is narrowing. Further, because of marital postponement, the proportion of young women who are unmarried has risen greatly. These two trends—rising illegitimate fertility compared with legitimate fertility, and swelling proportions of young women who are unmarried—have given rise to a spectacular increase in the proportion of births out of wedlock. Table 12.1 shows the trend for the United States between 1940 and 1983. Until 1960 much of the rise was due to increasing fertility among unmarried as compared with married women, but since then it has been due more to marital postponement.

The figures furnish stark evidence that marriage is not only failing in procreation but is losing its monopoly of births. Traditionally the institution in which reproduction was expected and rewarded, lawful wedlock now competes in producing children with other kinds of sexual relationships (Carlson, 1986; Espenshade, 1986; Spanier, 1986). It should not be inferred, however, that these other relationships are highly prolific. If people are unwilling to commit themselves to a durable legal relationship (marriage), they are usually reluctant to commit themselves to parenthood in any other situation. In other words, a switch from marital to unorganized and unregulated mating will not result in high fertility, as people occasionally assume, but in low fertility. According to the second column of Table 12.1, unmarried women in the United States in 1965 (their peak year for fertility) were bearing children at a rate that would have resulted in less than one child per unmarried woman at the end of their childbearing years. If the nation had to depend exclusively on nonmarital reproduction, it would quickly become depopulated. This explains why

Table 12.1 Percentage of births that are illegitimate, and fertility rate of unmarried women, United States, 1940–83

	Percentage of all births illegitimate	Total fertility rate per unmarried woman
1940	3.8	.17
1950	4.0	.38
1955	4.5	.59
1960	5.3	.75
1965	7.7	.82
1970	10.7	.71
1975	14.3	.57
1980	18.4	.68
1983	20.3	.71

US National Center for Health Statistics, 1981, pp. 54–5; and 'Advance Report of Natality Statistics', 1980 & 1983.

Sweden, with the world's lowest proportion married and one of the world's highest divorce rates, also has one of the world's lowest birth rates. In this regard, the Swedish and American 'anti-marriage' indicators for 1981 are of interest (see Table 12.2).[2]

Table 12.2 Indicators of anti-marriage, Sweden and United States, 1981

	Sweden	United States
Percentage of women aged 20–39 not married	49.6	38.1
Divorces per thousand wives under age 50	24.7	42.2
TFR per woman	1.63	1.82

High Divorce Rates

Marriage formerly served as a reproductive institution in part because it was durable and therefore, with close kin, provided a stable milieu for rearing children. Today, as high divorce rates testify, that stability has been substantially lost. Although the rise in the divorce rate in the United States has ceased since 1977, the rate has stabilized at a very high level. In nearly all other advanced countries, it has continued to increase. Among 24 industrial countries selected because they had the necessary data, not one showed a decline in divorce during the 13 years between 1970 and 1983. The average number of divorces per thousand population for the 24 countries was 1.32 in 1970 and 2.29 in 1983. The unweighted average increase in the rate was therefore 4.3 per cent per year. At that pace of increase, the divorce rate would double every 16.5 years. It was back in 1956 that the United States had a divorce rate equal to the 1983 average divorce rate of the 24 countries (2.3 per thousand population); so the industrial countries as a whole are approximately 27 years behind the United States in divorce. It thus seems probable that in the industrialized countries the divorce rate will continue to climb, at least for the next quarter of a century. Already in the United States, over half of all marriages end in divorce (Weed, 1980, p. 19).[3]

Divorce tends to reduce fertility in various ways. First, it lessens the time that men and women spend in marriage. Using 1975 data, James Weed (1980, p. 13) finds that without divorce the average first marriage in the United States would last 41.4 years. Actually it lasts only 25.8 years. Thus 38 per cent of the potential first-marriage duration is lost to divorce. Second, a high divorce rate implies a high degree of marital instability. Hence decisions about childbearing, which necessarily involve long-run planning, must often be made in an atmosphere of apprehensive uncertainty. As a result, couples often postpone having a child, in which case divorce may intervene. Third, a high divorce rate diminishes the financial security that a wife gets through marriage (Weitzman, 1985, 1986, ch. 12). Young women consequently tend to work outside the home and to seek more education as a means of upgrading their marketable working skills.

Wives and Work

Less direct than marital postponement, divorce, and illegitimacy, but nevertheless influential is the high and rising participation of married women in the labour force. This phenomenon is well documented (Davis, 1984c; Pepitone-Rockwell, 1980; US Bureau of the Census, 1986), and it characterizes virtually all of the industrial nations. For a long time, single women normally entered employment, and when marriage was postponed, increasing the number of single women, the female labour supply grew. The expanding activity of married women, however, is relatively new. As late as 1910 in the United States, only 9 per cent of married women were gainfully employed; by 1985 the figure had climbed to 54.2 per cent. If we take only married women in the prime working ages (20–59), we find that the proportions are higher (see Table 12.3).

Wives' participation in the labour force outside the home has a chilling effect on fertility in several ways. To begin with, it motivates single women to seek

Table 12.3 Married women in the prime working ages (20–59)

	Percentage of married women aged 20–59 in labour force
United States (1985)	64.4
Norway (1980)	65.6
England and Wales (1981)	56.0
New Zealand (1981)	42.1

more education in order to get better jobs. To avoid entrapment in household duties, they postpone marriage, perhaps opting for cohabitation in the interim. Once married, having already been in the labour market, they appreciate having an income of their own. Men, in turn, experiencing increased competition from women for jobs, are motivated to get more education and to conserve their assets. They, too, are likely to postpone marriage, and if they do get married they are in no position to demand that their wives quit work. They may assume some household duties, but not enough to eliminate the 'double burden' confronting their working wives.

In addition to contributing to marital postponement, the employment of married women contributes to marital instability. By giving the wife an income of her own, it lessens her need for a husband; by providing social contacts at the workplace, it enables her to meet other men; and by focusing her attention on an occupation, it gives her a role—a personal identity—apart from that of childcare and household responsibility. For these reasons, a high divorce rate goes hand in hand with a high rate of married women's employment.

In addition, regardless of marital stability or instability, work outside the home takes time and energy that would otherwise go into domestic activities. Just as in a hunting-and-gathering regime, so in a present-day industrial society the wife's role in economic production makes low fertility necessary. Indeed, the conflict is even greater now, because a mother cannot carry her offspring to work with her

and because training the young in a complex society is more burdensome. If a young woman today has only two children, she can work out daycare arrangements, can minimize the time lost from work due to pregnancy and infant care, and can expect to spend less than a fifth of her postmarital life with children under age seven. Unlike the mother in a hunting-and-gathering regime, she experiences less difficulty if she bears her children close together rather than far apart. On the other hand, she has far more reason to limit the total number of offspring she bears. Also, while the work of husband and wife in a hunting-and-gathering regime was complementary, in modern industrial societies it is, normally at least, unrelated. For husband and wife, then, there is nothing in the modern workplace that encourages either marriage or reproduction.

Underlying Causes of Below-Replacement Fertility

I have chosen to discuss what is happening to marriage in industrial societies, because it is through the institution of marriage that most factors affect fertility. Certainly, the four major trends considered—marital postponement, nonmarital reproduction, divorce, and wives' employment—go far toward explaining the below-replacement fertility of industrial nations.

Explanation in terms of such causes, however, does not satisfy everybody. Some investigators seek the underlying causes. They want to know why the trends described have occurred. Why is it that advanced industrial societies penalize marriage and marital reproduction?

The best answer I can hazard is that there is an incompatibility, or tension, between the family on the one hand and the industrial economy on the other. The fundamental principle of the family is ascription of status. Members of the family are connected with one another and with extended kin through reproduction. Husband and wife, for example, are connected to each other through common offspring. Kinship has been a major basis of social organization throughout human history, but the family's role in status ascription goes beyond kinship. Insofar as societies are divided into groups, membership has tended to be based on who one's parents were. One is a Muslim, Jew, or Christian because one's parents were. In fact, the major cleavages in human societies today—tribal, caste, racial, religious, ethnic, linguistic—are between groups whose membership is overwhelmingly determined by birth. This is why radical social reformers, seeking to achieve equality and freedom, often want to abolish the family.

The principle of industrial society is the opposite. By rewarding people for achievement, for what they do rather than who they are, industrialism generates competition and mobility. The result is a system so powerful that it dominates the world and inspires the dreams of backward countries.

Replacement of the population, however—at least insofar as it depends on biological motives—has not been 'industrialized'. It has been left to the family, which remains much as it has always been, a centre of close personal contact, primal emotions, and (as we have seen) status ascription. In a sense, then, industrial societies have left the important function of population replacement to a unit that is not only alien in principle to industrialism but which is vestigial, a social fossil. Until recently, this arrangement worked well enough—too well in fact, for the population in the industrializing nations grew rapidly. But of late the encroachments of modernity have so demoralized the family that it is failing to fulfill its reproductive function.

Since the family includes people of different age and sex in close and durable contact, and since it involves appetitive and emotional behaviour, its existence requires strong normative controls. These tend to break down when people live in large cities, strive for social mobility, work in an impersonal environment, receive income as individuals rather than as family members, and acquire formal education in schools beyond parental control. Under these conditions family norms increasingly are violated with impunity, and an ideology arises that justifies the violations as being 'up to date' or 'modern', while

conformity is labelled as 'old-fashioned' or 'conservative'. Any catalogue of 'liberal' or 'enlightened' views will include numerous anti-family attitudes. Homosexuality is only a matter of 'sexual orientation' and must be accepted; no-fault divorce is a good thing because it reduces recrimination; women bearing children out of wedlock should not be blamed for their situation but given financial help and special attention; abortion is a matter for the woman and her doctor to decide (the husband is ignored); teenagers should have access to contraceptives and abortions without their parents' knowledge; cohabitation without marriage is acceptable.

Unavoidable Consequences

If industrial societies thus inherently discourage procreation, they are not likely to experience automatically a new baby boom. Despite some minor cyclical fluctuation, their very low fertility will probably persist unless it is changed by deliberate policy. Presumably, the purpose of pronatalist policy is to avoid the undesired consequences of below-replacement fertility. What are these?

One consequence, the much-discussed aging of the population, has perhaps been exaggerated (the problem depends more on policies with respect to the aged than on the number of the elderly), but almost any conceivable pronatalist policy, even if successful, would make the population younger by only a small degree. In a stable population with present-day mortality, raising the total fertility rate from 1.6 to 2.0 (a 25 per cent increase) lowers the proportion aged 65 and over from 26 to 20 per cent (Coale & Demeny, 1983, p. 104). At any reproduction rate below replacement, the age structure will be top-heavy. Further consequences arise from the confinement of very low fertility to the industrial nations. With fertility still high in the less developed countries, this creates in the advanced countries a new and powerful demographic vacuum.

The impulse of the advanced nations is to adopt pronatalist policies. Such policies, however, can be expected to boost the birth rate only moderately

(Frejka, 1980; McIntosh, 1981). If they should do more than that, the resulting population growth would add to the existing congestion and pollution. A more effective and humane policy would be to encourage very low fertility in the less developed world as well as at home. This, if successful, would bring the earth back to the virtually zero population growth it had before humans ventured into agriculture and industrialism.

Conclusion

From an evolutionary point of view, humans have been extremely successful. They now number about 5 billion and are increasing by some 80 million each year. For an insect, this would not be many, but for a large resource-consuming and environmentally destructive mammal, it is a big number. In the human case, however, success in an evolutionary sense is not viewed with equanimity by everyone. A sizable proportion of humans view the explosive multiplication of their species as a global catastrophe that has helped to expand poverty, to extinguish thousands of other species, to pollute the air, to waste resources, to create congestion. No wonder, then, that a substantial and increasing number of people are in favour of either fewer or at least no more people than there are now.

For many observers, then, the current below-replacement fertility in the industrial countries is a blessing, not a calamity. It is a solution to a major problem, not a problem in itself. Since these countries are in a minority, however, their self-restraint with respect to fertility reduces global population growth only slightly. Instead it gives the industrial countries aging populations and international complications. Like everything else, then, below-replacement fertility has its costs. While these costs are leading some governments to

pursue or consider pronatalist programs, they are hardly great enough to justify programs that will do much more than achieve zero growth (Vining, 1984; Tomlinson, 1984).

To evaluate the present below-replacement fertility of the industrial nations, one must recall the millions of years when humans, like other animals, hunted and foraged. Under those conditions, a rapid expansion of human numbers was suicidal, because it would lead to feedback mechanisms such as environmental exhaustion, tribal warfare, and disease. In some animals, population stabilization is achieved by very high mortality, but in others, including humans, it is achieved by moderate fertility, which fits the evolutionary niche that humans have carved for themselves—namely a reliance on culture and technology. This reliance has succeeded best when emphasis was placed on the training of offspring rather than the number of offspring.

With agriculture, however, man began to live by controlling rather than simply skimming his environment. The switch was so profound and sudden that normal feedback mechanisms restraining population growth became partially inoperable. As agriculture improved and spread, population increased many times faster than it had grown before.

By greatly expanding production in agriculture and in other sectors of the economy, and by finally inventing scientific medicine, industrialism lowered death rates dramatically, with consequent unbridled population growth. Since, however, an industrial system must invest ever more heavily in the training of the young, it soon exerts a downward pressure on fertility. With full industrialism, the family, which has survived up to this point, becomes a weak institution and the output of babies becomes inadequate to replace the population. When and if the whole world becomes industrialized, the growth of the human population may, mercifully, reverse itself.

Notes

1.   The term 'hominids' designates the human family after it separated from the ape family. The time of the

separation is variously estimated as between 7 and 30 million years ago. The hominids include several fossil species in addition to modem man. See Fagan, 1979, ch. 5; and Campbell, 1974, pp. 372–97.

2.   Calculated from data in United Nations, *Demographic Yearbook*, 1982–4 editions.

3.   Weed's finding is that 47.4 per cent of first marriages in

the United States and 48.9 per cent of remarriages will end in divorce, but his calculation uses 1975 data. The divorce rate rose by 12 per cent between 1975 and 1979, after which it stabilized. It is therefore safe to say that the probability of divorce now exceeds 50 per cent.

References

Acsàdi, Gy., & J. Nemeskéri. 1970. *History of Human Life Span and Mortality*. Budapest: Akádemiai Kiadó.

Campbell, Bernard G. 1974. *Human Evolution: An Introduction to Man's Adaptations* (2nd edn). Chicago, IL: Aldine Publishing Company.

Carlson, Elwood. 1986. 'Couples without children: Premarital cohabitation in France'. In Davis, 1986 (pp. 113–30).

Carr-Saunders, A.M. 1922. *The Population Problem: A Study in Human Evolution*. Oxford: Clarendon Press.

Coale, Ansley J., & Paul Demeny. 1983. *Regional Model Life Tables and Stable Populations* (2nd edn). New York: Academic Press.

Coale, Ansley J., & Melvin Zelnik. 1963. *New Estimates of Fertility and Population in the United States*. Princeton, NJ: Princeton University Press.

Chiglieri, Michael Patrick. 1984. *The Chimpanzees of Kibale Forest: A Field Study of Ecology and Social Structure*. New York: Columbia University Press.

Cohen, Mark Nathan, & George J. Armelagos (Eds). 1984. *Paleopathology at the Origins of Agriculture*. New York: Academic Press.

Corlett, William Thomas. 1935. *The Medicine-Man of the American Indians*. Baltimore, MD: Charles C. Thomas.

Daly, Martin, & Margo Wilson. 1980. 'Sociobiological analysis of human infanticide'. In Hausfater & Hrdy, 1984 (pp. 487–502).

Davis, Kingsley. 1984a (January). 'Declining birth rates and growing populations'. *Population Research and Policy Review, 36*.

———. 1984b. 'Demographic dilemmas in the mid-1980s'. In John H. Moore (Ed.), *To Promote Prosperity: US Domestic Policy in the Mid-1980s* (Ch. 21). Stanford, CA: Hoover Institution Press.

———. 1984c (September). 'Wives and work: The sex role revolution and its consequences'. *Population and Development Review, 10*(3), 397–417.

———(Ed.). 1986. *Contemporary Marriage: Comparative Perspectives on a Changing Institution*. New York: Russell Sage Foundation.

Eaton, Joseph W., & Albert J. Mayer. 1954. *Man's Capacity to Reproduce: The Demography of a Unique Population*. Glencoe, IL: The Free Press.

Espenshade, Thomas J. 1986. 'The recent decline of American marriage: Blacks and whites in comparative perspective'. In Davis, 1986 (pp. 53–90).

Fagan, Brian M. 1979. *World Prehistory: A Brief Introduction*. Boston, MA: Little, Brown and Company.

Frejka, Thomas. 1980 (March). 'Fertility trends and policies: Czechoslovakia in the 1970s'. *Population and Development Review, 6*(1), 65–93.

Goodall, Jane van Lawick. 1971. *In the Shadow of Man*. Boston, MA: Houghton Mifflin Company.

Hausfater, Glenn, & Sarah Blaffer Hrdy (Eds). 1984. *Infanticide: Comparative and Evolutionary Perspectives*. New York: Aldine Publishing Company.

Hayden, Brian. 1972 (October). 'Population control among hunter–gatherers'. *World Archaeology, 4*(2).

Hernandez, Donald J. 1984. *Success or Failure? Family Planning Programs in the Third World*. Westport, CT: Greenwood Press.

Howell, Nancy. 1979. *The Demography of the Dobe !Kung*. New York: Academic Press.

Johansson, S. Ryan, & S. Horowitz. 1985. 'Life expectancy and age at death in skeletal populations' (mimeo).

Jolly, Alison. 1972. *The Evolution of Primate Behavior*. New York: Macmillan.

Jones, F. Lancaster. 1965. 'The demography of the Australian aborigines'. *International Social Science Journal, 17*(2), 232–45.

Klein, Richard G. 1984. 'Mammalian extinctions and Stone Age people in Africa'. In Martin & Klein, 1984 (pp. 553–73).

Landy, David (Ed.), 1977. *Culture, Disease. and Healing: Studies in Medical Anthropology*. New York: Macmillan.

Lee, Richard B. 1979. *The !Kung San: Men, Women, and Work in a Foraging Society*. Cambridge: Cambridge University Press.

Lee, Richard B., & Irven DeVore (Eds). 1968. *Man the Hunter*. Chicago, IL: Aldine Publishing Company.

McIntosh, C. Alison. 1981 (June). 'Low fertility and liberal democracy in western Europe'. *Population and Development Review, 7*(2), 181–207.

Maddox, John Lee. 1923. *The Medicine Man*. New York: Macmillan.

Martin, Paul S. 1973 (March). 'The discovery of America,' *Science, 179,* 969–74.

Martin, Paul S., & Richard G. Klein (Eds). 1984. *Quaternary Extinctions: A Prehistoric Revolution*. Tucson, AZ: The University of Arizona Press.

Nitecki, Matthew H. 1984. *Extinctions*. Chicago, IL: University of Chicago Press.

Pepitone-Rockwell, Fran (Ed.). 1980. *Dual-Career Couples*. Beverly Hills, CA: Sage Publications.

Schaller, George B. 1965. 'The behavior of the mountain gorilla'. In Irven DeVore (Ed.), *Primate Behavior: Field Studies of Monkeys and Apes* (pp. 324–67). New York: Holt, Rinehart and Winston.

Scrimshaw, Susan C.M. 1984. 'Infanticide in human populations: Societal and individual concerns'. In Hausfater & Hrdy, 1984 (pp. 439–62).

Sklar, June. 1977 (December). 'Marriage and nonmarital fertility: A comparison of Ireland and Sweden'. *Population and Development Review, 3*(4), 359–75.

Smith, T.E. 1960 (November). 'The Cocos-Keeling Islands: A demographic laboratory'. *Population Studies, 14,* 94–130.

Spanier, Graham B. 1986. 'Cohabitation in the 1980s: Recent changes in the United States'. In Davis, 1986 (pp. 91–111).

Starr, Paul. 1982. *The Social Transformation of American Medicine*. New York: Basic Books.

Tomlinson, Richard. 1984 (Summer). 'The French population debate'. *The Public Interest, 76,* 111–20.

United Nations. 1984 and earlier. *Demographic Yearbook*. New York.

———. 1985. *World Population Trends. Population and Development Interrelations and Population Policies.* 1983 Monitoring Report, vol. 1. New York.

———. 1986 and earlier. *Population and Vital Statistics Report*, Series A, 1 January.

United States Bureau of the Census. 1970 (25 March). 'Marital status and family status: March 1969', Series P–20, No. 198.

———. 1986 and earlier. *Statistical Abstract of the United States*. Washington, DC.

United States National Center for Health Statistics. 1981. *Vital Statistics of the United States, 1980,* vol. 1: Natality.

———. 1985 (18 July). 'Advance report of final natality statistics, 1984'. *Monthly Vital Statistics Report, 34*(4).

Vining, Daniel R., Jr. 1984 (December). 'Family salaries and the East German birth rate: A comment'. *Population and Development Review, 10*(4), 693–6.

Washburn, Sherwood L., & C.S. Lancaster. 1968a. 'The evolution of hunting'. In Lee & DeVore, 1968 (pp. 293–303).

Washburn, Sherwood L., & Jane B. Lancaster. 1968b. 'Human evolution'. In *International Encyclopedia Of the Social Sciences,* vol. 5 (pp. 215–21). New York: Macmillan.

Weed, James A. 1980 (November). 'National estimates of marriage dissolution and survivorship: United States'. *National Center for Health Analytical Studies, 3*(19).

Weitzman, Lenore J. 1985. *The Divorce Revolution: The Unexpected Social and Economic Consequences for Women and Children in America*. New York: The Free Press.

———. 1986. 'The divorce law revolution and the transformation of legal marriage'. In Davis, 1986 (Ch. 12).

CHAPTER 13

Explanations of the Fertility Crisis in Modern Societies: A Search for Commonalities

John C. Caldwell and Thomas Schindlmayr

Fertility declined in most of the industrialized world from the late nineteenth century until the 1930s, when much of western Europe recorded, for the first time in history, total fertility below two, with net reproduction only three-quarters of replacement levels (Keyfitz & Flieger, 1968). At that time some observers forecast that advanced industrial societies would experience a decline in population numbers (see Charles, 1934), but this prediction was subsequently discarded as birth rates rose and analysis showed its flaws. It was found that many births had been deferred, and that completed family size had fallen below replacement level for few birth cohorts and by only a modest amount. Furthermore, it had required the dire economic conditions of the World Depression to produce even these modest changes. Consequently, demographic transition theorists gave little thought to the possibility that the end of demographic transition would see shrinking populations.

Nevertheless, the high birth rates after the Second World War were ultimately followed by fertility decline—from the early 1960s in the USA and from the late 1960s in most other Western countries. This decline ceased in the USA in the late 1970s, to be succeeded by a persistent rise to replacement-level fertility. But in much of the West the decline came to a halt only in the late 1980s, to be followed by continued low fertility with some very limited rises. The exception was Germany, where fertility fell during the 1990s largely because it did so steeply in East Germany, as it had elsewhere in eastern Europe.

The result was the new phenomenon of very low fertility, defined here as a continuing total fertility of under 1.5 until 2002. Table 13.1 shows that, with some overlapping of dates, very low fertility was achieved in central Europe in the early 1980s, in southern Europe in the late 1980s, in parts of East Asia in the early 1990s, and in eastern Europe and ex-USSR western Asia as the 1990s progressed. By omission, Table 13.1 also throws further valuable light on what was happening in that it excludes some of the leaders in the fertility decline of the 1930s, namely Britain, Sweden, France, and Belgium, where total fertilities at the end of the twentieth century were in the range of 1.6–1.9. It also excludes what Maddison (2001) calls the 'Western Offshoots' (the English-speaking countries of overseas European settlement—USA, Canada, Australia, and New Zealand) where the range was 1.5–2.l.

This paper will explore whether the extreme fertility decline that resulted in very low cross-sectional fertility rates with little likelihood of cohort fertility reaching replacement levels was a single irreversible change and whether current theories are sufficient to explain what happened across the range of affected countries. We are concerned about conclusions reached from what may prove to be the short-term heterogeneity in the fertility levels of these countries, and we stress the need for a longterm perspective on population replacement

Table 13.1 Countries with continuing total fertility below 1.5, by region, period when it first fell below 1.5, and total fertility in 2002[1]

Region[2]	1980–5	1985–90	1985–90	1995–2000	2000–5
Central Europe	Germany (1.3)	Austria (1.3)			Switzerland (1.4)
Southern Europe		Italy (1.3)	Greece (1.3)		
Eastern Europe			Bulgaria (1.3)	Belarus (1.3)	Moldova (1.3)
			Slovenia (1.3)	Czech R. (1.1)	Croatia (1.4)
				Estonia (1.3)	
				Hungary (1.3)	
				Latvia (1.2)	
				Lithuania (1.3)	
				Poland (1.3)	
				Romania (1.2)	
				Russian Fed. (1.3)	
				Slovakia (1.2)	
				Ukraine (1.1)	
Ex-USSR Asia				Armenia (1.1)	Georgia (1.2)
Other Asia		Hong Kong (0.9)	Japan (1.3)	Macau (0.9)	Singapore (1.4)
					Taiwan (1.4)

[1] Continuing means the period, no matter how short, that encompasses the time spent up to and including 2002 with the annual total fertility not exceeding 1.5. Total fertility for 2002 shown in parentheses.

[2] Eastern Europe includes all ex-Communist European countries.
United Nations (2001a), Population Reference Bureau (2002).

based on a single explanation for very low fertility. In general terms the paper will address the question of whether rich countries have inherent problems in replacing their population. In specific terms it will try to throw light on such issues as the following: (a) Is the present explanation of the causes of very low fertility in Italy (or Italy and Spain) suited to a more general treatment of the phenomenon of very low fertility? (b) Is something being missed by ignoring the situation in Central Europe, given that Germany and Austria were the first societies to attain very low fertility and may well achieve the lowest completed cohort fertility? (c) Are the current emphases on the type of welfare state or kind of family structure appropriate as explanations, or should we be stressing the lifestyles of postmodern societies or family building in a regime of liberal economics? . . .

The Regional Fit of Very-Low-Fertility Theory

In the theoretical discussion we have so far considered, the arguments have usually been based on a comparison between countries or regions with different fertility levels. The process is usually selective and would gain, though perhaps become less clear cut, by being more comprehensive. Accordingly, we now survey the very-low-fertility populations. In searching for reasons for the lowest fertility recorded, one has to be conscious of the date. In the mid-eighteenth century we would focus on England, in the mid-nineteenth century on France, in the 1950s on Sweden, in the 1960s on eastern Europe, in the 1970s on such western European countries as Germany and the UK. Even if we rigidly confine ourselves to total fertilities below 1.5 (as in Table 13.1) there are five different regions: central Europe, southern Europe, eastern Europe, ex-USSR Asia (the Caucasus), and other Asia (Japan and two special areas) comprising 26 countries. Do the dominant explanations worked out for southern Europe, and specifically Italy and Spain, fit these other regions, and indeed do the explanations completely fit all of southern Europe?

Southern Europe

From the following sources, a clear picture is emerging of the forces that have created current very low fertility in the countries of southern Europe: for Italy, Pinnelli (1995), Dalla Zuanna, et al. (1998), Palomba (2001), Dalla Zuanna & Mencarini (2002); for Spain, Reher (1997), Delgado & Castro Martin (1999), Holdsworth & Dale (1999), Irazoqui Solda (2000), Puy (2001); for Italy and Spain, Delgado Pérez & Livi-Bacci (1992), Billari, et al. (2000), Dalla Zuanna (2001); for Greece, Georges (1996), Hondroyiannis & Papapetrou (2001), Symeonidou (2002); for all southern European countries, sometimes in a general European comparison, Bettia & Villa (1998), Reher (1998), Bagavos & Martin (2001), Pinnelli & De Rose (2001).

All stress the following features: a spectacular rise in incomes and the emergence of a consumer society; rapid rises in educational levels with girls catching up with boys and a consequent increased demand by young women for employment; household work and childcare undertaken almost exclusively by women, thus creating a clash with working outside the home; and the young—especially females—finding it hard to gain employment, and ill-supported by employers or the state in taking time off to give birth or care for children, or in returning to the workplace. On the other hand young adults are welcome, almost forced, to stay with their parents, not only until employed but until married. This situation may be somewhat restrictive, and it is much more comfortable than living alone on unemployment relief as is so often the case in English-speaking countries. These circumstances may well encourage some of the young

to remain unemployed until a good or secure job is found and an acceptable and (at least in the case of women) an employed spouse is identified. There is evidence that employment hastens a man's marriage but delays that of a woman (Billari, et al., 2000). Once married, a wife has to undertake nearly all the housework and childcare, as well as providing meals for the families of her husband's brothers and care for the husband's parents, all of whom usually live close by. This makes it hard to work and have a large family, not only when the children are young but also when they continue staying at home as young adults. This is a continuing situation insofar as few marriages end in divorce—10 per cent in Italy, Spain, and Greece compared with several times that proportion in northern Europe (Pinnelli, 1995, p. 82). There is little premarital cohabitation and births out of wedlock are rare. Age at first sexual intercourse in Italy, and possibly elsewhere in the Mediterranean yet in contrast to northern Europe, has risen moderately for men but more steeply for women (De Sandre, 2000, pp. 23, 32*ff.*). Unemployment is greater among women than men and among the young than the old, and is greatest among young women. Employers have little compunction about turning down job applications from women who are or appear to be pregnant or have already had a child. The extended family still expects parenthood from young couples yet will now settle for only two children or even one. Ahn and Mira (2001) reported that in Spain, with its low premarital fertility rate, deferred marriage wholly explained the fertility decline.

Some qualifications must be made. Portugal, a southern European but not a Mediterranean country, fits only loosely into the above description (Bettio & Villa, 1998, p. 166) and this probably partly explains its total fertility of 1.5. Cohabitation and ex-nuptial pregnancy are more tolerated in Greece provided that birth out of wedlock does not follow (Symeonidou, 2002, pp. 26–7). Women marry earlier in Greece and Portugal, the majority before 25 years of age, than in Italy and Spain. In all these countries, the extended family expects to house young adults whether employed or unemployed or still being educated, and older women expect to look after their grandchildren while their daughters or daughters-in-law are working. There appears to be little demand for unemployment relief payments for young adults or for state childcare facilities for the very young, although a high level of Italian 3–5 year olds attend pre-school (Gauthier, 1996, p. 181), and there is little evidence that such assistance would raise the birth rate. On the other hand, there is strong evidence that women's birth strike is caused by employer unwillingness to introduce flexible working hours, and to employ or re-employ pregnant women or those who are mothers. Legislation or pressure on employers could probably help here. So should a continued improvement of the economy from the harsh days of the early 1990s, helped by the fact that wages and employee benefits are still among the lowest in the European Union (*Economist*, 2002a). There is also strong evidence that more help from husbands within the home might mitigate the pressure against childbearing, although husbands, after long years of their mothers meeting every domestic need, might well acquiesce instead in settling for a single child. Eventually, social pressure or working grandmothers might lead to change.

Nevertheless, the Mediterranean family will probably continue to be distinctive as it has been for centuries. Indeed, little convergence may at present be taking place as both Billari and Kohler (2000) and Billari, et al. (2000) argue. Evidence of its stability is that even in Australia, where Mediterranean immigrants share the same industrial and formal childcare framework as people originating in northern Europe, convergence has been slow. The rates of in-marriage among Australian Greeks and Italians have consistently been considerably higher than for those of northern European origin (Penny & Khoo, 1996; Price, 1994). Australian Greek girls and young women are constantly, and largely successfully, harassed not to take up northern European sexual mores, and, although there is some resentment, there is also conformity to their own traditions and even pleasure that the family cares for them and will continue to embrace them (Packer, et al., 1976). All southern European families are prepared to have low fertility and, if necessary, to settle for a single successful child (Santow & Bracher, 1999), and, by 1987–91 the total fertility of Australian Greeks was 1.5, and of Australian Italians and Yugoslavs 1.6, compared with 1.8 for the native born (Abbasi-Shavazi & McDonald, 2002, p. 61).

Eastern Europe

The decline to very low fertility in eastern Europe and the former USSR began in the early 1990s, and became precipitous in the late 1990s, with laggards after 2000 (see Table 13.1). They now form the majority of very-low-fertility countries both in number and combined population, and, apart from the two cities now termed Chinese Special Administrative Regions, include the three lowest-fertility countries in the world, the Czech Republic, Ukraine, and Armenia, all with total fertility of 1.1. Until now comparatively little attention has been paid to the causes of their fertility decline, and almost none to whether they fit into the southern European very-low-fertility model. The explanation may have been merely the belief that this was a reaction, perhaps temporary, to a fearful crisis. Sources used here in seeking explanations for fertility change include the following: for East Germany, Eberstadt (1994), Witte & Wagner (1995), and Conrad, et al. (1996); for the Czech Republic, Kalibová (2001), and Rychta iková & Kraus (2001); for Hungary, Kamarás (1999); for Bulgaria, Philipov (2001); for Latvia. Zvidrins, et al. (1998); for Poland, Holzer & Kowalska (1997); for Armenia, DHS (2001); and for eastern Europe as a whole, Standing (1996), and Sobotka (2001).

In one sense, that of changes in real income per head, the eastern European crisis remains very variable. Maddison (2001, p. 185), employing fixed US dollars on a parity purchasing power basis, showed that between 1990 and 1998, although average income in the old USSR had fallen by 43 per cent, that of the rest of eastern Europe was at about the same level at the end of the decade as at the beginning. There were exceptional cases in both areas. In the ex-USSR, Georgia's average income had fallen 64 per cent and that of Ukraine and Moldova by 58 per cent. In Romania, Bulgaria, and ex-Yugoslavia it had declined by only 15–22 per cent, while the Czech Republic and Hungary altered little and Poland's income rose substantially. What is noteworthy is that the extent of average income change had little differentiating association with fertility. For in nearly all cases total fertility plummeted to the 1.1–1.3 range (see Table 13.1). This means that if economic factors are important, we must look for other changes such as increased job insecurity and unemployment, a changed distribution of incomes, the loss of benefits for those newly married or newly pregnant, and a marked rise in the cost of health and educational services. Eberstadt (1994, p. 150) wrote that 'the path back from Communism is *terra incognita*' and that the 'transition to a liberal market order might be expected to entail far-reaching, often traumatic adjustments. . . .' He supported the argument of trauma in East Germany by attempting to demonstrate steep rises in mortality (p. 146) even though there (alone among eastern European countries) health services had actually improved because of immediate coverage by West Germany's system (p. 149). Later analysis of more complete data showed that the mortality rise had not occurred (Conrad, et al., 1996, p. 332). We shall argue here that the fertility declines in eastern Europe and the former Soviet Union were a rational adjustment to a new situation and may prove to be partly transient.

Standing (1996, p. 230) reported that the crisis in eastern Europe had been caused by the removal of the three pillars of the former system: guaranteed employment from the time when full-time education was complete, social protection by stable low prices achieved through government subsidies, and enterprise-based social benefits, mostly in the form of goods and services. The sudden changes were shaped by international financial agencies that, even if they were not trying to traumatize the populations, believed in 'shock therapy' for previously 'overprotected populations' (Standing, 1996, pp. 230–1). The preceding protection included massive

assistance, especially after low fertility in the late 1960s and 1970s, to encourage early marriages and childbearing. Sobotka (2001, p. 2) described this as a totally distinct social system characterized by 'limited opportunities, uniformity, and a high degree of "familism"'. The latter had historical roots and it had been furthered by cheap formal childcare, progressive child payments, and housing linked both to childbearing and to marriage (pp. 25*ff.*). It was this system that kept the average age of women at last birth in eastern Europe at 23 years during the 1980s while that in the rest of Europe rose from 25 to 28 years (p. 10). As the system was dismantled in the 1990s, ex-nuptial births rose to northwestern European levels. Nonmarital pregnancy levels rose even higher and those pregnancies that were not aborted were usually followed by marriage, thus limiting the rise in marriage age yet placing great stress on not having a second child (pp. 10ff). Throughout the region there is anxiety over the future, especially about employment prospects for males and females, and also about the health, education, housing, and other costs that children will incur. There appears to be little employment discrimination against women who are pregnant or have children, and instead a tradition of their returning to the workforce.

We will now fill out this picture, starting with the case of East Germany which, although different in many ways, is the best documented. The East German government, in an at least partly successful attempt to raise the birth rate, provided massive assistance to young married couples, especially if they had children, and even to unmarried women who bore children. By 1989, the state paid around 80 per cent of the costs of children, through such direct and indirect measures as childcare, holiday facilities, and many subsidies (Ostner, 1997, p. 39). With the birth of a child a young woman could obtain an apartment and, with comprehensive childcare, enter the labour force or continue her education (Witte & Wagner, 1995, p. 393). In contrast to the position in West Germany, the 1949 constitution prohibited discrimination against illegitimate children, and subsequent legislation such as the 1950

Law for the Protection of Mothers and Children emphasized non-discrimination as one of its guiding principles. With unification, the generous support for single mothers disappeared, maternity benefits for all declined sharply, the organized childcare system disappeared, employment conditions became less flexible, unemployment levels soared, and workforces were put on shortened hours (Witte & Wagner, 1995, p. 394). By 1994 the marriage rate had fallen by 57 per cent and total fertility by 51 per cent. Eberstadt (1994), Witte & Wagner (1995), and Conrad, et al. (1996) tend to regard these changes as a rational reaction to a change in economic regimes. The ages at marriage and first birth moved upward toward those of West Germany. Total fertility fell below that of West Germany, but, given that it had earlier been higher, it is not yet certain that completed cohort fertility will be lower.

The situation in, and explanations for, the rest of eastern Europe are similar, except that these countries do not have the economic and social guarantees that came automatically to East Germany by its fusion with rich, stable West Germany. The Czech Republic is an interesting case because external investment—mostly German into a neighbouring country with a tradition of good workmanship meant that incomes actually rose and unemployment was minimal. Nevertheless, there was a fear of greater unemployment and a deep apprehension about the loss of certainty of continued employment. Family benefits were abandoned in 1990 to be partly restored in 1995. Rychta iková and Kraus (2001, p. xi) explain the fertility decline as being a reaction to 'the new phenomenon of unemployment and an appalling—and until quite recently unknown—feeling of uncertainty and insecurity'. In Hungary, state help at the start of marriage and childbearing, especially in the form of housing, had produced a 'baby boom' for several years from the mid-1970s, but even before 1990 there was some drop in fertility rates and a rise in divorce rates and cohabitation (Carlson & Omori, 1998; Kamarás 1999). Thereafter, marriage and fertility rates collapsed. Poland, in spite of its large Catholic

population, has followed a similar path, with rapid fertility decline during the 1990s and a rise in ex-nuptial births as marriage prospects became bleaker (Holzer & Kowalska 1997).

The situation was more acute in those countries where income levels had fallen more steeply, and the fall in fertility was similar. Philipov (2001) provides an interesting description of Bulgaria, where in the 1960s and 1970s pronatalism had taken the form not only of help to young married couples but also of an effort to change mindsets. 'There were attempts to create intolerance toward couples who had no children or had only one child, as well as toward unmarried persons. These groups were characterized as "consumerists", and they had to pay a "bachelor tax"' (Philipov, 2001, p. 17). After 1990 the pronatalist policies collapsed, child allowances were rendered almost worthless by inflation, and charges rose steeply in the previously low-cost nurseries. Armenia experienced a similar collapse in health and care facilities, as well as in employment, and, like the other trans-Caucasian state, Georgia, it experienced a steep fertility decline (DHS, 2001, pp. 4, 56).

Zvidrins, et al. (1998) present a revealing portrait of Latvia, a country originally predominantly Protestant with substantial Catholic and Orthodox minorities. Before its incorporation into the USSR in 1940, it was characterized by late marriage and substantial birth control; indeed, the Lutheran north and west had achieved a net reproduction rate of one by 1914 (Zvidrins, et al., 1998, p. 14). After 1940, with the adoption of Soviet social services, the proportions marrying increased and the age at marriage fell, and pronatalist measures in the 1980s lifted fertility above longterm replacement level. After 1990, average income fell more steeply than anywhere else in eastern Europe and in 5 years the number of employed persons declined by 18 per cent (pp. 3–5). Abortions exceeded births. Zvidrins, et al. concluded: 'Naturally, in a period of economic crisis, values related to the subjective appreciation of life and most indicators of demographic development have been falling. Marriage and fertility rates have dropped very sharply' (p. x).

The situation in eastern Europe has some ingredients of socioeconomic shock and what has happened is an enormous transformation in the populations' circumstances, a rapid change from a super-welfare state with guaranteed employment to regimes of particularly liberal economics. The reaction has been to halt or postpone marriages and births. Marriage age is moving towards 30 years as in much of the rest of Europe, use of contraception is increasing, and abortion levels remain high. In short, Latvians have moved to marriage ages and proportions that the rest of Europe has found to be required in an age of liberal economics. Because the situation is new there is a greater feeling of insecurity than in the West, even in former Czechoslovakia and Hungary where the economic collapse has been limited and where there are attempts to rebuild some of the welfare state. The ancient familism of eastern Europe, reinforced by Communism, is splintering. Because of the quick transition from moderate to very low fertility it is not certain how far completed cohort fertility will go below replacement level but it may need faster economic growth and the rebuilding of some of the welfare state to reverse the demographic situation.

The complexity of the situation is revealed by recent microeconomic research on the Russian situation by Kohler and Kohler (2002), which shows that unemployed women or those in areas of exceptionally high unemployment are the most likely to bear a child. Although the authors appear to think that this is at odds with the insecurity explanation of low fertility, it may merely mean that those with a job are terrified of pregnancy, while those who judge that it will be long before there is an employment opportunity conclude that childbearing should take place before it conflicts with holding down a job.

Central Europe

The greatest test of low-fertility theory is provided by central Europe: West Germany, Austria, and (and especially the German-speaking majority in) Switzerland. These are among the richest populations in the world, with, in the 1980s, low unemployment and only moderate change towards further liberalizing their economies. That change had been slowly proceeding and there had been no great social and economic jolts since the period after the Second World War, which was characterized by rising fertility with total fertility reaching 2.5 in Germany and 2.8 in Austria in the 1960s. Nevertheless, they were the first populations to attain very low fertility (see Table 13.1), and have been close to that situation since the early 1970s. Germany's cohort fertility is probably the lowest in Europe (Prioux, 2002, p. 721). A central question is how their society and welfare systems differ from those of the rest of northern Europe where moderately low fertility prevailed. Their near omission from theoretical analysis of the causes of very low fertility justifies a disproportionate concentration here.

Reher (1998), drawing partly on Hajnal (1982), concluded that there were individualistic societies in northwest Europe and familial ones in southern Europe, and that Germany and France were intermediate between the two (Reher, 1998, p. 212). Although holding that some differences went back a millennium or more, he stressed the importance of the Protestant reformation, with Germany split and France secularizing, and regarded the Industrial Revolution both as a product of the Reformation and as strengthening its effect on socially differentiating Europe into a north and a south (p. 214). Delgado Pérez and Livi-Bacci (1992, p. 162) pointed out that pre-transitional fertility levels in Germany, as well as in Belgium and the Netherlands, had been higher than those not only of Sweden, Denmark, and Britain but also of Italy and Spain. Among European migrants to Australia at the beginning of the twentieth century, the German and Irish arrivals alone were shown by the census to be maintaining high fertility (Coghlan 1903).

The family has long been the cornerstone of German society and the institution of marriage was long considered sacrosanct. Both were enshrined into the 1949 *Grundgesetz* (Basic Law), in the only sections not drafted by the victorious Allies. The Christian Democrats formulated Article 6, which places marriage, motherhood, and the family under state protection. Article 6(5) states that illegitimate children should receive the same opportunities as legitimate children, yet does not offer them equal rights. These articles rest uneasily with the socialist-inspired Article 3(2) giving women equal status with men. This contradiction in the constitution was for long unresolved and implicitly maintained sex differences.

The state stressed conservative family values, a response to the abuse of the family under the Nazis (Lawson, 1996, p. 35), and the perception that the family as repository of German values was at risk. Newly found female emancipation, as well as long separations, difficulties of post-war reunions, and a large number of non-returning soldiers fuelled the notion of a 'family crisis' (Moeller, 1995, p. 150). The state regularly focused its efforts on married women at the expense of unmarried women. Evidence for this mindset is found in a number of pieces of legislation such as the 1950 Housing laws offering housing only to married couples. The large *Frauenüberschu* (female surplus) at the end of the Second World War did not condemn a whole cohort of women to be without a husband, for by the early 1960s three-quarters of women born between 1915 and 1925 were married. Heinemann (1999, p. 211), however, contends that the surplus of women had a 'dramatic influence on single women's life-style'. The Civil Code was brought into line with the Basic Law in 1969 with the introduction of the *Gesetz über die rechtliche Stellung nichtehelicher Kinder* (Illegitimate Children's Act).

Arguably, by addressing social inequalities between various types of families, West Germany's welfare provisions benefited only low- and high-income earners, not the middle-class majority (Ostner, 1997, p. 41). Kaufmann (1993, p. 151) maintains that this significantly contributed to lower fertility. Family policies were purposively Christian, formulated by Christian Democratic administrations which governed for most of the past half-century (Lawson 1996, p. 32). Successive governments felt it was inappropriate for them to intervene in marriage and family issues. As a result childcare is scarce and expensive, employers do

not provide flexible working hours, and the restriction of school hours to mornings only means that childcare problems stretch into school-going ages (see Huinink & Mayer, 1995, p. 195). Eligibility rules for *Kindergeld* (child support), for example, changed. When it was first introduced in 1954 only those with three or more children were entitled. In 1961 this was changed to include two children and in 1975 to one (Kohler & Zacher 1981, pp. 147–8). The significant changes were in place before very low fertility was attained. Chesnais (1996, p. 736) described this as 'a socio-psychological environment . . . not conducive to childbearing'.

There is no parallel to the rise of ex-nuptial births in the rest of Europe north of the Alps, partly because of restricted welfare payments to single mothers. Esping-Andersen (1996, p. 68) described Germany and Italy as the extreme examples of the 'Southern Europe [or Catholic] social welfare model' in contrast to the universalistic systems of Britain and Scandinavia and the partly universalistic systems (at least in terms of child allowances) that developed in France and Belgium.

Certainly West Germany's fertility was low, with the 1950–4 birth cohorts of females having Europe's highest level of childlessness at 21 per cent, and with 48 per cent having 0–1 children compared with 27 per cent in Norway, 29 per cent in England and France, and 31–34 per cent in Sweden, Denmark, and the Netherlands (Bettio & Villa, 1998, p. 153). Heilig, et al. (1990) described modern Germany's fertility as having a 'turbulent past, uncertain future', yet despite their German and Austrian nationalities, they offered no explanation. German cultural practices encourage women to care for children aged under 3, rather than seek employment. This poses problems for those mothers wishing to work and needing care for children under 3 years of age (Ondrich & Spiess, 1998), and, in spite of those who draw parallels between Germany and Italy, there is in Germany no equivalent of the Mediterranean extended family expecting and expected to look after young children of working mothers. Childcare for children under 3 has long been in short supply

(Kreyenfeld & Hank, 2000, p. 321; Schaffer, 1981, p. 103), and this remains a reason why women do not have children. Until the 1970s, only a limited number of preschoolers attended kindergarten and studies suggested that low-income families used them least. As most kindergartens were non-public institutions they were either too expensive or as cooperatives required the mother to help as a part-time volunteer (Schaffer 1981, p. 103). Since then there have come into being many more places run by local communities, but still not enough of them to meet demand (Kreyenfeld & Hank, 2000, p. 334). Nevertheless, in recent years welfare payments have risen, especially those paid to religious and other organizations to provide childcare.

Germany, then, has a welfare and social system that does not make it easy for women to combine work with motherhood. However, there is evidence that the decision to have a second child depends less on the wife's characteristics than on those of the husband, so that it is couples where husbands are more qualified and better providers that go on to have a second child (Kreyenfeld, 2002). Bagavos and Martin (2001, p. 22) add that German mothers remain in employment only if highly educated. This suggests that very low fertility in Germany is related to an orientation toward a consumption society with the lifestyle of the married couple being paramount, although there has been a skewed welfare system that offered assistance for educated mothers. It is possible that both Germany and Austria are unique in that their long period of insecurity on the frontier of the cold war led to a 'live for the present' mentality. Their marriages are essentially partnerships of the northern European type that, in a consumerist age, can be regarded as a family even without children. So it is possible that the Germanic pattern may be typical of future very affluent countries.

Northwest Europe and the English-Speaking World

The models explaining very low fertility in Europe depend upon a comparison between very low fertility in southern, eastern, and central Europe and higher fertility in northwest Europe and the English-speaking European Offshoots. The dividing line is not clear cut: in 2002 total fertility in Canada was 1.5 and in Britain and Sweden 1.6. These are lower levels than in some countries with intermediate-type families or welfare systems: Belgium and the Netherlands 1.7 and France 1.9 (Population Reference Bureau, 2002). There is a clearer comparison with the total fertility of Australia 1.7, New Zealand 2.0, and the USA 2.1, but the latter two incorporate the higher fertility of the indigenous minority and recent Hispanic immigrants, respectively. The explanation given for higher fertility in Scandinavia is support for unmarried mothers, good and cheap childcare services, and the fact that the first pregnancy often occurs outside marriage (see Granstrom, 1997 on Sweden; Carneiro & Knudsen, 2001 on Denmark; Frejka & Calot, 2001 on Scandinavia). The explanation implied for the English-speaking countries is partly a universalistic welfare system, although that argument is hard to sustain for the USA (Myles, 1996). Perhaps more important is the implication that their economies are more liberal both in the changes that occurred over the last three decades and in a tradition stretching back to Adam Smith and David Ricardo. This system at present provides lower unemployment and a greater chance of the young finding jobs. Yet there is an anomaly here because the application of liberal economics has been blamed for causing greater uncertainty and hence lower birth rates everywhere. One could argue that this uncertainty now characterizes English-speaking peoples for a working lifetime in contrast to the relative security of central and southern Europe once a secure job is obtained, or that their populations have become inured to being economic and demographic risk takers. France remains a problem for the model builders. Its labour structure is fairly rigid and current unemployment relatively high, but it has moderately high fertility, perhaps explained by single-parent allowances, means-tested housing assistance, paid maternity leave, and subsidized childcare (Toulemon & de Guibert-Lantoine, 1998, pp. 17–18).

Asia

The development of models to explain very low fertility has been further confused by the attainment of such levels in non-Western societies—Japan, Taiwan, Hong Kong, and Macau (with South Korea's total fertility at 1.5). The explanations tend to mirror those for the Mediterranean except that none of these societies has experienced the trauma of high unemployment levels. In contrast, it is the availability of female employment that has provided explanations.

Most of those explanations have concentrated on Japan. Retherford, et al. (2001, p. 65) focused on the rising age of marriage: the singulate mean age for the marriage of females (SMAM) was stable for about 20 years before 1975 at around 24.5 years and then rose in the next 20 years by 3.2 years to 27.7 years, while over the same period the SMAM for males climbed from 27.6 to 30.7 years. By 1995, 5 per cent of women and 9 per cent of men were remaining unmarried for at least their reproductive lifetimes and these figures were likely to rise to 10 and 20 per cent, respectively, by 2010 (Retherford, et al., 2001, pp. 69–70). These changes were driven by huge increases in the proportion of women working before marriage, from 50 to 96 per cent between 1955 and 1995, and the proportion working for pay from perhaps 30 to 90 per cent (pp. 79–81). These changes in turn were the product of massive urbanization and a steep increase in education, among females from 7 per cent completing either junior college or university in 1965 to 40 per cent in 1997. Retherford, et al. (1996, p. 25) concluded that 'Many of the more important value changes affecting fertility are bound up with major educational and job gains by women, which have led to greater economic independence and increasing emphasis on values of individualism and equality between the sexes'. By 2001 Retherford, et al. had drawn the conclusion that the rising age of marriage for women in Japan could be attributed to the collapse of arranged marriages, the increasing acceptability of premarital sexual relations for females, and the fact that single women (and men) could continue to live in the parental family home

and enjoy a good lifestyle. The increased sexual freedom did not extend to cohabitation and ex-nuptial births (Dalla Zuanna, et al., 1998, pp. 187–8). As in the Mediterranean too, but perhaps even more so, Japanese women receive little help from husbands in household maintenance and childcare, so there are advantages in the postponement of marriage or its non-occurrence (Tsuya & Mason 1995, p. 162).

Japan's social welfare system was originally fashioned after that of Bismarck's Germany and has been sustained by a strong feeling that the multi-generation family should be the main provider of welfare. This is the model now adopted widely in Asia, notably in Japan, Taiwan, South Korea, Hong Kong, and Singapore, where a full welfare state is seen as essentially a Western necessity (Goodman & Peng, 1996, pp. 200–4). It is noteworthy that very low fertility was postponed in Singapore and probably avoided in Malaysia by government exhortation and action.

Toward a Comprehensive Theory of Very Low Fertility

As industrialization spreads and incomes rise, the evidence grows that rich, highly urbanized and educated countries with few families working in agriculture may not reproduce themselves. Simply, the family is no longer the production unit. The explanatory models showing why the postmodern values of northern Europe led to low fertility, and how the high rates of unemployment among Italian and Spanish young adults did the same, are impressive. But northern Europe is now being used, somewhat dubiously, as an example of relatively high fertility, and the fact is ignored that the huge mid-1990s unemployment differentials between Spain (and, to a lesser extent, Italy) and northern Europe have largely disappeared (*Economist*, 2002b). They may never return, for demographic reasons: in Italy, for example, new entrants to the labour force constituted annually about 2.5 per cent of the total in 1960 and 1.5 per cent in 2000, compared with a probable 1.0 per cent in 2030, while their ratio to retirements for those three dates can be calculated as 2.1, 1.0, and 0.9 per cent, respectively (United Nations, 2001b).

Too many problems arise from using a single model based on welfare systems or family type. Central Europe and Japan do not easily fit the Italian model, and the fertility differential between north-western Europe and the rest of Europe is too small to be taken very seriously. Perhaps what needs explanation is the curiously high fertility of the USA, and even that may be largely ascribable to a highly fertile immigration stream from Latin America.

It is clear that rich, well-educated, urbanized countries do not necessarily exhibit replacement-level fertility, and many may never do so again. Consumerism, a focus on job satisfaction, increasing need for dual incomes, a perception among many young people that raising children is simply too expensive, and a tendency for partnering rather than parenting to provide the family core are likely to reduce fertility. Better contraception and easier access to sterilization and abortion have provided the means for achieving any level of fertility, no matter how low. The population debate of the second half of the twentieth century provided the young with justification for not replacing themselves. Fertility has not been declining particularly smoothly, but then forces supporting replacement fertility are no longer strong enough to resist sudden crises. All young adults were affected by the contraceptive and attitudinal revolutions of the 1960s. Most were jolted by the economic crisis of the 1970s and have been left insecure by the liberal economic revolution that attempted to answer that crisis. This solution, together with the continuing integration into the European Union, led to widespread unemployment in southern Europe as did the even more severe economic solutions that provided shock therapy for post-Communist eastern Europe. Some of these crises may prove to be temporary, but fertility is unlikely to return to the pre-crisis level. One guarantee of that is the probable survival of liberal economics, seemingly necessary to provide the continuing economic growth expected by all societies, and the associated limitations placed on the welfare state and the consequent widespread

feeling of insecurity among young adults. And young adults are not more likely to be listened to by politicians, as the fertility decline ensures that they are a diminishing proportion of the electorate. The new economic order is unlikely to divert the proportion of national income that eastern Europe found necessary to raise its fertility modestly in the 1970s and 1980s. It is possible that the temptations of the consumer society, a sufficiently emotionally fulfilling partnership between husband and wife, and societal insecurity arising from the Second World War with a long subsequent period next to the Iron Curtain are all that is needed to explain Germany's descent into very low fertility.

It would be unwise to overemphasize sexual or generational conflict in the path to overcoming very low fertility. Mediterranean and East Asian husbands are probably more reluctant to undertake housework and childcare or to forgo their wives' earnings than they are to argue for more children. Similarly, parents are often more likely to take pride in their daughters' successful careers than to demand grandchildren.

In the long run Davis & van den Oever (1982, p. 511) may be right in stating that a social order that does not reproduce itself will be replaced by another, and it may be, as Westoff maintained (1983, p. 103), that some institutional solution will emerge. If the required major institutional change occurs it will probably do so only as the result of promoted national hysteria about the passing of peoples and cultures and the dire consequences for national security, accompanied by fairly lucrative rewards for childbearing. This is not at all certain, since conservationists' claims, with varying degrees of proof, of an overuse of resources or deteriorating lifestyles may provide sufficient offsetting resistance.

At present, there is little public consensus on whether low fertility is a concern and how best to confront it, if at all. A study for the years 1998–99 of 417 newspapers and magazines in 11 countries (USA, UK, Australia, New Zealand, Germany, Austria, Switzerland, France, Spain, Italy, and Japan) showed that as yet there is only limited discussion of low fertility, but more on the impact of women working, changing lifestyles, limited government support for families, and controversy about the move towards liberal economics (Stark & Kohler, 2002). People used to living for the here and now may have difficulties appreciating the longterm consequences beyond their immediate horizon.

Furthermore, if the explanations provided by the Mediterranean, largely the Italian model, centred on patriarchy and the breadwinner, are correct, then the tendency to fall below replacement-level fertility as incomes rise will eventually occur throughout much of the rest of the world because patriarchy is widespread throughout Asia and Africa,

More generally, a global economy governed by liberal economics creating a high degree of economic individual insecurity may be incompatible with societal replacement. Cohort fertility levels are quite likely to move to ever-lower plateaus, each transition being governed by some severe shock to the system. The mechanisms may be ever fewer couples planning to have more than two children, some deliberately remaining childless or settling for one child, but more failing to achieve a two-child family because of intervening temptations for education, occupational advance, travel, companionate pleasures, or expensive housing.

There are too many different groups of countries with very low fertility and different specific explanations for their situations for us not to conclude that there must be a common deeper explanation for all their conditions. Overarching conditions common to all developed countries determine fertility decline, but local and sometimes transient idiosyncrasies shape the timing and tempo (see Watkins, 1990). That explanation at its broadest must be the creation of a world economic system where children are of no immediate economic value to their parents. Related integral factors include, among other things, rising educational attainment for women and labour force participation. Yet, differences at the national level in legislation, policies, and the response of the population to these institutional settings, as well as family structures, partner relations, childcare expenses, and attitudes towards children determine the shape of the decline. Certainly at present the situation is aggravated by many peoples feeling the cold blasts of liberal economics to a greater extent than previously, but the acceptance of liberal economic policies is largely the outcome of the decision to award economic growth a higher priority than demographic growth. It may be a system to which the world will adjust, much as it is claimed the Anglo-Saxon world has.

The broadest explanation would echo the 1937 view of Kingsley Davis (1997) that ultimately the reproduction of the species is not easily compatible with advanced industrial society. This is a consequence of that society's rewards in the form of a career for women outside the home and the almost measureless temptations of the modern consumer society. The example of the richest countries, and the impact of modern advertising in the context of a global economy and a near-global political system, makes people in poorer countries yearn for the same possessions, especially motor cars, often giving the desire for such possessions priority over children. There is an extraordinary simultaneity in the contemporary world. Children do not easily fit in with a great deal of travel, and the entertainment they provide can be replaced by the electronic media and other pleasures. Yet couples will probably continue to regard two children as 'ideal', partly because they provide a unique and different kind of fulfillment, and usually admire even parents who make little impression on their peers. There is an awareness too that children will ultimately build up a network of relatives, the only adequate network many people may possess; and that, even in a well-insured welfare state, children may be needed in old age for company as well as physical and financial assistance. These advantages may prove to be sufficient to raise fertility to replacement level or higher in nationalistic states facing declining numbers and with a mandate from their electorate to spend hugely to overcome the difficulties faced by women or couples who want all the modern world can provide but who, if that provision can be maintained, are willing to have children as well. This time may not come for decades but it is likely that prototypes will begin to develop.

References

Abbasi-Shavazi, Mohammed Jalal & Peter McDonald. 2002. A comparison of fertility patterns of European immigrants in Australia with those in the countries of origin. *Genus 58*(1), 53–76.

Ahn, Namkee & Pedro Mira. 2001. Job bust, baby bust? Evidence from Spain. *Journal of Population Economics 14*(3), 505–21.

Anderson, Michael. 1998. Highly restricted fertility: Very small families in the British fertility decline. *Population Studies 52*(2), 177–199.

Aries, Philippe. 1962. *Centuries of Childhood*. London: Jonathan Cape.

———. 1980. Two successive motivations for the declining birth rate in the West. *Population and Development Review 6*(4), 645–650.

Bagavos, Christos & Claude Martin. 2001. Low fertility, family and public policies. Synthesis Report of the Annual Seminar of the European Observatory on Family Matters, Seville, Spain, 15–16 September 2001. Vienna: Austrian Institute for Family Studies.

Banfield, Edward C. 1958. *The Moral Basis of a Backward Society*. Glencoe, IL: The Free Press.

Bernhardt, Eva M. 1993. Fertility and employment. *European Sociological Review 9*(1), 25–47.

Bettio, Francesca & Paola Villa. 1998. A Mediterranean perspective on the breakdown of the relationship between participation and fertility. *Cambridge Journal of Economics 22*, 137–71.

Billari, Francesco C., Maria Castiglioni, Teresa Castro Martin, Francesca Michielin, & Fausta Ongaro. 2000. Household and union formation in a Mediterranean fashion: Italy and Spain. In E. Klijking & M. Corijn (Eds), *Fertility and Partnership in Europe: Findings and Lessons from Comparative Research* (vol. 2, pp.17–41). New York/Geneva: United Nations.

Billari, Francesco C. & Hans-Peter Kohler. 2000. The impact of union formation dynamics on first births in West Germany and Italy: are there signs of convergence? In E. Klijking & M. Corijn (Eds), *Fertility and Partnership in Europe: Findings and Lessons from Comparative Research* (vol. 2, pp. 43–58). New York/Geneva: United Nations.

Bongaarts, John. 2001. Fertility and reproductive preferences in post-transitional societies. In R.A. Bulatao & J.B. Casterline (Eds), *Global Fertility Transition*, Supplement to *Population and Development Review 27*, 260–81.

———. 2002. The end of fertility transition in the developed world. *Population and Development Review 28*(3), 419–43.

Bongaarts, John & Griffith Feeney. 1998. On the quantum and tempo of fertility. *Population and Development Review 24*(2), 271–91.

Caldwell, John C. 1982. An explanation of the continued fertility decline in the West: stages, succession and crisis. In John C. Caldwell, *Theory of Fertility Decline* (pp. 233–66). London: Academic Press.

Caldwell, John C. 2001. The globalization of fertility behavior. In R.A. Bulatao & J.B. Casterline (Eds), *Global Fertility Transition*, Supplement to *Population and Development Review 27*, 93–115.

Caldwell, John C., Pat Caldwell, Michael Bracher, & Gigi Santow. 1988. The contemporary marriage and fertility revolutions in the West: the explanations provided by Australian participants. *Journal of the Australian Population Association 5*(2), 113–45.

Caldwell, John C., Pat Caldwell, & Peter McDonald. 2002. Policy responses to low fertility and its consequences: a global survey. *Journal of Population Research 19*(1), 1–24.

Carneiro, Isabella & Lisbeth B. Knudsen. 2001. *Denmark: Comparable FFS-data*. Country Report, Fertility and Family Surveys in Countries of the ECE Region, Economic Studies No. 10t. Geneva: United Nations Economic Commission for Europe, and New York: United Nations Population Fund.

Carlson, Elwood & Megurni Omori. 1998. Fertility regulation in a declining state economy: Bulgaria, 1976–1995. *International Family Planning Perspectives 24*(4), 184–7.

Castles, Francis G. 1994. On religion and public policy: does Catholicism make a difference? *European Journal of Political Research 25*(1), 19–40.

———. 2002. The world turned upside down: below replacement fertility, changing preferences and family-friendly public policy in 21 OECD countries. Seminar paper, Demography Program, Australian National University, Canberra, 23 July 2002.

Charles, Enid. 1934. *The Menace of Under-population*. London: Watts.

Chesnais, Jean-Claude. 1996. Fertility, family and social policy in contemporary western Europe. *Population and Development Review 22*(4), 729–39.

————. 2001. Comment: a march toward population recession. In R.A. Bulatao & J.B. Casterline (Eds), *Global Fertility Transition* (pp. 255–9).

Coghlan, Timothy A. 1903. *The Decline of the Birth-rate in New South Wales and Other Phenomena of Childbirth: An Essay in Statistics.* Sydney: New South Wales Government Printer.

Conrad, Christoph, Michael Lechner, & Wolf Werner. 1996. East German fertility after unification: crisis or adaption? *Population and Development Review* 22(2), 331–58.

Dalla Zuanna, Gianpiero. 2001. The banquet of Aeolus: a familistic interpretation of Italy's lowest low fertility. *Demographic Research* 4(5), 133–62.

Dalla Zuanna, Gianpiero, Makoto Atoh, Maria Castiglioni, & Katsuhisa Kojima. 1998. Late marriage among young people: the case of Italy and Japan. *Genus* 54(3–4), 187–232.

Dalla Zuanna, Gianpiero & Letizia Mencarini. 2002. Gender dynamics on sex within young Italian couples. Paper presented to Seminario Internazionale di Studio, Milazzo, 20–22 June 2002.

Davis, Kingsley. 1984. Wives and work: consequences of the sex role revolution. *Population and Development Review* 10(3), 397–417.

————. 1997 [1937]. Reproductive institutions and the pressure for population. *Sociological Review* July 1937: 289–306, reprinted as 'Kingsley Davis on reproductive institutions and the pressure for population', Archives, *Population and Development Review* 23(3), 611–24.

Davis, Kingsley & Pietronella van den Oever. 1982. Demographic foundations of new sex roles. *Population and Development Review* 8(3), 495–511.

Delgado, Margarita & Teresa Castro Martin. 1999. *Spain.* Standard Country Reports, Fertility and Family Surveys in Countries of the ECE Region. Economic Studies No. 10i. Geneva: United Nations Economic Commission for Europe, and New York: United Nations Population Fund.

Delgado Pérez, Margarita & Massimo Livi-Bacci. 1992. Fertility in Italy and Spain: the lowest in the world. *Family Planning Perspectives* 24(4), 162–7, 171.

Demeny, Paul. 1997. Replacement-level fertility: the implausible endpoint of the demographic transition. In G.W. Jones, et al. (Eds), *The Continuing Demographic Transition* (pp. 94–110). Oxford: Clarendon Press.

————. 2003. Population policy dilemmas in Europe at the dawn of the twenty-first century. *Population and Development Review* 29(1), 1–28.

Demographic and Health Surveys (DHS). 2001. *Armenia: Demographic and Health Survey 2000.* Yerevan: National Statistical Service and Ministry of Health, and Calverton, MD: ORC Macro.

De Sandre, Paolo. 2000. Patterns of fertility in Italy and factors of its decline. *Genus* 56(1–2), 19–54.

Dumont, Arsène. 1890. *Depopulation et Civilisation.* Paris: Lecrosnier et Babé.

Eberstadt, Nicholas. 1994. Demographic shocks after communism: Eastern Germany, 1989–93. *Population and Development Review* 20(1), 137–52.

Economist, The. 2002a. Employment costs. Unemployment, 365(8299), 92.

Economist, The. 2002b. Unemployment, 365(8301), 92.

Esping-Andersen, Gøsta. 1996. Welfare states without work: the impasse of labour shedding and familialism in Continental European social policy. In G. Esping-Andersen (Ed.), *Welfare States in Transition: National Adaptions in Global Economics* (pp.66–87). London: Sage.

Frejka, Tomas & Gérard Calot. 2001. Cohort reproductive patterns in the Nordic countries. *Demographic Research* 5, 125–86.

Frejka, Tomas & John Ross. 2001. Paths to subreplacement fertility: the empirical evidence. In R.A. Bulatao & J.B. Casterline (Eds), *Global Fertility Transition* (pp. 213–14).

Gallup Organization. 1997. Global study of family values. Special Reports, Gallup Poll News Service.

Gauthier, Anne H. 1996. *The State and the Family: A Comparative Study of Family Policies in Industrialized Countries.* Oxford: Clarendon Press.

————. 2002. Family policies in industrialized countries: is there convergence? *Population* (English edition) 57(3), 447–74.

George, Vic. 1996. The future of the welfare state. In V. George & P. Taylor-Gooby (Eds), *European Welfare Policy: Squaring the Welfare Circle* (pp.1–30). New York: St Martin's Press.

Georges, Eugenia. 1996. Abortion policy and practice in Greece. *Social Science and Medicine* 42(4), 509–519.

Goldstone, J.A. 1986. The demographic revolution in England: a re-examination. *Population Studies* 40(1), 5–33.

Goodman, Roger & Ito Pengo. 1996. The East Asian welfare states: peripatetic learning, adaptive change and nation building. In G. Esping-Andersen (Ed.), *Welfare States in Transition: National Adaptions in Global Economics* (pp. 192–224). London: Sage.

Goody, Jack. 1976. *Production and Reproduction: A Comparative Study of the Domestic Domain.* Cambridge: Cambridge University Press.

———. 1983. *The Development of the Family and Marriage in Europe.* Cambridge: Cambridge University Press.

———. 1996. Comparing family systems in Europe and Asia: are there different sets of rules? *Population and Development Review 22*(1), 1–20.

Granstrom, Fredrik. 1997. *Sweden.* Standard Country Report, Fertility and Family Surveys in Countries of the ECE Region, Economic Studies No. 10b. Geneva: United Nations Economic Commission of Europe, and New York: United Nations Population Fund.

Hajnal, John. 1965. European marriage patterns in perspective. In David V. Glass & David E.C. Eversley (Eds), *Population in History* (pp. 101–43). London: Edward Arnold.

———. 1982. Two kinds of preindustrial household formation system. *Population and Development Review 8*(3), 449–94.

Hakim, Catherine. 1991. Grateful slaves and self-made women: fact and fantasy in women's work orientations. *European Sociological Review 7*(2), 101–21.

———. 1998. Developing a sociology for the twenty-first century: Preference Theory. *British Journal of Sociology 40*(1), 137–43.

Heilig, Gerhard, Thomas Buttner, & Wolfgang Lutz. 1990. Germany's population: turbulent past, uncertain future. *Population Bulletin 45*(4), 1–46.

Heinemann, Elizabeth D. 1999. *What Difference Does a Husband Make?* Berkeley: University of California Press.

Hobcraft, John. 1996. Fertility in England and Wales: a fifty-year perspective. *Population Studies 50*(3), 485–524.

Holdsworth, Clare & Angela Dale. 1999. Working mothers in Great Britain and Spain: a preliminary analysis, *CCSR Occasional Paper 14.* Manchester: Cathie Marsh Centre for Census and Survey Research, Faculty of Economics, University of Manchester.

Holzer, Jerzy Z. & Irena Kowalska. 1997. *Poland.* Standard Country Report, Fertility and Family Surveys in Countries of the ECE Region, Economic Studies No. 10d. Geneva: United Nations Economic Commission for Europe, and New York: United Nations Population Fund.

Hondroyiannis, George & Evangelia Papapetrou. 2001. Demographic changes, labor effort and economic growth: empirical evidence from Greece. *Journal of Policy Modeling 23*, 169–81.

Huinink, Johannes & Karl Ulrich Mayer. 1995. Gender, social inequality, and family formation in West Germany. In K.O. Mason & A.M. Jensen (Eds), *Gender and Family Change in Industrialized Countries* (pp.168–194). Oxford: Clarendon Press.

Irazoqui Solda, Mariana. 2000. Nest leaving and housing: a comparison between the Netherlands and Spain. Amsterdam Study Centre for the Metropolitan Environment. Amsterdam.

Jones, Catherine (Ed.). 1993. *New Perspectives on the Welfare State in Europe.* London and New York: Routledge.

Kaelble, Hartmut. 1989. *A Social History of Western Europe*, Daniel Bird (Trans.). Dublin: Gill & Macmillan.

Kalibová, Kveta. 2001. Changes in fertility patterns in the Czech Republic and Slovakia in the period of transition (1990–1999). Paper presented at European Association for Population Study (EAPS) Population Conference, Helsinki, 7–9 June 2001.

Kamarás, Ferenc. 1999. *Hungary.* Standard Country Report. Fertility and Family Surveys in Countries of the ECE Region, Economic Studies No. 10. Geneva: United Nations Economic Commission for Europe, and New York: United Nations Population Fund.

Kaufmann, Franz Xaver. 1993. Familienpolitik in Europa. In Bundesministerium für Familie und Senioren (Ed.), *40 Jahre Familienpoitik in der BRD* (pp. 141–67). Neuwied: Luchterhand.

Keyfitz, Nathan & Wilhelm Flieger. 1968. *World Population: An Analysis of Vital Data.* Chicago: University of Chicago Press.

Kohler, Hans-Peter, Francesco C. Billari, & José Antonio Ortega. 2001. Towards a theory of lowest-low fertility. MPIDR Working Paper 2001–032. Rostock: Max Planck Institute for Demographic Research.

———. 2002. The emergence of lowest-low fertility in Europe during the 1990s. *Population and Development Review 28*(4), 641–80.

Kohler, Hans-Peter & Iliana Kohler. 2002. Fertility decline in Russia in the early and mid-1990s: the role of economic uncertainty and labour market crises. *European Journal of Population 18*(3), 233–62.

Kohler, Hans-Peter & Jose A. Ortega. 2002. Tempo-adjusted period parity progression measures, fertility postponement and completed cohort fertility. *Demographic Research 6*(6), 91–144.

Köhler, Peter A. & Hans F. Zacher. 1981. *Ein Jahrhundert Sozialversicherung in der Bwtdesrepllblik Deutschland. Frankreich, Großbritannien. Österreich und der Schweiz*, Schriftenreihe für Internationales und Vergleichendes Sozialrecht Band 6. Berlin: Duncker & Humboldt.

Kreyenfeld, Michaela. 2002. Time squeeze, partner effect or self-selection. An investigation into the positive effect of women's education on second birth risks in West Germany. *Demographic Research 7*(2), 15–47.

Kreyenfeld, Michaela & Karsten Hank. 2000. Does the availability of child care influence the employment of mothers? Findings from western Germany. *Population Research and Policy Review 19*(4), 317–37.

Kuijsten, Anton C. 1996. Changing family patterns in Europe: a case of divergence. *European Journal of Population 12*(2), 115–43.

Lawson, Roger. 1996. Germany: maintaining the middle way. In V. George & P. Taylor-Gooby (Eds), *European Welfare Policy: Squaring the Welfare Circle* (pp. 31–50). New York: St Martin's Press.

Lesthaeghe, Ron. 1995. The second demographic transition in Western countries: an interpretation. In K.O. Mason & A-M. Jensen (Eds), *Gender and Family Change in Industrialized Countries* (pp.17–62). Oxford: Clarendon Press.

Lesthaeghe, Ron. 1977. *The Decline of Belgian Fertility, 1800–1970*. Princeton, NJ: Princeton University Press.

———. 1980. On the social control of human reproduction. *Population and Development Review 6*(4), 527–48.

———. 1983. A century of demographic and cultural change in western Europe. *Population and Development Review 9*(3), 411–35.

Lesthaeghe, Ron & Dominique Meekers. 1986. Value changes and the dimension of familism in the European Community. *European Journal of Population 2*, 225–268.

Lesthaeghe, Ron & John Surkyn. 1988. Cultural dynamics and economic theories of fertility change. *Population and Development Review 14*(1), 1–45.

Lesthaeghe, Ron & Paul Willems. 1999. Is low fertility a temporary phenomenon in the European Union? *Population and Development Review 25*(2), 211–28.

Lesthaeghe, Ron & Chris Wilson. 1986. Modes of production, secularization, and the pace of the fertility decline in Western Europe, 1870–1930. In A.J. Coale & S.C. Watkins (Eds), *The Decline of Fertility in Europe* (pp. 261–92). Princeton, NJ: Princeton University Press.

Maddison, Angus. 2001. *The World Economy: A Millennial Perspective*. Paris: OECD.

McDonald, Peter. 2000a. Gender equity. social institutions and the future of fertility. *Journal of Population Research 17*(1), 1–16.

———. 2000b. The 'toolbox' of public policies to impact on fertility—a global view. Paper presented at Low Fertility, Families and Public Policies, Annual Seminar of the European Observatory on Family Matters, Seville, 15–16 September 2000.

———. 2002. Sustaining fertility through public policy: the range of options. *Population* (English edition) *57*(3), 417–46.

Moeller, Robert G. 1995. Equality, difference, and the Grundgesetz. In Reiner Pommerin (Ed.), *The American Impact on Postwar Germany* (pp. 149–163). Providence: Bergbahn Books.

Morgan, S. Philip. 1991. Late nineteenth- and early twentieth-century childlessness. *American Journal of Sociology 97*(3), 779–807.

Murphy, Michael. 1993. The contraceptive pill and female employment as factors in fertility change in Britain 1963–80: a challenge to the conventional view. *Population Studies 47*(2), 221–43.

Myles, John. 1996. When markets fail: social welfare in Canada and the United States. In G. Esping-Anderson (Ed.), *Welfare States in Transition: National Adaptions in Global Economics* (pp. 116–40). London: Sage.

Notestein, Frank W. 1945. Population: the long view. In Theodore Schultz (Ed.), *Food for the World*. Chicago (pp. 36–57). University of Chicago Press.

———. 1953. Economic problems of population change. In *Proceedings of the 8th International Conference of Agricultural Economists, 1952* (pp.13–31). London: Oxford University Press.

Ondrich, Jan & C. Katharina Spiess. 1998. Care of children in a low fertility setting: transition between home and market care for pre-school children in Germany. *Population Studies 52*(1), 35–48.

Ostner. Ilona. 1997. Lone mothers in Germany before and after unification. In Jane Lewis (Ed.), *Lone Mothers in European Welfare Regimes*. London: Jessica Kingsley.

Packer, Rita, Pat Caldwell, & John Caldwell. 1976. Female Greek group interviews in Melbourne. In John Caldwell, et al. (Eds), *Towards an Understanding of Contemporary Demographic Change: A Report on Semi-structured Interviews*. Australian Family Formation

Project Monograph No.4. Canberra: Department of Demography, Australian National University.

Palomba, Rossella. 2001. Postponement in family formation in Italy, within the southern European context. Paper presented at IUSSP Seminar on International Perspectives on Low Fertility: Trends, Theories and Policies, Tokyo, 21–23 March 2001.

Penny, Janet & Siew-Ean Khoo. 1996. *Intermarriage: A Study of Migration and Integration*. Canberra: Australian Government Publishing Service.

Peristiany, J.G. 1965. *Honour and Shame: The Values of Mediterranean Society*. London: Weidenfeld & Nicolson.

——— (Ed.). 1976. *Mediterranean Family Structures*. Cambridge: Cambridge University Press.

Philipov, Dimiter. 2001. *Bulgaria*. Standard Country Report, Fertility and Family Surveys of Countries in the ECE Region, Economic Studies No. 10u. Geneva: United Nations Economic Commission for Europe, and New York: United Nations Population Fund.

Pinnelli, Antonella. 1995. Women's condition, low fertility, and emerging union patterns in Europe. In K.O. Mason & A-M. Jensen (Eds), *Gender and Family Change in Industrialized Countries* (pp. 82–101). Oxford: Clarendon Press.

Pinnelli, Antonella & Alessandra De Rose, 2001. Delayed fertility in Europe: determinants and consequences. Paper presented at European Association for Population Study (EAPS) Population Conference, Helsinki. 7–9 June 2001.

Pollard, Michael S. & Zheng Wu. 1998. Divergence of marriage in Quebec and elsewhere in Canada. *Population and Development Review 24*(2), 329–56.

Population Reference Bureau. 2002. *2002 World Population Data Sheet*. Washington, DC.

Price, Charles. 1994. Ethnic intermixture in Australia. *People and Place 2*(4); 8–11.

Prioux, France. 2002. Recent demographic developments in France. *Population* (English edition) *57*(4–5), 689–728.

Puy, Jimena. 2001. Socio-economic determinants of fertility in Spain: 1975–2000. Paper presented at European Association for Population Study (EAPS) Population Conference, Helsinki, 7–9 June 2001.

Reher, David S. 1997. *Perspectives on the Family in Spain, Past and Present*. Oxford: Clarendon Press.

———. 1998. Family ties in western Europe: persistent contrasts. *Population and Development Review 24*(2), 203–234.

Retherford, Robert D., Naohiro Ogawa, & Rikiya Matsukura. 2001. Late marriage and less marriage in Japan. *Population and Development Review 27*(1); 65–102.

Retherford, Robert D., Naohiro Ogawa, & Satomi Sakamoto. 1996. Values and fertility change in Japan. *Population Studies 50*(1), 5–25.

Rindfuss, Ronald R., Karin L. Brewster, & Andrew L. Kavee. 1996. Women, work and children: behavioral and attitudinal change in the United States. *Population and Development Review 22*(3); 457–82.

Ruzicka, Lado T. & John C. Caldwell. 1977. *The End of Demographic Transition in Australia*, Family Formation Project Monograph, No.5. Canberra: Department of Demography, Australian National University.

Rychta iková, Jitka & Jaroslav Kraus. 2001. *Czech Republic*. Standard Country Report, Fertility and Family Surveys in Countries of the ECE Region, Economic Studies No. l0v. Geneva: United Nations Economic Commission for Europe, and New York: United Nations Population Fund.

Ryder, Norman B. 1979. The future of American fertility. *Social Problems 26*(3), 359–70.

Santow, Gigi & Michael Bracher. 1999. Traditional families and fertility decline: lessons from Australia's Southern Europeans. In Richard Leete (Ed.), *Dynamics of Values in Fertility Change* (pp. 51–77). Oxford: Oxford University Press.

Schaffer, Harry G. 1981. *Women in the Two Germanies*. New York: Pergamon Press.

Simons, John. 1986. Culture, economy and reproduction in contemporary Europe. In David Coleman & Roger Schofield (Eds), *The State of Population Theory: Forward from Malthus* (pp. 256–78). Oxford: Blackwell.

Sobotka, Tomas. 2001. Ten years of rapid fertility changes in European post-Communist countries: evidence and interpretation. Paper presented at European Association for Population Study (EAPS) Population Conference, Helsinki, 7–9 June 2001.

Standing, Guy. 1996. Social protection in Eastern and Central Europe: a tale of slipping anchors and torn safety nets. In G. Esping-Andersen (Ed.), *Welfare States in Transition: National Adaptions in Global Economics* (pp. 225–55). London: Sage.

Stark, Laura & Hans-Peter Kohler. 2002. The debate over low fertility in the popular press: a cross-national comparison, 1998–1999. *Population Research and Policy Review 21*(6), 535–74.

Symeonidou, Haris. 2002. *Greece.* Standard Country Report, Fertility and Family Surveys in Countries of the ECE Region, Economic Studies No. 10w. Geneva: United Nations Economic Commission for Europe, and New York: United Nations Population Fund.

Teitelbaum, Michael S. & Jay M. Winter. 1985. *The Fear of Population Decline.* London: Academic Press.

Therborn, Garan. 1995. *European Modernity and Beyond: The Trajectory of European Societies, 1945–2000.* London: Sage.

Toulemon, Laurent & Catherine de Guibert-Lantoine. 1998. *France.* Standard Country Report, Fertility and Family Surveys of Countries in the ECE Region, Economic Studies No. 10e. Geneva: United Nations Economic Commission for Europe, and New York: United Nations Population Fund.

Tsuya, Noriko O. & Karen Oppenheim Mason. 1995. Changing gender rates and below-replacement fertility in Japan. In K.O. Mason & A.-M. Jensen (Eds), *Gender and Family Change in Industrialized Countries* (pp. 139–67). Oxford: Clarendon Press.

United Nations. 2001a. *World Population Prospects: The 2000 Revision*, Volume 1, *Comprehensive Tables.* New York.

———. 2001b. *World Population Prospects: The 2000 Revision*, Volume 2, *Sex and Age.* New York.

van de Kaa, Dirk J. 1987. Europe's second demographic transition. *Population Bulletin 42*(1), 1–57.

———. 1996. Anchored narratives: the story and findings of half a century of research into the determinants of fertility. *Population Studies 50*(3), 389–432.

———. 1997. Options and sequences: Europe's demographic patterns. *Journal of the Australian Population Association 14*(1), 1–30.

———. 2001. Postmodern fertility preferences: from changing value orientation to new behavior. In R.A. Bulatao & J.B. Casterline (Eds), *Global Fertility Transition* (pp. 290–331).

Van Nimwegen, Nico, Marika Blommesteijn, Hein Moors, & Gijs Beets. 2002. Late motherhood in the Netherlands. Current trends, attitudes and policies. *Genus 58*(2), 9–34.

Watkins, Susan Colts. 1990. From local to national communities: the transformation of demographic regimes in Western Europe, 1870–1960. *Population and Development Review 16*(2), 241–72.

Westoff, Charles F. 1983. Fertility decline in the West: causes and prospects. *Population and Development Review 8*(1), 99–110.

Witte, James C. & Gert G. Wagner. 1995. Declining fertility in East Germany after Unification: a demographic response to socioeconomic change. *Population and Development Review 21*(2), 387–97.

Wrigley, E. Anthony & Roger Schofield. 1981. *The Population History of England, 1541–1871.* Cambridge: Cambridge University Press.

Wulf, Deirdre. 1982. Low fertility in Europe: a report from the 1981 IUSSP meeting. *International Family Planning Perspectives 8*(2), 63–9.

Zvidrins, Peteris, Ligita Ezera, & Aigars Greitans. 1998. *Latvia.* Standard Country Report, Fertility and Family Surveys of Countries in the ECE Region, Economic Studies No. 10f. Geneva: United Nations Economic Commission for Europe, and New York: United Nations Population Fund.

CHAPTER 14

Fertility Transitions in Developing Countries: Progress or Stagnation?

John Bongaarts

In recent decades, fertility has declined at a rapid pace in a majority of developing countries. Overall, the total fertility rate (TFR) of the developing world dropped from 6.0 births per woman in the late 1960s to 2.9 births in 2000–5 (United Nations, 2007). Declines have been most rapid in Asia, North Africa, and Latin America—regions where social and economic development have also been relatively rapid. Sub-Saharan Africa also experienced significant declines despite its lagging development. On average, these changes occurred more rapidly than demographers had anticipated, as is evident from the fertility projections made in the 1970s and 1980s, which were generally higher than the subsequent trends (National Research Council, 2000). The most recent projections made by the United Nations (2007) assume that the fertility levels of countries that are in transition will continue their decline until fertility drops slightly below replacement level.

Fertility in the developing world declined less rapidly in the 1990s than in earlier decades, however, and a few countries (for example, Bangladesh and Egypt) experienced fertility stalls or near stalls in mid-transition (United Nations, 2002). The possibility of a pause during an ongoing fertility transition was first raised in the mid-1980s by Gendell (1985), yet the issue was given little attention until recently because in the past stall have been relatively rare. Interest in the topic is now increasing as new survey data for additional countries emerge on stalls

in fertility and on contraceptive prevalence during the 1990s (Bongaarts, 2006; Eltigani, 2003; Ross, et al., 2004; Shapiro & Gebreselassie, 2007; United Nations, 2002; Westoff & Cross, 2006).

The main objective of this study is to analyze recent trends in the pace of fertility transitions in developing countries since 1990 to determine whether these transitions are decelerating and how widespread stalling or near stalling had become around 2000. After a description of the data sources, a regional overview of levels and trends in fertility is provided using estimates from Demographic and Health Surveys (DHSs) followed by a more detailed assessment of country-level trends. Country estimates of the pace of fertility decline are examined for a set of 40 countries in which at least two DHS surveys have been conducted (to assess the prevalence of stalling fertility) and for a subset of 29 countries in which three DHS surveys have been conducted (which permit analysis of change in the pace over time).

Data

This analysis relies on fertility estimates from countries with multiple Demographic and Health Surveys (excluding the former Soviet republics, because of their unique demographic and political history). For 40 countries presented in Table 14.1 at least two such surveys are available since the early 1990s.

Table 14.1 Years in which Demographic And Health Surveys were conducted in the 40 countries with more than one survey, by region

Region/country	Survey year		
	Third most recent DHS	Second most recent DHS	Most recent DHS
Sub-Saharan Africa			
Benin	—	1996	2001
Burkina Faso	1992–3	1998–9	2003
Cameroon	1991	1998	2004
Chad	—	1996–7	2004
Côte d'Ivoire	1994	1998–9	2005
Ethiopia	—	2000	2005
Ghana	1993	1998	2003
Guinea	1992	1999	2005
Kenya	1993	1998	2003
Madagascar	1992	1997	2003–4
Malawi	1992	2000	2004
Mali	1987	1995–6	2001
Mozambique	—	1997	2003
Namibia	—	1992	2000
Niger	1992	1998	2006
Nigeria	—	1990	2003
Rwanda	1992	2000	2005
Senegal	1992–3	1997	2005
Tanzania	1996	1999	2004
Uganda	1988	1995	2000–1
Zambia	1992	1996	2001–2
Zimbabwe	1994	1999	2005–6

Asia/North Africa

Bangladesh	1996–7	1999–2000	2004
Egypt	1995	2000	2005
India	—	1992–3	1998–9
Indonesia	1994	1997	2002–3
Jordan	1990	1997	2002
Morocco	1987	1992	2003–4
Nepal	1996	2001	2006
Philippines	1993	1998	2003
Turkey	—	1993	1998
Vietnam	—	1997	2003
Yemen	—	1991–2	1997

Latin America

Bolivia	1994	1998	2003
Colombia	1995	2000	2005
Dominican Republic	1991	1996	2002
Guatemala	1987	1995	1998–9
Haiti	1994–5	2000	2005–6
Nicaragua	—	1997–8	2001
Peru	1996	2000	2004–5

— = no third survey

The dates of the surveys vary, with the latest having been conducted around 2003 (on average) and the previous one around 1997 (on average), yielding an average interval of 5.8 years between surveys. In a subgroup of 29 countries, a third survey was available, and the years of the three successive surveys in this subgroup averaged 1992, 1998, and 2004. The availability of three surveys permits the examination of trends during two successive periods: the first period from about 1992 to about 1998 and the second period from about 1998 to about 2004.

The DHS uses standardized procedures and questionnaires for collecting data; therefore, estimates of measures from different surveys are highly comparable. Nevertheless, Eritrea is deliberately excluded here because the Eritrea 1999 survey was conducted shortly after a war with Ethiopia, and the fertility rate that was derived from the reported births in the three years before this survey was depressed as a result of the separation of spouses during this conflict (Blanc, 2004). In addition, the 1999 surveys conducted in the Dominican Republic and in Nigeria are not used. The 2000 survey of the Dominican Republic had a much smaller sample size than is typical for the DHS, resulting in unusually large sampling errors. The first country report for the 1999 survey in Nigeria presents persuasive evidence of substantial underreporting of events, resulting in the underestimation of levels of fertility and child mortality (National Population Commission [Nigeria], 2000). Fortunately, trends in reproductive behaviour in the Dominican Republic and Nigeria are available from earlier and later DHSs conducted in these two countries.

Estimates of fertility, as measured by the total fertility rate in the three years before the survey, are taken from DHS first country reports (www.measuredhs.com). The main indicator used below is the pace of fertility decline, defined as the absolute decline per year in the TFR between two successive observations. Fertility declined over time in most countries and intersurvey periods, and the corresponding pace is, therefore, usually positive. Unless otherwise noted, the determination of statistical significance of results presented below relies on one-tailed t-tests.

Results

Aggregate Trends in Fertility

Figure 14.1 plots regional trends in the (unweighted) average total fertility rate based on data for the 29 countries with three surveys in sub-Saharan Africa (n = 16), Asia/North Africa (n = 7), and Latin America (n = 6). For each set of countries three observations are plotted, giving estimates from successive surveys conducted in about 1992, about 1998, and about 2004. (The distances between years for successive surveys plotted in Figure 14.1 are proportional to the average time elapsed between the surveys.) Average fertility is higher in sub-Saharan African countries than in Asian/North African and Latin American countries throughout the observed period. Fertility declines are evident in all three regions, both in the most recent period and in the earlier period. In Asia/North Africa and in Latin America, the downward trend is steady throughout the two periods, and in sub-Saharan Africa the decline is slower in the later period compared with the earlier one. This finding is surprising because fertility declines tend to be most rapid in the early phases of the transition and to slow down after countries have reached midtransition (National Research Council, 2000), and sub-Saharan Africa

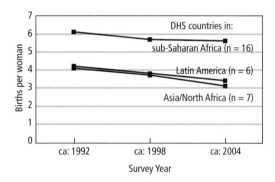

Figure 14.1 Unweighted average TFRs for three regional sets of countries across three successive DHS surveys

Demographic and Health Surveys

is earlier in the transition than Asia/North Africa and Latin America.

These results are confirmed in Figure 14.2, which plots the (unweighted) average pace of decline in the TFR for two successive time periods for DHS countries in three regions. For each regional set of countries, the first estimate is the pace during the interval between about 1992 and about 1998, and the second estimate is for the period between about 1998 and 2004. In the first period, the average pace of the TFR decline (in births per woman per year) varied little, from 0.07 in sub-Saharan Africa to 0.08 in Latin America. For reference, Figure 14.2 plots a dashed horizontal line at a value of 0.09 fewer births per woman per year, which equals the average pace of decline in all developing countries (excluding China) between 1965 and 1990 (United Nations, 2007). DHS countries in all regions in the first period show declines slightly (but not significantly) below this past aggregate pace. The results for the earlier period are, therefore, unsurprising and consistent with the pace of fertility decline in recent decades in the developing world overall (excluding China).

In contrast, in the more recent intersurvey interval, the average pace of fertility decline decelerated significantly in sub-Saharan Africa, dropping from 0.07 births per woman per year in the earlier

period to 0.02 in the later period ($p < 0.05$). The changes in pace in the decline in births per woman per year in Latin America and in Asia/North Africa are much smaller and not statistically significant. The average pace in the more recent period in Latin America and sub-Saharan Africa is lower than the average experienced between 1965 and 1990 in the developing world (excluding China), but the difference is significant only for sub-Saharan Africa.

Country-Level Trends in Fertility

The averages presented in the preceding section conceal wide variations in the levels and trends of fertility between countries. The analysis now turns to individual country data and in particular to the country variation in the pace of fertility decline. This section focuses on the set of 29 countries for which three successive surveys are available, thus allowing a comparison of the pace between the first two surveys with the pace between the two most recent surveys. This comparison can, therefore, shed light on the question of whether fertility transitions are decelerating.

Table 14.2 presents the TFR for three points in time and presents pace estimates for the decline in births per woman per year for the corresponding two successive intervals for countries with surveys. In the first interval, one country (Niger) had a negative pace, which indicates a rise in the TFR, whereas in the second interval TFR increases occurred in six countries (Cameroon, Guinea, Kenya, Mali, Rwanda, and Tanzania), all in sub-Saharan Africa. Small changes in fertility are often not statistically significant, however. This issue is examined further below.

Figure 14.3 plots the two successive estimates for the pace of decline in TFR for all 29 countries having three surveys. The vertical axis plots the pace during the interval between the DHS survey conducted approximately in 1992 and the one from approximately 1998; the horizontal axis plots the pace for the period between the two most recent surveys. The 45-degree diagonal represents observations for which the pace in the last interval equals the pace in the prior interval. Countries located below this

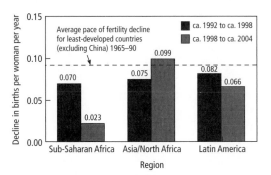

Figure 14.2 Unweighted average pace of TFR decline between ca. 1992 and ca. 1998 (DHS-2 & DHS-1) between ca. 1998 and ca. 2004 (DHS-1 & DHS-0) in three developing country regions

Demographic and Health Surveys

Table 14.2 TFR and pace of fertility decline for 29 countries for which three Demographic and Health Surveys are available

Country/region	Total fertility rate			Pace of fertility decline	
	ca. 1992	ca. 1998	ca. 2004	ca. 1992 to ca. 1998	ca. 1998 to ca. 2004
Sub-Saharan Africa					
Burkina Faso	6.5	6.4	5.9	0.02	0.11
Cameroon	5.8	4.8	5.0	0.14	−0.03
Côte d'Ivoire	5.7	5.2	4.6	0.10	0.11
Ghana	5.2	4.4	4.4	0.16	0.00
Guinea	5.7	5.5	5.7	0.03	−0.03
Kenya	5.4	4.7	4.9	0.14	−0.04
Madagascar	6.1	6.0	5.2	0.02	0.12
Malawi	6.7	6.3	6.0	0.05	0.08
Mali	7.1	6.7	6.8	0.05	−0.02
Niger	7.4	7.5	7.1	−0.02	0.05
Rwanda	6.2	5.8	6.1	0.05	−0.06
Senegal	6.0	5.7	5.3	0.07	0.05
Tanzania	5.8	5.6	5.7	0.07	−0.02
Uganda	7.4	6.9	6.9	0.07	0.00
Zambia	6.5	6.1	5.9	0.10	0.04
Zimbabwe	4.3	4.0	3.8	0.06	0.03
Asia/North Africa					
Bangladesh	3.3	3.3	3.0	0.00	0.07
Egypt	3.6	3.5	3.1	0.02	0.08
Jordan	5.6	4.4	3.7	0.17	0.14
Indonesia	2.9	2.8	2.6	0.03	0.04
Morocco	4.6	4.0	2.5	0.12	0.13
Nepal	4.6	4.1	3.1	0.10	0.20
Philippines	4.1	3.7	3.5	0.08	0.04
Latin America					
Bolivia	4.8	4.2	3.8	0.15	0.08
Colombia	3.0	2.6	2.4	0.08	0.04
Dominican Republic	3.3	3.2	3.0	0.02	0.03
Guatemala	5.5	5.1	5.0	0.05	0.03
Haiti	4.8	4.7	4.0	0.02	0.13
Peru	3.5	2.8	2.4	0.18	0.10

Demographic and Health Surveys

diagonal are experiencing a deceleration in the pace, and countries located above the diagonal are experiencing an acceleration. The dashed line represents the best-fitting line for the observation using an ordinary least squares regression.

This figure leads to two main findings. First, the relationship between the pace during the last and the next-to-last survey interval is not statistically significant ($p = 0.50$).[1] This relationship either does not exist or is too weak to detect in the available data sets, which contain inevitable measurement errors. Second, the number of countries below the diagonal exceeds the number of countries about the diagonal (17 versus 12), indicating that deceleration is more prevalent than acceleration.

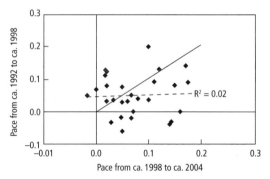

Figure 14.3 Relationship between pace of fertility decline from ca. 1992 to ca. 1998 (DHS-2 & DHS-1) and from ca. 1998 to ca. 2004 (DHS-1 & DHS-0) in 29 countries

Demographic and Health Surveys

To determine whether a change in the pace of a country's fertility is statistically significant, we must take into account the sampling errors in estimates. The DHS provides such estimates for the TFR.[2] A statistically significant deceleration in the pace of TFR decline ($p < 0.05$) occurred in four countries: Cameroon, Ghana, Kenya, and Peru. The presence or absence of a significant deceleration provides no information about the pace itself, nor does it indicate whether a fertility decline is or is not different

from zero. As shown below, a country can be stalling even though it exhibits no significant deceleration in the pace.

Stalling Fertility

The preceding analysis of changes in the pace of the TFR indicators was limited to the 29 countries with three DHS surveys. An analysis of the pace for one survey interval can be undertaken for a larger set of 40 countries with two successive surveys. The issue of whether fertility decline is stalling in these 40 countries is examined below.

Table 14.3 lists the 40 countries with at least two surveys. This set is divided into two groups: those with and those without a statistically significant decline in fertility in the most recent inter-survey period ($p < 0.05$). Among these 40 countries, 17 had no significant fertility decline. Notably, two-thirds (15 of 22) of the sub-Saharan countries show no significant decline, which is a much larger proportion than among Asian/North African and Latin American countries. Significant fertility declines occurred in all but one Asian/North African country (Turkey) and in all but one Latin American country (Guatemala).

The absence of a decline in fertility is often observed in pre- and post-transitional countries, yet it has been a rare occurrence in countries that are in the midst of a fertility transition. A period of no decline in countries in transition is usually referred to as a 'stall' in fertility. A stall implies that an ongoing fertility transition is interrupted by a period of no significant change in fertility before the country reaches the end of the transition.

To identify the stallers among the 17 countries with no significant fertility decline in Table 14.3, pre- and post-transitional countries in which the absence of decline is not a stall must be eliminated from the group. Countries are generally considered post-transitional when their fertility reaches replacement level or below. Only one country falls in this category: Vietnam, which had a TFR of 1.9 births per woman at the time of the last survey. The identification of pre-transitional countries is

Table 14.3   Significance of the pace of fertility decline between the last two DHS surveys, by region, 40 countries

	Sub-Saharan Africa	Asia/North Africa	Latin America
Pace not significant*	Cameroon (Chad) Côte d'Ivoire Ethiopia Ghana (Guinea) Kenya (Mali) Mozambique Nigeria Rwanda Tanzania Uganda Zambia Zimbabwe	Turkey	Guatemala
Pace significant*	Benin Burkina Faso Madagascar Malawi Namibia Niger Senegal	Bangladesh Egypt India Indonesia Jordan Morocco Nepal Philippines (Vietnam) Yemen	Bolivia Colombia Dominican Republic Haiti Nicaragua Peru

* Significant at $p < 0.05$, one-tailed t-test.
Parentheses indicate pre- or post-transitional societies

Demographic and Health Surveys

less straightforward. Historical studies often used a fertility decline of 10 per cent from pre-transitional levels as an indication of the onset of the transition. This approach cannot be used here because historical data are lacking, and the level of pre-transitional fertility cannot be determined accurately. Instead, a country is considered pre-transitional here if contraceptive prevalence among married women is 10 per cent or less.[3] By this criterion, three countries were pre-transitional at the time of the last survey: Chad, Guinea, and Mali. Pre- and post-transitional countries are indicated in parentheses in Table 14.3.

After excluding the pre- and post-transitional countries, 36 of the 40 countries remain and are considered to be in transition. Among these transitional countries, 14 (39 per cent) are in a stall, meaning that they did not experience a significant fertility decline between the two most recent surveys. More than half of the sub-Saharan countries with very small TFR declines (less than about 0.25 births per woman) are considered to have stalled because these declines are too small to be statistically significant.

This examination of the stalling of fertility decline was repeated for the earlier interval (between the DHSs conducted in or around 1992 and those conducted around 1998) (not shown). During this period, 9 of 25 transitional countries had no significant fertility decline: Bangladesh, Burkina Faso, Dominican Republic, Egypt, Haiti, Indonesia, Madagascar, Senegal, and Tanzania. All but one of the countries with a stall in the earlier period experienced a significant TFR decline in the next period (Tanzania is the exception). The pace of fertility decline in the inter-survey period following a stall is modest, however, with an average of 0.07 births per woman per year for these nine countries. This pace is lower than the average of 0.09 births for the developing world (excluding China) between 1965 and 1990. These findings suggest that stalls tend to be temporary and that after a stall the pace of fertility decline remains relatively low. Nevertheless, the number of countries for which a survey is available after a stall is too small to allow for a more definite conclusion.

Conclusion

Nearly all developing countries had high fertility levels in the 1950s. Since then, most of these countries have experienced substantial declines, and a growing number have reached replacement fertility. The record of fertility trends in the developing world suggest that once a fertility decline is underway it often continues without significant interruption until the replacement level of around two births per woman is reached. Stalls in midtransition before the 1990s (such as in Argentina, Chile, and Uruguay) were rare.

This study examines trends in fertility after 1990 using data from Demographic and Health Surveys. The main conclusion is that the average pace of fertility decline slowed significantly in sub-Saharan African countries from the first (about 1992 to about 1998) to the second (about 1998 to about 2004) interval between surveys. Two-thirds of sub-Saharan countries experienced no significant decline between the two most recent surveys compared with only one Asian/North African country and one Latin American country. Among countries in transition, more than half are in a stall.

The causes of the slowing pace of fertility change in sub-Saharan Africa are not examined here, but two factors may have played a role. First, according to conventional theory, socioeconomic development is a key driver of fertility decline (Bulatao & Lee, 1983; Caldwell, 1982; Easterlin, 1975; Notestein, 1953). During the 1990s, much of the world experienced substantial economic growth, yet the gross domestic product per capita in sub-Saharan Africa declined (World Bank, 2005). Moreover, life expectancy declined in sub-Saharan Africa owing to a rapidly spreading AIDS pandemic, while the rest of the world enjoyed rapid improvements in longevity (United Nations, 2007). Poorly performing economies and rising mortality are plausible factors contributing to the stalling of fertility in many sub-Saharan countries. Second, the fertility stalls may be attributable in part to the lower priority assigned to family planning programs in recent years in these countries (Blanc & Tsui, 2005; Cleland, et al., 2006).

The unexpected slowing of the pace of fertility decline around 2000 in sub-Saharan Africa has implications for future demographic trends, because minor variations in fertility trends have large effects on the future size and age structure of populations (Casterline, 2001). For example, according to the medium-variant estimate of the United Nations (2007), the population of sub-Saharan Africa is expected to more than double in size between 2005 and 2050, from 769 million in 2006 to 1.76 billion (this projection takes into account the large impact of the AIDS pandemic). The UN's high-variant projection estimates a population of 2.02 billion in 2050 because it assumes a slightly slower pace of fertility decline than the medium variant (reaching a TFR of 3.0 instead of 2.5 births per woman in 2050). If the recent slow pace of fertility transition persists, sub-Saharan Africa's population size could approach the high variant. This trend will likely have adverse effects on the region's prospects for social and economic development, food security, and the sustainability of natural resources (Alexandratos, 2005; Demeny & McNicoll, 2006).

Notes

1. Significance is calculated with a two-tailed *t*-test.
2. The standard error for the TFR is provided in an appendix to most DHS first country reports. For a few countries, this error was not available, and an estimate was obtained from a regression equation. In this regression, the log of the relative error (LRE) was the dependent variable, and the square root of the number of respondents (N) and the TFR were the independent variables:

   $$LRE = -0.014 \times N - 0.10 \times TFR - 2.14 \ (R^2 = 0.55).$$

3. The threshold of 10 per cent for overall contraceptive prevalence is used because on average it corresponds to a fertility decline of about 10 per cent according to regressions calculated by Ross and his colleagues (2005) and the United Nations (2003).

References

Alexandratos, Nikos. 2005. Countries with rapid population growth and resource constraints: Issues of food, agriculture, and development. *Population and Development Review 31*(2), 237–58.

Blanc, Ann K. 2004. The role of conflict in the rapid fertility decline in Eritrea and prospects for the future. *Studies in Family Planning 35*(4), 236–45.

Blanc, Ann K., & Amy O. Tsui. 2005. The dilemma of past success: Insiders' views on the future of the international family planning movement. *Studies in Family Planning 36*(4), 263–76.

Bongaarts, John. 2006. The causes of stalling fertility transitions. *Studies in Family Planning 37*(1), 1–16.

Bulatao, Rodolfo A., & Ronald D. Lee (Eds). 1983. *Determinants of Fertility in Developing Countries* (2 vols). New York: Academic Press.

Caldwell, John C. 1982. *Theory of Fertility Decline*. New York: Academic Press.

Casterline, John B. 2001. The pace of fertility transition: National patterns in the second half of the twentieth century. In Rodolfo A. Bulatao, & John B. Casterline (Eds), *Global Fertility Transition* (pp. 17–52). Supplement to *Population and Development Review 27*. New York: Population Council.

Cleland, John, Stan Bernstein, Alex Ezeh, Anibal Faundes, Anna Glasier, & Jolene Innis. 2006. Family planning: The unfinished agenda. *Lancet 368*(9549), 1810–27.

Demeny, Paul, & Geoffrey McNicoll. 2006. The political demography of the world system, 2000–2050. In Demeny, & McNicoll (Eds), *The Political Economy of Global Population Change, 1950–2050* (pp. 254–87). Supplement to *Population and Development Review*. New York: Population Council.

Easterlin, Richard A. 1975. An economic framework for fertility analysis. *Studies in Family Planning 6*(3), 54–63.

Eltigani Eltigani. 2003. Stalled fertility decline in Egypt, why? *Population and Environment 25*(1), 41–59.

Gendell, Murray. 1985. Stalls in the fertility decline in Costa Rica, Korea, and Sri Lanka. *World Bank Staff Working Paper* No. 693. Washington, DC: World Bank.

National Population Commission [Nigeria]. 2000. *Nigeria Demographic and Health Survey 1999*. Calverton, MD: National Population Commission and ORC/Macro.

National Research Council. 2000. *Beyond Six Billion: Forecasting the World's Population*. Panel on Population Projections, John Bongaarts, & Rodolfo Bulatao, Eds. Committee on Population, Commission on Behavioral and Social Sciences and Education. Washington, DC: National Academy Press.

Notestein, Frank W. 1953. Economic problems of population change. In *Proceedings of the Eighth International Conference of Agricultural Economics* (pp. 13–31). Oxford: Oxford University Press.

Ross, John, Edward Abel, & Katherine Abel. 2004. Plateaus during the rise of contraceptive prevalence. *International Family Planning Perspectives 30*(1), 39–44.

Ross, John, John Stover, and Demi Adelaja. 2005. *Profiles for Family Planning and Reproductive Health Programs: 116 Countries*. (2nd edn). Glastonbury, CT: The Futures Group.

Shapiro, David, & Tesfayi Gebreselassie. 2007. Fertility transition in sub-Saharan Africa: Falling and stalling. Paper presented at the session on 'Fertility declines: Rapid, slow, stalled' at the Annual Meeting of the Population Association of America, New York, 28–31 March.

United Nations. 2002. Fertility levels and trends in countries with intermediate levels of fertility. In *Completing the Fertility Transition*, Report of the

Expert Group Meeting on Completing the Fertility Transition, Department of Economic and Social Affairs, Population Division. ESA/P/WP.172/Rev.1. New York: United Nations. Retrieved from www.un.org/esa/population/publications/completing-fertility/completingfertility.htm

———. 2003. *Levels and Trends of Contraceptive Use as Assessed in 2002.* Department of Economic and Social Affairs New York: United Nations. ST/ESA/SER.A/190

———. 2007. *World Population Prospects: The 2006 Revision.* Department of Economic and Social Affairs, Population Division. New York: United Nations.

Westoff, Charles, & Anne Cross. 2006. The stall in the fertility transition in Kenya. *DHS Analytic Studies 9.* Calverton, MD: ORC Macro.

World Bank. 2005. *Economic Growth in the 1990s: Learning from a Decade of Reform.* Washington, DC: World Bank.

Basis Demographic Measures

Period measures of fertility are computed on the basis of current information, usually for a given year or some other specified interval. *Cohort measures* are derived from information based on specific generations of women. For example, we may speak of the cohort of women born in 1950 who completed their fertility in the year 2000 at the age of 50. Cohort fertility measures give the completed childbearing experience of women at the end of the cohort's reproductive lifespan.

1. Crude Birth Rate (CBR)

The *crude birth rate* (CBR) measures the number of births for a specified period per 1,000 population (for this and subsequent examples below, assume the interval is one year):

$$CBR = \frac{B}{P} \times 1,000$$

where B represents the number of births in a given year, and P is the corresponding mid-year population.

A number of drawbacks with the CBR make it unfavourable for comparative analysis. Two of them may be mentioned here. First, fertility is an age-specific phenomenon, but the CBR overlooks this. Second, since children are born to women only, the inclusion of the whole population in the denominator is problematic. The mid-year population includes women in the childbearing ages but also segments of the population with no risk of childbearing, notably men, children and the elderly.

2. General Fertility Rate (GFR)

The simplest age-limited measure of fertility is the *general fertility rate* (GFR). It expresses the number of births in a given year per 1,000 women aged 15–49:

$$GFR = \frac{B}{P_f^{15-49}} \times 1,000$$

where B is the total number of births born in a given year, and P_f^{15-49} corresponds to the mid-year population of females aged 15–49.

3. Age-Specific Fertility Rates (f_x)

The formula for the age-specific fertility rate can be written as follows:

$$f_x = \frac{B_x}{W_x} \times 1,000$$

where f_x symbolizes the age-specific fertility rate for a given age category x; B_x is the number of births to women aged x; and W_x is the mid-year female population aged x.

This formula reflects the number of births to women of a given age category in a given period per 1,000 women in the same age group. A clear advantage of age-specific fertility rates is that they can serve as the basis for the computation of other important fertility measures. One such measure is the total fertility rate.

4. Total Fertility Rate (TFR)

The *total fertility rate* (TFR) is a summary value of the total reproductive output for a given population during a specific point in time (such as a calendar year). As a single index of fertility, the TFR has the attraction of being easy to compute and interpret. It is a pure fertility measure that is not affected by age composition. It is also one of the few aggregate-level period measures of fertility that can be interpreted in terms of an individual woman's expected reproductive experience over her lifetime.

The TFR is the expected average number of children ever born to a randomly selected woman who survives to the end of her reproductive span (i.e. menopause or some suitably advanced age, such as 50 years), given that the current age-specific fertility rates in the population remain constant. To illustrate, we can think of a hypothetical cohort of 1,000 women who start reproducing at age 15, and who will eventually end their childbearing once they reach age 49. If this hypothetical cohort were to bear children in accordance with the age-specific fertility rates of a real population at present, then at the end of their childbearing years these hypothetical women would end up with a certain average number of children. That eventual average is the TFR. In terms of its computation, the TFR is the sum of age-specific fertility rates during a given calendar year for women aged 15 to 49:

$$\text{TFR} = \sum_{15}^{49} f_x$$

where f_x represents age-specific fertility *per woman*.

Age-specific fertility rates are often computed in five-year age categories (15–19, 20–24, 25–29, . . . , 45–49). In such cases the formula looks slightly different: the sum of age-specific birth rates is multiplied by 5 to take into account the width of the five-year age interval:

$$\text{TFR} = 5 \times \sum_{15-19}^{45-49} f_x$$

5. Cohort Fertility Rate (CFR)

We can assemble retroactive information for generations of women that have already passed through their reproductive lifespans, and with that information, compute their average completed family size for these specific generations of women. The input data for this would be period age-specific fertility rates over many years, beginning at some point in the past as far back as data are available, up to the most recent year of observation for which data are available. For instance, in Canada, vital statistics data are available from 1921. For each of the years since 1921 the age-specific fertility rates can be assembled into a matrix juxtaposing age and calendar year. The diagonal elements in such a matrix would represent the age-specific fertility rates of different cohorts of women. For each cohort, we would then compute the average completed fertility in the same manner described for the period TFR. The formula for the average completed fertility rate for cohort k is as follows:

$$\text{CFR}_K = \sum_{15}^{49} f_x$$

This says to sum all the age-specific fertility rates for women in cohort k. If the data are grouped into five-year age categories, then the formula is modified to take this into account, as described earlier in connection with the period TFR.

Questions for Critical Thought

1. Why are high birth rates in poor developing countries quite low in demographic terms?

2. What explains the persistence of low fertility in the most advanced countries of the world? Will fertility in these countries ever rise to the replacement level? Under what societal conditions might this happen?

3. How is the societal view of the child relevant to the explanation of either low or high fertility regimes?

Websites of Interest

Fertility and other reproductive health data are available online for the countries that have been participating in the *Demographic Health Surveys* (DHS). Visit the DHS website for statistical tables and maps based on data from over 200 surveys in over 75 countries: www.measuredhs.com/countries/

CANSIM is Statistics Canada's database of socioeconomic statistics, updated daily. Annual births by age of mother for 1991 to the latest year available can be obtained via the website: http://cansim2.statcan.ca/

Another useful StatsCan resource is its annual publication *Births*. The latest volume, for 2008, can be obtained from the website: www.statcan.gc.ca/pub/84f0210x/84f0210x2008000-eng.pdf

An important centre for demographic research is the *Vienna Institute of Demography*, which publishes studies on a variety of demographic topics, including fertility. Their website provides links to their publications: www.oeaw.ac.at/vid/index.html. Among these is the *European Fertility Data Sheet*.

Further Reading

Agyei-Menshah, Samuel. (1999). *Fertility decline in developing countries, 1960–1997*. Westport, CT: Greenwood.

Andorka, Rudolph. (1978). *Determinants of fertility in advanced societies*. London: Methuen.

Bentley, Gillian R., & Mascie-Taylor, C.G. Nicholas (Eds). (2000). *Infertility in the modern world: Present and future prospects*. Oxford: Oxford University Press.

Bledsoe, Caroline H., Lerner, Susana, & Guyer, Jane I. (2000). *Fertility and the male life-cycle in the era of fertility decline*. Oxford: Oxford University Press.

Derosas, Renzo, & van Poppel, Frans (Eds). (2006). *Religion and the decline of fertility in the Western world*. Dortrecht: Springer.

Dodoo, F. Nii-Amoo, & Frost, Ashley E. (2008). Gender in African population research: The fertility/reproductive health example. *Annual Review of Sociology, 34*, 431–52.

Eaton, J.W., & Meyer, A.J. (1953). The social biology of very high fertility among the Hutterites: The demography of a unique population. *Human Biology, 25*, 206–64.

Gustafsson, Siv, & Kalwij, Adriaan (Eds). (2006). *Education and postponement of maternity: Economic analyses for industrialized countries*. Dordrecht: Kluwer Academic Publishers/Springer.

Johnson-Hanks, Jennifer. (2006). *Uncertain honor: Modern motherhood in an African crisis*. Chicago: University of Chicago Press.

———. (2007). Natural intentions: Fertility decline in the African Demographic Health Surveys. *American Journal of Sociology, 112*(4), 1008–43.

Leving, Martin L., Xu, Xiaohe, & Bartokowski, Johan P. (2002). Seasonality of sexual debut. *Journal of Marriage and Family 64*, 871–84.

Menken, Jane, Trussell, James, & Larsen, Ulla. (1986). Age and infertility. *Science, 233*: 1289–94.

Myrskyla, Mikko, Kohler, Hans-Peter, & Billari, Francesco C. (2009, August 6). Advances in development reverse fertility declines. *Nature 460*, 741–3.

Morgan, Philip S., & Taylor, Miles G. Low fertility at the turn of the twenty-first century. *Annual Review of Sociology, 32*, 379–99.

Oppenheim Mason, Karen. (1997). Explaining fertility transitions. *Demography, 34*(4), 433–54.

Potts, Malcolm, & Campbell, Martha. (2008). The origins and future of patriarchy: The biological background of gender politics. *Journal of Family Planning and Reproductive Health Care, 34*(3), 171–4.

Potts, Malcolm, Diggory, Peter, & Peel, John. *Abortion.* Cambridge: Cambridge University Press.

Potts, Malcolm, & Selman, Peter. (1979). *Society and fertility.* London: Macdonald and Evans.

Udry, Richard J. (1996). Biosocial models of low-fertility societies. In John B. Casterline, Ronald D. Lee, & Karen A. Foote (Eds), *Fertility in the United States: New patterns, new theories,* pp. 325–36. Supplement to *Population and Development Review, 22.*

Yakibu, Scott T., & Gager, Constance T. (2009). Sexual frequency and the stability of marital and cohabiting unions. *Journal of Marriage and Family, 71*, 983–1000.

SECTION VII
Mortality and Health

Learning Objectives

By the end of this section, students should understand and be able to discuss the following:

- the epidemiological transition and its four stages
- the social determinants of health inequalities
- the sex differential in mortality and its biological and sociological determinants.

Introduction

Mortality Change through History

Throughout prehistory and until fairly recently in the long spectrum of human history, conditions for human beings were harsh and unpredictable. Life was punctuated by recurring famines, wars, and waves of epidemic diseases. As Preston reminds us, even though the world has seen gradual socioeconomic improvements through the ages, it wasn't until about the middle of the eighteenth century that death rates started to fall notably. Since then, the world has seen periodic setbacks—for example, during the two world wars and the global influenza epidemic of 1919–20—but in the overall sense, life expectancy has increased substantially. The gains humans have made since the start of the twentieth century have exceeded all the gains achieved since prehistoric times. In their recent study of highest observed life expectancies across the most developed countries, Vallin and Meslé (2010) show that between 1750 and the late 1700s, improvements in life expectancy were minimal; however, from 1790 to 1885, human life expectancy increased by about one-tenth of a year per annum, and in the period between 1886 and 1960, the gains rose to nearly one-third of a year per annum. Since 1960, the pace of increase in life expectancy has been just over one-fifth of a year per annum.

In the most advanced countries, the rapid increases in life expectancy since the start of the twentieth century involved a substitution of degenerative causes of death for deaths that, in the past, were caused by infectious and pathogenic diseases. This shift over time in cause-of-death structure represents what has been described as an *epidemiological transition*. In the less developed world, improvements since 1900 have also been substantial; unfortunately, a significant portion of the developing world is gaining less impressively in the fight against death. In some developing regions, improvements have stagnated or reversed in recent

years as a result of massive epidemics of infectious disease, famine, war, widespread poverty, and deteriorating living conditions. In this regard, two regions stand out: Africa, where the continuing HIV/AIDS epidemic has reached crisis proportions, and the former Soviet Union, where socioeconomic crises over the past five decades have led to reversals of life expectancy gains, particularly among men (Moser, Shkolnikov, & Leon, 2009). In parts of Africa, mortality improvements among children under 5 have been small compared with gains in other regions, and well short of targets that must be met in order to achieve the Millennium Development goal of reducing under 5 mortality by two-thirds between 1990 and 2015 (You, et al., 2010).

Epidemiological Transition

In 1971, Abdel Omran presented a systematic account of the historical shift in the pattern of disease and mortality based on the experience of the West. His explanation covers three stages that describe change in patterns of health and disease in the context of socioeconomic modernization. During prehistory, the leading killers were infectious and parasitic diseases (e.g. cholera, typhus, smallpox), along with famine, pestilence, and war. Today, chronic and degenerative diseases (such as cancer and heart disease) are the leading causes of premature mortality.

The Age of Famine and Pestilence (Prehistory to about 1750)

From earliest times up until the mid-eighteenth century, the pattern of population growth was cyclic, with minute net increments. Mortality and fertility rates were very high, fluctuating radically from year to year, and accounting for very little natural increase. The population in this stage of history was rural, with a 'few crowded, unsanitary, war-famine-epidemic–ridden cities of small and medium size' (Omran, 1971). Society was traditional, with a fatalistic orientation, sustained by rigid, hierarchical sociopolitical structures. The economy was based on an agrarian system, heavily dependent on manual, labour-intensive production. The leading causes of death and disease during this time were the epidemic scourges of parasitic and deficiency diseases, pneumonia-diarrhea-malnutrition complex in children, and tuberculosis-puerperal-malnutrition complex in females. Famines were frequent, and severe malnutrition was an underlying cause of most forms of disease and death. There were no medical care systems and few decisive therapies. People tended to rely on indigenous healing and witchcraft.

The Age of Receding Pandemics (about 1750 to the early 1920s)

Omran (1971) divided the age of receding pandemics into two sub-stages: an early stage and a late stage. The early stage saw improvements in agriculture and land use, coupled with modest developments in transportation and communication networks, which together served to encourage industrialization. The standards of living remained quite low, with some improvement toward the end of the period. Nutrition began to improve as a result of improved agricultural methods (e.g. crop rotation) and new technology designed to enhance yields, though children and women were still at a considerable disadvantage in terms of nutrition. Mortality remained high but showed signs of declining, as the fluctuations that had characterized the previous age became less pronounced. Average life expectancy increased to the low thirties, but females continued to be at high risk of dying in the adolescent and fertile years, while infant and childhood mortality were high. Urban mortality was higher than rural. The leading causes of death were endemic, parasitic, and deficiency diseases, epidemic scourges, and childhood and maternal complexes. Industrial disease increased. With regard to disease prevalence, tuberculosis peaked with industrialization and was generally more virulent in young females. Smallpox was chiefly a disease of childhood. Heart disease was still low, and death from starvation was less frequent. There were still no healthcare systems and few decisive therapies, the only hospitals of the time were seen as 'death traps'. People continued to rely on indigenous systems of healing, but personal hygiene and nutrition were starting to improve—slowly.

The late phase of the age of receding pandemics is described as characteristic of explosive population growth due to a sustained pattern of mortality decline coupled with high fertility, with a relatively young population. The 'takeoff' of sustained economic growth can often be traced to sharp stimuli such as scientific discovery or political revolution, which galvanize business and labour to reinforce gains in gross, real, and per capita income through reinvestment and speculation. This particular era of rising expectations touched nearly all segments of society. Continued improvements to agricultural practices led to greater availability of food and better nutrition. Industrialization brought more people to work in the cities. Hygiene and sanitation improved except in city slums, where poor living conditions grew worse. Gradually, life expectancy increased to around 40 years. Mortality declines favoured children under 15 and women in the reproductive ages. Infant mortality progressively dropped below 150 per thousand births. Pandemics of infection, malnutrition, and childhood disease receded during this stage, and although cholera swept through Europe in waves before disappearing, plagues declined dramatically. Infection remained the leading cause of death, but non-infectious diseases became more significant. Heart disease increased. Death from starvation was now rare, and many deficiency diseases, such as scurvy, started to disappear. Epidemics and famine receded, while childhood diseases and maternal death decreased in incidence. Environmental controls such as water filtration and refuse pickup began to be implemented in cities. A few decisive therapies and prophylactic measures were devised. Personal hygiene and nutrition improved.

The Age of Human-Made and Degenerative Causes of Death (early 1920s to the 1960s)

In sharp contrast to their ancestors in earlier ages, populations in the third age enjoyed relatively high life expectancy, approaching 60 years by the 1940s (though the sex differential in longevity favoured women increasingly with time). Infant mortality rates fell below 100 per thousand live births by the 1930s, and maternal death rates also declined substantially. Crude death rates in this stage declined rapidly to below 20 per thousand population. Fertility dropped to below 20 per thousand, with the occasional rise (for instance, during the postwar baby boom of the 1950s and 1960s). A progressive aging of the population saw more people survive to middle and old age. The leading killers during this stage were cancer, heart disease, and stroke. Infectious and parasitic diseases accounted for relatively few deaths on an annual basis; however, pneumonia, bronchitis, influenza, and some viral diseases persisted. Polio tapered off after a brief rise, while scarlet fever started to disappear. Tuberculosis, now low, persisted in slum populations and among older disadvantaged individuals. Smallpox was rare, and when it did occur, it was a disease of adults.

The society of this time was predominantly urban, with rural-to-urban migration, international migration, and natural increase in urban centres causing rapid population growth in cities. Scientific progress and technology helped produce considerable economic growth, leading to a consumerist society that was organized in accordance with rational bureaucratic principles. Public welfare and leisure spending grew, and large segments of the population enjoyed improvements in living conditions. Families were typically small, allowing women to strive for more options in their societal roles, including higher education and careers. In this context, people became extremely conscious of nutrition, especially as it affected the health of children and mothers. However, a tendency towards 'over-nutrition', thanks to increased consumption of rich and high-fat foods, contributed to increasing the risk of heart and metabolic diseases. Morbidity came to overshadow mortality as an index of health, as degenerative and chronic diseases prevailed, and mental illness, addiction, accidents, radiation hazards, and other pollution problems become more prevalent. As more decisive therapies became available, health systems gradually became oriented to preventive care. Against this backdrop, average age at death shifted out of childhood and young adulthood into older age brackets, with improvements in survival selectively favouring women more than men and the privileged more than the poor.

Sources of Epidemiological Transition

Opinions in the literature vary as to what factors were responsible for the transition away from pestilence and famine to the age of human-made and degenerative causes of death in European society. In this context, it is worth mentioning that one of the most lethal epidemics in history, the Black Death (or bubonic plague), after several outbreaks beginning in the fourteenth century, had receded and disappeared altogether by the end of the nineteenth century (Scott & Duncan, 2001). What caused the decline of plague and recurrent epidemics of other major infectious diseases? One perspective on this question considers the role of English physician Edward Jenner and his discovery in the late 1700s of the vaccine against smallpox, together with the practice of improved hygiene (Mercer, 1985, 1986, 1990; Razzel, 1974). Another view points to the role of modern medicine. A third hypothesis, attributed to Thomas McKeown and associates, is the *standards of living thesis* (McKeown, 1976; McKeown, Brown, & Record, 1972). It links the remarkable mortality declines that began midway through the nineteenth century to improvements in the standards of living and, most important, to improved nutrition, which we can assume allowed humans to better withstand infections and thus live longer. Yet in spite of its apparent reasonableness, this explanation continues to generate heated debates in the literature (see, for example, Hinde, 2003; Ostry & Franck, 2010).

What does the historical evidence have to say on the matter? While it is not unequivocal, it does indicate that modern medicine could not have been a major player until the third and fourth decades of the twentieth century, when germ theory was developed and, later, antibiotics (beginning with penicillin) were introduced. Further medical advances in the 1940s and 1950s included the introduction of blood transfusions and other therapies, which would save countless lives, especially those of women in their childbearing years (Berry, 1977). Neonatology, the study of infant health, was making important strides during this time, helping to reduce mortality rates among newborns. As well, significant public health interventions, such as new sanitation measures and the provision of clean water, must have contributed dramatically to the health of the population around the turn of the twentieth century, when these practices were introduced (Cutler and Miller, 2005; Preston, 1975; White & Preston, 1996). Overall, public health played an increasingly important role over the course of the twentieth century. Preston (1975), in a study reprinted here, shows that between 1905 and 1965, less than half of the mortality decline in the world can be attributed to rising per capita incomes and their indirect effects on health; the remaining survival gains can be attributed to the spread of medical and public health measures, first among the developed countries themselves, and later in the developing world. Some of the examples he cites are improvements in water supply and sewage disposal, campaigns to combat malaria, and immunization programs.

A Fourth Stage: The Age of Delayed Degenerative Diseases

In the United States and other high-income countries, death rates from heart disease declined by more than 30 per cent between 1968 and 1982. Most of this decline occurred among people in their late middle ages and older ages (Salomon & Murray, 2002; Vallin, 2006; White, 2002). In the view of

Olshansky and Ault (1986), this new trend heralded a fourth stage of epidemiological change: the 'age of delayed degenerative diseases'. It is characterized by the following principal features:

1. the continuation of slow and often fluctuating mortality declines that are increasingly concentrated in the later stages of life
2. a variable pattern of change in the average onset and duration of major chronic ailments, most notably cardiovascular diseases and, to a lesser degree, cancer.

This new epidemiological stage in the advanced societies points, on the one hand, to the continued dominance of chronic and degenerative diseases, but on the other hand, to the tendency for the onset of major disability from chronic diseases, especially vascular diseases, to occur later in life (thus 'delayed'). People afflicted by these chronic diseases are able to live longer on average as a result of advanced medical therapies. Rogers and Hackenberg (1987) add that in the fourth stage, many of the causes of premature mortality involve unhealthy lifestyles and behaviours, such as smoking and physical inactivity (see also Mokdad, et al., 2004).

Beyond the Fourth Stage

Vallin and Meslé (2010) note that the record for highest life expectancy has been held by different countries over the years. Around 1750, Sweden was the leader in life expectancy, whereas in 1850, Norway held the pole position. Today, Japanese life expectancy exceeds that of all other nations in the world. In these advanced societies, mortality rates have fallen to such low levels that today's newborns can expect to live well into their eighth decade of life or beyond. That is, mortality rates for children and for adults under 65 have fallen so low in these countries that further improvement in life expectancy at birth will depend almost completely on survival improvements among seniors (Hill, 1995). Demographers such as Vallin and Meslé have questioned whether indefinite gains in life expectancy are in fact possible for such advanced societies. According to Christensen and associates (in this volume), if the pace of life expectancy in developed countries over the past two centuries continues through the twenty-first century, most babies born since 2000 in countries such as France, Germany, Italy, Britain, the United States, Canada, and Japan (as well as most other countries with long life expectancies) will live to celebrate their hundredth birthdays.

A question remains: will these ever-extending lifespans be matched by a delay in the decrepitude that usually accompanies old age? Will society be able to provide sufficient care, assistance, and resources for the swelling population of ultra-citizens? Clearly, if future centenarians are able to stay healthy enough to continue working, they could help reduce the pressure on social services otherwise strained by increased demand for medical services just as the working population shrinks (due to recent trends of low fertility).

In 1980, James Fries proposed that the future pattern of mortality and morbidity in advanced societies will be characterized by a 'compression' phenomenon, whereby major disability and death would occur within an increasingly compressed period of advanced age; in other words, individuals would be generally healthy throughout most of their lives, but as they approached the maximum average age (which Fries estimated to be about 86) they would begin to experience major disability and illness. Under this scenario, the time spent in a state of debilitating infirmity, according to Fries, would be compressed into a relatively short period, very close to death.

Fries's theory has not gone unchallenged. Manton and Singer (1994), for example, found no empirical evidence for a 'compression' of survival probabilities among what they judged to be the healthiest subset of the human population: white American women. Their analysis across several historical periods is consistent with an 'expansion of survival' phenomenon rather than 'compression'. Manton and Singer found that life table survival probabilities of middle-aged and older American women had been improving over time (i.e. expanding into older and older ages). This challenges Fries's notion of a fixed upper limit to average human lifespan. More recently, Manton (2008) has shown that among the elderly in the United States there has been a continuation of survival improvements as well as notable declines in major disability. This suggests that recent generations of elderly people are healthier than previous cohorts of seniors and are living longer. This, too, runs counter to the 'compression' theory.

According to Vaupel (2010), there is mounting evidence for optimism surrounding these kinds of questions. Scientific evidence shows that over the past 20 years, human senescence (i.e. biological aging) has been delayed by a decade. Also remarkable is the fact that notwithstanding this trend, the rate of deterioration with age seems to be constant across individuals and over time. For Vaupel, this indicates that death is actually being delayed because people are reaching old age in better health. Further scientific progress is likely to help advance the frontier of survival and, in particular, healthy survival to even greater ages. Christensen and associates add that in the light of these trends, societies must plan for a growing elderly population living longer. Among other things, society will need to provide more healthcare services for an aging population and adopt a restructured model of working lives (see also Vaupel, 2010, on this point).

Health and Mortality Inequalities

Two of the chapters in this section deal with inequalities in health and mortality. Marmot addresses the social determinants of disparities in health, while Trovato and Lalu report on the narrowing sex differential in life expectancy at birth across industrialized countries. This long-established differential in favour of females widened considerably over the twentieth century; however, it has begun to narrow, in some countries as early as the 1970s and in many others since the early 1980s. Marmot, in his selection in this volume, examines the huge spread in life expectancy between the most disadvantaged and the most advantaged countries in the world—37 years in Sierra Leone versus 81.9 years in Japan. He notes that within some societies, the longevity gap between the most advantaged and the most disadvantaged can be as great as 20 years or more (examples: the Torres Straight Aborigines of Australia compared with the Australian population overall; the poor versus the rich in the US). A large body of research has identified nine key social determinants of what Wilkinson and Marmot (2003) refer to as 'the social gradient' in health:

1. *Stress damages health.* Circumstances that make people feel worried, anxious, and unable to cope (e.g. lack of control over work and home) are damaging to health and may lead to premature death.

2. *Early life conditions determine health in adulthood.* Important foundations of adult health are laid in early childhood. Ensuring that children have a good start in life means supporting mothers as well as their young children. The health impact of early development and education lasts a lifetime.

3. *Social exclusion and poverty are detrimental to good health.* Life is short where its quality is poor. Poverty, social exclusion, and discrimination, which cause hardship and resentment, cost lives. For example, people living on the street suffer the highest rates of premature death.

4. *Work conditions are important to health.* Stress in the workplace increases the risk of disease. People who have more control over their work have better health. For example, it is known that the incidence of coronary heart disease in men and women is highest among those having the lowest levels of control over their work.

5. *Unemployment and job insecurity damage health.* Job security increases wellbeing, health, and satisfaction. Higher rates of unemployment cause illness and premature death. The families of unemployed people suffer a higher risk of premature death.

6. *Social support is an important factor in health.* Belonging to a social network makes people feel cared for. Friendships, good social relations, and strong support networks improve health at home, at work, and in the community.

7. *Addictions are influenced by the social setting.* Individuals' use of alcohol, drugs, and tobacco is influenced by the wider social setting. People turn to these addictive substances to numb the pain of harsh economic and social conditions.

8. *Healthy food is important for good health.* Because global markets control the food supply, food is a political issue. Access to fresh vegetables and fruits is essential to reducing the risk of coronary heart disease.

9. *Transport.* Healthy transportation means less driving and more walking and cycling, supplemented with efficient methods of public transportation.

The Sex Differential in Health and Mortality

The female advantage in mortality and life expectancy is one of the most entrenched differentials across human populations (Lopez, 1983; Luy, 2003; Madigan, 1957; Stolnitz, 1955; Vallin, 1983). Only few exceptions have been noted (see Das Gupta & Shuzhuo, 2000; D'Souza & Chen, 1980; El-Badry, 1969; Mishra, Roy, & Retherford, 2004; Murphy, 2003; Nadarajah, 1983). Historical evidence for western Europe confirms that during the late nineteenth century, female life expectancy exceeded male expectancy by a margin of about two or three years, at a time when life expectancy was well below what it is today (Preston, 1976). This small female advantage in life expectancy in the past could have been greater were it not for women's high death rates from complications associated with giving birth (Henry, 1989).

Stolnitz (1955) established that the sex differential in mortality started to widen after about the second decade of the twentieth century, and that by the 1940s, females had gained an average of about

4 years of life over males. Preston (1976) confirmed that prior to large-scale modernization, the sex differential in mortality generally favours males, but that with increasing levels of modernization, the balance gradually shifts in favour of females. By the 1950s, the sex gap in the industrialized countries had grown to approximately 5 or 6 years, and by the 1970s, it had reached an apex of 7 or 8 years across most industrialized countries (Lopez, 1983). After the 1970s came a reversal of this trend, and the differential began to narrow. In Canada and Austria, for example, the sex difference in life expectancy at birth peaked around the mid-1970s and then began to decline, so that today the sex differentials in life expectancy in these two countries are virtually identical to the levels they had recorded in the mid-1950s—roughly 5.5 years in favour of females (Trovato, 2006).

This pattern of divergence and narrowing has been observed across a large number of industrialized countries (Glei & Horiuchi, 2007; Pampel, 2002, 2003; Trovato & Lalu, 1996a, 1996b). (A notable exception is Japan, where the difference favours women and continues to expand—see Trovato & Heyen, 2005.) Notwithstanding the recent narrowing trend, there are reasons to expect that the disparity in the average length of life between men and women will not close completely in the future. This raises two important questions. First, why should one expect an indefinite advantage by females? And second, why did the differential favour women for so much of the twentieth century and then begin to decline?

Biological and genetic differences between the sexes may provide part of the answer to the first question (Madigan, 1957; Perls & Fretts, 1998; Verbrugge, 1976; Waldron, 1976). The remainder of the puzzle is in large measure related to sex differences in acquired risks due to differences in the way males and females are socialized and therefore differences in behaviour (Hannerz, 2001; Veevers & Gee, 1986; Verbrugge, 1976; Waldron, 1976, 2000). Kramer (2000), in his review of the literature, describes the many behavioural risk factors that underlie the sex

differential in longevity. One of the most important is smoking (see also Case & Paxon, 2005; Doll & Peto, 1981; Lopez, 1995; Pampel, 2002, 2003; Peto, et al., 1992, 1996; Retherford, 1975; Waldron, 1986). While the smoking epidemic started earlier in history for men than for women, over recent decades (and particularly after 1960) there have been major declines in tobacco use among men, whereas smoking among women has increased. This divergence in smoking patterns has certainly contributed to the recent narrowing of the sex differential in life expectancy. Men have experienced significant reductions in smoking-related death, most notably from lung cancer and vascular diseases. For women, because of increased smoking, their gains in life expectancy over recent years have not been as large as those of men (Nathanson, 1995). Another key factor that has helped to narrow the sex gap in life expectancy is a significant reduction in male mortality from accidents and violence, except suicide (Trovato & Heyen, 2006; Trovato & Lalu, 1996b).

On the question of inherent sex differences underlying the male–female differential in mortality and health, Kramer writes that males' greater vulnerability begins very early in life—from the moment of conception, in fact—due to 'the biological fragility of the male fetus' (Kramer, 2000, p. 1609). Maleness seems to have intrinsic risks that are genetic/biological in origin. One of these intrinsic risks is thought to be hormonal in nature. It is believed that male mammals experience low immunocompetence—an organism's all-round ability to avoid the harmful effects of parasites—owing to the effect of the hormone testosterone, which is an immunosuppressant (Owen, 2002). Basically, testosterone is thought to alter the way that males allocate resources among competing physiological needs. Males may be unable to mount an effective immune response because the testosterone in their bodies has directed physical resources from the activity of fending off disease towards other metabolic activities (Owen, 2002). Thus, sex differences in immunocompetence may underlie the higher levels of male deaths from parasitic infections. But testosterone has also been implicated in higher rates of male deaths from other causes, including accidents and violence. Indeed, some biological scientists have called testosterone a 'toxic hormone' because of its supposed link to higher levels of risk-taking and aggression (Perls & Fretts, 1998).

A further reason for women's longevity advantage over men may be the inherently stronger female immune system (Pido-Lopez, Imami, & Aspinall, 2001). Males have higher rates of death from vascular diseases, especially coronary heart disease, and as this is a leading cause of death, this factor could account for a significant portion of the overall male disadvantage in mortality risk (Rogers, Hummer, & Nam, 2000). In both men and women, the mortality rate from coronary heart disease increases exponentially with age; however, the age-related rate rise in women lags behind the corresponding rate in men by 5 to 10 years (Smith, 1993). The female advantage in staving off vascular disease has been ascribed to the protective effects of female hormones, which account for differences in the way cholesterol is modulated in men and women (Smith, 1993). However, the incidence of cardiovascular disease in women rises sharply after the menopausal transition, when female hormones (most notably, estrogen) decline. With menopause comes a drop in the levels of HDL (high-density lipoprotein) cholesterol and a rise in LDL (low-density lipoprotein) cholesterol, which is associated with health problems including cardiovascular disease. Hormone replacement therapy has been shown to lower women's risk of heart disease. All of this reinforces the idea that estrogen plays an important protective role in women (Mendelsohn & Karas, 2005).

Works Cited

Acsadi, Gy, & Nemeskéri, J. (1970). *History of human life span and mortality.* Budapest: Akademia Kiado.

Berry, Linda G. (1977). Age and parity influences on maternal mortality: United States, 1919–1969. *Demography, 14*(3), 297–310.

Bobadilla, José Luis, & Costello, Christine A. (1997). Premature death in the New Independent States: An overview. In José Luis Bobadilla, Christine A. Costello, & Faith Mitchell (Eds), *Premature death in the new independent states* (pp. 1–33). Washington, DC: National Academy Press.

Caldwell, John C. (1986). Routes to low mortality in poor countries. *Population and Development Review, 12*(2), 171–220.

Case, Anne, & Paxson, Christina. (2005). Sex differences in morbidity and health. *Demography, 42*(2), 189–214.

Caselli, Graziella, Meslé, F., & Vallin, J. (2002). Epidemiologic transition theory exceptions. *Genus, 58*(1), 9–52.

Christensen, Kaare, Doblhammer, Gabriele, Rau, Roland, & Vaupel, James W. (2009, October 3). Aging populations: The challenges ahead. *The Lancet, 374*, 1196–208.

Coale, Ansley J. (1996). Age patterns and time sequence of mortality in national populations with the highest expectation of life at birth. *Population and Development Review, 22*(1), 127–36.

Cutler, David, & Miller, Grant. (2005). The role of public health improvements in health advances: The twentieth-century United States. *Demography, 42*(1), 1–22.

Das Gupta, Monica, & Shuzhuo, Lee. (2000). Gender bias in China, South Korea and India 1920–1990: Effects of war, poverty and fertility. In Shahra Razavi (Ed.), *Gendered poverty and well-being* (pp. 205–38). Oxford: Blackwell Publishers.

Doll, R., & Peto, R. (1981). The causes of cancer: Quantitative estimates of avoidable risks of cancer in the United States today. *Journal of the National Cancer Institute, 66*, 1191–308.

D'Souza, Stan, & Chen, Lincoln C. (1980). Sex differential in mortality in rural Bangladesh. *Population and Development Review, 6*(2), 257–70.

El-Badry, M.A. (1969). Higher female than male mortality in some countries of South Asia: A digest. *Journal of the American Statistical Association, 64*, 1234–44.

Fogel, Robert W. (2004). *The escape from hunger and premature death, 1700–2100.* Cambridge: Cambridge University Press.

Fries, James F. (1980). Aging, natural death and the compression of morbidity. *New England Journal of Medicine, 303*, 130–5.

Gauri, Varun, & Khaleghian, Peyvand. (2002). Immunization in developing countries: Its political and organizational determinants. *World Development, 30*(12), 2109–32.

Gjonca, Arjan. (2001). *Communism, health and lifestyle: The paradox of mortality transition in Albania, 1950–1990*. Westport, RI: Greenwood Press.

Gjonca, Arjan, Wilson, Christopher, & Falkingham, Jane. (1997). Paradoxes of health transition in Europe's poorest country, Albania 1950–1990. *Population and Development Review, 23*(3): 585–609.

Glei, Dana A., & Horiuchi, Shiro. (2007). The narrowing sex differential in life expectancy in high-income populations: Effects of differences in the age pattern of mortality. *Population Studies, 61*(2), 141–59.

Goldstone, Jack A. (2008). Capitalist origins, the advent of modernity, and coherent explanation: A response to Joseph M. Bryant. *Canadian Journal of Sociology, 33*(1), 119–33.

Hannerz, Harald. (2001, May). Manhood trials and the law of mortality. *Demographic Research, 4*(7), 185–202.

Haynes, Michael, & Husan, Rumy. (2003). *A century of state murder? Death and policy in twentieth-century Russia*. London: Pluto Press.

Henry, Louis. (1989). Men's and women's mortality in the past. *Population, 44*(1, English Selection), 177–201.

Heuveline, Patrick, Guillot, Michel, & Gwatkin, Davidson R. (2002). The uneven tides of the health transition. *Social Science and Medicine, 55*, 313–22.

Hill, Kenneth. (1995). The decline of childhood mortality. In Julian Simon (Ed.), *The state of humanity* (pp. 36–50). Oxford: Blackwell.

Hinde, Andrew. (2003). *England's population: A history since the Domesday survey*. New York: Oxford University Press.

Keyfitz, Nathan, & Flinger, Wilhelm. (1990). *World population growth and aging: Demographic trends in the late twentieth century*. Chicago: The University of Chicago Press.

Kinugasa, Tomoko, & Mason, Andrew. (2007). Why countries become wealthy: The effects of adult longevity on saving. *World Development, 35*(1), 1–23.

Kramer, Sebastian. (2000, December 23–30). The fragile male. *British Medical Journal, 321*, 1609–12.

Lamptey, Peter, Johnson, Jami L., & Khan, Maria. (2006). The global challenge of HIV and AIDS. *Population Bulletin, 67*(1). Washington: Population Reference Bureau.

Leon, David A., Chenet, Laurent, Shkolnikov, Vladimir M., Zakharov, S., et al. (1997, August 9). Huge variation in Russian mortality rates 1984–94: Artefact, alcohol, or what? *The Lancet, 350*, 383–8.

Livi-Bacci, Massimo. (1997). *A concise history of world population* (2nd edn). Oxford: Blackwell.

Lopez, Alan D. (1983). The sex mortality differential in developed countries. In Alan D. Lopez & Lado T. Ruzicka (Eds), *Sex differentials in mortality: Trends, determinants and consequences*. Canberra: Australian National University.

———. (1995). The lung cancer epidemic in developed countries. In Alan D. Lopez, Graziella Caselli, & Tapani Valkonen (Eds), *Adult mortality in developed countries: From description to explanation* (pp. 111–34). Oxford: Clarendon Press

Luy, Marc. (2003). Causes of male excess mortality: Insights from cloistered populations. *Population and Development Review, 29*(4), 647–76.

McKeown, Thomas. (1976). *The modern rise of population*. London: Arnold.

McKeown, Thomas, Brown, R.G., & Record, R.G. (1972). An interpretation of the modern rise of populating in Europe. *Population Studies, 26*(3), 345–54.

Madigan, Francis C. (1957). Are sex mortality differentials biologically caused? *Milbank Memorial Fund Quarterly, 35*(2), 202–23.

Manton, Kenneth G. (2008). Recent declines in chronic disability in the elderly US population: Risk factors and future dynamics. *Annual Review of Public Health, 29*, 91–113.

Manton, Kenneth G., & Singer, Burton. (1994). What's the fuzz about compression of mortality? *Chance, 7*(4), 21–30.

Marmot, Michael. (2005, March 19). Social determinants of health. *The Lancet, 365*, 1099–104.

Mendelsohn, Michael E., & Karas, Richard H. (2005, June 10). Molecular and cellular basis of cardiovascular gender differences. *Science, 308*, 1583–7.

Mercer, Alex J. (1985). Smallpox and epidemiological-demographic change in Europe: The role of vaccination. *Population Studies, 39*, 287–307.

———. (1986). Relative trends in mortality from related respiratory and airborne infectious diseases. *Population Studies, 40*, 129–45.

———. (1990). *Disease, mortality and population in transition: Epidemiological-demographic change in England since the eighteenth century as part of a global phenomenon*. Leicester, UK: Leicester University Press.

Mishra, Vionod, Roy, T.K., & Retherford, Robert D. (2004). Sex differentials in childhood feeding, health care, and nutritional status in India. *Population and Development Review, 30*(2), 269–96.

Mokdad, Ali H., Marks, James S., Stroup, Donna F., & Gerberding, Julie L. (2004, March 10). Actual causes of death in the United States, 2000. *Journal of the American Medical Association, 291*(10), 1238–45.

Moser, Kath, Shkolnikov, Vladimir, & Leon, David A. (2009). World mortality 1950–2005: Divergence replaces convergence from the late 1980s. *Bulletin of the World Health Organization, 83*, 202–9.

Murphy, Rachel. (2003). Fertility and distorted sex ratios in a rural Chinese county. *Population and Development Review, 29*(4), 595–626.

Nadarajah, T. (1983). The transition from higher female to higher male mortality in Sri Lanka. *Population and Development Review, 9*(2), 317–25.

Nathanson, Constance. (1995). The position of women and mortality in developed countries. In Caselli Lopez, & Tapani Valkonen (Eds), *Adult mortality in developed countries: From description to explanation* (pp. 135–57). Oxford: Oxford University Press.

Notkola, Veijo, Timaeus, Ian M., & Siiskonen, Harri. (2000). Mortality transition in the Ovamboland region of Namibia, 1930–1990. *Population Studies, 54*(2), 153–67.

Olshansky, S. Jay, & Ault, Brian A. (1986). The fourth stage of the epidemiologic transition: The age of delayed degenerative diseases. *The Milbank Quarterly, 64*(3), 355–91.

Omran, Abdel. (1971). The epidemiologic transition. *Milbank Memorial Quarterly, 49*(1), 509–38.

Ostry, Aleck S., & Franck, John. (2010). Was Thomas McKeown right for the wrong reasons? *Critical Public Health, 20*(2), 233–43.

Owen, Ian P.F. (2002, September 20). Sex differences in mortality rate. *Science, 297*, 2008–9.

Pampel, Fred C. (2002). Cigarette use and the narrowing sex differential in mortality. *Population and Development Review, 28*(1), 77–104.

———. (2003). Declining sex differences in mortality from lung cancer in high-income nations. *Demography, 40*(1), 45–65.

Perls, Thomas T., & Fretts, Ruth C. (1998). Why women live longer than men. *Scientific American Presents, 9*, 100–4.

Peto, Richard, Lopez, Alan D., Boreham, Jillian, & Thun, Michael. (1992). Mortality from tobacco in developed countries: Indirect estimation from national vital statistics. *Lancet 399*, 1268–78.

Peto, Richard, Lopez, Alan D., Boreham, Jillian, Thun, Michael, Clarke, Heath, & Doll, Richard. (1996). Mortality from smoking worldwide. *British Medical Bulletin 1*, 12–21.

Pido-Lopez, J., Imami, N., & Aspinall, R. (2001). Both age and gender affect thymic output: More recent thymic migrants in females than males as they age. *Clinical Experimental Immunology, 125*, 409–13.

Population Reference Bureau. (2010). *World population data sheet for 2010*. Washington, DC.

Preston, Samuel H. (1975). The changing relation between economic development and mortality. *Population Studies, 29*, 331–48.

———. (1976). *Mortality patterns in national populations*. New York: Academic Press.

———. (1995). Mortality through history and prehistory. In Julian Simon (Ed.), *The state of humanity* (pp. 30–5). Oxford: Blackwell.

Preston, Samuel H., Keyfitz, Nathan, & Schoen, Robert. (1972). *Causes of death: Life tables for national populations*. New York: Seminar Press.

Razzel, P.E. (1974). An interpretation of the modern rise of population in Europe. *Population Studies, 28*, 5–17.

Retherford, Robert D. (1975). *The changing sex differential in mortality*. Westport, CT: Greenwood Press.

Rogers, Richard G., & Hackenberg, R. (1987). Extending epidemiologic transition theory: A new stage. *Social Biology, 34*(3–4), 234–43.

Rogers, Richard G., Hummer, Robert A., & Nam, Charles B. (2000). *Living and dying in the USA: Behavioral, health, and social differentials of adult mortality*. New York: Academic Press.

Salomon, Joshua A., & Murray, Christopher J.L. (2002). The epidemiologic transition revisited: Compositional models for causes of death by age and sex. *Population and Development Review, 28*(2), 205–28.

Schultz, Paul T. (1993). Mortality decline in the low-income world: Causes and consequences. *American Economic Association Papers and Proceedings, 83*(2), 337–42.

Scott, Susan, & Duncan, Christopher J. (2001). *Biology of plagues: Evidence from historical populations*. Cambridge: Cambridge University Press.

Shkolnikov, Vladimir M., Meslé, France, & Vallin, Jacques. (1997). Recent trends in life expectancy and causes of death in Russia, 1970–1993. In José Luis Bobadilla, Christine A. Costello, & Faith Mitchell (Eds), *Premature death in the new independent states* (pp. 34–65). Washington, DC: National Academy Press.

Smith, David W.E. (1993). *Human longevity.* New York: Oxford University Press.

Stolnitz, George J. (1955). A century of international mortality trends. Part I. *Population Studies, 9,* 24–55.

———. (1955). A century of international mortality trends. Part II. *Population Studies, 10,* 17–52.

Trovato, Frank. (2005). Narrowing sex differential in life expectancy in Canada and Austria: Comparative analysis. *Vienna Yearbook of Population Research 2005* (pp. 17–52).

Trovato, Frank, & Heyen, Nils B. (2005). A varied pattern of change of the sex differential in survival in the G7 countries. *Journal of Biosocial Science, 38*(3), 301–401.

Trovato, Frank, & Lalu, N.M. (1996a). Narrowing sex differentials in life expectancy in the industrialized world: Early 1970s to early 1990s. *Social Biology, 43*(1–2), 20–37.

———, & ———. (1996b). Causes of death responsible for the changing sex differential in life expectancy between 1970 and 1990 in thirty industrialized nations. *Canadian Studies in Population, 23*(2), 99–127.

Vallin, Jacques. (1983). Sex patterns of mortality: A comparative study of model life tables and actual situations with special reference to the case of Algeria and France. In Alan D. Lopez & Lado T. Ruzicka (Eds), *Sex differentials in mortality: Trends, determinants and consequences* (pp. 443–76). Canberra: Australian National University, Department of Demography.

———. (2006). Europe's demographic transition, 1740–1940. In Graziella Caselli, Jacques Vallin, & Guillaume Wunsch (Eds), *Demography, analysis and synthesis: A treatise in population studies* (pp. 41–66). Amsterdam: Elsevier.

Vallin, Jacques, & Meslé, France. (2010, December). Will life expectancy increase indefinitely by three months every year? *Population and Societies, 473.* Paris: Institut National D'Études Demographiques (INED).

Vallin, Jacques, Meslé, France, & Valkonen, Tapani. (2001). Trends in mortality and differential mortality. *Population Studies, 36.* Strasbourg: Council of Europe Publishing.

Vaupel, James W. (2010, March 25). Biodemography of human ageing. *Nature, 464,* 536–42. doi:10.1038/nature08984

Veevers, Jane E., & Gee, Ellen M. (1986). Playing it safe: Accident mortality and gender roles. *Sociological Focus,* 19 (4), 349–360.

Verbrugge, Lois M. (1976). Sex differentials in morbidity and mortality in the United States. *Social Biology, 34*(4), 275–96.

Waldron, Ingrid. (1976). Why do women live longer than men? *Social Science and Medicine,* 10, 349–362.

———. (1983). Sex differences in human mortality: The role of genetic factors. *Social Science and Medicine, 17*(6), 321–33.

———. (1986). The contribution of smoking to sex differences in mortality. *Public Health Reports, 101*(2), 163–73.

———. (1993). Recent trends in sex mortality ratios for adults in developed countries. *Social Science and Medicine, 36*(4), 451–62.

———. (2000). Trends in gender differences in mortality: Relationships to changing gender differences in behavior and other causal factors. In E. Annandale & K. Hung (Eds), *Gender inequalities in health* (pp. 150–81). Buckingham: Open University Press.

White, Kevin M. (2002). Longevity advances in high-income countries, 1955–96. *Population and Development Review, 28*(1), 59–76.

White, Kevin M., & Preston, Samuel H. (1996). How many Americans are alive because of twentieth-century improvements in mortality? *Population and Development Review, 22*(3), 415–29.

Wilkinson, Richard, & Marmot, Michael. (2003). *Social determinants of health: The solid facts.* Geneva: World Health Organization.

You, Danzhen, Wardlaw, Tessa, Salama, Peter, & Jones, G. (2010, January 9). Levels and trends in under-5 mortality. *The Lancet, 375,* 100–3.

CHAPTER 15

Human Mortality Throughout History and Prehistory

Samuel H. Preston

Accurate data for estimating life expectancy at birth in sizable populations do not become available until the sixteenth century. For earlier times, the analyst must rely on sources of questionable quality or representativeness: skeletal remains, burial inscriptions, and, after 1300 or so, records of unusual groups such as the European aristocracy or members of religious orders.

Most of these records suggest that life expectancy from prehistoric times until 1400 or so was in the range of 20–30 years. A detailed and comprehensive account of life expectancy estimates through classical antiquity is found in Acsadi and Nemeskeri (1970). The most satisfactory collection of skeletal remains is drawn from the Maghreb peninsula (North Africa, between Egypt and the Atlantic) during the Neolithic period. This population evidently had a life expectancy at birth of about 21 years. Its age pattern of mortality was remarkably similar to that of modern populations at similar levels of mortality (Acsadi & Nemeskeri, 1970, p. 173).

Burial inscriptions, mummies, and skeletons drawn from the Roman Empire suggest that life expectancy was in the twenties for most of the geographic and occupational subgroups falling under its sovereignty. Few of these sources provided an adequate representation of infant deaths, so that some extrapolation to this age is required based on typical age patterns of mortality observed more recently.

Confidence in the range of 20–30 for life expectancy in the era before 1600 is enhanced by the use of demographic models. Since the world's population was growing very slowly during this period, life expectancy at birth was, to a very close approximation, the reciprocal of the birth rate. Given the age pattern of fecundity and the apparent absence of significant antinatal practices, the birth rate was quite unlikely to have fallen outside the range of 0.033–0.050 births per capita per year, implying life expectancies in the range of 20–30 years.

Mortality rates among members of religious orders provide a very useful bridge between antiquity and the advent of modern death statistics. In an unusually well-documented study, Hatcher (1986) shows that mortality among Benedictine monks in Canterbury, England from 1395 to 1505 corresponded to a life expectancy at birth of 22 years. He notes that nutrition, clothing, sanitation, and shelter were much better for this group than for the population as a whole, although its denser living conditions were undoubtedly a negative factor in its survivorship.

The earliest satisfactory series achieving national coverage is based on demographic reconstructions by a group of scholars at Cambridge. Using a large sample of parish registers and adjusting their data to achieve national representativeness, Wrigley and Schofield (1981) provide estimates of life expectancy at birth in England from 1541 to 1875. Their quinquennial series of life expectancies is plotted in Figure 15.1. It is clear that, by the middle of the sixteenth century, life expectancy was typically in the mid-thirties, with substantial fluctuation from period to period. Some mild secular deterioration, possibly associated with increasing population density and repeated visitations of the plague, is evident for a century and a half, followed by a slow advance. At the dawn of the nineteenth century, life expectancy was about 37 years, much the same level as it had been two centuries earlier. Life expectancy in France in 1800 was about 30 years, a disparity that Fogel (1989) attributes to poorer nutritional standards in France than in England.

The series of English life expectancies in figure 15.1 is completed by using life tables computed from national vital statistics and censuses for England and Wales. It is clear that a steady advance begins

just after the turn of the nineteenth century, and accelerates after about 1871–5. After the 1860s, there is no instance in which life expectancy declines from one period to the next. Not only were average conditions improving rapidly, but there was also less slippage from the gains that had been secured.

The first nation to produce reliable measures of mortality based on complete national counts of deaths and population is Sweden. A quinquennial series of Swedish life expectancies at birth beginning in 1778–82 is also plotted in Figure 15.1. While its series begins at a level similar to that of England, Sweden gains an advantage in the course of the nineteenth century, probably because of much less rapid urbanization (urban areas exposed people more frequently to infectious diseases through direct personal contact and indirectly through contamination of water and food supplies). As the urban health

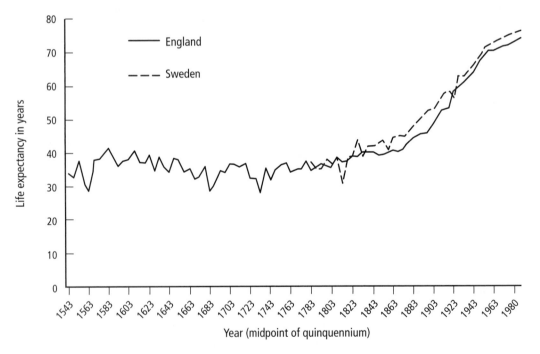

Figure 15.1 Life expectancy, England and Sweden, 1541–1985

For England and Wales: 1741–1875, Wrigley & Schofield (1981, table 7.15); 1876–1970, Case, et al. (1970); 1970–85 (individual years), Keyfitz & Flieger (1990). For Sweden: 1778–1962, Keyfitz & Flieger (1968); 1965–85, Keyfitz & Flieger (1990).

disadvantage is removed through public works during the twentieth century, the series for the two countries converge. As in England, life expectancy advances accelerate in the 1870s; the only instance of backsliding reflects the influenza epidemic after World War I. It has been argued that the acceleration in rates of mortality decline after the 1870s reflects primarily the implementation of personal and public health practices that took advantage of much clearer understandings of the nature of infectious diseases (Ewbank & Preston, 1990; Preston & Haines, 1991).

Thus far in the twentieth century, life expectancy in Sweden has increased by 24 years and in England and Wales by 27 years. These gains are typical for western European countries and areas of overseas European settlement. Increases were larger in southern and eastern Europe, which began the century at lower levels. Italian life expectancy has increased by 32 years, from 43.0 to 74.7, and Czechoslovakian life expectancy by 31 years, from 40.3 to 71.1 (Keyfitz & Flieger, 1990; Preston & Haines, 1991, table 2.3). If we set prehistoric life expectancy at a midrange value of 25 years, it is clear that about half of the progress in European populations since prehistoric times has occurred during the short span of the twentieth century. The only notable setbacks have been the influenza epidemic after World War I and mild reversals in male mortality in eastern Europe during the past two decades associated with alcohol consumption and other factors (Eberstadt, 1989).

The United States completed its death registration system in 1933, the last industrialized country to do so. Nevertheless, it is evident from partial statistics that the course of mortality during this century was quite similar to that of England. In an innovative and convincing analysis, Lee and Carter (1992) show that the pace of decline in American age-specific death rates during the century has been virtually constant right through the 1980s. Projections by the US Census Bureau and Social Security Administration have repeatedly been too conservative about future gains in life expectancy, and it appears that these errors are being repeated in recent forecasts (Preston, 1993).

Developing Countries

Mortality improvements in developing countries during the twentieth century have been even more dramatic than in industrialized countries. The data base is less secure but there is little doubt that turn-of-the-century life expectancy for the aggregate of developing countries was less than 30 years, i.e. in the range that appears applicable to prehistoric populations. In China around 1930, a valuable demographic survey suggests, life expectancy was around 24 years (Barclay, et al., 1976). Intercensal analysis in India indicates a life expectancy of 24–25 years during 1901–11 (Bhat, 1987). Life tables for Taiwan in 1920 give a life expectancy of 27.9 years and for Chile in 1909—one of the most advanced countries of the developing world—a life expectancy of 30.6 years (Preston, et al., 1972).

According to United Nations' (1991) estimates for 1985–90, China has a life expectancy of 69.4 years, India of 57.9, and Chile of 71.5. Taiwan's life expectancy, not available in UN sources, was 73.6 in 1985 (Keyfitz & Flieger, 1990). Thus, the mean increase from a level recorded earlier in this century for these four countries is about 42 years. Life expectancy more than doubled during the century for each of them. Since life expectancy for developing countries as a whole is estimated by the United Nations to be 61.4 years in 1985–90, it is apparent that this doubling also pertains to the aggregate of developing countries. Figure 15.2 presents a regional breakdown of the UN's life expectancy estimates. Even the poorest region, Africa, has a life expectancy (52.0 years) that would have been the envy of Europe at the turn of the century.

In 1909, impressed by recent discoveries in bacteriology and their application to health practices, economist Irving Fisher declared that 'the crowning achievement of science in the present century should be, and probably will be, the discovery of practical methods of making life healthier, longer, and happier than before' (p. 64). As the century closes, there is no doubt about the accuracy of Fisher's prophesy.

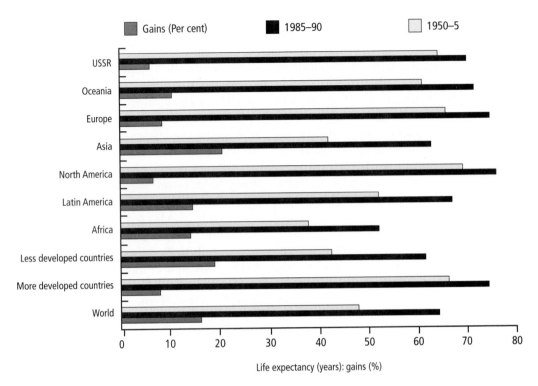

Figure 15.2 Life expectancy around the world, 1950–5, 1985–90, and gains

United Nations (1991, p. 28).

References

Acsadi, George, & Nemeskéri. J. (1970). *History of human life span and mortality.* Budapest: Akademiai Kiado.

Barclay, George, Coale, Ansley, Stoto, Michael, & Trussell, James. (1976). A reassessment of the demography of traditional rural China. *Population Index, 42*(4), 606–35.

Bhat, Mari (1987). *Mortality in India: Levels, trends, and patterns.* Dissertation in Demography, University of Pennsylvania. Ann Arbor, MI: University Microfilms International.

Case, R.A.M., Coghill, Christine, Harley, Joyce, & Pearson, Joan. (1970). *The Chester Beatty Research Institute serial abridged life tables. England and Wales 1841–1960* (supplemented 2nd edn). London: Chester Beatty Research Institute.

Eberstadt, Nicholas. (1989). Health and mortality in eastern Europe, 1965 to 1985. Joint Economic Committee, 101st Congress, first session. Vol. 1. *Pressures for reform in the East European economy.* Washington, DC: Government Printing Office.

Ewbank, Douglas, & Preston, Samuel. (1990). Personal health behavior and the decline of infant child mortality: The United States, 1900–1930. In John Caldwell (Ed.), *What we know about health transition* (pp. 116–49). Canberra: Australian National University Printing Service for the Health Transition Centre, Australian National University.

Fisher, Irving. (1909). Report on national vitality, its wastes and conservation. Bulletin of the Committee of One Hundred on National Health. Prepared for the National Conservation Commission, Washington, DC: Government Printing Office.

Fogel, Robert W. (1989). Second thoughts on the European escape from hunger: Famines, price elasticities, entitlements, chronic malnutrition, and mortality rates. National Bureau of Economic Research Working Paper on Historical Factors in Long Term Growth, no. 1. Cambridge, MA: National Bureau of Economic Research.

Hatcher, John (1986). Mortality in the fifteenth century: Some new evidence. *Economic History Review (second series), 39*(1), 19–38.

Keyfitz, Nathan, & Flieger, Wilhelm. (1968). *World population: An analysis of vital data.* Chicago: University of Chicago Press.

———, & ———. (1990). *World population growth and aging.* Chicago: University of Chicago Press.

Lee, Ronald, & Carter, Lawrence. (1992). Modeling and forecasting US mortality. *Journal of the American Statistical Association, 87*(419), 659–71.

Preston, Samuel. (1993). Demographic change in the United States, 1970–2050. In A.M. Rappaport & S.J. Scheiber (Eds), *Demography and retirement: The 21st century.* Westport, CT: Praeger.

Preston, Samuel, & Haines, Michael. (1991). *Fatal years: Child mortality in late nineteenth century America.* Princeton University Press.

Preston, Samuel, Keyfitz, Nathan, & Schoen, Robert. (1972). *Causes of death: Life tables for national populations.* New York: Academic Press.

United Nations. (1991). *World population prospects: 1990.* Population Study no. 120. New York: United Nations.

Wrigley, E.A., & Schofield, R.S. (1981). *The population history of England, 1541–1871.* Cambridge, MA: Harvard University Press.

CHAPTER 16

Aging Populations: The Challenges Ahead

Kaare Christensen, Gabriele Doblhammer, Roland Rau, and James W. Vaupel

Introduction

The remarkable gain of about 30 years in life expectancy in western Europe, the USA, Canada, Australia, and New Zealand—and even larger gains in Japan and some western European countries, such as Spain and Italy—stands out as one of the most important accomplishments of the twentieth century. According to the Human Mortality Database, death rates in life-expectancy leaders such as Japan, Spain, and Sweden imply that even if health conditions do not improve, three-quarters of babies will survive to celebrate their seventy-fifth birthdays. Most babies born since 2000 in countries with long-lived residents will celebrate their one-hundredth birthdays if the present yearly growth in life expectancy continues through the twenty-first century (see Table 16.1). This forecast is based on the assumption that mortality before age 50 years will remain at 2006 levels. At age 50 years and older, probability of dying decreases by a rate that yields yearly improvements in period life expectancy of 0.2 years. More complex methods can be developed on the basis of the assumption that life expectancies will increase linearly;[12] however, such models produce similar estimates to those given in Table 16.1.

These scenarios are projections, but we do not have to look to the future for challenges of an

Table 16.1 Oldest ages at which at least 50 per cent of a birth cohort is still alive in eight countries

	2000	2001	2002	2003	2004	2005	2006	2007
Canada	102	102	103	103	103	104	104	104
Denmark	99	99	100	100	101	101	101	101
France	102	102	103	103	103	104	104	104
Germany	99	100	100	100	101	101	101	102
Italy	102	102	102	103	103	103	104	104
Japan	104	105	105	105	106	106	106	107
UK	100	101	101	101	102	102	103	103
USA	101	102	102	103	103	103	104	104

Data are ages in years. Baseline data were obtained from the Human Mortality Database and refer to the total population of the respective countries.

aging population: the oldest-old group (aged > 85 years) have over past decades been the most rapidly expanding segment of the population in developed countries. This group is also the most susceptible to disease and disability.[13–18] Development of mortality, disease, and disability rates in elderly people will therefore have a fundamental effect on sustainability of modern society.

Mortality

Life expectancy is lengthening almost linearly in most developed countries, with no sign of deceleration. In 2002, Oeppen and Vaupel[12] showed that best-practice life expectancy—i.e. the highest value recorded in a national population—has risen by 3 months per year since 1840 (see Figure 16.1). Data for a further 7 years have since become available, and life expectancy keeps rising. In the record-holding country, Japan, female life expectancy was 86.0 years in 2007,[19] surpassing the 85-year limit to human life expectancy that was proposed by Fries[20] in 1980, and later elaborated on by Olshansky and colleagues.[21] Although with lower life expectancies than that of Japan, most developed countries have had similar yearly increases in life expectancy since 1950 (Figure 16.1). The linear increase in record life expectancy for more than 165 years does not suggest a looming limit to human lifespan. If life expectancy were approaching a limit, some deceleration of progress would probably occur. Continued progress in the longest-living populations

suggests that we are not close to a limit, and further rise in life expectancy seems likely.

Life-expectancy improvements over the past 165 years were not propelled by uniform reductions in mortality at all ages. Until the 1920s, improvements in infant and childhood survival contributed most to the increase in record life expectancies. After successful combatting of infectious diseases at young ages, gains in record life expectancy were fuelled by progress at older ages (see Table 16.2). This reduction in old-age mortality was unprecedented and unexpected.[20,21] Since the 1950s, and especially since the 1970s, mortality at ages 80 years and older has continued to fall, in some countries even at an accelerating pace.[14,22–26]

Data from more than 30 developed countries[26] showed that in 1950 the probability of survival from age 80 years to 90 years was on average 15–16 per cent for women and 12 per cent for men. In 2002, these values were 37 per cent and 25 per cent. Even in the country with the lowest probability (the Czech Republic), the situation improved remarkably. In Japan—which is the country with residents having the best chances of survival—the probability of surviving from age 80 years to 90 years now exceeds 50 per cent for women. Figure 16.2 plots the probabilities of survival to their next birthday of people who lived to age 80 or 90 years in seven large developed countries.[27] With a few exceptions, mortality generally keeps falling in all selected countries for both sexes at both ages. In 1950, about one in

Table 16.2 Age-specific contributions to the increase in record life expectancy in women from 1850 to 2007 (%)

	1850–1900	1900–25	1925–50	1950–75	1975–90	1990–2007
0–14 years	62.13	54.75	30.99	29.72	11.20	5.93
15–49 years	29.09	31.55	37.64	17.70	6.47	4.67
50–64 years	5.34	9.32	18.67	16.27	24.29	10.67
65–79 years	3.17	4.44	12.72	28.24	40.57	37.22
>80 years	0.27	−0.06	−0.03	8.07	17.47	41.51

Data derived from reference [12] and the Human Mortality Database.

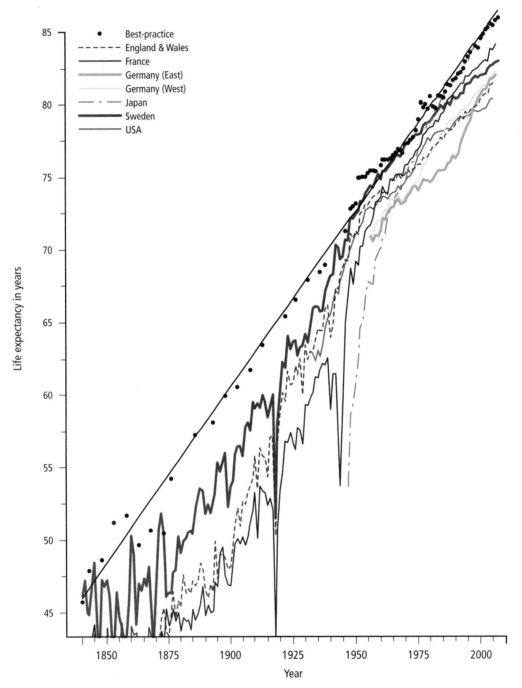

Figure 16.1 Best-practice life expectancy and life expectancy for women in selected countries from 1840 to 2007. Linear regression trend depicted by solid black line with a slope of 0.24 per year.

Data from supplementary material of reference [12] and the Human Mortality Database.

ten 80-year-old women died before their eighty-first birthdays. About 50 years later, this number was typically less than one in twenty. In Japan, it was less than 3 per cent. Male mortality was also halved. The probability of dying for men aged 80 years in the early 1950s was about 14 per cent, and only about 7 per cent half-a-century later. Deaths of children and young adults are rare in high-income countries. If the pace of increase in life expectancy is to continue, progress in mortality reduction needs to be made in the elderly population and oldest-old

groups. A continuous decrease in mortality at old age is reported in most developed countries, but not all (Figure 16.2).

In 1980, remaining life expectancy for people aged 80 years was higher in the USA than it was in Sweden, France, England and Wales, and Japan. Manton and Vaupel suggested that elderly Americans were receiving better healthcare than were elderly citizens of other developed countries.[28] However, through the 1980s and 1990s, mortality improvements stagnated for US women (Figure 16.2), not only for the

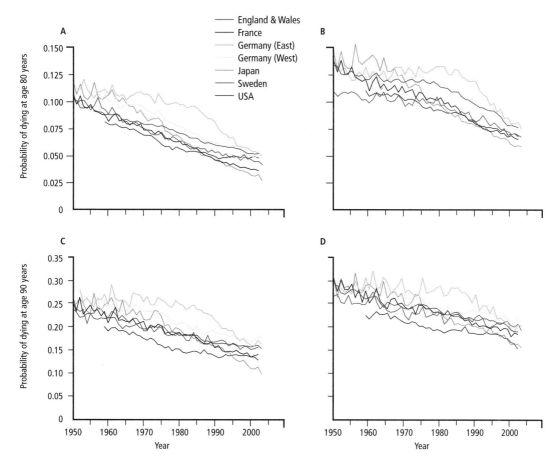

Figure 16.2 Probability of dying for elderly men and women in selected countries from 1950 to 2003: (A) Women aged 80 years; (B) Men aged 80 years; (C) Women aged 90 years; (D) Men aged 90 years.

Data from reference [27].

oldest-old population but also for younger elderly people. This stagnation was not due to immigration, because survival of US women is largely unaffected by place of birth. Wang and Preston[29] investigated the relation between cohort smoking patterns and adult mortality, and reported that smoking accounts for important anomalies in the recent age and sex pattern of mortality change in the USA. They concluded that because of reductions in smoking that have already occurred, mortality could decrease much faster than was previously projected.

Smoking also seems to be the main underlying reason for divergent trends in Denmark. In the 1950s, mean life expectancy in Denmark was among the highest in the world, a position that was maintained until around 1980, when an extended period of stagnation began, which was most pronounced for women. Denmark's position fell from third rank of 20 Organisation for Economic Cooperation and Development (OECD) countries in the 1950s to rank 17 for men and 20 for women at the beginning of the new millennium; life expectancy was 3 years lower than in neighbouring Sweden. Cause-specific mortality and morbidity data suggest that the Danish stagnation was caused by lifestyle factors, especially smoking.[30,31]

Analysis of life disparity in Denmark shows that slowing of progress in reduction of differentials in lifespans occurred at about the same time as did slowing of progress in increasing life expectancy— i.e. Danish life expectancy might have stagnated, at least in part, because inequalities in health-related factors did not fall in the 1970s and 1980s. Differing lifespans among Danes are attributable in part to differences in smoking behaviour. Generally, countries that have the least disparity in lifespans are those that enjoy the longest life expectancies.

The new demography of low fertility and, to an even greater extent, low mortality[32] produces population aging. Figure 16.3 summarizes the change in age structure of the German population in the half-century up to 2006 and the next half-century.[33] Because of Germany's losses in the two world wars, the panel for 1956 is jagged. About one person in ten was aged 65 years or older in Germany in the mid-1950s. Only

1.3 per cent of the population were aged 80 years or older. Fifty years later, the proportion of people aged 65 years and older almost doubled (19 per cent), and the proportion of octogenarians, nonagenarians, and centenarians more than tripled (4.4 per cent). On the assumption of a constant total fertility rate that is slightly higher than at present, more immigration than on average during the past 10 years, and the low scenario for increase in life expectancy, the age structure of the German population in 2050 will be substantially older and smaller than it is nowadays. Future trends in morbidity and disability rates will be crucial determinants of societies' ability to meet the challenges of population aging.

Health

Because health is a multidimensional notion, several indicators are needed to capture trends. On the basis of Verbrugge and Jette's[34] framework, health deterioration can be described by risk factors that lead to diseases and conditions that can cause loss of function, and, dependent on the environmental context, can result in disability. To assess trends in health, investigators have to analyze trends in these different levels of health, bearing in mind that different indicators show different phases of the disease and disability processes, and thus might follow different trends. Studies of health trends are complex because (1) indicators of morbidity, functional limitations, and disability have been applied inconsistently; (2) study designs, participation rates, and wording of questions have changed over time; and (3) institutional populations are excluded from many health surveys despite the burden this population places on healthcare systems and despite changes in institutionalization rates.

We focus on trends and patterns in highly developed industrial countries, which have the most complete data for developments in health, despite difficulties with trend assessment. In view of the discussion by Vallin and Meslé[35] about convergences and divergences in health transition and mortality, we expect similar trends in these countries, with the addition, however, of latecomers and forerunners.

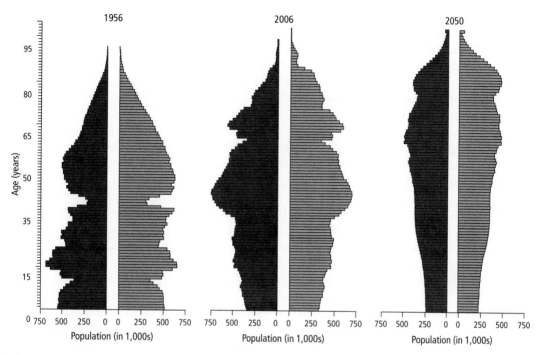

Figure 16.3 Population pyramids for Germany in 1956, 2006, and 2050. Horizontal bars are proportional to number of men (left) and women (right). Data for 2050 are based on the German Federal Statistical Office's 1-W1 scenario, which assumes a roughly constant total fertility rate of 1.4, yearly net migration of 100,000, and life expectancy in 2050 reaching 83.5 years for men and 88.0 years for women.

Data from reference [33] and the Human Mortality Database.

Disease

The prevalence of diseases in the elderly population has generally increased over time. Most survey data are based on self-reported morbidity. Although self-reported data are often assumed to underestimate true prevalence, investigators[36] report higher prevalences in a Dutch population of diabetes mellitus, cardiac disease, lower-back complaints, and asthma on the basis of self-reports than of medical records. However, increasing trends have generally been shown for both self-reports and medical records.[36–38] These trends might partly show improved medical knowledge and health service use in elderly

people, without changes in underlying conditions. For instance, initially silent diseases, such as type 2 diabetes, hypertension, and some cancers, now get diagnosed earlier and receive better treatment than they did previously. This progress leads to a longer period of morbidity, but with an improved functional status.[39]

A rise in prevalence of chronic diseases, including heart disease, arthritis, and diabetes, was recorded in elderly people between the 1980s and 1990s in the USA,[40,41] 12 OECD countries,[42] the Netherlands,[36] and Sweden.[37,43] Increases in pain and psychological distress,[44] general fatigue, dizziness, leg ulcers, heart problems, hypertension, and musculoskeletal pain,[36,45] and worsening lung function[34] have been reported for the elderly population in Sweden between 1991 and 2002. Reports suggest a general increase in multiple symptoms,[36,45] although in the Netherlands improvements have been noted for some diseases—e.g. prevalences of cardiac disease, asthma, osteoarthritis, depression based on family doctors' registers, and lower-back complaints.[36]

Total cancer incidence has been rising, mainly because of population aging, but also because of some cancers, such as prostate cancer in men, lung and breast cancer in women, and colorectal cancer and melanoma in both sexes. The most consistent decrease in Europe was noted for gastric and cervical cancers and male lung cancer. Survival rates for cancer have generally increased. Reduced exposure to carcinogens (e.g. tobacco smoke), earlier diagnosis, and therapeutic improvements account for part of this change, but overall the distribution of cancer has shifted towards less aggressive cancers, with the notable exception of lung cancer in women.[46]

An increase in disease and chronic conditions has been reported in people aged 65–69 years,[47] for example, in arthritis and chronic airways obstructions in the UK. At working ages in the USA, rises have been noted for asthma, chronic bronchitis, diabetes, congestive heart failure, and arthritis.[48] A comparison of baby boomers—i.e. people born during the post–World War II baby boom, between 1946 and 1966, dependent on country—with the preceding cohort[49] reveals fewer musculoskeletal conditions, but an increase in cardiovascular disease, lung problems, and diabetes.

The rise in prevalence of cardiovascular disease is thought to result from disparate trends in mortality versus incidence. Cardiovascular mortality fell more than did incidence of cardiovascular disease. Data for stroke incidence is mixed. Results of four studies showed increasing stroke incidence from the 1970s to the 1980s, five showed decreasing incidence from the late 1970s to the 1990s, and eight showed no change.[50] High prevalence of cardiovascular disease could be due to increased duration of time lived with the disease, potentially because of improved medical care, and possibly early diagnosis.[36]

Obesity is a widely discussed risk factor that threatens improvements in health.[51–54] It has been increasing in almost all populations,[38,42] with an estimated 3.8 per cent per year average rise in people aged 65 years or older during the 1990s in the Netherlands,[42] closely followed by the USA, UK, and Italy. Obesity increases probability of transition from good health to disability, reduces chance of recovery,[55,56] and increases risk of death,[56] although mortality in elderly people who are obese seems not to be raised, and could even be lower than in their non-obese counterparts.[55] Obesity is related to various poor health outcomes, including raised risk of diabetes, arthritis, and stroke. The number of diabetes cases, even if prevalence of obesity remains stable until 2030, is estimated to more than double worldwide[57] because of population aging, with the largest rise in people aged 65 years and older.

Definitions of obesity vary,[58] and the relation between obesity and disability is complex. The consequences of obesity can be modified by increased use of antihypertensives[59] and lipid-lowering drugs,[60] which reduce risk of cardiovascular disease and resulting disabilities. Reductions in disability reported in non-obese elderly individuals might not occur within an obese elderly population.[61]

Evidence about hypertension is mixed. Crimmins[1] reported a fall in the USA since the 1960s at ages 65–74 years. Conversely, Ostchega and colleagues[62] report a rise at ages 60 years and older. Lafortune and Balestat[42] report rates of increase in 12 OECD countries ranging from 3.9 per cent per year in Canada to 6.3 per cent per year in Italy. Rosen and Haglund[43] suggest an increase for Swedish men from the 1980s to 2000. In the USA, awareness and treatment of hypertension in elderly people has been growing over time;[59] however, elderly women (aged 70 years and older) are less aware and thus less often treated than are men.[62] Qureshi and colleagues[63] report different trends for severity of hypertension: prehypertension rose, stage I hypertension (140–159/90–99 mm Hg) remained constant, and stage II hypertension fell. Crimmins and colleagues[38] report increases in systolic blood pressure for the USA.

Little is known about trends in cognitive function and dementia. Freedman and colleagues[2] report a reduction in cognitive impairment in the mid-1990s in the USA. However, these results were contested by Rodgers and co-workers[64] using the same data with adjustments for learning effects and some methodological issues. Manton and colleagues[65] report a fall in severe cognitive impairment of 55 per cent in men and 45 per cent in women between 1982 and 1999, mainly because of a decrease in incidence of mixed dementia but not Alzheimer's disease. Langa and co-workers[66] reported a compression of cognitive morbidity between 1993 and 2004, in Americans aged 70 years or older, with a decreasing number of people reaching a threshold of significant cognitive impairment, and increasing mortality in those with cognitive impairment. A fall in prevalence of dementia is reported for Australia between 1998 and 2003, whereas data for Japan (1998–2004) and Sweden (1988–2004) suggest an increase.[42,45]

Functional Limitations and Disability

Improvements in mobility measured by single indices have been reported by many investigators in the USA.[2] The yearly rate of improvement is typically around 1 per cent. In Spain, between 1986 and 1999, improvements were reported on the basis of the Rosow-Breslau scale of items pertaining to stooping or kneeling, reaching or extending arms, pulling or pushing large objects, and handling or picking up of small objects.[67,68] A similar trend in the USA from the late 1970s to the late 1990s was reported in the Framingham Heart Study.[69] In Japan, in the 10 years from 1993 to 2002, the prevalence of functional limitations did not change at ages 66 years and older, with the exception of 16–17 per cent improvements in stooping, lifting, and the absence of any limitations.[70]

Investigators note a rise in severe hearing impairments for Sweden between 1991 and 2002,[37,71] a fall in hearing problems for Spain[67] between 1986 and 1999, and constant rates for the USA.[40,72] Vision has improved in Sweden,[71] Spain,[67] and the USA,[73,74] which is also the result of developments in cataract surgery—which is the most frequently done surgical procedure in developed countries. Few operations have changed so much in recent years.[75]

Table 16.3 shows yearly changes in mobility, based on indicators that are geared toward the highest level of physical functioning, such as walking and climbing stairs. Large improvements are reported for Spain,[67] the USA,[69] and the Netherlands,[36] smaller gains for Finland,[80] and stagnation for Japan.[70] In northern Europe there was stagnation, but improvements were reported in southern Europe.[77]

Disability is usually measured by a set of items on self-reported limitations with severity of disability ranked by the number of positively answered items. Disabilities in activities of daily living (ADL) show dependence of an individual on others, with need for assistance in daily life. The activities of feeding, dressing, bathing or showering, transferring from bed and chair, and continence are central to self-care and are called basic ADL. Disability in instrumental ADL refers to disabilities affecting a broad range of activities, such as telephone use, shopping, housekeeping, preparation of food, doing laundry, use of various types of transport, handling of drugs, and management of finances. Some international surveys use only a short general question on being hampered or disabled.[9]

Increasing evidence exists that disability prevalence, measured by these indices, has been falling (see Table 16.4). During the 1980s and 1990s, reductions in disability have been reported as 0.4–2.7 per cent per year.[2] Parker and Thorslund[11] conclude that most ADL indices are improving, although some evidence is mixed, and that indices for instrumental ADL are mostly improving or stagnating. National datasets have often reported conflicting evidence about severe forms of personal-care disability, such as limitations of bathing, dressing, and moving. Taking into account differing wording, sampling strategies, and inclusion of institutional populations in four US health surveys, a general reduction

Table 16.3 Studies of yearly changes in mobility-related disabilities in high-income countries

	Region	Age (years)	Length of follow-up (years)	Institutional population included?	Sample size	Indicator	Yearly change (age-adjusted) (%)	p value
1987–2001[36]	Netherlands	>55	14	No	2,708–3,474	Men: walking up stairs, carrying 5–10 kg, lifting object while standing, walking 400 m	−4.86	0.05
1987–2001[36]	Netherlands	>55	14	No	2,708–3,474	Women: walking up stairs, carrying 5–10 kg, lifting object while standing, walking 400 m	−3.64	0.05
1986–1999[67]	Spain	>65	13	Part	750,192 men	Walking up stairs, walking out of house, chairfast, bedfast, serious difficulty standing up or getting out of bed or chair	−3.56	...
1986–1999[67]	Spain	>65	13	Part	1,323,261 women	Walking up stairs, walking out of house, chairfast, bedfast, serious difficulty standing up or getting out of bed or chair	−2.57	...
1991/2–1996/7[47]	UK	65–69	5	Yes	689–687	Walking up stairs, chairfast, bedfast	5.00	0.09
1985/9–1993/9[76]	Finland	65–79	8	Yes, but under-represented	2,213–2,911	Men: use of stairs	−1.70	...
1985/9–1993/9[76]	Finland	65–79	8	Yes, but under-represented	2,213–2,911	Men: walking outside	−3.29	...
1985/9–1993/9[76]	Finland	65–79	8	Yes, but under-represented	2,251–2,934	Women: use of stairs	−0.52	...
1985/9–1993/9[76]	Finland	65–79	8	Yes, but under-represented	2,251–2,934	Women: walking outside	−1.88	...
1993–2002[70]	Japan	>66	9	No	1,786–2,391	Walking 200–300 m	−1.47	ns
1993–2002[70]	Japan	>66	9	No	1,786–2,391	Standing	−0.37	ns
1993–2002[70]	Japan	>66	9	No	1,786–2,391	Walking up stairs	−1.83	ns
1993–2002[70]	Japan	>66	9	No	1,786–2,391	Use of stairs or walking	−1.74	ns
1988–2000[77]	Europe	>70	12	No	3,496	Men: moving outdoors, walking up stairs, walking 400 m, carrying 5 kg	−0.17	ns

Period	Country	Age	Years	Reduction	N	Description	Value	Sig.
1988–2000[77]	Europe	>70	12	No	3,496	Women: moving outdoors, walking up stairs, walking 400 m, carrying 5 kg	−0.33	ns
1992–2002[37,44,45,78*]	Sweden	>77	10	Yes	537–561	Walking 100 m, walking up stairs, rising from chair, standing	4.00	0.01
1977–1999[69]	USA	79–88	22	No	177–174	Women: walking up stairs to 2nd floor	−3.34	0.01†
1977–1999[69]	USA	79–88	22	No	177–174	Women: walking 0.5 miles	−2.62	0.01†
1977–1999[69]	USA	79–88	22	No	103–119	Men: walking up stairs to 2nd floor	−4.55	0.01†
1977–1999[69]	USA	79–88	22	No	103–119	Men: walking 0.5 miles	−0.61	0.01†
1895 cohort vs 1905 cohort[79]	Denmark	>100	10	Yes	50–78	Community-dwelling women: walking indoors	−7.50	0.01
1895 cohort vs 1905 cohort[79]	Denmark	>100	10	Yes	50–78	Community-dwelling women: getting outdoors	−5.13	0.01
1895 cohort vs 1905 cohort[79]	Denmark	>100	10	Yes	50–78	Community-dwelling women: walking up stairs	−4.50	0.01
1895 cohort vs 1905 cohort[79]	Denmark	>100	10	Yes	110–107	Women in institutions: walking indoors	−1.82	0.23
1895 cohort vs 1905 cohort[79]	Denmark	>100	10	Yes	110–107	Women in institutions: getting outdoors	−4.19	0.01
1895 cohort vs 1905 cohort[79]	Denmark	>100	10	Yes	110–107	Women in institutions: walking up stairs	−2.67	0.01

Calculation of yearly change based on prevalences: (last year−first year)/first year×100. Calculation of yearly change based on odds ratio: −(1−OR)/number of years in follow-up×100. Positive values show an increase in disability. Negative values show a reduction in disability.

ns = not significant

* data are derived from reference [3]

† significant for any limitations of the Rosow-Breslau scale: heavy work around the house, walk up or down stairs to 2nd floor, walk 0.5 miles

Table 16.4   Studies of yearly changes in disabilities affecting activities of daily living in high-income countries

	Region	Age (years)	Length of follow-up (years)	Institutional population included?	Sample size	Indicator	Yearly change (age-adjusted) (%)	p value
1984–1996[51]	USA	40–59	12	No	NHIS	Unable to attend to personal care needs: severe disability	1.20	ns
1984–1996[51]	USA	40–59	12	No	NHIS	Unable to attend to or restricted in personal care needs: severe and moderate disability	1.62	0.05
1997/8–2005/6[49]	USA	40–59	8	No	NHIS	ADL	2.17	0.01
1997/8–2005/6[49]	USA	40–59	8	No	NHIS	IADL	−0.97	ns
1984–1996[51]	USA	60–69	12	No	NHIS	Unable to attend to personal care needs: severe disability	−0.09	ns
1984–1996[51]	USA	60–69	12	No	NHIS	Unable to attend to or restricted in personal care needs: severe and moderate disability	−0.31	ns
1991/2–1996/7[47]	UK	65–69	5	Yes	689–687	IADL/ADL	6.80	0.06
1987–2001[36]	Netherlands	>55	14	No	2,708–3,474	Men: ADL	−4.57	0.05
1987–2001[36]	Netherlands	>55	14	No	2,708–3,474	Women: ADL	−4.29	0.05
1993–1999[68]	Spain	>64	6	No	1,283	ADL	−9.54	0.05
1980/1–1991/2[81]	France	>65	11	No	5,000	Being hampered or disabled	−1.60	…
1991/2–2002/3[81]	France	>65	11	No	5,000	Being hampered or disabled	−5.50	…
1982–1994[82]	USA	>65	12	Yes	NLTCS	ADL low disability levels	−0.90	…
1994–2004/5[82]	USA	>65	10	Yes	NLTCS	ADL low disability levels	−1.70	…
1982–1994[82]	USA	>65	12	Yes	NLTCS	ADL high disability levels	−1.40	…
1994–2004/5[82]	USA	>65	10	Yes	NLTCS	ADL high disability levels	−2.40	…
1986–1999[67]	Spain	>65	13	Part	750,192 men	ADL and function	−3.97	…

1986–1999[67]	Spain	>65	13	Part	1,323,261 women	ADL and function	-3.29	...
1986–1999[67]	Spain	>65	13	Part	750,192	Men: BADL	0.50	...
1986–1999[67]	Spain	>65	13	Part	1,323,261	Women: BADL	1.92	...
1993/5–2001/3[80]	Finland	65–84	8	Yes	1,972–1,905	Women: BADL	-6.25	0.05
1993/5–2001/3[80]	Finland	65–84	8	Yes	2,021–1,908	Men: BADL	-5.13	0.05
1993–2002[70]	Japan	>66	9	No	1,786–2,391	Any IADL/ADL	-3.99	0.00
1993–2002[70]	Japan	>66	9	No	1,786–2,391	Any limitation	-1.94	0.10
1988–2000[77]	Europe	>70	12	No	3,496	Women: self-care disability	-7.20	0.03
1988–2000[77]	Europe	>70	12	No	3,496	Men: self-care disability	-2.60	0.05
1982–2001[83]	USA	>70	19	Yes	7,500–12,000	Difficulty, needs/receives help	1.0–2.5	...
1982–2003[84]	USA	>70	21	No	178,384 (all waves)	ADL/IADL	-1.38	0.01
1995–2004[85]	USA	>75	9	No	23,229 (all waves)	ADL	-1.46	0.01
1995–2004[85]	USA	>75	9	No	23,229 (all waves)	IADL	1.06	ns
1992–2002[37]	Sweden	>77	10	Yes	537–561	IADL	-0.70	ns
1992–2002[37]	Sweden	>77	10	Yes	537–561	ADL	0.70	ns
1977–1999[69]	USA	79–88	22	No	177–174	Women: ADL and function	-2.43	0.00
1977–1999[69]	USA	79–88	22	No	103–119	Men: ADL and function	-2.10	0.00
1895 cohort vs 1905 cohort[79]	Denmark	>100	10	Yes	162–189	Women: BADL	-1.19	0.01
1895 cohort vs 1905 cohort[79]	Denmark	>100	10	Yes	45–36	Men: BADL	0.61	ns

Calculation of yearly change based on prevalences: (last year–first year)/first year/number of years in follow-up×100. Calculation of yearly change based on odds ratio: –(1–OR)/number of years in follow-up×100. Positive values show an increase in disability. Negative values show a reduction in disability.

NHIS = National Health Interview Survey

ns = not significant

ADL = activities of daily living

IADL = instrumental activities of daily living

NLTCS = National Long Term Care Survey

BADL = basic activities of daily living

of 1.0–2.5 per cent per year is evident in the community-based elderly population with reported difficulties with ADL.[83] A series of studies, some in populations with the highest reported life expectancies, have lent support to this evidence.

In Japan, between 1993 and 2002, six of ten indices for ADL and instrumental ADL improved substantially after adjustment for age. Deterioration was mainly in disabilities affecting instrumental ADL. The proportion of people reporting any disability fell by 4.4 per cent per year.[70] For a general disability question about being hampered or disabled, a large yearly fall of 5.5 per cent between 1991 and 1992, and between 2002 and 2003, was reported for France,[81] after a smaller fall of 1.6 per cent in the previous decade. Changes in survey design, methods of data collection, and exact wording of the question might have caused acceleration of the trend in the later period.

Two studies in Spain had contradictory results— i.e. large yearly reductions of about 10 per cent in prevalence of disabilities affecting ADL,[68] and a worsening of an index of basic ADL by 0.5 per cent for men and 1.9 per cent for women per year,[67] in the presence of strong improvements in functional limitations. Finland benefited from large reductions in risk disability affecting basic ADL. Between 1993 and 1995, and 2001 and 2003, the index decreased yearly by 6.3 per cent for women and 5.1 per cent for men.[76] Small improvements are documented for the Netherlands[36] and the USA.[69,84,85] Contrary to the results of most studies, increases in disabilities affecting ADL and functional limitations are reported for elderly Swedish people, starting from the mid-1990s,[71] after decreases between the 1980s and 1990s. Disabilities affecting ADL and instrumental ADL might be increasing in young-old people in the UK[47] and in baby boomers in the USA.[49]

Health Expectancies

Health expectancies combine information about life expectancy and prevalence of good health, and thus directly address whether the period of morbidity or disability at the end of life is shortening or lengthening. Dependent on the measure of health, several health expectancies can be estimated:[86] disease-free health expectancy, life expectancy in perceived good health, and disability-free life expectancy. Trends in these three measures differ. Life years with morbidity have been increasing in parallel with the increase in some diseases and conditions. Life years in good self-perceived health have been generally rising,[87] whereas trends in life years with disability have evolved differently dependent on severity of disability: a decrease for the most severe levels of disability and an increase for the least severe levels.[9] Additionally, several one-country studies exist, but comparative analysis has been hampered by scarcity of harmonized longterm surveys that include health measures.

The European Health Expectancy Monitoring Unit is developing a common indicator of disability-free life expectancy named healthy life years (HLY). Time trends are available for 14 European countries between 1995 and 2003. People whose answers to the European Community Household Panel question, 'Are you hampered in your daily activities by any physical or mental health problem, illness, or disability?' were 'moderate' or 'severe' are defined as disabled. On the basis of this measure, differences in HLY in European countries are large. Even among countries with similar yearly rates of increase in life expectancy, some countries show a rise (men: Austria, Belgium, Italy, Finland, Germany; women: Belgium, Italy, Sweden), others stagnation (men: France, Greece, Ireland, Spain; women: Austria, Denmark, UK, Finland, France, Spain, UK) or reduction (men: Denmark, Portugal, Netherlands, Sweden, UK; women: Germany, Greece, Ireland, Netherlands, Portugal) in the proportion of life spent disability-free at ages 65 years and older.[88]

Inequalities in HLY are even larger if all 25 countries of the EU are considered:[89] at age 50 years the range is 14.5 years in men, and 13.7 years in women. A meta-regression with various macro-level indicators that cover the broad areas of wealth and expenditure, labour-force participation, and number of years of education shows that gross domestic product and expenditure on care for elderly people were positively associated with HLYs at age 50 years for both sexes, whereas for men only longterm employment was negatively and lifelong learning positively associated. A series of studies have reported larger improvements in disability-free life expectancy than in life expectancy.[1,39,67,90–92] A comparison of four health surveys in France[93] concludes that gains in life expectancy over recent decades might have added years with moderate difficulties but not years with severe difficulties. This finding is lent support by reports from Germany[94,95] and Belgium.[92]

Notably, almost all research about trends in health has been addressed to population averages that need not be typical of individual experience. Research in health has thus turned towards individual trajectories of health;[96] application to time trends, however, is still missing. Continued improvement of health trajectories depends on improvement in elderly people, although the foundation for this progress might partly be based on enhanced living conditions and lifestyle early in life. Progress towards improvement of health is likely to depend on public health efforts to, for example, combat smoking, obesity, low levels of exercise, poor diets, and excess drinking, and to provide improved living conditions and care for elderly people with several ailments.[97]

Although mortality is higher for men than for women at all ages, women have more functional limitations and more difficulties with ADL and instrumental ADL. For women compared with men, both incidence and prevalence of limitations are higher at all ages. The male advantage has been substantiated by results of physical performance tests up to the highest ages, and is larger in nonagenarians and centenarians than in octogenarians.[98] Sex differences in morbid conditions and diseases are more complex. For example, the increase in incidence of coronary heart disease starts about 10 years earlier in men than in women, but the male–female gap decreases after age 60 years and is small after 80 years. Women tend to have more reported symptoms, more non–life-threatening diseases, and more physical and psychological symptoms.[98] The most common explanations

of the health disadvantage of women pertain to differences in biology between men and women, illness and health behaviour and reporting, physicians' diagnostic patterns, and healthcare access, treatment, and use.

Time trends in disability and functional limitations usually apply to both sexes. With respect to disability affecting ADL or instrumental ADL, studies for the Netherlands,[36] Spain,[67] Finland,[80] and Europe[77] report larger reductions for women than for men, whereas in the USA[69] equal trends are reported, although for mobility limitations men generally fared better than did women.

Consequences of Mortality, Disease, and Disability

Are we living not only longer, but also better? Most evidence for people aged younger than 85 years suggests postponement of limitations and disabilities, despite an increase in chronic diseases and conditions. This apparent contradiction is at least partly accounted for by early diagnosis, improved treatment, and amelioration of prevalent diseases so that they are less disabling.[1,6,11,99] An estimated 14–22 per cent of the overall fall in disability can be attributed to reductions in disabilities associated with cardiovascular diseases.[100] Trends in disability might also show underlying trends in other domains. The rising use of assistive technology and improvements in housing standards, public transport, accessibility of buildings, changes in social policies, shifting gender roles, and the social perception of disability also might have contributed to loosening of the link between disease and functional limitation or disability.[4,11] Finally, increasing levels of educational attainment and income in elderly people, improved living and workplace conditions, reduced poverty, changes in marital status towards a rising proportion of couples in elderly people, and improvements in early childhood conditions might have contributed to the fall in disability.[6,56] Hence, people aged younger than 85 years are living longer and, on the whole, are able to manage their daily activities for longer than were previous cohorts.

For people aged older than 85 years, the situation is less clear. Data are sparse, and widespread concern exists that exceptional longevity has grim results both for individuals and for societies. The 'failure of success' hypothesis states that a cohort with a rising proportion of individuals surviving to some late age will have increased disease and disability at that age. The alternative hypothesis is that exceptionally old people generally enjoy the success of success—i.e. increases in the proportion of the population surviving to the highest ages are accompanied by concurrent postponements of physical and cognitive disability.

Data for exceptionally old people are few and inconsistent. Comparisons between centenarians from the Danish 1895–6 and 1905 cohorts suggest that although nearly 50 per cent more people from the 1905 cohort reached age 100 years than did people in the 1895–6 cohort, no increase was reported in physical or cognitive disability level and, on the contrary, some improvement was detected for women.[78,101] This finding is in agreement with research in young-elderly people (aged younger than 85 years) showing that prevalence of disability is decreasing and that individuals are not only living longer than they did in previous years, but also have improved functional states in successive cohorts because of prevention of disease and disabilities in addition to treatments and environmental changes compensating for consequences of disease.[2,5,8,37,38,77,102,103]

Other researchers have reported less encouraging results for exceptionally old people. Data from Japan, the country with the highest proportion of people surviving to age 100 years, suggest that more recent cohorts of Japanese centenarians have worse health than did previous cohorts.[104] Cross-country and cross-sex comparisons also suggest that increased survival to the highest ages is associated with worse health; Danish centenarians have worse physical function than do Chinese centenarians, and female centenarians have worse function than do male centenarians.[105] These findings are consistent with the common view in clinical medicine and among some gerontologists that the substantial rise in proportion of exceptionally long-lived individuals in successive birth cohorts is the result of help given to an increasing proportion of frail and ill people into advanced old age, with huge personal and societal costs.[106]

Even pediatric progress has generated worry. Gruenberg[107] suggested that survival of frail children could lead to a geriatric failure of pediatric success. However, on the basis of analyses of US trends in self-reported health, Waidmann[108] asserted that there was an illusion of failure: mortality reduction did not necessarily mean worsening of health in the population. Whether continued increases in survival to exceptionally old age will lead to a failure of success or a success of success in the health of the oldest-old population remains to be seen.

Traditionally, man has three major periods of life: childhood, adulthood, and old age. Old age is now evolving into two segments, a third age (young-old) and a fourth age (oldest-old). Some students of aging have asserted that the prospects for healthy longevity are poor.[21,109,110] For example, Baltes and Smith[106] envisioned that in the third age, functioning and dignity are usually conserved, whereas the fourth age will generally be characterized by vulnerability, with little identity, psychological autonomy, and personal control. The expectation is that developments will lead to an increasing number of individuals in successive birth cohorts reaching their tenth and eleventh decades in frail states of health, with many existing in a vegetative state. In other words, exceptional longevity within a cohort is expected to lead to exceptional levels of oldest-old disability.

This hypothesis was tested in the Danish 1905 Cohort Survey, which longitudinally assessed the entire Danish 1905 cohort from 1998 to 2005.[14] In the aggregate, this cohort had only a small reduction in the proportion of independent individuals at four assessments between age 92 and 100 years: 39 per cent, 36 per cent, 32 per cent, and 33 per cent—a nearly constant proportion of individuals in the cohort were independent over the 7–8 years of follow-up. However, for participants who survived until 2005, prevalence of independence fell by more than a factor of two—from 70 per cent in 1998 to 33 per cent in 2005. Similar results were obtained for other functional outcomes, such as grip strength, cognitive composite score, and symptoms of depression. Additional analyses of missing data due to death and non-response suggest that the discrepancy between population trajectory and individual trajectory is due to increased mortality in dependent individuals. Frail and disabled people die first, leaving the most robust in the cohort. Hence, overall characteristics of the cohort remain nearly unchanged.

The finding that 30–40 per cent of a contemporary cohort of nonagenarians is independent from age 92–100 years might also be valid beyond age 100 years. In a study of 32 US supercentenarians (age 110–119 years), about 40 per cent needed little assistance or were independent,[111] suggesting that supercentenarians are not more disabled than are people aged 92 years. These studies do not accord with the prediction that the fourth age for man is in a vegetative state. On the contrary, findings suggest that the characteristics of a cohort do not change much between ages 92 and 100 years (and maybe even 119 years) in central domains, such as physical and cognitive functions.

The levelling off in disability level for a cohort at the highest ages suggests that care costs per individual do not increase in the tenth and eleventh decades of life. Lubitz and colleagues[112] showed that the expected cumulative lifetime health expenditures for individuals in good health at age 70 years were not greater than were expenditures for less healthy people, despite greater longevity of healthier elderly people. Thus, health promotion efforts aimed at people aged 65 years and younger might improve health and longevity of elderly people without increasing health expenditure. Individuals who survive longest have a health profile that is, in many respects, similar to that of individuals who are a decade or so younger. This finding suggests that most individuals can expect to deteriorate physically before death, but postponement of this process enables people to live to advanced ages without great disability.

Population aging poses severe challenges for the traditional social welfare state. An often used indicator is

the old age dependency ratio, which divides the number of people at retirement ages (> 65 years) by the number of people at working ages (15–64 years). In Germany in 1956, there were about 15–16 pensioners for every 100 people at working ages. Half-a-century later, there were 29 people aged older than 65 years for every 100 people aged 15–64 years. The German Federal Statistical Office[33] projects another doubling of this index, to about 60, half-a-century from now. Large increases in both number and proportion of elderly individuals are forthcoming not only in Germany but also in other European countries, Japan, the USA, and many other countries. Population aging is a worldwide occurrence.

A reasonable strategy to cope with the economic implications of population aging is to raise the typical age of retirement, and most governments are moving in this direction. Improvements in health and functioning along with shifting of employment from jobs that need strength to jobs needing knowledge imply that a rising proportion of people in their sixties and seventies are capable of contributing to the economy. Because many people in their sixties and seventies would prefer part-time work to full-time labour, an increase in jobs that need 15, 20, or 25 hours of work per week seems likely. If part-time work becomes common for elderly people, then more opportunities for part-time work might open up for young people. If people in their sixties and early seventies worked much more than they do nowadays, then most people could work fewer hours per week than is currently common—if they worked correspondingly more years of their longer lives. The average amount of work per year of life could stay at about the same as it is at present.[113]

The twentieth century was a century of redistribution of income. The twenty-first century could be a century of redistribution of work. Redistribution would spread work more evenly across populations and over the ages of life. Individuals could combine work, education, leisure, and childrearing in varying amounts at different ages. This vision is starting to receive some preliminary attention.[113] Preliminary evidence suggests that shortened working weeks over extended working lives might further contribute to increases in life expectancy and health. Redistribution of work will, however, not be sufficient to meet the coming challenges. Even if the health of individuals at any particular age improves, there could be an increased total burden if the number of individuals at that age rises sufficiently. Healthcare often needs service sector or family-member labour by individuals; this labour is not easily substituted by machines, although assistive technology is likely to reduce the need for personal care in high-income countries.[114,115]

Very long lives are not the distant privilege of remote future generations—very long lives are the probable destiny of most people alive now in developed countries (Table 16.1).[12] Increasing numbers of people at old and very old ages will pose major challenges for healthcare systems. Present evidence, however, suggests that people are not only living longer than they did previously, but also they are living longer with less disability and fewer functional limitations.

References

1. Crimmins, E.M. (2004). Trends in the health of the elderly. *Annual Review of Public Health, 25*, 79–98.
2. Freedman, V.A., Martin, L.G., & Schoeni, R.F. (2002). Recent trends in disability and functioning among older adults in the United States: A systematic review. *Journal of the American Medical Association, 288*, 3137–246.
3. Spillman, B.C. (2004). Changes in elderly disability rates and the implications for health care utilization and cost. *Milbank Quarterly, 82*, 157–94.
4. Wolf, D.A., Hunt, K., & Knickman, J. (2005). Perspectives on the recent decline in disability at older ages. *Milbank Quarterly, 83*, 365–95.
5. Manton, K.G. (2008). Recent declines in chronic disability in the elderly US population: Risk factors and future dynamics. *Annual Review of Public Health, 29*, 91–113.
6. Schoeni, R.F., Freedman, V.A., & Martin, L.G. (2008). Why is late-life disability declining? *Milbank Quarterly, 86*, 47.
7. Jacobzone, S., Cambois, F., & Robine, J.M. (2000). Is the health of older persons in OECD countries improving fast enough to compensate for population ageing? *OECD Economic Studies, 30*, 149–90.
8. Robine, J.M., & Michel, J.P. (2004). Looking forward to a general theory on population aging. *Journals of Gerontology—Series A: Biological Sciences & Medical Sciences, 59*, M590–7.
9. Robine, J.-M., Romieu, I., & Michel, J.P. (2003). Trends in health expectancies. In J.-M. Robine, C. Jagger, C.D. Mathers, E.M. Crimmins, & R.M. Suzman (Eds), *Determining health expectancies*, pp. 75–104. Chichester: John Wiley & Sons.
10. Wen, X. (2004). Trends in the prevalence of disability and chronic conditions among the older population: Implications for survey design and measurement of disability. *Australian Journal of Ageing, 23*, 3–6.
11. Parker, M.G., & Thorslund, M. (2007). Health trends in the elderly population: Getting better and getting worse. *Gerontologist, 47*, 150.
12. Oeppen, J., & Vaupel, J.W. (2002). Broken limits to life expectancy. *Science, 296*, 1029–31.
13. Engberg, H., Oksuzyan, A., Jeune, B., Vaupel J.W., & Christensen, K. (2009). Centenarians—A useful model for healthy aging? A 29 year follow-up of hospitalizations among 40 000 Danes born in 1905. *Aging Cell, 8*, 270–6.
14. Christensen, K., McGue, M., Petersen, I., Jeune, B., & Vaupel, J.W. (2008). Exceptional longevity does not result in excessive levels of disability. *Proceedings of the National Academy of Science USA, 105*, 13274–9.
15. Vaupel, J.W., Carey, J.R, Christensen, K., et al. (1998). Biodemographic trajectories of longevity. *Science, 280*, 855–60.
16. Suzman, R.M., Willis, D.P., & Manton, K.G. (1992). *The oldest old.* New York: Oxford University Press.
17. Smith, J. (2001). Well-being and health from age 70 to 100 years: Findings from the Berlin Aging Study. *European Review, 9*, 461–77.
18. Suzman, R., & Riley, M.W. (1985). Introducing the 'oldest old'. *Milbank Memorial Fund Quarterly: Health and Society, 63*, 177–86.
19. Ministry of Health, Labour, and Welfare, Japan. (2009). Life tables. Retrieved from www.mhlw.go.jp/english/database/db-hw/vs02.html

20. Fries, J.F. (1980). Aging, natural death and the compression of morbidity. *New England Journal of Medicine, 303*, 130–5.

21. Olshansky, S.J., Carnes, B.A., & Désesguelles, A. (2001). Prospects for longevity. *Science, 291*, 1491–2.

22. Kannisto, V. (1994). *Development of oldest-old mortality, 1950–1990: Evidence from 28 developed countries* (Monographs on population aging 1). Odense: Odense University Press.

23. Kannisto, V. (1996). *The advancing frontier of survival* (Monographs on population aging 3). Odense: Odense University Press.

24. Kannisto, V., Lauritsen, J., Thatcher, A.R., & Vaupel, J.W. (1994). Reductions in mortality at advanced ages: Several decades of evidence from 27 countries. *Population and Development Review, 30*, 793–810.

25. Vaupel, J.W. (1997). The remarkable improvements in survival at older ages. *Philosophical Transactions of the Royal Society of London—Series B: Biological Sciences, 352*, 1799–804.

26. Rau, R., Soroko, F., Jasilionis, D., & Vaupel, J.W. (2008). Continued reductions in mortality at advanced ages. *Population Development Review, 34*, 747–68.

27. Max Planck Institute for Demographic Research. Kannisto-Thatcher Database on Old Age Mortality. Retrieved from www.demogr.mpg.de ?/http://www.demogr.mpg.de/databases/ktdb

28. Manton, K.G., & Vaupel, J.W. (1995). Survival after the age of 80 in the United States, Sweden, France, England, and Japan. *New England Journal of Medicine, 333*, 1232–5.

29. Wang, H., & Preston, S.R. (2009). Forecasting United States mortality using cohort smoking histories. *Proceedings of the National Academy of Science USA, 106*, 393–8.

30. Juel, K., Sørensen, J., & Brønnum-Hansen, H. (2008). Risk factors and public health in Denmark. *Scandinavian Journal of Public Health, 36*(1), 11–227.

31. Juel, K. (2008). Life expectancy and mortality in Denmark compared to Sweden. What is the effect of smoking and alcohol? *Ugeskr Laeger, 170*, 2423–7.

32. Preston, S.H., Himes, C., & Eggers, M. (1989). Demographic conditions responsible for population aging. *Demography, 26*, 691–704.

33. Statistisches Bundesamt, Wiesbaden, Germany. (2006). *Statistisches Bundesamt 2006.*

Bevölkerung Deutschlands bis 2050. Ergebnisse der 11 koordinierten Bevölkerungsvoraus-berechnung.

34. Verbrugge, L.M., & Jette, A.M. (1994). The disablement process. *Social Science and Medicine, 38*, 1–14.

35. Vallin, J., & Meslé, F. (2005). Convergences and divergences: An analytical framework of national and sub-national trends in life expectancy. *Genus, 61*, 83–123.

36. Puts, M.T.E., Deeg, D.J.H., Hoeymans, N., Nusselder, W.J., & Schellevis, F.G. (2008). Changes in the prevalence of chronic disease and the association with disability in the older Dutch population between 1987 and 2001. *Age and Ageing, 37*, 187–93.

37. Parker, M.G, Ahacic, K., & Thorslund, M. (2005). Health changes among Swedish oldest old: Prevalence rates from 1992 and 2002 show increasing health problems. *Journals of Gerontology—Series A: Biological Sciences & Medical Sciences, 60*, 1351–5.

38. Crimmins, E.M., Alley, D., Reynolds, S.L., Johnston, M., Karlamangla, A., & Seeman, T. (2005). Changes in biological markers of health: Older Americans in the 1990s. *Journals of Gerontology—Series A: Biological Sciences & Medical Sciences, 60*, 1409–13.

39. Jeune, B., & Brønnum-Hansen, H. (2008). Trends in health expectancy at age 65 for various health indicators, 1987–2005, Denmark. *European Journal of Ageing, 5*, 279–85.

40. Crimmins, E.M., & Saito, V. (2000). Change in the prevalence of diseases among older Americans: 1984–1994. *Demographic Research, 3*, 9.

41. Freedman, V.A., & Martin, L.G. (2000). Contribution of chronic conditions to aggregate changes in old-age functioning. *Journal of the American Public Health Association, 90*, 1755–60.

42. Lafortune, G., & Balestat, G. (2007). *Trends in severe disability among elderly people: Assessing the evidence in 12 OECD countries and the future implications* (OECD health working paper, no. 26), Paris: Organisation for Economic Co-operation and Development.

43. Rosen, M., Haglund, B. From healthy survivors to sick survivors—Implications for the twenty-first century. *Scandinavian Journal of Public Health, 33*, 151–5.

44. Fors, S., Lennartsson, C., & Lundberg, O. (2008). Health inequalities among older adults in Sweden

1991–2002. *European Journal of Public Health, 18,* 138–43.

45. Meinow, B., Parker, M., Kåreholt, I., & Thorslund, M. (2006). Complex health problems in the oldest old in Sweden 1992–2002. *European Journal of Ageing, 3,* 98–106.

46. Karim-Kos, H.E., de Vries, E., Soerjomataram, I., Lemmens, V., Siesling, S., & Coebergh, J.W.W. (2008). Recent trends of cancer in Europe: A combined approach of incidence, survival and mortality for 17 cancer sites since the 1990s. *European Journal of Cancer, 44,* 1345–89.

47. Jagger, C., Matthews, R., Matthews, F., et al. (2007). Cohort differences in disease and disability in the young-old: Findings from the MRC Cognitive Function and Ageing Study (MRC-CFAS). *BMC Public Health, 7,* 156.

48. Bhattacharya, J., Choudhry, K., & Lakdawalla, D. (2008). Chronic disease and trends in severe disability in working age populations. *Medical Care, 46,* 92–100.

49. Martin, L.G., Freedman, V.A., Schoeni, R.F., & Andreski, P.M. (2009). Health and functioning among baby boomers approaching 60. *Journal of Gerontology—Series B: Psychological Science and Social Science, 64,* 369–77.

50. Paul, S.L., Srikanth, V.K., & Thrift, A.G. (2007). The large and growing burden of stroke. *Current Drug Targets, 8,* 786–93.

51. Lakdawalla, D.N., Bhattacharya, J., & Goldman, D.P. (2004). Are the young becoming more disabled? *Health Affairs, 23,* 168–76.

52. Peeters, A., Barendregt, J.J., Willekens, F., Mackenbach, J.P., Mamun, A.A., & Bonneux, L. (2003). Obesity in adulthood and its consequences for life expectancy: A life-table analysis. *Annals of Internal Medicine, 138,* 24–32.

53. Sturm, R., Ringel, J.S., & Andreyeva T. (2004). Increasing obesity rates and disability trends. *Health Affairs, 23,* 199–205.

54. Olshansky, S.J., Passaro, D.J., Hershow, R.C., et al. (2005). A potential decline in life expectancy in the United States in the 21th century. *New England Journal of Medicine, 352,* 1138–45.

55. Doblhammer, G., Hoffmann, R., Muth, E., Westphal, C., & Kruse, A. (2009). A systematic literature review of studies analyzing the effect of sex, age, education, marital status, obesity, and smoking on health transitions. *Demographic Research, 20,* 37–64.

56. Reynolds, S.L., Saito, Y, & Crimmins, E.M. (2005). The impact of obesity on active life expectancy in older American men and women. *Gerontologist, 45,* 438–44.

57. Wild, S., Roglic, G., Green, A., Sicree, R., & King, H. Global prevalence of diabetes: Estimates for the year 2000 and projections for 2030. *Diabetes Care, 27,* 1047–53.

58. Zamboni, M., Mazzali, G., Zoico, E., et al. (2005). Health consequences of obesity in the elderly: A review of four unresolved questions. *International Journal of Obesity, 29,* 1011–29.

59. Ong, K.L., Cheung, B.M.Y., Man Y.B., Lau, C.P, & Lam, K.S.L. (2007). Prevalence, awareness, treatment, and control of hypertension among United States adults 1999–2004. *Hypertension, 49,* 69–75.

60. Alley, D.E, Chang, V.W, Doshi, J. (2008). The shape of things to come: obesity, aging, and disability. *LDI Issue Brief, 13,* 1.

61. Alley, D.E., & Chang, V.W. (2007). The changing relationship of obesity and disability, 1988–2004. *Journal of the American Medical Association, 298,* 2020–7.

62. Ostchega Y., Dillon, C.F., Hughes, J.P., Carroll, M., & Yoon, S. (2007). Trends in hypertension prevalence, awareness, treatment, and control in older US adults: Data from the National Health and Nutrition Examination Survey 1988 to 2004. *Journal of the American Geriatric Society, 55,* 1056.

63. Qureshi A.I., Sun, M.F.K, Kirmani, J.F., & Divani, A.A. (2005). Prevalence and trends of prehypertension and hypertension in United States: National Health and Nutrition Examination Surveys 1976 to 2000. *Medical Science Monitor, 11,* CR403–9.

64. Rodgers, W.L., Ofstedal, M.B., & Herzog, A.R. (2003). Trends in scores on tests of cognitive ability in the elderly US population, 1993–2000. *Journal of Gerontology—Series B: Psychological Science and Social Science, 58,* S338–46.

65. Manton, K.G., & Lamb, V.L. (2005). Mortality and disability trajectories above age 90 in the US 1982–2004. International Union for the Scientific Study of Population, XXV International Population Conference; Tours, France; July 18–23.

66. Langa, K.M., Larson, E.B., Karlawish, J.H., et al. (2008). Trends in the prevalence and mortality of cognitive impairment in the United States: Is there evidence of a compression of cognitive morbidity? *Alzheimers and Dementia, 4,* 134–44.

67. Sagardui-Villamor, J., Guallar-Castillon, P., Garcia-Ferruelo, M., Banegas, J.R., & Rodriguez-Artalejo, F. (2005). Trends in disability and disability-free life expectancy among elderly people in Spain: 1986–1999. *Journals of Gerontology— Series A: Biological Sciences & Medical Sciences, 60,* 1028–34.

68. Zunzunegui, M.V., Nunez, O., Durban, M., García de Yébenes, M.-J, & Otero, Á. (2006). Decreasing prevalence of disability in activities of daily living, functional limitations and poor self-rated health: A 6-year follow-up study in Spain. *Aging Clinical and Experimental Research, 18,* 352–8.

69. Murabito, J.M., Pencina, M.J., Zhu, L., Kelly-Hayes, M., Shrader, P., & D'Agostino, R.B., Sr. (2008). Temporal trends in self-reported functional limitations and physical disability among the community-dwelling elderly population: The Framingham Heart Study. *American Journal of Public Health, 98,* 1256–62.

70. Schoeni, B., Liang, J., Bennett, H., Sugisawa, H., Fukaya, T., & Kobayash, E. (2006). Trends in old-age functioning and disability in Japan 1993–2002. *Population Studies* (Cambridge), *60,* 39–54.

71. Parker, M.G., Schön, P., Lagergren, M., & Thorslund, M. (2008). Functional ability in the elderly Swedish population from 1980 to 2005. *European Journal of Ageing, 5,* 299–309.

72. Desai, M., Pratt, L.A., Lentzner, H., & Robinson, K.N. (2001). Trends in vision and hearing among older Americans. *Aging Trends, 2,* 1–8.

73. Freedman, V.A, & Martin, L.G. (1998). Understanding trends in functional limitations among older Americans. *American Journal of Public Health, 88,* 1457–62.

74. Freedman, V.A., Schoeni, R.F., Martin, L.G., & Cornman, J.C. (2007). Chronic conditions and the decline in late-life disability. *Demography, 44,* 459–77.

75. Spalton, D., & Koch, D. (2000). The constant evolution of cataract surgery. *British Medical Journal, 321,* 1304.

76. Sulander, T.T., Rahkonen, O.J., & Uutela, A.K. (2003). Functional ability in the elderly Finnish population: Time period differences and associations, 1985–1999. *Scandinavian Journal of Public Health, 31,* 100–6.

77. Äijänseppä, S., Notkola, I.-L., Tijhuis, M., van Staveren, W., Kromhout, D., & Nissinen, A. (2005). Physical functioning in elderly Europeans—10 year changes in the north and south: The HALE project. *Journal of Epidemiology and Community Health, 59,* 413–19.

78. Ahacic, K., Parker, M.G., & Thorsland, M. (2003). Mobility limitations 1974–1991: Period changes explaining improvement in the population. *Social Science and Medicine, 57,* 2411–22.

79. Engberg, H., Christensen, K., Andersen-Ranberg, K., Vaupel, J.W., & Jeune, B. (2008). Improving activities of daily living in Danish centenarians— but only in women: A comparative study of two birth cohorts born in 1895 and 1905. *Journals of Gerontology—Series A: Biological Sciences & Medical Sciences, 63,* 1186–92.

80. Sulander, T., Martelin, T., Sainio, P., Rahkonen, O., Nissinen, A., & Uutela, A. (2006). Trends and educational disparities in functional capacity among people aged 65–84 years. *International Journal of Epidemiology, 35,* 1255–61.

81. Cambois, E., Robine, J.M., & Mormiche, P. (2007). Did the prevalence of disability in France really fall sharply in the 1990s? A discussion of questions asked in the French Health Survey. *Population, 62,* 315–38.

82. Manton, K.G, Gu, X., & Lamb, V.L. (2006). Change in chronic disability 1982 to 2004/2005 as measured by long-term changes in function and health in the US elderly population. *Proceedings of the National Academy of Science USA, 103,* 18374–9.

83. Freedman, V.A., Crimmins, E., Schoeni, R.F., et al. (2004). Resolving inconsistencies in trends in old-age disability: Report from a technical working group. *Demography, 41,* 417–41.

84. Martin, L.G., Schoeni, R.F., Freedman, V.A., & Andreski, P. (2007). Feeling better? Trends in general health status. *Journals of Gerontology—Series B: Psychological Science and Social Science, 62,* S11–21.

85. Freedman, V.A., Martin, L.G., Schoeni, R.F., & Cornman, J.C. (2008). Declines in late-life disability: The role of early-and mid-life factors. *Social Science and Medicine, 66,* 1588–602.

86. Robine, J.M. (2002). A new health expectancy classification system. In C.J.L. Murray, J.A. Salomon, C.D. Mathers, & A.D. Lopez (Eds), *Summary measures of population health,* pp. 205–12. Geneva: World Health Organization.

87. Doblhammer, G., & Kytir, J. (2001). Compression or expansion of morbidity? Trends in healthy-life

expectancy in the elderly Austrian population between 1978 and 1998. *Social Science and Medicine, 52,* 385–91.

88. Van Oyen H. (2005). Living longer healthier lives, comments on the changes in life expectancy and disability free life expectancy in the European Union since 1995. In J.-M. Robine, C. Jagger, H. van Oyen, et al. (Eds), *Are we living longer healthier lives in the EU? Disability-free life expectancy (DFLE) in EU countries from 1991 to 2003 based on the European Household Panel (ECHP) EHEMU Technical Report 2,* pp. 1–29. Montpellier: EHEMU.

89. Jagger, C., Gillies, C., Moscone, F., et al, and the EHLEIS team. (2008). Inequalities in healthy life years in the 25 countries of the European Union in 2005: A cross-national meta-regression analysis. *The Lancet, 372,* 2124–31.

90. Mathers, C.D., Sadana, R., Salomon, J.A, Murray, C.J.L., & Lopez, A.D. (2001). Healthy life expectancy in 191 countries, 1999. *The Lancet, 357,* 1685–91.

91. Robine, J.M. (2006). Trends in population health. *Aging Clinical Experiments and Research, 18,* 349–51.

92. Van Oyen, H., Cox, B., Demarest, S., Deboosere, P., & Lorant, V. (2008). Trends in health expectancy indicators in the older adult population in Belgium between 1997 and 2004. *European Journal of Ageing, 5,* 137–46.

93. Cambois, E., Clavel, A., Romieu, I., & Robine, J.M. (2008). Trends in disability-free life expectancy at age 65 in France: Consistent and diverging patterns according to the underlying disability measure. *European Journal of Ageing, 5,* 287–98.

94. Doblhammer, G., & Ziegler, U. (2006). Future elderly living conditions in Europe: Demographic aspects. In G.M. Baltes, V. Lasch, & K. Reimann (Eds), *Gender, health and ageing: European perspectives on life course, health issues and social challenges.* Alter(n) und Gesellschaft ed.

95. Unger, R. (2006). Trends in active life expectancy in Germany between 1984 and 2003—A cohort analysis with different health indicators. *Journal of Public Health, 14,* 155–63.

96. Doblhammer, G., & Hoffmann, R. (2009, June 29). Gender differences in trajectories of health limitations and subsequent mortality. A study based on the German socioeconomic panel 1995–2001 with a mortality follow-up 2002–2005. *Journals of Gerontol—Series B: Psychological Science and Social Science.* DOI:10.1093/geronb/gbp051

97. Riley, J.C. (2001). *Rising life expectancy: A global history.* New York: Cambridge University Press.

98. Oksuzyan, O., Juel, K., Vaupel, J.W., & Christensen, K. (2008). Men: Good health and high mortality. Sex differences in health and aging. *Aging Clinical Experiments and Research, 20,* 91–102.

99. Perenboom, R.J.M., Van Herten, L.M., Boshuizen, H.C., & Van Den Bos, G.A.M. (2004). Trends in disability-free life expectancy. *Disability and Rehabilitation, 26,* 377–86.

100. Cutler, D.M., Landrum, M.B., & Stewart, K. (2006). *Intensive medical care and cardiovascular disease disability reductions* (NBER working paper no. 12184). New York: National Bureau of Economic Research.

101. Engberg, H., Christensen, K., Andersen-Ranberg, K., & Jeune, B. (2008). Cohort changes in cognitive function among Danish centenarians. A comparative study of 2 birth cohorts born in 1895 and 1905. *Dementia and Geriatric Cognitive Disorders, 26,* 153–60.

102. Manton K.G., Corder, L., & Stallard, E. (1997). Chronic disability trends in elderly United States populations: 1982–1994. *Proceedings of the National Academy of Science USA, 94,* 2593–8.

103. Manton, K.G., & Gu, X. (2001). Changes in the prevalence of chronic disability in the United States black and nonblack population above age 65 from 1982 to 1999. *Proceeding of the National Academy of Science USA, 98,* 6354–9.

104. Suzuki, M., Akisaka, M., Ashitomi, I., Higa, K., & Nozaki, H. (1995). Chronological study concerning ADL among Okinawan centenarians. *Nippon Ronen Igakkai Zasshi, 32,* 416.

105. Wang, Z., Zeng, Y., Jeune, B., & Vaupel, J.W. (1997). A demographic and health profile of centenarians in China. In J.M. Robine, J.W. Vaupel, B. Jeune, & M. Allard (Eds), *Longevity: To the limits and beyond,* pp. 91–104. New York: Springer.

106. Baltes, P.B., & Smith, J. (2003). New frontiers in the future of aging: From successful aging of the young old to the dilemmas of the fourth age. *Gerontology, 49,* 123–35.

107. Gruenberg, E.M. (1997). The failures of success. *Milbank Memorial Fund Quarterly: Health and Society, 55,* 3–24.

108. Waidmann, T., Bound, J., & Schoenbaum, M. (1995). The illusion of failure: Trends in the self-reported health of the US elderly. *Milbank Quarterly, 73,* 253–87.

109. Hayflick, L. (2003). Living forever and dying in the attempt. *Experiments in Gerontology, 38,* 1231–41.

110. Hayflick, L. (2007). Entropy explains aging, genetic determinism explains longevity, and undefined terminology explains misunderstanding both. *PLoS Genetics, 3,* e220.

111. Schoenhofen, E.A., Wyszynski, D.F., Andersen, S., et al. (2006). Characteristics of 32 supercentenarians. *Journal of the American Geriatric Society, 54,* 1237–40.

112. Lubitz, J., Cai, L., Kramarow, E., & Lentzner, H. (2003). Health, life expectancy, and health care spending among the elderly. *New England Journal of Medicine, 349,* 1048–55.

113. Vaupel, J.W., & Loichinger, E. (2006). Redistributing work in aging Europe. *Science, 312,* 1911–13.

114. Agree, E.M., Freedman, V.A., Cornman, J.C., Wolf, D.A., & Marcotte, J.E. (2005). Reconsidering substitution in long-term care: When does assistive technology take the place of personal care? *Journal of Gerontology—Series B: Psychological Science and Social Science, 60,* S272–80.

115. Freedman, V.A., Agree, E.M., Martin, L.G., & Cornman, J.C. (2006). Trends in the use of assistive technology and personal care for late-life disability, 1992–2001. *Gerontologist, 46,* 124–7.

CHAPTER 17

Social Determinants of Health Inequalities

Michael Marmot

There are gross inequalities in health between countries. Life expectancy at birth, to take one measure, ranges from 34 years in Sierra Leone to 81.9 years in Japan.[1] Within countries, too, there are large inequalities—a 20-year gap in life expectancy between the most and least advantaged populations in the USA, for example.[2] One welcome response to these health inequalities is to put more effort into the control of major diseases that kill and to improve health systems.[3,4]

A second, belated response is to deal with poverty. This issue is the thrust of the Millennium Development Goals.[5,6] These goals challenge the world community to tackle poverty in the world's poorest countries. Included in these goals is reduction of child mortality, the health outcome most sensitive to the effects of absolute material deprivation.

To reduce inequalities in health across the world there is need for a third major thrust that is complementary to development of health systems and relief of poverty: to take action on the social determinants of health. Such action will include relief of poverty, but it will have the broader aim of improving the circumstances in which people live and work. It will, therefore, address not only the major infectious diseases linked with poverty of material conditions but also non-communicable diseases—both physical and mental—and violent deaths that form the major burden of disease and death in every region of the world

outside Africa and add substantially to the burden of communicable disease in sub-Saharan Africa.

To understand the social determinants of health, how they operate, and how they can be changed to improve health and reduce health inequalities, WHO is setting up an independent Commission on Social Determinants of Health, with the mission to link knowledge with action (see Panel 1). Public policy—both national and global—should change to take into account the evidence on social determinants of health and interventions and policies that will address them.

This introduction to the Commission's task lays out the problems of inequalities in health that the Commission will address and the approach that it will take. This report will argue that health status should be of concern to all policy makers, not merely those within the health sector. If health of a population suffers it is an indicator that the set of social arrangements needs to change. Simply, the Commission will seek to have public policy based on a vision of the world where people matter and social justice is paramount.

Inequalities in Health between and within Countries: Poverty and Inequality

A catastrophe on the scale of the Indian Ocean tsunami rightly focuses attention on the susceptibility

Panel 1

The Commission on Social Determinants of Health

The Commission will not only review existing knowledge but also raise societal debate and promote uptake of policies that will reduce inequalities in health within and between countries.

The Commission's aim is, within three years, to set solid foundations for its vision: the societal relations and factors that influence health and health systems will be visible, understood, and recognized as important. On this basis, the opportunities for policy and action and the costs of not acting on these social dimensions will be widely known and debated. Success will be achieved if institutions working in health at local, national, and global levels will be using this knowledge to set and implement relevant public policy affecting health. The Commission will contribute to a longterm process of incorporating social determinants of health into planning, policy, and technical work at WHO.

of poor and vulnerable populations to natural disasters. It is no less important to keep on the agenda the more enduring problem of inequalities in health among countries.

Children

Under-5 mortality varies from 316 per 1,000 live births in Sierra Leone to 3 per 1,000 live births in Iceland, 4 per 1,000 live births in Finland, and 5 per 1,000 live births in Japan.[1] In 16 countries (12 in Africa), child mortality rose in the 1990s,[7] by 43 per cent in Zimbabwe, 52 per cent in Botswana, and 75 per cent in Iraq.[8]

Figure 17.1 shows under-5 mortality rates for four countries with households classified according to socioeconomic quintile. Child mortality varies among countries.[9] Within countries, not only is child mortality highest among the poorest households, but also there is a social gradient: the higher the socioeconomic level of the household, the lower the mortality rate.

Adults

Differences in adult mortality among countries are large and growing. Figure 17.2 shows probability of death between ages 15 and 60 by region of the world

between 1970 and 2002. Mortality rose in Africa and in the countries of central and eastern Europe, whereas it declined in the world as a whole. By 2002, for example, men in the high mortality countries of Europe had more than 40 per cent probability of death between ages 15 and 60 compared to a 25 per cent probability in Southeast Asia. These data are for regions. Among countries, the differences are even more dramatic. The probability of a man dying between 15 and 60 years of age is 8.3 per cent in Sweden, 82.1 per cent in Zimbabwe, and 90.2 per cent in Lesotho.[7]

A particularly telling example of health inequalities within countries is the 20-year gap in life expectancy between Australian Aboriginal and Torres Strait Islander peoples—life expectancy is 56.3 years for men and 62.8 years for women—and the Australian average.[10] The men in this population would look unhealthy in India (male life expectancy 60.1 years), whereas Australian life expectancy is among the highest in the world, marginally behind Iceland, Sweden, and Japan. The poor health of Aboriginal and Torres Strait Islander peoples is not the result of a high rate of child deaths. Infant mortality is 12.7 per 1,000 live births. This figure is high by Australian standards, but on a scale from Iceland to Sierra Leone, it is much closer to Iceland than to Sierra Leone. The shortened life expectancy of

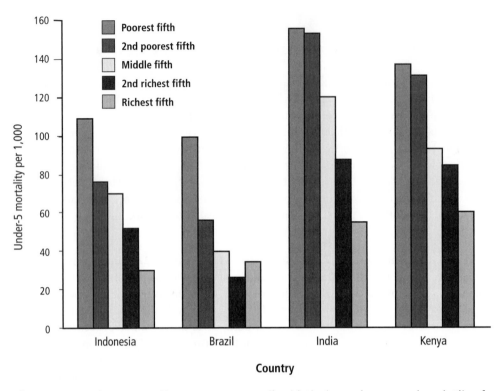

Figure 17.1   Under-5 mortality rates per 1,000 live births by socioeconomic quintile of household

Reprinted from reference [9] with permission of Elsevier.

Aboriginal and Torres Strait Islander peoples results from mortality in adults from non-communicable disease and injury. In this sense, the population is typical of the world health picture. Of the 45 million deaths among adults aged 15 years and older in 2002, 32 million were due to non-communicable disease and a further 4.5 million to violent causes.[7]

Aboriginal and Torres Strait Islander peoples are a socially excluded minority within their country. But poor health is not confined to poor populations or those who are socially excluded. As with child mortality, there is a socioeconomic gradient in adult mortality rates within countries. Figure 17.3 shows that in Bangladesh, adult mortality rates vary inversely with level of education.[11] This gradient in mortality is quite remarkable. Within rich countries, with strikingly different material conditions from Bangladesh, there is a social gradient in mortality prompting consideration of the causal links between status and health.[12] Whether the social gradient in poor countries can be attributed to the same causal pathways is an urgent task for review. It is especially important because, in many countries, inequalities in health have been increasing.[13–15] In Russia for example, where life expectancy is low, social inequalities have grown (Figure 17.4).[16]

Mortality statistics are readily available. They should not, however, lead to ignorance of the burden of nonfatal disease. In particular, mental illness causes much suffering, but its effect is not clear by inspection of mortality data. Worldwide, the second-highest cause of disease burden among adults age 15–59 years is unipolar depressive disorder.[7]

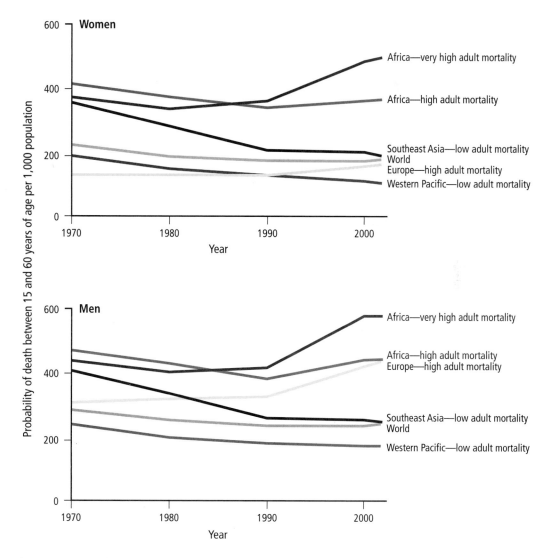

Figure 17.2 Trends in adult mortality by sex in regions of the world, 1970–2002. The graphs show the probability of death between 15 and 60 years of age per 1,000 population.

Reprinted from reference [7] with permission of the World Health Organization.

The Aging of the World's Population

It is convenient, but quite wrong, to think that the greying of the world's population is an issue only for the rich countries. Figure 17.5 shows the projected increase between 2000 and 2030 in the population older than 65 years in selected countries.[17] The fastest rates of increase are in countries at an intermediate level of human development, starting from a low base. The social determinants of the health of older people claim attention alongside those of health at younger ages.

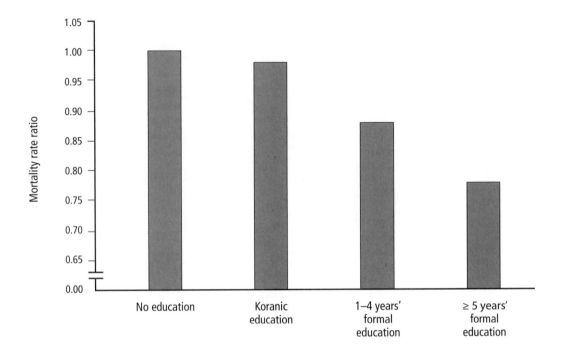

Figure 17.3   Mortality and education in men aged 45–90 years in Matlab, Bangladesh, 1982–98[11]

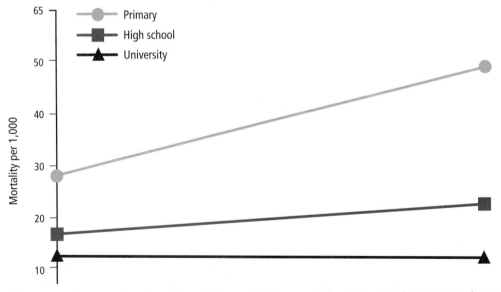

Figure 17.4   Increase in educational differentials in mortality between the 1980s and 1990s in St Petersburg men[16]

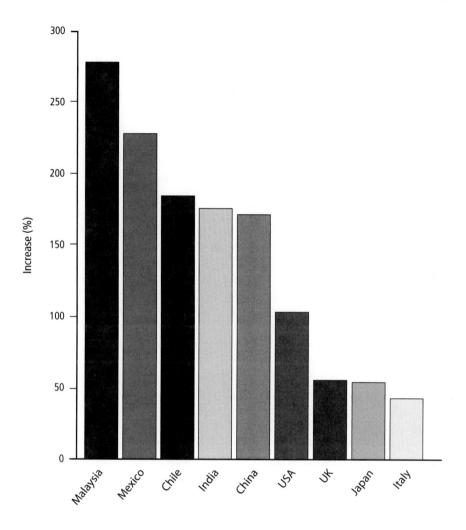

Figure 17.5 Projected percentage increase in the elderly population (older than 65 years) from 2000 to 2030 in selected countries

Adapted from reference [17] with permission of the US census Bureau.

Social Determinants: Poverty, Inequality, and the Causes of the Causes

In consulting widely in developing the plan for the Commission on Social Determinants of Health, a common question was: 'What's new? We know that poverty is bad for health. Does that need a Commission?'

It is not difficult to understand how poverty in the form of material deprivation—dirty water, poor nutrition—allied to lack of quality medical care can account for the tragically foreshortened lives of people in Sierra Leone. Such understanding is insufficient in two important ways. First, it fails properly to take into account that relief of such material deprivation is not simply a technical matter of providing clean water or better medical care.

Who gets these resources is socially determined.[18] Second, and related, international policies have not been pursued as if they had people's basic needs in mind. The critics of the policies pursued by the International Monetary Fund in the global South have argued eloquently that the economic policies pursued under structural adjustment have not benefited disadvantaged people in poor countries.[19] Recognizing the health effects of poverty is one thing. Taking action to relieve its effects entails a richer understanding of the health effects of social and economic policies.

Dirty water, lack of calories, and poor antenatal care cannot account for the 20-year deficit in life expectancy of Australian Aboriginal and Torres Strait Islander peoples. On a world scale, their infant mortality rate, at 12.7 per 1,000 live births, is low. Their high rate of adult mortality is from cardiovascular diseases, cancers, endocrine nutritional and metabolic diseases (including diabetes), external causes (violence), respiratory disorders, and digestive diseases.[10] This fact is not to deny that poverty is important. But the form that poverty takes and its health consequences are quite different when considering chronic disease and violent deaths in adults, compared to deaths from infectious disease in children. It entails a richer understanding of the social determinants of health.

The health experience of Aboriginal and Torres Strait Islander peoples has relevance for the health of disadvantaged people worldwide. While in Africa the major contributor to premature mortality is communicable disease, in every other region of the world it is non-communicable disease.[1] Careful analysis of the global burden of disease has pointed to the importance of risk factors, such as being overweight, smoking, alcohol, and poor diet.[20] These are indeed potent causes. But would it be helpful to go into a deprived Australian Aboriginal population and point out that they should really take better care of themselves—that their smoking and obesity were killing them; and if they must drink, please do so in moderation? Unlikely. To borrow Geoffrey Rose's term, we need to examine the causes of the causes:[21]

the social conditions that give rise to high risk of non-communicable disease whether acting through unhealthy behaviours or through the effects of impossibly stressful lives[12] (see Panel 2).

A further answer to the *What's new?* question: although it might be obvious that poverty is at the root of much of the problem of infectious disease, and needs to be solved, it is less obvious how to break the link between poverty and disease. Income poverty provides, at best, an incomplete explanation of differences in mortality among countries or among subgroups within countries. It is well known that among rich countries, there is little correlation between gross national product (GNP) per person and life expectancy. Greece for example, with a GNP at purchasing power parities of just more than US$17,000, has a life expectancy of 78.1 years; the USA, with a GNP of more than $34,000, has a life expectancy of 76.9 years. Costa Rica and Cuba stand out as countries with GNPs less than $10,000 and yet life expectancies of 77.9 years and 76.5 years.[23]

There are many examples of relatively poor populations with similar incomes but strikingly different health records.[8] Kerala and China, famously, have good health, despite low incomes.[24] The social processes that lead to this beneficial state of health need not wait for the world order to be changed to relieve poverty in the worst-off countries. A social determinants perspective is crucial. It is also important to inquire whether the action that is taking place to relieve poverty is having the desired effect not only on average incomes but also on income distribution and hence on the poorest people.

The social gradient in health is a particular challenge. Where material deprivation is severe, a social gradient in mortality could arise from degrees of absolute deprivation. In rich countries with low levels of material deprivation the gradient changes the focus from absolute to relative deprivation.[25] Relative deprivation relates to a broader approach to social functioning and meeting of human needs[12]—'capabilities' in the words of Amartya Sen,[26] 'spiritual resources' to use Robert Fogel's term.[27] It is likely that both material or physical needs and capability, spiritual, or

Panel 2

The Solid Facts

Because the causes of the causes are not obvious, the WHO Regional Office for Europe asked a group at University College London to summarize the evidence on the social determinants of health, published as *The Solid Facts*.[22] It had 10 messages on the social determinants of health based on:

- the social gradient
- stress
- early life
- social exclusion
- work
- unemployment
- social support
- addiction
- food
- transport.

As an indication that there was a ready audience for these messages, in the first 12 months after publication of the second edition, it was downloaded from the Internet 218,000 times.

The Solid Facts reviewed evidence from Europe, aimed mainly at reducing inequalities in health within countries. The task of the Commission will be to review evidence on the social determinants of health that are relevant to global health: inequalities among countries and within.

psychosocial needs are important to the gradient in health, which will, therefore, be an important focus.

A focus on material conditions and control of infectious disease must not be to the exclusion of social determinants. The circumstances in which people live and work are as important for communicable as they are for non-communicable disease. Social conditions powerfully influence both the onset and response to treatment of the major infectious diseases that kill.[28,29]

The Commission on Social Determinants of Health will need to have in its sights poverty of the sub-Saharan African sort and the social determinants that account for Bolivia having 14 fewer years of life expectancy than Costa Rica, or Aboriginal and Torres Strait Islander peoples having 20 years fewer than other Australians. As these examples illustrate, it will examine inequalities in health between countries and inequalities within.

Action Is Possible and Necessary

A review of policies in European countries identified several that took action on the social determinants of health.[30] Although the reason for the policies was not necessarily to improve health they were nevertheless relevant to health: taxation and tax credits, old-age pensions, sickness or rehabilitation benefits, maternity or child benefits, unemployment benefits, housing policies, labour markets, communities, and care facilities.

In Sweden, the new strategy for public health is 'to create social conditions that will ensure good health for the entire population'.[31] Of 11 policy domains, 5 relate to social determinants: participation in society, economic and social security, conditions in childhood and adolescence, healthier working life, and environment and products. These are in addition to health-promoting medical care and the usual health behaviours. The UK set reduction of health inequalities as a key aim of health policy. It assembled evidence and expert judgments on areas suitable for policy development.[32] These then formed the basis of a plan of action to reduce health inequalities.[33]

These are examples from rich countries. There are further encouraging examples. *Familias en Acción* in Colombia transfers cash to poor families. To qualify, families must ensure their children receive preventive healthcare, enrol in school, and attend classes. The results are encouraging: favourable growth of children and fewer episodes of diarrhea.[34] The *Oportunidades* program in Mexico had somewhat similar aims with similarly encouraging results.[35]

Meeting Human Needs

Two linked themes provide the rationale for the Commission on Social Determinants of Health. First, there is no choice. If the major determinants of health are social, so must be the remedies. Treating existing disease is urgent and will always receive high priority but should not be to the exclusion of taking action on the underlying social determinants of health. Disease control, properly planned and directed, has a good history, but so too does social and economic development in combating major disease and improving population health. Wider social policy will be crucial to reduction of inequalities in health.

There is a second theme that relates to the question of how one can tell if a population is thriving.

One standard answer is to measure economic well-being with measures such as GNP, average income, or consumption patterns. A better answer is to measure health status.[36] There is no difficulty in convincing medical and health personnel that health is important—that is what we do. It is more challenging, but necessary, to convince policy makers and others that the health of the population is important precisely because it is a measure of whether, in the end, a population is benefiting as a result of a set of social arrangements.

In other words, action on the social determinants of health is necessary not only to improve health but also because such improvement will indicate that society has moved in a direction of meeting human needs.[37] There is a great deal of dogmatic dispute about the rights and wrongs of economic and social policies. People use labels—globalization, neoliberal economic policies—as badges of allegiance and terms of abuse. The Commission will have one basic dogma: policies that harm human health need to be identified and, where possible, changed. From this perspective, globalization and markets are good or bad in so far as the way they are operated affects health.

Inequalities in health between and within countries are avoidable.[38] There is no necessary biological reason why life expectancy should be 48 years longer in Japan than in Sierra Leone, or 20 years shorter in Australian Aboriginal and Torres Strait Islander peoples than in other Australians. Reducing these social inequalities in health, and thus meeting human needs, is an issue of social justice.

References

1. WHO. *The world health report 2004: Changing history.* (2004). Geneva: World Health Organization.
2. Murray, C.J.L., Michaud, C.M., McKenna, M.T., & Marks, J.S. (1998). *US patterns of mortality by county and race: 1965–94.* Cambridge: Harvard Center for Population and Development Studies.
3. WHO. (2003). Treating 3 million by 2005: Making it happen. In *The WHO strategy—The WHO and UNAIDS global initiative to provide retroviral therapy to 3 million people with HIV/AIDS in developing countries by the end of 2005.* Geneva: World Health Organization.
4. The Global Fund to fight AIDS, tuberculosis, and malaria. Retrieved from www.theglobalfund.org
5. United Nations Development Group. Millennium Development Goals. Retrieved from www.undp.org/mdg/index.shtml
6. Sachs, J.D., & McArthur, J.W. (2005). The Millennium Project: A plan for meeting the Millennium Development Goals. *The Lancet, 365,* 347–53.

7. WHO. (2003). *World health report 2003: Shaping the future*. Geneva: World Health Organization.

8. United Nations. (2004). *Human development report 2004*. New York: United Nations Development Programme.

9. Victora, C.G., Wagstaff, A., Schellenberg, J.A., Gwatkin, D., Claeson, M., & Habicht, J.P. (2003). Applying an equity lens to child health and mortality: More of the same is not enough. *The Lancet, 362*, 233–41.

10. Aboriginal and Torres Strait Commissioner, Statistics Human Rights and Equal Opportunity Commission. A statistical overview of Aboriginal and Torres Strait Islander peoples in Australia. Retrieved from www.humanrights.gov.au/social_justice/statistics/index.html

11. Hurt, L.S., Ronsmans, C., & Saha, S. (2004). Effects of education and other socioeconomic factors on middle age mortality in rural Bangladesh. *Journal of Epidemiology and Community Health, 58*, 315–20.

12. Marmot, M. (2004). *Status syndrome*. London: Bloomsbury.

13. Donkin, A., Goldblatt, P., & Lynch, K. (2002). Inequalities in life expectancy by social class 1972–1999. *Health Statistics Quarterly, 15*, 5–15.

14. Mackenbach, J.P., Bos, V., Andersen, O., et al. (2003). Widening socioeconomic inequalities in mortality in six western European countries. *International Journal of Epidemiology, 32*, 830–7.

15. Crimmins, E.M., & Saito, Y. (2001). Trends in healthy life expectancy in the United States, 1970–1990: Gender, racial, and educational differences. *Social Science and Medicine, 52*, 1629–41.

16. Plavinski, S.L., Plavinskaya, S.I., & Klimov, A.N. (2003). Social factors and increase in mortality in Russia in the 1990s: Prospective cohort study. *British Medical Journal, 326*, 1240–2.

17. Kinsella, K., & Velkoff, V.A. (US Census Bureau). (2001). *An aging world: 2001* (series P95/01-1). Washington: US Government Printing Office.

18. Kim, J.Y., Mitten, J.V., Irwin, A., & Gershman, J. (2000). *Dying for growth: Global inequality and the health of the poor*. Monroe, ME: Common Courage Press.

19. Stiglitz, J.E. (2002). *Globalization and its discontents*. London: Allen Lane.

20. WHO. (2002). *Reducing risks, promoting healthy life: World Health Report 2002*. Geneva: World Health Organization.

21. Rose, G. (1992). *Strategy of preventive medicine*. Oxford: Oxford University Press.

22. Wilkinson, R., & Marmot, M. (2003). *The solid facts*. Copenhagen: World Health Organization.

23. United Nations Development Programme. (2003). *Human development report*. New York: Oxford University Press.

24. Sen, A. (1999). *Development as freedom*. New York: Alfred A. Knopf.

25. Wilkinson, R.G. (2005). *The impact of inequality: How to make sick societies healthier*. London: Routledge.

26. Sen, A. (19992). *Inequality reexamined*. Oxford: Oxford University Press.

27. Fogel, R.W. (2000). *The fourth great awakening and the future of egalitarianism*. Chicago: University of Chicago Press.

28. Farmer, P. (1999). *Infections and inequalities*. Berkeley: University of California Press.

29. Farmer, P. (2003). *Pathologies of power: Health, human rights, and the new war on the poor*. Berkeley: University of California Press.

30. Crombie, I.K., Irvine, L., Elliott, L., & Wallace, H. (2004). *Closing the health inequalities gap: An international perspective*. Dundee: NHS Health Scotland and University of Dundee.

31. Hogstedt, H., Lundgren, B., Moberg, H., Pettersson, B., & Agren, G. (2004). The Swedish public health policy and the National Institute of Public Health. *Scandinavian Journal of Public Health, 32*(64), 1–64.

32. Acheson, D. (1998). *Inequalities in health: Report of an independent inquiry*. London: HMSO.

33. Department of Health. (2003). *Tackling health inequalities: A programme for action*. London: Department of Health.

34. Attanasio, O., & Vera-Hernandez, M. (2004). *Medium and long run effects of nutrition and child care: Evaluation of a community nursery programme in rural Colombia* (IFS working papers EWP04/06). London: Institute for Fiscal Studies.

35. World Bank. Mexico's Oportunidades program. Retrieved from http://web.worldbank.org/WBSITE/EXTERNAL/TOPICS/EXTPOVERTY/EXTPA/0,,contentMDK:20269019~menuPK:443285~pagePK:148956~piPK:216618~theSitePK:430367,00.html

36. Sen, A. (1995, March 3). Mortality as an indicator of success and failure: Innocenti inaugural lecture 1995. Instituto degli Innocenti, Florence, Italy.

37. Doyal, L., & Gough, I. (1991). *A theory of human need*. London: Macmillan.

38. Whitehead, M. (1990). *The concepts and principles of equity and health*. Copenhagen: World Health Organization.

CHAPTER 18

Narrowing Sex Differentials in Life Expectancy in the Industrialized World: Early 1970s to Early 1990s

Frank Trovato and N.M. Lalu

Since the turn of the twentieth century, the sex gap in life expectancy has widened in all Western countries from approximately two to three years in favour of women, to the current difference in the range of about four to seven years (Lopez, 1983; Nathanson, 1984; Nathanson & Lopez, 1987; Tomason, 1984; Waldron, 1976; Wingard, 1984). However, between the early 1970s and the early part of the 1990s, some highly industrialized nations experienced, for the first time, a narrowing of their sex differences in life expectancy at birth. In another set of countries the differential has not yet reached a stage of convergence, but over the last two decades the female advantage appears to be increasing at a slower pace than ever before. By its very nature, this unprecedented development falls in the same class of phenomena as the baby boom and baby bust of the post-war years and the unanticipated reductions in old-age mortality since the early part of the 1970s (Fries, 1980; Manton, 1982; Olshansky & Ault, 1986; Stone & Fletcher, 1993). Common to these demographic events was their unexpectedness, such that few scholars had predicted *a priori* their developments.

As far as we can determine, on an international scale there is no sign of convergence prior to the early part of the 1970s. For instance, in his analysis of 30 nations in the interval between 1950 and 1978, Lopez (1983) presents data that indicate that only between the quinquennial periods of 1970–4 and 1975–8 do we see some evidence of narrowing sex differences in life expectation, with five countries (Japan, Austria, England–Wales, Northern Ireland, and Scotland) showing a 0.10 of a year reduction in their differentials. Although Lopez paid no attention to this numerical fact, in his concluding comments he stated that there exists 'the [eventual] possibility of a stabilization, if not reduction, in the size of the sex mortality differential' (p. 106).

Olshansky and Ault (1986) noted that in the early part of the 1980s the United States had entered a new stage of epidemiological development, which they call the 'age of delayed and degenerative diseases', characterized by (among other things) a general delay of the ages at which chronic and degenerative diseases tend to kill. An important corollary of this stage of epidemiological transition is that future gains in longevity will be made increasingly at older ages, since gains at the younger ages have become smaller over time and may be reaching a plateau in terms of further improvements. In this context, the authors project that 'the historical pattern of a widening gap in longevity between the sexes . . . [will come] to an end during the fourth stage of epidemiological transition in the United States' (p. 364). They do not elaborate the reasons underlying this prediction, nor do they offer any indication as to whether the same trend will prevail in other nations.

Only very recently have there been systematic attempts at documenting the possibility that male–female mortality differences in the industrialized countries may be declining. In her investigation of sex differences in mortality for adults, Waldron (1993) discovered that across 22 nations between 1977 and 1979, male–female mortality ratios continued to increase for persons in the age group 25–34, but at the older ages the pattern is mixed. For example, death ratios went up for 55–64-year-olds in southern Europe, eastern Europe, and Japan, but declined in some northern European societies and among Anglo-Saxon nations. In Canada, Gee and Veevers (1988) examined changes in sex ratios in mortality for the period 1966–85 for the age groups 45–54 and 55–64. They showed some evidence of a middle-aged reduction in the sex differential.

Given the recency of this phenomenon and its generality across a significant portion of the industrialized countries, analysis is timely and will be of practical value to those interested in establishing parameters for sex differences in life expectancy in the context of mortality projections (e.g. Bulatao & Bos, 1990; Coale, 1990; Krishnan, 1992; Lee & Carter, 1990; Manton, Stallard, & Tolley, 1991; McNown and Rogers, 1990; Olshansky, 1986; Valkonen, 1990). Theorists will want to consider the implications of this new trend for its sociological and social-psychological underpinnings in the context of rapid social and demographic change. We feel that this development is part of a larger configuration of social and demographic evolution witnessed by highly industrialized societies in the later part of the twentieth century.

The onset of narrowing sex differences in life expectancy may be closely associated with convergence in gender-based behaviours and lifestyles in recent decades (Nathanson, 1992; Waldron, 1993; Wister & Gee, 1994). For example, it has been hypothesized that sex differences in mortality have begun to decrease in the industrialized countries due to decreasing sex differences in several behaviours which have contributed to men's higher mortality in the past. The rise in smoking among women and their increased participation in the labour force have been cited as two possible interrelated processes contributing to this development (Waldron, 1993).

Materials and Methods

Unlike previous studies, such as Waldron (1993) and Gee and Veevers (1988), our investigation is based not on changing sex ratios in mortality but on the changing sex differential in life expectancy at birth from the early 1970s to the early 1990s. Our approach conveniently summarizes the mortality experience of the sexes over the complete age span as opposed to presenting mortality ratios of target age groups only. A desirable feature of our procedure is that life expectancy is a standardized measure of survival that takes into account age and sex compositional differences across populations. In another section of our analysis we examine the association of age–sex-specific changes in death rates to the amount of variance explained in the dependent variable in order to infer the relative importance of changes in sex mortality differences within age groups to the narrowing of the sex differential in longevity at birth.

In addition to covering a roughly twenty-year span of observations, and a more recent end point of analysis, we examine a larger set of industrialized countries (38 as opposed to the 22 of Waldron's study, and the single one in the case of Gee and Veevers) comprising both eastern and western European nations, the USSR, Canada, the United States, Australia, New Zealand, Japan, Singapore, Hong Kong, and Israel. These societies are diverse in terms of their histories, cultures, and social structures, but are commonly related by virtue of their industrialized economies and their being in the advanced stages of demographic and epidemiological transitions.

We investigate three questions. The first deals with the association of men's and women's changes in life expectation over time to convergence in life expectancy at birth. We hypothesize that in countries where there is evidence of convergence, this is mostly a function of men's greater rates of improvement in life expectancy over the roughly twenty-year interval from 1970 to 1990. We base this prediction on the assumption that in the industrialized world female life expectation may be approaching a plateau in terms of its rate of gain, whereas men, by virtue of their lower levels of life expectancy, still have considerable room for further improvements.

A second objective is to study the association between country levels of socioeconomic development (as measured by GNP [gross national product] in US dollars; Population Reference Bureau, 1975, 1994), and the amount of convergence in life expectancy between men and women. We surmise that convergence should be more pronounced in the most advanced nations of the world. We do not have data to test for the many causal mechanisms involved in this relationship, but we assume that countries in the advanced stages of epidemiologic and demographic transitions have social and economic structures that might be conducive to a narrowing of the long-established sex differential in life expectation. Our sense is that a large part of this new phenomenon is related to changes in lifestyles among men and women in recent decades, particularly in the adult working ages.

Therefore, if behavioural factors are germane to the phenomenon under investigation, as has been suggested by a number of authors (e.g. Gee & Veevers, 1983; Nathanson, 1992; Veevers and Gee, 1986; Waldron, 1990, 1993), important mortality changes should be noticed for those in the age range from young adulthood to late middle age. Thus, a third aspect of this study is to explore this possible relationship by examining changes in age–sex-specific death rates over time and their association with changes in life expectancy.

Data

Country data for the periods around 1970 and 1990 with respect to sex-specific life expectancies at birth, as well as corresponding age–sex-specific death rates (ages 0–15, 15–24, 25–59, 60+, and 85+) were compiled from published tables in the United Nations *Demographic Yearbooks* (1992, 1993). A more refined classification of age-specific death rates is not available from the published tabulations in the yearbooks.[1]

We tried as much as possible to include data for the same two periods consistently—that is, for 1970

and 1990—but for some countries the observations are one or two years prior to or after these time points; and on a number of occasions, the information for the most recent time point is for the early to mid-1980s (see Table 18.1), thus making it impossible to incorporate into our statistical analysis an intervening period of observation (i.e. for the early 1980s) between the two principal end points.[2]

Measurement

A variety of numerical methods could be applied to examine the phenomenon under investigation, but after a careful overview of the alternatives, we decided that the most appropriate and straightforward measure for our purposes is the second-order difference of period-specific differences in male and female life expectations at birth. This measure can be shown as follows:

$$\Delta^e0^{(1)} = f^e0^{(1)} - m^e0^{(1)} \qquad (1)$$
$$\Delta^e0^{(2)} = f^e0^{(2)} - m^e0^{(2)} \qquad (2)$$
$$\Delta(\Delta^{(2)-(1)}) = \Delta^e0^{(2)} - \Delta^e0^{(1)} \qquad (3)$$

where $\Delta^e0^{(1)}$ and $\Delta^e0^{(2)}$ represent symbols for sex difference in life expectancy at birth for the periods around 1970 (time point 1) and 1990 (time point 2), respectively, and the letters m and f pertain to males and females.

Equation (3) provides a simple measure of change over time. A negative value would indicate a narrowing of the sex gap in survival, while a positive value would denote the opposite development. Within these two possible outcomes we can also take note of the degree of convergence or divergence in male and female survival rates between the two time points under observation.

Results

Table 18.1 lists in rank order the amount of convergence or divergence in the sex gap in life expectancy for 38 industrialized nations over a roughly twenty-year interval between 1970 and 1990 (specific points of observations for each country are shown in parentheses). Hong Kong shows a change in its gender gap in longevity of −1.85 years, which happens to be the largest change among the countries in this analysis. It is followed by Iceland (−1.32), Austria (−0.63), the United States (−0.60), Scotland and the United Kingdom (both with values of −0.59), Canada (−0.49), Australia (−0.37), Finland (−0.27), the USSR (−0.26), New Zealand (−0.03), and Switzerland (−0.02).

Some of the countries with positive values in our measure of the changing sex gap in average length of life display larger divergences than others, indicating that over time they have experienced a greater degree of expansion in female advantage in longevity over males. This tendency can be demonstrated with the examples of Hungary, Romania, Albania, Bulgaria, Spain, and Yugoslavia, where the differential widened by a range of 2.81 (Hungary) to 1.04 years (Yugoslavia). At the other end of this continuum, the difference grew to only 0.19, 0.18, and 0.14 in the cases of Israel, Norway, and West Germany, respectively.

A number of patterns can be discerned from Table 18.1:

- Among the nations with positive values in their changing sex differences in life expectancy, the largest gaps appear to be typical of eastern European countries, with the notable exception of the USSR, where a narrowing has occurred.
- Of those nations with positive differences between values of 1.00 and 0.14, with the exception of Japan, all are situated in Europe.
- With the exceptions of Hong Kong and the USSR, all nations displaying a narrowing of their sex differentials are either in western Europe or in North America.

These tendencies suggest that country differences in the level of socioeconomic development may be related to the degree and direction of change over time in the sex gap in life expectancy. In this regard,

it is not surprising that the largest divergences tend to prevail among the relatively less affluent nations of eastern Europe, while the largest convergences tend to occur in some of the most wealthy societies of the world.

We correlated the life expectancies of men and women across all societies in the early and later periods of observation, separately, with the dependent variable. The zero-order association was −0.24 with a probability (p) of 0.11 when the male expectancies in period 1 (i.e. around 1970) were entered as the independent variable.[3] The correlation becomes significant and increases to −0.54 ($p < 0.01$) when female life expectancies in the early period were substituted as the independent variable. Thus, societies with relatively high female life expectancies at the beginning of the study period (around 1970) are more likely to experience larger reductions in their sex differences in life expectation over time.

When the two sets of sex-specific life expectancies around 1990 are put into the analysis, the resulting correlation goes up to −0.60 ($p < 0.01$) if the male expectancy is the independent variable; and it is −0.57 ($p < 0.01$) if female expectation is treated as the predictor variable.

In Table 18.2, we computed zero-order correlations between period-specific male and female life expectancies and the dependent variable for only those 12 countries that display a narrowing of the sex gap in longevity. Again, all the correlations are negative, but smaller in magnitude in comparison to the ones computed earlier for all the countries combined. As was true of the previous correlational analysis, the male coefficients become more pronounced over time than do those of females (i.e. the male coefficient increased all the way from −0.172 to −0.403, while that of females went up from −0.285 to just −0.303).

Another set of correlations in Table 18.2 involves those countries with positive differences in the dependent variable. The corresponding coefficients in the table are larger in magnitude than in the previous analyses. Both gender-specific coefficients tend to increase in magnitude over time, but the

Table 18.1 Sex differential in life expectancy and its change between early 1970s and early 1990s

Country and periods	Early 1970s (Period 1) Male	Female	Early 1990s (Period 2) Male	Female	$e^f_0 - e^m_0$ Period 1 (A)	Period 2 (B)	$\Delta(\Delta^{(2)} - {}^{(1)})$ (A)–(B)
Hong Kong (1971, 1989)	67.36	75.01	74.25	80.05	7.65	5.80	−1.85
Iceland (1973, 1989)	71.60	77.50	75.71	80.29	5.90	4.58	−1.32
Austria (1971, 1990)	66.57	73.72	72.50	79.02	7.15	6.52	−0.63
United States (1971, 1989)	67.40	74.80	71.80	78.60	7.40	6.80	−0.60
Scotland (1971, 1985)	67.17	73.54	70.05	75.83	6.37	5.78	−0.59
United Kingdom (1972, 1988)	69.00	75.20	72.42	78.03	6.20	5.61	−0.59
Canada(1971, 1991)	69.34	76.36	74.41	80.94	7.02	6.53	−0.49
Australia (1966, 1990)	67.63	74.15	73.86	80.01	6.52	6.15	−0.37
Finland (1971, 1989)	65.89	74.21	70.85	78.90	8.32	8.05	−0.27
USSR (1970, 1986)	65.00	74.00	65.04	73.78	9.00	8.74	−0.26
New Zealand (1971, 1989)	68.55	74.60	71.94	77.96	6.05	6.02	−0.03
Switzerland (1971, 1989)	70.15	76.17	74.00	80.00	6.02	6.00	−0.02
Germany West (1971, 1986)	67.41	73.83	71.81	78.37	6.42	6.56	0.14
Norway (1971, 1990)	71.24	77.43	73.44	79.81	6.19	6.37	0.18
Israel (1971, 1989)	70.08	73.44	74.54	78.09	3.36	3.55	0.19
Belgium (1970, 1989)	67.79	74.21	72.43	79.13	6.42	6.70	0.28
Malta (1973, 1989)	68.10	72.02	73.79	78.04	3.92	4.25	0.33
Sweden (1971, 1990)	72.00	77.25	74.81	80.41	5.25	5.60	0.35
Luxembourg (1972, 1986)	67.00	73.90	70.61	77.87	6.90	7.26	0.36
Northern Ireland (1971, 1983)	67.63	73.67	69.25	75.65	6.04	6.40	0.36
Netherlands (1971, 1989)	71.00	76.70	73.67	79.88	5.70	6.21	0.51
Denmark (1970, 1989)	70.70	75.90	71.98	77.70	5.20	5.72	0.52
Japan (1971, 1990)	70.17	75.58	75.86	81.81	5.41	5.95	0.54
France (1971, 1990)	68.50	76.10	72.75	80.94	7.60	8.19	0.59
Italy (1971, 1988)	68.97	74.88	73.19	79.70	5.91	6.52	0.61
Portugal (1970, 1990)	64.18	70.50	70.13	77.17	6.32	7.04	0.72
Germany East (1970, 1988)	68.85	74.19	70.03	76.23	5.34	6.20	0.86

Ireland (1971, 1986)	68.77	73.52	71.01	76.70	4.75	5.69	0.94
Yugoslavia (1971, 1989)	65.42	70.22	68.64	74.48	4.80	5.84	1.04
Spain (1970, 1986)	69.69	74.96	73.27	79.69	5.27	6.42	1.15
Bulgaria (1975, 1989)	68.68	73.91	68.12	74.77	5.23	6.65	1.42
Greece (1970, 1990)	70.13	73.64	75.00	80.00	3.51	5.00	1.49
Czechoslovakia (1970, 1990)	66.23	72.94	67.25	75.81	6.71	8.56	1.85
Poland (1971, 1990)	66.83	73.80	66.51	75.49	6.97	8.98	2.01
Ukraine (1970, 1989)	67.00	74.00	66.10	75.20	7.00	9.10	2.10
Albania (1972, 1988)	66.00	69.50	69.60	75.50	3.50	5.90	2.40
Romania (1971, 1988)	66.27	69.82	66.56	72.65	3.55	6.09	2.54
Hungary (1970, 1990)	66.28	72.05	65.13	73.71	5.77	8.58	2.81

Table 18.2   Zero-order correlation between change in sex differential in life expectancy over time and expectation of life at birth of males and females in early 1970s and early 1990s

Variable	All countries	Correlation with $\Delta(\Delta^{(2)-(1)})$	
		Countries where the difference is negative	Countries where the difference is positive
e_0 of male in early 1970s	−0.240	−0.172	−0.495
e_0 of females in early 1970s	−0.541	−0.285	−0.545
e_0 of males in early 1990s	−0.595	−0.403	−0.743
e_0 of females in early 1990s	−0.574	−0.303	−0.687

male one increased more and is the larger one in the later period of observation. This pattern of results suggests that there is considerable variability in the extent of change in the sex gap in longevity within those nations where the direction of change is still positive. That is, where the gender gap is widening, some countries are experiencing less divergence than others. Stated differently, in those nations where the second-order difference is positive, the higher the male or female life expectancy in either early 1970s or early 1990s, the lower the degree of divergence in the male–female gap in survival.

Noteworthy is the fact that in both groups of nations the male coefficients increased more over time than those corresponding to females. This finding suggests support for the notion that it may be the temporal change in male life expectancy which largely explains the amount of convergence in the sex differential in survival across countries. We explore this question in greater detail below by examining the varying contribution of the sexes to the change

in the male–female gap in longevity over time.

Table 18.3 contains 10 regression equations, 7 of which are directed to testing the effects of national variations in each gender's life expectation at the earlier or later point in time on the dependent variable. Female life expectancy in the early 1970s is a significant predictor of the change in the sex gap in the average length of life (equation [2]), while male life expectancy during this period has no significant effect (equation [1]).

Equations (3) and (4) in Table 18.3 correspond to the same analysis using gender-specific life expectations for the later period of observation (i.e. around the early 1990s) as separate predictors of the change in the sex gap in survival. In this case, the male coefficient is statistically significant and the respective equation explains 35 per cent of the variance in the dependent variable. The contribution of female life expectancy around 1990 to explaining the dependent variable is slightly lower, with an R^2 of 0.330. Therefore, level of male expectancy in around

Table 18.3 Regression analysis of change in sex difference in expectation of life at birth between early 1970s and early 1990s*

Independent variable	Constant	Regression coefficient	R^2	Significance level of F for regression
(1) e_0 of male in early 1970s	9.388	−0.1302	0.057	0.1464
(2) e_0 of females in early 1970s	21.931	−0.2890	0.293	0.0004
(3) e_0 of males in early 1990s	15.231	−0.2063	0.354	0.0001
(4) e_0 of females in early 1990s	20.426	−0.2559	0.330	0.0002
(5) Change in male expectation of life	1.486	−0.3055	0.389	0.0000
(6) Change in female expectation of life	0.895	−0.1047	0.028	0.3080
(7) ln(GNP, early 1970s)	7.637	−0.9368	0.285	0.0006
(8) ln(GNP, early 1990s)	6.725	−0.6739	0.511	0.0000
(9) Change in ln(GNP)	1.8662	−0.8407	0.382	0.0000
(10) Multiple regression	5.608	...	0.568	0.0000
Change in male e_0	...	−0.1472	...	...
ln(GNP, early 1990s)	...	−0.5016	...	...

* dependent variable used in the regression analysis is $\Delta(\Delta^{(2)-(1)})$
ln(GNP) is the natural logarithm of the gross national product

1990 is slightly more important in predicting convergence in male and female life expectancy.

Equations (5) and (6) assess which gender-specific change in expectation of life accounts for more of the variance in the dependent variable. As shown in the table, the change in male expectancy is more significant than the corresponding change in female life expectancy. Moreover, the male regression coefficient is larger than that of females ($b = -0.306$ $vs -0.105$), and the associated R^2 is also greater (0.389 vs 0.028). The female equation fails to reach statistical significance.

In Table 18.3 equations (7) to (9) have positive intercepts and negative slopes, which implies that the change in sex difference is positive (i.e. sex difference increases) at lower levels of the independent variable (GNP or change in the natural logarithm of GNP), and becomes negative (i.e. sex difference decreases) at higher levels of the predictor variable. In general, a rise in GNP is associated with a reduction in the sex gap in longevity, as denoted by the negative regression coefficients for both periods. Equations (7) and (8) show that the GNPs of periods 1 and 2, respectively, explain 29 and 51 per cent of the variation in the dependent variable, whereas equation (9) indicates that the larger the gain in GNP over time, the larger the degree of convergence in the sex gap in longevity ($b = -0.841$, $R^2 = 0.382$).

Equation (10) considers both GNP around the early 1990s and change in male life expectancy over time simultaneously for their independent contributions to explaining cross-national changes in the survival gap between the sexes. These two variables emerged as the most powerful predictors in previous regressions, thus justifying their inclusion in equation (10).

Both variables are statistically significant and explain 57 per cent of the variance in the dependent variable. It would appear, therefore, that an important condition for reducing the male disadvantage in longevity at the aggregate level would be a significant rise in national levels of GNP. A critical mechanism in this relationship may be the GNP's positive association with male improvements in lifestyle (e.g. reduction in smoking and increased exercise)

and also in the availability of and access to good healthcare (Waldron, 1993). The more prosperous and socially advanced the nation, the more likely that men will benefit from further developments in healthcare because the gains in survival for women in such countries may have already reached close to a maximum; consequently, men have more to gain from any improvements in healthcare. One may also hypothesize that in the most advanced nations, a recent consequence of changing gender roles is that women have been increasing their levels of tobacco consumption; this changing behavioural difference may be of some relevance in reducing the gender gap in life expectancy by virtue of raising female death rates from lung cancer (Waldron, 1993).

It would seem unlikely that all age groups would contribute equally to the changing sex differential in life expectancy. In recent years scholars have observed that the elderly have made gains in survival probabilities (Crimmins, Hayward, & Saito, 1994; Fries, 1980; Manton, 1982; Olshansky & Ault, 1986; Olshansky & Carnes, 1994; Olshansky, Carnes, & Cassel, 1990; Stone & Fletcher, 1993). It has also been indicated that men and women in their middle ages have made notable gains in survival (Levy, 1981; Myers, 1989; Olshansky & Carnes, 1994; Rothenberg & Koplan, 1990). Therefore, most of the observed narrowing in the sex gap in expectation of life across the 12 nations in Table 18.1 may turn out to be a function of decreasing sex differences in mortality at the older ages and possibly within the interval between the young adulthood years and retirement age. It is also possible that a narrowing in life expectancy at age zero may result as a function of relatively larger male reductions in infant mortality over the time interval being considered. Clearly, if this last condition is a factor, it would preclude gender role explanations for the phenomenon being investigated.

Table 18.4 shows three equations involving the dependent variable regressed on the change in male–female age-specific death rates between the early 1970s and the early 1990s. Here the number of countries is reduced to 33 (from 38) because appropriate data concerning age–sex-specific death rates is unavailable for five of the nations included in Table 18.1. In equation (2), we substitute the death rate for age 60+ with the rate corresponding to 85+ to better assess the possible importance of change in the sex mortality difference in old age mortality on the narrowing of the sex differential in life expectancy at age zero. [4]

As in our preceding analyses, we rely on ordinary least squares regression and use the nation as the unit of analysis in the interpretation of parameters. Thus, a given coefficient measures the relative effect of male–female differences in the amount of change in age-specific death rates (per 1,000 population) on the dependent variable, thereby allowing us to answer the substantive question of which age group or groups show(s) the strongest association with the dependent variable. A positive coefficient would indicate that the age-specific difference in the rate of change in death rate for men and women is related to a divergence in the male–female difference in life expectancy at age zero, which is the same as saying that in a given age class males in comparison to females have made relatively lower improvements over time in reducing their mortality risk. A negative coefficient would indicate that the effect of a differential rate of change in age-specific mortality serves to reduce the sex gap in life expectation over time, and that therefore men would be making larger improvements than women in reducing their death risk. This can be seen as follows:

$$\Delta(\Delta^{(2)-(1)})$$
$$= \alpha + b\,[(m_{ASDR}^{(1)} - m_{ASDR}^{(2)})$$
$$- (f_{ASDR}^{(1)} - f_{ASDR}^{(2)})] + \epsilon ij \;\; (4)$$

where $\Delta\,(\Delta^{(2)-(1)})$ represents the expected difference of the sex differential in life expectancy over time points 1 and 2 (i.e. between the early 1970s and the early 1990s); the letter b denotes the unstandardized regression coefficient; α is the intercept term of the equation; and ϵij is a residual term.

From equation (1) in Table 18.4, the zero-order correlations indicate that two age classes may

Table 18.4 Regression analysis of change in male–female life expectancy from early 1970s to early 1990s, based on male–female change in age-specific death rates in industrialized nations

		$y = \Delta\,(\Delta^{(2)-(1)})$					
		(1)		(2)		(3)	
Predictor	r	ß	b	ß	b	ß	b
Δ_{t1-t2} (m–f:0–14)	0.13	−0.12	−0.750	−0.12	−0.762	...	...
Δ_{t1-t2} (m–f:15–24)	−0.17	−0.12	−0.521	−0.15	−0.612	...	...
Δ_{t1-t2} (m–f:25–59)	−0.82*	−0.78	−0.705*	−0.85	−0.773*	−0.82	−0.742*
Δ_{t1-t2} (m–f:60+)	−0.54*	−0.14	−0.031	...	...	...	...
Δ_{t1-t2} (m–f:85+)	...	...	...	−0.02	−0.000	...	...
Constant	...	0.9154*	...	0.8495*	...	0.5965	...
R^2	...	0.72	...	0.70	...	0.67	...

r is the zero-order correlation coefficient between the dependent variable and the predictor
ß is the standardized regression coefficient
b is the unstandardized regression coefficient
* $p < 0.01$

account for the phenomenon under investigation: age groups 25–59 and 60+. Equation (2) gives further indication that age group 85+ is not statistically significant in its contribution to variance explained in the dependent variable. The multivariate results, however, show that it is mainly male–female differences in the amount of change in death risk among those aged 25–59 that accounts for most of the explained variations in male–female change in life expectancy at age zero. The effect of the 25–59 sex mortality differential is to reduce the sex gap in life expectancy by 0.705 on average (or by 0.78) in standard units). Stated differently, since the early part of the 1970s, men's relatively greater improvements in mortality within the ages 25–59 have significantly reduced the sex gap in longevity across nations in this analysis.

Given the overlap between the 60+ and 85+ age groups, we decided to delete the former age class and include the latter in a separate equation to better assess the relative effect of change in gender-specific death rates in old age to the phenomenon under investigation. As it turns out, there is only a marginal additional influence of this predictor to the change in male–female differences in life expectancy across countries ($b = -0.000$; $\beta = -0.02$). It is clear, however, that this is a minor effect in relation to the impact of age class 25–59, which now in this last equation shows an increased contribution over the previous one ($b = -0.742$, $\beta = -0.82$). In fact, the changing sex mortality differential within this age group alone accounts for 67 per cent of the variance in the dependent variable (total variance explained is 72 per cent).

It appears that a significant part of the recent observed convergence in the sex gap in longevity can be accounted for by the differential speed at which the sexes have been reducing their respective mortality rates within the period from young adulthood to late middle age (i.e. between ages 25 and 59). This is the age range within which industrial nations vary significantly in explaining the narrowing of sex variance in survival. Countries where males in this age range have made faster gains in reducing their death risk in comparison to females experience a larger degree of convergence in the sex

Table 18.5 Regression analyses of change in male–female age-specific death rates based on GNP in early 1970s and early 1990s across industrialized nations

Predictor	Dependent variable				
	Δ_{t1-t2} (m–f:0–14)	Δ_{t1-t2} (m–f:15–24)	Δ_{t1-t2} (m–f:25–59)	Δ_{t1-t2} (m–f:60+)	Δ_{t1-t2} (m–f:85+)
(1) ln(GNP, $t1$)	−0.081*	0.097	0.833**	2.342*	−10.38*
	(−0.29)	(0.23)	(0.43)	(0.29)	(−0.26)
R2	0.084	0.054	0.190	0.09	0.069
(2) ln(GNP, $t2$)	−0.010	0.025	0.793**	1.240	−6.80*
	(−0.05)	(0.10)	(0.71)	(0.27)	(−0.30)
R2	0.00	0.01	0.51	0.07	0.09
(3) ln(GNP, $t2$ / GNP, $t1$)	0.037	−0.014	0.984**	0.886	−6.42
	(0.17)	(−0.04)	(0.64)	(0.14)	(0.20)
R2	0.03	0.00	0.41	0.02	0.04

ln(GNP) is the natural logarithm of the gross national product
  * $p < 0.10$
 ** $p < 0.01$
zero-order correlation coefficients in parentheses.

gap in life expectancy than in those countries where males within the same age group have been less successful in making mortality improvements.

A question worth posing is whether across countries the male–female difference in age-specific rates of mortality reductions vary by level of GNP. Table 18.5 concerns itself with three bivariate regressions involving three different measures of GNP as predictors of the male–female change in age-specific death rates over time. As displayed in the table, country variations in GNP explain a relatively small part of the sex difference in the rate of change in age-specific mortality. This finding is true irrespective of whether GNP is measured at the beginning of the study period or at the end. The only case where GNP seems to make any real difference is in connection with the explanation of sex differences in death rates in the age group 25–59, where the amount of variance explained ranges from 19 per cent in the period around 1970 to 51 per cent in the later period, and where 41 per cent of the variability is explained if the predictor is the temporal change in GNP (i.e. $\ln(\text{GNP}, t2 \, / \, \text{GNP}, t1)$.

The results indicate that for 25–59-year-olds, on the aggregate a rising GNP would decrease men's death rates faster than those of women within this age range ($b = 0.833$ and 0.793 at time points 1 and 2, respectively). Moreover, a rise in a nation's GNP over time is associated with greater benefits for men in reducing mortality risk ($b = 0.984$). The data also indicate that if nations had relatively high levels of GNP at the beginning of the study period, men aged 60 and older would experience larger declines in mortality in relation to women ($b = 2.342$, $r = 0.29$). On the other hand, the opposite is suggested among those aged 85+, where male gains have occurred at a slower pace ($b = -10.38$, $r = -0.26$); however, these last two effects are not significant in statistical terms ($p < 0.10$).

Conclusions

Since the early 1970s or so, the industrialized world has witnessed the beginning of an unprecedented narrowing of the long-established sex differential in life expectancy. When exactly this trend began is not possible to identify, as it started earlier in some countries and later in others, but it is clear that around the early part of the 1970s, some nations were approaching an apex in their sex gaps in longevity, and by the early 1990s, 12 countries had experienced varying degrees of convergence. Some of these countries have reduced their sex gaps in life expectancy by as much as 1.85 years (Hong Kong), while others by as little as 0.02 of a year (e.g. Switzerland). In another set of nations, situated mostly in western Europe but also including Israel and Japan, the male–female difference in longevity has not yet reached a point of convergence, but this may happen not long in the future. There is a third group of countries, situated mainly in eastern Europe, where the male disadvantage in the average length of life has actually increased by as much as two to almost three years (e.g. Albania, Romania, Hungary). The substantive reasons for this phenomenon in this part of the industrialized world need to be explored systematically in subsequent research. Our observations suggest that an important basis for this development is cross-national discrepancies in level of social and economic development, as measured by GNP. How exactly country differences in GNP translate into a reduction in the sex gap in life expectancy in some nations while in others it produces divergence remains a question worthy of further empirical exploration.

An important finding in this analysis pertains to the contribution of temporal change in age–sex-specific differences in death rates across nations to the changing sex gap in life expectancy. Our results indicate that a significant portion of the change in male–female survival differences is due to changing death rates in the age group 25–59. The larger the male improvement in this age range in terms of mortality reductions, the larger a country's degree of convergence in its sex gap in life expectation. We found little support for the proposition that much of this convergence would result from changing sex mortality differences in the very young (i.e. ages 0–14) and in those of older ages (i.e. 60+). Of course, this finding does not in any way refute the fact that within many industrialized nations old age mortality has improved. Indeed, there is evidence that this is the case (Krishnan, 1992; Manton, 1982; Myers, 1989; Nagnur, 1990; Olshansky & Ault,1986; Olshansky, Carnes, & Cassel, 1990). What we are saying is that the differences across countries with respect to sex variation in mortality in old age do not appear to be statistically relevant in explaining a narrowing of the sex gap in life expectancy at birth across industrialized societies.

What implications can be drawn from our results? Earlier, we advanced the notion that recently the industrialized world may have entered a new phase of epidemiological evolution. This proposition will undoubtedly receive further attention, but at this point it is clear that for a significant number of industrialized nations there is now evidence of a reversal in the long-established trend in the sex differential in survival. This situation seems to be permanent and is not likely the result of data errors. The phenomenon has occurred in some of the most advanced nations of the world, which are known to possess excellent vital statistics registration and systems of data collection. This phenomenon has taken place in not one or two countries, but in at least 12, making it difficult to accept the hypothesis that the observed development is solely a function of vagaries in the data. In the next several decades more industrial nations will likely witness the onset of convergence in the sex gap in life expectancy.

In some of the recent literature on sex differences in mortality, researchers have hypothesized that as women increase their levels of labour force participation toward those of men and approximate the same occupational distribution, they will begin to experience similar patterns of mortality (Bouvier-Colle, 1983; Hazuda, et al., 1986; Pampel & Zimmer, 1989; Passannante & Nathanson, 1985; Waldron, 1990). Others have added that in recent decades women have been increasingly taking on 'masculine' roles and thus may soon start to approximate a correspondingly 'masculine' configuration of death (Gee & Veevers, 1983; Veevers & Gee, 1986; Waldron, 1993).

Furthermore, it has been argued that the sex gap in death rates has begun to narrow in the industrialized world partly owing to women's adoption of several behaviours that have contributed to men's higher mortality in the past. The rise of smoking among women and the concomitant reduction of tobacco use among men during the past few decades is an example of this trend (Nathanson, 1992). Women may also be consuming more alcohol than in previous times. Also, with their increased independence due to their labour force participation combined with the growing affordability of cars, women are driving more and are hence more likely to be involved in fatal motor vehicle accidents (Veevers & Gee, 1986).

In societies where these trends prevail, a minimum value for the sex differential in life expectancy at birth should eventually be attained. What that minimum difference will be and when it will be reached are open to speculation, however. We surmise that women will always enjoy one to two additional years of life expectancy over men, for it seems highly unlikely that men will ever attain parity with women. Even in high mortality conditions, the differential in life expectation favours women. This assertion can be verified in part by the Coale and Demeny (1983) model life tables at the highest mortality levels. It seems likely that a two- to three-year gap may represent a natural lower limit for the amount of eventual convergence in the male–female gap in longevity.

From a theoretical point of view, the evidence presented in this study is not inconsistent with the thesis proposed by Rogers and Hackenberg (1991). They argue that the industrialized nations of the world have in recent years entered the 'Hybristic' stage of epidemiological transition, whereby the morbidity and mortality patterns of men and women are now largely a function of individual behaviours and lifestyles.

The beginning of convergence in the sex gap in longevity in some industrialized countries may be partly associated with developments in the social worlds of men and women. Some indication that this may be true is provided by our finding that a significant portion of the phenomenon we investigated is a function of the mortality conditions prevailing among those aged 25–59, the group most affected by major life-style changes in contemporary society during the past 20–30 years. Thus, the recent gains in male survival in comparison to females, albeit modest in most cases, may be linked to convergence in behaviours among the sexes, such as the relative rise of cigarette smoking among women and the concomitant declines in such behaviours among men, possibly resulting in

differential rates of mortality from major killers such as lung cancer (Waldron, 1993).

Further study is needed to develop a more complete picture of the interrelationships between changing individual behaviours among men and women, changes in gender differences in morbidity, cause-specific death rates, and convergence in male/female life expectancy.

Notes

1. The 1992 and 1993 United Nations *Demographic Yearbooks* contain the most exhaustive listing of life expectancy by sex for the nations of the world. These sources also contain data on age–sex-specific death rates; however, the age groupings are not as refined as we would have liked. Notwithstanding this limitation, the classification provided sufficient information to allow us to execute an adequate investigation of the phenomenon.
2. The countries for which data do not correspond closely to 1970 are Bulgaria (1975) and Iceland and Malta (1973). The nations for which data do not correspond closely to 1990 are Scotland (1985), the USSR (1986), West Germany (1986), Northern Ireland (1983), Luxembourg (1986), and the Republic of Ireland (1986).

3. Typically, a statistical result is considered significant if the p value is less than or equal to 0.05. Sometimes, however, depending on the nature of the data (e.g. if it is highly aggregated), significance may be tentatively established with a p value of less than or equal to 0.10. Values of p greater than 0.10 are always considered statistically insignificant.
4. Out of the 38 countries listed in Table 18.1, 5 nations (Albania, Northern Ireland, Romania, Scotland, and the USSR) had to be excluded from this part of the analysis because data on death rates by age groups were unavailable in the data sources.

References

Bouvier-Colle, Marie-H. (1983). Mortalité et activité professionelle chez les femmes. *Population, 1*, 107–36.

Bulatao, Rodolfo A., & Bos Eduard. (1990). Projecting mortality for all countries. Paper presented at the annual meetings of the Population Association of America, Toronto, ON, May 3–6.

Carnes, Bruce, & Olshansky, S. Jay. (1993). Evolutionary perspectives on human senescence. *Population and Development Review, 19*(4), 793–806.

Coale, Ansley J. (1990). The possible future of mortality in Europe and North America. Paper presented at the annual meetings of the Population Association of America, Toronto, ON, May 3–6.

Coale, Ansley J., & Demeny, Paul. (1983). *Regional model life tables and stable populations* (2nd edn). New York: Academic Press.

Crimmins, Eileen M., Hayward, Mark D., & Saito, Y. (1994). Changing mortality and morbidity rates and the health status and life expectancy of the older population. *Demography, 31*(1), 159–75.

Fries, James F. (1980). Aging, natural death. and compression of mortality. *New England Journal of Medicine, 303*, 130–5.

Gee, Ellen M., & Veevers, Jane E. (1983). Accelerating differentials in mortality: An analysis of contributing factors. *Social Biology, 30*(1), 75–85.

———, & ———. (1988). Recent trends in Canadian sex differentials in mortality: The middle-aged turnaround. In P. Krishnan, F. Trovato, & G. Fearn (Eds), *Contributions to demography: Methodological and substantive, essays in honour of Dr Karol J. Krotki*, vol. 1, pp. 435–56. Department of Sociology, University of Alberta, Edmonton, AB.

Hazuda, H., Hefner, P., Stern, S.M., et al. (1986). Employment status and women's protection against coronary heart disease. *American Journal of Epidemiology, 123*(4), 623–40.

Krishnan, Parameswara. (1992). Predicting old age mortality in Canada. Research Discussion Paper No. 90, Population Research Laboratory, The University of Alberta, Edmonton.

Lee, Ronald D., & Carter, Lawrence. (1990). Modeling and forecasting US mortality. Paper presented at the annual meetings of the Population Association of America. Toronto, ON, May 3–6.

Levy, Robert L. (1981). The decline in cardiovascular disease mortality. *Annual Review of Public Health, 2*, 49–70.

Lopez, Alan D. (1983). The sex differential in mortality in developed countries. In Alan D. Lopez & Lado T. Ruzicka (Eds), *Sex differentials in mortality: Trends, determinants, and consequences*, pp. 53–120. Canberra, Australia: Australian National University Printing Press.

Manton, K.G. (1982). Changing concepts of mobility and mortality in elderly population. *Milbank Memorial Fund Quarterly/Health and Society 60*, 183–244.

Manton, K.G., Stallard, Eric, & Tolley, H.D. (1991). Limits to human life expectancy: Empirical and theoretical evidence. Paper presented at the annual meetings of the Population Association of America, Washington, DC, March 22.

McNown, Robert, & Rogers, Andrei. (1990). Forecasting cause-specific mortality using time series methods. Paper presented at the annual meetings of the Population Association of America, Toronto, ON, May 3–6.

Myers, George C. (1989). Mortality dynamics at older ages. In Lado Ruzicka, Guillaume Wunsch, & Penny Kane (Eds), *Differential mortality*, pp. 189–214. Oxford: Oxford University Press.

Nagnur, Drhuva. (1990). Epidemiologic transition in the context of demographic change: The evolution of Canadian mortality patterns. *Canadian Studies in Population, 17*, 1–24.

Nathanson, Constance A. (1984). Sex difference in mortality. *Annual Review of Sociology, 10*, 191–213.

———. (1992). The position of women and mortality in developed countries. Paper presented at the IUSSP Seminar on Premature Adult Mortality in Developed Countries: From Description to Explanation, Taormina, Italy, June 1–5.

Nathanson, Constance A., & Lopez, Alan D. (1987). The future of sex mortality differentials in the industrialized countries: A structural hypothesis. *Population Research and Policy Review, 6*, 123–36.

Olshansky, S.J. (1986). On forecasting mortality. *Milbank Quarterly, 66*(3), 482–530.

Olshansky, S.J., & Ault, A.B. (1986). The fourth stage of epidemiologic transition: The age of delayed degenerative diseases. *Milbank Quarterly, 46*(3), 355–91.

Olshansky, S.J., & Carnes, Bruce A. (1994). Demographic perspectives on human senescence. *Population and Development Review, 20*(1), 57–80.

Olshansky, S.J., Carnes, Bruce A., & Cassel, C. (1990). In search of Methuselah: Estimating the upper limits to human longevity. *Science, 250*, 634–40.

Omran, Abdel R. (1971). The epidemiological transition: A theory of epidemiology of population change. *Milbank Memorial Fund Quarterly, 49*, 509–38.

Pampel, Fred C., & Zimmer, C. (1989). Female labour force activity and the sex differential in mortality: Comparisons across developed nations, 1950–1980. *European Journal of Population, 5*, 281–304.

Passannante, Marion R., & Nathanson, Constance A. (1985). Female labor force participation and female mortality in Wisconsin, 1974–1978. *Social Science and Medicine, 21*(6), 655–65.

Population Reference Bureau. (1975). World population data sheet, 1975. Washington, DC.

———. (1993). World population data sheet, 1993. Washington, DC.

———. (1994). World population data sheet, 1994. Washington, DC.

Preston, Samuel H. (1976). *Mortality patterns in national populations with special reference to recorded causes of death*. New York: Academic Press.

Ravenholt, R.T. (1984). Addiction mortality in the United States, 1980: Tobacco, alcohol, and other substances. *Population and Development Review, 10*(4), 697–724.

Retherford, Robert D. (1975). *The changing sex differential in mortality*. Westport/London: Greenwood Press.

Rogers, Richard G., & Hackenberg, Robert. (1991). Extending epidemiologic transition theory: A new stage. *Social Biology, 34*(3–4), 234–43.

Rothenberg, Richard B., & Koplan, J.P. (1990). Chronic diseases in the 1990s. *Annual Review of Public Health, 11*, 267–96.

Stone, Leroy O., & Fletcher, Susan. (1993). *The seniors boom: Dramatic increases in longevity and prospects for better health*. Ottawa: Ministry of Industry, Science and Technology.

Tomason, Richard F. (1984). The components of the sex differential in mortality in industrialized populations. *Comparative Social Researach, 7*, 287–311.

United Nations. (1992). *Demographic yearbook, 1992*. New York: UN.

————. (1993). *Demographic yearbook, 1993.* New York: UN.

Valkonen, Tapani. (1990). Assumptions about mortality trends in industrialized countries: A survey. In Wolfgang Lutz (Ed.), *Future demographic trends in Europe and North America: What can we assume today?*, pp. 3–26. London: Academic Press.

Veevers, Jane E., & Gee, Ellen M. (1986). Playing it safe: Accident mortality and gender roles. *Sociological Focus, 19*(4), 349–60.

Verbrugge, Lois M. (1976). Sex differentials in morbidity and mortality in the United States. *Social Biology, 23*(4), 275–96.

————. (1980). Recent trends in sex mortality differentials in the United States. *Women's Health, 5*(3), 17–37.

————. (1989). The twain meet: Empirical explanations of sex differences in health and mortality. *Journal of Health and Social Behavior, 30*(3), 282–304.

Waldron, Ingrid. (1976). Why do women live longer than men? *Social Science and Medicine, 10*, 349–62.

————. (1983). The role of genetic and biological factors in sex differences in mortality. In A.D. Lopez & L.T. Ruzicka (Eds), *Sex differentials in mortality: Trends, determinants and consequences*, pp. 141–64. Canberra, Australia: Australian National University Printing Press.

————. (1986). The contribution of smoking to sex differences in mortality. *Public Health Report, 101*(2), 163–73.

————. (1990). Effects of labor force participation on sex differences in mortality and morbidity. Paper presented at the meetings of the Population Association of America, Toronto, ON, May 3–6.

————. (1993). Recent trends in sex mortality ratios for adults in developed countries. *Social Science and Medicine, 36*(4), 451–62.

Waldron, Ingrid, & Johnston, Susan. (1976, June). Why do women live longer than men? Part II. *Journal of Human Stress*, pp. 19–29.

Wingard, Deborah L. (1984). The sex differential in morbidity, mortality, and life style. *Annual Review of Public Health, 5*, 433–58.

Wister, Andrew V., & Gee, Ellen. (1994). Age at death due to ischemic heart disease: Gender differences. *Social Biology, 41*(1–2), 110–26.

Basic Demographic Measures

1. Crude Death Rate (CDR)

The crude death rate (CDR) is defined as the number of deaths in a given interval (let us assume the interval is one year for this and subsequent measures), divided by the mid-point population (i.e. the population at midyear). This rate is usually expressed per thousand population:

$$CDR = \frac{D}{P} \times 1{,}000$$

where D is the number of deaths observed in the interval, and P refers to the midyear population.

2. Age-Specific Death Rate (M_x)

Mortality varies considerably by age. Therefore, it is important to compute age-specific death rates. The age-specific death rate is defined as the number of deaths to persons of a given age divided by the midyear population at risk in that same age category. Age-specific death rates are calculated for separate age categories. The general formula for the age-specific death rate (Mx) takes the form

$$M_X = \frac{D_x}{P_x} \times 1{,}000$$

where the letter x indexes age category, and D_x and P_x correspond to the number of deaths and midyear population for age category x, respectively.

3. Infant Mortality Rate (IMR)

Infant mortality is defined as deaths occurring between birth and one year of life. For analytical purposes infant deaths are often subdivided into three categories:

1. *early neonatal mortality* – deaths in infants from birth up to one week after birth
2. *late neonatal mortality* – deaths that occur from the seventh day after birth to the end of the twenty-seventh day after birth
3. *post-neonatal mortality* – deaths from 28 days after birth up to one year after birth.

Early and late neonatal deaths are sometimes combined in a single category, *neonatal mortality*. In calculating infant mortality, it is customary to include late fetal deaths (explained below) with early neonatal deaths to form a fourth category of infant mortality, *perinatal mortality*.

The infant mortality rate (IMR) is calculated as the number of infant deaths in a given year divided by the number of live births in the same year. It is usually multiplied by 1,000. The formula is expressed as follows:

$$IMR = \frac{D_0}{B} \times 1{,}000$$

where D_0 is the number of infant deaths in a given year, and B is the number of live births during the same year.

4. Cause-Specific Death Rate

Different populations can experience the wide range of fatal diseases and conditions quite differently. In the industrialized nations, for instance, three frequent killers are cardiovascular disease, cancer, and accidents and violence. The World Health Organization (WHO) collects on a regular basis country-level mortality statistics by age, sex, period, country, and cause of death, which it then publishes on a period basis. The official coding of causes of death is based on the *International Classification of Diseases* (ICD) system, which involves a detailed listing of all known diseases and medical conditions that can result in death.

In the ICD, each disease or condition is assigned a letter and numerical code. For example, in the latest ICD revision (ICD-10), the code for breast cancer is C50. Prostate cancer has a code of C61. Suicide encompasses codes X61 to X88, as there are various methods of suicide. The letter in front of the numerical code represents a 'chapter', which reflects a given category of disease or circumstance responsible for death. For instance, the first chapter in the ICD-10 is 'Certain Infectious and Parasitic Diseases', containing information on specific diseases such as cholera, typhoid fever, and other infectious viral and bacterial diseases. There is a separate chapter called 'Neoplasms', which contains all the specific cancers arranged by their anatomical site (e.g. cancer of the lung, cancer of the prostate, cancer of the breast). In total, the ICD-10 consists of 22 chapters.

The general form of the cause-specific death rate is

$$\text{cause-specific death rate} = \frac{D_c}{P} \times 1{,}000$$

where D_c is deaths due to a particular disease or 'cause' c, occurring in the population during a specified interval (e.g. one year). P is the midyear population exposed to the risk of dying from the disease or condition during the interval.

Since mortality data are usually tabulated by age and sex, it is also possible to compute cause-specific death rates by age for males and females separately.

5. The Life Table and Life Expectancy

Life tables are used frequently in the biological and social sciences, as well as in many applied situations. In order to understand the life table and its uses in mortality analysis, we need to see what it is, how it works, and what its fundamental assumptions are.

Demographers commonly view the life table as a tool to describe the mortality experience of a population using period cross-sectional age-specific death rates. In this sense, the life table describes the survival experience of a fictitious cohort (also known as a *synthetic cohort*) subjected to the current age-specific death rates of an actual population over the cohort's fictional lifetime. This is the generally accepted definition of the *period life table*. There is also the *cohort* (or *generational*) *life table*, which is computed from retroactive historical data for a specific birth cohort that was born many years ago and that is now extinct.

One of the most frequently used measures derived from the life table is *life expectancy*. Life expectancy refers to the average number of years remaining for someone aged x, where x represents any age category in the life table from birth to some upper age (e.g. 110). For example, if we wanted to determine the life expectancy of a newborn baby boy in Canada based on mortality rates in 2010, we would first compute 2010 age-specific death rates for males, and then from these rates generate the corresponding life table. With the information contained in the life table we would then be able to answer this question by looking at the life expectancy figure corresponding to male infants. We might find that on the basis of 2010 death rates the life expectancy for a newborn baby boy in Canada is 78 years. This tells us that on the average, a male born in 2010 can expect to live 78 years, assuming of course that current mortality rates remain unchanged (i.e. that death rates do not change from what they are in 2010).

Questions for Critical Thought

1. How do the epidemiological transitions of more developed and less developed countries differ?
2. What is the future of human longevity in the advanced societies of the world?
3. In what ways do social factors produce inequalities in health and mortality?
4. Will sex differences in mortality ever converge between men and women? Why or why not?

Websites of Interest

The World Health Organization has posted the *International Classification of Diseases* manual (ICD-10) and a history of its origins on their website: www.who.int/classifications/icd/en/index.html

The *World Health Report* is yet another useful source of information on global health trends. It is also available on the World Health Organization's website: www.who.int/whr/en/index.html

Harvard Health Publications is a set of links to Harvard Medical School's periodic health bulletins, which cover a range of important health-related topics from skin care to stress management. These bulletins can be accessed free of charge by registering at www.health.harvard.edu/special_health_reports/

Further Reading

Ananth, Cande V., Liu, Shiliang, Joseph, K.S., & Kramer, Michael S. (2009). A comparison of foetal and infant mortality in the United States and Canada. *International Journal of Epidemiology, 38*, 480–9.

Berkman, Lisa F., & Kawachi, Ichiro (Eds). (2000). *Social epidemiology.* Oxford: Oxford University Press.

Caselli, Graziella, & Lopez, Alan D. (Eds). (1996). *Health and mortality among elderly populations.* Oxford: Clarendon Press and Oxford University Press.

Drevenstedt, Greg L., Crimmins, Eileen M., Vasunilashorn, Sarinnapha, & Finch, C.E. (2008). The rise and fall of excess male infant mortality. *Proceedings of the National Academies of Science, 105*(13), 5016–21.

Easterlin, Richard A. (2004). How beneficent is the market? A look at the modern history of mortality. In Richard A. Easterlin, *The reluctant economist* (pp. 101–138). Cambridge: Cambridge University Press.

Gavrilov, Leonid A., & Gavrilova, Natalia S. (1991). *The biology of life span: A quantitative approach.* Chur, Switzerland: Harwood Academic Publishers.

Gracey, Michael, & King, Malcolm. (2009). Indigenous health. Part 1: Determinants and disease patterns. *The Lancet, 374*, 65–75.

Hayflick, Leonard. (2007). Biological aging is no longer an unsolved problem. *Annals of the New York Academy of Sciences, 1100*, 1–13.

Kirby, David. (2008). Changes in sexual behavior leading to the decline in the prevalence of HIV in Uganda: Confirmation from multiple sources of evidence. *Sexual Transmitted Infections 84*(II), ii35–41.

Kunitz, Stephen J. (2007). *The health of populations: General theories and particular realities.* Oxford: Oxford University Press.

Marmot, Michael, & Wilkinson, Richard G. (Eds). (2006). *Social determinants of health* (2nd edn). Oxford: Oxford University Press.

McNeill, William H. (1976). *Plagues and peoples.* New York: Doubleday.

Olshansky, S. Jay, Carnes, Bruce A., & Butler, Robert N. (2001, March). If humans were built to last. *Scientific American*, pp. 50–5.

Oeppen, Jim, & Vaupel, James W. (2002). Broken limits to life expectancy. *Science, 296*, 1029–31.

Pison, Gilles. (2010, January). Child mortality reduction: A contrasting picture across the world. *Population and Societies, 463.* Paris: Institut National D'Études Demographiques (INED).

Porter, Roy. (1997). *The greatest benefit to mankind: A medical history of humanity from antiquity to the present.* London: Harper Collins.

Stuckler, David. (2008). Population causes and consequences of leading chronic diseases: Comparative analysis of prevailing explanations. *The Milbank Quarterly, 86*(2), 273–326.

SECTION VIII
Migration and Urbanization

Learning Objectives

By the end of this section, students should understand and be able to discuss the following:

- the historical forces behind the process of urbanization
- the relationship between population aging and internal migration in industrialized societies
- shifts over time in trends and regional origins of international migration to major receiving countries
- the complex nature of international migration since the 1960s.

Introduction

Internal migration is the movement of people across administrative/political boundaries within a given territory, such as a country. This type of movement is closely linked to two interrelated processes: industrialization (the development of an economic system based on industrial production) and urbanization (the increasing concentration of a country's population in towns and cities). The development of an industrial economy (first in western Europe and then throughout the rest of the world) is responsible for the displacement of the population away from rural areas to towns and cities, otherwise known as urbanization. In essence, urbanization involves three interrelated processes:

1. a progressive concentration of people and economic activity in cities and towns, which alters the general scale of population settlement;
2. a shift in the national or regional economy to a model in which the dominant mode of production is non-agricultural; and
3. the spread of technological advancement down the urban hierarchy of a country, so that it eventually reaches the rural areas; in the advanced stages of urbanization the urban and the rural become increasingly similar in the extent and intensity of technological adoption as well as in the social psychological dimensions of lifestyles, values, and attitudes.

The world's developed countries have progressed through all these stages, and the majority of their populations are situated in urban areas. The less developed countries, although lagging behind in these processes, are urbanizing rapidly and account for an increasing share of the total urban population of the world. For developing countries, the shift toward an increasingly urban population brings with it both positive and negative consequences. For example, on the one hand urbanization is strongly correlated with fertility declines and rising national incomes (Weil, 2009); on the other, it introduces massive challenges for governments responsible for providing sufficient housing and basic services and for creating sufficient jobs for a rapidly expanding urban population while also ensuring economic development in the rural sector (Brokerhoff, 2000; Brokerhoff & Brennan, 1998; Gugler, 2004; Henderson, 2010; National Research Council, 2003).

The latest figures from the United Nations' *World Urbanization Prospects* indicate that the overall level of urbanization in the world has reached just over 50 per cent (see Table VIII.1). In absolute terms this amounts to nearly 3.5 billion people living in areas classified as urban. By 2025, this figure is anticipated to reach almost 60 per cent, and nearly 70 per cent by 2050 (United Nations Department of Economic and Social Affairs, Population Division, 2010).

Table VIII.1 Urban versus rural population by major world area, 2009

	Population (billions)			Percentage		
Region	Urban	Rural	Total	Urban	Rural	Total
World	3.42	3.41	6.83	50.1	49.9	100.0
More developed countries	0.92	0.31	1.23	74.9	25.1	100.0
Less developed countries	2.50	3.10	5.60	44.6	55.4	100.0

Adapted from United Nations Economic and Social Affairs Population Division, 2010, pp. 3–4.

As might be expected given the varying levels of economic development found across countries, urbanization has occurred unevenly across the regions. Northern America (i.e. Canada and the US), Latin America and the Caribbean, and Europe and Oceania are highly urbanized, with the proportions of urban dwellers ranging from 70 per cent in Oceania to 82 per cent in Northern America. These regions are expected to see their urbanization levels continue to rise, even if slowly, so that by 2050, all of them (except Oceania) are expected to be more than 84 per cent urbanized. In contrast, Africa and Asia remain mostly rural, with just 40 per cent and 42 per cent of their respective populations living in urban settlements in 2010. By 2050 they are expected to be significantly less urbanized than the other major regions, attaining urbanization levels of 62 per cent in Africa and 65 per cent in Asia (United Nations Department of Economic and Social Affairs, Population Division, 2010).

Mobility and Migration

What counts as migration? Are all moves migrations? How does one define a move from one neighbourhood to another within the same community? What about the routine commute of people from home to their workplaces on a daily basis—is this considered migration?

The term *mobility* (as in 'geographic mobility') denotes any type of geographic move by either an individual or a group. As a demographic concept, *migration* is understood to mean mobility across a significant political/administrative boundary, such as a region, a province, a state, or a municipality. These types of moves are distinct from *local mobility* (also referred to as *residential mobility*), which encompasses movements within a particular community (Morrison, Bryan, & Swanson, 2004, p. 493). An example of residential, or local, mobility would be moving from one house to another within the same city.

Migration, then, is distinguished by three main criteria:

1. the crossing of significant administrative boundaries
2. travel over long distances
3. a permanent or semi-permanent change of residence (Yaukey & Anderton, 2001, pp. 271–2).

In actual research findings, these three criteria are seldom met. For example, not all migrations entail long distance travel; some migrations happen over relatively short distances (e.g. cross-border moves between Windsor, Ontario, and Detroit, Michigan). And as to the third criterion, in most cases researchers cannot ascertain the intentions of individuals regarding the permanency of their moves (Morrison, Bryan, & Swanson, 2004; Ritchey, 1976; Shaw, 1975). In fact, of the three criteria, perhaps the only one that is unambiguous is the crossing of administrative boundaries. Therefore, in practice researchers commonly apply operational definitions of what constitutes migration for the purposes of their investigations, the most widely applied criterion being a change of place of usual residence from one administrative area to another. This definition is especially common in aggregate-level studies of migration. Survey data, being based on individual responses, presents researchers with a wider choice of operational definitions.

The Mobility Transition

Wilbur Zelinsky's *hypothesis of the mobility transition* describes how geographic mobility patterns change in the context of the socioeconomic modernization of societies. In this sense, Zelinsky's theory complements the ideas expressed earlier in theories of demographic and epidemiological transition. The mobility transition as a spatio-temporal process can be viewed as evolving in concert, or in parallel, with these other two transitions in the historical experience of the Western world.

Zelinsky's thesis encompasses five successive phases, each reflecting progressively higher levels of urbanization, societal complexity, and associated shifts in geographical mobility patterns. In the *premodern traditional society*, there is little residential migration. During this period, residential moves are mainly connected to land use, social visits, commerce, warfare, and religious observances. The *early transitional society* and the *late transitional society*, successive phases in the mobility transition, are closely connected to industrialism. In response to newly emerging opportunities, people from the countryside flock to the industrial towns and cities. Major outflows of international migration to new colonies also characterize these phases. As the population becomes increasingly urbanized there is a slackening of movement from the countryside to the city. Economic and commercial activity becomes increasingly concentrated in cities and towns. As the society becomes increasingly complex, there is a significant increase in 'circulation mobility' (repeated movements, such as from home to work). In the *advanced society*, the population is mostly urban; therefore the predominant type of geographic mobility is between urban places. In the *super-advanced society*, a great deal of potential mobility is absorbed by new communication technologies, which by their very nature reduce the friction of distance for people. For example, in the world of work, transactions that at one time needed to be carried out face-to-face can now be performed instantaneously through the medium of highly advanced electronic technologies (e.g. computers). Nations during this phase become increasingly concerned with immigration controls and formulate restrictive policies to safeguard their borders.

The Future of Urbanization in the Super-Advanced Societies

We live in an urbanizing world (Brockerhoff, 2000), and for an increasing portion of the world's population, life takes place in the hustle and bustle of expanding cities. Some of these cities—the 'global cities'—exert a dominant influence on the global economy and therefore, indirectly, on virtually all significant aspects of daily life for the average citizen (Friedman, 1986; Sassen, 2000). So, what is

the future of urbanization? For Champion (2001), the advanced economies of the world have moved to a stage which can be best defined as 'beyond urbanization'. That is, the traditional concept of urbanization, which is based on the proportion of population in urban areas, no longer seems a fruitful concept, given that the vast majority of the population is now urbanized. A likely future scenario for the highly urbanized societies is urbanization beyond the suburbs, or *exurbanization*—the growth of smaller remote areas beyond the suburbs of cities. This process appears to be underway in Canada. According to the 2006 census, the fastest growing areas in the country are peripheral settlements surrounding the central municipalities of Canada's 33 census metropolitan areas (Statistics Canada, 2007; Turcotte & Vézina, 2010). Although this emerging phenomenon clearly needs further investigation, it may be surmised that it reflects the growing cost of real estate and housing in the cities. Land and housing in the more remote areas are more affordable, and many people find it advantageous to take up residence in such localities. The presence of efficient roadways and communication systems connecting remote localities to the metropolis allow residents of more distant places to commute easily to work on a daily basis.

Internal Migration in Advanced Societies

Within highly advanced societies an important area of study is the geographical mobility of labour. This type of movement can be seen as a response to the supply of and demand for workers across regions with varying levels of socioeconomic development. More developed regions attract skilled and unskilled labour from the less prosperous areas of a country. This process helps to redistribute human capital skills in accordance with regional differences in demand for these skills. Correspondingly, we can expect the intensity of labour migration to fluctuate closely with the business cycle: times of intense economic activity are likely to see increased migration, while economic downturns bring a reduction in geographic mobility (Hiller, 2009; Lowry, 1966; Plane & Rogerson, 1994; Shaw, 1975).

One of the characteristics of contemporary society is the high degree of geographic dispersal of families (Silverstein, 1995; Smith, 1998). This phenomenon has important social and economic implications for the movers themselves, their families, and society at large. One of the most important concerns associated with the situation today is the possible implications for intergenerational relationships and, in particular, the ability for different generations of families to be available to each other to provide support when it is needed. For example, Silverstein (1995) describes the problems many aging parents face in gaining access to their children as a result of the geographic distance that often separates the generations. This matter is bound to become an increasingly serious concern in demographically mature societies with rapidly aging populations.

Rogerson and Kim address this interesting problem in the American context as it relates to the very large baby boom generation born between 1946 and 1964. The sheer size of this cohort means that it exerts a powerful influence on many aspects of society, including its regional population trends. The sociological literature has described this cohort as a 'sandwich generation' because its members are simultaneously caught between obligations to their own immediate families and to their aging parents. It isn't difficult to see how geographic dispersal can lead to complications for this generation and, especially, for its intergenerational relations.

Rogerson and Kim found that in 1990, members of the baby boom cohort comprised a large proportion of the population in a small number of dynamic metropolitan areas of the United States. By 2003, the locations with large percentages of baby boomers had become primarily areas surrounding large metropolitan regions found especially in northern parts of the country, notably New England, the northern Rocky Mountain region, and the northern parts of Wisconsin and Minnesota. Much of this redistribution resulted from net in-migration of baby boomers to these areas and by net out-migration away

from their bicoastal and metropolitan locations of 1990. (The Midwest also witnessed a proportionate growth of baby boomer population, though this was mainly a function of the high out-migration of younger cohorts from this region.) To some extent, these relocation patterns might reflect spatial patterns of retirement for the boomer generation.

Although the boomer generation is experiencing dual obligations to their immediate and parent families, it seems that in the majority of cases the geographic distance moved is not very large, and therefore intergenerational caregiving should not be a major issue. Interestingly, though, the authors of the study argue that this is the case mostly for the less educated members of the boomer generation, many of whom are not relocated very far from their aging parents. Those most affected, according to Rogerson and Kim, will be the more educated baby boomers, because these individuals on average move greater distances away from their parents.

Another interesting point raised by Rogerson and Kim is that the future demands for simultaneous intergenerational caregiving are likely to be even greater for the children of baby boomers, since the baby boomers themselves have had fewer children than their parents did. Therefore, from a research point of view, the spatial redistribution of aging baby boomers and the nature of their spatial separation from their (relatively few) children should become an important focus of attention.

International Migration

When examined in the context of the broad spectrum of history, migration is a core feature of our existence as a species. Human civilization arose out of migrations, beginning with the movement of our earliest ancestors out of Africa and their eventual spread throughout Asia, Europe, Oceania, and the Americas (Cavalli-Sforza & Cavalli-Sforza, 1995; Diamond, 1999). From well back in antiquity, societies have been transformed by the intermingling of peoples of diverse cultures, their migratory movements stimulated by the quest for commerce, the exploration and conquest of new lands, wars, persecution, and even the enslavement of one people by another (Hoerder, 2002; McNeill, 1984).

International Migration in Modern History

Historians consider the year 1500 the start of the *Modern Era* (Barzun, 2001, p. xxi). In his review of immigration history through the Modern Era, Massey (1999) identifies four distinct periods: (1) the mercantile period; (2) the industrial period; (3) a period of limited migration between the world wars; and (4) the post-industrial period beyond the 1960s.

1. The Mercantile Period (1500-1800)

The main impetus for transnational movements during this period was European colonization of the New World—the Americas and parts of Africa, Asia, and Oceania. As these areas developed, their new economies required abundant labour. According to Massey (1999), emigrants from Europe generally fell into three categories: a relatively large number of agrarian settlers; a smaller number of administrators and artisans; and an even smaller number of entrepreneurs who founded plantations to produce raw materials for Europe's growing mercantile economies. The rise of plantations and the concomitant near-destruction of the indigenous peoples of the Americas after European contact meant that an outside source of cheap labour had to be found to maintain the colonial economy. The slave trade and a system of indentured workers emerged in response to this need. During this time, about 10 million West Africans were forcibly taken to the Americas and the Caribbean, many of them ultimately arriving in the United States. This period of history has left an indelible mark on American society, most notably reflected in its ongoing problem with race relations (Petersen, 1978).

2. The Industrial Period (1800–1914)

The industrial period represents an especially important part of modern migration history. During the nineteenth century, New World nations—in particular, the United States, Canada, Australia, New Zealand, Argentina, and South Africa—were eager to receive Europeans to help populate and develop frontier lands within their territories. This was a period of intense nation building by these emerging economies. One of the most significant migratory flows in human history took place during this period, one not likely to be replicated by virtue of its sheer magnitude, intensity, and impact on sending and receiving areas. According to Petersen (1975, p. 279), about 60 million Europeans crossed the oceans between 1800 and 1950 to settle in the Americas, and perhaps another 7 million relocated to Australia and New Zealand. The key sending countries were Britain, Italy, Norway, Portugal, Spain, and Sweden. According to Easterlin (1961), between 1850 and 1914, emigration accounted for a cumulative loss of more than one-tenth of Europe's population.

A number of interrelated forces—demographic, economic, and social—helped spark the nineteenth-century European migration to the New World. Easterlin (1961) has proposed that population pressure (i.e. a high rate of natural increase in a country) was an important force underlying European emigration, as were cross-country variations in gross national product (i.e. wage differentials). Complementing these push factors was a strong pulling effect in the promise of economic prosperity in the New World, most notably in the economically strong United States. These factors were thought by Easterlin to be of prime importance in stimulating mass European emigration. The Industrial Revolution also played a major role by destabilizing the rural economies of European countries. As the economy shifted farther away from agriculture in favour of manufacturing, many rural inhabitants were left without a stable source of income. Some managed to find work in the factories, but a large number of them, seeing few prospects in Europe, left to seek opportunities overseas (Hatton & Williamson, 1994, 1998; B. Thomas, 1954; D. Thomas, 1941). As the number of people leaving Europe rose, this stimulated even more emigration to the New World—once a substantial number of emigrants became established in their adoptive countries, these settled migrants would sponsor their families and relatives to join them in the New World. This type of social networking helped lower the financial and psychological costs of migration for prospective European migrants.

As the nineteenth century approached its end, the stimulating effect on emigration of demographic pressure and economic conditions in Europe diminished in importance. European wages rose and the differential with New World societies shrunk, making emigration increasingly less desirable from mid-century right up until the start of World War I. Hatton and Williamson (1998, p. 51) also point out that as demographic transition in Europe eased and industrialization slowed, the forces of convergence began to dominate, aided by the weakening pull of the stock of previous emigrants as their numbers abroad levelled out, causing emigration rates to fall sharply, even before World War I.

Thus, in the early stages of European industrialization, it was differences in average wages and living standards between countries that stimulated massive emigration to the New World. But as industrialization reached a mature stage in Europe and living standards improved, the need for emigration by Europeans waned. Previous emigration contributed to the convergence in living standards between Europe and the New World by helping to reduce labour market inequalities in the source countries. At the same time it helped to accentuate socioeconomic inequalities in the destination countries of the New World because each new wave of immigrants took their place at the bottom of the income and occupational hierarchies of the host societies.

of limited international migration. In response to the two wars and the inter-war collapse of the world economy, major receiving countries like the United States and Canada implemented restrictive laws to limit immigration. During the Great Depression, opposition to receiving immigrants was based largely on the principle that nationals deserved to have priority over immigrants in obtaining whatever work was available under such dire economic conditions. Repatriation of immigrants during this period was a common policy. Some governments, such as those of the United States and France, encouraged and even assisted the voluntary return of foreigners to their own countries (Taft, 1936). The number of newcomers to Canada in 1931 had fallen to just 27,530, down from 135,982 in 1926. In 1941, at the start of the Second World War, immigration to Canada was a mere 9,329—the lowest total in Canadian history. However, the end of the war brought a rebound in immigration, so that in 1951, Canada welcomed over 194,000 newcomers, thus surpassing by a considerable margin the earlier figure for 1926 (McVey & Kalbach, 1995, p. 84).

Although this is known as a period of limited migration, the two world wars had the effect of uprooting and displacing massive numbers of people from their homelands in Europe and other parts of the world. In the aftermath of World War I, for example, there were major displacements of people from Asia Minor, the Russian empire, and the Balkans (Polian, 2004). In the 1930s, many fled from China because of the Japanese invasion, while a large number of Spaniards left Spain in response to the Fascist victory. In the context of World War II, an estimated 7 million Jews and others threatened by the Nazi regime fled their homelands (Kraft, 2005).

3. The Limited Migration Period (WW I, The Great Depression, and WW II)

Between World War I (1914–18) and World War II (1939–45), the world experienced the Great Depression (1929 through the 1930s). These consequential and protracted events provoked a period

4. The Post-Industrial Period (1960s and beyond)

The migration story following World War II can be subdivided into two sub-periods. During the years between the end of the war and 1970, when western European countries and overseas Western offshoot nations were in need of labour to help rebuild their economies, many immigrants from peripheral areas of the Mediterranean (i.e. Italy, Spain, Portugal, Greece, and Turkey) migrated to the industrialized north (i.e. West Germany, Belgium, France, Austria, Switzerland, Holland, England, and Wales). In contrast to this major migratory movement, which was principally motivated by the growing need for labour in the receiving countries of the industrialized world, the second sub-period was marked by the intensification of economic globalization, beginning in the 1970s. Early on in this second sub-period, a major worldwide economic recession, sparked by a severe deficit in the supply of oil, forced corporations throughout the industrialized countries to restructure in an effort to cut costs. One solution was to transport manufacturing to the developing countries. Here many of the leading corporations found a new source of mass labour, where a growing population with low economic prospects would welcome paid factory work at very low wages. These changes had a devastating effect on the early wave of migrants from the Mediterranean region (e.g. Italy, Turkey) resident in the prosperous countries of northern and western Europe (e.g. Germany, France). The immigrants of the 1950s and 1960s to these wealthy European countries were, for the most part, of low education and had limited skills beyond those used in their work, mainly in manufacturing and construction. Unemployment among these immigrants went up dramatically, and many among the older workers became permanently jobless (Therborn, 1987).

Global migration through the 1980s and 1990s intensified, so much so that authors have referred to this period as 'worlds in motion' (Massey, et al., 1998) and 'age of migration' (Castles and Miller, 2009). All regions of the globe are participating in one form or another today. Many movements have been peaceful in nature, generated by the growing demand for labour in a globalizing world; others have resulted from war and political unrest in some parts of the world (e.g. in Africa and, earlier, in the former Yugoslavia). International migration today is more diverse than in earlier times in history.

Emigration is an option for more people thanks to the increasing global demand for labour on the one hand, and the relative ease of global transportation on the other. The major supply of immigrants to receiving areas has shifted from Europe to the developing countries. Primary receiving countries, including the United States and Canada, Germany, France, Belgium, Switzerland, Sweden, and the United Kingdom, now attract the majority of their immigrants from Africa, Asia, Latin America, and the former Soviet countries of eastern Europe. At the same time, nations that traditionally exported immigrants—Italy, Spain, Greece, and Portugal, for example—have become countries of immigration (Koser, 2007; Therborn, 1987). And since the 1970s, oil-rich countries in the Gulf region (e.g. Saudi Arabia, the United Arab Emirates, Kuwait) have been attracting large waves of labour migrations to work in their oil-based economies. Finally, beginning in the 1980s, migration spread into the newly industrializing countries of Asia, specifically South Korea, Taiwan, Hong Kong, Singapore, Malaysia, and Thailand (Castles and Miller, 2009).

Contemporary International Migration Trends

According to the United Nations, in 2010 an estimated 214 million people—roughly 3 per cent of the world's population—were immigrants, that is, people living outside the country of their birth. As Table VIII.2 shows, a substantial proportion of international immigrants (60 per cent) are living in the developed countries. Between 1990 and 2010, the more developed regions gained about 45 million international migrants, according to the UN, representing an increase of 55 per cent. As of 2010, international migrants account for roughly 10 per cent of the total population residing in the more developed regions, up from 7.2 per cent in 1990. In the less developed regions, the migrant stock has increased by 13 million since 1990, a gain of 18 per cent (United Nations Department of Economics and Social Affairs, Population Division, 2009a).

Table VIII.2 Estimated international migrants and refugees for the world and major development regions, 1990–2010

Year	World total migrants	Migrants living in more developed regions	Migrants living in less developed regions	World total refugees	Refugees living in MDCs	Refugees living in LDCs
1990	155,518,065	82,354,728	73,163,337	18,481,171	2,010,446	16,470,725
1995	165,968,778	94,123,386	71,845,392	18,497,567	3,870,640	14,626,927
2000	178,498,563	104,433,692	74,064,871	15,645,933	3,198,489	12,447,444
2005	195,245,404	117,187,935	78,057,469	13,852,349	2,528,127	11,324,222
2010	213,943,812	127,711,471	86,232,341	16,345,740	2,370,691	13,975,049
Percentage						
1990	100	53	47	100	11	89
1995	100	57	43	100	21	79
2000	100	59	41	100	20	80
2005	100	60	40	100	18	82
2010	100	60	40	100	15	85
Percentage change 1990–2010	38	55	18	−12	18	−15

Adapted from United Nations Department of Social and Economic Affairs, Population Division, 2009a.

Table VIII.2 also shows the large number of refugees living worldwide; these are people displaced from their countries of birth because of well-founded fear of persecution in their homelands. Of the roughly 16 million refugees in 2010, most of them (85 per cent) were living in the less developed countries. This situation is linked to sociopolitical upheavals that have affected certain regions of the world over the past several decades, including the breakup of the Soviet Empire in the late 1980s, and civil unrest in parts of Africa, Asia, and eastern Europe. In some cases, this unrest has sparked refugee crises of significant proportions.

The intensification of migration in the second half of the twentieth century can be attributed in part to economic globalization and the consequent increased demand for labour in the world's wealthier countries. The United States leads in the number of migrants living within its borders, with almost 43 million (see Table VIII.3). The Russian Federation is a distant second, with just under 13 million migrants. The number of foreign-born residents in Canada is 7.2 million, just below the 7.3 million listed for Saudi Arabia.

The Complex Nature of International Migration

As described by Castles and Miller in their chapter of this volume, all regions of the globe are currently being affected, in one way or another, by the movement of people across national borders. The reasons behind this phenomenon are varied and complex. Undoubtedly, a critical factor remains the economic

Table VIII.3 Countries with the largest number of international migrants, 2010

Country	Number of migrants (millions)
United States	42.8
Russian Federation	12.3
Germany	10.8
Saudi Arabia	7.3
Canada	7.2
France	6.7
United Kingdom	6.5
Spain	6.4
India	5.4
Ukraine	5.3

United Nations, Department of Economic and Social Affairs, Population Division, 2009b.

divide between rich and poor countries. People from poor areas of the world aspire to a better life elsewhere, and as income inequality widens, migration intensifies. As a result of the demographic deficit stemming from protracted sub-replacement fertility rates and consequent high levels of demographic aging, the rich countries have become increasingly reliant on immigrant labour to support their economies. In many respects, immigrants are needed because native-born citizens in these countries are reluctant to accept low-paying jobs in the less desirable areas of the economy, such as agriculture, construction, and the service sector. For these reasons, capitalist societies have been described as possessing a chronic need for immigration (Piore, 1979).

There are other complex realities associated with the state of immigration today. Immigration entails gains and losses for both sending and receiving countries. Through emigration, rapidly growing countries afflicted by a Malthusian poverty trap of high rates of natural increase and poverty may relieve some of the pressure of overpopulation. At the same time, however, poor countries lose many of their most talented and educated people (e.g. physicians, scientists) to other countries that offer

better opportunities. This so-called 'brain drain' has many implications for the 'losing' countries, most significantly a slowing of economic growth and development. Meanwhile, although wealthy receiving countries benefit from the 'brain gain' at the expense of poorer countries, it is also true that the sending countries accrue huge benefits from the remittances immigrants disburse to their families back home. These remittances are often used by the families of immigrants to purchase goods and services in their local economy, thus helping to stimulate economic development.

The social consequences of immigration for receiving countries vary depending on the nature of the society. In countries that have been built on immigration, like Canada, the United States, and Australia, immigrants are seen as a key part of nation building, and they form an integral part of the society. But this situation is radically different elsewhere, where 'foreigners' are treated as outsiders by the mainstream host society (Parsons & Smeeding, 2006). Yet as the flow of immigration persists, these receiving societies inevitably change, often becoming increasingly heterogeneous along racial and ethnic dimensions. The change is most acutely felt in liberal democracies whose historical experiences with immigration have either been limited or been defined by sending emigrants to other parts of the globe rather than welcoming them from abroad. Countries such as Italy, Spain, and Greece are typical of this situation. For these countries, the old world has turned new: they are now destinations of choice for immigrants, many of whom are asylum seekers (Therborn, 1987). This new reality brings many challenges to these receiving societies, which must somehow develop ways to integrate newcomers both socially and economically. They may need to review their sense of nationhood, making inclusiveness and cultural diversity parts of the national identity.

Though these challenges may be less acute in countries that have been built on immigration, they may still require some adjustments. Canada and Australia have enacted official policies of multiculturalism; in doing so, they have embraced diversity, and for the most part, this approach is working. And although no such policy has been adopted by the United States, immigrants to that country tend to behave no differently than they do in Canada and Australia: they establish thriving ethnic communities and contribute to the life of their host society in significant ways, both economically and socially (Hirschman, 2005). In sharp contrast, in countries where immigrants have traditionally been viewed as outsiders, ethnic communities tend to form marginal enclaves, separated from the mainstream society, and therefore limited in their ability to contribute significantly to the host society. This situation, which represents a failure on the part of the host society, fosters the propagation of poverty and socioeconomic marginalization (Koser, 2007).

Works Cited

Barzun, Jacques. (2001). *From dawn to decadence: 1500 to the present. 500 years of western cultural life.* New York: Harper Collins.

Brockerhoff, Martin P. (2000). An urbanizing world. *Population Bulletin.* Washington, DC: Population Reference Bureau.

Brockerhoff, Martin P., and Brennan, Ellen. (1998). The poverty of cities in developing regions. *Population and Development Review, 24*(11): 75–114.

Cadwallader, Martin. (1992). *Migration and residential mobility: Micro and macro approaches.* Madison, WI: The University of Wisconsin Press.

Castles, Steven, & Miller, Mark J. (2009). *The age of migration: International population movements in the modern world* (4th edn). New York: The Guilford Press.

Cavalli-Sforza, Luigi L., & Cavalli-Sforza, Francesco. (1995). *Great human diasporas: The history of diversity and evolution.* Trans. Sarah Thorne. New York: Helix Books, Addison-Wesley.

Champion, Anthony H. (2001). Urbanization, suburbanization, counterurbanization and reurbanization. In Ronald Paddison (Ed.), *Handbook of urban studies* (pp. 143–61). London: Sage Publications.

Diamond, Jared. (1999). *Guns, germs, and steel: The fates of human societies.* New York: W.W. Norton.

Easterlin, Richard A. (1961). Influences in European overseas immigration before WWI. *Economic Development and Cultural Change, 9,* 331–51.

Friedman, John. (1986). The world city hypothesis. *Development and Change, 17*(1): 69–84.

Geyer, H.S., & Kontuly, T.M. (Eds). *Differential urbanization: Integrating spatial models.* London: Arnold.

Gugler, Joseph. (2004). *World cities beyond the West: Globalization, development and inequality.* Cambridge: Cambridge University Press.

Hatton, Timothy J., & Williamson, Jeffrey G. (1994). What drove the mass migrations from Europe in the late nineteenth century? *Population and Development Review, 20*(3): 503–31.

———, & ———. (1998). *The age of mass migration: Causes and economic impact.* New York: Oxford University Press.

Henderson, J. Vernon. (2010). Cities and development. *Journal of Regional Science, 50*(1): 515–40.

Hiller, Harry H. (2009). *Second promised land. Migration to Alberta and the transformation of Canadian society.* Montreal and Kingston: McGill–Queen's University Press.

Hirschman, Charles. (2005). Immigration and the American century. *Demography, 42*(4): 595–620.

Hoerder, Dirk. (2002). *Cultures in contact: World migrations in the second millennium.* Durham, NC: Duke University Press.

Koser, Khalid. (2007). *International migration: A very short introduction.* Oxford: Oxford University Press.

Kraft, Barbara Sarina. (2005). Refugee. In *Microsoft Encarta Encyclopaedia.* Microsoft Corporation.

Lewis, G.J. (1982). *Human migration: A geographical perspective.* London: Croom Helm.

Lowry, Ira. S. (1966). *Migration and metropolitan growth: Two analytical models.* Los Angeles, CA: Institute of Government and Public Affairs, University of California.

McNeill, David. (1984). Migration in historical perspective. *Population and Development Review, 10*(1), 1–18.

McVey, Wayne W., Jr, & Kalbach, Warren E. (1995). *Canadian population.* Toronto: Nelson.

Massey, Douglas S. (1999). Why does immigration occur? A theoretical synthesis. In Charles Hirschman, Philip Kasinitz, & Josh DeWind (Eds), *The handbook of international migration: The American experience* (pp. 34–53). New York: Russell Sage Foundation.

Massey, Douglas S., Arango, Jaoquin, Hugo, Graeme, Kouaouci, A., Pellegrino, A., & Taylor, J.E. (1998). *Worlds in motion: Understanding international migration at the end of the millennium.* Oxford: Oxford University Press.

Morrison, Peter A., Bryan, Thomas M., & Swanson, David A. (2004). Internal migration and short-distance mobility. In Jacob A. Siegel & David A. Swanson (Eds), *The methods and materials of demography* (2nd edn, pp. 493–451). Amsterdam: Elsevier.

National Research Council. (2003). Cities transformed: Demographic change and its implications in the developing world. Panel on urban population dynamics. In M.R. Montgomery, R. Stren, B. Cohen, & H.E. Reed (Eds), *Committee on Population, Division of Behavioral and Social Sciences and Education.* Washington, DC: The National Academies Press.

Parsons, Craig A., & Smeeding, Timothy M. (2006). What's unique about immigration in Europe? In Craig A. Parsons & Timothy M. Smeeding (Eds), *Immigration and the transformation of Europe* (pp. 1–29). Cambridge: Cambridge University Press.

Petersen, William. (1975). *Population* (3rd edn). New York: Macmillan.

———. (1978). International migration. *Annual Review of Sociology, 4,* 533–75.

Piore, Michael J. (1979). *Birds of passage: Migrant labour and industrial societies.* Cambridge: Cambridge University Press.

Plane, David A., & Rogerson, Peter A. (1994). *The geographical analysis of population with applications to planning and business.* New York: Academic Press

Polian, Pavel. (2004). *Against their will: The history and geography of forced migrations in the USSR.* Budapest and New York: Central European University Press.

Ravenstein, Ernst Georg. (1885 [1976]). The laws of migration (paper I). *Journal of the Statistics Society* 48(2), 167–235. Reprinted by Arno Press.

———. (1889 [1876]). The laws of migration (paper II). *Journal of the Statistics Society* 52 (2): 167–235 (with commentary). Reprinted by Arno Press.

Ritchey, Neil P. (1976). Explanations of migration. *Annual Review of Sociology, 2,* 363–404.

Rogerson, Peter A., & Kim, Daejong. (2005). Population distribution and redistribution of the baby-boom cohort in the United States: Recent trends and implications. *Proceedings of the National Academies of Science, 102*(43), 15319–24.

Sassen, Saskia. (2000). *Cities in a world economy.* Thousand Oaks, CA: Pine Forge Press.

Shaw, Paul R. (1975). *Migration theory and fact: A review and bibliography of current literature.* Philadelphia: Regional Science Research Institute.

———. (1985). *Intermetropolitan migration in Canada: Changing determinants over three decades.* Toronto: New Canada Publications.

Silverstein, Merril. (1995). Stability and change in temporal distance between the elderly and their children. *Demography, 32*(1): 29–45.

Smith, Geoffrey C. (1998). Residential separation and patterns of interaction between elderly parents and their adult children. *Progress in Human Geography, 22*(3), 368–84.

Statistics Canada. (2007). *Portrait of the Canadian population in 2006. Population and dwelling counts, 2006 census* (catalogue no. 97-550-XIE). Ottawa: Minister of Industry.

Stillwell, J., & Congdon, P. (Eds). (1991). *Migration models: Macro and micro approaches.* London: Belhaven Press.

Taft, Donald R. (1936). *Human migration.* New York: Ronald Press.

Therborn, Goran. (1987). Migration and western Europe: The old world turning new. *Science, 237,* 1183–8.

Thomas, Brinley. (1954). *Migration and economic growth.* Cambridge: Cambridge University Press.

Thomas, Dorothy S. (1941). *Social and economic aspects of Swedish population movements.* New York: Macmillan.

Tobler, Waldo. (1995). Migration: Ravenstein, Thornthwaite, and beyond. *Urban Geography 16*(4), 327–43.

Turcotte, Martin, & Vézina, Mireille. (2010, winter). Migration from central to surrounding municipalities in Toronto, Montreal and Vancouver. *Canadian Social Trends 90,* 2–24.

United Nations Department of Economics and Social Affairs, Population Division. (2009a, July). *Trends in international migrant stock: The 2008 revision* (POP/DB/MIG/Stock/Rev.2008). CD-ROM Documentation. New York: UN.

———. (2009b). International migration, 2009 wall-chart. *International migration 2009: Graphs and maps from the 2009 wallchart* (Sales No. E.09.XIII.8). Retrieved from www.un.org/esa/population/publications/2009Migration_Chart/IttMig_maps.pdf

———. (2010). *World urbanization prospects. The 2009 revision: Highlights* (ESA/P/WP/215). New York: UN.

Weil, N. David. (2009). *Economic growth* (2nd edn). Boston: Addison Wesley.

Yaukey, David, & Anderton, Douglas L. (2001). *Demography: The study of human population* (2nd edn). Prospect Heights, IL: Waveland Press.

CHAPTER 19

The Hypothesis of the Mobility Transition

Wilbur Zelinsky

Introduction

Social scientists are guided in their gropings towards pattern and regularity in human activities by their small hoard of paradigms. In the fields of geography and demography, such broad intellectual designs have been especially scarce.[1] Indeed, there are probably no more than three major geographical paradigms in active use today. The first, which might be called the geographic axiom, so basic and instinctive as to be seldom articulated, is the conviction that there is genuine significance in the spatial patterning of physical and social events on and near the surface of the earth. Next is the notion of the spatial diffusion of innovations, sired jointly by anthropologists and geographers and recently explored with highly interesting results. Finally, geographers have borrowed the principle of least effort, or economic optimization, from economists and have grafted it onto the geographic axiom. This hybridization has spawned a number of hypotheses concerning the territorial arrangement of economic and related activities.

In demography we can discern only two such axiomatic items: the theory of the demographic transition and the so-called laws of migration. The first is the assertion that, on attaining certain thresholds of socioeconomic development, every community will pass from a pre-modern near-equilibrium in which high levels of mortality tend to cancel out high levels of fertility, to a modern near-equilibrium, in which low fertility almost matches low mortality but with the decline in births lagging far enough behind the decline in deaths to ensure a substantial growth in numbers during the transitional phase.[2] The laws of migration, first enunciated by Ravenstein in 1885, later modified by Thomas and Stouffer, and most recently improved and codified by Lee,[3] are a set of loosely related general empirical statements describing migrational relationships between sources and destinations. After making certain assumptions about degree of attractiveness and repulsion of places of origin and destination and about intervening obstacles and personal factors, Lee offers 18 hypotheses: 5 concern absolute volume of migration, 6 deal with streams and counter-streams of migrants, and 7 have to do with characteristics of migrants. When all these have been carefully reviewed, it may be found that most are explicitly migrational cases of the broader principle of least effort, according to which actors reach decisions whether and whither to move on the basis of relative known costs and returns (material and nonmaterial), subject as always to various inertial anchors.

Given the hybrid vigour of the offspring from the union of the geographic axiom with the principle of least effort, further experiments in crossbreeding paradigms would seem worthwhile. I shall argue here that all the assumptions described above are compatible and that their polygamous marriage in the form of the 'hypothesis of the mobility transition' may prove fruitful. The fusion of the spatial with the temporal perspective would seem especially intriguing. Indeed, it is surprising how little effort has been made by geographers to treat the demographic transition as a process diffusing outward through space and time.[4] But perhaps this is understandable in the light of the tepid interest geographers have generally displayed towards developmental phenomena.[5]

What is attempted here is the application of the principle of the spatial diffusion of innovations to the laws of migration, and specifically to Lee's assertion that 'unless severe checks are imposed, both volume and rate of migration tend to increase with time'.[6] The results are set within the same sort of temporal structure that has been developed for the demographic transition, and in accordance with the geographic axiom, coherent spatial entities are identified.[7] The principle of least effort, though not specifically invoked, is embedded in much that follows. The hypothesis set forth here is original only to the degree that it makes visible the implicit and joins together a number of ideas already immanent in the literature.[8] The exposition is almost entirely at the descriptive level; no serious effort is made to plumb the processual depths.

In this reconnaissance voyage the route is both deductive and inductive. The proposed generalizations seem logical in the light of current geographic and demographic doctrine. They also survive testing with what fragmentary evidence is readily accessible, but a more searching examination of a greater range of data is clearly in order.

The Hypothesis of the Mobility Transition

The hypothesis of the mobility transition can he expressed most succinctly as follows: *There are definite, patterned regularities in the growth of personal mobility through space–time during recent history, and these regularities comprise an essential component of the modernization process.* But it is more useful, perhaps, to offer eight related statements that, taken together, more adequately elucidate the hypothesis.

1. A transition from a relatively sessile condition of severely limited physical and social mobility towards much higher rates of such movement always occurs as a community experiences the process of modernization.

2. For any specific community the course of the mobility transition closely parallels that of the demographic transition and that of other transitional sequences not yet adequately described. A high degree of interaction may exist among all the processes in question.

3. There are major, orderly changes in the form as well as in the intensity of spatial mobility at various stages of the transition—changes in function, frequency, duration, periodicity, distance, routing, categories of migrants, and classes of origin and destination.

4. There are concurrent changes in both form and intensity of social mobility and in the movement of information, and under certain conditions the potential migrant may exercise the option of changing his locus in social space or of exploiting a superior flow of information rather than engaging in a territorial shift.

5. At a fairly high level of generalization, which dampens out minor spatial and temporal irregularities, we can recognize in mobility conditions coherent patterns that propagate themselves onward through time as successive periods and outward through space as concentric zones emanating from successful growth points.

6. The processes in question tend to accelerate in spatial and temporal pace with time, apparently because of the steady accumulation and intensification of causative factors within any given community and because of information and effects transferred from more advanced to less advanced regions.

7. Thus, the basic spatiotemporal scenario of change may be preserved, yet be noticeably modified when a region initiates its mobility transition at a late date, so that absolute dating is a significant consideration.

8. Such evidence as we have indicates an irreversible progression of stages.

The progress of a community towards advanced developmental status can be gauged by its control over energy, things, and knowledge, as exercised both individually and collectively, and also by the attainment of personal mobility, that is, a widening range of options for locating and patterning one's life. Obviously, these two attributes are closely related. The two transitional sequences—the demographic and the mobility transitions, plus others yet to be specified—essentially chronicle the trajectory from low to high values. Growth in power can be quite literally construed as mastery and discharge of great quantities of chemical, kinetic, and nuclear energy. Even more basic is the power to control or to affect strongly the physical and biotic habitat, including human physiology, and to manipulate various social systems through scientific knowledge and ever more complex technology, and an elaborate network of organizations. Of immediate concern is the fact that through biological knowledge and increasingly effective policing of the environment, modern man has extended control over his own physiology, first in the form of death control and more recently by means of birth control. The resultant series of changes is more accurately termed the 'vital transition' than the 'demographic transition', since the concept is only concerned with births and deaths, without taking into account other population events and characteristics.

The accretion and manipulation of human power during recent times have attracted much scholarly attention, but the remarkable expansion of personal mobility has been largely overlooked, despite its rich potential for interpreting the larger phenomenon of modernization. The volume of work on migration is considerable,[9] but it is greatly overshadowed by analyses of fertility and other such popular topics. The essential reasons are to be found in the intrinsic nature of the phenomenon, in definitional problems, and in the difficulties of data procurement and analysis. Given an effective registration system, we can count births and deaths with the greatest of ease. But exactly who is a migrant, and what do we mean by migration? No general consensus is likely for some time, since we are confronted here by a physical–social transaction, not just an unequivocal biological event. Several subsidiary questions must be answered—for example, how far (or how rapidly) need one travel and for how long to be classed as a migrant? What are the purposes of the trip? How different are origin and destination? How do we handle repetitive trips? But the most profound difficulty is the intimate, yet ambiguous, liaison between territorial and social mobility. Clearly one is partly, but not fully, convertible into the other, so that one can be traded off against the other, up to a point; but the exact nature of the linkages has yet to be worked out.

Genuine migration obviously means a perceptible and simultaneous shift in both spatial and social loci, so that the student cannot realistically measure one kind of movement while he ignores the other. Which family is more migratory, the one transferred three thousand miles across the continent by an employer to be plugged into a suburb almost duplicating its former neighbourhood, or the black family that moves a city block into a previously white district? Ideally, we should observe shifts in both varieties of space in tandem, but given the dearth of techniques and data for handling purely social movement, we are forced to rely almost solely on territorial movements as a clumsy surrogate for total mobility. When a truly serviceable index of mobility is fabricated, it will certainly be composite, bringing together measures of several dimensions. The problem is comparable to that of gauging general socioeconomic advancement: no single number will do; a variety of indicators must be viewed simultaneously.[10] Thus, when we speak of changes in mobility in this essay, only rough orders of magnitude can be suggested.

The Recent Historic Transformation

The growth in individual mobility has been spectacular in modernizing societies. If we use sedentary peasant societies as our datum plane, the life patterns of all but a few privileged or exceptional persons are, or were, preordained by circumstances of birth. Options of activities were rigidly constrained by gender and by inherited class, caste, occupation, religion, and location. Barring disaster, the orbit of physical movement was severely circumscribed, and the feasible range of information and ideas was narrow and stagnant, changing almost imperceptibly from generation to generation.

Today, by contrast, many individuals in the most advanced societies, and not merely the lucky, determined, and gifted, are able to shift about with relative impunity in the social space among classes or to comparison-shop among jobs and careers. The socioeconomic and behavioural barriers between the sexes have been crumbling; marriage is no longer a life sentence: it is possible to switch without disastrous consequences from one religion to another, to alter political allegiance, or to seek membership in any of a vast array of voluntary associations; and the possibilities for travel or for any of a variety of spatial migrations have multiplied greatly.

But perhaps the greatest of the new mobilities is that of the mind. Perception and thought are no longer tethered to the living memory and to the here and now but have been stretched to virtual infinity. Through such instrumentalities as the printing press, camera, telephone, postal system, radio, television, phonograph, electronic computer, library, museum, school, theatre, and concert hall, as well as personal gadding about, there remain no effective boundaries beyond which the nimbler mind cannot penetrate. This intellectual mobility is not just outward to all parts of the earth and the observable universe or backward and forward through time but is into other dimensions as well—the psychological, the aesthetic, and the scientific. All these forms of motion are closely interrelated: increasing freedom of spatial movement is both cause and effect of other forms of enhanced mobility. On still another level, it is also true that the two dynamic processes, magnification of power and of mobility, though distinct at their cores, are also vigorously interactional, one feeding heartily on the other.

This newly won freedom of movement in a multidimensional physical-social-psychic space has not been achieved without paying a penalty. Greater mobility means shallower local attachment, and some would argue that rootlessness may be psychologically detrimental. There has been an erosion of kinship and place-dependent social ties; the individual's perception of and feeling for his immediate habitat, his whole sense of place, may be disintegrating. This matter is subsidiary to the larger issues of modernization. For all its vast momentum and seeming inevitability, no convincing proof exists that modernization has meant any real gain in the more inward, and presumably genuine, measures of welfare at the individual or social scale.

Territorial Mobility

The concept of territorial mobility—used here as a substitute for the totality of social and physical mobility—calls for close examination. The term 'territorial mobility' is comprehensive, combining conventional (that is, residential) migration with what, for lack of a better designation, can be called 'circulation'. As generally defined, migration is any permanent or semi-permanent change of residence; more meaningfully, perhaps, it is a spatial transfer from one social unit or neighbourhood to another, which strains or ruptures previous social bonds.[11] Because of shortcomings in data systems, the migrational movements actually analyzed are usually those that happen to cross census or political boundaries and that intercept the time intervals used by census enumerators. In effect, a considerable fraction of territorial mobility goes unrecorded.

Circulation denotes a great variety of movements, usually short term, repetitive, or cyclical in nature, but all having in common the lack of any declared intention of a permanent or long-lasting change in residence. Under this rubric, one can include such disparate items as weekend or seasonal movements by students; vacation and weekend travel; shopping trips; hospital and church visits; religious pilgrimages; travel to professional and business conventions; trips by government and business executives, salesmen, athletes, migratory farm workers, and the like; social visits; and much seemingly aimless or fun-seeking cruising by wheelborne youngsters.[12]

The conventional definition of migration may serve after a fashion for the totality of territorial mobility in the initial and intermediate stages of the mobility transition. But the volume, intensity, and nature of circulation in advanced communities is such that there is no realistic alternative to treating all territorial mobility as a single continuum, extending from the shortest, most routine of iterated motions to the most adventurous intercontinental journey.

The most difficult problem in defining mobility has been left for last. Throughout the migrational literature, space is almost always treated as an absolute, with distances between points reckoned as constant. Although this is valid in a physical sense, it is misleading in any functional approach to space.[13] Recent improvements in transportation technology, combined with a general rise in level of living, have caused the mile to shrink drastically in terms of time or cost or of any index combining the two. At the same time, a great broadening of information fields has contributed further to the implosion of functional space. A logical step in pursuing the mobility transition would be to convert physical space into the functional space of migrants and circulators, probably through some variety of map transformation.[14] But there are other elastic yardsticks to worry about. Are the ways in which we perceive and evaluate time and people any more immutable than distance is? Can we confidently say that an hour is equivalent to an hour, or one infant to one infant, when one society is being compared with another, or when we look at the same community at different dates? We may be boxed in by the spurious precision of numbers.

The number of potential demographic transitions has not been exhausted by the addition of a mobility transition to the vital (mistakenly known as *the* demographic) transition. The relatively early discovery of the vital transition may have been the natural consequence of its sharp impact on three of the most visible and significant of all statistical indexes, namely, total population, crude birth rate,

and crude death rate. An occupational transition, frequently implied in the literature but never fully spelled out, would comprise that series of changes whereby the industrial-occupational structure of pre-modern societies evolves from heavy concentration in the primary sector to an almost totally different modern mix, the upward shift into secondary, tertiary, and eventually quaternary occupations. Similarly, the literature is strewn with hints of an educational transition. The series of steps from a totally illiterate society to one in which most young adults attend college could be delineated and its relationships to other channels of socioeconomic development explored.

Much could also be gained by charting the progression in forms of morbidity and cause of death from the relatively primitive community to the highly advanced, or the changes in marital and family characteristics. It would fall largely to settlement and urban geographers, who already command much documentary evidence, to outline the residential transition, which might unite census-derived data with details of physical morphology and could also subsume the rank-size rule as one of the terminal conditions.[15] All such transitional sequences seem susceptible to treatment as diffusional phenomena, spreading upward and outward through space–time. Indeed, it seems strange to find so few serious attempts to treat the historical geography of modern urbanization in a diffusional framework by charting the spatial extension of cities and metropolitan areas at the national scale or beyond.[16]

The various strands of the modernization process represented by the individual transitions are mutually interdependent. The first serious attempt to document this supposition comes from Friedlander, who uses a strictly temporal, economic, and aspatial framework to analyze the interaction between fertility and migrational responses to rural population pressures over the past 200 years in France, Sweden, and England and Wales.[17] His argument, derived from Davis's hypothesis of a multiphasic response to population growth,[18] is essentially that the timing and rate of decline in fertility, especially among the rural populations of developing societies, are inversely correlated with the number of internal and external migrational opportunities. Friedlander's evidence is persuasive, and it would seem worthwhile to examine other ways in which population dynamics, fertility level, and migration rates may be interconnected and to do so in an explicitly spatial manner.[19]

As in all geographical discourse, the question of scale is crucial. The mobility transition is intended as a highly idealized, flexible scheme that affords a general overview of a variety of places and periods. It is aloof from 'accidents' or exceptional circumstances; it is of little help in describing or predicting specific patterns of migration or circulation for a particular small area or set of areas over a brief period; it is deliberately vague in indicated distances, elapsed time, and rates. But if geography and history are viewed in extremely soft focus through the lens of the hypothesis, it may have value in whatever broader insights are forthcoming.

The Changing Forms of Territorial Mobility

The temporal sequence of a five-stage mobility transition is set forth here in outline form (see Table 19.1) subject to the qualifications already mentioned and others to be introduced. A five-stage vital transition is placed in parallel position to indicate contemporaneity (and probable interdependence) between adjacent segments of the two columns, even though no suggestion of absolute date or duration can be offered. The model is set forth in highly schematic fashion which shows the mobility and the viral transitions as a kind of outward spatial diffusion of successively more advanced forms of human activity. Although both transitions are real-world phenomena, representing incremental power and mobility among modernizing communities, their rather arbitrary segmentation into phases is done largely to facilitate discussion.

The several different forms of mobility suggested in Table 19.1 would appear to vary considerably through time in their relative volumes and rates. Comparative time profiles for these rates are sketched in Figure 19.1. The progression of five phases of spatial mobility is indicated for an ideal nation (one that averages out the demographic history of the whole universe of currently advanced countries), in which the potential migrant enjoys a full range of options. In addition, the magnitude of movement that might have occurred but was obviated by the recent availability of superior transport and communications is hypothesized in Figures 19.1 (f) and (g). In all cases the vertical scale is nonnumerical, since only the roughest order of magnitude can be indicated. It is also meant to show total movement—that is, the algebraic sum of inward and outward shifts—rather than just net values. The first three curves—Figures 19.1 (a), (b), and (c)—largely chronicle the rural exodus among developing societies; all three curves dwindle sharply, and the movement towards internal frontiers vanishes completely, as a country progresses towards Phase IV.

The peaking of international and frontierward movements somewhat earlier than the peaking of countryside-to-city movements would seem at first to violate common sense, since they usually involve greater physical distances. However, scattered evidence and the deeper logic of socioeconomic history tend to support this scheme. Assuming that some adventurous migrants had established firm beachheads in a foreign land or along a frontier and started a flow of information back to the source region, the transfer to a comparably rudimentary economy in a far locality might mean less dislocation in social space than transfer to a nearby city. During the earlier phases of the mobility transition, the demand for workers at the more advanced occupational levels would have been quite moderate in the growing cities, with a correspondingly small supply in the countryside. A redundant rural labour force would then have found a better market for its services in the agricultural and extractive industries of frontier and other non-urban zones in domestic and foreign settings.[20] Later, of course, the situation changed. A sharp rise in urban-to-urban migration and in

Table 19.1 Two sequential spatio-temporal processes among modernizing populations

The vital transition	The mobility transition
Phase A – The pre-modern traditional society	**Phase I – The pre-modern traditional society**
1) a moderately high to quite high fertility pattern that tends to fluctuate only slightly 2) mortality at nearly the same level as fertility on the average, but fluctuating much more from year to year 3) little, if any, long-range natural increase or decrease	1) little genuine residential migration and only such limited circulation as is sanctioned by customary practice in land utilization, social visits, commerce, warfare, or religious observances
Phase B – The early transitional society	**Phase II – The early transitional society**
1) slight but significant rise in fertility, which then remains fairly constant at a high level 2) rapid decline in mortality 3) a relatively rapid rate of natural increase, and thus a major growth in size of population	1) massive movement from countryside to cities, old and new 2) significant movement of rural folk to colonization frontiers, if land suitable for pioneering is available within country 3) major outflows of emigrants to available and attractive foreign destinations 4) under certain circumstances, a small but significant immigration of skilled workers, technicians, and professionals from more advanced parts of the world 5) significant growth in various kinds of circulation
Phase C – The late transitional society	**Phase III – The late transitional society**
1) a major decline in fertility, initially rather slight and slow, later quite rapid, until another slowdown occurs as fertility approaches mortality level 2) a continuing but slackening decline in mortality 3) a significant but decelerating natural increase, at rates well below those observed during Phase B	1) slackening but still major movement from countryside to city 2) lessening flow of migrants to colonization frontiers 3) emigration on the decline or may have ceased altogether 4) further increases in circulation, with growth in structural complexity
Phase D – The advanced society	**Phase IV – The advanced society**
1) decline in fertility has terminated, and a socially controlled fertility oscillates rather unpredictably at low to moderate levels 2) mortality is stabilized at levels near or slightly below fertility with little year-to-year variability 3) there is either a slight to moderate rate of natural increase or none at all	1) residential mobility has levelled off and oscillates at a high level 2) movement from countryside to city continues but is further reduced in absolute and relative terms 3) vigorous movement of migrants from city to city and within individual urban agglomerations 4) if a settlement frontier has persisted, it is now stagnant or actually retreating 5) significant net immigration of unskilled and semiskilled workers from relatively underdeveloped lands 6) there may be a significant international migration or circulation of skilled and professional persons, but direction and volume of flow depend on specific conditions 7) vigorous, accelerating circulation, particularly the economic and pleasure-oriented, but other varieties as well

(cont.)

Table 19.1 Two sequential spatio-temporal processes among modernizing populations *(cont.)*

Phase E – A future superadvanced society	Phase V – A future superadvanced society
1) no plausible predictions of fertility behaviour are available, but it is likely that births will be more carefully controlled by individuals—and perhaps by new sociopolitical means 2) a stable mortality pattern slightly below present levels seems likely, unless organic diseases are controlled and lifespan is greatly extended	1) there may be a decline in level of residential migration and a deceleration in some forms of circulation as better communication and delivery systems are instituted 2) nearly all residential migration may be of the inter-urban and intra-urban variety 3) some further immigration of relatively unskilled labour from less developed areas is possible 4) further acceleration in some current forms of circulation and perhaps the inception of new forms 5) strict political control of internal as well as international movements may be imposed

aggregate circulation during Phases II and III, with a subsequent deceleration or levelling off, is implied by the available information.

The time profile for migration obviated by improved means for circulating people is hypothetical. The empirical evidence may eventually confirm the speculation that during Phase III and later the broadening out of the circulator's daily cruising range has offered so many new social and economic options that many potential switches in residence were aborted.[21] If such has been the case in the recent past, more of the same can be expected in the near future. Similarly an even greater amount of migration and circulatory movement may be cancelled out by better communications, as travel is rendered redundant by more efficient transmission of messages for business, social, and educational purposes. For example, the average weekly cinema attendance in the United States has declined from a peak figure of 110 million in 1930 to 46 million in 1965, in large part because of highly effective competition from television. As a result, a considerable number of passenger-miles (or pedestrian-miles)

have been subtracted from current circulatory movements. The volume of such vicarious motion promises to increase sharply in the next few years.

In summary, then, we have added to the viral transition a second sequential spatio-temporal process, the mobility transition, that is essential to the understanding of the modernization phenomenon. Both transitions identified thus far are irreversible; barring a truly major catastrophe, neither the world as a whole nor any single region can ever revert to anything resembling its pristine, pre-modern condition. Furthermore, they are highly time-specific: they have occurred only within a fraction (less than a thousand years) of the scores of millennia *Homo sapiens* has already endured, and the precise date at which the transition is initiated in a particular region is profoundly significant. Both transitions seem to have a fatalistic inevitability; all human communities have been launched upon them, and if they can surmount the developmental crisis that occurs in midstream, all appear destined to rush forward to whatever terminal conditions may be implied by extremely advanced demographic development.

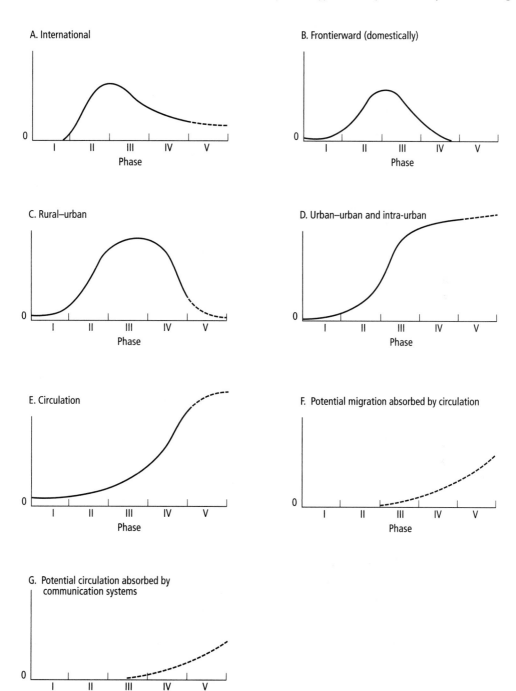

Figure 19.1   Comparative time profiles for the five phases of spatial mobility

Geographical Review, *61*(2), April 1971.

Notes

1. As far as demographic theory is concerned, there has been little recent improvement in the situation described in Rupert B. Vance, 'Is Theory for Demographers?', *Social Forces 31* (1952–3): 9–13. The theoretical landscape in geography is surveyed in David Harvey, *Explanation in Geography* (New York, 1969).

2. The demographic transition was apparently introduced into the demographic literature by Warren S. Thompson, 'Population', *American Journal of Sociology 34* (1929): 959–75, and since then has been treated in innumerable articles and books. A general description is to be found in Ralph Thomlinson, *Population Dynamics* (New York, 1965), 12–25. For an excellent theoretical exposition, see Donald O. Cowgill, 'Transition Theory as General Population Theory', *Social Forces 41* (1962–3): 270–9. The statistical evidence supporting the theory is examined in Maurice S. Satin, 'An Empirical Test of the Descriptive Validity of the Theory of Demographic Transition on a Fifty-three-Nation Sample'. *Sociological Quarterly 10* (1969): 190–203.

3. E.G. Ravenstein, 'The Laws of Migration', *Journal of the Royal Statistical Society 48*, Pt 2 (1885): 167–227, and 52 (1889): 241–301; Dorothy Swaine Thomas, 'Research Memorandum on Migration Differentials', *Social Science Research Council Bulletin 43* (1938); Samuel A. Stouffer, 'Intervening Opportunities: A Theory Relating Mobility and Distance', *American Sociological Review 5* (1940): 845–67; idem, 'Intervening Opportunities and Competing Migrants', *Journal of Regional Science 2* (1960): 1–26; Everett S. Lee, 'A Theory of Migration', *Demography 3* (1966): 47–57.

4. The only explicit treatment of this topic of which I am aware is Roy Chung, 'Space–Time Diffusion of the Transition Model: The Twentieth Century Patterns', in *Population Geography; A Reader*, ed. George J. Demko, Harold M. Rose, and George A. Schnell (New York, 1970), 220–39. The fertility phase of the transition is treated spatially by Emilio Casetti and George J. Demko, 'A Diffusion Model of Fertility Decline: An Application to Selected Soviet Data, 1940–1965', Ohio State University. Department of Geography, Discussion Paper No. 5, 1969, and by Gösta Carlsson, 'The Decline of Fertility: Innovation or Adjustment Process', *Population*

Studies 20 (1966): 149–74. The larger notion is implicit in a series of world maps showing viral indexes at various dates, in Jan O.M. Broek and John W. Webb, *A Geography of Mankind* (New York, 1968), 432, 433, 436, 437, and 442–5.

5. The only extensive published discussions of the problems of socioeconomic development by geographers of which I am aware are Norton Ginsburg, ed., 'Essays on Geography and Economic Development', Univ. of Chicago, Dept. of Geography, Research Paper No. 62 (Chicago, 1960); idem, *Atlas of Economic Development* (Chicago, 1961); Yves Lacoste, *Géographie du sous-développement* (Paris, 1965) and Edward W. Soja, *The Geography of Modernization in Kenya* (Syracuse, NY, 1968).

6. Lee, 'Theory of Migration', 53.

7. The theme of successively more advanced forms of a phenomenon—biological, social, or cultural—moving outward from a generative centre and thus creating concentric zones has been developed in the biological and anthropological literature (in essence, the age–area concept), but its only vocal champion among geographers was the late Griffith Taylor. Although he treated the notion vigorously and at some length, most fully perhaps in *Our Evolving Civilization* (Toronto, 1946), he was able to win few, if any, converts.

8. Cowgill, 'Transition Theory', suggested that the theory of the demographic transition is one of considerable generality and that changes in residential pattern might well be included, but he did not carry through with this idea. The diffusion of new forms of demographic behaviour through social space is discussed at some length in James M. Beshers, *Population Processes in Social Systems* (New York, 1967). Kingsley Davis in 'The Theory of Change and Response in Modern Demographic History', *Population Index 29* (1963): 345–66, put forward the notion of a multiphasic response to population growth in developing societies, including the option of outward migration. Interrelations among changes in population size, fertility, and rate of migration are elaborated in Dov Friedlander, 'Demographic Responses and Population Change', *Demography 6* (1969): 359–81. Five sequential stages in the demographic evolution of a community are postulated in Jack P. Gibbs, 'The Evolution of

Population Concentration', *Economic Geography 39* (1963): 119–29, who uses the relative urban and rural rates of change and degree of unevenness in territorial distribution as the basic criteria. In another sequential scheme, which encompasses all major dimensions of modernization (Gino Germani, 'Stages of Modernization', *International Journal 24* [1969]: 463–85), migrational characteristics are listed though not discussed. All the foregoing lack explicit spatial dimensions (with the partial exception of Gibbs). Adumbrations of the notion that the propensity to emigrate to foreign lands displays a wavelike motion through time and space are found in Adna Ferrin Weber, *The Growth of Cities in the Nineteenth Century* (New York, 1899), 254, and in Brinley Thomas, *Migration and Economic Growth: A Study of Great Britain and the Atlantic Economy* (Cambridge, UK, 1954), 224.

9. An excellent annotated bibliography of the migrational and other demographic literature through the mid-1950s is available in Hope T. Eldridge, *The Materials of Demography: A Selected and Annotated Bibliography* (New York, 1959), and earlier items are comprehensively and critically covered in Dorothy S. Thomas, 'Research Memorandum'. Virtually all English-language materials on migration appearing during a recent eight-year period are listed and abstracted in J.J. Mangalam, *Human Migration: A Guide to Migration Literature in English, 1955–1962* (Lexington, KY, 1968). Current publications in demography are covered in exemplary fashion in *Population Index*. Within the field of geography, the most useful summary statements concerning migration are probably Max Sorre, *Les migrations des peuples: Essai sur la mobilité géographique* (Paris, 1955); Edgar Kant, 'Classification and Problems of Migrations', in *Readings in Cultural Geography*, ed. Philip L. Wagner and Marvin W. Mikesell (Chicago, 1962), 342–54; and Brook and Webb, *Geography of Mankind*, 459–80.

10. For examples of such multidimensional approaches to classifying kinds and stages of development, see Brian J.L. Berry, 'Basic Patterns of Economic Development', in Ginsburg, ed., *Atlas of Economic Development*, 110–19; Bruce M. Russett, et al., *World Handbook of Political and Social Indicators* (New Haven, CT, 1964), 293–303; Bruce M. Russett, *International Regions and the International System: A Study in Political Ecology* (Chicago, 1967), 36–58; C.E. Black: *The Dynamics*

of Modernization (New York, 1966); and Germani, 'Stages of Modernization'.

11. Two of the many possible typologies of migration are proposed in Kant, 'Classification and Problems of Migration', and William Petersen, 'A General Typology of Migration', *American Sociological Review 23* (1958): 246–66.

12. Theodore Goldberg, 'The Automobile: A Social Institution for Adolescents', *Environment and Behavior 1* (1969): 157–85.

13. I am indebted to my colleague John S. Adams for fuelling this train of thought.

14. This approach is explored in Donald G. Janelle, 'Spatial Reorganization: A Model and Concept', *Annuals of the Association of American Geographers 59* (1969): 348–64.

15. There have been at least two experimental efforts in developing a sequential typology of cities: 'The "Seven Ages of Towns" as Exemplified by Toronto, Chicago, London, the Ruhr, Canberra', in Taylor, ed., *Our Evolving Civilization*, 222–47; and 'The Stages of Urban Growth', in Wilbur R. Thompson, *A Preface to Urban Economics* (Baltimore, 1965), 15–18. On a broader scale, sequential stages of change from rurality to vast conurbations are proposed in Constantinos A. Doxiadis, *Ekistics: An Introduction to the Science of Human Settlements* (New York, 1968), and Laurence G. Wolf, 'The Metropolitan Tidal Wave in Ohio, 1900–2000', *Economic Geography 45* (1969): 133–54.

16. Useful introductory sketches of the subject are to be found in Kingsley Davis, 'The Origin and Growth of Urbanization in the World', *American Journal of Sociology 60* (1954–5): 429–37; Kingsley Davis and Hilda Hertz, 'The World Distribution of Urbanization', *Bulletin of the International Statistical Institute 33* (1954): 227–43; idem: 'Urbanization and the Development of Pre-Industrial Areas', *Economic Development and Cultural Change 3* (1954–5): 6–24; and Eric E. Lampard, 'Historical Aspects of Urbanization', in *The Study of Urbanization*, ed. Philip M. Hauser and Leo F. Schnore (New York, 1965), 519–54.

17. Friedlander, 'Demographic Responses'.

18. Davis, 'Theory of Change and Response'.

19. Evidence has also been produced to show that the internal dynamics of a demographic system passing through the transitional experience are cybernetically controlled, aside from any exogenous factors, so that mortality decline may ultimately trigger a

major shrinkage in fertility (Harald Frederiksen, 'Feedbacks in Economic and Demographic Transition', *Science 166* [1969]: 837–47).

20. Census data for the 1810–20 period in the United States strongly suggest that something of this sort happened. Because of depressed business conditions in the Atlantic Seaboard cities, the overall urban growth rate fell below the rural. It is likely that rural-to-rural movements, many towards the frontier, far exceeded rural-to-urban movements. The same pattern seems to have materialized in Costa Rica during the 1950s, when a rapidly expanding settlement frontier may have drawn more rural migrants than the few cities did.

21. For detailed information on the widening areal range and increasing intensity of labour commutation through time, see Robert E. Dickinson, 'The Geography of Commuting: The Netherlands and Belgium', *Geographical Review 47* (1957): 521–38; and James E. Vance, Jr, 'Labor-Shed, Employment Field, and Dynamic Analysis in Urban Geography', *Economic Geography 36* (1960): 189–220.

CHAPTER 20

Population Distribution and Redistribution of the Baby Boom Cohort in the United States: Recent Trends and Implications

Peter A. Rogerson and Daejong Kim

The baby boom cohort, generally defined as the group of people born between 1946 and 1964, is now between 41 and 59 years old. The cohort currently has over 65 million individuals, representing close to one-fourth of the population of the United States. Much has been written about the baby boom; an annotated bibliography on the subject from two decades ago[1] contains more than 700 entries, on subjects ranging from consumption and marketing to retirement financing. Demographic and economic predictions were made for the cohort by Russell,[2] and Gillon[3] has recently expounded on how the generation has changed the country in myriad ways. Both the age and the size of the cohort portend dramatic changes in many social, economic, and demographic arenas.

Of the large volume of literature on the baby boom cohort, only a small fraction has been written from a geographic perspective. The focus of this article is on the geographical consequences of the aging of the baby boom cohort. We emphasize the recent, current, and future geographic distribution of the cohort, and we note some of the consequences for intergenerational caregiving. We first describe the recent geography of the baby boom in the United States, paying particular attention to recent changes in geographical distribution, and the migration trends of the cohort. We then focus upon temporal and geographical perspectives on intergenerational caregiving.

Recent and Current Distribution and Redistribution of the Baby Boom Cohort

What is the geographic distribution of the baby boom cohort in the United States? Is it spatially uniform, or are there clusters of high concentration in particular regions? It is of interest to examine both the current and recent geographic distribution and the recent redistribution of this large cohort.

Figure 20.1 depicts the relative size of the baby boom cohort consisting of individuals approximately 25 to 44 years old in 1990 county populations; it is similar to that given by Rogerson.[4] The main features of the figure include bicoastal and metropolitan concentrations (we focus our attention here on the 48 contiguous states, primarily for the sake of convenience in mapping and visualization). The bicoastal concentrations reflect longstanding migration patterns away from other parts of the country toward the coasts. Members of the baby boom cohort took place in, and in fact were the driving force behind, these population shifts, particularly during their migration-prone years of young adulthood. The emptying of the American breadbasket of its breadwinners has left the Midwest with a disproportionate share of its population in older age groups. The spatial concentration of the elderly in the Midwest strikes many as surprising; although Florida, Arizona, and other popular retirement destinations have large proportions

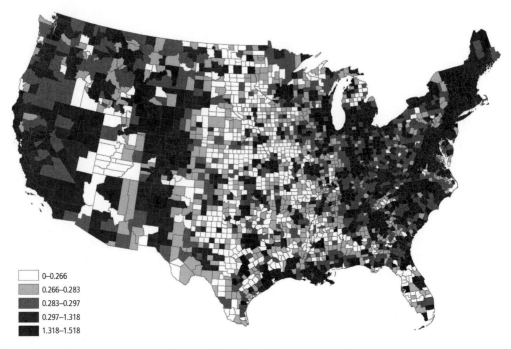

	0–0.266
	0.266–0.283
	0.283–0.297
	0.297–1.318
	1.318–1.518

Figure 20.1 Baby boom population as a fraction of total population, 1990

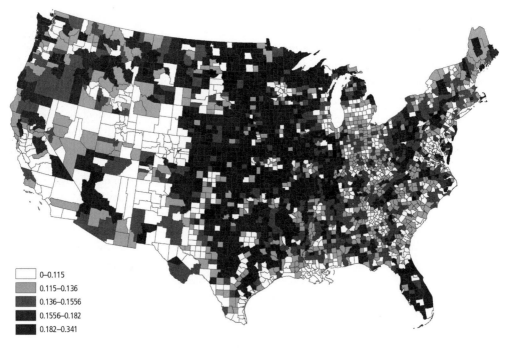

	0–0.115
	0.115–0.136
	0.136–0.1556
	0.1556–0.182
	0.182–0.341

Figure 20.2 Fraction of population aged 65 and over, 1990

of their populations in the older age groups, so too does the Midwest, and the latter region constitutes the more prominent visual feature when the focus is on the spatial distribution of the elderly (see Figure 20.2, which reveals the remarkable degree to which the elderly constitute the population of the Midwest).

Perhaps less apparent in Figure 20.1, but still clearly notable, is the relative demographic importance of the baby boom population in a small number of dynamic metropolitan areas, notably San Francisco, Portland (Oregon), Minneapolis, Denver, Dallas–Fort Worth, Washington, DC, Phoenix, and Atlanta. Rogerson[4] notes that these concentrations are the result of net in-migration of the cohort to these areas; the baby boom itself was a fairly uniform spatial event, with slightly higher 'production' of baby boomers in the Rocky Mountain region, the upper Midwest, and the Deep South.

Figure 20.3 essentially is an 'update' of Figure 20.1; it shows county populations aged 40–59 in 2003 as a fraction of total county population in 2003.

One caveat is that it does not perfectly match the baby boom cohort, whose members were between ages 38.5 and 57.5 at the time of the estimates. The figure reveals a distribution that is quite different from that in Figure 20.1 for 1990. In particular, New England, the northern parts of the Rocky Mountain (Wyoming, Montana, Idaho) and Pacific (Oregon, Washington) regions, and parts of Virginia and West Virginia all now have relatively high percentages of baby boomers in their populations. What are the demographic reasons for these changes in the spatial distribution of baby boomers?

Figure 20.4 highlights the changes by depicting the ratio between the 2003 and 1990 maps (figures 20.3 and 20.1, respectively). A ratio that is greater than one implies that the demographic importance of the baby boom generation in county populations has grown over time. Such areas are not common in large part because of the declining size of the cohort due to mortality. Figure 20.4 reveals that large portions of the Midwest, parts of western Pennsylvania,

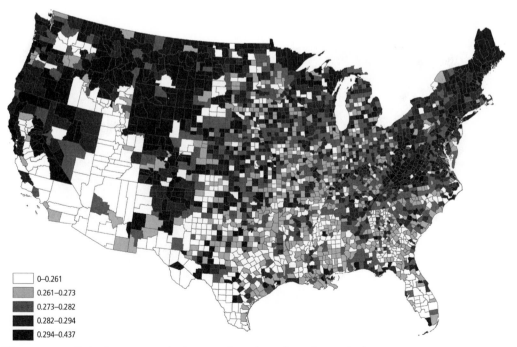

Figure 20.3   Baby boom population as a fraction of total population, 2003

western Virginia, and West Virginia, portions of Florida, and the Pacific Northwest all have witnessed increases in the percentage of their populations that is composed of baby boomers. The two possible reasons for such increases are net in-migration among baby boomers and/or net out-migration of other age cohorts. Similarly, the light-shaded areas in Figure 20.4, such as much of the Carolinas and Georgia, now have lower fractions of their populations in the baby boom years, perhaps because of baby boomer out-migration, but also perhaps because of the net in-migration of cohorts of other ages.

A somewhat different, yet complementary, perspective on spatial change is achieved by mapping the ratio of 40- to 59-year-olds in 2003 to 25- to 44-year-olds in 1990 (Figure 20.5). Again, the 'match' is not perfect. We are examining a 13-year time period (1990 to 2003) and are looking at a cohort that is 15 years older. Adjustments could be made, but adjustments would entail estimation that would introduce error; the imperfect match still

provides revealing insights into broad-scale demographic change.

Areas in Figure 20.5 with ratios greater than one imply a net increase in the number of individuals who are members of the baby boom cohort. These areas are not common because of mortality; the net in-migration of cohort members must exceed declines from mortality if the ratio is to be greater than one. Dark areas in this figure could occur in regions with either (*i*) relatively low mortality, (*ii*) relatively high net in-migration of individuals in this age cohort, or (*iii*) both. Because mortality is fairly uniform spatially, the majority of the geographic variation shown in the figure is due to the migration of the baby boom cohort. Net in-migration is evident in the Pacific Northwest, Florida, and selected areas of the South (e.g. the Ozark region and the western Carolinas). More generally, it seems that net in-migration has occurred in many of the areas surrounding the areas of high concentration in 1990 (portrayed in Figure 20.1). Thus, we see in Figure

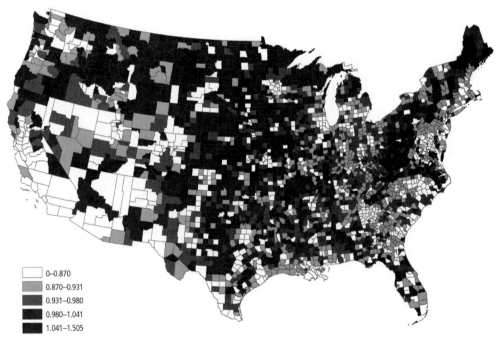

☐	0–0.870
▨	0.870–0.931
▨	0.931–0.980
■	0.980–1.041
■	1.041–1.505

Figure 20.4 Ratio of baby boom fraction in 2003 to baby boom fraction in 1990

Figure 20.5   Ratio of size of baby boom cohort in 2003 to size of baby boom cohort in 1990

0–0.948
0.948–1.006
1.006–1.069
1.069–1.176
1.176–2.613

20.5 that there has been net in-migration of the baby boom cohort in the vicinity of Washington, DC, Minneapolis, Atlanta, and Dallas. Unfortunately, the data are not detailed enough to show whether it is the same baby boomers who lived in these metropolitan areas in 1990 that have diffused outward into surrounding counties by 2003, but the maps suggest the possibility that such outward diffusion has occurred. In some cases, this diffusion seems to be confined to counties that are quite close to the metropolitan area; in other cases, diffusion may be taking place on larger spatial scales (for example, note that the dark areas in southern and central Michigan in Figure 20.1 have 'migrated' to the dark areas in northern Michigan in Figure 20.5).

These findings are broadly consistent with findings about specific regions (for example, Plane and Heins[5] note the popularity of both the Ozarks and northern Michigan as migrant destinations) and with more general observations regarding regional population change. With respect to the latter, Plane,

et al.[6] suggest the importance of older individuals moving down the urban hierarchy, and Garreau[7] and others have commented on the importance of 'edge cities' and the population growth that occurs near, but not in, major urban centres.

A caveat associated with these findings is that the effects of immigration have essentially been ignored here. Indeed, immigration to the coasts and immigration patterns that have bypassed the interior portions of the country have at least in part contributed to the patterns displayed in the figures. Still, the magnitude of internal migration at these spatial scales is greater than the magnitude of immigration, and the majority of the effects can likely be attributed to the former.

Geographical Perspectives on Intergenerational Relationships

The changing spatial distribution of the baby boom cohort has many social, economic, and demographic consequences. A consequence of particular importance concerns intergenerational relationships, because there have been several studies that have reported that the geographic distance between parents and their offspring is the primary determinant of interaction between them.[8,9] This section focuses upon the spatial and temporal dimensions of intergenerational relationships between the baby boomers and (*i*) their parents, and (*ii*) their children.

Spatial Dimensions of Intergenerational Relationships

Plane and Rogerson[10] have noted that, whereas the baby boom cohort exhibited lower than average mobility rates during their migration-prone, young-adult years, their migration efficiency (that is, their ability to effect regional population change through migration, as measured by the ratio of net to total migration) was relatively high. Despite such relatively high efficiency, the combination of low mobility rates and, more importantly, the fact that the majority of moves are short-distance moves (over half of all moves are <6–10 miles [≈10–16 km][11]) has meant that parents and their adult children are not separated by large distances. For example, Rogerson, et al.[12] found that more than half of married individuals with both parents alive and living together lived within 10 miles [≈16 km] of either their own parents or their in-laws, and two-thirds lived within 25 miles [≈40 km]. These spatial separations vary with education; those with a college education are separated from their parents by a median distance of 100 miles [≈161 km], whereas those without one have a median separation distance of just 15 miles [≈24 km], based on a sample size of >6,300. Spatial separation also varies with location; those living in the West live a median distance of 80 miles [≈129 km] from their parents, and individuals in the South and Midwest census regions live a median distance of 20 miles [≈32 km] from their parents. The corresponding figure for respondents from the Northeast is 15 miles [≈24 km].[12]

The consequences of these patterns for intergenerational relationships may be summarized as follows. For the majority of individuals, spatial separation between generations is not large, and therefore the effect of spatial separation on caregiving is not an important issue. This is not to diminish the importance of the significant impacts that distance can have on caregiving when it is an issue (e.g. for the college-educated). The relationship between spatial separation and distance also implies that a disproportionate share of caregiving falls upon those without a college education. It would be interesting to discern whether siblings provide complementary forms of assistance, with distant siblings providing more financial assistance and closer siblings providing relatively more assistance with physical and day-to-day tasks. Some evidence for this hypothesis comes from the National Survey of Families and Households (Lin and Rogerson[13]). Through interviews with individuals, Climo[14] has explored some of the emotional issues that accompany large geographical separations between generations.

The lack of a perfect correspondence between distance and caregiving should also be noted. Interestingly, Lin and Rogerson[13] report that daughters live no closer to parents than do sons, yet Brody[15] has shown that daughters are more likely than sons to provide care.

Temporal Perspectives: The Sandwich Generation and Stretched Periods of Caregiving

We next turn to the timing of caregiving. There is a general sense that delayed childbearing among baby boomers has increased the likelihood that they find themselves facing simultaneous caregiving demands from their parents and their children. To assess whether the duration of these demands is longer for baby boomers than for their parents, consider Figure 20.6, which is a schematic of the timing of caregiving. Figure 20.6a shows the years spent in potential caregiving for a baby boom member born when his or her parents were 25 (and, because boomers' parents were having children at earlier ages, this individual is likely to be roughly in the middle of the birth order). Members of the baby boom cohort typically had first children around age 25 and completed childbearing by age 35, implying that they were empty nesters at age 55. At this time, the individual's parents were ≈80 years old. If we take 75 to be the year at which caregiving begins,

there is a period of 5 years where simultaneous demands are placed on the baby boomer.

Contrast this picture with that in Figure 20.6b, where the individual began having children at age 20 and completed childbearing at age 30. This person, representing the parent of the baby boomer, started

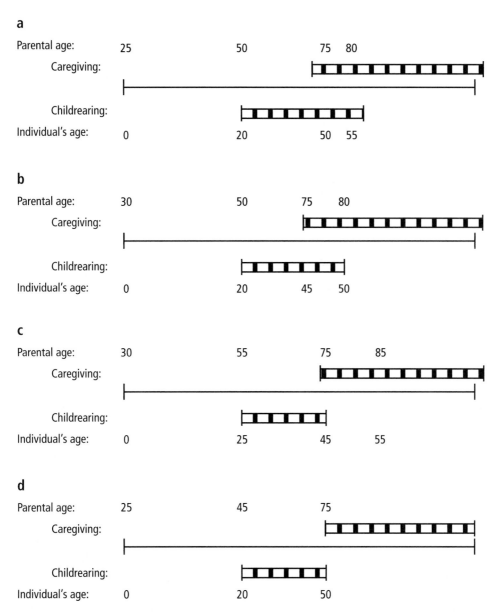

Figure 20.6 The timing of caregiving throughout the life course

childbearing at a relatively early age; she was born when her own parents were ≈30, which might be the case for a middle birth-order child as the baby boomers' grandparents delayed childbearing. This individual would also have simultaneous caregiving demands for a period of 5 years (from the time her parents turned 75, when she herself was 45, until she completed childrearing and became an empty nester at age 50).

This crude analysis reveals that the timing itself places no additional demands on baby boomers. Increasing life expectancies, however, have implied that baby boomers' parents are more likely to be alive and in need of caregiving, relative to the situation faced by the boomers' parents. With regard to the average burden per person, baby boomers have more potential for spreading out care for their parents across a larger number of siblings, in comparison with the parental care demands faced by their own parents, who were members of a smaller cohort and consequently had fewer siblings (the notion of 'burden' here should not necessarily be taken too literally, because selfless giving and reciprocity in intergenerational relationships are common).

Figure 20.6c considers the possibility that the children of the baby boomers will also delay having children. In this case, the middle birth-order child with a baby boomer parent who is ≈30 years older will begin having children around age 25 and become an empty nester at about age 55, when his parents are 85, thus creating the potential of a 10-year period of caring for children and parents. Thus, it is the children of the baby boomers who may find themselves truly sandwiched. In addition, the situation will be exacerbated by the fact that these individuals will have fewer siblings to share in the care of their baby boomer parents (relative to the situation faced by their baby boomer parents, who had relatively more siblings to share in the caregiving). The difficulties that might soon face baby boomers with respect to receiving care from their children could easily be as great as any difficulties imposed by feeling sandwiched. As with many other phenomena that have affected the baby boom, the popular 'crisis of the moment' that faces the generation changes as the generation ages. Without denying the sandwich demands placed on this generation, it is quite probable that these demands will be even greater on their children, and a looming crisis may be the relative difficulty in receiving support from their children.

To complete the picture, consider successive generations of individuals characterized by early childbearing (Figure 20.6d). Middle children have parents who are about age 25; they begin having children around age 20 and become empty nesters at about age 50. As the Figure 20.6d indicates, there is no period of simultaneous caregiving in this scenario.

The concept of the baby boom as sandwich generation caught between the simultaneous need to care for parents and children may therefore be slightly overstated. The concept of the sandwich generation has been around at least since the early 1980s,[16] and likely much longer (Miller[16] refers to the work of Litwak[17] in the mid-1960s). Interestingly, the oldest parents of the baby boomers were turning 75 at the time of Miller's article, and the members of the biggest bulge in the cohort, born in 1957, were in the middle of their childbearing years. Thus, at the time of Miller's article, the generation was at the initial stage of the sandwich.

Although the notion of a sandwich generation may be somewhat overstated, it is notable that caregiving occurs over such a stretched period. A stretched period of caregiving is particularly likely for successive cohorts characterized by early childbearing (Figure 20.6d), for whom the childrearing years are equal to ≈30 (from age 20 to age 50), plus the 12 years of life expected for a 75-year old (the parents of this cohort will be ≈75 when the cohort member becomes an empty nester and the assumption is that cohort members will care for their parents until their parents' deaths). Generations like the baby boom (Figure 20.6a) can expect the total number of caregiving years to be shorter, approximately equal to 30 for childrearing, plus the 9 years of life expected for an 80-year-old (because the individual's parent will be ≈80 years of age when the last child leaves home). Those born at the height of the baby boom in 1957 are now 48 years old; the modal age of their offspring is 23, and the modal age of their mothers is ≈70. Although the majority of baby boomers have become, or are about to become, empty nesters, they are just beginning to grapple with care issues associated with their parents. Finally, successive generations characterized by late childbearing, as may be the case with the children of the baby boomers, have a relatively lower expectation for the number of caregiving years (30, plus the 7 years of life expected for an 85-year-old), despite having the greatest number of years with simultaneous responsibilities. Perhaps more important than a 5- or 10-year period of simultaneous caregiving is the more basic fact that caregiving itself can easily be stretched >40 years or more.

Summary

We have examined the current and recent spatial distribution of the large baby boom cohort born between 1946 and 1964. In 1990, members of this cohort were clustered predominantly in county populations along the east and west coasts. A small number of metropolitan areas also had large percentages of baby boomers in their populations. By 2003, the locations with large percentages of baby boomers had shifted, primarily to areas surrounding large metropolitan areas and to many northern areas of the country, including New England, the northern Rocky Mountain region, and the northern parts of Wisconsin and Minnesota. Many of these changes were brought about by the net in-migration of baby boomers to these regions and by net out-migration away from their bicoastal and metropolitan locations of 1990. The Midwest also witnessed an increase in the fraction of their populations made up of baby boomers, but this increase was due more to the out-migration of younger cohorts.

These changes in spatial distribution have many consequences, and, in this article, we have focused upon both the spatial and temporal dimensions of intergenerational relationships. Although spatial separation between generations is not great because of the relatively short distances moved by the majority of movers, it is significant for many, particularly the college-educated and those living in the West. With regard to the timing of intergenerational caregiving, although it is true that members of the baby boom cohort are sandwiched between simultaneous support of children and parents, the demands of simultaneous caregiving are likely to be even greater for the children of baby boomers. In addition, because baby boomers have had fewer children than their parents, the spatial distribution of aging baby boomers and the nature of their spatial separation from their (relatively few) children will become even more important during the next few decades. Also important is the fact that intergenerational caregiving is stretched over a significant portion of the life course. Periods of 40 years of caregiving, first to children, then simultaneously to children and parents, and then to parents, are not uncommon, and the effects in social and economic terms deserve additional study from this perspective.

References

1. Byerly, G., & Rubin, R.E. (1985). *The baby boom: A selective annotated bibliography.* Lexington, MA: Heath.

2. Russell, C. (1987). *100 predictions for the baby boom.* New York: Plenum.

3. Gillon, S. (2004). *Boomer Nation: The largest and richest generation ever, and how it changed America.* New York: Simon and Schuster.

4. Rogerson, P. (1999). In K. Pandit & S.D. Withers (Eds), *Migration restructuring in the United States:* *A geographic perspective* (pp. 174–92). New York: Rowman and Littlefield.

5. Plane, D.A., & Heins, F. (2003). *Annals of Regional Science, 37,* 107–30.

6. Plane, D.A., Henrie, C.J., & Perry, M.J. (2005). *Proceedings of the National Academy of Science USA, 102,* 15313–18.

7. Garreau, J. (1991). *Edge City: Life on the new frontier.* New York: Doubleday.

8. Crimmins, E., & Ingegneri, D.G. (1990). *Research on Aging, 12,* 3–35.
9. Kivett, V.R., & Atkinson, M.P. (1984). *Journal of Gerontology, 39,* 499–503.
10. Plane, D., & Rogerson, P. (1991). *Professional Geographer, 43,* 416–30.
11. Rogerson, P. (1990). *Mathematical Population Studies, 2,* 229–38.
12. Rogerson, P., Weng, R.H., & Lin, G. (1993). *Annals of the Association of American Geographers, 83,* 656–71.
13. Lin, G., & Rogerson, P. (1995). *Research on Aging, 17,* 303–31.
14. Climo, J. (1992). *Distant parents.* New Brunswick, NJ: Rutgers University Press.
15. Brody, F. (1985). *The Gerontologist, 25,* 19–29.
16. Miller, D. (1981). *Social Work, 26,* 419–23.
17. Litwak, F. (1965). In F. Shanas & G.F. Streib (Eds), *Social structure and the family: Generational relations* (pp. 290–323). Englewood Cliffs, NJ: Prentice-Hall.

CHAPTER 21

The Age of Migration: International Population Movements in the Modern World

Stephen Castles and Mark J. Miller

On the surface, two series of major events in France in 2005 and in the USA in 2006 appeared unrelated. The rioting that convulsed much of France seemed quite unlike the generally peaceful mass rallies in support of migrant rights in the USA. In the French riots, bands of youths burned cars and battled police following the deaths of two boys who were being chased by the police. In the USA, the breathtaking scale of the demonstrations surpassed the wildest dreams of organizers.

Yet, the bulk of the participants in both series of events were young persons of migrant background, both citizens and non-citizens. The French protests expressed anger against the police, and against the discrimination and high unemployment experienced by young adults of African and North African background. The US protests reflected concerns about the progress of legislation, which was seen as hostile to immigrants, in the House of Representatives. At the same time, the demonstrators supported a bill before the US Senate that would have authorized a legalization of undocumented migrants—a bill that eventually failed to be enacted into law.

Both the French riots and the US demonstrations showed how international migration has re-forged societies in recent decades. As in most highly developed states, youth cohorts in France and the United States differ strikingly from older generations. Due to international migration, younger generations are much more diverse. Quite literally, international migration has changed the face of societies. The commonality of the two situations lies in the rapidly increasing ethnic and cultural diversity of immigrant-receiving societies, and the dilemmas that arise for states and communities in finding ways to respond to these changes. Most of the youths involved in the rioting in France were migrants or the children or grandchildren of migrants. In the USA, the massive participation of young persons of Latin American background, both legally and illegally resident, stood out. In both instances, young people were protesting against their perception of being excluded from the societies in which they had grown up (and often been born). By contrast, some politicians and elements of the media claimed that immigrants were failing to integrate, were deliberately maintaining distinct cultures and religions, and had become a threat to security and social cohesion.

Similar events were to be found in many places. In the Netherlands in 2004, the murder of the filmmaker Theo Van Gogh, who had made a film critical of Muslims and Islam, by a Dutch Muslim of Moroccan background produced a similar drama. The backlash against multicultural policies in the Netherlands led to changes in Dutch naturalization requirements, including an 'integration test' based on Dutch language knowledge and 'Dutch values'.

In Australia in late 2005, groups of white 'surfer' youths attacked young people 'of Middle Eastern appearance', claiming that they had harassed local girls at Cronulla, a beachside suburb of Sydney. In the following days, hundreds of Lebanese-origin youths came to Cronulla to retaliate. Right-wing radio talk show hosts called on white youth to mobilize, and the result was civil disturbances on a level unseen for years. The political fallout seemed likely to further isolate Australia's Lebanese Muslims—a community with high rates of unemployment and considerable experience of racial discrimination (Collins, et al., 2001). The Cronulla events strengthened the conservative Howard government's resolve to modify Australia's policies of multiculturalism.

Newer immigration countries were not immune to unexpected challenges. In Dubai in March 2006 foreign workers building the world's tallest building demonstrated against low wages, squalid dormitories, and dangerous conditions. Their main grievance was that employers often simply refused to pay wages. Dubai is one of the oil-rich United Arab Emirates, where the migrant workforce—mainly from India, Pakistan, and Bangladesh—far outnumbers the local population. Lack of worker rights, prohibition of unions, and fear of deportation have forced migrant workers to accept exploitative conditions. Women migrants, who often work as domestic helpers, are especially vulnerable. The Dubai government was forced to set up an inquiry and to insist that employers meet their obligations (DeParle, 2007).

The Challenges of Global Migration

Momentous events around the world increasingly involve international migration. This does not imply that migration is something new—indeed, human beings have always moved in search of new opportunities, or to escape poverty, conflict, or environmental degradation. However, migration took on a new character with the beginnings of European expansion from the sixteenth century. A high point was the mass migrations from Europe to North America from the mid-nineteenth century until World War I. Some scholars call this the 'age

of mass migration' (Hatton & Williamson, 1998) and argue that these international movements were bigger than today's. However, the 1850–1914 period was mainly one of transatlantic migration, while the movements that started after 1945 and expanded sharply from the 1980s involve all regions of the world. Mobility has become much easier as a result of recent political and cultural changes, as well as the development of new transport and communication technologies. International migration, in turn, is a central dynamic within globalization.

A hallmark of states in the modern era has been the principle of sovereignty, the idea that the government of a nation-state constitutes the final and absolute authority in a society, and that no outside power has the right to intervene in the exercise of this authority. The nation-state system is traced back by historians to the 1648 treaties of Westphalia, which ended the devastating Thirty Years War in Europe. The 'Westphalian system' evolved from its European origins to become a global system of governments, first through European colonization of other continents, and then through decolonization and the formation of nation-states on the Western model throughout the world.

A defining feature of the age of migration is the challenge posed by international migration to the sovereignty of states, specifically to their ability to regulate movements of people across their borders. The extensiveness of irregular (also called undocumented or illegal) migration around the world has probably never been greater than it is today. Paradoxically, efforts by governments to regulate migration also are at an all-time high and involve intensive bilateral, regional, and international diplomacy. A second challenge is posed by 'transnationalism': as migration becomes easier and people become more mobile, many of them have important and durable relationships of a political, economic, social, or cultural nature in two or more societies at once. This is seen as undermining the undivided loyalty seen as crucial to sovereign nation-states.

While movements of people across borders have shaped states and societies since time immemorial, what is distinctive in recent years is their global scope, their centrality to domestic and international politics, and their enormous economic and social consequences. Migration processes may become so entrenched and resistant to governmental control that new political forms may emerge. This would not necessarily entail the disappearance of national states; indeed, that prospect appears remote. However, novel forms of interdependence, transnational societies, and bilateral and regional co-operation are rapidly transforming the lives of millions of people and inextricably weaving together the fate of states and societies.

For the most part the growth of transnational society and politics is a beneficial process, because it can help overcome the violence and destructiveness that characterized the era of nationalism. But it is neither inevitably nor inherently so. Indeed, international migration is sometimes linked to conflict. Major determinants of historical change are rarely profoundly changed by any single event. Rather, singular events like 9/11 (the 2001 terrorist attacks on the World Trade Center in New York and the Pentagon in Washington, DC) reflect the major dynamics and determinants of their time. It is scarcely coincidental that migration figured so centrally in the chain of events leading up to the terrorist attacks.

The US response to such events, the 'war on terror' announced by President Bush in 2001, and the attacks on Afghanistan and Iraq, have exacerbated the ideological rifts that provide a basis for violent fundamentalism. The attacks by Islamic radicals on trains, buses, and airports in Spain in 2004 and in the UK in 2005 and 2007 were a further upward twist in the spiral of violence. Some of the militants involved were immigrants or the offspring of post–World War II migrants. Initially, the attacks were thought to be 'home grown', indicating that al-Qaeda had succeeded in serving as a model for emulation in the West. However, as investigations progressed, several of the Islamic militants involved were found to have had links with al-Qaeda in Pakistan or Afghanistan. Through such events,

perceptions of threat to the security of states have come to be linked to international migration and to the problems of living together in one society for culturally and socially diverse ethnic groups.

These developments in turn are related to fundamental economic, social, and political transformations that shape today's world. Millions of people are seeking work, a new home, or simply a safe place to live outside their countries of birth. For many less developed countries, emigration is one aspect of the social crisis which accompanies integration into the world market and modernization. Population growth and the 'green revolution' in rural areas lead to massive surplus populations. People move to burgeoning cities, where employment opportunities are inadequate and social conditions miserable. Massive urbanization outstrips the creation of jobs in the early stages of industrialization. Some of the previous rural–urban migrants embark on a second migration, seeking to improve their lives by moving to newly industrializing countries in the South or to highly developed countries in the North.

The movements take many forms: people migrate as manual workers, highly qualified specialists, entrepreneurs, refugees, or as family members of previous migrants. Class plays an important role: destination countries compete to attract the highly skilled through privileged rules on entry and residence, while manual workers and refugees often experience exclusion and discrimination. New forms of mobility are emerging: retirement migration, mobility in search of better (or just different) lifestyles, repeated or circular movement. The barrier between migration and tourism is becoming blurred, as some people travel as tourists to check out potential migration destinations. Whether the initial intention is temporary or permanent movement, many migrants become settlers. Migratory networks develop, linking areas of origin and destination, and helping to bring about major changes in both. Migrations can change demographic, economic, and social structures, and bring a new cultural diversity, which often brings into question national identity.

This chapter is about contemporary international migrations, and the way they are changing societies. The perspective is international: large-scale movements of people arise from the accelerating process of global integration. Migrations are not an isolated phenomenon: movements of commodities and capital almost always give rise to movements of people. Global cultural interchange, facilitated by improved transport and the proliferation of print and electronic media, also leads to migration. International migration ranks as one of the most important factors in global change.

There are several reasons to expect the age of migration to endure: growing inequalities in wealth between the North and South are likely to impel increasing numbers of people to move in search of better living standards; political, environmental, and demographic pressures may force many people to seek refuge outside their own countries; political or ethnic conflict in a number of regions could lead to future mass flights; and the creation of new free trade areas will cause movements of labour, whether or not this is intended by the governments concerned. But migration is not just a reaction to difficult conditions at home: it is also motivated by the search for better opportunities and lifestyles elsewhere. It is not just the poor who move: movements between rich countries are increasing, too. Economic development of poorer countries can actually lead to greater migration because it gives people the resources to move. Some migrants experience abuse or exploitation, but most benefit and are able to improve their lives through mobility. Conditions may be tough for migrants but are often preferable to poverty, insecurity, and lack of opportunities at home—otherwise migration would not continue.

No one knows exactly how many international migrants there are. The United Nations Population Division (UNPD) estimate for midyear 2005 stood at nearly 191 million (UNDESA, 2005). By 2007, the figure approached 200 million or approximately 3 per cent of the world's population of 6.5 billion people. Migrants as a percentage of the world's population have remained fairly stable in recent years,

between 2 and 3 per cent. However, absolute numbers have doubled over the past quarter-century. Previous epochs have also been characterized by massive migrations. Between 1846 and 1939, some 59 million people left Europe, mainly for major areas of settlement in North and South America, Australia, New Zealand, and South Africa (Stalker, 2000, p. 9). Comparison of data on pre–World War I international migration with statistics on contemporary population movements suggests remarkable continuity in volume between the two periods (Zlotnik, 1999). However, credible statistics about international migration are lacking in some areas of the world. A great unknown involves the scope of illegal migration. Reliable estimates are lacking in most places. In the USA, however, an estimated 12 million were thought to reside illegally amidst a population of 300 million in 2006 (Passel, 2006).

Many of those who move are in fact 'forced migrants': people who have been forced to flee their homes and seek refuge elsewhere. The reasons for flight can include political or ethnic violence or persecution, development projects like large dams, or natural disasters like the 2004 Asian tsunami. In 2006 there were about 10 million officially recognized refugees in the world—a considerable decline from the peak figures of the early 1990s. But this decline was partly due to states' unwillingness to admit refugees. The number of internally displaced persons (IDPs)—forced migrants who remained in their country of origin because they found it impossible to cross an international border to seek refuge—grew to about 26 million.

In fact, the vast majority of human beings remain in their countries of birth. Migration is the exception, not the rule. Yet the impact of international migration is frequently much greater than is suggested by figures such as the UN estimates. People tend to move not individually, but in groups. Their departure may have considerable consequences for their area of origin. Remittances (money sent home) by migrants may improve living standards and encourage economic development. In the country of immigration, settlement is closely linked to

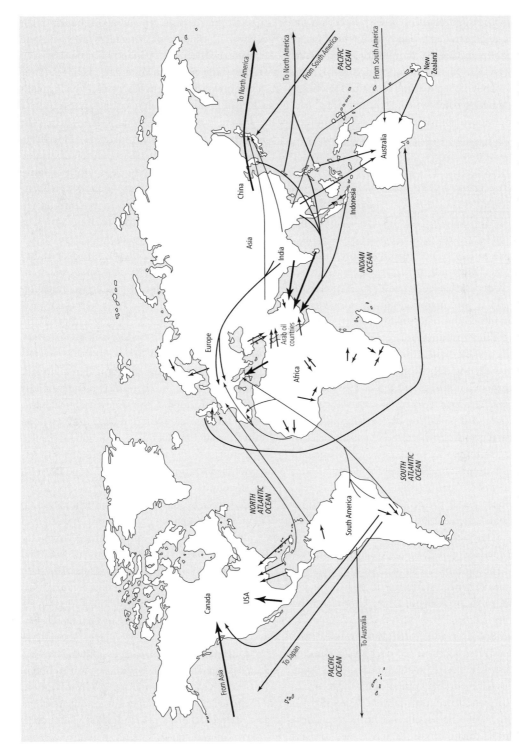

Figure 21.1   Global migratory movements from 1973. The arrow dimensions give only an approximate indication of the volume of flows. Exact figures are often unavailable.

employment opportunities and is almost always concentrated in industrial and urban areas, where the impact on receiving communities is considerable. Migration thus affects not only the migrants themselves but the sending and receiving societies as a whole. There can be few people in either industrial or less developed countries today who do not have personal experience of migration and its effects.

Contemporary Migrations: General Trends

International migration is part of a transnational revolution that is reshaping societies and politics around the globe. The old dichotomy between migrant-sending and migrant-receiving states is being eroded. Most countries experience both emigration and immigration (although one or the other often predominates), while some countries have taken on an important role as transit zones for migrants. The differing ways in which such trends have affected the worlds' regions is a major theme throughout this study. Areas such as the USA, Canada, Australia, New Zealand, and Argentina are considered 'classical countries of immigration'. Their current people are the result of histories of large-scale immigration—often to the detriment of indigenous populations. Today, migration continues in new forms. Virtually all of northern and western Europe became areas of labour immigration and subsequent settlement after 1945. Since the 1980s, southern European states like Greece, Italy, and Spain, which for a long time were zones of emigration, have become immigration areas. Today central and eastern European states, particularly Hungary, Poland, and the Czech Republic, are becoming immigration lands.

The Middle East and North Africa (MENA), the vast area stretching from Morocco to Pakistan, is affected by complex population movements. Some countries, like Turkey, Jordan, and Morocco, are major sources of migrant labour. The Gulf oil states experience mass temporary inflows of workers. Political turmoil in the region has led to mass

flows of refugees. In recent years, Afghanistan has been a major source of refugees, while Iran and Pakistan have been the main receiving countries. In Africa, colonialism and white settlement led to the establishment of migrant labour systems for plantations and mines. Decolonization since the 1950s has sustained old migratory patterns—such as the flow of mineworkers to South Africa—and started new ones, such as movements to Kenya, Gabon, and Nigeria. Africa has more refugees and IDPs relative to population size than any other region of the world. Asia and Latin America have complicated migratory patterns within the region, as well as increasing flows to the rest of the world.

Throughout the world, longstanding migratory patterns are persisting in new forms, while new flows are developing in response to economic, political, and cultural change, and violent conflicts. Yet, despite the diversity, it is possible to identify certain general tendencies:

1. *The globalization of migration.* The tendency for more and more countries to be crucially affected by migratory movements at the same time. Moreover, immigration countries tend to receive migrants from a larger number of source countries, so that most countries of immigration have entrants from a broad spectrum of economic, social, and cultural backgrounds.

2. *The acceleration of migration.* International movements of people are growing in volume in all major regions at the present time. This quantitative growth increases both the urgency and the difficulties of government policies. However, as indicated by the decrease in the global refugee total since 1993, international migration is not an inexorable process. Governmental policies can prevent or reduce international migration, and repatriation is a possibility.

3. *The differentiation of migration.* Most countries do not simply have one type of immigration, such as labour migration, refugees, or permanent settlement, but a whole range of types at once. Typically, migratory chains which start with one

type of movement often continue with other forms, despite (or often just because of) government efforts to stop or control the movement. This differentiation presents a major obstacle to national and international policy measures.

4. *The feminization of migration.* Women play a significant role in all regions and in most types of migration. In the past most labour migrations and many refugee movements were male-dominated, and women were often dealt with under the category of family reunion. Since the 1960s, women have played a major role in labour migration. Today women workers form the majority in movements as diverse as those of Cape Verdeans to Italy, Filipinos to the Middle East, and Thais to Japan. Some refugee movements contain a significant majority of women, as do certain networks of trafficked persons. Gender variables have always been significant in global migration history, but awareness of the specificity of women in contemporary migrations has grown.

5. *The growing politicization of migration.* Domestic politics, bilateral and regional relationships, and national security policies of states around the world are increasingly affected by international migration. There is increasing realization that migration policy issues require enhanced global governance, and co-operation between receiving, transit, and sending countries.

6. *The proliferation of migration transition.* This occurs when traditional lands of emigration become lands of transit migration and immigration as well. This is often the prelude to becoming predominantly immigration lands. States as diverse as Poland, Spain, Morocco, Mexico, the Dominican Republic, Turkey, and South Korea are experiencing various stages of a migration transition.

Ethnic Diversity, Racism, and Multiculturalism

Regulation of international migration is one of the two central issues arising from the population movements of the current epoch. The other is the effect of growing ethnic diversity on the societies of immigration countries. Settlers are often distinct from the receiving populations: they may come from different types of societies (for example, agrarian-rural rather than urban-industrial) with different traditions, religions, and political institutions. They often speak a different language and follow different cultural practices. They may be visibly different, through physical appearance (skin colour, features, and hair type) or style of dress. Some migrant groups become concentrated in certain types of work (often of low social status) and live segregated lives in low-income residential areas. The position of immigrants is often marked by a specific legal status: that of the foreigner or non-citizen. The differences are frequently summed up in the concepts of 'ethnicity' or 'race'. In many cases, immigration complicates existing conflicts or divisions in societies with longstanding ethnic minorities.

The social meaning of ethnic diversity depends to a large extent on the significance attached to it by the populations and states of the receiving countries. The classic immigration countries have generally seen immigrants as permanent settlers who were to be assimilated or integrated. However, not all potential immigrants have been seen as suitable: the USA, Canada, and Australia all had policies to keep out non-Europeans and even some categories of Europeans until the 1960s. Countries which emphasized temporary labour recruitment—western European countries in the 1960s and early 1970s, more recently the Gulf oil states and some of the fast-growing Asian economies—have tried to prevent family reunion and permanent settlement. Despite the emergence of permanent settler populations, such countries have declared themselves not to be countries of immigration, and have denied citizenship and other rights to settlers. Between these two extremes is a wealth of variations.

Culturally distinct settler groups almost always maintain their languages and some elements of their homeland cultures, at least for a few generations. Where governments have recognized permanent settlement, there has been a tendency to move from policies of individual assimilation to acceptance of some degree of longterm cultural difference. The result has been the granting of minority cultural and political rights, as embodied in the policies of multiculturalism introduced in Canada, Australia, and Sweden since the 1970s. However, as previously noted, the post-9/11 era has witnessed a retreat from multiculturalism in many democracies that espoused it in the 1970s or 1980s. Governments which reject the idea of permanent settlement also oppose pluralism, which they see as a threat to national unity and identity. In such cases, immigrants tend to turn into marginalized ethnic minorities. In other cases (France, for example), governments may accept the reality of settlement, but demand individual cultural assimilation as the price for granting of rights and citizenship.

Whatever the policies of the governments, immigration may lead to strong reactions from some sections of the population. Immigration often takes place at the same time as economic restructuring and far-reaching social change. People whose conditions of life are already changing in an unpredictable way often see the newcomers as the cause of insecurity. One of the dominant images in the highly developed countries today is that of masses of people flowing in from the poor South and the turbulent East taking away jobs, pushing up housing prices and overloading social services. Similarly, in immigration countries of the South, such as Malaysia and South Africa, immigrants are blamed for crime, disease, and unemployment. Extreme-right parties have grown and flourished through anti-immigrant campaigns. Racism is a threat, not only to immigrants themselves, but also to democratic institutions and social order. Analysis of the causes and effects of racism must therefore take a central place in any discussion of international migration and its effects on society.

International migration does not always create diversity. Some migrants, such as Britons in Australia or Austrians in Germany, are virtually indistinguishable from the receiving population. Other groups, like western Europeans in North America, are quickly assimilated. 'Professional transients'—that is, highly skilled personnel who move temporarily within specialized labour markets—are rarely seen as presenting an integration problem. But these are the exceptions; in most instances, international migration increases diversity within a society. This presents a number of problems for the state. The most obvious concerns social policy: social services and education may have to be planned and delivered in new ways to correspond to different life situations and cultural practices.

More serious is the challenge to national identity. The nation-state, as it has developed since the eighteenth century, is premised on the idea of cultural as well as political unity. In many countries, ethnic homogeneity, defined in terms of common language, culture, traditions, and history, has been seen as the basis of the nation-state. This unity has often been fictitious—a construction of the ruling elite—but it has provided powerful national myths. Immigration and ethnic diversity threaten such ideas of the nation, because they create a people without common ethnic origins. The classical countries of immigration have been able to cope with this situation most easily, since absorption of immigrants has been part of their myth of nation building. But countries which place common culture at the heart of their nation building process have found it difficult to resolve the contradiction. Movements against immigration have also become movements against multiculturalism, which have led to a retreat from multicultural policies in many places.

One of the central ways in which the link between the people and the state is expressed is through the rules governing citizenship and naturalization. States which readily grant citizenship to immigrants, without requiring common ethnicity or cultural assimilation, seem most able to cope with ethnic diversity. On the other hand, states which link citizenship to cultural belonging tend to have exclusionary policies which marginalize and disadvantage immigrants. Continuing international population movements will increase the ethnic diversity of more and more countries. This has already called into question prevailing notions of the nation-state and citizenship.

Debates over new approaches to diversity will shape the politics of many countries in coming decades.

Bibliography

Collins, J., Noble, G., Poynting, S., & Tabar, P. (2001). *Kebabs, kids, cops and crime: Youth, ethnicity, and crime.* Sydney: Pluto Press Australia.

DeParle, J. (2007, August 6). Fearful of restive foreign labor, Dubai eyes reforms. *New York Times.*

Hatton, T.J., & Williamson, J.G. (1998). *The age of mass migration: Causes and economic effects.* Oxford and New York: Oxford University Press.

Passel, J.S. (2006). *Size and characteristics of the unauthorized migrant population in the US. Pew Hispanic Center report.* Washington, DC: Pew Hispanic Center. Retrieved from http://pewhispanic.org/reports

Stalker, P. (2000). *Workers without frontiers: The impact of globalization on international migration.* Geneva, London, and Boulder, CO: International Labour Office and Lynne Rienner Publishers.

UNDESA. (2005). *Trends in total migrant stock: The 2005 revision.* New York: United Nations Department of Economic and Social Affairs.

Zlotnik, H. (1999). Trends of international migration since 1965: What existing data reveal. *International Migration, 37*(1), 21–62.

Basic Demographic Measures

1. Migration Rates

A general migration rate takes the following form:

$$\text{migration rate} = \frac{\text{number of persons moving in a given period}}{\text{population at risk of moving in the period}} \times 1{,}000$$

This equation appears to define the migration rate the same way as any other demographic rate. But this is not exactly so, because in the case of migration—unlike fertility or mortality, for example—migration can take place in two opposite directions. For any given area, people can move either in or out. (Fertility and mortality are, of course, irreversible processes.) Since every move must have a population of origin and a population of destination, two rates must be considered for any given area: a rate of in-migration and a rate of out-migration.

$$\text{out-migration rate for area } i = \frac{\text{number of out-migrants from area } i \text{ in a given period}}{\text{population of area } i \text{ in the beginning of the period}} \times 1{,}000$$

This formula says that the out-migration rate for area i is the number of persons that leave area i during a given period, divided by the population of area i at the beginning of the period. In actuality, in most cases it is not possible to obtain the population at risk at the beginning of the interval because published census data are usually based on the census population at midyear. In usual practice, then, the denominator is the midyear census population rather than the population at the beginning of the interval.

Using abbreviated notation, we can now write:

$$\text{out-migration rate for area } i = \frac{O_i}{P_i} \times 1{,}000$$

where O_i is the number of out-migrants from area i in a given period, and P_i is the midyear population at risk of leaving area i. By convention, the rates are expressed as per thousand population.

A complication arises in connection with the in-migration rate. Specifically, what should be the population at risk? In theory this should be everyone who is *not* living in area i at the beginning of the period. But how does one obtain this information? In the majority of cases, it is simply not possible. The solution is to use the same denominator as for the out-migration rate. So, if I_i is the number of in-migrants to area i in a given period, then

$$\text{in-migration rate for area } i = \frac{I_i}{P_i} \times 1{,}000$$

Since both the in- and out-migration rates now have the same denominator, this introduces an advantage, in that we may also compute two additional rates used frequently in the literature: the *gross migration rate* (GMR) and the *net migration rate* (NMR).

The *gross migration rate* is a sum of two directional migratory flows for a given area: in-migration and out-migration. Stated differently, it is the total in-migration to area i plus the out-migration from area i, divided by the midyear population of area i. It is expressed as follows:

$$\text{GMR}_i = \frac{I_i + O_i}{P_i} \times 1{,}000$$

The usefulness of this measure lies in its providing an indication of how much migration turnover there is in a given locality in total during a specified period.

The *net migration rate* is simply the difference in the number of in- and out-migrants for a given area during a given period. It is a useful descriptor of the relative impact of migration on a locality's degree of population change. A positive net migration rate means that the population is gaining people through net migratory exchanges. A negative rate would imply the population is losing people. The net migration rate is computed as follows:

$$\text{NMR}_i = \frac{I_i - O_i}{P_i} \times 1{,}000$$

2. Estimation of Net Migration: Residual Method

It is not always possible to compute actual rates of migration because the frequencies of in- and out-migration are not available. In such circumstances, one can rely on indirect estimation. An example of this is the estimation of net migration through the *demographic balancing equation*. With this equation, net migration can be estimated from information on the numbers of births and deaths during a given interval and the total population sizes for the beginning and the end of the period. Net migration can be worked out as follows:

$$\text{net migration} = (P_1 - P_0) - (B - D)$$

where B and D represent the number of births and deaths during the interval, and P_1 and P_0 are corresponding populations at the end and the start of the period.

3. Urban Proportion

The *urban proportion* of a country is simply the percentage of a country's population that resides in areas designated as 'urban':

$$\text{\% urban} = \left(\frac{\text{urban population}}{\text{urban population} + \text{rural population}} \right) \times 100$$

4. Percentage Change in Urban Proportion

In many applications the analyst is interested in looking at the extent of change over time in the percentage of the population that lives in urban areas. Specifically, the *percentage change in urban proportion* measures the magnitude of increase or decrease (in percentage terms) of the population that lives in urban areas between any two points in time. Usually this calculation is made over two or more time points, most typically between census periods. For a case involving two periods of observation, t_0 and t_1, the formula for this index of urbanization is as follows:

$$\text{\% change in urban proportion} = \left(\frac{\text{\% urban } t_1 - \text{\% urban } t_0}{\text{\% urban } t_0} \right) \times 100$$

Questions for Critical Thought

1. Why are young adults more geographically mobile than citizens of other ages? What explains the age pattern of geographic mobility?

2. How will the aging of the population affect internal migration trends in advanced societies? Will internal migration decline as the population becomes increasingly older?

3. Why are immigrants welcomed as potential citizens by some receiving countries and not wanted as citizens by other host countries?

4. What is unique about international migration patterns since the 1970s as compared to international migratory movements in the past? What does the future hold?

Websites of Interest

Le Centre—Urbanisation Culture Société, operated by the Institute National de la Recherche Scientifique (INRS), is an important Montreal-based research centre focusing on urbanization and internal migration, with special reference to the province of Quebec province. Information on their research—in French and English—is available from their website: www.ucs.inrs.ca/

The Government of Alberta's *Finance and Enterprise* page provides links to updated figures on interprovincial migration in Canada: www.finance.alberta.ca/

The *Development Research Centre on Migration, Globalization and Poverty* at the University of Sussex, England, undertakes policy-oriented research on migration, including internal migration, in poor countries. More information is available from their website: www.migrationdrc.org/index.html

Graphs and maps based on the latest information on internal migration may be obtained from the website of the *United Nations Department of Economic and Social Affairs, Population Division*: www.un.org/esa/population/publications/2009Migration_Chart/IttMig_maps.pdf

International migration data can be downloaded from the following UN website: http://esa.un.org/migration/index.asp?panel=1

The website of the *Migration Policy Institute* (MPI) is a useful source of information on international migration and refugees: www.migrationpolicy.org/. Especially useful are their World Migration Map and Global City Migration Map, both available from their Immigration Data Hub: www.migrationinformation.org/datahub/index.cfm

The website for the *United Nations High Commissioner for Refugees* is a useful source of information on refugees: www.unhcr.org/cgi-bin/texis/vtx/home

Further Reading

Bloemraad, Irene, Korteweg, Anna, & Yurdakul, Gokce. (2008). Citizenship and immigration: Multiculturalism assimilation, and challenges to the nation-state. *Annual Review of Sociology, 34*, 153–79.

Borjas, George J. (1999). *Heaven's door: Immigration policy and the American economy.* Princeton: Princeton University Press.

Champion, Anthony H., & Hugo, Graham. (2004). *New forms of urbanization: Beyond the urban–rural dichotomy.* London: Ashgate.

Cornelius, Wayne A., Tsuda, Takeyuki, Martin, Philip L., & Hollifield, J.F. (2004). *Controlling immigration: A global perspective* (2nd edn). Stanford, CA: Stanford University Press.

Davis, Kingsley. (1970). The urbanization of the human population. In *Cities* (special issue, *Scientific American*), pp. 3–24. New York: Alfred Knopf.

Davis, Kingsley. (1974). The migrations of human populations. In *The human population* (special issue, *Scientific American*), pp. 53–65. San Francisco: W.H. Freeman.

Dutt, Ashok K., Noble, Allen G., Venugopal, G. & Subbiah, S. (Eds). (2006). *Challenges to Asian urbanization in the 21st century.* Dordrecht: Kluwer Academic Publishers.

Edmonston, Barry, & Michalowski, Margaret. (2004). International migration. In Jacob S. Siegel & David A. Swanson (Eds), *The methods and materials of demography* (2nd edn , pp. 455–92). Amsterdam: Elsevier.

Frey, William H., & Speare, Alden, Jr. (1988). *Regional and metropolitan growth and decline in the United States.* New York: Russell Sage Foundation.

Gilbert, Alan. (1993). Third World cities: The changing national settlement system. *Urban Studies, 30*(4/5), 721–40.

Heath, Anthony F., Rothon, Catherine, & Kilpi, Elian. (2008). The second generation in western Europe: Education, unemployment, and occupational attainment. *Annual Review of Sociology, 34*, 211–35.

Hoerder, Dirk. (1999). *Creating societies: Immigrant lives in Canada.* Montreal and Kingston: McGill–Queen's University Press.

Hooghe, Marc, Trappers, Ann, Meuleman, Bart, & Reeskens, T. (2008). Migration to European countries: A structural explanation of patterns. *International Migration Review, 42*(2), 476–504.

Hou, Feng. (2007). Changes in the initial destinations and redistribution of Canada's major immigrant groups:

Reexamining the role of group affinity. *International Migration, 41*(3), 680–705.

Jacobs, Jane. (2004). *Dark age ahead.* New York: Random House.

Jasso, Guillermina, Massey, Douglas S., Rosenzweig, Mark R., & Smith, James P. (2008). From illegal to legal: Estimating previous illegal experience among new legal immigrants to the United States. *International Migration Review, 42*(4), 803–43.

Kambur, Ravi, & Rapoport, Hillel. (2005). Migration selectivity and the evolution of spatial inequality. *Journal of Economic Geography 5*, 43–57.

Kasarda, John. (1991). Third World urbanization: Dimensions, theories and determinants. *Annual Review of Sociology, 71*, 467–501.

Keyfitz, Nathan. (1996). Internal migration and urbanization. In Bernardo Colombo, Paul Demeny, & Max F. Perutz (Eds), *Resources and population: Natural, institutional, and demographic dimensions of development* (pp. 269–85). Oxford: Clarendon Press.

Lee, Everet M. (1966). A theory of migration. *Demography, 3*, 47–57.

Legrain, Philippe. (2006). *Immigrants: Your country needs them.* London: Little-Brown.

Manning, Patrick. (2005). *Migration in world history.* New York: Routledge.

Martin, Philip, & Zurcher, Gottfired. (2008). Managing migration: The global challenge. *Population Bulletin, 63*(1). Washington, DC: Population Reference Bureau.

Massey, D.S., Arango, J., Hugo, G., Kouaouci, A., Pellegrino, A., & Taylor, J.E. (1993). Theories of international migration: A review and appraisal. *Population and Development Review, 19*(3), 431–66.

Massey, D.S., & Espana, F.G. (1987). The social process of international migration. *Science, 237*, 733–738.

Matusiz, Jonathan. (2010). Collapsing the global and the local through interscalar strategies: A glurbanization perspective. *Planning Theory, 9*(1), 6–27.

Meng, Xin, & Manning, Chris, with Li Shi & T.N. Effendi. (2010). *The great migration: Rural–urban migration in China and Indonesia.* Cheltenham, UK: Edward Elgar.

Portes, Alejandro, & De Wind, Josh (Eds). (2007). *Rethinking migration: New theoretical and empirical perspectives.* New York: Berghahn Books.

Portes, Alejandro, & Zhou, Min. (1993). The new second generation: Segmented assimilation and its variants.

Annals of the American Academy of Political and Social Science, 530, 74–96.

Segal, Uma A., Elliott, Doreen, & Mayadas, Nazneen S. (2010). *Immigration worldwide: Policies, practices, and trends.* Oxford: Oxford University Press.

Simmons, Alan B. (2010). *Immigration and Canada: Global and transnational perspectives.* Toronto: Canadian Scholars Press.

Smith, Stanley K., Tayman, Jeff, & Swanson, David A. (2001). *State and local population projections: Methodology and analysis.* New York: Kluwer Academic/Plenum Publishers.

Statistics Canada Demography Division. (2003). *Population and family estimation methods at Statistics Canada* (Cat. No. 91-528-XIE). Ottawa: Minister of Industry.

Taylor, Peter J., Derudder, Ben, Saey, Pieter, & Witlox, Frank (Eds). (2007). *Cities in globalization: Practices, Policies and theories.* London: Routledge.

Todaro, Michael P. (1969). A model of labour migration and urban unemployment in less developed countries. *American Economic Review, 59,* 138–48.

United Nations Economic and Social Affairs, Population Division. (2009). *International migration report 2006: A global assessment* (ESA/P/WP.209). New York: UN.

Wachter, Kenneth W. (2005). Spatial demography. *Proceedings of the National Academies of Science, 102*(43), 15299–300.

Worldwatch Institute. (2007). *State of the world 2007: Our urban future.* Washington, DC: Worldwatch Institute.

Zlotnik, Hania. (2006). Theories of international migration. In Graziella Caselli, Jacques Vallin, & Guillaume Wunsch (Eds), *Demography: Analysis and synthesis* (vol. II, pp. 293–306). Amsterdam: Elsevier.

SECTION IX

Population, Environment, and Resources

Learning Objectives

By the end of this section, students should understand and be able to discuss the following:

- classical and contemporary perspectives on population, the environment, and resources
- the interrelationship of population growth with resources and environmental sustainability in the world.

Introduction

Concern about the role of population in matters of societal wellbeing can be found in the works of philosophers and other intellectuals from ancient times to the present (Demeny & McNicolls, 2003; Overbeek, 1974; Petersen, 1979; Stangeland, 1904). Two dominant themes have characterized this literature. The first perspective views curbing population growth as an essential requirement for maintaining a healthy balance between human numbers and resources. This is the *neo-Malthusian* position, based on the ideas of Thomas Malthus (1766–1834), who in 1798 published one of the most influential and debated works in the social sciences, *An Essay on the Principle of Population*. The second school of thought considers population as a minor or inconsequential factor in human welfare. This viewpoint is closely associated with *neo-Marxist* scholars, studying in the tradition of Karl Marx (1818–1883), whose principal work, *Das Kapital* (volume I published in 1867; volumes II and III published posthumously in 1885 and 1894 and edited by Friedrich Engels), entails a fervent critique of capitalism.

Influenced by Malthus's notion that population growth, if unchecked, leads eventually to the depletion of essential resources and, in particular, the ability of a society to grow sufficient food for its expanding population, neo-Malthusians believe fundamentally that the world's population has already surpassed tenable levels of growth and that, as a consequence, the planet is close to critical ecological limits, thus posing potentially disastrous consequences for the future of humankind. Prominent neo-Malthusian scholars (e.g. Ehrlich, 1968; Ehrlich, Ehrlich, & Holdren, 1977; Hardin, 1968; Leslie, 1996; Meadows, et al., 1972; Tobias, 1994) have argued for the desirability of reducing population growth, especially in the rich countries, whose inhabitants have disproportionate per capita impacts on the environment and resources. Scholars in this tradition have also called for a limit on wasteful consumption and the development of more environmentally benign technologies and cultural practices that would reduce strain on the earth's limited resources. Implicit in the neo-Malthusian view is the belief that the world would be better and safer if it contained fewer people and if population were growing more slowly. Neo-Malthusians regard contraception and family planning as crucial to achieving population control.

While neo-Malthusians attribute many human and ecological problems to unchecked population growth, neo-Marxist scholars downplay the role of population in human predicaments. Fixing on population as the root of human suffering obscures the reality that the world is divided into wealthy and relatively poor regions, and that this divide is widening rather than narrowing. Neo-Marxists would argue that the population 'crisis' of poor developing nations is largely a function of their relative economic deprivation and continued dependency on rich industrialized nations that exert overwhelming influence and control over the world's economy. Thus, the root of the problem in the world's poorer countries is not overpopulation but poverty and underdevelopment. In response to Malthus's view that population grows geometrically and the food supply arithmetically, Marxist scholars would argue that scientific and technological progress also follow a geometric pace of growth, and that the important challenge is to redistribute benefits of scientific and technological progress equitably to all peoples of the world. The elimination of poverty and inequality in the world is then a foremost priority for the neo-Marxists. In keeping with this orientation, neo-Marxist research often focuses on regional inequalities in resources, and the political and economic dependence of developing countries on the developed nations (see, for example, Frank, 1969, 1991; Wallerstein, 1974). The globalization of capital, seen by many writers as the key to helping developing countries emulate the 'success story' of the West, is thought by neo-Marxists to exacerbate rather than diminish socioeconomic disparities within and across nations (Wimberly, 1990).

Pessimists, Optimists, and Neutralists

Although the ideas of Malthus and Marx remain important and continue to stimulate serious thought among students of population, the contemporary literature can best be categorized as representative of three conceptual frameworks, labelled by Bloom, Canning, and Sevilla as the *pessimist*, the *optimist*, and the *neutralist*. Bloom and colleagues are principally interested in examining how these different schools of thought perceive the role of population growth in economic development, a question that remains a subject of debate among economists and demographers. The chief disagreement concerns whether population growth restricts, promotes, or is independent of economic growth. As we shall see in the chapter written by these authors, the ideas of Malthus and Marx, although not at centre stage in this debate, are never completely out of the picture.

The pessimistic perspective traces its lineage to Malthus. Scholars in this theoretical camp promote the ideas advocated by the neo-Malthusians, and for all intents and purposes, the pessimists are indistinguishable from the neo-Malthusians. They remain deeply concerned about the rapid growth of the world's population (now at nearly 7 billion and projected to surpass 9 billion by 2050) and the negative impact this will have on the environment and resources. For them, population growth can only lead to reduced levels of economic development and increased pressures on fixed resources.

The optimists reject these pessimistic concerns. They point to the fact that even though between 1960 and 2000 the world's population doubled and continues to grow, per capita incomes have not fallen worldwide but have actually increased significantly. Moreover, they point out, the prices of raw materials have been declining while overall standards of living are improving. Finally, they argue that many of society's undesirable features, which are often blamed on population growth, are actually related not to population but to inefficient government policies and institutions.

The neutralist (or revisionist) school looks at the empirical evidence concerning population growth and economic development and finds little correlation between the two. In general, countries with rapidly growing populations do typically show slower rates of economic growth, but this negative correlation tends to disappear, or even change direction (i.e. the correlation becomes positive), once other relevant factors are brought into the equation (e.g. country size, openness to trade, quality of civic and political institutions, and overall level of education).

A further point can be raised in favour of the neutralist perspective. In principle, one might expect to find that countries with booming populations are worse off than less densely populated places with endless arable acres. In practice, though, there is no empirical relationship at all. There are poor, densely populated places whose environments are degraded (e.g. Bangladesh, Haiti), and there are rich, overcrowded countries (e.g. the Netherlands); at the same time, there are sparsely populated countries across the whole spectrum of income categories: poor, middle-income, and high-income—consider Chad, Brazil, and the US ('Green view', 2007). This is not to deny in any way that in some parts of the world population pressure can cause social, economic, and environmental problems. But across the board, the empirical evidence is not strongly supportive of a close link between population growth, economic development, and environmental damage.

Although these three perspectives differ in significant ways, it is important to point out that each offers something of value toward a better understanding of the issues. But according to Bloom and associates, all three perspectives overlook an important dimension in the debate: they fail to consider the role of evolving age structure as an intermediary between population growth, economic development, and resources. Population growth in essence means that the age structure of the population is changing. The change in age structure in turn affects dependency ratios. And depending on the relative sizes of the working-age population and the dependent population in a society, this change in age structure can ultimately affect economic development, either adversely or positively.

Revisiting the Limits to Growth

In their chapter of this volume, Hall and Day revisit an important Malthusian question, one first raised in the *Limits to Growth* study in the early 1970s (Meadows, et al., 1972). It concerns the interdependence of population growth, energy production (particularly oil), and agricultural output (i.e. food supply). The authors note that while in the 1970s a rising world population and the finite resources available to support it were hot topics, interest in this concern has faded since then. They argue that it is time to take another look at the question of whether we may run out of resources to sustain population growth. First, they acknowledge that the Malthusian prediction made by adherents of the *Limits* school has not come true. Indeed, the world thus far has avoided wholesale famine, and most of the earth's people have access to an adequate supply of food. This is so because the use of fossil fuels as a source of energy has expanded geometrically (like population growth). Increased access to fossil fuels—most notably oil—has provided the world plenty of energy for use in agricultural production, which in turn has helped increase the food supply for an expanding population.

The authors, however, point to a number of trends over the past several decades that suggest that the *Limits to Growth* school may have been correct in their early pronouncements about the precarious interconnections between population growth, resource depletion, and eroding environment. For instance, Hall and Day alert us to the following facts:

- The 1973 oil crisis that paralyzed the industrial world brought to the forefront our heavy dependence on oil as a source of energy.
- Peak oil production occurred in 1970, while natural gas production peaked in 1973; since then, consumption of these resources has been increasing as discovery of new supply sources

(particularly for oil) has been dropping.
- Even though oil prices have seen ups and downs over the years, the overall trend in the cost of oil has been generally upward.
- Meanwhile, over recent decades the world has experienced higher levels of acid rain owing to increased pollutants in the earth's atmosphere, and the reality of global warming owing to the depletion of the earth's protective ozone layer, all while experiencing significant biodiversity loss.

To Hall and Day, the evidence taken on a global scale indicates that as of 2008, the early predictions of the *Limits to Growth* model are actually on target. In other words, population, pollution, and resources are at just about where they are expected to be under the assumptions of the *Limits* model. They do concede, however, that there are no guarantees that the predictions of this model will hold true in the future.

Population and Environment: The Geography of Poverty

A country's natural endowments, its location, and its climate can help explain part of the longstanding 'puzzle' first introduced by Adam Smith in his *Inquiry into the Nature and Causes of the Wealth of Nations* (1937 [1776]): basically, why are some nations wealthy and others not? David Landes (1999) has devoted considerable attention to this question. He suggests that the success of Europe in the world economy has much to do with good fortune in terms of geography, which gave this part of the world the natural attributes to catapult it to economic prominence: a temperate climate, warm winds from the Gulf Stream, gentle rains, water in all seasons, and low rates of evaporation, all of which have provided Europeans with large, dense forests, good crops, and healthy livestock. Added to these endowments are Europe's many navigable rivers, seaports, and abundant mineral resources.

Sachs, Mellinger, and Gallup (2001) expand on this theme, arguing that nations in tropical climates and desert zones generally face higher rates of infectious diseases and lower agricultural productivity than do nations in temperate zones. The very poorest regions of the world are those saddled with both handicaps: distance from sea trade and a tropical or desert ecology. Tropical areas are susceptible to persistent endemic diseases such as malaria, whose pathogen is transmitted to humans by mosquitoes, which thrive in tropical environments. Malaria, a debilitating illness for millions in such areas and a major killer, can significantly reduce a nation's productivity by affecting a large part of the working population; it is a disease that is seldom seen in temperate climates. Economic disparities between nations can thus be attributed, at least in part, to geography and its indirect relationships to factors detrimental to economic growth.

Coastal countries with temperate climates, such as Germany, enjoy lower transportation costs and higher farm productivity than landlocked tropical countries such as Uganda. Among the high-income economies of the world, only Hong Kong, Singapore, and part of Taiwan are in the tropical climate zone. Sachs and associates also note that almost all the temperate-zone countries have either high-income economies (as the cases of North America, western Europe, Korea, and Japan illustrate) or middle-income economies burdened by a history of socialist policies (evident in eastern Europe, the former Soviet Union, and China). In addition, there is a strong temperate–tropical divide within countries that straddle both types of climates. Most of Brazil, for example, lies within the tropical zone, but the richest part of the nation, comprising the southernmost states, is in the temperate zone.

A final point made by Sachs, Mellinger, and Gallup: geography and climate affect food production. Tropical environments are plagued by diverse infestations of pests and parasites that can devastate crops and livestock. And environmental variables correlated with geographic location determine a country's ability to exploit its resources. Nations enjoying an advantage in geographic location, climate, and resources are able to develop institutions that bolster social wellbeing and productivity—free markets, equitable tax laws, protection and promotion of private property rights, and universal education and healthcare.

Works Cited

Demeny, Paul, & McNicoll, Geoffrey. (Eds). (2003). *Encyclopedia of population* (2 vols). New York: Macmillan Reference USA.

Ehrlich, Paul R. (1968). *The population bomb.* London: Pan Books.

Ehrlich, Paul R., & Ehrlich, Anne. (1990). *The population explosion.* London: Hutchinson.

Ehrlich, Paul R., Ehrlich, Anne, & Holdren, John P. (1977). *Ecoscience: Population, resources, environment.* San Francisco: W.H. Freeman and Co.

Frank, Andre Günter. (1969). *Capitalism and underdevelopment in Latin America.* New York: Monthly Review Press.

———. (1991). The underdevelopment of development. *Scandinavian Journal of Development Alternatives, 10*(3), 5–72.

Green view. Population and its discontents. Lighten the footprint, but keep the feet. (2007, September 10). *The Economist.*

Hardin, Garrett. (1968, December 13). The tragedy of the commons. *Science, 162*(3859), 1243–8.

Landes, David S. (1999). *The wealth and poverty of nations: Why some are so wealthy and others poor.* New York: W.W. Norton.

Leslie, John. (1996). *The end of the world: The science and ethics of human extinction.* London: Routledge.

Meadows, Donella H., Meadows, Dennis L., Randers, J. & Behrens, W.W. III. (1972). *The limits to growth: A report for the Club of Rome's project on the predicament of mankind.* New York: Universe Books.

Overbeek, Johan. (1974). *History of population theories.* Rotterdam: Rotterdam University Press.

Petersen, William. (1979). *Malthus.* Cambridge: Harvard University Press.

Sachs, Geoffrey, Mellinger, Andrew D., & Gallup, John L. (2001, March). The geography of poverty and wealth. *Scientific American*, pp. 70–5.

Smith, Adam. (1937 [1776]). *Inquiry into the nature and causes of the wealth of nations.* New York: The Modern Library, Random House.

Stangeland, Charles E. (1904). *Pre-Malthusian doctrines of population: A study in the history of economic theory.* New York: The Columbia University Press.

Tobias, Michael. (1994). *World War III: Population and the biosphere at the end of the millennium.* Santa Fe, NM: Bear and Company Publishing.

Wallerstein, Immanuel. (1974). *The modern world-system* (2 vols). New York: Academic Press.

Wimberley, Dale W. (1990). Investment dependence and alternative explanations of Third World mortality. *American Sociological Review, 55*(1), 75–91.

CHAPTER 22

The Debate Over the Effects of Population Growth on Economic Growth

David E. Bloom, David Canning, and Jaypee Sevilla

The relationship between population change and economic growth remains a subject of debate among economists and demographers. They continue to disagree about whether population growth (a) restricts, (b) promotes, or (c) is independent of economic growth. Proponents of each view can point to research evidence to support their cases.

The utility of this debate has been hampered by its almost exclusive focus on population *size* and *growth*. Little attention has been paid to a critical variable: the *age structure* of the population (that is, the way in which the population is distributed across different age groups) and how it changes when populations grow.

This report attempts to address this limitation. It reviews the debate over the effects of demographic change on economic growth and examines the evidence for the relevance of changes in age structure for economic growth. It also examines the relationship between population change and economic development in particular regions of the world. Finally, it discusses key policies that, combined with reduced fertility and increases in the working-age population, have contributed to economic growth in the developing world.

Understanding the relationship between population change and economic growth has taken on immense significance in recent years because of demographic trends in the developing world. The world's developing countries—home to the vast majority of the world's population—are in varying stages of a demographic transition from high to low rates of mortality and fertility. This transition is producing a boom generation that is gradually working its way through nations' age structures. In conjunction with the right kinds of policies, this phenomenon creates opportunities for economic growth in developing countries. For this reason, policy makers should benefit from a clearer understanding of the relationship between economic development and the shifting age structure that results from the unfolding demographic transition.

The 'Pessimistic' Theory: Population Growth Restricts Economic Growth

After World War II, rapid population growth, resulting from the gap between declining mortality and continuing high fertility, began occurring in much of Asia. By the mid-1960s, more countries, including a number in Latin America and the Middle East, were experiencing unprecedented rates of population growth. At such rates, their populations would double in less than 25 years.

Concerns about rapid population growth voiced by demographers, social scientists, and others were based largely on the assumption that such growth would 'serve as a brake' on economic development.[1] In the late 1940s, conservationists began to write about excessive population growth as a threat to food supplies and natural resources. Concerns about the impact of rapid population growth and high fertility motivated the widespread implementation of family planning programs in many areas of the developing world (see Seltzer, 2002). Policy makers presumed that by helping to reduce high fertility, family planning programs would slow population growth, which in turn would contribute to improved economic performance by freeing resources that otherwise would be devoted to child-rearing and by reducing strains on infrastructure and the environment.

The 'pessimistic' theory traces its lineage to Thomas Malthus. Writing in the 1790s, Malthus asked whether 'the future improvement of society' was possible in the face of ever larger populations. He reached his famously dismal conclusion:

> Taking the population of the world at any number, a thousand millions, for instance . . . the human species would increase in the ratio of 1, 2, 4, 8, 16, 32, 64, 128, 256, 516, etc. and subsistence as 1, 2, 3, 4, 5, 6, 7, 8, 9, 10, etc. In two centuries and a quarter the population would be to the means of subsistence as 512 to 10; in three centuries as 4096 to 13, and in two thousand years the difference would be incalculable. (Malthus, 1798)

In a world with fixed resources for growing food, and slow technical progress, Malthus theorized, food production would quickly be swamped by the pressures of a rapidly growing population. The available diet would then fall below subsistence level, until population growth was halted by a high death rate. Living standards could only ever improve in the short term—before they set in motion more rapid population growth. The balance between population and income growth was the 'great law of our nature'. Accordingly,

> No fancied equality, no agrarian regulations in their utmost extent, could remove the pressure of it even for a single century. And it appears, therefore, to be decisive against the possible

existence of a society, all the members of which should live in ease, happiness, and comparative leisure; and feel no anxiety about providing the means of subsistence for themselves and families. (Malthus, 1798)

Malthus's pessimism has remained with us. In 1968, for instance, Paul Ehrlich opened his influential book *The Population Bomb* with the words, 'The battle . . . is over. In the 1970s hundreds of millions of people are going to starve to death' (Ehrlich, 1968). More measured studies undertaken by the US National Academy of Sciences (NAS) in 1971 and the United Nations in 1973 also predicted that the net effect of population growth would be negative (National Academy of Sciences, 1971; United Nations, 1973). Rapid population growth continues to press on the modern consciousness. The world's population has grown sixfold since 1800, when it stood at about 1 billion. It took less than 130 years to add another billion. Things have quickened considerably since. The 6 billionth baby was born in October 1999—and world population is forecast to reach 9.3 billion by the year 2050.

With the population of many developed countries decreasing by 2050, all of this explosive population growth is happening in developing countries (United Nations, 2001) (see Figure 22.1)—most rapidly in those geographic regions that are most fragile and least hospitable (due to adverse climate, lack of resources, or unfavourable location) to economic growth (Sachs, Mellinger, & Gallup, 2001)—encouraging predictions of demographic catastrophe.

For a time, it seemed the pessimists had the right answer. Innovations in agriculture, such as irrigation in China and potato cultivation in Ireland, were accompanied by vast increases in population that hampered improvements in living standards. Until 1700, income gaps between countries were fairly small and, even in 1820, real income levels in the advanced European nations were only about two to three times those found in Africa, Asia, and Latin America (see Figure 22.2).

In addition to the effect of population numbers on the demand for fixed resources, there is also a

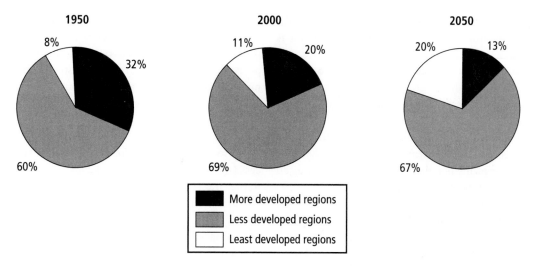

Figure 22.1 Shares of the world population by level of regional development, 1950, 2000, and 2050. The UN defines least-developed nations to be a subset of less-developed nations. By contrast, these charts completely separate the two categories, removing the least-developed nations from the less-developed.

United Nations (2001).

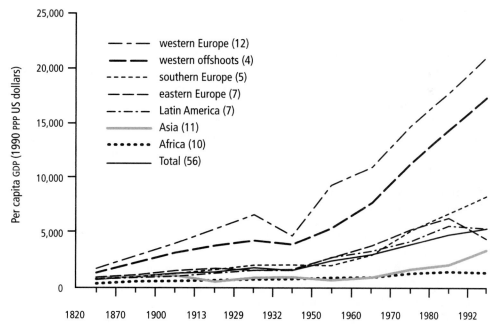

Figure 22.2 Economic growth, 1820–1992 (by major region). (*n*) = number of countries; PPP = purchasing power parity; Western offshoots = the United States, Canada, Australia, and New Zealand.

Maddison (1995).

potentially negative impact of population growth on capital intensity. In principle, higher population numbers require more homes, factories, and infrastructure to house, employ, and provide for their needs. In the long run, such capital can be constructed, but periods of rapid population growth may well lead to reductions in capital per worker and lower living standards. When population growth is rapid, a large part of investment is used to supply the needs of the growing population rather than enabling an increase in the level of provision per capita.

Both these theories give grounds for pessimism. However, by the early 1980s, economists were beginning to reject the pessimist view. Empirical research had weakened the pessimists' case; economic theory had begun to give increasing importance to technology and human capital accumulation rather than to the old key growth factor of physical capital; and demographic theory started to look to the intermediate and long term, where the short-term effects of population growth were likely to have at least partly smoothed out.[2] In response to these developments, organizations such as the National Academy of Sciences began to revise their earlier views, as economists' voices, with their greater faith in markets' ability to respond to population growth, no longer took a backseat to those of the social and biological scientists who previously dominated population thinking (National Research Council, 1986).

The 'Optimistic' Theory: Population Growth Can Fuel Economic Growth

Recent history has cast further doubt on the pessimists' theory. In the last 30 years—during which the world's population has doubled—per capita incomes have increased by about two-thirds. Famines have occurred, but Ehrlich's 'hundreds of millions' of people have not starved. The famines that have occurred were largely caused by poverty and lack of funds within a section of the population to buy food rather than by any absolute shortage of food.

(As Amartya Sen has noted, there has never been a famine in a functioning democracy, whatever its population growth rate [Sen, 1999].) Technological progress, in both agriculture and industry, has been more rapid than during any other time in human history. There have been equally dramatic social and institutional innovations: in the way people work, the standard of their education and health, and the extent to which they participate in the political process (Bloom, Craig, & Malaney, 2001; Sen, 1999). Rather than being constrained by fixed resources, the prices of many raw materials are in long-term decline, and some parts of the economy are becoming 'dematerialized' as knowledge becomes an increasingly vital asset (Task Force on Higher Education and Society, 2000; World Bank, 1997).

These trends have supported the views of a group of 'population optimists' who have sought to promote the idea that population growth can be an economic asset. Simon Kuznets and Julian Simon, for example, argued (separately) that as populations increase, so does the stock of human ingenuity. Larger societies—with the capacity to take advantage of economies of scale—are better positioned to develop, exploit, and disseminate the increased flow of knowledge they receive (Kuznets, 1960, 1967). Simon, in his influential book *The Ultimate Resource* (1981), showed that rapid population growth can actually lead to positive impacts on economic development (Simon, 1981). As one example, he cites the tendency of natural resource prices to decline in the long term because of technological progress induced by the growing demands of rising populations. Ester Boserup uses similar arguments to turn the Malthusian worldview around. Population growth creates pressure on resources. People are resourceful and are stimulated to innovate, especially in adversity. When rising populations swamped traditional hunter–gatherer arrangements, slash-burn-cultivate agriculture emerged. When that, too, became inadequate, intensive multi-annual cropping was developed (Boserup, 1965, 1981). More recently the Green Revolution, which has almost quadrupled world food production since 1950 using just 1 per cent more land, was a direct reaction to population pressure. 'Without high yield agriculture,' comments Norman Borlaug, an initiator of the Green Revolution, 'either millions would have starved or increases in food output would have been realized through losses of pristine land a hundred times greater than all losses to urban and suburban expansion' (Department for International Development, 1997).

The Optimists, while refuting the alarmist tendencies of the Pessimists' theory, were not dogmatic about the positive impacts of population growth. Instead, they took a broader view, suggesting that a multiplicity of external factors was responsible for the consequences of population growth. These factors could have either positive or negative economic consequences; as T.N. Srinivasan said, 'Many of the alleged deleterious consequences result more from inappropriate policies and institutions than from rapid population growth' (Srinivasan, 1988). This broadening of the discussion on population growth eventually led to population *neutralism* emerging as the dominant view in the demographic debate.[3]

The 'Neutralist' Theory: Population Growth Has No Significant Effect on Economic Growth

In his pathbreaking *Inquiry into the Nature and Causes of the Wealth of Nations*, Adam Smith (1776) asked why some countries were richer than others. He found his answer in the division of labour, which allowed workers to become more productive by honing their skills at ever more specialized tasks. In recent years, economists considering the economic effects of demographic change have been more interested in Adam Smith, and in his narrative of the power of the market, than in Thomas Malthus's dire predictions about population.

Most economic analysis has examined the statistical correlation between population and economic growth and found little significant connection. Though countries with rapidly growing populations

tend to have more slowly growing economies (see Figure 22.3), this negative correlation typically disappears (or even reverses direction) once other factors such as country size, openness to trade,[4] educational attainment of the population, and the quality of civil and political institutions are taken into account. Figure 22.4 shows the portion of economic growth unexplained by these other factors. It shows that this 'residual' growth bears little correlation to population growth rates. In other words, when controlling for other factors, there is little cross-country evidence that population growth impedes or promotes economic growth.[5] This result seems to justify a third view: population neutralism.

The neutralist theory has been the dominant view since the mid-1980s (Bloom & Freeman, 1986). Although there are some variations within the neutralist school—with the NAS concluding in 1986 that '*on balance . . .* slower population growth would be beneficial to economic development of *most* developing countries' (National Research Council, 1986; italics added), and many World Bank economists suggesting that in some countries bigger populations can boost economic growth[6]—the overall tendency is to accord population issues a relatively minor place in the context of the wider policy environment.

Allen Kelley has suggested that population neutralism has in fact been the predominant school in thinking among academics about population growth for the last half-century; for example, the academic background papers to even the most pessimistic UN and NAS reports are much more moderate in tone than the reports themselves (Kelley, 2001). Kelley cites three major research areas that influenced the rise of population neutralism in the 1980s:

- *Natural resources.* Exhaustion of natural resources was found not to be as strongly affected by population growth as the Pessimists thought. Technology, conservation, and efficient market allocation of resources all play a part in preserving natural resources, and per capita income has been shown to be a key determinant of supply and demand for these resources.

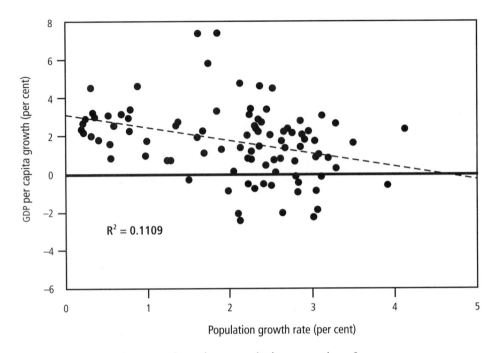

Figure 22.3 GDP per capita growth against population growth, 1965–1990

Authors' calculations, based on GDP data from Heston and Summers (1995) and on population growth rate data from United Nations (2001).

- *Saving.* The negative impact of population growth on savings (and a consequent negative effect on economic growth) was not borne out by studies.
- *Diversification of resources.* Whereas the Pessimists had thought that population growth would lead to a diversion of resources from the formation of physical capital (which would yield quick returns) to the formation of social capital (e.g. child health and education, whose returns would take longer to be realized), multi-country studies showed that this did not in fact happen to any great extent.

According to Kelley, these studies, coupled with the impact of Julian Simon's *The Ultimate Resource* on extending demographers' view into the longer term, were crucial in bringing neutralism to the fore, and the theory has since had an enormous influence on policy makers in developing countries and on the international development community. The Reagan administration and several donor agencies sought to limit support of population programs and simultaneously appealed to neutralist theory.[7]

The Importance of Age Structure

Proponents of population pessimism, optimism, and neutralism can all fall back on theoretical models and more or less robust data to support their positions.

All of these theories, however, tend to ignore a critical dimension of population dynamics: populations' evolving *age structure*. Economists have tended to focus on population *growth*, ignoring the changing age distribution within populations as they grow.[8] Yet these changes are arguably as important

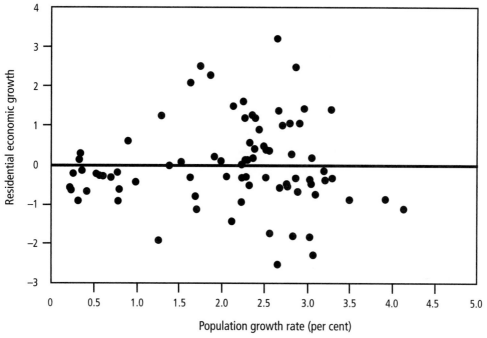

Figure 22.4 Overall population growth rate and the economic growth residual

Authors' calculations, based on GDP data from Heston and Summers (1995) and on population growth rate data from United Nations (2001).

as population growth. Each age group in a population behaves differently, with distinct economic consequences: The young require intensive investment in health and education, prime-age adults supply labour and savings, and the aged require healthcare and retirement income (Figure 22.5 is a schematic representation of life cycle income and consumption). When the relative size of each of these groups in a population changes, so does the relative intensity of these economic behaviours. (Figure 22.6 illustrates the period of high population growth preceding the period during which there is a high share of working-age people.) This matters significantly to a country's income growth prospects. Policy makers with a broad view of development and the complex relation between economic and human development must factor these effects of changing age structure into decisions about their countries' future.

This challenge is especially pressing in the developing world. In those countries whose mortality and fertility rates are beginning to fall (South-Central Asia and much of sub-Saharan Africa, for example), there is an opportunity for governments to capitalize on the consequent demographic transition, where the number of working-age adults grows large relative to the dependent population and potentially acts as a major economic spur. Conversely, if the appropriate policy environment is not in place, unemployment and instability may result, and health, education, and social welfare systems may undergo unbearable strain. Those developing countries whose transition is advanced, on the other hand (Southeast Asia and Latin America), need to look to the future, adopting policies to cope with an aging population and optimize the remaining years of low dependency ratios.

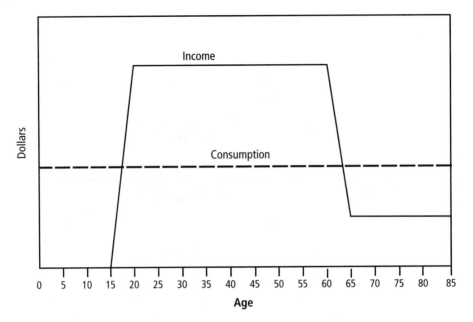

Figure 22.5 Life cycle income and consumption

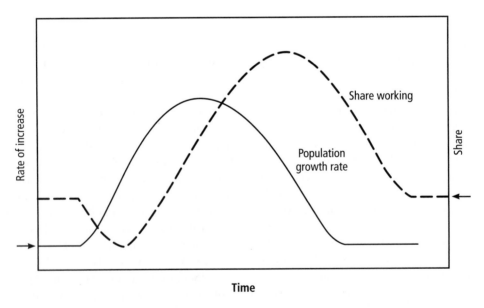

Figure 22.6 Population growth and age structure

Notes

1. For one interesting discussion of trends in global population growth since the 1950s and the development implications of family planning, see Bulatao (1998), pp. 3–20.

2. On the importance of human capital in explaining differences in standards of living across countries, see Mankiw, Romer, and Weil (1992). On demographics, see A.C. Kelley (2001).

3. A more recent position is that of Galor and Weil (1999), who propose that the Malthusian and growth regimes should not be seen as competitors but rather, respectively, the beginning and end of a historical process. The world begins in the Malthusian regime and eventually evolves from an intermediate stage they call post-Malthusian into the current Modern Growth Regime.

4. Sachs and Warner (1995) judge openness to trade on the basis of tariffs, quotas and licensing, black-market premia, and export taxes.

5. This result refers to the average experience across countries. The economic performance of any specific country, however, will be determined by many forces.

6. See Easterly (2001), especially Chapter 5.

7. World Bank economists had long thought that the macroeconomic case for population lending was weak (Steven W. Sinding, Professor of Clinical Public Health, Columbia University, personal communication), and excluded population issues from most policy discussions (Tom Merrick, Senior Population and Reproductive Health Adviser, World Bank, personal communication). The Reagan administration's Mexico City policy in 1984 stated that 'population is neither a positive nor a negative factor' in development, but is neutral. This statement was associated with the new policy of denying federal funding to NGOs that performed or promoted abortion as a means of fertility regulation in other nations. This policy, which had been overturned by President Clinton in 1993, was reinstated by the George W. Bush administration in January 2001.

8. The most famous exception was the seminal Coale–Hoover study, which used India and Mexico as case studies to emphasize the costs associated with a high dependency ratio in the early stage of the demographic transition. See Coale and Hoover (1958). See also Bloom and Freeman (1988).

References

Bloom, D.E., Craig, P.H., & Malaney, P.N. (2001). *The quality of life in rural Asia.* Hong Kong: Oxford University Press.

Bloom, D.E., & Freeman, R. (1986, September). The effects of rapid population growth on labor supply and employment in developing countries. *Population and Development Review,* pp. 381–414.

Boserup, E. (1965). *The conditions of agricultural progress.* London: Allen and Unwin.

———. (1981). *Population and technological change: A study of long-term trends.* Chicago: University of Chicago Press.

Department for International Development. (1997). Poverty and the environment. uk@earth.people, United Kingdom.

Ehrlich, P. (1968). *The population bomb.* New York: Ballantine.

Heston, A., & Summers, R. (1995). Penn World Tables v 5.6. Data update to Heston and Summers, 1991, available at www.nber.org/pub/pwt56/

Kelley, A. (2001). The population debate in historical perspective: Revisionism revised. In N. Birdsall, A.C. Kelley, & S.W. Sinding (Eds), *Population matters: Demographic change, economic growth, and*

poverty in the developing world, pp. 24–54. Oxford: Oxford University Press.

Kuznets, S. (1960). Population change and aggregate output. In Universities—National Bureau Committee for Economic Research, *Demographic and economic changes in developed countries.* Princeton, NJ: Princeton University Press.

———. (1967). Population and economic growth. *Proceedings of the American Philosophical Society, 111,* 170–93.

Maddison, A. (1995). *Monitoring the world economy: 1820–1992.* Paris: OECD.

Malthus, Thomas R. (1798). *An Essay on the Principle of Population As It Affects the Future Improvement of Society, with Remarks on the Speculations of Mr. Godwin, M. Condorcet, and Other Writers.* London: J. Johnson, in St. Paul's Church-yard.

National Academy of Sciences. (1971). *Rapid population growth: Consequences and policy implications* (2 vols). Baltimore, MD: Johns Hopkins Press for the National Academy of Sciences.

National Research Council. (1986). *Population growth and economic development: Policy questions.* Washington, DC: National Academy Press.

Sachs, J.D., Mellinger, A.D., & Gallup, J.L. (2001, March). The geography of poverty and wealth. *Scientific American.*

Seltzer, J. (2002). *The origins and evolution of family planning programs in developing countries.* Santa Monica, CA: RAND MR-1276.

Sen, A. (1999). *Development as freedom.* New York: Oxford University Press.

Simon, J. (1981). *The ultimate resource.* Princeton, NJ: Princeton University Press.

Smith, A. (1776). *Inquiry into the nature and causes of the wealth of nations.*

Srinivasan, T.N. (1988, spring). Population growth and economic development. *Journal of Policy Modeling, 10*(1), 7–28.

Task Force on Higher Education and Society. (2000). Higher education and developing countries: Peril and promise. World Bank/UNESCO. Retrieved from www.tfhe.net

United Nations. (1973). The determinants and consequences of population trends. In Department of Economic and Social Affairs, *Population studies, 50* (2 vols). New York: United Nations.

———. (2001). *World population prospects: The 2000 revision.* Retrieved from CD-ROM.

World Bank. (1997). *World development report 1997: The state in a changing world.* Oxford: Oxford University Press.

CHAPTER 23

Revisiting the Limits to Growth After Peak Oil

Charles A.S. Hall and John W. Day, Jr

In recent decades there has been considerable discussion in academia and the media about the environmental impacts of human activity, especially those related to climate change and biodiversity, but far less attention has been paid to the diminishing resource base for humans. Despite our inattention, resource depletion and population growth have been continuing relentlessly. The most immediate of these issues appears to be a decline in oil reservoirs, a phenomenon commonly referred to as 'peak oil' because global production appears to have reached a maximum and is now declining. However, a set of related resource and economic issues are continuing to come home to roost in ever greater numbers and impacts—so much so that author Richard Heinberg speaks of 'peak everything'. We believe that these issues were set out well and basically accurately by a series of scientists in the middle of the last century, and that events are demonstrating that their original ideas were mostly sound. Many of these ideas were spelled out explicitly in a landmark book called *The Limits to Growth*, published in 1972.

In the 1960s and 1970s, during our formative years in graduate school, our curricula and our thoughts were strongly influenced by the writings of ecologists and computer scientists who spoke clearly and eloquently about the growing collision between increasing numbers of people—and their enormously increasing material needs—and the finite resources of the planet. The oil price shocks and long lines at gasoline stations in the 1970s confirmed in the minds of many that the basic arguments of these researchers were correct and that humans were facing some sort of limits to growth. It was extremely clear to us then that the growth culture of the American economy had limits imposed by nature, such that, for example, the first author made very conservative retirement plans in 1970 based on his estimate that we would be experiencing the effects of peak oil just about the time of his expected retirement in 2008.

These ideas have stayed with us, even though they largely disappeared, at least until very recently, from most public discussion, newspaper analyses, and college curricula. Our general feeling is that few people think about these issues today, but even most of those who do so believe that technology and market economics have resolved the problems. The warning in *The Limits to Growth*—and even the more general notion of limits to growth—are seen as invalid.

Even ecologists have largely shifted their attention away from resources to focus, certainly not inappropriately, on various threats to the biosphere and biodiversity. They rarely mention the basic resource/human numbers equation that was the focal point for earlier ecologists. For example, the February 2005 issue of the journal *Frontiers in Ecology and the Environment* was dedicated to 'Visions for an ecologically sustainable future', but the word 'energy' appeared only for personal 'creative energy'—and 'resources' and 'human population' were barely mentioned.

But has the limits-to-growth theory failed? Even before the financial collapse in 2008, recent newspapers were brimming with stories about energy and food price increases, widespread hunger and associated riots in many cities, and various material shortages. Subsequently, the headlines have shifted to the collapse of banking systems, increasing unemployment and inflation, and general economic shrinkage. A number of people blamed at least a substantial part of the current economic chaos on oil price increases earlier in 2008.

Although many continue to dismiss what those researchers in the 1970s wrote, there is growing

Parameter	Predicted	Actual
Population	6.9 billion	6.7 billion
	values vs 1970 levels	
Resources	0.53	
Copper		0.50
Oil		0.50
Soil		0.70
Fish		0.30
Pollution	3.00	
CO^2		2.10
Nitrogen		2.00
Per capita industrial output	1.80	1.90

Figure 23.1 The values predicted by the limits-to-growth model and actual data for 2008 are very close. The model used general terms for resources and pollution, but current, approximate values for several specific examples are given for comparison. Data for this long a time period are difficult to obtain; many pollutants such as sewage probably have increased more than the numbers suggest. On the other hand, pollutants such as sulphur have largely been controlled in many countries.

evidence that the original 'Cassandras' were right on the mark in their general assessments, if not always in the details or exact timing, about the dangers of the continued growth of human population and their increasing levels of consumption in a world approaching very real material constraints. It is time to reconsider those arguments in light of new information, especially about peak oil.

Early Warning Shots

A discussion of the resource/population issue always starts with Thomas Malthus and his 1798 publication *First Essay on Population*:

> I think I may fairly make two postulata. First, that food is necessary to the existence of man. Secondly, that the passion between the sexes is necessary, and will remain nearly in its present state. . . . Assuming then, my postulata as granted, I say, that the power of population is indefinitely greater than the power in the earth to produce subsistence for man. Population, when unchecked, increases in a geometrical ratio. Subsistence increases only in an arithmetical ratio. A slight acquaintance with numbers will shew the immensity of the first power in comparison of the second.

Most people, including ourselves, agree that Malthus's premise has not held between 1800 and the present, as the human population has expanded by about seven times, with concomitant surges in nutrition and general affluence—albeit only recently. Paul Roberts, in *The End of Food*, reports that malnutrition was common throughout the nineteenth century. It was only in the twentieth century that cheap fossil energy allowed agricultural productivity sufficient to avert famine. This argument has been made many times before—that our exponential escalation in energy use, including that used in agriculture, is the principal reason that we have generated a food supply that grows geometrically as the human population has continued to do likewise. Thus since Malthus's time we have avoided wholesale famine for most of the earth's people because fossil fuel use also expanded geometrically.

The first twentieth-century scientists to raise again Malthus's concern about population and resources were the ecologists Garrett Hardin and Paul Ehrlich. Hardin's essays in the 1960s on the impacts of overpopulation included the famous *Tragedy of the Commons*, in which he discusses how individuals tend to overuse common property to their own benefit even while it is disadvantageous to all involved. Hardin wrote other essays on population, coining such phrases as 'freedom to breed brings ruin to all' and 'nobody ever dies of overpopulation', the latter meaning that crowding is rarely a direct source of death, but rather results in disease or starvation, which then kill people. This phrase came up in an essay reflecting on the thousands of people in coastal Bangladesh who were drowned in a typhoon. Hardin argued that these people knew full well that this region would be inundated every few decades but stayed there anyway because they had no other place to live in that very crowded country. This pattern recurred in 1991 and 2006.

Ecologist Paul Ehrlich argued in *The Population Bomb* that continued population growth would wreak havoc on food supplies, human health, and nature, and that Malthusian processes (war, famine, pestilence, and death) would sooner rather than later bring human populations 'under control', down to the carrying capacity of the world. Meanwhile agronomist David Pimentel, ecologist Howard Odum, and environmental scientist John Steinhart quantified the energy dependence of modern agriculture and showed that technological development is almost always associated with increased use of fossil fuels. Other ecologists, including George Woodwell and Kenneth Watt, discussed people's negative impact on ecosystems. Kenneth Boulding, Herman Daly, and a few other economists began to question the very foundations of economics, including its dissociation from the biosphere necessary to support it and, especially, its focus on growth and infinite substitutability—the idea that something

will always come along to replace a scarce resource. These writers were part and parcel of our graduate education in ecology in the late 1960s.

Meanwhile Jay Forrester, the inventor of a successful type of computer random-access memory (RAM), began to develop a series of interdisciplinary analyses and thought processes, which he called system dynamics. In the books and papers he wrote about these models, he put forth the idea of the coming difficulties posed by continuing human population growth in a finite world. The latter soon became known as the limits-to-growth model (or the 'Club of Rome' model, after the organization that commissioned the publication). The models were refined and presented to the world by Forrester's students Donella Meadows and Dennis Meadows and their colleagues. They showed that exponential population growth and resource use, combined with the finite nature of resources and pollution assimilation, would lead to a serious decline in the material quality of life and even in the numbers of human beings.

At the same time, geologist M. King Hubbert predicted in 1956 and again in 1968 that oil production from the coterminous United States would peak in 1970. Although his predictions were dismissed at the time, US oil production in fact peaked in 1970 and natural gas in 1973.

These various perspectives on the limits to growth seemed to be fulfilled in 1973 when, during the first energy crisis, the price of oil increased from $3.50 to more than $12 a barrel. Gasoline increased from less than $0.30 to $0.65 per gallon in a few weeks while available supplies declined, because of a temporary gap of only about 5 per cent between supply and projected demand. Americans became subject for the first time to gasoline lines, large increases in the prices of other energy sources, and double-digit inflation with a simultaneous contraction in total economic activity. Such simultaneous inflation and economic stagnation was something that economists had thought impossible, as the two were supposed to be inversely related. Home heating oil, electricity, food, and coal also became much more expensive. Then it happened again: oil increased to $35 a barrel and gasoline to $1.60 per gallon in 1979.

Some of the economic ills of 1974, such as the highest rates of unemployment since the Great Depression, high interest rates, and rising prices, returned in the early 1980s. Meanwhile, new scientific reports came out about all sorts of environmental problems: acid rain, global warming, pollution, loss of biodiversity, and the depletion of the earth's protective ozone layer. The oil shortages, the gasoline lines, and even some electricity shortages in the 1970s and early 1980s all seemed to give credibility to the point of view that our population and our economy had in many ways exceeded the ability of the earth to support them. For many, it seemed like the world was falling apart, and for those familiar with the limits to growth, it seemed as if the model's predictions were beginning to come true and that it was valid. Academia and the world at large were abuzz with discussions of energy and human population issues.

Our own contributions to this work centred on assessing the energy costs of many aspects of resource and environmental management, including food supply, river management, and, especially, obtaining energy itself. A main focus of our papers was *energy return on investment* (EROI) for obtaining oil and gas within the United States, which declined substantially from the 1930s to the 1970s. It soon became obvious that the EROI for most of the possible alternatives was even lower. Declining EROI meant that more and more energy output would have to be devoted simply to getting the energy needed to run an economy.

The Reversal

All of this interest began to fade, however, as enormous quantities of previously discovered but unused oil and gas from outside the US were developed in response to the higher prices and then flooded into the country. Most mainstream economists, and a lot of other people too, did not like the concept that there might be limits to economic growth, or indeed

human activity more generally, arising from nature's constraints. They felt that their view was validated by this turn of events and new gasoline resources.

Mainstream (or neoclassical) economics is presented mostly from the perspective of 'efficiency'—the concept that unrestricted market forces seek the lowest prices at each juncture, and the net effect should be the lowest possible prices. This would also cause all productive forces to be optimally deployed, at least in theory.

Economists particularly disliked the perspective of the absolute scarcity of resources, and they wrote a series of scathing reports directed at the scientists mentioned above, especially those most closely associated with the limits to growth. Nuclear fusion was cited as a contender for the next source of abundant, cheap energy. They also found no evidence for scarcity, saying that output had been rising between 1.5 and 3 per cent per year. Most importantly, they said that economies had built-in, market-related mechanisms (the invisible hand of Adam Smith) to deal with scarcities. An important empirical study by economists Harold J. Barnett and Chandler Morse in 1963 seemed to show that, when corrected for inflation, the prices of all basic resources (except for forest products) had not increased over nine decades. Thus, although there was little argument that the higher-quality resources were being depleted, it seemed that technical innovations and resource substitutions, driven by market incentives, had and would continue indefinitely to solve the longer-term issues. It was as if the market could increase the quantity of physical resources in the earth.

The new behaviour of the general economy seemed to support their view. By the mid-1980s the price of gasoline had dropped substantially. The enormous new Prudhoe Bay field in Alaska came online and helped mitigate to some degree the decrease in production of oil elsewhere in the US, even as an increasing proportion of the oil used in America was imported. Energy as a topic faded from the media and from the conversations of most people. Unregulated markets were supposed to lead to efficiency, and a decline in energy used per unit of economic output in Japan and the US seemed to provide evidence for that theory. We also shifted the production of electricity away from oil to coal, natural gas, and uranium.

In 1980 one of biology's most persistent and eloquent spokesmen for resource issues, Paul Ehrlich, was 'trapped', in his words, into making a bet about the future price of five minerals by economist Julian Simon, a strong advocate of the power of human ingenuity and the market, and a disbeliever in any limits to growth. The price of all five went down over the next 10 years, so Ehrlich (and two colleagues) lost the bet and had to pay Simon $576. The incident was widely reported through important media outlets, including a disparaging article in the *New York Times Sunday Magazine*. Those who advocated for resource constraints were essentially discredited and even humiliated.

So indeed it looked to many as though the economy had responded with the invisible hand of market forces through price signals and substitutions. The economists felt vindicated, and the resource pessimists beat a retreat, although some effects of the economic stagnation of the 1970s lasted in most of the world until about 1990. (They live on still in places such as Costa Rica as unpaid debt from that period.) By the early 1990s, the world and US economies basically had gone back to the pre-1973 model of growing by at least 2 or 3 per cent a year with relatively low rates of inflation. Inflation-corrected gasoline prices, the most important barometer of energy scarcity for most people, stabilized and even decreased substantially in response to an influx of foreign oil. Discussions of scarcity simply disappeared.

The concept of the market as the ultimate objective decider of value and the optimal means of generating virtually all decisions gained more and more credibility, partly in response to arguments about the subjectivity of decisions made by experts or legislative bodies. Decisions were increasingly turned over to economic cost–benefit analysis where supposedly the democratic collective tastes of all people were reflected in their economic choices.

For those few scientists who still cared about resource scarcity issues, there was not any specific place to apply for grants at the National Science Foundation or even the Department of Energy (except for studies to improve energy efficiency), so most of our best energy analysts worked on these issues on the weekend, after retirement or *pro bono*. With very few exceptions graduate training in energy analysis or limits to growth withered. The concept of limits did live on in various environmental issues such as disappearing rain forests and coral reefs, and global climate change. But these were normally treated as their own specific problems, rather than as a more general issue about the relationship between population and resources.

A Closer Look

For a distinct minority of scientists, there was never any doubt that the economists' debate victory was illusory at best, and generally based on incomplete information. For example, Cutler J. Cleveland, an environmental scientist at Boston University, reanalyzed the Barnett and Morse study in 1991 and found that the only reason that the prices of commodities had not been increasing—even while their highest-quality stocks were being depleted— was that for the time period analyzed in the original study, the real price of energy had been declining because of the exponentially increasing use of oil, gas, and coal, whose real prices were simultaneously declining. Hence, even as more and more energy was needed to win each unit of resources, the price of the resources did not increase because the price of energy was declining.

Likewise, when the oil shock induced a recession in the early 1980s, and Ehrlich and Simon made their bet, the relaxed demand for all resources led to lower prices and even some increase in the quality of the resources mined, as only the highest-grade mines were kept open. But in recent years energy prices increased again, demand for materials in Asia soared, and the prices of most minerals increased dramatically. Had Ehrlich made his bet with Simon over the past decade, he would have made a small fortune, as the price of most raw materials, including the ones they bet on, had increased by 2 to 10 times in response to huge demand from China and declining resource grades.

Another problem is that the economic definition of efficiency has not been consistent. Several researchers, including the authors, have found that energy use—a factor that had not been used in economists' production equations—is far more important than capital, labour, or technology in explaining the increase in industrial production of the US, Japan, and Germany. Recent analysis by Vaclav Smil found that over the past decade the energy efficiency of the Japanese economy had actually decreased by 10 per cent. A number of analyses have shown that most agricultural technology is extremely energy intensive. In other words, when more detailed and systems-oriented analyses are undertaken, the arguments become much more complex and ambiguous, and show that technology rarely works by itself but instead tends to demand high resource use.

Likewise oil production in the US has declined by 50 per cent, as predicted by Hubbert. The market did not solve this issue for US oil because, despite the huge price increases and drilling in the late 1970s and 1980s, there was less oil and gas production then, and there has been essentially no relation between drilling intensity and production rates for US oil and gas since.

There is a common perception, even among knowledgeable environmental scientists, that the limits-to-growth model was a colossal failure, since obviously its predictions of extreme pollution and population decline have not come true. But what is not well known is that the original output, based on the computer technology of the time, had a very misleading feature: there were no dates on the graph between the years 1900 and 2100. If one draws a timeline along the bottom of the graph (see Figure 23.2) for the halfway point of 2000, then the model results are almost exactly on course some 35 years later in 2008 (with a few appropriate assumptions). Of course, how well it will perform in the future

when the model behaviour gets more dynamic is not yet known. Although we do not necessarily advocate that the existing structure of the limits-to-growth model is adequate for the task to which it is put, it is important to recognize that its predictions have not been invalidated and in fact seem quite on target. We are not aware of any model made by economists that is as accurate over such a long time span.

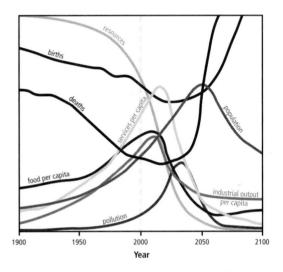

Figure 23.2   The original projections of the limits-to-growth model examined the relation of a growing population to resources and pollution, but did not include a time scale between 1900 and 2100. If a halfway mark of 2000 is added, the projections up to the current time are largely accurate, although the future will tell about the wild oscillations predicted for upcoming years.

Avoiding Malthus

Clearly even the most rabid supporter of resource constraints has to accept that the Malthusian prediction has not come true for the earth as a whole, as human population has increased some seven times since Malthus wrote his article, and in many parts of the world it continues to grow with only sporadic and widely dispersed starvation (although often with considerable malnutrition and poverty). How has this been possible?

The most general answer is that technology, combined with market economics or other social incentive systems, has enormously increased the carrying capacity of the earth for humans. Technology, however, is a two-edged sword, whose benefits can be substantially blunted by *Jevons's paradox*, the concept that increases in efficiency often lead to lower prices and hence to greater consumption of resources.

And technology does not work for free. As originally pointed out in the early 1970s by Odum and Pimentel, increased agricultural yield is achieved principally through the greater use of fossil fuel for cultivation, fertilizers, pesticides, drying, and so on, so that it takes some 10 calories of petroleum to generate each calorie of food that we eat. The fuel used is divided nearly equally between the farm, transport and processing, and preparation. The net effect is that roughly 19 per cent of all of the energy used in the United States goes to our food system. Malthus could not have foreseen this enormous increase in food production through petroleum.

Similarly, fossil fuels were crucial to the growth of many national economies, as happened in the United States and Europe over the past two centuries, and as is happening in China and India today. The expansion of the economies of most developing countries is nearly linearly related to energy use, and when that energy is withdrawn, economies shrink accordingly, as happened with Cuba in 1988. (There has been, however, some serious expansion of the US economy since 1980 without a concomitant expansion of energy use. This is the exception, possibly due to the US's outsourcing of much of its heavy industry, compared to most of the rest of the world.) Thus, most wealth is generated through the use of increasing quantities of oil and other fuels. Effectively each person in the United States and Europe has on average some 30 to 60 or more 'energy slaves', machines to 'hew their wood and haul their water', whose power output is equal to that of many strong people.

Thus a key issue for the future is the degree to which fossil and other fuels will continue to be abundant and cheap. Together oil and natural gas supply nearly two-thirds of the energy used in the world, and coal another 20 per cent. We do not live in an information age, or a post-industrial age, or (yet) a solar age, but a petroleum age. Unfortunately, that will soon end: it appears that oil and gas production has reached, or soon will reach, a maximum (see Figure 23.3). We reached that point for oil in the US in 1970 and have also now reached it in at least 18, and probably the majority, of the 50 most significant oil-producing nations. The important remaining questions about peak oil are not about its existence, but rather, when it occurred for the world as a whole, what the shape of the peak will be and how steep the slope of the curve will be as we go down the other side.

The other big question about oil is not how much is left in the ground (the answer is a lot) but how much can be extracted at a significant energy profit. The EROI of US petroleum declined from roughly

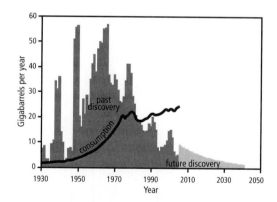

Figure 23.3 The rate at which oil is discovered globally has been dropping for decades, and is projected to drop off even more precipitously in future years. The rate of worldwide consumption, however, is still continuing to rise, as the consumption line shows. Thus, the gap between supply of and demand for oil can be expected to widen.

Data courtesy of the Association for the Study of Oil and Gas.

100:1 in 1930, to 40:1 in 1970, to about 14:1 in 2000 (see Figure 23.4). Even these figures are relatively positive compared to EROI for finding brand-new oil in the US, which, based on the limited information available, appears likely to approach 1:1 within a few decades.

Historically most of the oil supplies in the world were found by exploring new regions for oil. Very large reservoirs were found rather quickly, and most of the world's oil was found by about 1980. According to geologist and peak-oil advocate Colin Campbell, 'The whole world has now been seismically searched and picked over. Geological knowledge has improved enormously in the past 30 years and it is almost inconceivable now that major fields remain to be found.'

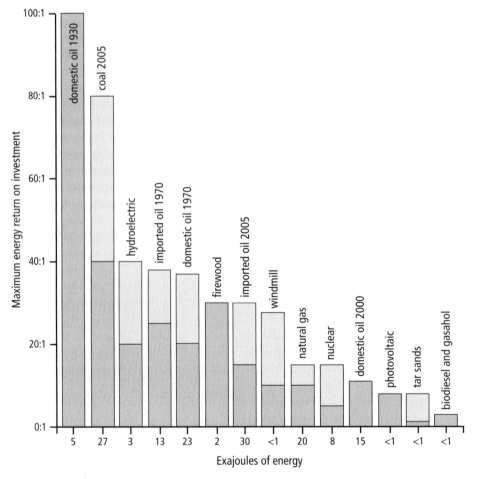

Figure 23.4 The energy return on investment (EROI) is the energy cost of acquiring an energy resource; one of the objectives is to get out far more than you put in. Domestic oil production's EROI has decreased from about 100:1 in 1930, to 40:1 in 1970, to about 14:1 today. The EROI of most 'green' energy sources, such as photovoltaics, is presently low.

Note: Lighter shading represents the range of possible EROI due to varying conditions and uncertain data. EROI does not necessarily correspond to the total amount of energy in exajoules produced by each resource.

Energy Scarcity

The world today faces enormous problems related to population and resources. These ideas were discussed intelligently and, for the most part, accurately in many papers from the middle of the last century, but then they largely disappeared from scientific and public discussion, in part because of an inaccurate understanding of both what those earlier papers said and the validity of many of their predictions. Most environmental science textbooks focus far more on the adverse impacts of fossil fuels than on the implications of our overwhelming economic and even nutritional dependence on them. The failure today to bring the potential reality and implications of peak oil, indeed of peak everything, into scientific discourse and teaching is a grave threat to industrial society.

The concept of the possibility of a huge, multifaceted failure of some substantial part of industrial civilization is so completely outside the understanding of our leaders that we are almost totally unprepared for it. For large environmental and health issues, from smoking to flooding in New Orleans, evidence of negative impacts has historically preceded general public acceptance and policy actions by several decades.

There are virtually no extant forms of transportation, beyond shoe leather and bicycles, that are not based on oil, and even our shoes are now often made of oil. Food production is very energy-intensive, clothes and furniture and most pharmaceuticals are made from and with petroleum, and most jobs would cease to exist without petroleum. But on our university campuses one would be hard pressed to have any sense of that beyond complaints about the increasing price of gasoline, even though a situation similar to the 1970s gas shortages seemed to be unfolding in the summer and fall of 2008 in response to three years of flat oil production, assuaged only when the financial collapse decreased demand for oil.

No substitutes for oil have been developed on anything like the scale required, and most are very poor net energy performers. Despite considerable potential, renewable sources (other than hydropower or traditional wood) currently provide less than 1 per cent of the energy used in both the US and the world, and the annual increase in the use of most fossil fuels is generally much greater than the total production (let alone increase) in electricity from wind turbines and photovoltaics. Our new sources of 'green' energy are simply increasing along with (rather than displacing) all of the traditional ones.

If we are to resolve these issues, including the important one of climate change, in any meaningful way, we need to make them again central to education at all levels of our universities, and to debate and even stand up to those who negate their importance, for we have few great intellectual leaders on these issues today. We must teach economics from a biophysical as well as a social perspective. Only then do we have any chance of understanding or solving these problems.

Bibliography

Barnett, H., & Morse, C. (1963). *Scarcity and growth: The economics of natural resource availability.* Baltimore: Johns Hopkins University Press.

Campbell, C., & Laherrere, J. (1998, March). The end of cheap oil. *Scientific American*, pp. 78–83.

Cleveland, C.J. (1991). Natural resource scarcity and economic growth revisited: Economic and biophysical perspectives. In R. Costanza (Ed.), *Ecological economics: The science and management of sustainability.* New York: Columbia University Press.

Day, J., et al. (2007). Restoration of the Mississippi delta: Lessons from hurricanes Katrina and Rita. *Science*, 315, 1679–84.

Ehrlich, P.R. (1968). *The population bomb.* New York: Ballantine.

Ehrlich, P.R., & Holdren, J.P. (1971). Impact of population growth. *Science*, 171, 1212–17.

Forrester, J.W. (1971). *World dynamics.* Cambridge: Wright-Allen Press.

Hall, C. 2004. The myth of sustainable development: Personal reflections on energy, its relation to neoclassical economics, and Stanley Jevons. *Journal of Energy Resources Technology*, 126, 86–9.

Hall, C.A.S., & Cleveland, C.J. (1981). Petroleum drilling and production in the United States: Yield per effort and net energy analysis. *Science*, 211, 576–9.

Hall, C.A.S., et al. (2001). The need to reintegrate the natural sciences with economics. *BioScience*, 51, 663–73.

Hardin, G. (1968). The tragedy of the commons. *Science*, 162, 1243–48.

Hubbert, M.K. (1969). Energy resources. In the National Academy of Sciences—National Research Council, *Committee on resources and man: A study and recommendations*. San Francisco: W.H. Freeman.

Meadows, D., Meadows, D., & Randers, J. (2004). *Limits to growth: The 30-year update*. White River, VT: Chelsea Green Publishers.

Odum, H.T. (1973). *Environment, power and society*. New York: Wiley Interscience.

Smil, V. (2007, April 2). *Light behind the fall: Japan's electricity consumption, the environment, and economic growth*. Japan Focus.

Tierney, J. (1990, December 2). Betting the planet. *New York Times Magazine*, pp. 79–81.

CHAPTER 24

The Geography of Poverty and Wealth

Jeffrey D. Sachs, Andrew D. Mellinger, and John L. Gallup

Why are some countries stupendously rich and others horrendously poor? Social theorists have been captivated by this question since the late eighteenth century, when Scottish economist Adam Smith addressed the issue in his magisterial work *The Wealth of Nations*. Smith argued that the best prescription for prosperity is a free market economy in which the government allows businesses substantial freedom to pursue profits. Over the past two centuries, Smith's hypothesis has been vindicated by the striking success of capitalist economies in North America, western Europe, and East Asia, and by the dismal failure of socialist planning in eastern Europe and the former Soviet Union.

Smith, however, made a second notable hypothesis: that the physical geography of a region can influence its economic performance. He contended that the economies of coastal regions, with their easy access to sea trade, usually outperform the economies of inland areas. Although most economists today follow Smith in linking prosperity with free markets, they have tended to neglect the role of geography. They implicitly assume that all parts of the world have the same prospects for economic growth and longterm development, and that differences in performance are the result of differences in institutions. Our findings, based on newly available data and research methods, suggest otherwise. We have found strong evidence that geography plays an important role in shaping the distribution of world income and economic growth.

Coastal regions and those near navigable waterways are indeed far richer and more densely settled than interior regions, just as Smith predicted. Moreover, an area's climate can also affect its economic development. Nations in tropical climate zones generally face higher rates of infectious disease and lower agricultural productivity (especially for staple foods) than do nations in temperate zones. Similar burdens apply to the desert zones. The very poorest regions in the world are those saddled with both handicaps: distance from sea trade and a tropical or desert ecology.

A skeptical reader with a basic understanding of geography might comment at this point, 'Fine, but isn't all of this familiar?' We have three responses. First, we go far beyond the basics by systematically quantifying the contributions of geography, economic policy, and other factors in determining a nation's performance. We have combined the research tools used by geographers—including new software that can create detailed maps of global population density—with the techniques and equations of macroeconomics. Second, the basic lessons of geography are worth repeating, because most economists have ignored them. In the past decade the vast majority of papers on economic development have neglected even the most obvious geographical realities. Third, if our findings are true, the policy implications are significant. Aid programs for developing countries will have to be revamped to specifically address the problems imposed by geography. In particular, we have tried to formulate new strategies that would help nations in tropical zones raise their agricultural productivity and reduce the prevalence of diseases such as malaria.

The Geographical Divide

The best single indicator of prosperity is gross national product (GNP) per capita—the total value of a country's economic output, divided by its population. A map showing the world distribution of GNP per capita immediately reveals the vast gap between rich and poor nations (see Figure 24.1). Notice that the great majority of the poorest countries lie in the geographical tropics—the area between the tropic of Cancer and the tropic of Capricorn. In contrast, most of the richest countries lie in the temperate zones.

A more precise picture of this geographical divide can be obtained by defining tropical regions by climate rather than by latitude. Map 24.2 divides the world into five broad climate zones based on a classification scheme developed by German climatologists Wladimir P. Köppen and Rudolph Geiger. The five zones are tropical-subtropical (hereafter referred to as tropical), desert-steppe (desert), temperate-snow (temperate), highland, and polar. The zones are defined by measurements of temperature and precipitation. We excluded the polar zone from our analysis because it is largely uninhabited.

Among the 28 economies categorized as high-income by the World Bank (with populations of at least 1 million), only Hong Kong, Singapore, and part of Taiwan are in the tropical zone, representing a mere 2 per cent of the combined population of the high-income regions. Almost all the temperate zone countries have either high-income economies (as in the cases of North America, western Europe, Korea, and Japan) or middle-income economies burdened by socialist policies in the past (as in the cases of eastern Europe, the former Soviet Union, and China). In addition, there is a strong temperate–tropical divide within countries that straddle both types of climates. Most of Brazil, for example,

lies within the tropical zone, but the richest part of the nation—the southernmost states—is in the temperate zone.

The importance of access to sea trade is also evident in a world map of GNP per capita. Regions far from the sea, such as the landlocked countries of South America, Africa, and Asia, tend to be considerably poorer than their coastal counterparts. The differences between coastal and interior areas show up even more strongly in a world map delineating GNP density—that is, the amount of economic output per square kilometre. We produced such a map based on a detailed survey of global population densities in 1994. Geographic information system software was used to divide the world's land area into five-minute-by-five-minute sections (about 100 square kilometres at the equator). One can estimate the GNP density for each section by multiplying its population density and its GNP per capita. Researchers must use national averages of GNP per capita when regional estimates are not available.

To make sense of the data, we have classified the world's regions in broad categories defined by climate and proximity to the sea. We call a region 'near' if it lies within 100 kilometres of a seacoast or a sea-navigable waterway (a river, lake, or canal in which oceangoing vessels can operate) and 'far' otherwise. Regions in each of the four climate zones we analyzed can be either near or far, resulting in a total of eight categories. Table 24.1 shows how the world's population, income, and land area are divided among these regions.

The breakdown reveals some striking patterns. Global production is highly concentrated in the coastal regions of temperate climate zones. Regions in the 'temperate-near' category constitute a mere 8.4 per cent of the world's inhabited land area, but they hold 22.8 per cent of the world's population and produce 52.9 per cent of the world's GNP. Per capita income in these regions is 2.3 times greater than the global average, and population density is 2.7 times greater. In contrast, the 'tropical-far' category is the poorest, with a per capita GNP only about one-third of the world average.

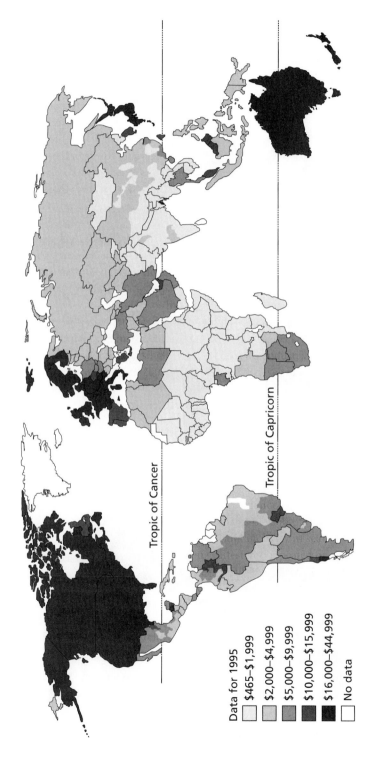

Figure 24.1 GNP per capita. Wealth and climate are inextricably linked. By comparing world maps showing GNP per capita (Figure 24.1) and climate zones (Figure 24.2), one notices that temperate zone countries are generally much more prosperous than tropical zone nations. And in each climate zone, the regions near seacoasts and waterways are richer than the hinterlands (see Table 24.1).

Data for 1995
$465–$1,999
$2,000–$4,999
$5,000–$9,999
$10,000–$15,999
$16,000–$44,999
No data

Tropic of Cancer

Tropic of Capricorn

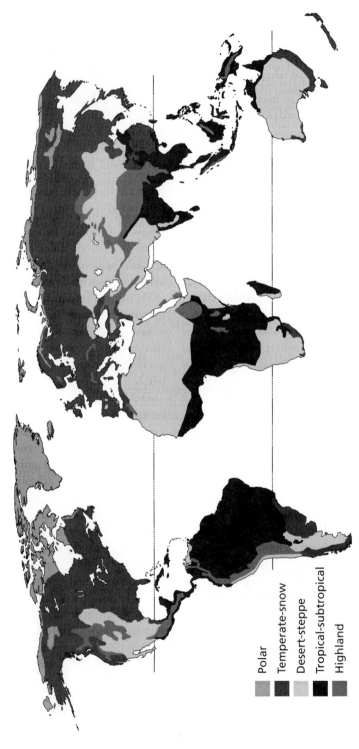

Figure 24.2   Climate zones

Polar
Temperate-snow
Desert-steppe
Tropical-subtropical
Highland

Table 24.1 The wealth of regions

	Climate zone (percentage of world total)	Near (%)	Far (%)
Tropical			
Land area	19.9	5.5	14.4
Population	40.3	21.8	18.5
GNP	17.4	10.5	6.9
Desert			
Land area	29.6	3.0	26.6
Population	18.0	4.4	13.6
GNP	10.1	3.2	6.8
Highland			
Land area	7.3	0.4	6.9
Population	6.8	0.9	5.9
GNP	5.3	0.9	4.4
Temperate			
Land area	39.2	8.4	30.9
Population	34.9	22.8	12.1
GNP	67.2	52.9	14.3

Note: 'Near' means within 100 kilometres of the seacoast or any sea-navigable waterway; 'far' means otherwise.

Interpreting the Patterns

In our research we have examined three major ways in which geography affects economic development. First, as Adam Smith noted, economies differ in their ease of transporting goods, people, and ideas. Because sea trade is less costly than land- or air-based trade, economies near coastlines have a great advantage over hinterland economies. The per-kilometre costs of overland trade within Africa, for example, are often an order of magnitude greater than the costs of sea trade to an African port. Here are some figures we found recently: the cost of shipping a six-metre-long container from Rotterdam, the Netherlands, to Dar-es-Salaam, Tanzania—an air distance of 7,300 kilometres—was about $1,400.

But transporting the same container overland from Dar-es-Salaam to Kigali, Rwanda—a distance of 1,280 kilometres by road—cost about $2,500, or nearly twice as much.

Second, geography affects the prevalence of disease. Many kinds of infectious diseases are endemic to the tropical and subtropical zones. This tends to be true of diseases in which the pathogen spends part of its life cycle outside the human host: for instance, malaria (carried by mosquitoes) and helminthic infections (caused by parasitic worms). Although epidemics of malaria have occurred sporadically as far north as Boston in the past century, the disease has never gained a lasting foothold in the temperate zones, because the cold winters naturally control the mosquito-based transmission of the disease. (Winter could be considered the world's most effective public health intervention.) It is much more difficult to control malaria in tropical regions, where transmission takes place year-round and affects a large part of the population.

According to the World Health Organization, 300 million to 500 million new cases of malaria occur every year, almost entirely concentrated in the tropics. The disease is so common in these areas that no one really knows how many people it kills annually—at least 1 million and perhaps as many as 2.3 million. Widespread illness and early deaths obviously hold back a nation's economic performance by significantly reducing worker productivity. But there are also longterm effects that may be amplified over time through various social feedbacks.

For example, a high incidence of disease can alter the age structure of a country's population. Societies with high levels of child mortality tend to have high levels of fertility: mothers bear many children to guarantee that at least some will survive to adulthood. Young children will therefore constitute a large proportion of that country's population. With so many children, poor families cannot invest much in each child's education. High fertility also constrains the role of women in society, because childrearing takes up so much of their adult lives.

Third, geography affects agricultural productivity. Of the major food grains—wheat, maize, and rice—wheat grows only in temperate climates, and maize and rice crops are generally more productive in temperate and subtropical climates than in tropical zones. On average, a hectare of land in the tropics yields 2.3 metric tons of maize, whereas a hectare in the temperate zone yields 6.4 metric tons. Farming in tropical rain forest environments is hampered by the fragility of the soil: high temperatures mineralize the organic materials, and the intense rainfall leaches them out of the soil. In tropical environments that have wet and dry seasons—such as the African savannah—farmers must contend with the rapid loss of soil moisture resulting from high temperatures, the great variability of precipitation, and the ever-present risk of drought.

Moreover, tropical environments are plagued with diverse infestations of pests and parasites that can devastate both crops and livestock.

Many of the efforts to improve food output in tropical regions—attempted first by the colonial powers and then in recent decades by donor agencies—have ended in failure. Typically the agricultural experts blithely tried to transfer temperate zone farming practices to the tropics, only to watch livestock and crops succumb to pests, disease, and climate barriers. What makes the problem even more complex is that food productivity in tropical regions is also influenced by geologic and topographic conditions that vary greatly from place to place. The island of Java, for example, can support highly productive farms because the volcanic soil there suffers less nutrient depletion than the non-volcanic soil of the neighbouring islands of Indonesia.

Moderate advantages or disadvantages in geography can lead to big differences in longterm economic performance. For example, favourable agricultural or health conditions may boost per capita income in temperate zone nations and hence increase the size of their economies. This growth encourages inventors in those nations to create products and services to sell into the larger and richer markets. The resulting inventions further raise economic output, spurring yet more inventive activity. The moderate geographical advantage is thus amplified through innovation.

In contrast, the low food output per farm worker in tropical regions tends to diminish the size of cities, which depend on the agricultural hinterland for their sustenance. With a smaller proportion of the population in urban areas, the rate of technological advance is usually slower. The tropical regions therefore remain more rural than the temperate regions, with most of their economic activity concentrated in low-technology agriculture rather than in high-technology manufacturing and services.

We must stress, however, that geographical factors are only part of the story. Social and economic institutions are critical to longterm economic performance. It is particularly instructive to compare the post–World War II performance of free-market and socialist economies in neighbouring countries that share the same geographical characteristics: North and South Korea, East and West Germany, the Czech Republic and Austria, and Estonia and Finland. In each case we find that free-market institutions vastly outperformed socialist ones.

The main implication of our findings is that policy makers should pay more attention to the developmental barriers associated with geography—specifically, poor health, low agricultural productivity, and high transportation costs. For example, tropical economies should strive to diversify production into manufacturing and service sectors that are not hindered by climate conditions. The successful countries of tropical Southeast Asia, most notably Malaysia, have achieved stunning advances in the past 30 years, in part by addressing public health problems and in part by moving their economies away from climate-dependent commodity exports (rubber, palm oil, and so on) to electronics, semiconductors, and other industrial sectors. They were helped by the high concentration of their populations in coastal areas near international sea lanes and by the relatively tractable conditions for the control of malaria and other tropical diseases. Sub-Saharan Africa is not so fortunate: most of its population is located far from the coasts, and its ecological conditions are harsher on human health and agriculture.

The World Bank and the International Monetary Fund, the two international agencies that are most influential in advising developing countries, currently place more emphasis on institutional reforms—for instance, overhauling a nation's civil service or its tax administration—than on the technologies needed to fight tropical diseases and low agricultural productivity. One formidable obstacle is that pharmaceutical companies have no market incentive to address the health problems of the world's poor. Therefore, wealthier nations should adopt policies to increase the companies' motivation to work on vaccines for tropical diseases. In one of our own initiatives, we called on the governments of wealthy nations to foster greater research and development by pledging to buy vaccines for malaria, HIV/AIDS, and tuberculosis from the pharmaceutical companies at a reasonable price. Similarly, biotechnology and agricultural research companies need more incentive to study how to improve farm output in tropical regions.

The poorest countries in the world surely lack the resources to relieve their geographical burdens on their own. Sub-Saharan African countries have per capita income levels of around $1 a day. Even when such countries invest as much as 3 or 4 per cent of their GNP in public health—a large proportion of national income for a very poor country—the result is only about $10 to $15 per year per person. This is certainly not enough to control endemic malaria, much less to fight other rampant diseases such as HIV/AIDS, tuberculosis, and helminthic infections.

A serious effort at global development will require not just better economic policies in the poor countries but far more financial support from the rich countries to help overcome the special problems imposed by geography. A preliminary estimate suggests that even a modest increase in donor financing of about $25 billion per year—only 0.1 per cent of the total GNP of the wealthy nations, or about $28 per person—could make a tremendous difference in reducing disease and increasing food productivity in the world's poorest countries.

Questions for Critical Thought

1. Can population growth be viewed as both a positive and a negative factor in human wellbeing?

2. How well does the Malthusian model explain the contemporary population situation of developed countries? Is the Malthusian model at all applicable in this part of the world?

3. How useful is the Marxist perspective in explaining the social, economic, and demographic conditions of contemporary Third World countries?

Websites of Interest

Action Bioscience is a non-commercial, educational website created to promote bioscience literacy by examining a host of issues related to ecology and resources: www.actionbioscience.org/

The *Organization for Economic Co-operation and Development* (OECD) publishes reports on matters pertaining to the intersections of population with environment and resources. Some of their publications are available via their homepage: www.oecd.org/home/

The *Worldwatch Institute* publishes a number of reports on global environmental issues, including its annual report on the 'state of the world'; details are available via their website: http://www.worldwatch.org/

The National Oceanic and Atmospheric Administration's National Climatic Data Center publishes annual reports on the *State of the Climate* for the Bulletin of the American Meteorological Society; the reports are available from the NOAA website: www.ncdc.noaa.gov/bams-state-of-the-climate/

Suggested Reading

Bailey, Ronald. (2002). *Global warming and other eco-myths: How the environmental movement uses false science to scare us to death*. Roseville, CA: Prima Publishing/Forum.

Brown, Lester, Gardner, Gary, & Halweil, Biran. (1999). Beyond Malthus: Nineteen dimensions of the population challenge. New York: Norton.

Bryant, Leo, Carver, Louise, Butler, Colin, & Anage, Ababu. (2009). Climate change and family planning: Least-developed countries define the agenda. *Bulletin of the World Health Organization, 87*(11), 852–7.

Climate change. Warming world. A clearer picture of global warming since the 1850s. (2010, July 29). *The Economist*.

Cohen, Joel. (1997). Population, economics, environment and culture: an introduction to human carrying capacity. *Journal of Applied Ecology, 34*, 1325–33.

Costello, Anthony, Abbas, Mustafa, Allen, Adriana, et al. (2009, May 16). Managing the health effects of climate change. *The Lancet, 373*, 1693–1733.

De Sherbinin, Alex, Schiller, Andrew, & Pulsipher, Alex. (2007). The vulnerability of cities to climate hazards. *Environment and Urbanization, 19*(1), 39–64.

Homer-Dixon, Thomas F., Boutwell, J.H., & Rathjens, G.W. (1993, February). Environmental change and violent conflict. *Scientific American, 268*(2), 38–45.

Kahn, Matt. (2010). Climatopolis: *How our cities will thrive in the hotter future*. New York: Basic Books.

Leridon, Henri. (2008). Human populations and climate: Lessons from the past and future scenarios. Comptes Rendus Geoscience, *340*, 663–9.

Linner, Bjorn-Ola. (2003). *The return of Malthus: Environmentalism and post-war population-resources crises*. Strond, Isle of Harris, UK: The White Horse Press.

Lomborg, Bjorn. (2001). *The skeptical environmentalist.* Cambridge: Cambridge University Press.

McKee, Jeffrey K. (2002). *Sparing nature: The conflict between human population growth and Earth's biodiversity.* New Brunswick, NJ: Rutgers University Press.

Meadows, Donella H. (1993). Seeing the population issue whole. In Laurie Ann Mazur (Ed.), *Beyond the numbers: A reader on population, consumption, and the environment,* pp. 23–32. Washington, DC: Island Press.

Meadows, Donella H., Meadows, Dennis L., & Randers, Jorgen. (1992). *Beyond the limits: Confronting global collapse, envisioning a sustainable future* (2nd edn). Post Mills, VT: Chelsea Green Publishing.

Pearce, Fred. (2010). The coming population crash: And our planet's surprising future. Boston: Beacon Press.

Pebley, Ann R. (1998). Demography and the environment. *Demography, 35*(4): 377–89.

Pimentel, David, & Pimentel, Marcia. (2006). Global environmental resources versus world population growth. *Ecological Economics, 59,* 195–8.

Rockstrom, Johan, et al. (2009). Feature: A safe operating space for humanity. *Nature, 461*(24), 472–5.

Rogers, Peter. (2008, August). Facing the freshwater crisis. *Scientific American,* pp. 46–53.

Sachs, Geoffrey. (2008). *Common wealth.* New York: The Penguin Press.

Satterthwaite, David, McGanahan, Gordon, & Tacoli, Cecilia. (2010). Urbanization and its implications for food and farming. *Philosophical Transactions of the Royal Society B, 365,* pp. 2809–20.

Schellnhuber, Hans Joachim, Molina, Mario, Stern, Nicholas, Huber, Veronika, & Kadner, Susanne (Eds).

(2010). *Global sustainability: A Nobel cause.* Cambridge: Cambridge University Press.

Simon, Julian (Ed.). (1998). *The economics of population: Classic writings.* New Brunswick, NJ: Transaction Publishers.

Slack, Paul (Ed.). (1999). *Environments and historical change.* Oxford: Oxford University Press.

Smil, Vaclav. (2008). *Global catastrophes and trends: The next fifty years.* Cambridge, MA: The MIT Press.

Spidel, Joseph J., Weiss, Deborah C., Ethelston, Sally A., & Gilbert, S.M. (2009). Population policies, programmes and the environment. *Philosophical Transactions of the Royal Society B, 364,* 3049–65.

Raleigh, Clionadh, & Urdal, Henrik. (2007). Climate change, environmental degradation and armed conflict. *Political Geography, 26,* 674–94.

Vorosmarty, C.J., McIntyre, P.B., Gessner, M.O., Dudgeon, D., Prusevich, A., et al. (2010, September 30). Global threats to human water security and river biodiversity. *Nature, 467,* 555–61.

Wackernagel, Mathis, & Rees, William. (1996). *Our ecological footprint: Reducing human impact on the earth.* Gabriola Island, BC: New Society Publishers.

Weart, Spencer R. (2003). *The discovery of global warming.* Cambridge, MA: Harvard University Press.

Zhang, David D., Brecke, Peter, Lee, Harry F., He, Yuan-Qing, & Zhang, Jane. (2007). Global climate change, war, and population decline in recent human history. *Proceedings of the National Academies of Science, 104*(49), 19214–19.

SECTION X
Population Change and Policy Concerns

Learning Objectives

By the end of this section, students should understand and be able to discuss the following:

- population policy options for countries that are growing too fast and those with very low population growth rates
- the concept of 'demographic divide' and the Millennium Development Goals
- the effectiveness of policies intended to increase fertility in low-fertility countries
- the state of family planning programs in poor countries and the 'unmet need' for family planning in such countries.

Introduction

Population policy may be defined as an objective plan formulated by government to reduce, increase, or stabilize population growth rates over some specified period of time. Usually, the aim of population policy is to affect quantitative change in order to reduce or increase the rate of population growth through change in fertility, mortality, or migration. Policies intended to influence change in one of these variables directly can be thought of as *direct population policies*. An example of a direct policy approach is the implementation of family planning programs aimed at reducing fertility rates in developing countries. Programs intended to affect non-demographic variables in order to impact any of these three demographic variables indirectly would be examples of *indirect policies*. For example, programs to improve health, such as immunization and anti-malaria campaigns in poor countries, have been shown to lower mortality among infants and children and to bring about fertility declines because as child survival probabilities improve, parents eventually begin to desire smaller families. Likewise, policies applied to improve the status of women in less developed countries would be expected to achieve similar effects on fertility rates: as the status of women is raised women gain greater autonomy over their personal lives; this then translates into delayed marriage, later timing of childbearing, and consequently lower birth rates.

In liberal democracies, population policies must be developed around the principle of voluntary participation. Thus, governments often create incentives to encourage citizens to participate in demographic change. Baby bonuses and extended maternity leave are examples of incentives that may be offered as means to stimulate fertility increases. By contrast, non-democratic states have much greater leeway in the kinds of polices they are able to apply, since they are not bound by such democratic principles as guaranteeing freedom of choice to the individual. Indeed, history provides us many examples of authoritarian regimes imposing draconian

policies on their people in order to control population. One is the 1966 anti-abortion decree in Romania, where the communist regime headed by Nicolae Ceausescu suddenly banned abortion on demand, allowing pregnancies to be terminated only under very limited circumstances (e.g. the pregnancy would risk the life of the mother). The abrupt turn in Romania's abortion law had immediate and far-reaching effects on the country, and the implications of it are still being felt today. In the year following the anti-abortion decree there was a dramatic rise in the birth rate. Many of the births were unwanted, and countless infants were abandoned in orphanages. Romania has had to confront a series of related issues arising from the unanticipated baby boom, beginning with the need to provide adequate schooling for a large cohort of children, and then, as the cohort passed through its life stages, the need to ensure sufficient productive work for a large influx of entry-level workers. As this cohort reaches old age, there will be other kinds of societal adjustments to be made, particularly in the areas of public pensions and healthcare (Berelson, 1979).

Like the Romanian anti-abortion law, China's one-child policy exemplifies elements of a coercive system. Although in recent years the Chinese government has relaxed some of its stringent rules governing this policy, there is little doubt that the program continues to be enforced largely through penalties and elements of coercion (Attané, 2002; Greenhalgh, 1986; Winckler, 2002). Clearly, both the Chinese one-child policy and the Romanian anti-abortion decree would be inconceivable in a liberal democracy.

Demographic Divide

As we enter the second decade of the new millennium, rapid population growth may seem less of a concern than it was during the latter half of the twentieth century. This perception could not be further from the truth. Owing to their different demographic histories, the world's developed and developing countries are separated by a vast demographic divide, most visible in the disparate fortunes of the poorest and the most developed nations. Developing countries have relatively high birth and death rates and low life expectancies, with population growth rates above the world average. At the other end of the spectrum, the wealthy countries maintain their patterns of sub-replacement fertility, high life expectancy, increasing levels of demographic aging, and growth rates well below the global average. A related concern is the growing disparity in standards of living, health conditions, and socioeconomic wellbeing of the two sets of countries (Kent & Haub, 2005; Suttcliffe, 2001; Therborn, 2006).

The Millennium Development Goals

In 2000, the United Nations initiated the Millennium Development Goals (MDGs), a multiyear program to help poor countries improve their standards of living and advance their social and economic development (Sachs & McArthur, 2005). The MDGs were established to provide tangible benchmarks for measuring progress in eight areas, with a target date of 2015 for most of them. The goals are as follows:

1. Eradicate extreme hunger and poverty by halving the proportion of people living on less than a dollar a day and halving rates of malnutrition.
2. Achieve universal primary education by ensuring that all children are enrolled in and are able to complete a full course of primary schooling.
3. Promote gender equality and empower women by eliminating gender disparity in primary and secondary schooling, preferably by 2005 and no later than 2015.
4. Reduce child mortality by cutting the death rate of children under five by two-thirds.
5. Improve maternal health by reducing the maternal mortality rate by three-quarters.
6. Combat HIV/AIDS, malaria, and other diseases by halting and reversing their spread.

7. Ensure environmental stability by halving the proportion of people without sustainable access to safe drinking water and sanitation.
8. Develop a global partnership for development by reforming aid and trade with special treatment for the poorest countries.

The year 2007 was the midway point between the adoption of the MDGs and the 2015 deadline for achieving them. The UN's *Millennium Development Goals Report 2007* announced that progress toward meeting the goals has been mixed. There have been some gains, but many more are needed to achieve the MDG targets by 2015. On the positive side, the world as a whole has made progress in reducing poverty from its 1990 levels. Almost 32 per cent of people in the developing world lived on less than one US dollar per day in 1990; by 2004, that figure had dropped to 19.2 per cent, and it is expected to fall below 16 per cent by 2015. Part of the decline in poverty (as measured by the 'one dollar a day' standard) can be attributed to growing economic prosperity in China and India, the two most populous countries in the world. Extreme poverty has also been falling in sub-Saharan Africa, a region that has been experiencing some success in economic growth and in the advancement of education for children.

The rate of extreme poverty in Africa has fallen from approximately 46 per cent in 1999 to 41 per cent in 2004. However, this pace of poverty reduction is considered slow and is insufficient to meet the 2015 goal of a 22 per cent poverty level. Unfortunately, there are other problems plaguing the region, most notably hunger and malnutrition: the proportion of children under five who are underweight has declined only marginally, from 33 per cent in 1990 to 29 per cent in 2005. Rapid population growth has exacerbated these problems, meaning that, among other things, although more children in Africa are attending school today, there are still many who do not, and this situation is only likely to grow worse in the future. In 1990 there were 237 million Africans under the age of 14; today, the figure is 348 million. By 2015, this number is expected to reach 400 million.

Governments in Africa will find it increasingly difficult to provide for such a large population of children.

Policy Responses in Low-Fertility Settings

Unlike many contemporary developing countries, where the predominant policy issue is the reduction of population growth rates, today's advanced societies have reached a state of demographic maturity and find themselves progressing—inexorably, though at varying rates—towards a state of demographic stagnation. In *The Fear of Population Decline*, Teitelbaum and Winter (1985) called the prospect of sustained population decline a new concept in the histories of societies. So how are these advanced societies responding to their demographic situation? What kinds of policies are possible to counteract the looming prospect of demographic stagnation and decline?

As noted earlier, liberal democracies aiming to boost fertility rates are limited to incentive-based programs, such as family-friendly policies and baby bonuses. However, as Anne Gauthier explains in her chapter of this volume, these kinds of policy approaches in highly developed countries are not only costly to taxpayers but also of limited success. Gauthier found that while many of the studies she reviewed indicate that family policies have a small positive effect on fertility, many other studies produced only weak statistical evidence or none at all. Furthermore, where studies revealed a positive relationship between policy approaches and fertility, the effect of the policy was mainly to promote a shift in the timing of childbearing (i.e. to reduce the interval between children) and not to increase completed family size over women's reproductive years. There are at least three possible reasons for the limited efficacy of policy incentives designed to increase fertility. First, democracies are based on the principle of freedom for the individual, making it impossible for governments to interfere in the private matters of their citizens, particularly in the areas of sexuality and reproduction. Second, truly effective monetary incentives (i.e. large baby bonuses) would be economically prohibitive for governments and taxpayers. Third, in highly advanced societies, the small family norm is pervasive and too deeply entrenched to be destabilized by incentive-based pronatalist policies (Alwin, 1996; McIntosh, 1986).

So what can governments of liberal democracies do to stimulate fertility? Research has shown that those countries with the highest fertility rates (albeit below replacement levels) are countries in which women are most fully empowered (Chesnais, 1996; Pinelli, 1995). As Peter McDonald (2000) has argued, women living in these countries enjoy equality in both the family institution and the workplace. Thus, liberal democracies, to the extent that they are able to ensure these conditions, may achieve higher levels of fertility.

Controlled immigration is another policy option capable of boosting population growth rates in low-fertility populations. Through immigration, governments can control population growth while at the same time dealing with emerging labour force exigencies. But as Stephen Castles (2007) argues in a perceptive essay, this option poses its own set of challenges. Among other things, raising immigration targets might invite negative social responses from a resident population concerned about changing economic opportunities, especially in times of recession. Governments of receiving countries must find ways to integrate newcomers effectively into the new society. Yet the historical experiences of many highly developed receiving nations show that immigration can transform the receiving population from a culturally homogeneous society to a multicultural/multiracial one. Australia and Canada are perfect illustrations of this. At one time these nations were predominantly Anglo-Saxon (and French, in the case of Canada); today, they are two of the most ethnically diverse populations in the world. Of course, history also shows that some societies cope better with the challenges associated with immigration than others do. Nations that have been built on immigration and whose national identities are grounded in that historical context are much more likely to accommodate immigrants than countries that have, throughout history, viewed themselves as ethnically and culturally distinct.

Castles (2007) acknowledges that international migration is an extremely complex phenomenon that is difficult for liberal democracies to manage effectively through their immigration policies. There are many instances in which such policies have failed to achieve their stated goals or—even worse—have had consequences radically opposite to what the policies were intended to achieve. For an immigration policy to be effective, writes Castles, governments must first come to understand that international migration is a complex multidimensional process involving social, economic, and political factors, all acting together, and that these interrelated processes are often very difficult to manage. Liberal democratic states cannot assume that immigration allowed on a temporary basis (e.g. to supplement the labour force) will remain temporary. The case of West Germany following the Second World War is one such example. The West German government enacted a policy to admit immigrant workers on a temporary basis to help the country rebuild its post-war economy; however, many of the immigrants settled permanently, forming entrenched ethnic communities of their own and changing the cultural makeup of the country.

Many forces associated with liberal democracies make immigration a self-sustaining process, regardless of policy changes intended to discourage further immigration. Castles (2007) cites the phenomenon known as *chain migration*, in which an initial cohort of immigrants facilitates the arrival of new migrants from their country of origin, thus helping to establish a transplanted community in the new society. Once started, this process is virtually irreversible. The migrants are typically young people in the prime working ages. Eventually they will marry in the new country and then have children. These developments make it virtually impossible for a policy of temporary migration to be enforced. Strengthening the case for permanent settlement is the fact that in liberal democracies, all people, including immigrants, have rights, including the right of citizenship for the children of immigrants born in the new country (Koser, 2007).

How, then, can liberal democracies learn from past policy failures regarding immigration? Castles (2007) discusses a number of guiding principles that governments should bear in mind:

- Migration is a social process, with dynamics that occasionally put it at odds with the goals of immigration policy (e.g. immigrants have agency; immigration is self-sustaining; there are structural dependencies between sending and receiving countries that reinforce immigration).
- Migration is an integral part of North–South relations in a globalizing world. Rich countries share an increasing need for labour, and poor countries have an increasing supply of labour owing to high rates of population growth. Therefore, immigration serves two important functions in the global economy: it relieves population pressure in poor countries and is a source of labour for rich countries.
- Within states there are competing interests (e.g. big business *vs* government) at play in the formulation of immigration policy; this can lead to inconsistent or even contradictory policies that may produce unforeseen outcomes.
- States may enact policies to conceal unpopular or undeclared immigration objectives. For example, a government might impose restrictive policies aimed at controlling the inflows of undocumented workers while quietly allowing practices that permit such workers to enter. At the same time, the state will argue that illegal immigration is beyond its control. Consequently, the state gains favour both with business interests at home, who exploit the immigrant workers, and with the sending countries.
- Non-migration policies are often more powerful in shaping migration than are migration policies themselves; for example, in the long term, trade relationships between countries of the North and South can reduce South–North migrations

more effectively than explicit immigration policies can.

Policy Responses in High-Fertility Settings

The Chinese family-planning program—the one-child policy—is one of the most talked about examples of a successful antinatalist policy. Viewed strictly in terms of its demographic objectives, there is little doubt it has been successful. Rates of population growth in China have slowed considerably since the inception of the law in the late 1970s. As of 2010, China's population is almost 1.34 billion, projected to reach approximately 1.48 billion by 2025, and to decline thereafter to about 1.44 billion by the year 2050 (Population Reference Bureau, 2010). This expected decline in population growth can be attributed directly to the longterm consequences of the one-child policy. However, demographic success may not equal success in the broader social sense. One far-reaching implication (among many) is that a large number of Chinese family lineages may eventually become extinct, since couples having a girl as the sole progeny will fail to ensure extension of the family name to the next generation. In a society that places considerable importance on family and lineage, this situation could create widespread resentment. Some critics believe that this situation is largely responsible for a rise in sex-selective abortions in China since the institution of the one-child policy (Coale & Bannister, 1994; Potts, 2006; Zhu, Lu and Hesketh, 2009).

It is interesting to note that according to some calculations, the Chinese government could perhaps have avoided these kinds of social problems had they followed a different, yet equally effective, policy approach to achieve the desired demographic goals. Greenhalgh and Bongaarts (1987) estimated that the demographic objectives of the Chinese government could have been attained through less coercive policies involving start, spacing, and stop rules for childbearing. For example, a policy that allowed women to bear two children, the first at age 25, the second following a minimum five-year interval, would produce the same longterm target population as projected under the present one-child policy.

In many other settings in the developing world, voluntary family planning programs have been in place for quite some time. The empirical evidence accumulated over the last four or five decades indicates that these countries have had varying degrees of success in lowering their fertility rates (Bongaarts & Sinding, 2009; Lapham & Mauldin, 1972, 1984; Locoh & Vandermeersch, 2006; Mauldin & Ross, 1991; Ross & Mauldin, 1996; Tsui, 2001). Just as important is the fact that, as Sinding (2009, p. 3030) notes, those countries that have had success with family planning programs have also 'achieved high and sustained rates of economic growth and . . . significant reductions in poverty'.

Yet despite decades of documented success in introducing family planning programs, many women in developing countries still bear more children than they desire (Dodoo & Frost, 2008; Westoff & Bankole, 1998), and as Ndola Prata argues in her assessment of the situation (in this volume), there remains a large unmet need for effective family planning services in these low-resource settings. The situation is most severe in the poorest nations of sub-Saharan Africa, where, unless women gain better control over their fertility, rates of population growth will remain high and will, over the long term, exacerbate existing economic, environmental, and health crises. Moreover, as Prata notes, it is in these resource-poor areas where maternal and child mortality is the highest. Greater access to family planning in such settings is essential not just to lowering high rates of population growth but to reducing rates of premature death among mothers and their children.

Regrettably, effective contraceptives are either too expensive or simply unavailable to those who need them most. In order to increase access to family planning in resource-poor areas, Prata proposes four critical steps for governments to take: (1) increase knowledge about the safety of family planning methods; (2) ensure contraception is genuinely affordable to the poorest families; (3) ensure that there is an adequate supply of contraceptives by making family planning a permanent line item in government budgets for healthcare; and (4) take immediate action to remove barriers hindering access to family planning.

Works Cited

All Party Parliamentary Group on Population Development and Reproductive Health. (2007). *Return of the population growth factor: Its impact on the Millennium Development Goals.* London: HMSO.

Alwin, Dwayne F. (1996). From childbearing to childrearing: The link between declines in fertility and changes in the socialization of children'. In John B. Casterline, Ronald D. Lee, & Karen A. Foote (Eds), *Fertility in the United States: New patterns, New theories* (pp. 176–96). Supplement to *Population and Development Review, 22.*

Attané, Isabelle. (2002). China's family planning policy: An overview of its past and future. *Studies in Family Planning, 33*(1). In John C. Caldwell, James F. Phillips, & Barkat-e-Khuda (Eds), *Family planning programs in the twenty-first century* (special issue).

Berelson, Bernard. (1979). Romania's 1966 abortion decree: The demographic experience of the first decade. *Population Studies, 33*(2), 205–22.

Bongaarts, John, & Sinding, Steven W. (2009). A response to critics of family planning programs. *International Perspectives on Sexual and Reproductive Health, 35*(1), 39–44.

Castles, Steven. (2007). The factors that make and unmake migration policies. In Alejandro Portes & Josh DeWind (Eds), *Rethinking migration: New theoretical and empirical perspectives* (pp. 29–61). New York: Bergahahn Books.

Chesnais, Jean-Claude. (1996). Fertility, family and social policy in contemporary western Europe. *Population and Development Review, 22*(4), 729–39.

Coale, Ansley J., & Bannister, Judith. (1994). Five decades of missing females in China. *Demography, 31*(3), 459–79.

Demeny, Paul. (2003). Population policy. In Paul Demeny & Geoffrey McNicoll (Eds), *The encyclopedia of population* (vol. 2, pp. 752–763). New York: Macmillan Reference USA Thompson/Gale.

Dodoo, F. Nii-Amoo, & Frost, Ashley E. (2008). Gender in African population research: The fertility/reproductive health example. *Annual Review of Sociology, 34*, 431–52.

Gauthier, Anne. (2007). The impact of family policies on fertility in industrialized countries: A review of the literature. *Population Research and Policy Review, 26*, 323–46.

Greenhalgh, Susan. (1986). Shifts in China's population policy. *Population and Development Review, 12*(3), 491–516.

Greenhalgh, Susan, & Bongaarts, John. (1987). Fertility policy in China: Future options. *Science, 235,* 1167–72.

Kent, Mary M., & Haub, Carl. (2005). Global demographic divide. *Population Bulletin, 60*(4). Washington, DC: Population Reference Bureau.

Koser, Kalid. (2007). *International migration: A very short introduction.* Oxford: Oxford University Press.

Lapham, R.J., & Mauldin, W.P. (1972). National family planning programs: Review and evaluation. *Studies in Family Planning, 3*(3), 29–52.

———, & ———. (1984). Family planning program effort and birth rate decline in developing countries. *International Family Planning Perspectives, 10*(4), 109–18.

Locoh, Thérése, & Vandermeersch, Céline. (2006). Fertility control in Third World countries. In Graziella Caselli, Jacques Vallin, & Guillaume Wunsch (Eds), *Demography: Analysis and synthesis* (pp. 95–127). Amsterdam: Elsevier.

McDonald, Peter. (2000). Gender equity in theories of fertility. *Population and Development Review, 26*(3), 427–39.

McIntosh, Allison C. (1986). Recent pronatalist policies in western Europe. In Kingsley Davis, Mikhail S. Berstam, & Rita Ricardo-Campbell (Eds), *Below-replacement fertility in industrial societies: Causes, consequences, policies*, pp. 318–34. Supplement to *Population and Development Review, 12.*

Mauldin, W. Parker, & Ross, John A. (1991). Family planning programs: Efforts and results, 1982–89. *Studies in Family Planning, 22*(6), 350–67.

Pinelli, Antonella. (1995). Women's condition, low fertility, and emerging union patterns in Europe. In Karen Oppenheim Mason & An-Magritt Jensen (Eds), *Gender and family change in industrialized countries* (pp. 82–101). Oxford: Clarendon Press.

Population Reference Bureau. (2010). *World population data sheet for 2010.* Washington, DC.

Potts, Malcom. (2006). China's one child policy. *British Medical Journal, 333*, 361–2.

Ross, John A., & Mauldin, W. Parker. (1996). Family planning programs: Efforts and results, 1972–94. *Studies in Family Planning, 27*(3), 137–47.

Sachs, Geoffrey D., & McArthur, J.W. (2005, January 22). The millennium project: A plan for meeting the Millennium Development Goals. *The Lancet, 365*, 47–353.

Sinding, Steven W. (2009). Population, poverty, and economic development. *Philosophical Transactions of the Royal Society, B 364*, 3023–30.

Suttcliffe, Bob. (2001). *100 ways of seeing an unequal world.* London: Zed Books.

Teitelbaum, Michael S., & Winter, Jay M. (1985). *The fear of population decline.* San Diego, CA: Academic Press.

Therborn, Goran. (2006). Meaning, mechanisms, patterns, and forces: An introduction. In Goran Therborn (Ed.), *Inequalities of the world: New theoretical frameworks, multiple empirical approaches* (pp. 1–60). London: Verso.

Tsui, Amy Ong. (2001). Population policies, family planning programs, and fertility: The record. In Rudofo A. Bulatao & John B. Casterline (Eds), *Global fertility transition* (pp. 184–203). Supplement to *Population and Development Review, 27.* New York: The Population Council.

United Nations. (2007). *The Millennium Development Goals report 2007.* New York: UN. Retrieved from http://mdgs.un.org/unsd/mdg/Resources/Static/Products/Progress2007/UNSD_MDG_Report_2007e.pdf

Westoff, Charles F., & Bankole, Akinrinola. (1998). The time dynamics of unmet need: An example from Morocco. *International Family Planning Perspectives, 24*(1), 12–14, 24.

Winckler, Edwin A. (2002). Chinese reproductive policy at the turn of the millennium: Dynamic stability. *Population and Development Review, 28*(3), 379–418.

Zhu, Wei Xing, Lu, Li, & Hesketh, Therese. (2009). China's excess males, sex selective abortion, and one child policy: Analysis of data from 2005 national intercensus survey. *British Medical Journal, 338*(b1211). doi:10.1136/bmj.b1211

CHAPTER 25

The Impact of Family Policies on Fertility in Industrialized Countries: A Review of the Literature

Anne H. Gauthier

Introduction

Public policies have an undeniable effect on families. Among other things, they regulate the conditions of employment, define eligibility to welfare benefits, provide education and health services, and define the rights and responsibilities of parents. Public policies thus shape family life in defining rights, responsibilities, opportunities, and constraints. Yet public policies have been claimed to have a much more pervasive effect on families. They have been claimed to be encouraging some types of family structures over others, and to be providing incentives or disincentives to cohabit, marry, divorce, and to have children in or outside wedlock. For instance, according to Popenoe (1988), generous social and welfare policies have destroyed traditional family values, have encouraged nontraditional family forms, and have thus contributed to the decline of families.

The links between public policies and demographic behaviour are, however, very complex. They depend on the type of policies, the levels of benefits, the conditions of eligibility, and the income and opportunity sets of individuals, as well as the norms, stigma, and sanctions associated with the receipt of benefits. Isolating the impact of social and welfare benefits on demographic behaviour (from other determinants) is therefore a difficult exercise, and not surprisingly, one that has led to contradictory findings.

This paper reviews the theoretical premises and empirical evidence linking policies and demographic behaviour. As such, the paper expands and updates the reviews by Chesnais (1996), Demeny (1987), Gauthier (1996), Hecht and Leridon (1993), McNicoll (1998), and Sleebos (2003). Because of the vastness of this field of research, I confine the discussion to the impact of policies on fertility. I consequently leave aside the impact of policies on other demographic phenomena including marriage, divorce, immigration, and mortality. I also leave aside the impact of policies on fertility in the context of high fertility. As to female labour force participation, I examine it as an intermediate mechanism in the process linking policies and fertility.

As to the type of policies covered in this paper, I restrict the review to policies directly targeted at families with children, such as direct and indirect cash transfers for families with children, means-tested child welfare benefits, maternity and parental leave benefits, and childcare facilities and related subsidy programs.[1] I thus exclude other labour market policies, monetary and fiscal policies, education policies and subsidies, social security policies, family law, etc., even though some of these policies (including policies without a specific demographic target) may potentially affect demographic behaviour (see Ermisch, 1986).

The paper is divided into four main sections. In Section 1, I discuss the theoretical framework at the basis of the analysis of the impact of policies on families. In Section 2, I review the empirical literature on the impact of policies on fertility, focusing on studies that have relied on public opinion data and on descriptive statistical analyses. In Section 3, I then move to the review of multivariate analyses, first focusing on the impact of cash benefits on fertility, and then on the impact of work-related policies. In Section 4, I conclude the paper by reflecting on various methodological issues and by identifying future avenues of research.

Theoretical Framework

In their analysis of the determinants of below-replacement fertility, Rindfuss and Brewster (1996) argue that: 'insofar as labor force participation acts as a constraint on fertility, we would expect fertility to rise in response to any easing of the worker–mother conflict' (p. 263). By extension, they furthermore argue that: 'We would expect, other things being equal, that improvements in childcare availability, acceptability, and quality, and decreases in its cost would have a positive impact on fertility' (p. 271). At the core of these hypotheses is the assumption that childbearing is a rational decision, and that parents weigh the costs and benefits of having children against their income, career expectations, own standards concerning the quality of care for children, etc.

Variants of rational choice theory, including the new home economics theory, have in fact been used by most authors to study the relationship between policies and fertility. Thus, according to the neoclassic economic theory of fertility, the decision to have a child is subject to an economically rational decision (a utility maximization process), and is a function of the economic cost and benefits of children, subject to an income constraint and to individuals' preferences for children (as opposed to other goods). According to this model, any reduction in the cost of children (as a result of public subsidy) or any increase in income (as a result of transfer payments) is therefore expected to increase the demand

for children (Becker, 1981; Cigno, 1991). Policies such as child and family cash allowances, tax relief for children, subsidies to childcare, and maternity and parental leave benefits are consequently all expected to have a positive impact on fertility by reducing the direct or indirect (opportunity) cost of children or by increasing individuals' income.

This economic model has been very influential in the literature and is at the core of the assumed relationship between policies and demographic behaviour.[2] It relies, however, on five key assumptions, each having potential implications for the relationship between policies and fertility, and each possibly explaining some of the unexpected or inconsistent findings in the empirical literature.

First, while in its original formulation an increase in income was expected to result in an increase in the demand for children (i.e. the number of children), as discussed by Becker and Lewis (1973), an increase in income may alternatively result in children of higher quality (i.e. higher cost). The consequence for policies is important as it suggests that a measure, such as a child benefit, while increasing income, may not necessarily result in an increase in fertility. For instance, a parent who is receiving monthly child benefits for his/her only child may decide to use this money to buy more expensive toys or clothes or to send the child to a higher-quality childcare instead of having a second child.[3] As will be seen in the empirical section of the paper, this quality–quantity tradeoff may explain why cash benefits are usually found to have a very small impact on fertility.

The second assumption behind the economic model of fertility is that individuals make the decision to have or not to have children based on full information on the cost and benefits of various alternatives. This assumption has been questioned by numerous scholars on the basis that it is doubtful that individuals have full information concerning the cost and benefits of children (Goldthorpe, 2000).[4] Imperfect information is more likely to be the case. Consequently, more recent variants of rational choice theory have relaxed the full information requirement, and have formulated a 'milder' requirement, namely, that individuals make their decisions based on the situational information available to them, regardless of whether or not this information is accurate or complete (Goldthorpe, 2000). For example, it could be argued that individuals make their decisions to have or not to have children based on the perceived cost of children, which may not necessarily correspond to the actual cost of children. While rational choice theory may easily accommodate the relaxation of the information assumption, the consequence for the possible impact of policies is unclear: it may increase the impact of cash benefits if individuals are underestimating the real cost of children (cash benefits may appear to be more generous than they actually are), or it may decrease the impact of cash benefits if individuals are overestimating the real cost of children.

The third assumption is that having a child, marrying, or divorcing is the result of an economically rational decision. Again, scholars have questioned this assumption and have framed it in more general terms. As argued by Goldthorpe (2000), an action may be rational 'simply in the sense of being "appropriate" or "adequate" given actors' goals and given their situation of action which is taken to include their beliefs' (p. 120).[5] If this is the case, the actual level of child benefits, or the actual duration of parental leave, may not necessarily be assessed at face value by individuals (in terms of their dollar amount), but may be assessed more generally in terms of whether or not they are adequate or sufficient to allow them to reach their goals (for example, family size goals and/or career goals). It is not clear *a priori* whether such a decision making process would increase or decrease the possible impact of policies, but it is likely to introduce some noise in the relationship between policies and fertility (because individuals will vary in their perception of what constitute adequate benefits).

Fourth, in its original formulation, the economic model of fertility assumed that policies can impact fertility by reducing the cost of children or by increasing income. Preferences for children, in this model, are taken for granted and are not seen as being potentially influenced by policies. Recent work on the formation of preferences has, however, questioned this assumption and has instead stressed the importance of factors such as peers, neighbours, habits, traditions, and publicity in the formation of preferences and values (see, for example, Becker, 1996; Becker & Murphy, 2000). Drawing from this work, it could be posited that certain types of family policies (e.g. cash bonus) may be influencing fertility by valorizing children, and thus by influencing individuals' preferences for children. Similarly, policies such as parental leave may be influencing fertility by making it more socially and professionally acceptable to take time off to look after newborns.

The final assumption of the economic model of fertility is that preferences regarding children are homogeneous among household members. This unitary assumption has been questioned by numerous scholars who have instead proposed that preferences may differ among household members (Rasul, 2002). Without entering into the details of the other theoretical models proposed, suffice it to say that the heterogeneity of preferences has potentially large implications on the effect of policies on fertility in allowing spouses to have different preferences for children and, by extension, different perceived costs of childbearing and different views about family, careers, etc. The gender theory proposed by McDonald (2000) makes a similar point in arguing that gender inequalities are responsible for countries' low levels of fertility. While this theory suggests that policies that promote gender equality could have an impact on fertility, it has not been systematically tested empirically.

It follows from the above discussion that family policies may therefore be posited to affect fertility through three different channels: through their influence on the cost of children (e.g. subsidies), individuals' income (e.g., cash transfers), and/or individuals' preferences. Such a model also allows for the possibility of 'imperfect' information, non-economic costs and benefits, and the role of societal or community norms and sanctions (see Blossfeld

& Prein 1998; Brewster 1994; Goldthorpe 2000; Hechter 1994; Sucoff & Upchurch 1998). As will be seen below, it is not easy to test this model empirically, especially due to a lack of a consistent and comprehensive database on family policies.[6]

Empirical Evidence I

I begin the review of the empirical literature by first examining the empirical evidence linking policies and fertility, which is based on public opinion data and descriptive statistical analyses. While these studies are based on relatively simple methodologies (not controlling for other possible determinants of fertility), they continue to be widely cited in the literature as evidence of the positive impact of policies on fertility. In the next section, I then move to studies based on multivariate analyses.

Evidence Based on Public Opinion Data

The discrepancy between the ideal and the actual number of children has often been used to identify the window of opportunity of policies. People, it has been argued, have fewer children than what they considered as being ideal because of barriers to fertility, including the high cost of children and the incompatibility between family and work responsibilities.[7] For example, Chesnais (1996) states that: 'the gap between the ideal and the reality (in terms of number of children) demonstrates that public policies have failed to remove the obstacles to the realization of fertility desires' (p. 736). Relevant data collected in the European Communities in the late 1980s suggest that the gap between ideal and actual fertility is around 0.55 children per woman, a gap that has been interpreted by some scholars as the possible window of opportunities of policies (European Commission, 1990). This line of argument is convincing, to some extent, when we consider the fact that the gap between ideal and actual fertility is highest in countries such as Greece and Italy, where limited governmental support for family is provided, and lowest in countries such as France

with more supportive family policies. It is less convincing in view of numerous counter-examples, for instance, the fact that the gap between ideal and actual fertility is also low in the UK despite a much less supportive family policy than in France.

Obviously, there are well-known problems associated with the use of data on the ideal number of children in order to capture the possible impact of policies (Bongaarts, 1998). Among other things, data on the ideal or expected number of children tend to be highly volatile (Goldberg, et al., 1959; Westoff & Ryder, 1977). Furthermore, when asked about the ideal number of children, people tend to refer to global norms and expectations rather than what they themselves consider as ideal (Livi Bacci, 2001). In particular, responses to questions about the ideal number of children tend to cluster around the two-child norm, and very few people tend to report having zero or one child as the ideal. Interestingly, a recent study by Goldstein, et al. (2003) reports evidence of the beginning of a decline in ideal family size below the two-child norm. This is important as it suggests that the window of opportunity that some saw in the gap between ideal and actual fertility may be decreasing.[8]

The other type of data that has been used to assess the possible impact of policies on fertility is public opinion on the perceived causes of low fertility and about preferred family policy measures. For instance, in a Eurobarometer survey carried out in 1989, about one-third of respondents stated that reasons related to housing and childcare can influence fertility, and about one-fifth gave reasons related to the level of child allowance (European Commission, 1990). If inadequate policies are identified by respondents as the cause of low fertility, more generous policies could potentially motivate individuals to have an additional child, but there is no assurance in these data that it would be the case. Interestingly, respondents in the nine-country Population Policy Acceptance Survey carried out in the early 1990s were asked whether or not they would have an additional child if their preferred family policy measures were introduced. Results suggest that only one or two respondents out of ten would have another child if their preferred policy measures were introduced, thus translating into an increase in fertility of 0.1–0.2 children per woman (Kamaras, et al., 1998).[9] This impact of 0.1–0.2 children per woman may in fact be a much more realistic estimate of the policies' window of opportunity than the 0.5–0.6 children per woman estimated on the basis of the gap between ideal and actual number of children.[10]

Evidence Based on Descriptive Time-Series Analyses

The other type of studies that has attempted to assess the impact of policies on fertility is studies that have examined the historical trends in fertility in relation to the countries' policies. For example, the higher level of fertility observed in France as compared to other western European countries in recent decades has been argued to be the result of France's higher level of support for families (Dumont & Descroix, 1988). For example, fertility rates in France remained higher than those observed in Belgium and Germany, especially in the immediate post–World War II period. Between 1940 and 1999, France's total fertility has exceeded that observed in Belgium by an average of 0.2 children per woman. This figure matches that estimated by Ekert (1986), who concluded that the higher family benefits provided in France have resulted in a higher fertility of about 0.2 children per woman.

The case of Germany has often been cited as evidence of a positive effect of policies on fertility. The evidence lies in the fact that until 1976 the fertility rates in East and West Germany followed similar trends. But starting in 1977, the difference between them, which was until then negligible, began to increase to reach 0.4–0.5 children per woman. It is argued that the higher fertility observed in East Germany was the result of a series of family policy measures introduced from 1976–7, including an extended maternity leave and a paid childcare leave (Chesnais, 1987; Vining, 1984). More recent analyses carried out by Monnier (1990) and Buttner and

Lutz (1990) confirmed the positive impact of the East German family policy package on fertility: an impact corresponding to an increase of roughly 20 per cent of the total fertility rate. As noted by Buttner and Lutz (1990), part of this increase was, however, the result of earlier births rather than additional births, but the impact was still significant five to ten years after the implementation of policies. Interestingly, since the end of the socialist regime and the country's reunification, not only has the East German state support for families been substantially reduced, fertility has also plummeted to unprecedented low levels (Witte & Wagner, 1995).

While the above examples provide convincing evidence of a positive impact of policies on fertility, other examples are less convincing. For example, fertility in Britain has been tracking very closely that of France in recent decades, despite a much less supportive family policy. Similarly, while the province of Quebec in Canada provides a much more supportive family policy than the other provinces, its fertility has remained at a level that is either lower than or equal to that of the rest of Canada since the mid-1960s—and this despite the adoption of a series of pronatalist measures from the late 1980s, including a generous baby bonus for the second and third child. However, econometrics evidence discussed in the next section suggests that fertility in Quebec may have been even lower in the absence of policies (Milligan, 2002). Of course, numerous other factors may explain the similarity in fertility trends in France and Britain, and the lower fertility in Quebec as compared to the rest of Canada. What these counter-examples suggest, however, is that cross-national and cross-provincial differences in policies do not completely match differences in fertility, and that other determinants of fertility have to be taken into account in order to isolate the impact of policies.

Evidence Based on Bivariate Cross-Sectional Analyses

Cross-national differences in the level of state support for families provide a natural experiment to test the impact of policies on fertility. From a cross-sectional perspective, and using countries as the unit of analysis, some studies have shown a positive relationship between policies and fertility. For example, Finch and Bradshaw (2003) showed the relatively strong bivariate correlation between an index of child benefit package (which includes various cash benefits and tax relief for children) and the total period fertility rate for 2000, and between the child benefit package for a poor family and the total period fertility rate.[11] No statistically significant correlation was found however between the child benefit package for a large family and fertility. A series of bivariate correlation analyses between various policy indicators and fertility for twenty OECD countries by Castles (2003) revealed no statistically significant correlation between indicators of cash benefits and fertility but a statistically significant one with a composite index of work and family reconciliation policies.

The other piece of evidence provided in the literature in support of the thesis of a positive impact of policies on fertility has come from the bivariate correlation between female labour force employment and fertility. As has been documented in the literature, while this correlation was negative in the 1970s, it became positive in the 1990s. In other words, countries that display a high level of female labour force participation nowadays are also those that display a higher level of fertility (Billari & Kohler, 2004; Brewster & Rindfuss, 2000). This positive correlation between female employment and fertility runs counter to the economic model of fertility discussed earlier, which posits that when women are active in the labour market, they face a higher opportunity cost of children and should consequently have a lower fertility—unless of course their opportunity cost is reduced by specific policies. This is exactly what numerous authors have argued, namely, that the reversal of the correlation between fertility and female employment provides evidence that policies can ease the incompatibility between work and family responsibilities and can indirectly affect fertility (Rindfuss, et al., 2003). Such a conclusion has

however been refuted by Kogel (2004) on the basis of econometrics evidence. Using panel data techniques with data from 21 OECD countries over the period 1960–2000, he concluded that the negative relationship between fertility and female labour force participation persisted throughout the period. The apparent reversal in sign was instead explained by 'the combination of country effects and country-heterogeneity in the magnitude of the negative time-series association' (p. 50). And while the time-series association between fertility and female labour force participation appeared to have weakened in some countries after 1985, he nonetheless concluded that 'changes in public policies or labor market developments cannot have caused that a rising female labor force participation increases the total fertility rate within countries over time' (p. 47).

To summarize, while descriptive styles of studies provide some evidence of a positive impact of policies on fertility, and while they have been widely cited in the literature, their lack of statistical controls for other determinants of fertility make their case much less reliable. In the next section, I turn to studies based on multivariate statistical analyses in an attempt at better isolating the impact of policies on fertility from other possible determinants.

Empirical Evidence II

I first review the literature regarding the impact of cash benefits on fertility, and then review the literature regarding the impact of work-related benefits (e.g. parental leave and childcare). The studies reviewed here use either macro-level or micro-level data. And as will be seen, although most of these studies suggest a positive relationship between policies and fertility, the impact tends to be small.

The Impact of Family Cash Benefits on Fertility

I begin with studies based on macro-level data, that is, studies that exploit cross-national and/or historical variations in family policies in order to assess their impact on fertility.[12] These studies are summarized in Table 25.1. They typically use a global measure of fertility, such as the total period fertility rate, as the dependent variable, and various independent variables, including specific policy indicators, male and female wages, etc. All of the studies listed in Table 25.1 have concluded that there is a positive impact of policies on fertility, that is, higher family or child benefits are associated with higher levels of fertility. This is the case for studies based on a cross-national design, and for those based on a single-country design. Family cash benefits, such as family and child allowances and tax credit for dependent children, appear to have a positive impact on aggregate indices of fertility. This impact tends however to be small. On the basis of a pooled time-series and cross-national dataset, Blanchet and Ekert-Jaffé (1994), for instance, estimate the impact of family policies to be 0.2 children per woman. Using a similar research design, Gauthier and Hatzius (1997) estimate that a 25 per cent increase in family allowances would result in an increase of the total fertility rate of 0.07 children per woman.

Very importantly, studies using macro-level data have furthermore concluded that the impact of policies on fertility is most likely on the timing of births rather than on the total number of children. For example, Ermisch (1988), using data on age- and parity-specific fertility rates, found that more generous child allowances in Britain increased the likelihood of higher-parity births, but also encouraged young motherhood. A tempo effect of policies was also observed in Sweden by Hoem (2005) and Andersson, et al. (2006) with respect to parental-leave allowance. According to Lutz and Skirbekk (2005), such a tempo effect of policies should not be neglected. Instead, they argue that policies that may increase the period fertility rate may also eventually have an indirect effect on cohort fertility. This hypothesis has not been tested empirically in the literature, especially its connection to a possible threshold effect, the so-called 'low fertility trap' (Lutz & Skirbekk, 2005).

Studies based on micro-level data have also generally concluded that policies have a positive impact on fertility (see Table 25.2). The results are, however, more complex, showing varying impact of policies by birth order. For example, a comparison of French and British family policies by Ekert-Jaffé, et al. (2002) showed that the French family policy appears to have a positive impact on the probability of a third birth. In contrast, a study by Laroque and Salanie (2004) based on Labor Force Survey data concluded that cash benefits in France have an effect on the probability of having a first birth but not on the probability of having a third one. Inversely, a study of the impact of the Finnish child home care allowance concluded that the take-up of the allowance increases the probability of having a third birth, but not a second one (Vikat, 2004). I have already referred to the province of Quebec with its generous family policy. The study by Milligan (2002) and based on census data revealed that the cash benefits offered in Quebec significantly increased the probability of having a second child. Interestingly, while the strong support provided to large families in France could be viewed as evidence of the positive impact of policies, counter-examples are significant. As pointed out by Breton and Prioux (2005), proportions of births of parity three and above close to the French ones were also observed in Finland, Norway, Sweden, and the UK—despite policies targeted at large families.

These results are obviously complex and likely reflect differences in the nature and design of policies by birth order (e.g. level of benefits, eligibility criteria) but possibly also differences in the processes associated with the decision to have a first, second, or third child, including the cost of birth of different parities.

The Impact of Work-Related Policies on Fertility

Studies summarized in Table 25.3 use fertility as the dependent variable; as independent variables they use various work-related policies such as maternity or parental leave and childcare characteristics. All of these studies, with one exception, use micro-level

Table 25.1 Overview of studies on the impact of policies on fertility (macro-level [aggregate] data): Cash benefits and general indices of family policy

Country	Author(s) (year)	Data	Method of analysis	Dependent variable	Policy variables	Findings
International	Gauthier & Hatzius (1997)	Official statistics, 22 OECD countries, 1970–96	Pooled cross-national and time-series regression	Total period fertility rate	Family cash benefits	Small positive effect of cash benefits on fertility
International	Castles (2003)	Official statistics, 21 OECD countries, 1998	Correlation and ordinary least-squares regression	Total period fertility rate	Various measures of family policies	The average level of formal childcare has a positive impact on fertility
International	Blanchet & Ekert-Jaffé (1994)	Official statistics, 11 western European countries, 1969–83	Ordinary least-squares regression and two-stage least-squares regression	Total period fertility rate	Index of family policy	Positive and significant effect of family policy on fertility
International	Ekert (1986)	Official statistics, 8 western European countries, 1971–83	Ordinary least-squares regression	Total period fertility rate	Index of family policy	Positive effect of family policy on fertility
Canada	Brouillette, et al. (1993)	Survey of consumer finances, 1985–8	Maximum likelihood method	Conditional fertility probabilities	Direct and indirect cash transfers to families	Direct and indirect cash transfers to families have a positive but small effect on fertility
Canada	Zhang, et al. (1994)	Official statistics, 1971–83	Generalized least-squares	Total period fertility rate	Tax exemption, child tax credit, family allowances, maternity leave	Tax exemption, child tax credit, and family allowances have significant positive effects on fertility
Canada	Duclos, et al. (2001)	Vital statistics and survey of consumer finances, 1981–97	Ordinary least-squares	Proportion of women giving birth to a first, second, or third child	Cash benefits measured indirectly through a dummy variable for the province of Quebec	Cash benefits have an effect on fertility transition rates; however, it is unclear whether the effect is on the tempo of fertility or on the total family size.

Country	Study	Data	Method	Fertility measure	Policy measure	Findings
Germany	Buttner & Lutz (1990)	Official statistics, 1964–87	Age-period-cohort analysis	Age-specific fertility rates	Pronatalist policy introduced in 1976	Statistically significant positive effect of policy on birth rate up to 5 years after implementation
Sweden	Walker (1995)	Official statistics, 1955-1990	Time-series analysis	Total period fertility rate	Sweden's social insurance programs	Parental benefits, public childcare availability, and child allowances have reduced the price of fertility since the early 1970s and thus, had a pronatalist effect. However, these effects were small compared to the larger and negative effects of trends in female wages and return to human capital.
Sweden	Bjorklund (2006)	Official statistics, cohort born 1917-1958	Difference-in-differences approach	Completed cohort fertility rate	Overall measure of family policy measured indirectly by comparing Sweden's fertility rates with those of other countries	Positive effect of family policy on fertility, although stable fertility for women born 1930-60 could be explained by other factors
UK	Ermisch (1988)	Official statistics, 1971-1986	Time-series regression	Parity- and age-specific birth rates	Child allowances	More generous child allowances increase the chance of third and fourth births, and also encourage early motherhood
USA	Georgellis and Wall (1992)	Official statistics, 1913-1984	Generalized least-squares method	Birth rate	Real tax value of dependent exemption	Tax exemption has a positive impact, but small, on fertility
USA	Whittington et al. (1990)	Official statistics, 1913-1984	General least-squares regression	General fertility rate	Real tax value of the personal exemption	Personal exemption has a positive and significant effect on the birthrate

Table 25.2 Overview of studies on the impact of policies on fertility (micro-level): Cash benefits and general indices of family policy

Country	Author(s) (year)	Data	Method of analysis	Dependent variable	Policy variables	Findings
Canada	Milligan (2005)	Canadian 1991 and 1996 Census: Public-Use Microdata Files on Families	Probit regression	Presence of a child under the age of six	The Allowance for Newborn Children measured indirectly through a dummy variable for the province of Quebec	The cash benefit increases the probability of having a second child by 20.5 percentage points
Finland	Vikat (2004)	Register data, 1988–2000	Proportional hazard model	Probability of first, second, and third birth	Child home care allowance	The take-up of child home care allowance is related to a higher risk of third birth but not to a second-birth risk
France	Laroque & Salanie (2004)	Enquête Emploi (Labour Force Survey) in January, 1999–2000	Log-likelihood function and probit model	Probability of giving birth	Cash benefits	Cash benefits have an effect on the probability of having a first birth, but not the probability of having a third birth
France	Laroque & Salanie (2005)	Enquête Emploi (Labour Force Surveys), 1997, 1998, 1999	Full information maximum likelihood	Probability of first, second, and third birth	Cash benefits	Cash benefits have an impact on all parities, but especially for parity 2 and higher
France and UK	Ekert-Jaffé, et al. (2002)	France: INSEE échantillon démographique permanent (EDP); UK: ONS Longitudinal Study	Logistic regression	Probability of first, second, and third birth	Overall family policy measured indirectly by comparing French and UK probability of birth	The French family policy appears to have an impact on the probability of a third birth
Sweden and Hungary	Oláh (2003)	Swedish Survey of Family and Working Life of 1992–3 and Hungarian Fertility and Family Survey of 1992–3	Piecewise-constant proportional-hazards model	Probability of second birth	Overall family policy measured indirectly by comparing Swedish and Hungarian probability of birth	Couples who share family responsibilities more equally have higher second-birth intensity than others in Sweden
UK	Cigno & Ermisch (1989)	1980 Women and Employment Survey	Ordered probit model	Completed fertility	Tax and child benefits	Increases in women's hourly earnings net of tax reduce birth rates, higher child benefits raise completed fertility

Table 25.3 Overview of studies on the impact of policies on fertility: Work-related policies (maternity and parental leave and childcare)

Country	Author(s) (year)	Data	Method of analysis	Dependent variable	Policy variables	Findings
Macro-level data						
Sweden	Hoem (1993)	Official statistics 1961–1990	Indirect standardization	Parity-specific birth rate	Parental leave policy	Positive impact of policies on the total fertility rate
Canada	Hyatt & Milne (1991)	Official statistics, 1948–86	Ordinary least-squares regression	Total period fertility rate (log)	Maternity benefits	Maternity benefits have a significant but small effect on fertility. A 1% increase in maternity benefits would result in a 0.26% increase in fertility.
Micro-level data						
Austria	Hoem, Prskawetz, & Neyer (2001)	Austrian Family and Fertility survey, 1995–6	Hazard regression	Probability of third birth	Parental leave	No overall effect of changes in parental leave on fertility apart from an increase in the tempo of third births following the changes in parental leave in the mid-1990s
Austria	Lalive & Zweimuller (2005)	Austrian social security dataset, 1990	Regression discontinuity analysis	Probability of having a child within the 3 years following the change in policies	Parental leave	The extension of the parental leave in 1990 increased the probability of having an additional child (both the tempo of birth and completed fertility)

Table 25.3 *(continued)*

Country	Author(s) (year)	Data	Method of analysis	Dependent variable	Policy variables	Findings
Denmark, (West) Germany, Italy, UK, USA	Diprete, et al. (2003)	Panel surveys	Descriptive analysis	Parity progression ratio	Cost of childcare	Institutionally driven childcare costs affect the fertility pattern
Denmark, Italy, Netherlands, Spain	Del Boca, et al. (2003)	European Community Household Panel	Fixed effect and random effect models	Whether or not the woman had a child in the last two years	Childcare availability	Childcare availability has a positive effect on fertility
Finland and Norway	Ronsen (1999)	1988 Norwegian Family and Occupation Survey and the 1989 Finnish Population Survey (cohorts 1943–65)	Hazard-rate analysis	Probability of birth	Parental leave	Parental leave has had a small positive effect on fertility in these two countries. The impact is stronger in Finland.
Finland and Norway	Ronsen (2004)	Norwegian Family and Occupation Survey and the 1989 Finnish Population Survey	Hazard model	Probability of first, second, and third birth	Parental leave, public daycare coverage, and child benefits	Parental leave has a positive effect on fertility. The provision of daycare has no effect on fertility. Child benefits have no effect on fertility.
Germany	Hank & Kreyenfeld (2003)	German Socio-Economic Panel Study (GSOEP), 1984–95	Multilevel discrete-time logit models	Probability of a first birth	Availability of public daycare	No statistically significant effect
Italy	Del Boca (2002)	Bank of Italy's Survey of Households' Income and Wealth, 1991–5	Cross-sectional and pooled logit model	Whether or not the woman had a child in the last two years	Childcare availability	The availability of childcare increases the probability of having a child

Norway	Kravdal (1996)	Family and Occupation Survey 1988	Logistic regression	Probability of first-, second-, and third-birth	Daycare facilities	The provision of daycare facilities has a weak positive effect on fertility. A 20% increase in childcare enrolment rate would result in an increase in cohort fertility of 0.05 children per woman.
Sweden	Andersson, Duvander, & Hank (2004)	Register data, 1997–8	Event-history analysis	Probability of second and third birth	Regional childcare characteristics	No effect
USA	Blau & Robins (1989)	Employment opportunity pilot projects, 1980	Hazard rate model	Birth probability	Childcare cost	Higher childcare costs result in a lower birth rate for non-employed women but not for employed women

data. Results are mixed, with some concluding that work-related benefits have a small positive impact on fertility, and others finding no evidence of an impact of policies on fertility.[13]

With regard to parental and maternity leave, Hyatt and Milne (1991) estimated, on the basis of Canadian data, that a 1 per cent increase in the real value of maternity benefit would result in an increase in the total fertility rate between 0.09 per cent and 0.26 per cent. Studies by Ronsen (1999, 2004) on Finland and Norway and by Hoem (1993) on Sweden also concluded there was a positive impact of parental leave on fertility. In contrast, a study by Hoem, et al. (2001) on Austrian data revealed no overall effect of changes in parental leave on fertility apart from an increase in the tempo of third births.

With regard to childcare cost and availability, mixed results are also found. On the basis of Norwegian macro-level data, Kravdal (1996) estimated that a twenty percentage point increase in the provision of childcare would result in an increase of no more than 0.05 children per women in completed cohort fertility. A positive impact of reduced childcare cost and increased childcare availability on fertility was also observed by Diprete, et al. (2003) and Del Boca, et al. (2003) on the basis of their multi-country analyses. No statistically significant impact of childcare characteristics (cost and availability) on fertility was however reported by Ronsen (2004) for Norway and Finland, by Hank and Kreyenfeld (2003) for Germany, and by Andersson, et al. (2004) for Sweden. The explanations given for these mixed findings are varied including the concomitant increase in female labour force participation and childcare supply (in some countries), the heterogeneity of parents in terms of childcare needs, the structure of the childcare system in terms of opening hours, and the relationship between the public daycare system and other social and welfare state institutions.

Discussion and Conclusion

I started this paper by referring to beliefs by some scholars and politicians that policies have an undeniably negative impact on families, in encouraging single-parenthood and births outside wedlock, and in discouraging employment. The analysis presented in this paper suggests that policies may indeed have an effect on families, but that the effect tends to be of a small magnitude and that it may possibly have an effect on the timing of fertility rather than on completed family size. In view of these results, the popularity of baby bonus schemes among governments, as a way of encouraging fertility, is difficult to understand. While the additional financial support is bound to be welcomed by parents, the overall effect on fertility is likely to be small.[14]

What is also clear from this review of the literature is that it is very difficult to accurately measure policies and to adequately model the various ways by which policies may impact fertility. In this last section of the paper, I reflect further on some of these methodological challenges in an attempt at outlining some future avenues of research (including data collection).

The Measurement of Family Policies

The measurement of policies is a major challenge in all studies. As pointed out, and because of data limitations, studies tend to be restricted to only some type of policies and to neglect others that may be equally—if not more—important. In particular, because of data limitations, studies seldom include a comprehensive measure of the total support provided by government to families. For example, while not providing econometrics evidence, Hoem (2005) claims that it is the whole political culture of Sweden, as opposed to specific policies, that makes the country more family-, child-, and woman-friendly, a situation that may have an impact on fertility. Calls for the adoption of a system of monitoring and of comprehensive reporting of governmental expenditures on families and children have in fact been made (the so-called family impact statement), but few countries have adopted such a system (Cuyvers & Kiely 2000). This means that governmental support for housing is often excluded from empirical analysis of the effect of policies on fertility, as is governmental support for health and education.

Another limitation is that studies usually rely on global measures of family policies while failing to consider individual variations in access to, and receipt of, benefits. Eligibility criteria, benefit caps, etc. are often overlooked and flat rate benefits instead assumed. For example, maternity cash benefits are subject to ceilings in several countries, but these ceilings are often ignored in demographic studies. Similarly, studies often ignore employer-provided benefits, which tend to highly vary within and between countries. For example, data from the OECD suggests that a non-negligible proportion of employees have access to extra-statutory maternity and parental leave, employer-provided childcare, and flexi-time and/or part-time work opportunities (OECD, 2001). Such benefits may also have an effect on fertility and on the combination of work and family responsibilities, but they are usually not included in demographic analyses.

The Modelling of Family Policies and Demographic Behaviour

In the theoretical section of this paper, three channels by which policies may be influencing fertility were identified: one channel operating through a reduction of the cost of children (e.g. governmental subsidies or the provision of services), another operating through an increase in families' incomes (e.g. cash benefits), and a third one operating through an increase in the preference for children. Other factors may, however, be operating through the same channels, thus making it very difficult to isolate the impact of policies from other determinants. For instance, in his analysis of the impact of public policies on fertility in Sweden, Walker (1995) concludes that: 'Its (parental benefit) strong connection to the female wage, combined with the large movement in income tax rates and other factors connected to wages, makes it impossible to estimate the separate effects of parental benefits' (p. 246). Concomitant variations, and strong links between policies, wages, and female labour force participation, thus complicate the modelling of family policies and demographic behaviour.

Another modelling issue that has not been fully discussed in the literature is the possibility of a non-linear effect of policies on fertility. For example, instead of the assumed linear effect, it may be possible that fertility is subject to a threshold effect, which either requires benefits to reach a certain minimum level before having an effect, or which implies that the effect of benefits reaches a plateau beyond a certain level. None of the studies reviewed above explored this possibility.

The Possible Polarization of Families

All of the econometric evidence reviewed in this paper acknowledges the heterogeneity in the population and consequently controls for various individual-level factors that may affect the cost of children and/or the preference for children including personal wages. However, one may question whether or not these statistical controls are sufficient to capture heterogeneity and whether or not more complex interaction models are instead needed. For example, it is possible that individuals located at different points of the income distribution may respond differently to flat-rate child benefits simply because such benefits increase household income differently in relative terms. Similarly, the ceiling often imposed on maternity and parental leave benefits may make them more or less attractive depending on the parents' income. In fact, studies that have documented the take-up rate of paternity and parental leave conclude that it varies significantly with the parents' socioeconomic status. For example, the take-up rate of parental leave by Finnish fathers tends to be curvilinear, being lowest at the low and high ends of the income distribution (Salmi & Lammi-Taskula, 1999).

This possible polarization of families is further complicated by the fact that in numerous countries high earners and those in high-level occupations are also those who are more likely to have access to supplementary employer-provided benefits (Evans 2002).

Social and economic differences in fertility behaviour and in response to policies have been extensively examined in the USA for welfare mothers. However, this has not been examined for the entire population and especially with respect to individuals' positions in the income distribution and their types of occupation. A recent study by Ekert-Jaffé and others (2002) points to large occupational inequalities in fertility behaviour in England, more so than in France. In their study, the link with policies was, however, examined only indirectly. Interestingly, recent changes announced by the French government to its cash benefit scheme have been interpreted by the press as having a strong socioeconomic bias in offering incentives to middle-class women to have more babies (Randall, 2005).[15] And while it may be politically sensitive to examine social class differences in fertility behaviour and in policy response, this is an area of research that warrants more study, especially if policy schemes contribute to the polarization of families.

Conclusion

This paper provides some evidence of the impact of family policies on fertility. However, the impact tends to be small and also to vary highly depending on the type of data used and on the type of policies. For example, while data on ideal and actual fertility suggest a policy's window of opportunity of around 0.5 children per woman, multivariate analyses suggest instead an impact of less than 0.2 children per woman. The results of the empirical literature are, however, often contradictory, especially when it comes to the magnitude of the impact of policies and on the differential impact by birth order. The results are also puzzling, if not disconcerting, in view of numerous counter-examples including the persistence of higher fertility levels in some countries despite lower levels of state support for families and/or despite the absence of policies targeted at higher-parity births.

What this paper has also made clear is that the absence of a comprehensive database on state support for families has prevented researchers from identifying which type of public policy has had the largest impact on fertility, and what would be the price tag of such a policy. Similarly, little is known about the impact of employer-provided policies on fertility (and on the inequalities that they introduce).

During the last decade, governments in industrialized countries have tended to pursue two main directions in policies: a move away from universal cash benefits in order to tackle child poverty, and a greater emphasis on policies that reduce the barriers to the combination of work and family responsibilities (Gauthier, 2005). The studies reviewed in this paper provide some information as to the potential impact of such policies on people's fertility desires, timing of fertility, and completed family size. However, knowledge on this matter is still limited and calls for complex modelling of the causal relationship between policies, female labour force participation, and fertility.

Notes

1. I use the term 'family policies' to encompass these different types of policies. However, one should bear in mind that very few countries have in place an explicit and comprehensive family policy. Instead, the responsibility for these various policies tends to be scattered across various ministries or departments.
2. From the onset, the economic theory of fertility has also been criticized for its consumerist view of children. The discussion of this aspect of the theory is beyond the scope of the paper. For more information, see Blake (1968).
3. The model is unclear with regard to the actual sequencing of events. In the above case it could be argued that the individual had a first child knowing that by becoming a parent he/she would start receiving child benefits. Alternatively, it could be argued that once the individual has a child and is receiving benefits, he/she could decide to have a second child because he/she is already receiving benefits.
4. Goldthorpe (2000) does not raise the issue of imperfect information in the context of fertility decision. His argument applies generally to rational action theory.

5. In the case of teenagers, this may mean that having a child may be a rational decision, not in economic terms, but because it provides the teenage mother with a sense of personal worth and responsibilities, and may provide her with a higher status in her immediate neighbourhood. This appears to be the case in some deprived communities. For example, the high teenage pregnancy rate in remote communities of northern Canada has been linked with the perceived elevated social status of being a mother (George, 2000).

6. It should be noted that numerous studies on the impact of policies on fertility do not discuss in detail their theoretical model and underlying mechanisms. Some of the complex mechanisms described above may account for some of the unexpected findings.

7. For example, such an argument has been used in Japan to explain the gap between ideal and actual number of children (Japan Ministry of Health, Labor, and Welfare, 1999). The gap between ideal and actual number of children was also noted in Switzerland although without reference to policies (Switzerland Statistics, 1997).

8. Aware of the measurement biases associated with the use of fertility ideals, the data used by Goldstein, et al. (2003) attempted at better distinguishing between perceived societal ideals and the respondents' own personal ideals.

9. For a discussion of policy acceptance and their potential impact on fertility, see also Palomba, et al. (1989).

10. Results from the second round of the Population Policy Acceptance Survey (PPA2) in Slovenia suggest a potentially larger impact of policies. However authors such as Stropnik (2001) have been critical of these results, arguing that the hypothetical nature of the questions on policies make them an unreliable source of information to capture their potential effect on policies.

11. The analysis was based on 17 OECD countries but excluded Austria, New Zealand, and the USA. While the reasons for excluding these three countries are unclear in the study, it is clear that their inclusion would have considerably altered (i.e., weakened) the correlation between fertility and policies.

12. There is a large literature (mainly American) on the impact of means-tested benefits on teenage fertility, births outside wedlock, and births by welfare recipient mothers. I am not covering this subtopic here. Interested readers are referred to Duncan and Hoffman (1990), Plotnick (1990), Tanisha Dyer and Fairlie (2005), and Joyce, et al. (2005) for more information.

13. There is a substantial literature on the impact of family policies on female labour force participation. This literature is not discussed here in view of our focus on fertility. Examples include Gustafsson and Stafford (1992) on Swedish data, and Kreyenfeld and Hank (2000) on German data.

14. In recent years, baby bonus schemes were introduced in Australia, Italy, and Poland (Mathieson, 2003; Kennedy, 2003; Easton, 2005). In the UK, a child savings scheme (the Child Trust Fund) was introduced in 2005, but with no pronatalist motive (Ross, 2005).

15. 'Middle-class French women are to be offered cash incentives to have third babies amid growing concern that too few children are being born to professional couples' (Randall, 2005).

References

Andersson, G., Duvander, A.-Z., & Hank, K. (2004). Do child care characteristics influence continued childbearing in Sweden? An investigation of the quantity, quality and price dimension. *Journal of European Social Policy*, 14, 407–18.

Andersson, G., Hoem, J.M., & Duvander, A.-Z. (2006). Social differentials in speed-premium effects in childbearing in Sweden. *Demographic Research*, 14(4), 51–70.

Becker, G.S. (1981). *A Treatise on the family*. Cambridge, MA: Harvard University Press.

———. (1996). *Accounting for tastes*. Cambridge, MA: Harvard University Press.

Becker, G.S., & Lewis, H.G. (1973). On the interaction between the quantity and quality of children. *Journal of Political Economy*, 81(2), S279–88.

Becker, G.S., & Murphy, K.M. (2000). *Social economics: Market behavior in a social environment*. Cambridge, MA: Harvard University Press.

Billari, F., & Kohler, H.-P. (2004). Patterns of low and lowest-low fertility in Europe. *Population Studies*, 58(2), 161–76.

Bjorklund, A. (2006). Does family policy affect fertility? Lessons from Sweden. *Journal of Population Economics*, 19(1), 3–24.

Blake, J. (1968). Are babies consumer durables? A critique of the economic theory of reproductive motivation. *Population Studies*, 22, 5–25.

Blanchet, D., & Ekert-Jaffé, O. (1994). The demographic impact of fertility benefits: Evidence from a micro-model and from macro-data. In J. Ermisch & N. Ogawa (Eds), *The family, the market and the state in ageing societies*, pp. 79–104. Oxford, UK: Clarendon Press.

Blau, D.M., & Robins, P.K. (1989). Fertility, employment, and child care costs. *Demography*, 26(2), 287–299.

Blossfeld, H.P., & Prein, G. (Eds). (1998). *Rational choice theory and large-scale data analysis*. Boulder, CO: Westview Press.

Bongaarts, J. (1998). Fertility and reproductive preferences in post-transitional societies. *Population Council*. Retrieved from www.popcouncil.org/pdfs/wp/114.pdf

Breton, D., & Prioux, F. (2005). Deux ou trois enfants? Influence de la politique familiale et de quelques facteurs socio-demographiques. *Population*, 4(juillet–aôut), 489–524.

Brewster, K.L. (1994). Race differences in sexual activity among adolescent women: The role of neighborhood characteristics. *American Sociological Review*, 59(June), 408–24.

Brewster, K.L., & Rindfuss, R.R. (2000). Fertility and women's employment in industrialized nations. *Annual Review of Sociology*, 26, 271–96.

Brouillette, L., Felteau, C., & Lefebvre, P. (1993). The effects of financial factors on fertility behavior in Quebec [Les effets de la fiscalité sur les comportements de fecondité au Québec]. *Canadian Public Policy / Analyse de Politiques*, 19(3), 260–78.

Buttner, T., & Lutz, W. (1990). Estimating fertility responses to policy measures on the German Democratic Republic. *Population and Development Review*, 16(3), 539–55.

Castles, F.G. (2003). The world turned upside down: Below replacement fertility, changing preferences and family-friendly public policy in 21 OECD countries. *Journal of European Social Policy*, 13(3), 209–27.

Chesnais, J.-C. (1987). When one people becomes two: One Germany and the other [Quand un peuple en devient deux: Une Allemagne et l'autre]. *Population et Sociétés*, 209, 1–4.

———. (1996). Fertility, family, and social policy. *Population and Development Review*, 22(4), 729–39.

Cigno, A. (1991). *Economics of the family*. Oxford, UK: Clarendon Press.

Cigno, A., & Ermisch, J. (1989). A microeconomic analysis of the timing of births. *European Economic Review*, 33, 737–60.

Cuyvers, P., & Kiely, G. (2000). The family rollercoaster ride. *Family Observer*, 2, 4–12.

Del Boca, D. (2002). The effect of child care and part time opportunities on participation and fertility decisions in Italy. *Journal of Population Economics*, 15(3), 549–73.

Del Boca, D., Aaberge, R., Colombino, U., Ermisch, J., Francesconi, M., Pasqua, S., & Strom, S. (2003). Labour market participation of women and fertility: The effect of social policies. Paper presented at the FRDB Child conference. Alghero (June).

Demeny, P. (1987). Pronatalist policies in low-fertility countries: Patterns, performance, and prospects. In K. Davis, M.S. Bernstam, & R. Ricardo-Campbell (Eds), *Below-replacement fertility in industrial societies: Causes, consequences, policies. Population and development review* (vol. 12, Supplement), pp. 335–58.

Diprete, T.A., Morgan, P.S., Engelhardt, H., & Pacalova, H. (2003). Do cross-national differences in the costs of children generate cross-national differences in fertility rates? *Population Research and Policy Review*, 22(5–6), 439–77.

Duclos, E., Lefebvre, P., & Merrigan, P. (2001). A natural experiment on the economics of storks: Evidence on the impact of differential family policy on fertility rates in Canada. Center for Research on Economic Fluctuations and Employment, working paper no. 136. Université du Québec à Montréal.

Dumont, G.-F., & Descroix, P. (1988). La spécificité du comportement démographique de la France: Mesure de la surfécondité relative de la France par rapport aux autres pays industriels à faible fécondité précoce de 1963 à 1986. *Histoire, Economie et Société*, 419–32.

Duncan, G.J., & Hoffman, S.D. (1990). Welfare benefits, economic opportunities, and out-of-wedlock births among black teenage girls. *Demography*, 27(4), 519–35.

Easton, A. (2005). Polish women offered baby bonus. *BBC News*. Retrieved from http://news.bbc.co.uk/go/pr/fr/-/2/hi/europe/4567224.stm

Ekert, O. (1986). Effets et limites des aides financières aux familles: Une expérience et un modèle. *Population*, 2, 327–48.

Ekert-Jaffé, O., Joshi, H., Lynch, K., Mougin, R., & Rendall, M. (2002). Fécondité, calendrier des naissances et milieu social en France et en Grande-Bretagne: Politiques sociales et polarisation socioprofessionnelle. *Population-F*, 57(3), 485–518.

Ermisch, J. (1986). Impacts of policy actions on the family and household. *Journal of Public Policy*, 6(3), 297–318.

————. (1988). The econometric analysis of birth rate dynamics in Britain. *The Journal of Human Resources*, 23(4), 563–76.

European Commission. (1990). European public opinion on the family and the desire for children. Eurobarometer 32. Brussels, Belgium: Commission of the European Communities.

Evans, J.M. (2002). Work/family reconciliation, gender wage equity and occupational segregation: The role of firms and public policy. *Canadian Public Policy*, 28(Supplement), 187–216.

Finch, N., & Bradshaw, J. (2003). Fertility and supporting the costs of children. Paper presented at the conference Recent fertility trends in Northern Europe, Oslo, Norway, May 2003.

Gauthier, A.H. (1996). The measured and unmeasured effects of welfare benefits on families: Consequences for Europe's demographic trends. In D. Coleman (Ed.), *Europe's population in the 1990s*, pp. 297–331. Oxford, UK: Oxford University Press.

Gauthier, A.H. (2005). Trends in policies for family-friendly societies. In M. Macura, A.L. MacDonald, & W. Haug (Eds), *The new demographic regime: Population challenges and policy responses*, pp. 95–110. New York: United Nations.

Gauthier, A.H., & Hatzius, J. (1997). Family benefits and fertility: An econometric analysis. *Population Studies*, 51, 295–306.

George, J. (2000, May 19). Babies having babies: An explosion of infants born to teenage mothers. *Nunatsiaq News*. Retrieved from http://www.nunatsiaq.com/archives/nunavut000531/nvt20519_01 html

Georgellis, Y., & Wall, H.J. (1992). The fertility effect of dependent tax exemptions: Estimates for the United States. *Applied Economics*, 24(10), 139–45.

Goldberg, D., Sharp, H., & Freedman, R. (1959). The stability and reliability of expected family size data. *The Milbank Memorial Fund Quarterly*, 37, 368–85.

Goldstein, J., Lutz, W., & Testa, M.R. (2003). The emergence of subreplacement family size ideals in Europe. *Population Research and Policy Review*, 22, 479–96.

Goldthorpe, J. (2000). *On sociology; Numbers, narratives, and the integration of research and theory*. Oxford, UK: Oxford University Press.

Gustafsson, S., & Stafford, F. (1992). Child care subsidies and labour supply in Sweden. *Journal of Human Resources*, 27(1), 204–30.

Hank, K., & Kreyenfeld, M. (2003). A multilevel analysis of childcare and women's fertility decisions in Western Germany. *Journal of Marriage and the Family*, 65(3), 584–96.

Hecht, J., & Leridon, H. (1993). Fertility policies: A limited influence? In D. Noin & R. Woods (Eds), *The changing population of Europe*, pp. 62–75. Cambridge MA: Blackwell.

Hechter, M. (1994). The role of values in rational choice theory. *Rationality and Society*, 6, 318–33.

Hoem, J.M. (1993). Public policy as the fuel of fertility: Effects of a policy reform on the pace of childbearing in Sweden in the 1980s. *Acta Sociologica*, 36(1), 19–31.

————. (2005). Why does Sweden have such high fertility? *Demographic Research*, 13(22), 559–72.

Hoem, J.M., Prskawetz, A., & Neyer, G. (2001). Autonomy or conservative adjustment? The effect of public policies and educational attainment on third births in Austria, 1975–96. *Population Studies*, 55(3), 249–61.

Hyatt, D.E., & Milne, W.J. (1991). Can public policy affect fertility? *Canadian Public Policy / Analyse de Politiques*, 27(1), 77–85.

Japan, Ministry of Health, Labor and Welfare (1999). Annual reports on Health and Welfare 1998–1999: Social Security and National Life. Tokyo, Japan.

Joyce, T., Kaestner, R., Korenman, S., & Henshaw, S. (2005). Family cap provisions and changes in births and abortions. *Population Research and Policy Review*, 23(5–6), 475–511.

Kamaras, F., Kocourkova, J., & Moors, H. (1998). The impact of social policies on reproductive behavior. In R. Palomba & H. Moors (Eds), *Population, family and welfare: A comparative survey of European attitudes* (vol. 2), pp. 242–61. Oxford, UK: Clarendon Press.

Kennedy, F. (2003). Italy offers families baby cash. BBC News. Retrieved from http://news.bbc.co.uk/go/pr/fr/-/2/hi/europe/3252794.stm

Kogel, T. (2004). Did the association between fertility and female employment within OECD countries really change its sign? *Journal of Population Economics*, 17, 45–65.

Kravdal, O. (1996). How the local supply of day-care centers influences fertility in Norway: A parity-specific approach. *Population Research and Policy Review*, 15(3), 201–18.

Kreyenfeld, M., & Hank, K. (2000). Does the availability of child care influence the employment of mothers? Findings from Western Germany. *Population Research and Policy Review*, 19, 317–37.

Lalive, R., & Zweimuller, J. (2005). Does parental leave affect fertility and return-to-work? Evidence from a 'true natural experiment'. IZA (Institute for the Study of Labor). Discussion paper no.1613. Retrieved from http://www.iza.org/publications/dps/

Laroque, G., & Salanie, B. (2004). Fertility and financial incentives in France. *CESifo Economic Studies*, 50(3), 423–50.

———, & ———. (2005). Does fertility respond to financial incentives? Retrieved from http://www.columbia.edu/~bs2237/FertilityMay08.pdf

Livi Bacci, M. (2001). Comment: Desired family size and the future of fertility. In R.A. Bulatao & J.B. Casterline, (Eds), *Global fertility transition*, Supplement to *Population and Development Review 27*, 282–9.

Lutz, W., & Skirbekk, V. (2005). Policies addressing the tempo effect in low-fertility countries. *Population and Development Review*, 31(4), 699–720.

McDonald, P. (2000). Gender equity, social institutions and the future of fertility. *Journal of Population Research*, 17(1), 1–16.

McNicoll, G. (1998). Government and fertility in transitional and post-transitional societies. Population Council Working Paper. Retrieved from www.popcouncil.org/pdfs/wp/113.pdf

Mathieson, S. (2003). Labor pledges new baby bonus plan. *The Age*. Retrieved from www.theage.com.au/articles/2003/12/14/1071336812201.html

Milligan, K. (2002, January 24). Quebec's baby bonus: Can public policy raise fertility? C.D. Howe Institute. *Backgrounder*. Retrieved from www.cdhowe.org/pdf/Milligan_Backgrounder.pdf

———. (2005). Subsidizing the stork: New evidence on tax incentives and fertility. *Review of Economics and Statistics*, 83(3), 539–55.

Monnier, A. (1990). The effects of family policies in the German Democratic Republic: A re-evaluation. *Population: An English Selection*, 2, 127–40.

Oláh, L.S. (2003). Gendering fertility: Second births in Sweden and Hungary. *Population Research and Policy Review*, 22(2), 171–200.

Organization for Economic Cooperation and Development [OECD]. (2001). Balancing work and family life: Helping parents into employment. *OECD Employment Outlook, June*, 129–66.

Palomba, R., Bonifazi, C., & Menniti, A. (1989). Demographic trends, population policy and public opinion. *Genus*, 45(3/4), 37–54.

Plotnick, R. (1990). Welfare and out of wedlock childbearing: Evidence from the 1980s. *Journal of Marriage and the Family*, 52, 735–46.

Popenoe, D. (1988). *Disturbing the nest: Sweden and the decline of families in modern society*. New York: Aldine de Gruyter.

Randall, C. (2005, September 20). Educated French paid to have more babies. *The National Post*.

Rasul, I. (2002). Household bargaining over fertility: Theory and evidence from Malaysia. Job market paper, London School of Economics.

Rindfuss, R.R., & Brewster, K.L. (1996). Childbearing and fertility. *Population and Development Review*, 22(Supplement), 258–89.

Rindfuss, R.R., Guzzo, K.B., & Morgan, S.P. (2003). The changing institutional context of low fertility. *Population Research and Policy Review*, 22(5/6), 411–38.

Ronsen, M. (1999). Impacts on fertility and female employment of parental leave programs: Evidence from three Nordic countries. Paper presented at the European Population Conference, The Hague, Netherlands, August/September 1999.

———. (2004). Fertility and public policies—Evidence from Norway and Finland. *Demographic Research*, 10, 143–70.

Ross, C. (2005, September 21). Saving for your children. BBC News. Retrieved from: http://news.bbc.co.uk/go/pr/fr/-/1/hi/business/3112942.stm

Salmi, M., & Lammi-Taskula, J. (1999). Parental leave in Finland. In P. Moss & F. Deven (Eds), *Parental leave: Progress or pitfall?*, pp. 85–122. Brussels, Belgium: CBGS.

Sleebos, J. (2003). *Low fertility rates in OECD countries: Facts and policy responses*. OECD social, employment and migration working papers no.15. Paris, France: OECD.

Stropnik, N. (2001). Reliability of a policy acceptance and attitude survey for formulating family and population policy. Paper presented at the IUSSP General Population Conference, Salvador, Bahia, Brazil, 20–24 August 2001.

Sucoff, C.A., & Upchurch, D.M. (1998). Neighborhood context and the risk of childbearing among metropolitan-area black adolescents. *American Sociological Review*, 63, 571–85.

Switzerland Statistics. (1997, February 13). La famille en Suisse: Tradition et transitions. Press release. Retrieved from: www.statistik.admin.ch/news/archiv97/fp97005.htm

Tanisha Dyer, W., & Fairlie, R.W. (2005). Do family caps reduce out-of-wedlock births? Evidence from Arkansas, Georgia, Indiana, New Jersey and Virginia. *Population Research and Policy Review*, 23(5–6), 441–73.

Vikat, A. (2004). Women's labor force attachment and childbearing in Finland. *Demographic Research*, Special collection 3, article 8.

Vining, D.R., Jr. (1984). Family salaries and the East German birth rate: A comment. *Population and Development Review*, 10(4), 693–6.

Walker, J.R. (1995). The effect of public policies on recent Swedish fertility behavior. *Journal of Population Economics*, 8(3), 223–51.

Westoff, C.F., & Ryder, N.B. (1977). The predictive validity of reproductive intentions. *Demography*, 14(4), 431–53.

Whittington, L.A., Aim, J., & Peters, H.E. (1990). Fertility and the personal exemption: Implicit pronatalist policy in the United States. *The American Review*, 80(3), 545–56.

Witte, J.C., & Wagner, G.G. (1995). Declining fertility in East Germany after unification: A demographic response to socioeconomic change. *Population and Development Review*, 21(2), 387–97.

Zhang, J., Quan, J., & Van Meerbergen, P. (1994). The effect of tax-transfer policies on fertility in Canada, 1921–88. *The Journal of Human Resources*, 29(1), 181–201.

CHAPTER 26

Making Family Planning Accessible in Resource-Poor Settings

Ndola Prata

Introduction

Family planning programs in resource-poor settings are usually fragile, show signs of poor performance, and are both dependent on international funding and constrained by existing policies or lack thereof. However, it is exactly in those settings where family planning programs are most needed if countries aim to reduce inequalities in health, reduce maternal and child mortality rates, alleviate poverty, and foster economic development.

Voluntary family planning is an effective way of controlling fertility within a human rights framework by giving couples the ability to have their desired family size (Prata, 2007). In the 1993 *World Development Report* entitled *Investing in Health*, the World Bank considered family planning a highly cost-effective public health intervention (World Bank, 1993). As Cleland, et al. (2006) write, 'The promotion and availability of family planning in resource-poor settings represents one of the most significant public health success stories of the past century. . . . Family planning is unique among health interventions in the breadth of its benefits—family planning decreases maternal and child mortality, empowers women, reduces poverty, and it lessens stress on the natural and political environment.'

In many resource-poor settings, the growing unmet need for contraception is astounding. Couples who wish to have fewer children are unable to determine the size of their families, as family planning funding continues to become scarce and existing programs and services fail to meet the concerns and desires of their users. It is important to emphasize not telling women how many children they should have, but underscore that they have a right and the freedom to choose how to control their own fertility. To control fertility effectively, women and couples need to have access to correct information about contraceptive methods and be able to afford the method of their choice. The end result at the family level will positively impact the health of women and children, easing pressure on family resources and increasing a family's chances to escape the trap of poverty (Cleland, et al., 2006).

The poorest economic quintiles in resource-poor settings are often more likely to turn to the private sector than to government services, which often fail to reach those in greatest need (Prata, et al., 2005). In this paper, I am including not only the work of public, private, and faith-based health facilities but social marketing, output-based assistance, and franchised service providers who meet the need for family planning information and services.

The report by the UK's All Party Parliamentary Group on Population, Development and Reproductive Health entitled *Return of the Population Growth Factor: Its Impact upon the Millennium Development Goals* shows clearly that poverty and socioeconomic disparities are closely linked to unchecked population growth. The poorest of the poor tend to have not only the lowest contraceptive prevalence, but the highest total fertility rate (TFR) and the highest unmet need for family planning (Prata, 2006, 2007). Population growth also remains a significant issue with respect to increasing levels of education or improving the income gap. The *Return of the Population Growth Factor* report analysis shows that, as a result of rapid population growth, the developing world must train 2 million additional teachers every year to keep education levels at where they are today—with no level of improvement. With increasing population levels, however, even this will not be enough.

A large part of the burden of disease linked to maternal health which poor countries are facing today is also reflective of undesired fertility. It is unjust that women are dying simply because of unmet need for contraception, and yet this remains to be the case. Cleland, et al. (2006) estimate that promotion of family planning in high-fertility countries has the potential to avert 32 per cent of all maternal deaths and nearly 10 per cent of childhood deaths. It is estimated that 25 per cent of HIV-positive women have an unmet need for family planning. Unfortunately, even though contraception is also more cost-effective than Niverapine to prevent mother-to-child-transmission (Reynolds, et al., 2006), family planning is often not an integral part of HIV prevention programs.

Health disparities are increasing over time, and this in turn poses a significant problem for quickly growing populations living on extremely scarce resources (Ezeh, et al., 2009). Low-resource settings are already suffering from water scarcity, food shortages, and inadequate sanitation. Furthermore, internal conflict and/or civil unrest that affects poor countries has often also been a direct result of desperation over the need for resources such as arable land that continue to remain at crisis levels (Thayer, 2009). Until family planning is made accessible to address the large burden of unmet need for contraception, countries will be unable to provide their citizens with even their basic human needs.

In this paper, I propose four critical steps that can help increase access to family planning in low-resource settings, especially those in sub-Saharan Africa. In support of the proposed solutions, I present evidence on current status and recent trends in family planning in poor countries. I argue that family planning services are greatly needed and discuss the health and socioeconomic benefits at individual, family and community levels.

Greater Accessibility to Family Planning

To address the issue of high fertility in low-resource settings, it is imperative that family planning is made accessible to all. Given the current socioeconomic and demographic indicators in poor countries and the slow progress in the last decade, four critical steps should be undertaken: (i) increase knowledge about the safety of family planning methods; (ii) ensure contraception is genuinely affordable to the poorest families; (iii) ensure supply of contraceptives by making family planning a permanent line item in healthcare systems' budgets; and (iv) take immediate action to remove barriers hindering access to family planning methods.

(i) Use of Family Planning Methods

Sub-Saharan Africa has the lowest family planning use in the developing world. The use of modern methods by married women is higher in Latin America (63 per cent), followed by Asia (48 per cent excluding China) and sub-Saharan Africa (18 per cent). The current contraceptive level in sub-Saharan Africa represents a modest increase from 13 per cent registered around the late 1990s to the beginning of 2000 (Population Reference Bureau, 2002, 2008). According to recent available data from 31 countries with Demographic and Health Surveys (DHS), on average 30 per cent of women in sub-Saharan Africa have an unmet need for modern family planning methods. Nineteen of the 31 countries have a reported unmet need for family planning up to 49 per cent. On average, sub-Saharan Africa has not seen a reduction in the unmet need for family planning in the last decade. As a result, there are more women (25 million) with an unmet need for family planning than women currently using modern methods (18 million) (Westoff, 2006; Population Reference Bureau, 2008).

Directly associated to this low family planning use and high unmet need is very high fertility and rapid population growth. In sub-Saharan Africa, the TFR is 5.5, considerably higher than the TFR of Latin America (2.5) and Asia (2.4 excluding China). Fifteen of the 31 sub-Saharan African countries with a recent DHS have TFRs that exceed 6.0 (Population Reference Bureau, 2007). This level is essentially unchanged from the late 1990s, when the region's overall TFR was 5.6 (Population Reference Bureau, 2002). It is estimated that in 2008 sub-Saharan Africa's population was 828 million and is expected to increase by nearly a billion people (1,761 million) by 2050 (United Nations Population Division, 2007).

The use of family planning methods is inherently related to correct knowledge and access to available methods. Correct knowledge should include how the various methods work, family planning methods' safety and side effects, and address the issues of misinformation.

Incorrect knowledge can be addressed in the information, education, and communication campaigns by using simple, single messages that empower women and families, such as 'Family Planning Is Safe' or 'Family Planning Is Safe and Works'. A study of eight developing countries showed that 50–70 per cent of women thought the use of oral contraceptive pills was a considerable health risk, even though in a low-resource setting, having a baby can be up to 1,000 times as dangerous as taking oral contraceptives (Grubb, 1987). Family planning programs should take primary responsibility for disseminating accurate information and correcting misinformation. A couple's acceptance of modern methods is all too often limited because they do not know how modern methods work or they think methods have an adverse influence on their ability to conceive later.

(ii) Family Planning Must Be Affordable

The need for making family planning more accessible is also compelling from the standpoint of alleviating the burden of poverty. Seven of every 10 sub-Saharan Africans live in poverty (less than US$2 per day), with 4 of every 10 sub-Saharan Africans living in extreme poverty (less than US$1 per day) (Chen & Ravallion, 2007). Examples of sub-Saharan African countries where the vast majority of people live in poverty include Uganda with 97 per cent, Nigeria with 91 per cent, and Zambia with 87 per cent (World Bank, 2005).

Poverty is likely to increase markedly in absolute terms in the next few decades in sub-Saharan Africa, because by 2050 the population of almost every country in western, eastern, and middle Africa will be double the 2000 level (United Nations Population Division, 2008). For example, Uganda's population will have more than tripled, from 25 million (32 million in 2008) to 93 million in 2050, and Nigeria's population will have grown by an additional 164 million people to 289 million. Thus, if poverty rates do not decline, in 2050 over 350 million people—more than the entire population of the USA today—will be living in poverty in these two countries alone, with more than 280 million of them living in extreme poverty. This compares to 135 million living in poverty between 1999 and 2003 in these two countries.

The implications of such high levels of population growth, coupled with the even more rapid urban growth, are stark. Three of every four urban dwellers in sub-Saharan Africa today already live in slum conditions. Hundreds of millions more people—more than 1.25 billion people overall—will be living in poverty in 2050, and sub-Saharan African countries will thus have even greater difficulty elevating their level of socioeconomic development and maintaining their often-tenuous political stability.

Given the current and rising levels of people living in poverty, it cannot be expected that consumers will pay the increasing costs of family planning services. The poor are very sensitive to price changes, and the results could be a decline in contraceptive use (Prata, et al., 2001). Sub-Saharan Africa poses the greatest threat with 77 per cent of its population in 2002 unable to pay for the price of the commodities (Prata, 2006) (see Table 26.1).

The current costs of family planning commodities should be examined critically, and prices should be adjusted making affordability and necessary subsidies a primary concern. The poorest quintile of the

Table 26.1 Fertility indicators for selected sub-Saharan African countries: Respective national DHS final reports

Country		TFR	Wanted fertility rate	Met need for FP (modern-method CPR)	Unmet need for FP
Ghana	2003	4.4	3.7	18.7	34.0
	1998	4.6	3.7	13.3	24.3
	1993	5.5	4.2	10.1	38.6
	1988	6.4	5.3	5.2	
Kenya	2003	4.9	3.6	31.5	24.5
	1998	4.7	3.5	31.5	23.9
	1993	5.4	3.4	27.3	36.4
	1989	6.7	4.4	17.9	
Malawi	2004	6.0	4.9	28.1	27.6
	2000	6.3	5.2	26.1	29.7
	1992	6.7	5.7	7.4	36.3
Nigeria	2003	5.7	5.3	8.2	16.9
	1999	5.2	4.8	8.6	17.5
	1990	6.0	5.8	3.5	20.8
Senegal	2005	5.3	4.5	10.3	31.6
	1997	5.7	4.6	8.1	32.6
	1992–3	6.0	5.1	4.8	27.9
Tanzania	2004	5.7	4.9	20.0	21.8
	1999	5.6	4.8	16.9	21.8
	1996	5.8	5.1	13.3	23.9
	1992	6.2	5.6	6.6	30.1
Uganda	2006	6.7	5.1	17.9	40.6
	2000–1	6.9	5.3	18.2	34.6
	1995	6.9	5.6	7.8	29.0
	1988	7.5	6.4	2.5	53.7

Note: CPR data refer to women aged 15–49 who are currently married or in union and are currently using a modern contraceptive method. TFR, total fertility rate. FP, family planning. CPR, contraceptive prevalence rate.

population suffers from the highest unmet need for family planning and shoulders the largest burden of maternal and child mortality. To reduce rising inequalities that place a high burden on society as a whole, family planning methods must be supplied to the poor at a cost they can afford. The overall, long-term burden for any country is ultimately higher if a large proportion of the poor cannot afford to determine the size of their own families. Therefore, it is important to ensure that contraception is genuinely affordable to the poorest families.

(iii) Importance of a Steady Supply of Contraceptives

Trends in modern contraceptive use in resource-poor settings seem to be associated with the level of the international community's support for family planning and local resources, thus affecting the pace of fertility decline in such settings. For example, in sub-Saharan Africa, many countries experienced substantial gains in contraceptive prevalence rates (CPR) in the 1980s and 1990s, followed by a diminished or stalled progress in the 2000s (see Figure

26.1). In the 1990s, modern method use almost quadrupled in Malawi, substantially increasing in all wealth quintiles, despite the widespread poverty, and more than doubled in Tanzania and Uganda. However, subsequent increases were more modest in Malawi, Senegal, and Tanzania, and the rise in CPR that ceased altogether in Kenya, Uganda, and Nigeria has yet to achieve double-digit levels of modern contraceptive use.

The solid declines in TFR that accompanied the increased modern methods in the 1980s and 1990s, of 0.6 births per woman or more from DHS to the next DHS, have subsequently diminished in Ghana, Malawi, and Uganda and ceased in Kenya, Nigeria, and Tanzania, with TFRs remaining at quite high levels. Yet, as seen in Table 26.1, all seven countries have higher total fertility than wanted fertility, which, along with their high unmet need for family planning, suggests missed programmatic opportunity. These results could also be showing programmatic challenges in these countries due to lack of steady funding for family planning, the effects of healthcare workforce dynamics, and/or health sector reform and decentralization.

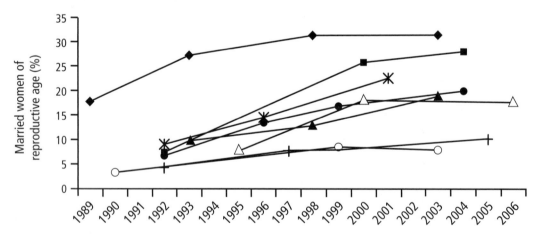

Figure 26.1 Modern contraceptive use in Ghana, Kenya, Malawi, Nigeria, Senegal, Tanzania, Uganda, and Zambia, 1989–2006. Filled triangle, Ghana; filled diamond, Kenya; filled square, Malawi; open circle, Nigeria; plus, Senegal; filled circle, Tanzania; open triangle, Uganda; star, Zambia.

It is well known that Africa suffers more than 24 per cent of the global burden of disease, yet it has only 3 per cent of the world's health workers and less than 1 per cent of the world's financial resources, even with loans and grants from abroad (World Health Organization, 2006). Although international population assistance, much of which went to sub-Saharan Africa, more than doubled worldwide from 2001 to 2004, increasing from $2.5 billion to $5.6 billion, this was largely due to increased funding for HIV/AIDS prevention, treatment, and care programs. The share of international population assistance devoted to family planning declined from 30 per cent in 2001 to less than 10 per cent in 2004 (Ethelston, et al., 2004; Leahy, 2007), which represents a decline in both absolute and per capita terms (Speidal, 2009). Although donors often have shifted their priorities and resources to other health problems and other development sectors, in pursuit of the UN Millennium Development Goals (MDGs), 'the MDGs are difficult or impossible to achieve with current levels of population growth in the least developed countries and regions, unless attention is paid to the population growth factor' (All Party Parliamentary Group, 2007)—an issue that can be dealt with if family planning is made easily available.

In the resource-poor settings common in sub-Saharan Africa, family planning programs are further challenged by the unintended consequences of health sector reform and decentralization, which have devolved programmatic authority to lower levels. At that level, family planning programs have to compete for the insufficient human and financial resources of other pressing priority health programs, such as malaria, tuberculosis, and HIV/AIDS. As a result, the health, social, and economic benefits that family planning confers on individuals, communities, and nations are not as widely appreciated as they should be at the sites where the funding and human resource allocation decisions that affect family planning are being made.

The devastating AIDS pandemic in sub-Saharan Africa has not only been diverting programmatic attention and resources, but it has also been affecting the healthcare workforce itself through disability and death. Reductions in the skilled workforce available to provide family planning are further occurring because of other negative factors: out-migration to more developed countries; low pay, especially in the public sector; uneven distribution, deployment, and use of existing staff; retirement and diminished programmatic investment in pre-service education (World Health Organization, 2006).

Thus, contraceptive security is essential. Ensuring a steady flow of family planning commodities should be part of the healthcare system's responsibility—it cannot allow the supply of products, which are so essential to protecting the health of the populations, to get disrupted. Currently, most governments are relying on donors to provide funding for family planning, but donor support has been unsteady and difficult to predict. Outside funding should be sought as a supplement to a healthcare system's commitment but should never be the sole source. A promising new 'South–South' supply of contraceptives is arising, and recently the government of Peoples Republic of China has donated contraceptives to Partners in Population and Development for distribution in Africa. It is important to ensure the supply of contraceptives by making family planning a permanent line item in healthcare systems' budgets.

(iv) Remove Barriers Hindering Access to Family Planning

Programs committed to reduce unmet need for family planning can take concrete steps to remove barriers that hinder access to family planning (Campbell, et al., 2006). Legal, facility-based, and provider-based barriers must be addressed to improve access. *Legal barriers* include formal laws and restrictions that deny females of reproductive age easy access to family planning services. For example, keeping oral contraceptive pills on prescription disallows the ability to socially market the pills—an important distribution and financing mechanism in low-resource settings. Other restrictions include what level of provider can/should provide certain contraceptive methods.

For example, rural women in many parts of Africa receive services from community-based distributors (CBDs), but CBDs are only allowed to distribute pills and condoms. However, it is exactly in rural areas of sub-Saharan Africa that women prefer injectable contraceptives. Depo-provera provision by community-based workers was used in many parts of Asia and Latin America, and it was recently demonstrated in pilot projects in Uganda, Madagascar, and Ethiopia. However, in most of sub-Saharan Africa, Depo-provera provision is restricted to skilled providers, despite the evidence showing its safety, feasibility, and acceptability at the community level (Stanback, et al., 2007). Similarly, the satisfactory provision of IUD insertion by non-physicians has been established since the 1970s (Eren, et al., 1983; Farr, et al., 1998), but today these services are provided mostly by physicians and in some places selected mid-level providers such as clinical officers when, in fact, provision of non-surgical longterm methods of contraception should be an integral part of pre-service training for all levels of health workers, not only those working in higher-level facilities. The reproductive rights of all women of reproductive age, regardless of age, marital status, and place of residence, need to be protected and facilitated by non-restrictive laws.

Facility-based barriers are not codified in law, but their *de facto* practice creates unnecessary barriers to accessing family planning services, such as clinics refusing to see adolescent patients or only providing contraceptive services on specific days of the week. In addition, provision of services of poor quality, including limited contraceptive choice and inability to switch methods if unsatisfied with the prescribed one, are all facility restrictions imposed on clients that hinder access. Moreover, to make family planning more accessible, all family planning methods except tubal ligation and vasectomy should be provided by community outreach workers whom women trust, outside of a facility.

Finally, *provider-based barriers* prevent women from accessing certain methods of contraception through discouragement or non-evidence-based clinical practices that emerge from personal biases and beliefs. Providers have been widely documented to discourage individuals from accessing hormonal methods by insisting on costly and medically unnecessary pelvic examinations, blood tests, or making it difficult (or impossible) for women to obtain the method of their choice if they are nulliparous, have recently had an abortion, or are of a certain age. Moreover, women using oral contraceptives are often required to visit the provider every month.

Family planning program planners, particularly in sub-Saharan Africa, could greatly benefit from removing the above-mentioned barriers. They are in a position to demonstrate strong leadership by taking on this important policy commitment which will pave the way for improved health and prosperity in future generations.

Conclusions

Increasing access to family planning is an urgent priority for low-resource settings. It is both a feasible and achievable intervention that can be implemented immediately. To ensure that populations living in resource-poor settings have the freedom and the choice to control their own fertility, current family planning programs will benefit from focusing on the four proposed strategies. This requires continued political and programmatic commitment to increase financial and human resources for family planning, from both governments and international foreign aid.

Addressing the fertility and population growth crisis can be done only when program planners consider the revitalization of their current family planning program within a human rights framework. Evidence shows that the poorest couples have the highest fertility, the lowest contraceptive use, and the highest unmet need for contraception. Not only would making family planning accessible in low-resource settings help decrease the existing inequities in achieving desired fertility, it could also increase contraceptive use, decrease fertility, and help slow population growth within a human rights framework. In addition, family planning can contribute to improvements in maternal and child health.

Failure to pay concerted attention to making family planning accessible in low-resource settings will probably result in couples having higher than desired fertility. Continued high fertility will hinder efforts to decrease maternal and infant mortality as well as poverty. As a result, development goals will become difficult to achieve and in some cases impossible.

The health rationale alone is a compelling reason for making family planning more accessible. Sub-Saharan Africa, for example, has not experienced a significant reduction in maternal mortality (Hill, et al., 2007). In all, 205 million pregnancies occur annually worldwide, 35 per cent of which are unintended and 22 per cent of which end in an induced abortion. Most of these pregnancies (182 million) happen in the developing world. Two-thirds of these pregnancies occur among women who are not using any method of contraception, making family planning a significant contributor to maternal health (Prata, et al., 2009). A sub-Saharan African woman today has a 1-in-22 lifetime chance of maternal death, and for every 109 births, a woman dies in pregnancy or childbirth (UNICEF, 2009). By contrast, among the European and other industrialized nations where women have good access to family planning services, fewer than 1 in 16,400 will die of complications of pregnancy and childbirth, an almost 750-fold difference (UN Working Group at Women Deliver, 2007). In addition to mortality, for every woman who dies, approximately 30 women suffer infections, injuries, and/or disabilities. Ensuring access to family planning in sub-Saharan Africa could avert thousands of maternal deaths (Prata, et al., 2009) and prevent hundreds of thousands of children from losing their mothers every year. When a mother dies in a low-resource setting, the risk of death in children who survive their mother's death also rises. Furthermore, family planning prevents more mother-to-child transmission of HIV than do antiretroviral drugs (US AID, 2006).

The largest cohorts of young people in sub-Saharan Africa's history are entering and moving through their reproductive years. Forty-three per cent of sub-Saharan Africa's population is below the age of 15 (Population Reference Bureau, 2007). Given the current population growth rate and the projected rise in female population 15–49 years old, family planning programs will have to run much faster just to keep the current low modern contraceptive use. The certain large increase in future need and demand for family planning that the incoming young and growing cohorts represent will be intensified further by sub-Saharan Africa's rapidly increasing urbanization.

Sub-Saharan Africa's 5 per cent annual urban growth rate is the highest in the world, and twice its overall annual population increase of 2.4 per cent, also the world's highest (United Nations Population Fund, 2007). According to recent estimates by the United Nations Population Division, whereas 28 per cent of sub-Saharan Africans lived in cities in 1990, 37 per cent of them lived in cities in 2006, and this proportion will rise to 48 per cent by 2030 and 60 per cent by 2050 (United Nations Population Division, 2007). The additional pressure for family planning that such urbanization will impose may be inferred from the current urban–rural differentials in CPR that are found in various countries. For example, data from recent DHS surveys show that some of the lowest differentials are found in Malawi (35 per cent modern CPR in urban areas versus 27 per cent in rural areas) and Nigeria (14 per cent urban versus 6 per cent rural) and the highest in Zambia (39 per cent urban versus 14 per cent rural) and Uganda (43 per cent urban versus 21 per cent rural).

The United Nations Population Division projections for the year 2050 vary between a high of 10.6 and a low of 7.4 billion. Making family planning easily accessible to all today could make a difference of billions in the world's population in 2050.

References

All Party Parliamentary Group on Population Development and Reproductive Health. (2007). *Return of the population growth factor: Its impact on the Millennium Development Goals.* London: Development and Reproductive Health, All Party Parliamentary Group on Population.

Campbell, M., Sahin-Hodoglugil, N.N., & Potts, M. (2006). Barriers to fertility regulation: A review of the literature. *Studies in Family Planning*, 37, 87–98. doi:10.1111/j.1728-4465.2006.00088.x

Chen, S., & Ravallion, M. (2007). *Absolute poverty measures for the developing world, 1981–2004.* Washington, DC: World Bank, Development Research Group.

Cleland, J., Bernstein, S., Ezeh, A., Faundes, A., Glasier, A. & Innis, J. (2006). Family planning: The unfinished agenda. *The Lancet*, 368, 1810–27. doi:10.1016/ S0140-6736(06)69480-4

Eren, N., Ramos, R., & Gray, R.H. (1983). Physicians vs auxiliary nurse-midwives as providers of IUD services: A study in Turkey and the Philippines. *Studies in Family Planning*, 14, 43–7. doi:10.2307/1965401

Ethelston, S., Bechtel, A., Chaya, N., Gibb Vogel, C., & Kanter, A. (2004). *Progress & promises: Trends in international assistance for reproductive health and population.* Washington, DC: Population Action International.

Ezeh, A.C., Mberu, B.U., & Emma, J.O. (2009). Stall in fertility decline in Eastern African countries: Regional analysis of patterns, determinants and implications. *Philosophical Transactions of the Royal Society, B 364*, 2991–3007. doi:10.1098/rstb.2009.0166

Farr, G., Rivera, R., & Amatya, R. (1998). Non-physician insertion of IUDs: Clinical outcomes among TCu38OA insertions in three developing-country clinics. *Advances in Contraception*, 14, 45–57. doi: 10.1023/A:1006575610716

Grubb, G. (1987). Women's perceptions of the safety of the pill: A survey in eight developing countries. *Journal of Biosocial Science*, 19, 313–21. doi:10.1017/50021932000016965

Hill, K., Thomas, K., AbouZahr, C., Walker, N., Say, L., Inoue, M., Suzuki, E., & Maternal Mortality Working Group. (2007). Estimates of maternal mortality worldwide between 1990 and 2005: An assessment of available data. *The Lancet*, 370, 1311–19. doi:10.1016/50140-6736(07)61572-4

Leahy, E. (2007). *Update: Trends in international assistance for reproductive health and population in 2004.* Washington, DC: Population Action International.

Population Reference Bureau. (2002). *Family planning worldwide.* Washington, DC: Population Reference Bureau.

———. (2007). *2007 world population data sheet.* Washington, DC: Population Reference Bureau.

———. (2008). *Family planning worldwide 2008 data sheet.* Washington, DC: Population Reference Bureau.

Prata, N. (2006). Assistance to international family planning programs. *UC Davis Journal of International Law and Policy*, 13, 19–33.

———. (2007). The need for family planning. *Population and Environment*, 28, 212–22. doi:10.1007/ s11111-007-0042-9

Prata, N., Marceau, S., Walsh, J., Townes, E., & Wade, T. (2001). *How much are consumers willing to pay for family planning?* Bay Area International Group.

Prata, N., Montagu, D., & Jeffrey, E. (2005). Private sector human resources and health franchising in Africa. *Bulletin of the World Health Organization*, 83, 274–9.

Prata, N., Sreenivas, A., Vahidnia, F., & Potts, M. (2009). Saving maternal lives in resource-poor settings: Facing reality. *Health Policy (Amsterdam, Netherlands)*, 89, 131–48.

Reynolds, H.W, Janowitz, B., Homan, R., & Johnson, L. (2006). The value of contraception to prevent perinatal HIV transmission. *Sexually Transmitted Diseases*, 33, 350–6.

Speidal, J.J. (2009). Food, water, & population. Presentation at *The world in 2050: A scientific investigation of the impact of global population changes on a divided planet.* Berkeley, CA, January 2009.

Stanback, J., Mbonye, A.K., & Bekiita, M. (2007). Contraceptive injections by community health workers in Uganda: A nonrandomized community trial. *Bulletin of the World Health Organ, 85*, 768–73. doi:10.2471/BLT.07.040162

Thayer, B.A. (2009). Considering population and war: A critical and neglected aspect of conflict studies. Presentation at *The world in 2050: A scientific investigation of the impact of global population changes on a divided planet.* Berkeley, CA, January 2009.

UNICEF. (2009). *The state of the world's children 2009.* New York, NY: UNICEF. Retrieved from www.unicef. org/sowc09/report/report.php

United Nations Population Division. (2007). *World population prospects: The 2006 revision population database.* New York, NY: United Nations Population Division. Retrieved from www.un.org/esa/population/publications/wpp2006/English.pdf

———. (2008). *World urbanization prospects: The 2007 revision population database.* New York, NY: United Nations Population Division. Retrieved from http://esa.un.org/unup/

United Nations Population Fund. (2007). *State of world population 2007: Unleashing the potential of urban growth.* New York, NY: United Nations Population Fund. Retrieved from www.unfpa.org/swp/2007/english/introduction.html

UN Working Group at Women Deliver. (2007). Maternal mortality scorecard. Women Deliver, Family Health International. Retrieved from www.womendeliver.org/assets/MM_Country_Rankings_factsheet_(A4).pdf

US AID. (2006). *Adding family planning to PMTCT sites increases PMTCT benefits.* Washington, DC: US AID. Retrieved from www.usaid.gov/our_work/global_health/pop/techareas/repositioning/briefs/adding_fp_pmtct.pdf

Westoff, C.F. (2006). *New estimates of unmet need and the demand for family planning.* Calverton, MD: Macro International Inc.

World Bank. (1993). *World development report 1993: Investing in health.* New York, NY: Oxford University Press.

———. (2005). *World development indicators 2005.* Washington, DC: World Bank. Retrieved from http://go.worldbank.org/DXDWYUKQA0

World Health Organization. (2006). *The world health report 2006: Working together for health.* Geneva, Switzerland: WHO.

Questions for Critical Thought

1. How can family planning services be better provided to women in the poorest countries of the world? What are the cultural, social, and economic barriers that prevent women in these countries from gaining access to adequate family planning?

2. Are pronatalist policies in advanced societies effective?

3. How can population policies be evaluated? What indicators would you suggest for this purpose?

Websites of Interest

Population Action International (PAI) is an independent policy advocacy group working to secure political and financial support for population programs grounded in individual rights. A private, non-profit group, it focuses on public policy and strategic initiatives, with an aim to improve individual wellbeing and preserve global resources by mobilizing political and financial support for population, family planning, and reproductive health policies and programs. Current research and projects are outlined on their website: www.populationaction.org/About_PAI/Index.shtml

The *Population Division* of the United Nations' Department of Economic and Social Affairs is the authoritative source on population policies across the world. Their work is described on their website: www.un.org/esa/population/

Further Reading

Berelson, Bernard. (1980). Romania's 1966 anti-abortion decree: The demographic experience of the first decade. *Population Studies, 32*(2), 209–22.

Berelson, Bernard. (1992). The great debate on population policy: An instructive entertainment. *Family Planning Perspectives, 16*(4), 126–38.

Boswell, Christina. (2007). Theorizing migration policy: Is there a third way? *International Migration Review, 41*(1), 75–100.

Gauthier, Anne H., & Philipov, Dimiter (Eds). (2008). *Can policies enhance fertility in Europe?* Special issue of *Vienna Yearbook of Population Research*.

Greenhalgh, Susan, & Winckler, Edwin A. (2005). *Governing China's population: From Leninist to neoliberal biopolitics.* Stanford, CA: Stanford University Press.

Halfon, Saul. (2007). *The Cairo consensus: Demographic surveys, women's empowerment, and regime change in population policy.* Lanham, MD: Lexington Books.

Jones, Gavin W., & Karim, Mehtab S. (Eds). (2005). *Islam, the state and population.* London: Hurst and Company.

Poston, Dudley L., Jr, Lee, Che-Fu, Chang, Chiung-Fang, McKibben, Sherry L., & Walther, Carol S. (Eds). (2006). *Fertility, family planning, and population policy in China.* New York: Routledge.

Sadik, Nafis (Ed.). (2002). *An agenda for the people: The UNFPA through three decades.* New York: New York University Press.

Credits

Chapter 1 'The space and strategy of demographic growth'. By Massimo Livi-Bacci (2007). *Concise History of World Population* (3rd edition), translated by Carl Ipsen, 5–9, 17–20. (Blackwell Publishing). Reproduced with permission.

Chapter 2 'How do we know the facts of demography?' By Nathan Keyfitz (1975). *Population and Development Review*, 1(2), 267–88 (Wiley, US). Reprinted by permission.

Chapter 3 'The structure of demographic action.' By Thomas K. Burch (1979). *Journal of Population*, 2(4), 279–93. Reprinted by permission.

Chapter 4 'Illustrating behavioral principles with examples from demography: The causal analysis of differences in fertility'. By Lincoln H. Day (1979). *Journal for the Theory of Social Behaviour*, 15(2), 189–201 (Wiley-Blackwell). Reprinted by permission.

Chapter 5 'The rising numbers of humankind'. By Jean-Noël Biraben (2003). *Population and Societies*, 394(October), 1–4. Reprinted by permission.

Chapter 6 'The demographic transition: Three centuries of fundamental change'. By Ronald Lee (2003). *Journal of Economic Perspectives*, 17(4), 167–90. Reprinted by permission.

Chapter 7 'How a population ages or grows younger'. By Ansley J. Coale. In Ronald Freedman, ed., *Population: The Vital Revolution*, copyright © 1964 by Doubleday, a division of Random House, Inc. Used by permission of Anchor Books, a division of Random House, Inc.

Chapter 8 'The coming acceleration of global population ageing'. By Wolfgang Lutz, Warren Sanderson and Sergei Scherbov (2008). *Nature*, 461(7 February), 716–19. Reprinted by permission.

Chapter 9 'Changes in conjugal life in Canada: Is cohabitation progressively replacing marriage?' By Céline Le Bourdais and Évelyne Lapierre-Adamcyk (2004). *Journal of Marriage and Family*, 66(November), 929–42 (Wiley). Reprinted by permission.

Chapter 10 'The role of cohabitation in family formation: The United States in comparative perspective'. By Patrick Heuveline and Jeffery M. Timberlake. (2004). *Journal of Marriage and Family*, 66, 1214–30 (Wiley). Reprinted by permission.

Chapter 11 Excerpt from 'Introduction and Overview' in *Fertility, Biology and Behavior: An Analysis of the Proximate Determinants*. By John Bongaarts and Robert G. Potter, copyright © 1983 (Academic Press). Reprinted by permission of the publisher.

Chapter 12 'Low fertility in evolutionary perspective'. By Kingsley Davis (1986), 48–65, in K. Davis, Mikhail S. Bernstam and Rita Ricardo-Campbell (eds.), *Below-Replacement Fertility in Industrial Societies: Causes, Consequences, Policies*. Population & Development Review. Supplement to Volume 12. New York: The Population Council. Reprinted by permission.

Chapter 13 'Explanations of the fertility crisis in modern societies: A search for commonalities'. By John C. Caldwell and Thomas Schindlmayr (2003). *Population Studies*, 57(3), 241–63. Reprinted by permission.

Chapter 14 'Fertility transitions in developing countries: Progress or stagnation?' By John Bongaarts (2008). *Studies in Family Planning*, 39(2), 105–10. Reprinted by permission.

Chapter 15 'Human mortality throughout history and prehistory'. By Samuel H. Preston (1995), 31–5. In Julian L. Simon (ed.), *The State of Humanity* (Oxford: Blackwell). Reprinted by permission.

Chapter 16 'Aging populations: The challenges ahead'. By Kaare Christensen, Gabriele Doblhammer, Roland Rau and James W. Vaupel (2009). *Lancet*, 374 (October 3), 1196–1208. Reprinted by permission.

Chapter 17 'Social determinants of health inequalities'. By Michael Marmot (2005). *Social Biology*, 41(1–2), 20–37. Reprinted by permission.

Chapter 18 'Narrowing sex differentials in life expectancy in the industrialized world: Early 1970s to early 1990s'. By Frank Trovato and N.M. Lalu. *Social Biology*, 41(1-2), 20–37. Reprinted by permission.

Chapter 19 'The hypothesis of the mobility transition'. By Wilbur Zelinsky (1971). *The Geographical Review*, 61 (2), 219–49 (The American Geographical Society). Reprinted by permission.

Chapter 20 'Population distribution and redistribution of the baby-boom cohort in the United States: Recent trends and implications'. By Peter A. Rogerson and Daejong Kim (2005). *Proceedings of the*

National Academies of Science 102(43), 15319–24. Reprinted by permission.

Chapter 21 *The Age of Migration: International Population Movements in the Modern World* (4th edn). By Stephen Castles and Mark A. Miller (2009), 1-19 (plus references). New York: The Guilford Press. Reprinted by permission.

Chapter 22 'The debate over the effects of population growth on economic growth'. By David E. Bloom, David Canning, and Jaypee Sevilla (2003), 1–23. In David E. Bloom, D. Canning, and J. Sevilla, *The Demographic Dividend: A New Perspective on the Economic Consequences of Population Change*. Santa Monica, CA: Rand Corporation. Reprinted by permission.

Chapter 23 'Revisiting the limits to growth after peak oil'. By Charles A.S. Hall and John W. Day, Jr (2009). *American Scientist*, 97(May–June), 230–37. Reprinted by permission.

Chapter 24 'The geography of poverty and wealth'. By Jeffrey D. Sachs, Andrew D. Mellinger, and John L. Gallup (2001). *Scientific American*, (March), 70–75. Reprinted by permission.

Chapter 25 'The impact of family policies on fertility in industrialized countries: A review of the literature'. By Anne Gauthier (2007). *Population Research and Policy Review*, 26, 323–46. Reprinted by permission.

Chapter 26 'Making family planning accessible in resource-poor settings'. By Ndola Prata (2009). *Philosophical Transactions of the Royal Society*, B 364, 3093–9. Reprinted by permission.